THE ILLUSTRATED HISTORY
— OF THE —
WORLD

Published in 2004 by Mercury Books London
An imprint of the Caxton Publishing Group
20 Bloomsbury Street, London WC1B 3JH

ISBN: 1-904668-47-X

THE ILLUSTRATED HISTORY OF THE WORLD
was created and produced by McRae Books,
Borgo Santa Croce, 8 – Florence (Italy)
e-mail: info@mcraebooks.com

PROJECT DIRECTOR: Anne McRae

ADVISORS: John Haywood, Simon Hall

TEXT: Neil Morris, Neil Grant, Lisa Isenman, Hazel Mary Martell, Lynn McRae, John Malam, Michael Pollard

ILLUSTRATORS: Giorgio Albertini, Daniela Astone, Alessandro Bartolozzi, Simone Boni, Alessandro Cantucci, Lorenzo Cecchi, Stefania Ciccarelli, Matteo Chesi, Fabiano Fabbrucci, Gian Paolo Faleschini, Ferruccio Cucchiarini, Luisa Della Porta, Sauro Giampaia, Sabrina Marconi, Leonardo Meschini, Federico Micheli, Antonella Pastorelli, Andrea Morandi, Paola Ravaglia, Ivan Stalio

EDITORS: Vicky Egan, Anne McRae

INDEX: Susan Kelly, Holly Willis

PICTURE RESEARCH: Loredana Agosta, Erika Barrow, Christie Cooper, Elzbieta Gontarska

GRAPHIC DESIGN: Marco Nardi
LAYOUTS: Ornella Fassio, Adriano Nardi, Laura Ottina

COLOR SEPARATIONS: Litocolor Florence (Italy), Color Plates, Milan (Italy)

Printed and bound in China

Neil Morris, Neil Grant, Lisa Isenman, Hazel Mary Martell,
Lynn McRae, John Malam, Michael Pollard

THE ILLUSTRATED HISTORY
— OF THE —
WORLD
FROM THE BIG BANG TO THE THIRD MILLENNIUM

Illustrated by Paola Ravaglia, Alessandro Cantucci, Andrea
Morandi, Fabiano Fabbrucci, Sauro Giampaia, Ivan Stalio

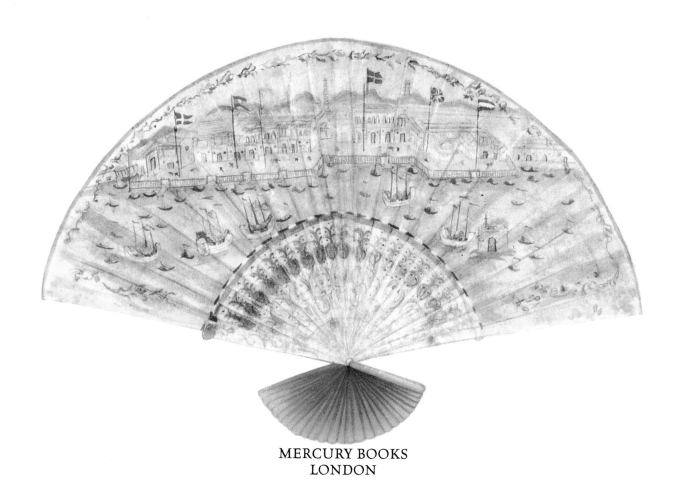

MERCURY BOOKS
LONDON

List of Contents

Introduction

When our earliest human ancestor first walked the African grasslands around 5 million years ago, the earth was already more than 4 billion years old. Since then, people have spread to every corner of the globe and developed every conceivable form of society. The sheer scope of human experience and the huge spans of time involved are sufficient to overawe historians, while the general reader will often be at a loss to explain all but the most recent events. *The Illustrated History of the World* is designed to fill those gaps, providing an overview of world history from the origins of the planet to the present day. Our approach is international, with many pages dedicated to the history of Islam, Africa, and the Far East, alongside the tumultuous histories of Europe and America. Maps on almost every page locate people and events geographically, and brief and accessible historical overviews are backed up with timelines, diagrams, and over 2,000 color illustrations each with captions to explain specific events, inventions, artifacts, and people. *The Illustrated History of the World* provides a digestible panorama of the great sweep of history on earth, from the Big Bang, right up to the dawn of the 21st century.

Origins

20 BYA–10,000 BC

Scientists have pieced together enough evidence to develop convincing theories to explain the origins of the universe and the formation of planet earth. Accounting for the beginnings of life on earth is more complicated; present-day life forms are so complex and interdependent that for a long time it seemed unlikely that they should have developed spontaneously. But new theories based on chemical research have shown that the building blocks of life were present when the first simple creatures appeared. It took almost 4 billion years for these life forms to evolve into the plants and animals our ancestors learned to farm.

The invention of tools

The development of tools was a fundamental stepping stone in the path of human evolution. It was a slow process, and early hominids probably used pointed sticks to obtain food in much the same way as chimpanzees do today. Gradually, they learned to fashion increasingly sophisticated tools.

The Age of Reptiles
p. 12 *The earliest reptiles developed about 300 million years ago. They reigned supreme on earth from about 235 to 65 million years ago, when the dinosaurs died out.*

Mammals and Primates
p. 13 *The first mammals lived alongside the dinosaurs but they did not become widespread until after the dinosaurs became extinct. The first primates appeared immediately after the demise of the ruling reptiles.*

Early Humans
p. 13 *The first human-like creatures, called hominids, evolved in Africa between 6 and 4 million years ago. They began to walk on two legs instead of four, and gradually learned to make and use stone tools for hunting and preparing food.*

Modern Humans
p. 15 *Modern humans, called Homo sapiens sapiens, first appeared in Africa about 100,000 years ago. They migrated out of Africa and peopled the entire planet. They are the ancestors of all the people living on earth today.*

The Birth of Farming
p. 18 *People learned to farm animals and plants around 10,000 years ago. Farming developed independently in different parts of the world.*

DISCOVERING OUR PAST

Our knowledge of the history of the world, and especially human history, is based on many separate discoveries made by specialists in different fields. Paleontologists find and study prehistoric remains that tell us a great deal about life before writing was invented. Archeologists specialize in ancient remains and especially the sites of early human civilizations. Modern historians interpret these findings, along with records and documents from ancient, medieval, and more recent times, to build up an overall picture of the past. Today they are helped by new techniques of dating and genetics. Our understanding of the past is growing all the time, but it is exciting to think how much we still have to discover and learn.

Fossils are revealed when the rock in which they formed wears away. Paleontologists chip away at likely sites to find the fossils.

Paleontology

Paleontologists are fossil hunters. They find and study fossils found in rocks to learn about prehistoric animals and plants. Animal fossils – such as those of huge dinosaurs or tiny shellfish – started to form many millions of years ago when animals died and were buried by sediment. Their bodies rotted, leaving only hard shells or bones. Over millions of years the sediment hardened into rock and the bones were replaced by minerals.

Genetic information

Our growing knowledge of the genetic make-up of all living material may help us find out more about past life on Earth. Scientists are able to extract DNA (deoxyribonucleic acid, shown in the diagram below) from human and animal remains. This allows them to see genetic relationships between individuals, families, or even entire populations.

Dendrochronology, or tree-ring dating, can be used to determine the age of wooden objects. Each year a living tree produces a new ring of wood, and these vary according to climate and changes in the seasons. By piecing together overlapping ring patterns, scientists have managed to establish a timeline stretching back over 7,000 years.

The potassium-argon method is often used to date hominid remains, such as this Homo ergaster skull, which is between 1.7 and 1.5 million years old. The method is based on the known rate at which potassium decays into argon gas.

Pottery is often dated using thermoluminescence. When a piece of pottery is heated, electrons are released as light. Measuring the amount of light allows scientists to determine how many years have passed since the pottery was originally fired. The method is effective on items up to 80,000 years old.

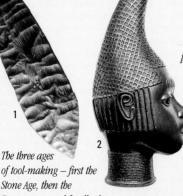

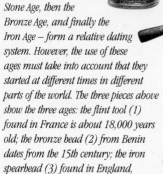

The three ages of tool-making – first the Stone Age, then the Bronze Age, and finally the Iron Age – form a relative dating system. However, the use of these ages must take into account that they started at different times in different parts of the world. The three pieces above show the three ages: the flint tool (1) found in France is about 18,000 years old; the bronze head (2) from Benin dates from the 15th century; the iron spearhead (3) found in England, however, may date back to 600 BC.

Dating methods

Archeologists use a range of different methods to date the objects they find, depending on the materials from which they are made. Some of the methods are radiometric, which means that they work by measuring radioactivity. The best known of these methods is radiocarbon dating, which can be used to date anything that was once alive, such as wood or bone. It measures amounts of carbon-14, which decays at a known rate after an organism dies. The potassium-argon method is similar, while other, less accurate dating systems are also useful to historians.

Stratigraphy is the study of the composition and sequence of strata, or layers, that build up over time. This helps archeologists establish the order in which objects were made or used. In sites that have been occupied for thousands of years, many layers of debris are uncovered as archeologists dig, each layer older than the one above it. Mounds that have built up from earlier remains, such as the one shown below, are known as tells.

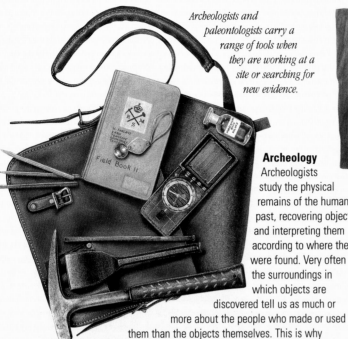

Archeologists and paleontologists carry a range of tools when they are working at a site or searching for new evidence.

Archeology

Archeologists study the physical remains of the human past, recovering objects and interpreting them according to where they were found. Very often the surroundings in which objects are discovered tell us as much or more about the people who made or used them than the objects themselves. This is why modern archeologists keep a very detailed and careful record of sites as they work.

Written records

People began to keep written records around 3500 BC, when the ancient Sumerians began to list items in the form of pictograms. These developed into the cuneiform script, and by 2700 BC there were libraries of clay tablets in Sumer. At the same time the Egyptians developed their hieroglyphic system, but this was last used in AD 394, and the script was only deciphered by modern historians in 1822. All written records pass on invaluable information to later generations.

Above: Part of an Egyptian coffin lid from the 4th century BC. The columns of hieroglyphic inscription are inlaid in multicolored glass.

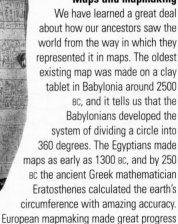

This broken fragment, called the Palermo Stone, dates to around 2400 BC. It lists all the kings of Egypt up to that time, as well as important religious festivals, military campaigns, and the level of the Nile River's annual flood.

Historical documents

All historical documents are important to historians in their attempts to piece together and understand our past. Some famous documents, such as the Domesday Book, give us detailed information – down to the number of plows and mills in a particular region. Others, such as the Magna Carta signed by King John of England in 1215, give us more general information on laws and customs. Pictorial images, such as the miniatures in medieval illuminated manuscripts, give us information on how people looked and what they wore.

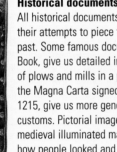

The Domesday Book was produced in 1086, twenty years after the Norman Conquest of England. William the Conqueror ordered it as a survey and record of the property holders in his realm. The original is kept in the British Public Record Office.

The 11th-century Bayeux Tapestry presents a wonderful pictorial record of the Norman Conquest of England in more than 70 scenes. It is kept and exhibited in a museum near the cathedral of Bayeux, in northwest France.

Maps and mapmaking

We have learned a great deal about how our ancestors saw the world from the way in which they represented it in maps. The oldest existing map was made on a clay tablet in Babylonia around 2500 BC, and it tells us that the Babylonians developed the system of dividing a circle into 360 degrees. The Egyptians made maps as early as 1300 BC, and by 250 BC the ancient Greek mathematician Eratosthenes calculated the earth's circumference with amazing accuracy. European mapmaking made great progress during the Middle Ages.

Two maps showing a geographical and a spiritual vision of the world. The map on the left, drawn by an Arab cartographer, shows Europe and Africa (note that south is at the top). The map below, made by a Christian monk in the Middle Ages, shows Jerusalem at the center of the world.

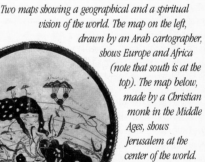

Calendars

Some ancient peoples had their own methods of dating events, and many had their own calendars based on astronomical observation or mythical beliefs. References to dating systems and finds of actual calendars have been of great help to modern historians. In Europe, Julius Caesar established the so-called Julian Calendar in 46 BC. This was amended by Pope Gregory XIII in 1582, to create the modern Gregorian Calendar.

This Aztec calendar stone dates from the 12th century. It shows the fifth sun, which the Aztecs believed to be the present era, surrounded by the four previous suns and signs for the 20 Aztec days.

c.20 BYA Big Bang – origin of
universe. c.4.6 BYA Formation of

planet earth. c.3.4 BYA
Development of stromatolites

and blue-green algae.
c.1.5 BYA Single-celled organisms

with nuclei appear.
c.590 MYA First multicelled

animals, including coelenterates,
annelid worms, and arthropods.

From the Big Bang to the Rise of Reptiles

Over the years there have been different theories about the origin of the universe, but today most scientists believe that it began with a colossal explosion around 20 billion years ago. Millions of years after the Big Bang, gases clustered into clouds, which eventually clumped together to form galaxies. Countless billions of stars formed within separate galaxies, as the universe continued to expand. Planets formed around one star, our sun, about 4.6 billion years ago. These included planet earth, where simple, single-celled forms of life developed around a billion years later. Over the next three billion years, life on earth developed, as marine animals filled the seas, and insects, amphibians, plants, and the first reptiles developed on land.

Early forms of life

The first living cells were probably similar to the bacteria that are still found today around hot springs and underwater volcanoes. Gradually cells began to trap the sun's energy in the process known as photosynthesis. One of the earliest forms of life was blue-green algae, which formed slimy layers on rocks. Over millions of years these simple, single-celled organisms developed into more complex, multicelled forms of life such as worms and jellyfish.

Birth of the universe

Most scientists believe that when the universe began billions of years ago, all its material was in one small lump. Then there was a massive explosion, which we call the "Big Bang." This blew energy and particles of matter out into space and produced an enormous, incredibly hot fireball.

As the fireball started to cool, the hydrogen and helium that made up most of the universe's material came together to form galaxies. These were made up of billions of stars.

Formation of the solar system

Our sun is an ordinary yellow star that formed within the Milky Way galaxy. As it formed, material around it made up a rotating disk. As bits of dust circled around the newborn sun, they collided and slowed down. Pieces of dust and rock came together to form bigger and bigger lumps that became the four rocky, inner planets of the solar system, including earth.

Farther away from the sun, dust sucked in hydrogen and helium to form the gas giants that make up the outer planets of the solar system.

The beginning of life

As the young earth cooled, steam condensed into water droplets and fell as rain, forming the oceans. Gases dissolved in the oceans and made a warm "soup" of chemicals. Over millions of years the sun's high-energy rays and lightning flashes acted on the "soup" to form more complex chemicals. Eventually DNA (deoxyribonucleic acid) formed, and this had the ability to make copies of itself and reproduce. DNA then mixed with other chemicals to make the first forms of life.

EON	ERA	PERIOD	EPOCH	START OF INTERVAL (millions of years ago)	LIFEFORMS
PHANEROZOIC	CENOZOIC	Quaternary	HOLOCENE	0.01 MYA	Spread of modern humans
			PLEISTOCENE	1.8	Humans appear
		Tertiary	PLIOCENE	5	Earliest hominids Apes and whales appear
			MIOCENE	24	
			OLIGOCENE	34	
			EOCENE	55	Early horse and camel appear
			PALEOCENE	65	First big mammals Dinosaurs die out
	MESOZOIC	Cretaceous	Upper		
			Lower	142	First flowering plants
		Jurassic		206	First birds and mammals
		Triassic		248	First dinosaurs and flying reptiles
	PALEOZOIC	Permian		290	First mammal-like tetrapods
					First reptiles
		Carboniferous		354	First forests and winged insects
		Devonian		417	First tree ferns and tetrapods
		Silurian		443	First land plants and insects
		Ordovician		495	First corals and freshwater animals
		Cambrian		545	First fish
PRECAMBRIAN	PROTEROZOIC			2,500	First soft-bodied invertebrates (jellyfish)
	ARCHEAN			3,800	First life: algae and bacteria
	HADEAN			4,600	

c.560 MYA First animals with external skeletons, including sponges, trilobites, and lamp shells.

c.420 MYA Jawed and shark-like fishes in sea; first plants on land.

c.360 MYA First amphibians.
c.300 MYA First reptiles.

c.250 MYA Mass extinction; trilobites die out.

Scientists believe that the universe was created with a Big Bang about 20 billion (or 20 thousand million) years ago. By about 100,000 years later there was a fireball with a temperature of about 8,000°F (4000°C), and the universe contained just hydrogen and helium.

About 1 to 2 billion years after the Big Bang, the galaxies were formed, and our solar system formed billions of years later. Our sun came into existence about 4.8 billion years ago, and the earth about 4.6 billion years ago. We call the first geological time period the Precambrian eon; it lasted for more than 4 billion

years. The early surface of the earth was covered with volcanoes, which spewed out gas and molten rock. Then steam condensed into water, which fell as rain and formed the oceans.

A warm "soup" of chemicals built up, leading eventually to the substance known as DNA, which was able to reproduce itself. The first record of life is in the form of stromatolites made up of blue-green algae and dating back 3.4 billion years. About 2 billion years ago eukaryotes (single-celled organisms with nuclei) appeared.

Toward the end of the Precambrian

period (about 590 MYA) the first multicelled animals – including coelenterates, such as jellyfish – appeared.

During the early Cambrian period (545–495 MYA) the evolution of external skeletons led to larger marine animals, and there was an explosion of new life-forms. In the Ordovician (495–443 MYA), sea urchins, starfishes, and jawless fishes developed, but there was a mass extinction at the end of the period. In the Silurian (443–417 MYA), the first plants appeared on land, and the first jawed and shark-like fishes swam in the sea.

Scorpions and wingless

insects appeared on land during the Devonian (417–354 MYA), as well as the first amphibian. Coal deposits developed in lowland swamps during the Carboniferous (354–290 MYA), when flying insects and the first reptiles appeared. During the final Paleozoic period, the Permian (290–248 MYA), conifers and cycads appeared, while trilobites died out.

1. A protozoan, a modern single-celled organism. The earliest forms of life were probably very similar to this.

2. A trilobite, an extinct marine creature that burrowed in sand and mud. It lived between 550 and 250 million years ago.

The Cambrian explosion

Early in the Cambrian period there was an amazing increase in the development of life. Many of the major groups of animals that we know today made their first appearance on earth. At this time there were large areas of warm, shallow water and soft mud, which made ideal conditions for life. The early forms of life then began to develop hard parts, such as shells, chalky tubes, and external skeletons.

Jellyfish were one of the earliest kinds of multicelled sea creatures. They are still found in all the oceans of the world.

Vertebrates

The development of backbones was a major development. Today vertebrates (animals with backbones) make up all the largest, most active animals on earth. The first vertebrates were jawless fishes, and many had heavy outer armor. Their internal skeleton anchored muscles and supported the body's organs.

Fossils of this jawless fish, called Arandapis, *have been found in Australia. They date to about 500 million years ago.*

Wandering continents

The Earth's crust is cracked into huge moving plates that fit together like a giant jigsaw puzzle. The continental landmasses are attached to these plates and they drift about with them. Toward the end of the Precambrian period most land masses came together to form a giant supercontinent. By the mid-Carboniferous period, the lower continent of Gondwanaland was made up of what would become Africa and Australia, as well as Antarctica.

NORTHERN CHINA
LAURENTIA
GONDWANA
SIBERIA
Impetus Ocean
GONDWANA
NORTHERN EUROPE

SIBERIA
LAURASIA
SOUTH AMERICA
AFRICA
AUSTRALIA
G O N D W A N A L A N D

The position of the continents early in the Cambrian period (above), and in the middle of the Carboniferous period (left).

The appearance of plants

The first plants, such as clubmosses, appeared on land during the Silurian period. By the Devonian they had grown into tall trees and been joined by ferns, horsetails, and the first seed plants. The first conifers appeared during the Carboniferous period, when much of the land that is now Europe, Asia, and North America was covered by tropical swamps.

Tree ferns still grow in moist, mountainous regions near the equator.

Eusthenopteron was a fish with a solid lobe of flesh at the bottom of its fins. This allowed it to crawl on land and gulp air as it went in search of a new pool.

Out of the water

Towards the end of the Devonian period some sea creatures crawled out onto land, where there were already many plants and wingless insects. These creatures could live on land as well as in water, and we call them amphibians (meaning "having a double life.") They laid their eggs in water, the eggs hatched into swimming creatures, and when they became adults and grew legs, they moved onto land – just as frogs and toads do today.

The first reptiles

The first reptiles appeared during the Carboniferous period, when most amphibians still lived mainly in the water. The early reptiles were small, lizard-like animals that fed on insects and worms. They were able to live on land all the time, and their eggs were protected by a leathery shell. Their young hatched into miniature versions of their parents, making a very different life cycle from amphibians.

Below: Skeleton of an Eryops, which was an amphibian that probably fed in the water and was quite similar to the reptiles that were soon to rule the land.

c.245 MYA Spread of mammal-like reptiles called synapsids.

c.230 MYA First dinosaurs appear.

c.200 MYA Pterosaurs take to the air.

c.150 MYA First known bird, *Archaeopteryx*.

c.65 MYA Dinosaurs die out in mass extinction.

From Dinosaurs to Hominids

The span of geological time known as the Mesozoic era was marked by the development of dinosaurs, as well as the appearance of the first mammals, birds, and flowering plants. Dinosaurs dominated the land for 165 million years, while other giant reptiles developed in the sea and took to the air. After the extinction of all these reptiles, the small mammals that already existed grew in size and number. During the Tertiary period many new, more complex species of mammals developed, culminating in the first humanlike creatures that walked on two legs. During this vast timespan the continents continued to drift apart, as plant life also developed on land.

1

The first dinosaurs appeared on earth about 230 million years ago, during the first period of the Mesozoic era, called the Triassic. They were to dominate the land for 165 million years, flourishing in the Jurassic period, and finally dying out quite suddenly at the end of the Cretaceous period. During the Triassic, and later, there were other giant reptiles as well as dinosaurs. In the world's oceans there were sea reptiles, such as plesiosaurs and ichthyosaurs, and many bony fishes first appeared. On land conifers, cycads, and ferns continued to dominate, and by the end of the Triassic all modern conifer families except pines were in existence.

The age of dinosaurs
Dinosaurs dominated the land for many millions of years. They adapted to a wide range of habitats and could live anywhere on earth. During their time the continents were slowly drifting apart, but early dinosaurs were able to cross from one continent to another by land. Some dinosaurs were meat-eaters, while others ate only plants. Some were huge – *Diplodicus* was almost 90 ft (27 m) long and weighed about 12 tons (12 tonnes) – while others were small – *Compsognathus* was about 3 ft (1 m) long and weighed about 7 lb (3 kg).

A group of meat-eating Herrerasaurus *dinosaurs, which lived in the Triassic period, are on the lookout for prey. They are in luck. A dead nothosaur (a large marine reptile) has been washed up on the shore.*

A vast crater has been found in the Gulf of Mexico. It was made at the end of the Mesozoic era by an object at least 6 mi. (10 km) wide. Many believe this was the cause of dinosaur extinction.

End of the dinosaurs
We are not sure why dinosaurs died out, but most scientists believe their extinction was caused by a natural catastrophe. The most likely explanation is that the earth was hit by a huge asteroid or comet at the end of the Mesozoic era, causing wildfires and a mass of dust that traveled around the globe and blocked out the sun for months or even years. There was also a great deal of volcanic activity at that time, which may have made the earth too hot for the dinosaurs and poisoned the air.

Flying reptiles
Reptiles called pterosaurs took to the air over 200 million years ago. They launched themselves from high cliffs and flew on wings of skin, which stretched out from their long, thin arms. They had light, delicate bones, which made it easy for them to stay in the air. While dinosaurs ruled the land, pterosaurs controlled the skies – millions of years before the first feathered birds appeared.

The largest pterosaur, called Quetzalcoatlus, *had a wingspan of about 40 ft (12 m). This huge reptile weighed over 220 lb (100 kg).*

SEE ALSO
p. 10 FROM THE BIG BANG TO THE RISE OF REPTILES • p. 14 HUMAN EVOLUTION

65–53 MYA Explosive spread of new mammals.

c.60 MYA First primates.

c.50 MYA First horse-like animal, *Hyracotherium*.

c.20 MYA Generally cooler climate and sea levels fall.

5 MYA End of the Miocene epoch; first hominids appear.

During the Jurassic period many new dinosaurs appeared, both meat-eating and plant-eating, while marine and freshwater turtles and crocodiles spread around the world. Flying pterosaurs took to the air; they had larger brains than many dinosaurs and some may have had fur, to keep them warm. The first known bird lived about 150 million years ago; scientists have named it *Archaeopteryx* ("ancient wing"), and they believe that it was closely related to the dinosaurs. Unlike modern birds, the first bird had teeth, clawed fingers, and a bony tail.

During the Cretaceous period, when the continent of South America separated from Africa, flowering plants arose. By the end of the period many of the world's forests were full of deciduous, broad-leaved trees, and the first grasses appeared. Then, about 65 million years ago, came a mass extinction: the dinosaurs died out, along with ichthyosaurs, pterosaurs, and ammonites.

Small mammals had existed throughout the Mesozoic era, and they grew bigger and flourished in the first epoch of the Tertiary period, (called the Paleocene). In the next epoch – the Eocene – elephants, whales, rodents, carnivores, and higher primates all appeared, as well as many orders of birds. There were large, flightless birds on land, while water birds caught fish in the sea. Monkeys appeared in the Oligocene epoch, and in the following Miocene apes and horses spread. At the end of the Miocene and beginning of the Pliocene epoch (6–4 MYA), by which time the world's flora (plant life) was similar to that of today, the first hominids appeared on earth.

1. Deinonychus ("terrible claw") was a meat-eating dinosaur that lived over 100 million years ago.

2. Flowering plants first appeared in the Cretaceous period.

3. The first platypus swam in streams more than 100 million years ago, and this egg-laying mammal still exists today.

The first mammals

During the Permian and early Triassic periods, a group of animals which we call mammal-like reptiles became dominant. Some were very small, but others were as large as a modern rhinoceros. The so-called mammal-like reptiles died out, to be replaced by their descendants – the first true mammals – by the end of the Triassic. These mammals were very small, and most probably stayed in burrows during the day. They came out to feed at night when the larger dinosaurs were asleep.

Continental drift: by the late Cretaceous period, the early Atlantic Ocean spread northward, and shallow seas covered parts of North America, eastern Europe, and northern Africa.

This strange hoofed mammal, called Macrauchenia, *lived in South America during the Pliocene epoch. The position of the nostril holes in its skull have led scientists to believe that it had a short, elephant-like trunk.*

Alphadon, *an early mammal that lived in the later Cretaceous period.*

Primates appear

Today's primates – the highest order of mammals – include lemurs, monkeys, apes, and humans. Scientists believe that the earliest animals in this order appeared during the first epoch of the Tertiary period. By about 50 million years ago early primates had the characteristic features of grasping hands, an enlarged brain area, a short snout, and eyes at the front of the skull.

The map below shows the shape and position of continents during the Miocene epoch (24–5 million years ago). During this period grasslands spread as the climate in many parts of the world became drier.

This restored skeleton shows the tree-climbing, lemur-like primate, Smilodectes, *which lived about 50 million years ago.*

Artwork reconstruction of an Ardipithecus.

Hominids

We call the humanlike creatures that belong to our animal family hominids. They became separate from other primate families some time between 6 and 4 million years ago. We call the earliest hominid an *Ardipithecus* ("ground ape"). It was about the size of a modern chimpanzee, with a shorter muzzle than other apes and a brain less than half the size of a modern human's. *Ardipithecus* probably still lived in the trees most of the time.

c.5 million years ago The first hominids appear, in Africa.

4.4 million years ago Age of the oldest hominid fossil found.

3.2 million years ago Age of the famous *Australopithecus* *afarensis* fossil named Lucy, found in Ethiopia, Africa.

2.3–1.9 million years ago *Homo habilis* makes tools.

Human Evolution

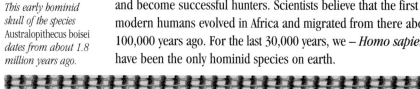

Modern humans are descended from apelike creatures that lived in Africa several million years ago. Some time between 6 and 4 million years ago, the humanlike creatures that we call hominids became separate from the apes, the family of primates that includes modern chimpanzees, gorillas, and orangutans. Hominids stood upright and walked on two legs; there were many different kinds. Over millions of years they learned to make stone tools, use fire, and become successful hunters. Scientists believe that the first modern humans evolved in Africa and migrated from there about 100,000 years ago. For the last 30,000 years, we – *Homo sapiens* – have been the only hominid species on earth.

This early hominid skull of the species Australopithecus boisei *dates from about 1.8 million years ago.*

This flint blade was made toward the end of the Paleolithic, or Old Stone Age, which finished about 70,000 years ago.

Most scientists believe that human beings and apes share a common ancestor. The ancestors of humans, called hominids, began evolving separately from the apes about 6 to 4 million years ago.

It is generally believed that all hominids first appeared in east Africa. The oldest-known hominid, *Ardipithecus ramidus*, lived 4.4 million years ago; its fossil remains were found in Ethiopia. It probably walked upright on two legs, as did the slightly later *Australopithecus afarensis* (4.2–3.9 million years ago). There were at least seven separate species of australopithecines (or "southern apes"). By 3 million years ago

1 *Ardipithecus ramidus*
2 *Australopithecus anamensis*
3 *Australopithecus afarensis*
4 *Australopithecus africanus*

5 *Australopithecus ethiopicus*
6 *Australopithecus garhi*
7 *Australopithecus boisei*
8 *Australopithecus robustus*

9 *Homo rudolfensis*
10 *Homo habilis*
11 *Homo ergaster*
12 *Homo erectus*

13 *Homo antecessor*
14 *Homo heidelbergensis / neanderthalensis*
15 *Homo sapiens*

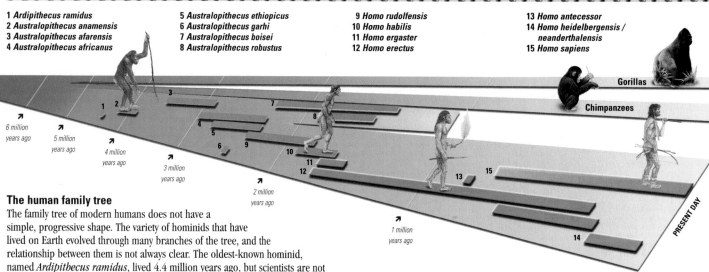

Gorillas

Chimpanzees

6 million years ago

5 million years ago

4 million years ago

3 million years ago

2 million years ago

1 million years ago

PRESENT DAY

The human family tree

The family tree of modern humans does not have a simple, progressive shape. The variety of hominids that have lived on Earth evolved through many branches of the tree, and the relationship between them is not always clear. The oldest-known hominid, named *Ardipithecus ramidus*, lived 4.4 million years ago, but scientists are not sure of its exact place in the family tree, or even if it definitely walked upright.

Early humans may often have gathered together to make their stone tools. A tool usually had a chipped sharp end for cutting, and a smooth blunt end for holding in the palm of the hand.

Making tools

Early hominids probably used pointed sticks and sharp stones to probe for insects and other food. Then, about 2.5 million years ago, according to the latest discoveries, they started making specialist tools from selected materials. The first choppers were made by hitting a core stone with a hammerstone so that flakes of the core were removed to create a sharp cutting edge. Other tools gradually appeared, including hand axes and knives. Later humans learned to attach wooden handles to the stones.

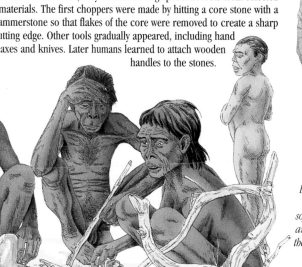

This beautiful spear-thrower was carved from a reindeer's antler. It was used as a hunting weapon for launching spears, sending them much farther than an unaided throw of the hand.

Double-sided choppers.

By about 500,000 years ago hominids had discovered that they could use a softer material than stone, such as bone, antler, or wood, to chip smaller flakes off the core stone. This enabled them to make a chopper, or hand ax, with a much sharper edge.

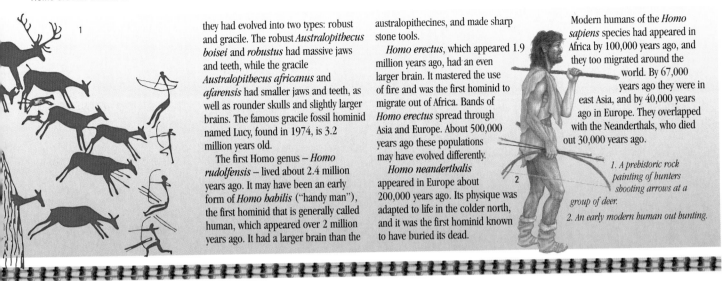

1.9 million–250,000 years ago
Homo erectus uses fire.

800,000 years ago Age of *Homo antecessor* fossils from Spain.

200,000 years ago Neanderthals appear in Europe.

100,000 years ago Modern humans migrate from Africa.

c.30,000 years ago Neanderthals die out.

they had evolved into two types: robust and gracile. The robust *Australopithecus boisei* and *robustus* had massive jaws and teeth, while the gracile *Australopithecus africanus* and *afarensis* had smaller jaws and teeth, as well as rounder skulls and slightly larger brains. The famous gracile fossil hominid named Lucy, found in 1974, is 3.2 million years old.

The first Homo genus – *Homo rudolfensis* – lived about 2.4 million years ago. It may have been an early form of *Homo habilis* ("handy man"), the first hominid that is generally called human, which appeared over 2 million years ago. It had a larger brain than the australopithecines, and made sharp stone tools.

Homo erectus, which appeared 1.9 million years ago, had an even larger brain. It mastered the use of fire and was the first hominid to migrate out of Africa. Bands of *Homo erectus* spread through Asia and Europe. About 500,000 years ago these populations may have evolved differently.

Homo neanderthalis appeared in Europe about 200,000 years ago. Its physique was adapted to life in the colder north, and it was the first hominid known to have buried its dead.

Modern humans of the *Homo sapiens* species had appeared in Africa by 100,000 years ago, and they too migrated around the world. By 67,000 years ago they were in east Asia, and by 40,000 years ago in Europe. They overlapped with the Neanderthals, who died out 30,000 years ago.

1. A prehistoric rock painting of hunters shooting arrows at a group of deer.

2. An early modern human out hunting.

Using fire

Homo erectus, or "upright man," who lived 1.9 million to 250,000 years ago, may have been the first hominid to master the use of fire. This major development must have greatly improved the hominids' quality of life. Fire provided warmth, which helped survival in colder climates. It was also used for cooking meat, making it more digestible. Fire also offered protection against ferocious animals such as lions and leopards. The hearth (left) would have been the focal point of a hominid shelter.

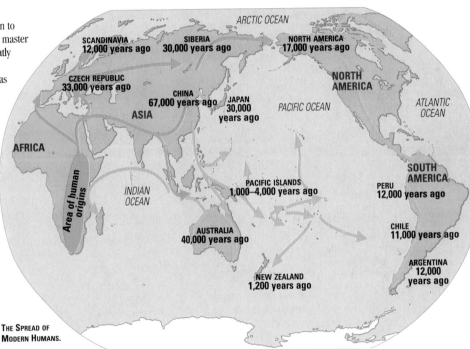

THE SPREAD OF MODERN HUMANS.

ARCTIC OCEAN

SCANDINAVIA **12,000 years ago**
SIBERIA **30,000 years ago**
NORTH AMERICA **17,000 years ago**

CZECH REPUBLIC **33,000 years ago**
NORTH AMERICA

CHINA **67,000 years ago**
JAPAN **30,000 years ago**
PACIFIC OCEAN
ATLANTIC OCEAN

ASIA

AFRICA

Area of human origins

INDIAN OCEAN

PACIFIC ISLANDS **1,000–4,000 years ago**

SOUTH AMERICA

PERU **12,000 years ago**

AUSTRALIA **40,000 years ago**

CHILE **11,000 years ago**

ARGENTINA **12,000 years ago**

NEW ZEALAND **1,200 years ago**

Right: An ape's skeleton has much longer forelimbs than a human's, and a more protruding muzzle.

Walking upright

The skeletons of humans and apes are very similar in their general distribution of bones. But when the early hominids (right) began to walk on two legs, some important changes occurred. The feet became arched so that they could absorb impact and keep balance when walking upright. The pelvis became shorter and wider, to help carry upper body weight, and the shallower ribcage suited the upright stance. The head was held high and was more rounded.

Peopling the world

Most scientists believe that early humans first appeared in Africa and migrated from there to populate the other continents. The first migration probably took place about 1.8 million years ago, when bands of *Homo erectus* began spreading across Asia and Europe. Their descendants all became extinct. *Homo sapiens* – modern humans – started migrating from Africa about 100,000 years ago and spread right across the globe.

Early homes

Some early humans lived in caves, especially near the mouths, where it was not too cold, dark, or damp. Others sheltered beneath overhanging rocks (right). They suspended a canopy of animal skins on a wooden framework, which was held in place using holes cut into the rock. Shelters were also made in the open air from brushwood and turf. In Africa a circle of stones that is thought to have marked the base of a brushwood hut built by early humans has been dated to about 1.8 million years ago.

SEE ALSO
p. 16 BECOMING HUMAN
p. 18 THE NEOLITHIC REVOLUTION

This pottery water jug decorated with a human head dates from the ancient Chinese Yangshao culture (c.3100–1700 BC).

MAJOR DATES

c.100,000 years ago Modern humans *(Homo sapiens)* migrate from Africa.

45,000 years ago Date of the oldest-known musical instrument (a flute) found in Africa.

c.40,000 years ago Modern humans *(Homo sapiens)* reach Europe from Asia.

c.35,000 years ago Humans called Cro-Magnons (after the location where their remains were first found, in France) live in Europe.

32,000–14,000 years ago Period of cave art in Europe, especially France and Spain.

c.30,000 years ago Paintings made in Chauvet cave, in France (found in 1994); the first Paleolithic Venuses are made.

20,000–17,000 years ago About 600 paintings and 1,500 engravings made in Lascaux cave, in France (found in 1940).

c.10,500 BC Jomon pottery made in Japan by hunter-gatherers.

c.6000 BC Farming villages develop in Mesopotamia.

c.3500 BC Towns expand into city-states in Sumer (southern Mesopotamia).

Below left: The so-called Venus of Willendorf *was found in Austria and dates from 30,000 to 25,000 BC. It was carved from limestone.*

Left: This dancing figure comes from the Predynastic Period in ancient Egypt (c.5500–3150 BC.)

BECOMING HUMAN

The development of many of the characteristics and abilities that we think of as human may have begun shortly before members of our species began moving from Africa to the rest of the world. The most intriguing of the abilities is the use of language, but little is known of when and how humans developed speech. About 40,000 years ago there was a rapid improvement in tool-making, as stone tools became more refined. Soon afterward, our ancestors began sculpting and painting the first works of art, many of which have only recently been rediscovered. Some of these artworks may have had religious meaning, as artifacts were soon being buried with the dead in graves. This suggests that humans were thinking about ideas beyond day-to-day survival.

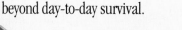

This pottery bowl was made in prehistoric times by the Mimbres people of present-day New Mexico, USA. Painted ceremonial bowls were placed in tombs, usually over the dead person's head.

Early religion

Rock paintings and evidence of burial ceremonies suggest that prehistoric humans held some kind of religious beliefs many tens of thousands of years ago. But experts believe that some form of religion was practiced in the lower period of the Old Stone Age, more than 80,000 years ago. The beginnings of religion may have arisen out of fear and wonder at natural events, such as storms, earthquakes, birth, and death. Our human ancestors may have explained these natural events as the actions of spirits, which they came to worship as gods.

People must have used some form of communication when they were out hunting or performing other tasks that required co-operation between several individuals. Communal activities helped the development of language.

In early burials the dead body was often laid on one side, with the legs drawn up.

Burial

Humans began to make special graves for their dead during the middle period of the Old Stone Age, which began about 80,000 years ago. Early graves were made by the Neanderthals, who died out about 30,000 years ago. The performance of burial is seen as an important advance for prehistoric humans because it suggests that they believed in some form of soul or life after death.

Figure of a sorcerer disguised as an animal, from the Trois Frères cave in France. The figure has an owl's face, a reindeer's antlers, and a horse's tail.

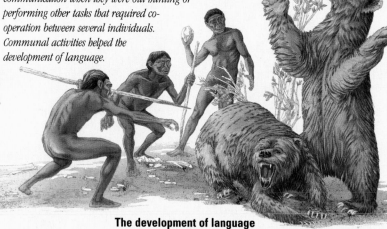

Mother goddesses

Some of the earliest works of art were small statues of women, which are often called Paleolithic Venuses. Dating from at least 25,000 years ago, they have been found at sites all over Europe, from the Pyrenees mountains to Russia. They are probably evidence of a widespread religious cult but their exact meaning and purpose is unknown.

The development of language

There is no record of prehistoric language. Language may have developed among early members of our species of modern humans from sounds such as grunts and hoots. Vocal communication then became more complex as human speech organs developed. Some experts believe that the close physical relationship between a mother and her child may have led her to use sounds to warn the child of danger.

This man, known as "Ginger" because of the color of his hair, was buried in the desert sands of Egypt more than 5,000 years ago.

During the last Ice Age a man was buried wearing this shell necklace.

Portable art

The experience of tool-making meant that early humans were expert carvers. About 30,000 years ago some prehistoric people began carving human and animal figures that they could carry around with them. Some of the earliest were the female figurines shown opposite. Other early artists decorated tools and weapons, such as the spear-thrower (lower right).

Grave goods

Many ancient tombs contain pots, jewelry, weapons, clothing, food, and many other objects. These grave goods show that early humans believed that a person continued to exist in some way after death, and they were probably placed there to help the dead person in the next life.

Right: This ivory statuette shows a figure with a cat's head and a human body. It was carved more than 30,000 years ago. The artist has shown great technical skill and the ability to express feelings.

Above: This horse, found in Germany, was carved in amber, which was often used to make ornaments and jewelry.

Reconstruction of a prehistoric painter's "palette," with a selection of instruments and colors. Minerals were crushed to powder and then mixed with water before being applied to a rock surface.

Left: This ironstone cobble was found in a cave that was inhabited by australopithecine hominids three million years ago. The stone was worn away by dripping water, and may have been carried to the cave by a hominid because it looked like a human face.

In prehistoric times, hunters carved decorated spear-throwers from reindeer antlers. This one was found in a cave in the Pyrenees mountains.

Prehistoric artists used flaming torches and animal-fat lamps to light up dark caves. They may have built wooden scaffolding to reach high walls.

Cave paintings

Humans first decorated the walls and roofs of caves at least 30,000 years ago. The earliest artists painted woolly mammoths, bison, deer, horses, and oxen. The animals were well observed and sensitively drawn. The human figure only started to appear about 12,000 years ago. The meaning of the cave paintings has intrigued scholars. Many believe that the paintings were connected with some form of religious or magical ceremony.

Sheep and goats were among the first animals to be domesticated.

KEY DATES

c.10,000 BC Hunter-gatherers in Syria harvest wild cereals.
c.9000 BC Flocks of wild sheep are managed in the Zagros mountains.
c.9000 BC Wild cereals cultivated in the Near East.
c.8000 BC End of the last Ice Age.
c.8000 BC Wheat and barley domesticated in the Near East.
c.6500 BC Rice is cultivated in the Yangtze valley in China.
c.6000 BC Copper and textiles being made in Çatal Hüyük.
c.5000 BC Irrigation first used by farmers in Mesopotamia.
c.3800 BC First bronze smelted in the Near East.
c.3000 BC Copper and silk being made in China.
c.2000 BC Farming begins in South America.

The origins of farming

The earliest farming sites have been found in the Near East: in Mesopotamia, the Zagros Mountains, Anatolia (modern Turkey), northern Syria, and along the Jordan River. Farming emerged in these areas around 10,000 to 12,000 years ago. Subsequently, agriculture also appeared in other regions, including the north China plain, the Indus River Valley in northern India, Southeast Asia, the Sahara, the Nile Valley, and parts of North and South America. Farming spread all over the world. It took on many different forms, depending on the plants and animals that were available locally.

THE NEOLITHIC REVOLUTION

By about 10,000 years ago some people had begun to cultivate plants for food rather than gathering wild varieties. They had also domesticated some animals, such as sheep and goats, which they kept to provide them with meat, milk, hides, and wool. These early farmers began to live in one place for long periods of time or even permanently. Their first small settlements were the world's first villages and, as these grew in size, they became the first towns. The change from living as nomadic hunters and gatherers to becoming settled farmers was a very gradual process, occurring over many thousands of years. Despite the slowness, archeologists refer to this time as a "revolution" because it radically changed how people lived, and eventually led to the development of civilization.

Grain
Pestle   Mortar

This painted and glazed pot was made in China by people of the Yangshao culture (c.3100–1700 BC).

Pottery

Pottery is heavy and easy to break, so it is not surprising that its appearance coincides with the origins of farming when people began to live in one place. The first potter's wheels were in use by about 6,500 years ago. Special kilns, like the reconstruction above, were dug into the ground so that the pots could be fired.

Wood was shaped into a sickle and pieces of flint or bone inserted into it to make an early sickle for harvesting crops.

Neolithic craftspeople produced tools for farming, utensils for daily life (such as pots and pans for cooking, and knives and scrapers for preparing animal skins), jewelry, and leather sandals, among other things. Many were highly skilled and made finely decorated items that were probably used for ceremonies. This flint knife (right) with a carved ivory handle was made in ancient Egypt over 6,000 years ago.

Early varieties of barley, wheat, and oats were cultivated in the Near East. In China, rice and millet were more common. The most suitable local plants were domesticated in each region.

A great leap forward took place in the Near East in about 6000 BC when people began to use metals to make tools. This early bronze vessel was found in the Judean desert in modern Israel.

Social organization

Farming is hard work. At planting and harvest times everybody had to work long hours in the fields to ensure that the group would produce enough food. The farmers also had to store their food and protect it from pests and thieves. They had to refrain from eating all their supplies when their was plenty, making them last from one season to the next. All of this called for planning, strict social organization, and personal and group discipline.

This Neolithic rock painting from Jordan shows three men herding their sheep into an enclosure.

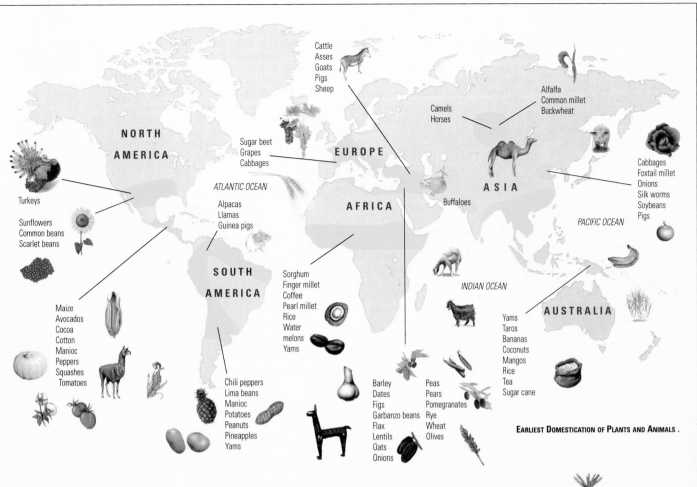

Cattle
Asses
Goats
Pigs
Sheep

Alfalfa
Common millet
Buckwheat

Camels
Horses

NORTH
AMERICA

Sugar beet
Grapes
Cabbages

EUROPE

Cabbages
Foxtail millet
Onions
Silk worms
Soybeans
Pigs

ATLANTIC OCEAN

ASIA

AFRICA

Buffaloes

PACIFIC OCEAN

Turkeys

Sunflowers
Common beans
Scarlet beans

Alpacas
Llamas
Guinea pigs

SOUTH
AMERICA

Sorghum
Finger millet
Coffee
Pearl millet
Rice
Water
melons
Yams

INDIAN OCEAN

Yams
Taros
Bananas
Coconuts
Mangos
Rice
Tea
Sugar cane

AUSTRALIA

Maize
Avocados
Cocoa
Cotton
Manioc
Peppers
Squashes
Tomatoes

Chili peppers
Lima beans
Manioc
Potatoes
Peanuts
Pineapples
Yams

Barley
Dates
Figs
Garbanzo beans
Flax
Lentils
Oats
Onions

Peas
Pears
Pomegranates
Rye
Wheat
Olives

EARLIEST DOMESTICATION OF PLANTS AND ANIMALS .

From village to city

As farming villages became more efficient at producing food, they grew in size and population. Gradually some people were freed from farming duties to take up specialized trades, such as tool-making and store-keeping. Over time, trading links were established, and these gradually produced even more wealth. Many villages grew into towns and a few of them became cities, with wealthy priest-kings and a small court ruling over a large population of mostly poor craftspeople in the city and farmers in the surrounding countryside. Some of these city-states became more and more powerful, eventually establishing refined civilizations and far-reaching empires.

Reconstruction of the Neolithic farming village of Banpo, in northern China. The thatched houses were grouped around a large central meeting house.

Çatal Hüyük

Çatal Hüyük, in present-day Turkey, was one of the oldest cities in the world. Founded about 8,000 years ago, it had a population of around 5,000 people and covered an area of about 26 acres (11 hectares). As the reconstruction (left) shows, the entrances to the houses were on the roofs and the different levels of the dwellings were connected by portable wooden ladders.

Household utensils found in the ruins of Çatal Hüyük.

Ancient Worlds

10,000 BC–AD 500

The earliest civilizations arose in river valleys in Africa and Asia. The Sumerians built some of the world's first cities between the Tigris and Euphrates rivers in western Asia over 6,000 years ago. Over the following millennia towns and cities appeared in the Nile Valley in Africa, along the Yellow River in China, and in the Indus Valley in present-day northern India and Pakistan. These "Old World" civilizations may well have been in contact with one another, exchanging merchandise and ideas along well-established trade routes. At slightly later dates, magnificent urban civilizations, including those of the Mayas, Aztecs, and Incas, arose in the Americas.

The Mediterranean World
Civilization in Europe was dominated by the peoples of the southeast for more than 2,500 years. It began with the Minoans on Crete in around 2200 BC. They were replaced by the Mycenaeans (c.1450 BC) from the Greek mainland. Their civilization ended abruptly around 200 years later and a "dark age" followed until the rise of the brilliant classical Greek civilization in 500 BC. The Greeks were replaced by the Romans whose empire controlled Europe for another 500 years.

Ancient India
p. 48 *The Indus Valley civilization developed in present-day northern India and Pakistan from around 2600 BC.*

Ancient China
p. 52 *Farming communities developed along the Yellow and Yangtze rivers in China from 6500 BC. The first Chinese dynasty – the Shang – ruled over a large area of China from about 1766 BC.*

The Americas
p. 60–62 *People crossed the land bridge from northern Asia into Alaska around 13,000 BC. They settled throughout North and South America, forming splendid civilizations in the central and southern regions.*

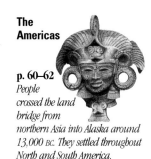

Ancient Africa
p. 64 *Farming began in the Sahara area (much wetter at that time) around 6000 BC. Ancient Egypt was the earliest African civilization, but other empires also developed farther south. Around 700 BC the Nok people made expressive figures of humans and animals.*

World Religions
p. 66 *Many of the world's major religions developed during this time. Judaism and Christianity began in western Asia, Hinduism and Buddhism in India, and Taoism and Confucianism in China.*

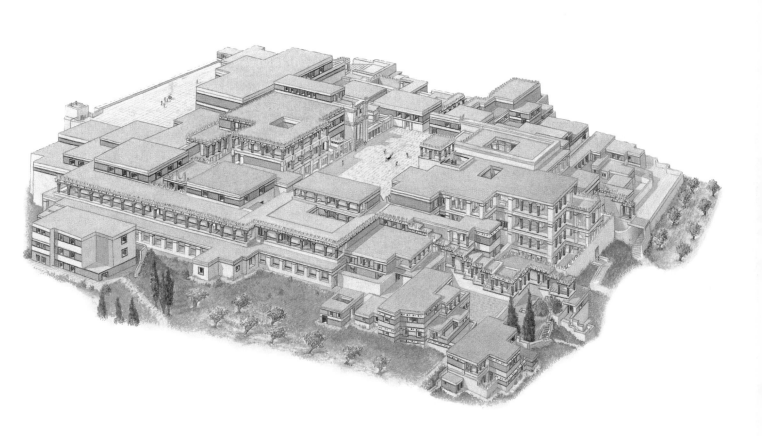

c.6000 BC First farmers in Mesopotamia.

c.4500 BC Farming villages develop into small towns.

c.3500 BC Towns expand into city-states.

Development of cuneiform script for keeping records.

c.2700 BC Kings become rulers of Mesopotamian cities.

Sumer and Akkad

About 8,000 years ago, people started to settle in the fertile region between the Euphrates and Tigris rivers. This area was later called Mesopotamia ("land between two rivers") by the ancient Greeks and is today part of Iraq. As the population grew, agricultural settlements developed into separate city-states, giving rise to the world's first urban civilization. The Sumerians were the first people to use wheels; they invented the cartwheel and the potters' wheel. They also developed one of the first writing systems and an early code of law. In time conflicts developed between the city-states and Sumer was conquered by the kingdom of Akkad to the north. Eventually the region was subdued by the expanding Babylonian Empire.

1

Agriculture created the wealth that led to the emergence of the first city-states. As farmers learned how to grow crops for the following year, settlements developed. People no longer needed to move each year to keep themselves and their families fed. They learned how to domesticate animals, store food, and grow surplus crops that could be traded for goods such as weapons, textiles, and pottery. The settlements grew and developed into city-states.

The oldest and largest Sumerian city was called Uruk. It was founded sometime before 3500 BC, by which time it had a population of 10,000. By 2700 BC this number had risen to about 50,000. Because the farmers were successful at producing more food than they immediately needed, other members of the community were able to practice specialized occupations. Uruk soon had sculptors, potters, bakers, stonemasons, bronze-casters, brewers, and weavers. Written records also first appeared in these settlements: by about 4000 BC a system of pictographic writing had developed in Mesopotamia. By 3000 BC there were at least 12 Sumerian city-states, including Ur, Lagash, Umma, and Kish.

Sumerian cities

The Sumerians lived in walled cities, which were surrounded by villages, small settlements, and farmland. Each city had its own temple, where people believed the city-state's main god lived. City dwellers lived in mud-brick houses that were grouped around an open courtyard. Sumerians were skilled craftworkers and traders. Textile workers wove fine cloth, while other craftsmen made pottery, jewelry, and weapons.

Ancient coastline

MESOPOTAMIA AND ITS MAJOR CENTERS.

A Mesopotamian winged demon.

A bas-relief showing the god Baal.

A four-winged king or god.

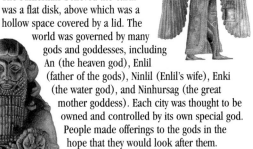

A reconstruction of the ziggurat of Ur, which was built about 2100 BC. The remains of earlier temples are almost certainly buried inside the structure.

Gods and goddesses

The Sumerians believed the earth was a flat disk, above which was a hollow space covered by a lid. The world was governed by many gods and goddesses, including An (the heaven god), Enlil (father of the gods), Ninlil (Enlil's wife), Enki (the water god), and Ninhursag (the great mother goddess). Each city was thought to be owned and controlled by its own special god. People made offerings to the gods in the hope that they would look after them.

Ziggurats

Early Sumerian temples were rectangular buildings erected on low platforms, all made of mud brick. When a new temple was needed, it was built on top of the ruins of the old one. Over the years the temples developed into stepped towers called ziggurats (from an Assyrian word meaning "pinnacle"). The ziggurat of Ur was built by King Ur-Nammu and dedicated to the Sumerian moon goddess, Nanna. At ground level it measures over 140 by 200 ft (62 by 43 m), and it is almost 65 ft (20 m) high.

Sargon of Akkad

According to legend, Sargon I of Akkad (reigned 2334–2279 BC) was born to a goddess who put him in the Euphrates River in a reed basket. He was supposedly found and raised by a gardener's family. This legend is very similar to the story of Moses. We do know that Sargon became cup-bearer to the king of the city of Kish, then overthrew him and took his place. His capital city of Akkad has not yet been identified by archeologists.

Left: This bronze head, found at Nineveh, is thought to represent Sargon, though it may be his grandson Naram-Sin.

Right: In this bas-relief, Gilgamesh is holding a whip and a lion, symbols of dominance and power.

Gilgamesh

Gilgamesh was probably the hero-king of Uruk about 2750 BC. So brave and strong was he reputed to be that legends about him were passed down the generations. He was immortalized in the epic poem *Gilgamesh*, composed around 2000 BC, thought to be the first great poem.

2334 BC Sargon unifies Akkad.
2200 BC Collapse of Akkad.

2112 BC Ur-Nammu founds Third Dynasty of Ur.

2034 BC Sumer attacked by Amorites.

2004 BC Ur sacked by Elamites.
1787 BC Hammurabi, Amorite

king of Babylon, conquers Uruk and Isin.

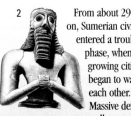

From about 2900 BC on, Sumerian civilization entered a troubled phase, when the growing cities began to war with each other. Massive defensive walls were built around the cities, and the most powerful centers – Kish, Lagash, Umma, Ur, and Uruk – conquered neighboring towns and villages and became small kingdoms.

The rulers of the city-states had both political and religious power and more authoritarian forms of leadership began to appear from about 2700 BC. When war broke out, a city's council of elders appointed a *lugal*, or "big man," to lead the city into war. As wars became more common, the "big men" began to control the daily life of their cities and in time became kings.

For some time Kish dominated the region; about 2600 BC power passed to Ur and Uruk; in 2500 BC Lagash became dominant; and then about 2350 BC King Lugalzagesi of Umma conquered the other cities and made his capital at Uruk. This unified the Sumerian cities for the first time.

In 2334 BC Sargon I of Akkad united the Akkadian cities to the north of Sumer and went on to conquer Sumer. Sargon became the first person to unite all of Mesopotamia into one great empire. This Akkadian Empire reached its peak under Sargon's grandson, Naram-Sin (reigned 2254–2218 BC), but it collapsed around 2200 BC. The cities regained their independence for about a hundred years, until King Ur-Nammu, who established the Third Dynasty of Ur in 2112 BC, founded a new empire in the region. In 2034 BC Sumer was attacked by nomadic Amorites from the Syrian desert. The empire finally fell in 2004 BC, when Ur was sacked by the Elamites, who came from the plains to the east of the Tigris River. The Amorites continued to dominate the region for the next two centuries, until Hammurabi, the Amorite king of Babylon, marched south and conquered the cities of Uruk and Isin in 1787 BC. Ancient Sumer was now part of the Babylonian Empire.

1. Tiny statue of a boat from Mesopotamia.

2. Statue of person praying, from the temple of Abu, god of vegetation, in southern Mesopotamia.

3. Bronze statue of a bull with a human head.

4. Ishtar, the Mesopotamian goddess of love, who fell in love with King Gilgamesh.

The King List

About 2000 BC a scribe made a list of all the kings of Sumer from earliest times. It begins: "When kingship was lowered from heaven, kingship was first in Eridu." Eridu was a Sumerian city near the Euphrates River and Ur. The Sumerians clearly thought that their kings were appointed by the gods. The King List also refers to a great flood, and this legend was later passed on to the Babylonians and the Hebrews.

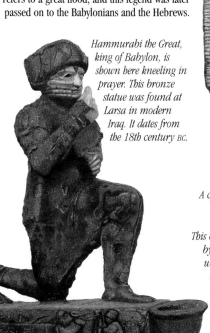

Hammurabi the Great, king of Babylon, is shown here kneeling in prayer. This bronze statue was found at Larsa in modern Iraq. It dates from the 18th century BC.

Above: This is one of several surviving copies of the Sumerian King List.

A cylinder seal from the 18th century BC.

This clay tablet has been rolled by a cylinder seal. The seals were made of carved stone, ivory, or metal. They were rolled across fresh clay, so that they left a relief of pictures and writing.

Below: The Standard of Ur, dating from 2600 BC, is decorated with mosaics made of shell and lapis lazuli. This panel shows a battle scene. The Sumerian chariots are being pulled by donkeys and wild asses.

The invention of writing

From about 4000 BC on, Sumerians used pictograms to keep records. Gradually these were replaced by symbols used to represent the sounds and syllables of a word rather than the idea it conveyed. The early pictograms were carved onto stone. Later, from about 3500 BC on, scribes kept records by making vertical, horizontal, and oblique strokes on a damp clay tablet using a wedgelike section of a reed. The tablets were then left to dry in the sun. The script is called cuneiform, meaning "wedge-shaped." By 2700 BC there were libraries of clay tablets in Sumer.

This early cuneiform tablet shows details of the amount of barley needed to make beer, malt, and other products.

SEE ALSO
p. 24 BABYLONIA AND ASSYRIA
p. 26 ANCIENT EGYPT
p. 28 THE ANCIENT HEBREWS
p. 36 ANCIENT PERSIA

War and peace

The Standard of Ur is a wooden box with inlaid panels. It was found in a royal tomb, but its purpose is unknown. It may have been part of a musical instrument. On one side, the standard shows scenes of Sumerian life during peacetime, including farmers bringing cattle to their rulers at a banquet. The other side shows scenes of war, like those below.

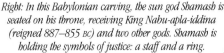

Right: In this Babylonian carving, the sun god Shamash is seated on his throne, receiving King Nabu-apla-iddina (reigned 887–855 BC) and two other gods. Shamash is holding the symbols of justice: a staff and a ring.

The Code of Hammurabi

King Hammurabi established a famous code of laws based on older collections of Sumerian and Akkadian laws, which he revised and expanded. In the code, Hammurabi promised to treat conquered peoples justly. The code also dealt with witchcraft, military service, land, family laws, and wages. Stone carvings of the code were found in the ruins of Susa, capital of the ancient kingdom of Elam. An Elamite king had taken them there as a war trophy.

Above: A stela, or stone pillar, on which the Code of Hammurabi is inscribed.

A bronze statuette from the city of Larsa, which was overpowered by Hammurabi in 1761 BC.

The Hanging Gardens of Babylon were built about 600 BC on the orders of King Nebuchadnezzar II. It was said that the king had them built for his homesick young wife, Amytis, to remind her of her homeland in the mountains of Media.

The god Marduk

Marduk was the chief god of the Babylonians. As the city became the most powerful in Mesopotamia, Marduk became the most important god. His power was said to lie in his wisdom, which he used to help good people and to punish evil. The king often visited Marduk's Temple to gain the god's approval.

Right: A Kudurru, sculpted with the symbols of the main gods of Mesopotamia in the 12th century BC.

The city of Babylon

In the 6th century BC, under Nebuchadnezzar II, Babylon was rebuilt and quickly became a wealthy, magnificent city. The Greek historian Herodotus visited Babylon in the following century and described it as a place of splendor and sophistication. The temples and palaces were decorated with colored, glazed bricks. The king's palace was built around five courtyards, near the Hanging Gardens.

PLAN OF ANCIENT BABYLON.

1 Ishtar Gate
2 Emah Temple
3 Ramparts
4 Euphrates River
5 Processional Way
6 Tower of Babel
7 Marduk's Temple
8 Lugalgirra Gate
9 Hadad Gate
10 Shamash Gate
11 Urash Gate
12 Enlil Gate
13 Zababa Gate
14 Marduk Gate
15 Sin Gate

The beautiful Ishtar Gate, main entrance to the city of Babylon, was decorated with glazed blue bricks. The bulls represent the weather god, Hadad, and the dragons are symbols of the chief god, Marduk.

The walls of Babylon

The city's fortified walls were built in the time of kings Nabopolassar and his son Nebuchadnezzar II, between 625 and 562 BC. The inner, double wall was surrounded by a moat. The outer wall was also double. Each of the two walls was 23 ft (7 m) thick and more than 7 mi. (12 km) long. The walls made a superb fortification. However, the invading Persians found a way through. They diverted the Euphrates River upstream of the city and entered along the riverbed when the water level was low.

The Hanging Gardens

These famous gardens were included in the ancient list of the Seven Wonders of the World. They were actually watered terraces, full of trees and plants from all over the Babylonian Empire. The top terrace may have been up to 130 ft (40 m) above the ground. Water from the Euphrates River was lifted to the top, possibly by a chain of buckets driven by slaves working a treadmill.

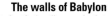

c.1894 BC Samuabum becomes first Amorite king of Babylon.

c.1813–1781 BC Shamshi-Adad rules Ashur, capital of Assyria.

1792–1750 BC Hammurabi reigns over Babylonia.

1595 BC Babylonia invaded by Hittites; Kassites take power.

Babylonia and Assyria

After the fall of Ur, the next 1,500 years of Mesopotamian history were dominated by the Babylonians and the Assyrians. Babylon became the dominant cultural and religious center of the region, though it was often overshadowed by the military might of Assyria. It was a magnificent city, built on the banks of the Euphrates River and protected by huge walls. The Assyrians, from northern Mesopotamia, were great fighters. They built up a huge military organization skilled in siege warfare. After many setbacks they succeeded in expanding their empire to cover a vast area from the Mediterranean to the Persian Gulf. For some time this included Babylonia and its wondrous capital, but in 612 BC they were defeated. Just 73 years later, Babylon fell to the invading Persians.

The ancient Babylonian and Assyrian empires began about 2000 BC. Over the next 1,500 years their histories were closely intertwined. After the fall of the city of Ur in 2004 BC, the city of Babylon, a provincial outpost, quickly grew to become the center of a small kingdom (established about 1894 BC). King Hammurabi (reigned 1792–1750 BC), the sixth king of the First Dynasty of Babylon, made the kingdom much more powerful. In 1787 BC he conquered Uruk and Isin, and 26 years later his army overpowered the city of Larsa. With this victory the Babylonians became rulers of all

This clay tablet, found at Nineveh, tells the Assyrian version of the great flood, in which all the world's evil people were drowned.

THE ASSYRIAN EMPIRE
AT ITS MAXIMUM EXTENT.
The Assyrian Empire expanded rapidly from the 9th century BC on. By 669 BC it extended from the Persian Gulf to the Nile River, covering all of fertile Mesopotamia.

This relief of a leaping lion comes from Nineveh. The Assyrians called the lion "the lord of the desert."

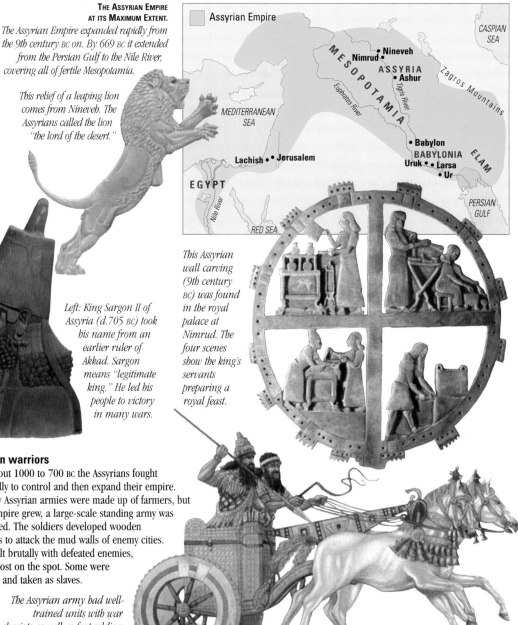

Assyrian Empire

CASPIAN SEA

MESOPOTAMIA

Nineveh
Nimrud
ASSYRIA
Ashur

Zagros Mountains

MEDITERRANEAN SEA

Euphrates River

Tigris River

Babylon
BABYLONIA
Uruk • Larsa
• Ur

ELAM

Lachish • Jerusalem

EGYPT

Nile River

RED SEA

PERSIAN GULF

Assyrian kings

The kings of Assyria believed they were chosen by the gods to rule, and that their land belonged to the sun god, Ashur. Their first capital city was named after Ashur, and the people were named after the city. Assyrian kings had many wives and children, and usually chose one son to be specially educated to rule after their deaths.

Left: King Sargon II of Assyria (d.705 BC) took his name from an earlier ruler of Akkad. Sargon means "legitimate king." He led his people to victory in many wars.

This Assyrian wall carving (9th century BC) was found in the royal palace at Nimrud. The four scenes show the king's servants preparing a royal feast.

Assyrian warriors

From about 1000 to 700 BC the Assyrians fought continually to control and then expand their empire. The early Assyrian armies were made up of farmers, but as the empire grew, a large-scale standing army was introduced. The soldiers developed wooden machines to attack the mud walls of enemy cities. They dealt brutally with defeated enemies, killing most on the spot. Some were captured and taken as slaves.

The Assyrian army had well-trained units with war chariots as well as foot soldiers. Later, cavalry units were introduced.

A reconstruction of the bronze armor plates that the Assyrians wore in battle. Most foot soldiers were armed with bows and arrows, slings, or lances.

c.1220 BC King Tukulti-Ninurta captures Babylon.

612 BC Nineveh sacked; end of Assyrian Empire.

605–562 BC Nebuchadnezzar II builds Hanging Gardens.

587 BC Jerusalem destroyed.

539 BC Cyrus the Great captures Babylon; end of Babylonian Empire.

the earlier Sumerian and Akkadian territory. After Hammurabi's death the empire declined, and in 1595 BC King Samsuditana was brought down by the Hittite invader Mursilis I. This allowed the Kassites from the east to gain power, which they held until 1150 BC.

During this period Assyria, formerly controlled by Babylonia, emerged as an independent state (about 1400 BC). Under King Ashuruballit (reigned 1363–1328) the Assyrians captured Nineveh from the crumbling Mittanian kingdom to the west. Then King Tukulti-Ninurta (reigned 1238–1197 BC)

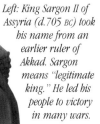

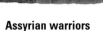

waged war on the Kassites and in about 1220 BC captured Babylon. The Assyrian Empire fell apart again when their king was murdered by his nobles.

Elam, to the east of Mesopotamia, had become powerful, and about 1160 BC conquered most of Babylonia. After a series of wars, a new dynasty of Babylonian kings was established. King Nebuchadnezzar I (reigned 1124–1103 BC) defeated Elam, and his successors worked hard to hold off the Assyrians and the Arameans.

From the 9th century BC on, Assyrian kings often ruled Babylonia, appointing

subkings to govern Babylon. The ferocious Assyrian king, Tiglath-pileser III (reigned 744–727 BC), united most of the region from Egypt to the Persian Gulf. The last Assyrian king, Ashurbanipal (668–627 BC), fought a civil war against his brother, who was subking. In 612 BC the Medes and Babylonians sacked the Assyrian capital of Nineveh, and the Assyrians vanished from history. The Chaldeans from the south took over Babylon and established a new Babylonian dynasty. King Nebuchadnezzar II (reigned 604–562 BC) expanded the kingdom, conquering Syria and

Palestine and destroying Jerusalem in 587 BC. Babylonia's last king, Nabonidus (reigned 555–539 BC), moved to an oasis in the Arabian Desert and left his son Belshazzar in charge. When the Persian king, Cyrus the Great, invaded in 539 BC, Babylon surrendered without a fight and the great empire of Babylonia came to an end.

1. Babylonian world map c.700 BC.

2. Boundary stone from Babylon, with records about land ownership.

3. Statue of the Assyrian god, Lahmu.

c.6000 BC Farming in Nile Valley.
c.3500 BC First towns appear.

c.3150–2686 BC Early Dynastic
Period; King Menes of Upper

Egypt subdues Lower Egypt.
c.2686–2181 BC Old Kingdom

(the age of pyramid building).
c.2181–2040 BC 1st Intermediate

Period. Much famine and chaos.
c.2040–1782 BC Middle Kingdom.

Ancient Egypt

The civilization of ancient Egypt would not have existed without the Nile River. Protected from invaders by deserts to the east and west, people settled along the river's fertile banks. Each year the river flooded, depositing on the sandy fields a thick, black layer of mud that nourished the soil. Farmers learned to plant their crops there. The Egyptians called the fruitful river valley *kemet,* "the black land," and they referred to themselves as *remet-en-kemet,* "the people of the black land." Most years the harvests were good, and the civilization thrived. Egyptian civilization lasted for nearly 3,000 years, and is traditionally divided into three kingdoms – the Old Kingdom, the Middle Kingdom, and the New Kingdom – and three intermediate periods during which 30 dynasties of kings reigned.

The ancient Egyptian civilization emerged in the Nile Valley over 5,000 years ago. During the Predynastic Period, Egypt was divided into Upper Egypt and Lower Egypt. Gradually the people of Lower Egypt adopted the customs of Upper Egypt, and the two were united politically by King Menes about 3150 BC.

During the Early Dynastic Period, rapid technological advances were made in metalworking and stonemasonry, and hieroglyphic writing was already in use. Living conditions also improved and the population increased.

By the beginning of the Old Kingdom, a powerful Egyptian monarchy was fully established. The kings built themselves great pyramids as tombs and monuments to their own power. Then came a period of erratic flooding of the Nile River and a decline in royal power, which led to the First Intermediate Period.

Strong, centralized power was soon restored, however, and during the Middle Kingdom irrigation schemes were extended, overseas trade flourished, and Egypt strengthened its

MEDITERRANEAN SEA

Nile Delta
• Tanis

LOWER EGYPT

Giza •
Memphis •
Saqqara •

RED SEA

Nile River

AUPPER EGYPT

The Nile River rises in the highlands of east Africa, south of the Equator, and flows northward to the Mediterranean Sea.

Thinis •

Thebes •
• Luxor

NUBIA
(to the south)

ANCIENT EGYPT.

The pharaoh

An Egyptian king, or "pharaoh," was all powerful, and his subjects believed he was a living god. His chief duty was to uphold the principles of justice, order, and truth, so that the country would prosper. As High Priest, he honored the gods and goddesses, and built temples to them. As military leader, he was responsible for defeating Egypt's enemies.

The Rosetta stone

The Egyptians invented a form of writing using hieroglyphs, or pictures that stood for objects or sounds. The ability to read Egyptian hieroglyphs was lost until, in AD 1822, a Frenchman named Jean-François Champollion compared three piéces of the same text that had been inscribed in Greek, demotic, and hieroglyphic, on the Rosetta stone (left). By comparing the two known scripts with the hieroglyphs, he was able to decipher them.

Scribes

Scribes, or writers, kept records of trade, crops, animals, and taxes for the government. From age five, boys (usually from wealthy families) went to scribal school, where they learned reading, writing, and math. When trained, they were expected to teach the younger boys.

A burial from the Predynastic Period. The body was placed in dry sand to prevent it from decaying. It was surrounded by pots and jewelry.

Women in ancient Egypt

Egyptian women led freer lives than women in many other places in the ancient world. They could inherit, own, and manage property, make loans, and run their own businesses. Most Egyptian women, however, worked in the home and cared for their children.

The army

A standing army was introduced during the New Kingdom. Soldiers carried a bow and arrows for long-range fighting, and a battle ax with a copper blade for hand-to-hand combat.

Agriculture

Egypt was an agricultural society. Most people worked on the land. Farmers grew flax, wheat, and barley, and made beer by fermenting grain. They also grew grapes to make wine. The grapes were pressed and the juice was left to ferment in large jars for several years. When the wine had matured, it was flavored using spices, honey, or dates.

c.1782–1570 BC 2nd Intermediate Period. The Hyksos seize power.

c.1570–1070 BC New Kingdom.
1279 BC Rameses II fights off

Hittites at Battle of Kadesh.
1182–1151 BC Rameses III rules;

defeats invading Sea Peoples.
1070–332 BC Late Dynastic Period.

332 BC Alexander the Great conquers Egypt.

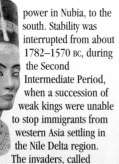

power in Nubia, to the south. Stability was interrupted from about 1782–1570 BC, during the Second Intermediate Period, when a succession of weak kings were unable to stop immigrants from western Asia settling in the Nile Delta region. The invaders, called Hyksos by the Egyptians, arrived in increasing numbers and took control of the Nile Valley for more than a hundred years. They were finally expelled, and the

New Kingdom began.

The strong warrior kings of the early New Kingdom established a large empire, ruling over Palestine and Syria to the northeast and Nubia. They fought off invading Hittites. Later warrior kings, including Rameses III (reigned c.1182–1151 BC), were fully occupied defending Egypt against attacks by bands of people, called "the Sea Peoples," from the north, and by the Libyans from the west. Egypt gradually lost control of its empire, and a period of decline set in.

By the end of the New Kingdom, Egypt was once again ruled from two centers: Tanis in the Nile Delta and Thebes in the

south. More fragmentation followed and the Nubians seized control, followed by the Persians. Then, in 332 BC, Alexander ("the Great") of Macedon (356–323 BC) swept in and annexed Egypt to Greece.

1. Statue of a dancing woman from the Predynastic Period.

2. King Menes, sometimes called Narmer, with the falcon god, Horus.

3. Queen Nefertiti, principal wife of Pharaoh Akhenaten (reigned c.1350–1334 BC).

4. A Middle Kingdom faïence hippopotamus, symbol of the Nile River's fertility.

Union of the gods Ra and Osiris, shown as a person with green skin and a ram's head.

Gods and goddesses

The Egyptians worshiped a great many gods and goddesses. Some, such as Osiris, Horus, Hathor, Isis, Anubis, Thoth, and Bes, were worshiped throughout Egypt. Others were local to Egypt's 42 districts, called "nomes." Each god was represented by a different symbol.

Structure of Khufu's pyramid at Giza.

Entrance.

Passageway later used by tomb raiders.

A chosen animal was often believed to be the living incarnation of a god or goddess. After a life of luxury, the animal was embalmed. This calf mummy comes from Thebes.

The age of pyramids

The Old Kingdom is known as the age of pyramids. Egypt's powerful kings, or pharaohs, prepared for death by building themselves a monumental tomb, usually in the form of a pyramid. They believed that, as gods, they would rule from their tombs and maintain world order after their death. Many of these 4,000-year-old tombs are still standing.

Preparing for the afterlife

The Egyptians believed that if they were good during their lives and respected the gods, they would have an afterlife. They also believed that it was important to preserve a dead person's body, because if the body decayed the person would not attain an afterlife. Priests performed ceremonies to preserve, or "mummify," a body. First they removed the internal organs. Then they covered the body in salt crystals for 40 days to dry it out. Finally it was washed in spices, wrapped in linen, and placed in a coffin, or mummy case.

Funeral goods

The tombs of Egypt's kings and queens were filled with food and treasures for the dead person to use during the afterlife. Over the centuries, tomb raiders have looted many Egyptian tombs.

Funeral mask of the young Pharaoh Tutankhamun (reigned 1334–1325 BC).

Step pyramids

The earliest pyramids were simple stepped structures. The step pyramid of Pharaoh Djoser (reigned 2668–2649) at Saqqara (below) was the first monument to be built of specially cut blocks of stone. The architect Imhotep was later worshiped as a god for this achievement.

Funeral rituals and ceremonies

Many rituals and ceremonies were carried out to ensure that the body passed through the Underworld to the afterlife. A priest wearing the mask of Anubis, the god of the dead, placed the dead person's heart on a scale balanced against a feather, which represented the goddess Maat. If the heart and the feather did not balance, it was believed the dead person was not pure enough to enter the afterlife.

The Great Pyramid at Giza is the largest of all the pyramids. It was built as a tomb for Pharaoh Khufu (Cheops, reigned 2590–2568 BC). In front of it stands the Sphinx.

A body's internal organs were preserved in separate containers, called canopic jars. These were placed next to the coffin in the tomb.

SEE ALSO
p. 28 THE ANCIENT HEBREWS
p. 36 ANCIENT PERSIA
p. 38 THE HELLENISTIC WORLD

c.2000 BC Abraham born in Ur; leads his people to Canaan.

c.1700 BC Hebrews leave Canaan for Egypt.

c.1300 BC Hebrew exodus from Egypt, led by Moses.

c.1200 BC Fighting between Philistines and Israelites.

c.1020 BC Kingdom of Israel formed; Saul chosen as king.

The Ancient Hebrews

The history and religion of the Bible Lands are closely bound together. They center on a tiny piece of land in the eastern Mediterranean now occupied by the states of Israel, Jordan, Lebanon, and Syria. In ancient times, the Holy Land was called Canaan. According to the Old Testament of the Bible, the forefathers of the nation of Israel were the patriarchs: Abraham, Isaac, and Jacob; and Jacob's sons were the ancestors of the 12 tribes of Israel. Many historians think the patriarchal stories are set about 2000 to 1750 BC. At this time there was a rebirth of towns and trade in Canaan, probably stimulated by contact with traders from the great cities of Mesopotamia and Egypt.

Nomadic herders

From ancient times, nomadic herders roamed the arid lands of Canaan with their sheep and goats in search of new pastures. They relied on their animals for milk, meat, and clothing. A traditional festival – the Day of Atonement (Yom Kippur) – dates from this time. On a special day each year Hebrew priests released a goat into the desert as a symbolic way of freeing the people from their sins.

Exodus from Egypt

The Hebrews lived peaceably in Egypt while it was governed by the Hyksos. Then, according to the Bible, a new pharaoh forced them to work as slaves. He ordered his soldiers to drown all Hebrew boys at birth. Moses, a Hebrew boy who was saved by the pharaoh's daughter, later led the Hebrews out of slavery in Egypt. He took them across the Sinai Desert (a 40-year journey) to Canaan, the "Promised Land." It is thought that this exodus (reconstruction, right) took place in the 13th century BC, when Hebrews came to Canaan and started to conquer its cities.

A tiny gold statue of a Hittite king or god, made c.1400 BC. The Hittites controlled the lands north of Canaan, and influenced ancient Hebrew culture.

Abraham and the founding fathers

Abraham's family came from Ur in southern Mesopotamia. About 2000 BC Abraham's father decided to move the family to Haran, to the northwest. There, the Bible tells us, God spoke to Abraham and told him to travel to a new land, where his descendants would become a great nation. Abraham and his son, Isaac, and grandson, Jacob, are known as the Hebrew patriarchs, or founding fathers of the Hebrew nation.

RECONSTRUCTION OF ABRAHAM'S PROBABLE ROUTE.

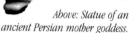

From Ur to Canaan

On his journey from Ur to Canaan, Abraham and his family took their herds of animals and traveled northwest along the Euphrates River to Haran. Then Abraham, his wife Sarah, his nephew Lot, and all their servants headed southwest to Canaan, setting up camp wherever they found water and pasture.

Below: Statue of the Canaanite god, Baal.

Above: Statue of an ancient Persian mother goddess.

Canaan and its gods

Canaan covered roughly the same area as the modern states of Israel, Jordan, Lebanon, and Syria. The Canaanites lived in small city-states. They worshiped many gods, the chief of whom was El, god of the sky. But the most popular god was El's son, Baal, the fertility and weather god, who brought welcome rains to the desert land. All the gods were worshiped at hilltop sites, known as "high places."

Below: A parchment scroll and a terra-cotta jar, in which scrolls were found.

According to the Old Testament, God gave Moses laws by which his people were to live their lives. These were based on Ten Commandments.

Above: This wall painting from about 1900 BC shows Hebrew nomads trading with Egyptians.

Dead Sea Scrolls

In 1947 manuscript scrolls were found in caves at Qumran, on the shores of the Dead Sea. They contained the texts of many Old Testament books, as well as psalms and prophecies. The scrolls were made and written by the members of a Jewish religious sect, probably the Essenes, for their monastery's library. The documents date from about 250 BC. In AD 68 the scrolls were put into terra-cotta jars and hidden from the invading Roman army. About 800 scrolls have now been found.

Ark of the Covenant

This sacred wooden chest, plated with gold (above left), was known as the Ark of the Covenant. Inside it the Hebrews kept the stone tablets inscribed with God's laws. The chest was eventually placed in Solomon's Temple in Jerusalem, the first Hebrew temple, built in the 10th century BC. The mosaic floor (above right) shows religious objects of the time.

Statue of a golden calf, a Canaanite idol that Moses forbade the Hebrews to worship.

SEE ALSO

p. 24 BABYLONIA AND ASSYRIA • p. 26 ANCIENT EGYPT
p. 36 ANCIENT PERSIA • p. 66 MYTH AND RELIGION

c.1006–965 BC David reigns; unites 12 tribes of Israel and makes Jerusalem capital. **c.965–928 BC** Solomon reigns.

928 BC Israel divides in two; Kingdom of Judah in south.

721 BC Assyrians conquer Kingdom of Israel.

587 BC Babylonians conquer Kingdom of Judah.

Palestine

Kingdom of Judah at its greatest extent

Kingdom of Israel at its greatest extent

The Philistines lived in southern Canaan. Another name for the Philistines is the Peleset, from which Palestine takes its name. The Philistines and Hebrews lived side by side for almost 200 years. Then the Hebrews united to defend themselves from Philistine attacks, and about 1020 BC formed a kingdom, called Israel.

The Philistines

After the Egyptians withdrew from Canaan about 1150 BC, the Philistines settled the coastal plain to the south. They took control of the local iron trade, crafting weapons that made them greatly feared. During the 10th century BC, however, King David finally defeated them. They were gradually absorbed into the kingdom of Israel, and by about 600 BC they were no longer a separate people.

Portrait of a Philistine with his people's distinctive headdress, from the Temple of Ramses III in Egypt.

This coffin was probably made by the Philistines, or by another of the "Sea Peoples."

The Phoenicians

The Phoenicians lived along the coast of northern Canaan. They were good sailors (left), trading all over the Mediterranean. During the 17th century BC the Phoenicians invented what is believed to be the earliest alphabet.

Jerusalem

King David made Jerusalem the capital of the Hebrew state of Israel. His son, Solomon, built a great temple and palaces there. After the Israelite kingdoms split, Jerusalem remained the capital of Judah. In 587 BC the Babylonians seized the city, destroyed Solomon's Temple, and took the Jews captive to Babylon. Over fifty years later, when the Persians conquered Babylonia, the Jews were allowed to return.

King David

David succeeded Saul and became the second king of Israel. As a young man he fought and killed the giant Philistine warrior, Goliath. Later his troops defeated the Philistines, among many others. David united the twelve tribes of Hebrews in Israel.

Statue of King David, who ruled Israel for about 40 years.

Reconstruction of Jerusalem during the reign of King Solomon.

Daily life

Most Israelites lived in villages or small towns and worked as farmers. Many families kept sheep and goats, which grazed in the surrounding countryside. Children often helped watch over the animals.

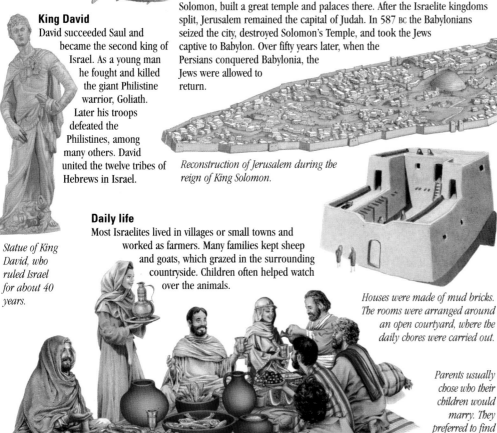

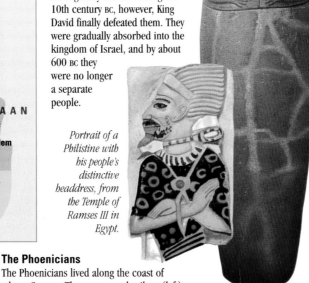

Houses were made of mud bricks. The rooms were arranged around an open courtyard, where the daily chores were carried out.

Parents usually chose who their children would marry. They preferred to find a partner within the same tribe. Weddings were celebrated with a feast.

About 2000 BC nomadic peoples came to Canaan from the east. Among them, according to the Bible, were the Hebrew patriarch Abraham and his tribe. Sometime during the 17th century BC there was famine in Canaan, so the Hebrews moved south along the Mediterranean coast to Egypt. At first they lived there in peace under the rule of the Hyksos, a nomadic people from Asia. When the Hyksos were driven northward, the Hebrews became slaves in Egypt. According to the Bible, they were forced to work for the Egyptian pharaohs until about 1300 BC when Moses helped them to escape, and they returned to conquer Canaan. About 100 years later, Canaan was attacked by the Philistines, one of the feared "Sea Peoples."

About 1020 BC the Hebrews formed a kingdom, called Israel. Their first king was Saul (reigned c.1020–1006 BC). Saul lost to the Philistines at the Battle of Mount Gilboa. He was succeeded by David (reigned c.1006–965 BC), who united the Hebrews and defeated the Philistines.

King Solomon (reigned 965–928 BC) made foreign alliances and traded with Egypt and Phoenicia. He also built a great temple and palaces in Jerusalem. When Solomon died, his kingdom split in two. The northern part, called Israel, existed for another 200 years, until it was conquered by the Assyrians in 722 BC. The smaller southern Kingdom of Judah continued under the rule of David's successors until 587 BC, when the Babylonians invaded, sacked Jerusalem, and carried its inhabitants off to Babylon.

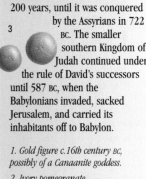

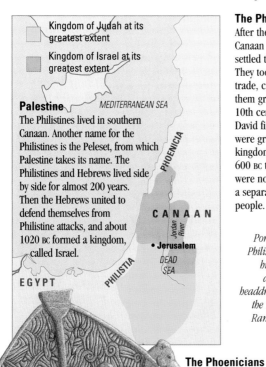

1. Gold figure c.16th century BC, possibly of a Canaanite goddess.

2. Ivory pomegranate c.8th century BC, found in Jerusalem.

3. Stone weights used as money in Canaan.

4. Man playing a Hebrew wind instrument called a shofar.

c.10,000–9000 BC Ice starts to melt as Ice Age ends.

c.6500 BC Farming underway in southeastern Europe.

c.6200 BC First farming villages in Sicily and southern Italy.

c.5000 BC Farming begins in southern France.

c.4500 BC Megalith building starts in western Europe.

This Bronze Age painting from Val Camonica in Italy shows a man using a wooden plow pulled by two oxen. The plow was able to scratch through the soil, but it was not strong enough to turn the soil over.

About 10,000 BC the climate began to warm up and the ice sheets that had covered northern Europe during the Ice Age began to melt and retreat toward the North Pole once more. Along the southern edge of the ice the land was covered in scrubland vegetation, called tundra. This started to grow farther north as the climate continued warming, and was replaced by coniferous forests. As the ice retreated still more, conifers grew farther north and into the mountains. They were replaced by thick forests of oak, elm, birch, and other deciduous trees. The forests were home to a wide variety of animals, such as red deer and wild pigs.

People moved farther north too, living in temporary camps and getting all the food they needed by hunting, fishing, and gathering the abundant wild fruits and nuts. As the number of people increased, however, they needed a more reliable source of food and the knowledge of farming gradually spread from the southeast to the northwest.

The first farmers belonged to the Neolithic (or New Stone) Age, which was characterized by its improved techniques for making tools and weapons from stone. The best of these were traded over long distances. In western Europe people lived mainly in small villages or hamlets, but by about 4500 BC their society was organized enough for them to be able to start building megalithic monuments, each of which needed many thousands of hours of work cutting, transporting, and erecting the massive stones.

Early Europe

During the Ice Age, much of central and northern Europe was covered with thick ice, making it impossible for people to live there. As the climate warmed up and the ice began to melt, however, people began to move farther and farther north. At first they survived by hunting wild animals and gathering seeds, nuts, and berries for food. Then, as conditions became more suitable, they began to settle down in small villages, herding wild animals such as cattle, pigs, and goats, and planting seeds in fields they had cleared from the thick forests that covered the land after the ice retreated. These first farmers made the tools and utensils they needed from stone, bone, and wood, but gradually they discovered how to make pottery and how to smelt the ores of tin and copper to make bronze for stronger tools and weapons. Some of them also built huge monuments from massive stones, called megaliths. They traded goods such as fine stone axheads and good quality flint for knives and arrowheads.

Dolmens, such as this one at Bari in Italy, were found in many parts of prehistoric Europe. Made of upright stone slabs supporting a stone roof, they were usually family or village tombs.

The first farmers

Farming in Europe started in the southeast and gradually spread from there as the climate improved. Using stone axes, farmers cleared the land of trees, then broke up the soil with picks before planting seeds of wheat, barley, lentils, and peas in small fields surrounded by wooden fences. Wild cattle, sheep, pigs, and goats were caught and domesticated to provide meat and skins for clothing. However, many farming families still relied on hunting, fishing, and gathering wild fruits and berries to add variety to their diet.

Antlers were shaped into picks like these and used to break up lumps in the soil. Tools were also made from wood, stone, and bone, but they quickly broke or wore out.

Domesticated animals (left) were not as big as the same animals in the wild (above). Their horns, tusks, and teeth were often smaller and their wool or hair was shorter.

Villages and towns

Just as they had hunted in groups, so most of the early peoples of Europe settled in groups when they started farming. Each family probably had its own house, built from wood, stone, wattle-and-daub (interlaced twigs plastered with mud), or mud bricks, depending on what was available. Everyone worked together at busy times, such as planting and harvesting, and in times of danger.

Many early farming villages, such as Sesklo, in Greece (shown here), were surrounded by a wall or fence to keep out enemies and wild animals.

c.**4400** BC Horses domesticated in eastern Europe. c.**4000** BC   Farming widespread in Europe. c.**2800** BC Building of Stonehenge   starts in Britain. c.**2300** BC Start of Bronze Age in Europe.   c.**1800** BC Defense towers built in Sardinia, Corsica, and Balearic   Islands. c.**1200** BC Last use of megalithic tomb in Ireland .

Pottery

The use of pottery made it easier to store and prepare food and drink, but, as early pottery was quite heavy and easily broken, it was not suitable for people who were always on the move. Its appearance in southeastern Europe from about 7000 BC indicates that people were starting to settle down. The earliest pots were made from thin coils of clay, which were smoothed and decorated before being briefly hardened on an open fire or inside a kiln or oven.

Below: Found in Denmark, this bronze horse-drawn chariot holds a gold-plated disk, which represents the Sun. It dates from about 1500 BC.

Neolithic pottery was decorated with geometric patterns that were either painted on or scratched into the wet clay.

MAJOR MEGALITHIC MONUMENTS IN EUROPE.

Megalithic monuments take several different forms. Some are single stones; others are set in long lines or in circles; others still were built as tombs. Although some tombs were still being used in 1200 BC, their use in most parts of Europe declined after 2000 BC.

Early craftworkers carved decorative figures in stone. This head of a fish is from Lepenski Vir, a settlement on the Danube, in southeastern Europe. It dates from around 5500 BC, and measures about 12 in. (30 cm) long.

Heel Stone

Metals

The first metals to be used were gold and copper, both of which are sometimes found as nuggets of pure metal that can be beaten and shaped without heating. In this pure form, however, the metals were too soft to be used for tools or weapons, and so were only used for decorative purposes. About 2300 BC people discovered that if they added tin to pure copper, a much harder metal was produced. This new metal, called bronze, was much more useful. At first it was used for decorative items, but from about 1200 BC people started using it to make everyday items, in place of stone and bone.

Monument builders

About 4500 BC the peoples of western Europe began to build monuments of huge standing stones, known as megaliths. Some of the monuments were graves, containing as many as 40 bodies, but the purpose of others is less certain. Some probably marked territorial boundaries, while others were used for ritual or religious purposes. The best known is Stonehenge in southwest England. Some of its stones were transported from a site over 125 mi. (200 km) away.

Left: This reconstruction of Stonehenge shows its encircling ditch and banks, which are broken by an avenue in which the Heel Stone stands. Stonehenge was a calendar as well as a possible temple. The Heel Stone, for example, marks the midsummer sunrise.

c.2200 BC Minoan palaces built on Crete at Knossos, Zakro, etc.   **c.1700 BC** Minoan palaces destroyed by fires. Knossos   becomes the main center on Crete. **c.1628 BC** Volcanic   eruption destroys settlements on Thera. **1650–1550 BC** Rise of   Mycenaean civilization on mainland Greece.

Minoans and Mycenaeans

The earliest major civilization on European soil appeared on the Mediterranean island of Crete about 2200 BC. It is known as the Minoan civilization, after the legendary King Minos, whose wife – according to Greek myth – gave birth to the Minotaur, a monster with a bull's head and a human body. The powerful Minoan kings ruled from huge palace-cities, overseeing local agriculture and trade. The Minoans prospered until about 1450 BC, when they were conquered by the Mycenaeans. The Mycenaean civilization had emerged on the Greek mainland between 1650 and 1550 BC. It was made up of a number of small kingdoms, each controlled from a well-defended hilltop town, or "citadel." This well-organized, warlike society was destroyed by invaders in about 1200 BC.

People were living on the wooded and mountainous island of Crete about 6000 BC. Some 3,000 years later, villages and towns appeared. The first palace at Knossos was built about 2200 BC. Over the years other palaces were built, including the ones at Phaistos, Mallia, and Zakro. The Cretan kings ruled over their small states from their palaces. Trade with Egypt created great wealth for the Minoans. Much of it was in raw materials such as copper and tin, used to make bronze.

Disaster struck about 1700 BC, when the Minoan palaces were destroyed by

fire, probably caused by warfare among the palace states. New ones were built to replace them, and these continued to function as centers of power. Then, in 1628 BC the flourishing Minoan settlements on the nearby island of Thera were buried by a volcanic eruption. Minoan civilization ended around 1450 BC when all the palace-cities were destroyed by the Mycenaeans from the Greek mainland.

After this control of Crete passed to the Mycenaeans. The Mycenaeans were an aggressive, warlike people, who had migrated into Greece from the north. They became the dominant power in the region, controlling and

The Cyclades

A rich culture flourished on the Cyclades before Minoan civilization reached the islands. It lasted from about 3000 to 2000 BC and left many statues of women (probably fertility goddesses) and other figures, such as this musician (left).

Wall painting called The Fisherman, *from the island of Thera.*

Bull leaping

Many traces of wall paintings from the Cretan palaces depict bull-leaping contests. It is not known whether this was a sport or part of a religious ceremony. The fragment below, from Knossos, shows a man (red figure) leaping over a bull. Two women are attending.

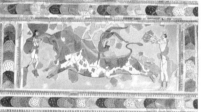

Wall paintings

The Cretan palaces were decorated with vivid wall paintings of fish, dolphins, sports, and religious rituals. Archeologists have learned much about Minoan clothing, hairstyles, jewelry, food, and daily life from these works.

MAJOR MINOAN PALACES AND MYCENAEAN CITADELS.

Minoan religion

The Minoans mainly worshiped female deities, including the mother goddess. There were some male gods, particularly associated with the figure of the bull, but they were probably introduced through contact with the Mycenaeans. The snake goddess (above) was a common household deity.

The palace at Knossos

Knossos was the largest of the palaces on Crete. During the 14th century BC about 4,300 people lived there. The palace had huge storerooms for oil, wine, and other farm products. It kept flocks of about 80,000 sheep.

Below: This reconstruction shows the palace of Knossos after it was rebuilt about 1700 BC.

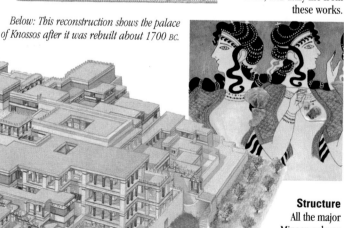

Structure

All the major Minoan palaces were three or four stories high and were built around a central courtyard. The royal apartments were on the second story. In basement workshops, skilled craftspeople made jewelry and other fine metalwork, eggshell-thin pottery, and carvings.

c.1450 BC Minoan civilization ends with Mycenaean invasion. **c.1200 BC** Mycenaean civilization ends, probably destroyed by the "Sea Peoples." **c.1200–900 BC** "Dark Ages." **c.1100 BC** Dorian people settle in Greece. **c.1000 BC** Gradual recovery of economy leads into Archaic period of Greek history.

colonizing the Cyclades, Crete, Cyprus, Sicily, and parts of Italy.

The Mycenaean economy was based on agriculture and breeding livestock. From oil, flax, and wool they produced cosmetics and cloth for home use and export. The Mycenaeans established far-reaching trade links east into Asia Minor and north into Europe. Their skilled artisans excelled in making gold and bronze jewelry, lavishly decorated with amber and precious stones. Much of what we know about the Mycenaeans comes from inscriptions written on clay tablets found at the palaces of Pylos, Knossos, Mycenae, Tiryns, and Thebes.

The civilization appears to have ended abruptly about 1200 BC. The palaces and walled citadels on the mainland were destroyed by fire, probably started by migrant peoples known as the "Sea Peoples," who terrorized all of the eastern Mediterranean at about this time. Within just a few decades trade stopped, and there is evidence of widespread destruction and impoverishment.

Greece entered a period known as the "Dark Ages," when the knowledge of writing was lost. The Greek poet Homer is thought to have lived at the end of the Mycenaean age, and the tales in his epic poems the *Iliad* and the *Odyssey* probably refer to events in that period. The Dorian people from the north are thought to have settled in Greece around 1100 BC. From about 1000 BC the economy gradually began to recover, new towns were built, and trade links were re-established.

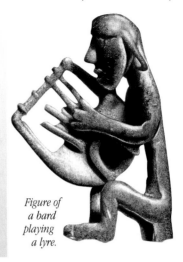

Figure of a bard playing a lyre.

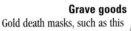

1. An engraved double-ax made of gold, possibly a symbol of the Minoan sky god.
2. A Mycenaean image of a sphinx.
3. A Mycenaean warrior's helmet made of boars' tusks.

Minoan influence on the Mycenaeans
The Mycenaeans were strongly influenced by the earlier Minoans. This head of a bull, decorated with a metal rosette ready for sacrifice, was found in a grave at Mycenae. The craftsmanship in the rosette shows strong Minoan influence.

Vase showing heavily armed Mycenaean soldiers going off to war. A woman on the left sadly waves them good-bye.

Reconstruction of a grave circle at Mycenae as it probably looked about 1200 BC.

Grave goods
Gold death masks, such as this magnificent one, were found in vertical shaft graves at Mycenae in Greece.

Mycenaean artifacts
Painted clay figures, usually female, such as this one (below right), are typical of Mycenae. They may have been kept in small shrines or in the home.

Mycenae
The citadel at Mycenae (from which the civilization takes its name) was a wealthy center during the 16th century BC. It occupied a commanding position on a major trade route in the northeastern Peloponnese.

Writing
Both the Minoans and the Mycenaeans had written scripts. The Minoan script, called Linear A, has still not been deciphered. Linear B, the Mycenaean script, is an ancient form of Greek. Clay tablets that have been deciphered from Linear B are administrative records.

The "Dark Ages"
Little is known of the 300 to 400 years that came after the Mycenaean civilization. Most historians agree that it was a period of migration and unrest. Peoples from the north, called Dorians, are thought to have settled in Greece at this time. Recent discoveries by archeologists have revealed that well-organized towns existed. In Lefkandi, in central Greece, they uncovered tombs of a man and a woman who were buried in great style about 950 BC.

Toward Classical pottery
The earliest Greek vases were decorated with geometric patterns, including bands of zigzags, triangles, and "Greek keys." New patterns developed slowly. Figures of animals and people began to appear during the 7th century BC.

Linear A script.   *Linear B script.*

Left: Clay centaur (half man, half horse) found in the tombs at Lefkandi.

Pottery and craft
The Mycenaeans were skilled potters, and many of their beautifully decorated vases have survived to the present day. This one (left) has typical coloring and patterns.

SEE ALSO
p. 26 ANCIENT EGYPT
p. 34 CLASSICAL GREECE
p. 38 THE HELLENISTIC WORLD

c.900 BC End of "Dark Ages." Archaic period begins.

776 BC First Olympic Games held at Olympia.

683 BC Athens replaces kings with elected *archons*.

c.594 BC Solon, *archon* of Athens, reforms laws.

510 BC Sparta is the leading Greek city.

Classical Greece

Ancient Greek civilization reached its peak in the 5th and 4th centuries BC, a time called the Classical period, when an early form of democratic government was invented and there was great economic growth and military success. Many Greeks were inspired to write plays and poetry, and to produce sculptures and art. They also enlarged their cities, building fine temples and public buildings. Philosophers, mathematicians, and scientists discussed new ideas and wrote them down in books and treatises, many of which are studied today. Greek civilization spread far beyond the frontiers of Greece; its language and culture were known throughout the Mediterranean world. Classical Greek civilization has also reached across time, influencing people and thought down to the present day.

Civilization in ancient Greece emerged from the "Dark Ages" that followed the collapse of the Mycenaean civilization during the 10th century BC. The first few centuries, from about 900 to 500 BC, are called the Archaic period. It was a time of growth and change, during which the Greek alphabet, based on an earlier Phoenician one, was developed, and written records were kept again. Homer's two great epic poems, the *Iliad* and the *Odyssey*, which probably record events that occurred in Mycenaean times, were first written down.

As the population increased, many Greeks emigrated, establishing colonies in southern Italy, northern Africa, and around the shores of the Black Sea. Trade in raw materials, craftwork, food, and wine flourished, and in the 7th century BC the Greeks invented coins to pay for goods.

Kings, aristocratic families, or military leaders ruled the burgeoning towns and surrounding countryside. These small, self-governing communities were known as *poleis*, or "city-states." By about 700 BC most of Greece was divided into city-states. Over the

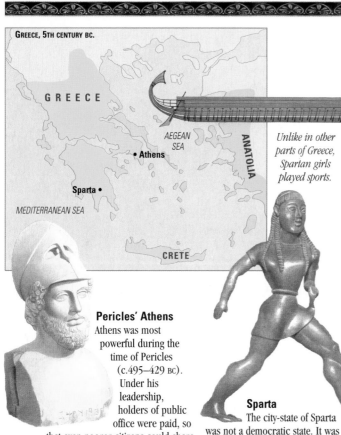

GREECE, 5TH CENTURY BC.

GREECE

AEGEAN SEA

• Athens

ANATOLIA

Sparta •

MEDITERRANEAN SEA

CRETE

Unlike in other parts of Greece, Spartan girls played sports.

Pericles' Athens

Athens was most powerful during the time of Pericles (c.495–429 BC). Under his leadership, holders of public office were paid, so that even poorer citizens could share in government. He also rebuilt Athens after the Persian Wars and enlarged the port of Piraeus.

The importance of sea travel

Greece is a mountainous land with many islands, so sea travel was the main means of transportation. Travel, trade, and warfare were usually maritime activities.

The Greeks were excellent sailors, and many city-states had large navies. In about 700 BC the trireme battleship (above left) was developed. Manned by 170 rowers, it was the mainstay of Greek navies for several hundred years and was later adopted by the Romans. Each trireme had five officers aboard. In battle, the rowers built up tremendous speed and smashed their ship against an enemy ship, inflicting damage with the metal battering ram on the front.

An early Greek coin.

Democracy in ancient Greece

Ancient Greece was the birthplace of democracy, or rule by the people. The term comes from two Greek words: *demos*, meaning "people," and *kratos*, meaning "rule." In Greek city-states all male citizens had a say in decision making. At a public meeting, each speaker was timed using a water clock (above).

Agriculture and trade

The cities of mainland Greece imported huge quantities of cereals, wine, olive oil, salt-fish, and other products to feed their growing populations. In exchange, they exported finely crafted pottery, jewelry, and other craftwork all over the Mediterranean world.

Sparta

The city-state of Sparta was not a democratic state. It was led by military leaders. All male citizens spent their lives as soldiers. Discipline, loyalty, and self-denial were the chief Spartan codes of conduct.

A TYPICAL *POLIS*.

Acropolis

Town walls

Agora

Town walls

Port

The *polis*, or "city-state"

There were several hundred city-states in Classical Greece. Each one was centered on a town, but included the surrounding countryside. Most of the towns had walls to protect them. Each one had an *acropolis*, or "citadel," on raised ground and an *agora*, or "marketplace." Most were situated on the coast or near a river so that there was easy access to transportation and a trading port.

Weighing farm products for export.

507 BC Kleisthenes' introduces democratic institution in Athens.   **492–448 BC** Persian Wars.
c.480 BC Classical period begins.   **c.460–429 BC** Pericles is the leading politician in Athens.   **405 BC** Spartans defeat Athenian fleet.   **334 BC** Alexander ("the Great") of Macedon controls Greece.

following centuries almost all of them (except Sparta) developed more democratic forms of government.

In Athens, the change from monarchy to aristocratic government to democracy took many years. Early in the 6th century BC Solon introduced reforms that limited the power of the aristocracy and slightly increased that of the poorer people. At the end of the century Kleisthenes introduced a democratic constitution that gave all 45,000 male citizens the right to vote.

By Classical times a typical city-state was made up of citizens (adult males), citizens without political rights (women, and children of male citizens), and non-citizens (foreigners and slaves). It was governed by elected male citizens, who met in the *agora* or "marketplace," to decide how the city-state should be run.

Although the Greek city-states were independent, they often formed alliances when threatened from abroad. A combined army fought the Persians from 492 to 448 BC. Athens and Sparta also fought each other in the Peloponnesian War (431–404 BC).

The Classical period ended in 334 BC

when Alexander, a warrior king from Macedon, a kingdom to the to the north, invaded. Alexander went on to conquer an empire that reached from Greece to northern India. The time after Alexander's conquest is known as the Hellenistic period; it continued until Greece was absorbed by the Roman Empire.

1. *An Athenian silver coin. Each city-state had its own coinage.*

2. *Statue of the giant Atlas, condemned by Zeus to carry the sky on his shoulders.*

3. *Statue of a Greek foot soldier, called a hoplite, with armor and shield.*

4. *A Greek coin showing the symbol of Athens.*

Theater
There were many great Greek playwrights, including Aeschylus, Sophocles, Euripides, and Aristophanes. Their plays were performed in steep-sided, semicircular theaters in the open air. The chorus stood in the orchestra at ground level, and the actors performed on a raised stage. Large theaters could hold up to 12,000 people.

Greek art
The Greeks have left a rich store of temples, statues, painted vases, jewelry, and craftwork. Over the centuries their art developed from the rather stiff but mysteriously beautiful work of the Archaic period, through the lifelike perfection of Classical art, to the expressive beauty of Hellenistic works. Greek art later inspired the artists of the European Renaissance.

Top: A 7th-century BC vase.
Above: A horse's head from the Parthenon.

Above: A Greek theater.
Right: The Parthenon in Athens.

Religion
The Greeks worshiped a large pantheon of male and female gods. Zeus was the leader of the gods, who were thought to dwell on Mount Olympus.

Philosophy and learning
The word "philosophy" means "love of wisdom." Thales of Miletus, who lived during the 6th century BC, is considered the first Greek philosopher. Other great thinkers, such as Socrates, Plato, and Aristotle, laid the foundations of Western philosophy and are still studied today.

Sports
The Greeks took sports very seriously, and all young males began training at an early age. The first Olympic Games were held in 776 BC. Athletes came from all over Greece to compete, and wars were even interrupted so that everyone could attend. The games lasted for seven days, and included religious ceremonies.

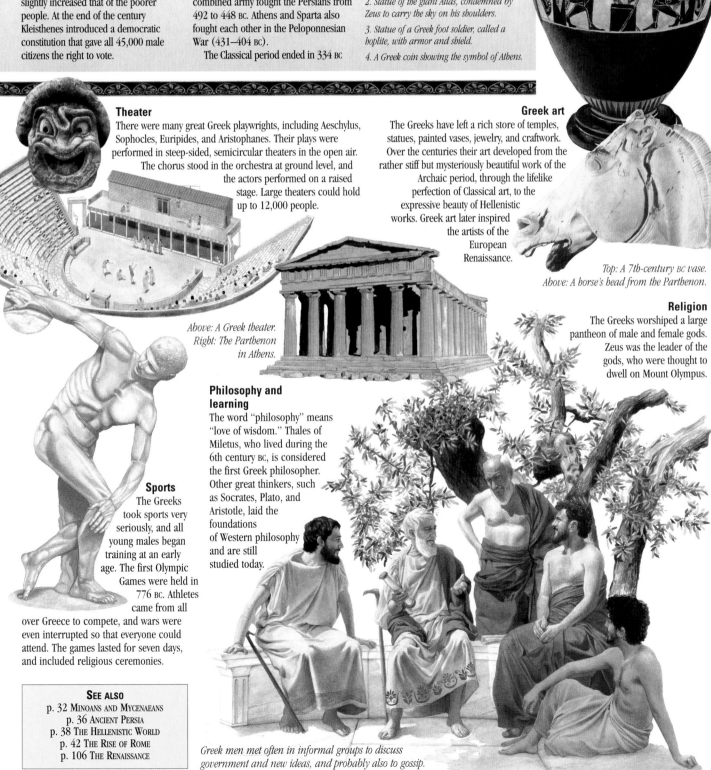

Greek men met often in informal groups to discuss government and new ideas, and probably also to gossip.

SEE ALSO
p. 32 MINOANS AND MYCENAEANS
p. 36 ANCIENT PERSIA
p. 38 THE HELLENISTIC WORLD
p. 42 THE RISE OF ROME
p. 106 THE RENAISSANCE

c.700 BC Medes create first state on the Persian plateau.

681 BC Achemenes leads his army against Assyria.

648 BC Persians seize eastern part of kingdom of Elam.

559 BC Cyrus the Great becomes king of Persia.

c.550 BC Cyrus the Great controls Media, Lydia and Ionia.

Ancient Persia

Cyrus the Great founded the Persian Empire about 550 BC when he overthrew the kingdom of Media and then conquered Lydia and Ionia. When, in 539 BC, he conquered Babylonia he created the largest empire known until that time. This mighty empire lasted for just over 200 years, reaching its greatest extent under King Darius I. The Persians had a strong army and they were highly organized. They divided their empire into provinces and built roads to link up the regions. These enabled them to trade with people in remote areas. The famous Royal Road covered more than 1,500 miles (2,400 km) between the capital, Susa, and Sardis, in Lydia. Tribute and taxes were brought to royal palaces at Susa and Persepolis. The Persians were tolerant rulers, permitting exiles to return to their homelands and also allowing a certain amount of religious freedom. Their own ancient gods were mainly replaced by Zoroastrianism in about 600 BC.

The Persians and Medes were originally nomads from Central Asia who came to the area of modern Iran in the 9th and 8th centuries BC. The Medes settled on the Iranian plateau, but the Persians pushed farther south and settled east of the ancient kingdom of Elam. Achemenes was the founder of the Persian monarchy, although little is known about his reign.

In 648 BC, the Persians – who were subject to the Medes – began their expansion by seizing eastern Elam. About 550 BC the Persian king, Cyrus the Great (reigned c.559–530 BC), defeated an invasion by the Median king, Astyages. Cyrus went on to enlarge the Persian Empire by seizing the kingdom of Lydia and defeating the Greek colonies in Ionia. In 539 BC he made his greatest conquest: Babylonia. Nine years later he was killed on campaign in Central Asia. His son, Cambyses (reigned 530–522 BC), added Egypt and Libya to the Persian Empire.

The next king, Darius I (reigned 522–486 BC), declared himself "King of Kings," and divided the empire into provinces. He sent an army into mainland Greece in 490 BC, but it was defeated by the Athenians at Marathon. Darius's son, Xerxes (reigned 486–465 BC), defeated the Spartans at Thermopylae in 480 BC, but then his fleet was defeated at Salamis, and his army at Plataea a year later. This brought the expansion of the Persian Empire to an end.

The empire weakened, and in 331 BC Alexander the Great defeated a huge Persian army at the Battle of Gaugamela. A year later he captured Persepolis and razed it to the ground.

1. A silver deer from Persepolis.

2. A gold coin showing the Persian warrior king, Darius.

3. A silver drinking horn c.400 BC. The griffin was a common image in Persian art.

This silver bull holding a vessel is from Elam. Early metalworkers in the region prized silver highly, thinking that it was a rare, white variety of gold.

A clay cylinder, called the Cyrus Cylinder, records how the Persian king, Cyrus the Great, conquered Babylon in 539 BC. It also tells how he restored various gods to their home cities. The Persians had developed a cuneiform system of writing, which was only used for royal inscriptions.

King of Kings

Persian rulers gave themselves the title "King of Kings," to show that they were more powerful than the monarch of any other region. The Persian king ruled over a court of powerful landowners, priests, and officials chosen from noble families. He usually had many wives. The king had absolute authority over the empire and its people, but there was a constant danger that he might be overthrown. Some kings had their male relatives killed so that they could not be threatened by them.

The tomb of Cyrus the Great still stands at Pasargadae, in modern Iran. The tomb was vandalized, but restored by Alexander the Great, who was an admirer of Cyrus.

Carvings on the great staircase at Persepolis show conquered peoples bringing offerings to the Persian king. These Elamites have brought a lioness and her two cubs.

Persepolis

In about 515 BC King Darius I ordered skilled workers from all over his empire to build a new palace at Persepolis. The palace stood within a heavily fortified citadel built on a massive limestone platform. It was probably used only on ceremonial occasions. Ambassadors from all over the empire would bring tributes to the king, presenting them to him in a huge room 360 ft (110 m) square, with stone columns 65 ft (20 m) high. Archeologists have learned a great deal about ancient Persia from carvings found at Persepolis.

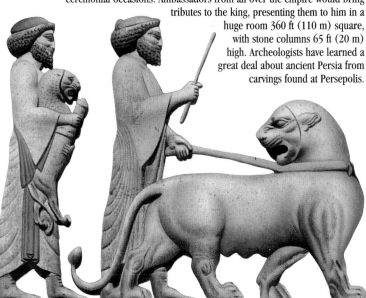

539 BC Cyrus the Great destroys the Babylonian Empire.

522 BC Darius I declares himself "King of Kings."

490 BC Persians defeated by Greeks at Marathon.

479 BC Persians defeated by Greeks at Plataea.

331 BC Persians defeated by Alexander the Great.

THE PERSIAN EMPIRE.

The Persian Empire

The empire extended from Egypt in the west to the Indus River in the east, and from the Caspian Sea in the north to the Indian Ocean in the south. This vast area was divided into 20 provinces, called *satrapies*, each ruled by a governor, or *satrap*. The king sent inspectors, called the "king's ears," to check that the *satrapies* were being well run and that his people were loyal.

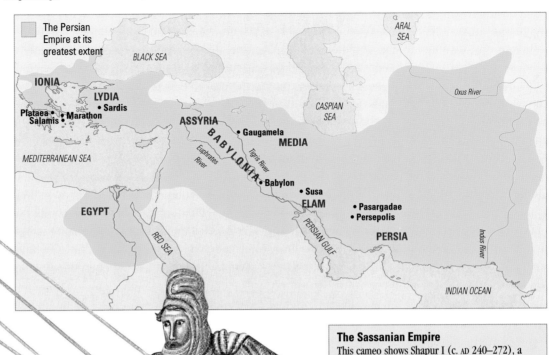

The Persian Empire at its greatest extent

King Darius III in his war chariot, fleeing from Alexander the Great at the Battle of Issus in 333 BC.

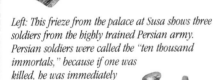

Left: This frieze from the palace at Susa shows three soldiers from the highly trained Persian army. Persian soldiers were called the "ten thousand immortals," because if one was killed, he was immediately replaced by another.

The Sassanian Empire

This cameo shows Shapur I (c. AD 240–272), a Persian king of the later Sassanian Dynasty that ruled Persia from AD 224 to 636, fighting the Roman Emperor Valerian. Shapur expanded the empire founded by his father, Ardashir I, by making war on Rome, conquering Nisibis and Carrhae (both in modern Turkey), and advancing deep into Syria. He defeated Valerian at Edessa in 260, keeping him prisoner for the rest of his life.

A double-headed griffin capital (the decorated top of a column) from Persepolis. It was used to support a roof beam.

The Persians were skilled metalworkers. This gold model of a four-horse chariot, with a charioteer and passenger, was part of a hoard of treasure found at the Oxus River.

Zoroaster and religion

The ancient Persians believed in many gods of nature, the most important of whom was Mithra. They did not build temples, but prayed and offered sacrifices on mountains. About 600 BC a priest named Zoroaster (or Zarathustra) had a vision of a supreme god of goodness, light, and truth, called Ahura Mazda (meaning "the Wise Lord"). The god asked Zoroaster to preach his faith and fight against Ahriman, the destructive force of greed and anger. Zoroastrians gradually spread the new faith throughout the Persian Empire. They reformed certain ancient rituals, but continued to practice animal sacrifice and the ancient fire cult.

Mithra, the Persian god of light, truth, and justice, is shown here slaying the bull whose blood, according to the myth, became the source of all animals and plants on Earth. Mithraism reached Rome in about 68 BC, and the god became known as Mithras.

SEE ALSO
p. 24 BABYLONIA AND ASSYRIA
p. 38 THE HELLENISTIC WORLD
p. 44 THE ROMAN EMPIRE
p. 66 MYTH AND RELIGION

359 BC Philip II becomes regent of Macedon.

356 BC Philip II becomes king. His son Alexander is born.

338 BC Philip and Alexander defeat the Greeks at Chaeronea.

336 BC Alexander III (the Great) becomes king of Macedon.

333 BC Alexander defeats Darius III of Persia at Issus.

The Hellenistic World

When Alexander succeeded his father, Philip II, as king of Macedon, he inherited a determination to expand the Macedonian empire eastward and defeat the Persians. During his short life Alexander achieved his aim by making a huge journey of conquest that lasted 11 years, covered more than 20,000 mi. (32,000 km), and later earned him the description "the Great." As he traveled, he spread Greek culture throughout his vast empire. After his death, the empire was split among his generals [1] into five kingdoms, and power moved to new capitals outside Greece, including Alexandria in Egypt, Antioch in Syria, and Pergamum in Asia Minor. The 300 years between Alexander's life and the fall of Egypt to the Romans is known as the Hellenistic age.

A lively sculpture of a young boy wrestling a goose. Its style is typical of Hellenistic art.

The kingdom of Macedon, north of Greece, was established c.640 BC, but played only a minor role in Greek history until Philip II (382–336 BC) became king in 356 BC. Philip transformed Macedon into a formidable power and expanded the kingdom's boundaries. In 338 BC he defeated the Greeks at Chaeronea. He then planned to lead a combined force against Persia, but his plans were thwarted when he was assassinated in 336 BC.

Philip's son, Alexander III (356–323 BC), took command of the army and determined to carry out the conquest of

MAP SHOWING ALEXANDER'S ROUTE THROUGH ASIA MINOR.

Alexander's journey started at his birthplace, Pella, in Macedon, which he left in 335 BC. He first defeated the Greeks at Thebes, before going on to conquer the entire Persian Empire, and finally the Punjab in 326 BC. There, his exhausted troops forced him to turn back, and he died at Babylon in 323 BC.

BLACK SEA · CASPIAN SEA · MACEDONIA · Pella · Oxus River · Alexandria Eschate · GREECE · PERSIAN EMPIRE · Halicarnassus · Issus · Gaugamela · Bactra · Ecbatana · Alexandria Bucephala · MEDITERRANEAN SEA · Euphrates River · Tyre · Babylon · Susa · Alexandria · Indus River · Alexandria · Memphis · Persepolis · EGYPT · PERSIAN GULF · RED SEA · Pattala · Nile River

Alexander's Empire — Alexander's journey of conquest

Alexander with his favorite horse, Bucephalus.

This fragment of a mosaic shows Alexander charging into battle at Issus, where he won a decisive victory over the Persian king, Darius III, in 333 BC.

Below: A Macedonian phalanx was made up of 16 rows of foot soldiers, each armed with a sarissa, or "pike," up to 20 ft (6 m) long.

The Macedonian army

Before Philip II came to power, the Macedonian army had been made up mainly of cavalry. Philip introduced a strong, well-armed infantry. Both the cavalry and the foot soldiers were armed with long pikes that were much more effective than the shorter Greek spears. Philip organized the foot soldiers into a new phalanx formation that was more maneuverable than the Greek version. Alexander inherited the army from his father and journeyed into Asia with about 32,000 foot soldiers and 5,000 cavalry.

Alexandria

When Alexander reached Egypt in 332 BC, he founded the city of Alexandria. Three years after his death in 323 BC, the new city replaced Memphis as the capital of Egypt. Alexandria's most famous buildings were its lighthouse (one of the Seven Wonders of the Ancient World), library, and museum. Alexander founded many other cities on his journey of conquest, some of which were originally also called Alexandria. Famous examples are Khojand in present-day Tajikistan, and Kandahar and Herat in Afghanistan.

Alexandria soon grew into a famous city. The world's first lighthouse, the Pharos (right), took about 20 years to build and was completed in about 280 BC.

This coin shows Alexander in the Punjab, fighting against the war elephants of King Porus at the Hydaspes River.

326 BC Macedonian army reaches Punjab; troops rebel.

323 BC Alexander the Great dies in Babylon, age 32.

312 BC Seleucus I governor of Babylonia.

285 BC Ptolemy II king of Egypt.

76 BC Antigonus II king of Macedon.

30 BC Romans take Egypt.

2

Persia. In 335 BC his army stormed the rebellious Greek city of Thebes and razed it to the ground; the rest of Greece was soon under his control. He then marched his army into Asia Minor. His route took him south through Anatolia (modern Turkey). He defeated the Persian king, Darius III, at Issus in 333 BC. Next he marched south through Phoenicia and captured Tyre. He went on to Egypt, where he was welcomed as the country's liberator from Persian rule. Alexander then marched back into the heart of the Persian Empire and defeated Darius III again, at Gaugamela in

331 BC. He went on to capture the cities of Babylon and Susa. The following year he destroyed Persepolis.

In 327 BC the army crossed the Indus River into the Punjab, where he won his last major battle. His troops, exhausted and homesick, refused to go on into India. Alexander returned to Babylon, where he died in 323 BC, age 32.

Alexander's vast empire split into five independent states: Egypt, the Seleucid kingdom, Macedon, Thrace, and Anatolia. They were ruled by Alexander's former generals and their successors.

Egypt under the Ptolemies achieved stability, and Alexandria became the largest and richest Greek city in the world. The Seleucid kingdom in Mesopotamia and the east covered a vast area that was difficult to control. In 263 BC it lost the city of Pergamum to Attalus I (reigned 241–197 BC), and in 191 and 190 BC it lost more ground, this time to the Romans, who were fast becoming the strongest power in the Mediterranean. Macedon had been annexed by Thrace in 285 BC, and invaded by Celts from central Europe in 279 BC. In 277 BC Antigonus II (reigned 277–239 BC) became king of Macedon, and defeated both Athens and Sparta. Then, between

214 and 168 BC, the Romans conquered Macedon. Finally, Ptolemaic Egypt fell to the Romans in 30 BC, signaling the end of the Hellenistic age.

1. An ivory statue of Philip II of Macedon.

2. A Roman copy of a bronze head of a philosopher or poet.

3. The inside of a cup, decorated with Hellenistic cameo art.

3

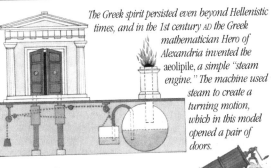

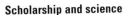

Scholarship and science

Greek ideas and academic life thrived throughout the Hellenistic period. The two greatest libraries of the ancient world were at Alexandria, which contained almost half a million book rolls, and Pergamum. Greek was the language of scholarship. In science, mathematicians such as Archimedes (c.287–212 BC) created workable machines, though greater progress was made in scientific theory. The Greek astronomer Aristarchos of Samos (c.300–250 BC) suggested that the earth moved around the sun, but his views did not seem to agree with observations of the naked eye, and were largely ignored.

The Greek spirit persisted even beyond Hellenistic times, and in the 1st century AD the Greek mathematician Hero of Alexandria invented the aeolipile, a simple "steam engine." The machine used steam to create a turning motion, which in this model opened a pair of doors.

Hellenistic sculpture was particularly expressive of emotions. This 1st-century BC sculpture of the Laocoön group shows a father and his sons struggling with a giant serpent.

This device for raising water is called an Archimedes' screw, because it is believed to have been invented by the Greek mathematician Archimedes, though it may have been known earlier. It was used to raise water for irrigation.

Above: In this statue from 203 BC, called the Nike of Samothrace, *the winged Greek goddess of victory alights in triumph on the prow of a ship.*

Below: The Dying Gaul is a Roman copy in marble of a bronze statue put up by King Attalus I (269–197 BC) of Pergamum to celebrate his victories over the Gauls in Galatia. It shows great respect for the fallen enemy and is a famous example of Hellenistic art.

The Hellenistic states

After about 285 BC, the Hellenistic world was divided into separate kingdoms. Ptolemy I's successors ruled in Egypt for nearly 300 years. In Asia Minor, a vast domain including Syria, Babylonia, and lands farther east was controlled by the Seleucid Dynasty, named after the Macedonian general Seleucus I (reigned 312–281 BC). Their capital was Antioch. Macedon itself was ruled by the Antigonids, named after Antigonus II (reigned 277–239 BC); during his reign the Macedonian court became a center of culture. The three kingdoms shared a rough balance of power – though many wars were fought between them – until they gradually lost control to the Romans.

THE HELLENISTIC KINGDOMS C.285 BC.

Celtic Europe

Celts are first known in Europe about 750 BC, when they were trading salt from Hallstatt (in present-day Austria) with the ancient Greeks. Their civilization gradually spread north, east, and west, reaching its greatest extent during the 3rd century BC. However, the Celts never had an empire, or even a single ruler. Instead they were divided into many different groups, each with its own leader and territory. Groups often fought against each other, but all were united by their way of life; among the things they shared were their language, beliefs, arts, and crafts. Most Celts lived as farmers, but they were also fierce warriors. They had learned how to smelt iron to make strong tools and weapons.

1 About 750 BC people from the Hallstatt region of central Europe (in present-day Austria) crossed the Alps to trade with the ancient Greeks. They took with them salt, which they mined from the mountains around Hallstatt, and which was used to preserve food. The Celts exchanged salt for luxury goods made by Greek craftworkers. The Greeks called them *Keltoi*, which was probably similar to the name they called themselves. Today we call them Celts.

As well as mining salt, the Celts dug iron ore from the ground and smelted it to make weapons and tools. Their

metal tools were stronger and cheaper to make than earlier bronze implements, enabling them to clear more land for farming than any previous peoples of central Europe. With more widespread farming, the Celts produced more food. This meant that people were less likely to die of hunger, and so the population began to increase. Soon there was not enough land for everyone and families moved farther away in search of new land to settle. 2

Burials

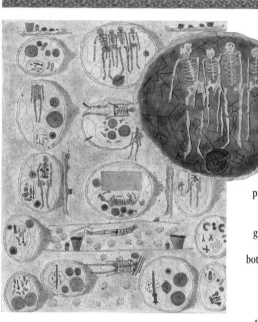

The Celts believed that when people died, they went to a place called the "Otherworld," which they thought was much like this world. As these graves (above) at Hallstatt show, they buried people with objects that they would need for the journey, and for their new life there. Items included plenty of food and drink, as well as weapons, tools, jewelry, and clothing. Rich people were even buried with horses, chariots, or wagons for the journey.

Gods and goddesses

The Celts had many different gods and goddesses, all of whom were closely linked to the natural world. Some were special to one group of Celts, or even to a place such as a river or a well. Others were worshiped by all the Celts, but known by different names in different areas. When they wanted favors from their gods, the Celts offered sacrifices to them. Sometimes these were animals or humans, but more often they were gifts of flowers, weapons, or jewelry.

Celtic houses were usually circular, but some were oblong or square. Their walls were quite low and made of wood, stone, or wickerwork, while the roofs were steeply sloping and thatched with reeds, straw, or leather.

Daily life

For most Celts life was centered on the home; one big room in which all the family ate, slept, and did their daily chores. An open fire in the middle of the room provided light and heat, and was also used for cooking. One important daily task was grinding grain into flour to make bread. Grain was also used to make porridge and beer, both of which were important in the diet. Stews and roast meat were also eaten.

Farming

The Celts grew the food they needed in the fields around their homes. Their main cereal crops were barley, oats, wheat, and rye. They also grew vegetables: beans, peas, onions, and lentils. They kept pigs for their meat and sheep for their wool and milk. Cattle also provided milk, as well as meat and hides to make into leather. Geese and hens provided feathers and eggs, and bees provided honey, which was used as a sweetener.

The Celts at war

The Celts were brave and ferocious warriors, but their armies were badly organized and they relied on surprise to defeat their enemies. Their weapons included swords, daggers, and spears, as well as bows and arrows and sling-shots, and they defended themselves with shields. The wealthiest wore metal helmets and shirts of chain-mail, but many fought naked except for a gold torc, or neck bangle.

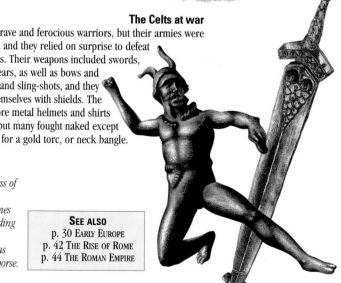

Epona was the goddess of horses and good harvests. Sometimes she was shown riding a horse and sometimes she was represented as a horse.

SEE ALSO
p. 30 EARLY EUROPE
p. 42 THE RISE OF ROME
p. 44 THE ROMAN EMPIRE

198–19 BC Romans conquer Spain.
58 BC Roman armies invade Gaul.

55 BC Roman armies go to Britain but fail to take control.

52 BC Gauls defeated at Alesia.
AD 43 Romans invade Britain.

60 British Celtic queen, Boudicca, defeated in revolt against Romans.

122 Hadrian's Wall built at northern border of Roman territory in Britain.

First they settled along the valleys of the Danube and Rhine rivers, but by the 6th century BC they had reached present-day France, Belgium, Spain, Portugal, Britain, and Ireland, as well as parts of Germany, central Europe, and northern Italy. About 390 BC the Celts were powerful enough to defeat the Romans at the Battle of Allia. After their victory they marched on Rome and looted the city.

By the 3rd century BC the Celtic civilization had spread as far east as Galatia in present-day Turkey. The time of expansion was almost over by then, however, as Germanic peoples prevented the Celts spreading farther north, and the Dacians of present-day Romania prevented them spreading farther east.

At the same time, the Romans were becoming more powerful and were expanding their territory. At the Battle of Telamon in central Italy in 225 BC, the Romans decisively defeated the Celts and began slowly to conquer their lands. By the end of the 1st century AD all the Celtic lands, apart from remote parts of Britain and Ireland, were ruled by the Romans (who called the Celts "Gauls.")

The Romans thought the Celts were uncivilized, because they did not live in towns and cities with large public buildings and grand temples. Instead the Celts lived in small villages, farmsteads, and hillforts, and made offerings to their gods in natural places such as lakes and rivers. But they made fine woolen cloth, which they traded with the Romans, and they were skilled metalworkers. They made beautiful jewelry and decorative objects, as well as tools and weapons. They were also great storytellers. They had no written language, and instead passed stories on by word of mouth. Their society was well organized and took care of people too old, poor, or sick to look after themselves.

1. A Celtic bronze helmet with two horn-shaped projections that made the wearer more frightening to the enemy.

2. A gold coin decorated with a prancing horse. It was made by Celts from northern Gaul (present-day France).

3. A glass figure of a dog. The Celts learned to make glass from Mediterranean peoples.

4. A horse trapping made from bronze and decorated with enamel.

Most Celtic warriors were brilliant horse riders. In times of peace they enjoyed horse racing and chariot racing.

Spread of the Celts

As the Celtic population increased, the civilization spread across Europe as people looked for new land to settle and farm. From present-day Austria, they moved along the valleys of the Danube and Rhine rivers, and by the 6th century BC they had reached present-day France, Belgium, Spain, Portugal, Britain, Ireland, and northern Italy. They also went east into the Balkans, and by the 3rd century BC they had reached Galatia in modern Turkey.

THE SPREAD OF THE CELTS IN EUROPE AND ASIA MINOR.

Celtic expansion northward in mainland Europe was prevented by the Germanic peoples, who themselves began to migrate southward and westward from about 500 BC.

Mining and metalwork

The Celts were skilled miners and metalworkers, using both iron and bronze to make their tools and weapons. The earliest Celts mined salt in the mountains around Hallstatt in Austria. They carried the salt out of the mines in leather rucksacks (right). As well as making iron tools, blacksmiths put hard-wearing iron rims onto the wooden wheels of their carts (right).

Clothing and jewelry

Celtic clothing was simple and practical. All the garments were made from either linen or wool, which was spun and woven by the women. They often used bright colors and wove patterns into the fabric. Brooches, belts, and buckles were used as fastenings. Warriors wore gold torcs, or bangles, around their necks. Other jewelry was made from gold (below), or copper decorated with glass or enamel (right).

Right: Vercingetorix (d. 46 BC) was chieftain of the Gallic tribe of the Averni. He led a revolt against the Romans in Gaul in 52 BC. Captured by Julius Caesar, he was taken to Rome and executed.

The decline of the Celtic world

The Celts and Romans often came into conflict as each tried to expand their territories. At first the Celts were victorious, but in time the Roman army became better organized, and after 225 BC the Romans defeated the Celts regularly, conquering the Celtic lands in mainland Europe. Most of the Celts there adopted a Roman way of life. Britain was conquered in AD 43, but Celtic strongholds survived in Ireland and Scotland.

c.900 BC Latins settle on hills near Tiber River, Italy.

c.800 BC Etruscan civilization begins in Italy.

753 BC Legendary founding of Rome by Romulus and Remus.

616 BC Etruscan kings in Rome.
509 BC Etruscan kings expelled;

Roman Republic begins.
270 BC Romans control all of

An Etruscan coffin from the 6th century BC showing a married couple reclining on a couch. They were probably the master and mistress of a large household.

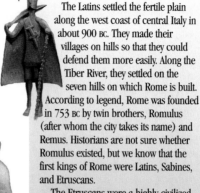

The Latins settled the fertile plain along the west coast of central Italy in about 900 BC. They made their villages on hills so that they could defend them more easily. Along the Tiber River, they settled on the seven hills on which Rome is built. According to legend, Rome was founded in 753 BC by twin brothers, Romulus (after whom the city takes its name) and Remus. Historians are not sure whether Romulus existed, but we know that the first kings of Rome were Latins, Sabines, and Etruscans.

The Etruscans were a highly civilized people who had settled the area north of Rome c.800 BC. It is thought that Rome's

Etruscan king, Tarquin I (reigned c.616–579 BC) turned Rome into a city. His grandson, Tarquin II (the Proud), became king c.534 BC. He refused to rule with the advice of the Senate (the assembly of leading citizens), and in 509 BC he was overthrown. Rome became a republic, run by two consuls elected by the citizens.

The Republic built up a strong, well-trained army and expanded rapidly. By 270 BC Rome had conquered all of Italy. The Romans then fought three long wars against Carthage, a city on the coast of North Africa, and

THE PEOPLES OF ITALY c.500 BC.

Metalworking

The Etruscans were skilled metalworkers and craftspeople. From gold and silver they made coins and jewelry, and from bronze (made by combining copper and tin from Etruria's rich deposits) they made figures such as this chimera (below) – a mythical fire-breathing creature in the shape of a lion, with a goat's head in the middle of its back, and a serpent's tail. The Etruscans also used iron from the island of Elba.

Etruscan language

Scholars have not yet found a way to decipher the Etruscan script. The language does not belong to the Indo-European group that includes Greek and Latin. However, the alphabet is similar to Greek, and the language may be related to those of Asia Minor, such as Lydian. A large number of inscriptions have been found, most of them fairly short. Experts believe the Etruscans had their own literature, but so far none has been discovered.

Telling the future

The Etruscans tried to learn the will of the gods by examining the entrails, including the liver, of sacrificed animals. This bronze model, found at Piacenza, Italy, is of a sheep's liver. It is divided into forty compartments, bearing the names of Etruscan and Roman gods.

Etruscan engineering

The Etruscans, like the Greeks whom they greatly admired, were superb engineers. They built walled cities with arched entrances, paved streets, and brick buildings. The region of Etruria was crisscrossed with underground water tunnels and sunken roads.

Above: An Etruscan arch at Volterra in Tuscany, Italy.

Left: Etruscan pottery vase. Below: Gold tablet with Etruscan inscription.

Left: Etruscan gold and silver coins. The Etruscans traded all over the Mediterranean.

Right: Pre-Roman objects:
1. Incense burner made by Villanovians. 2. Human shaped rock statue made by Ligurians. 3. Bronze vessel made by Veneti.

Etruscan tombs

The Etruscans believed in an afterlife, so rich people buried their dead in tombs with food, drink, cooking utensils, and weapons. Many tombs were decorated with wall paintings, and hundreds of these have been found. The Etruscans also staged duels to provide a human sacrifice at funeral ceremonies.

Before the Romans

A variety of peoples of different origins and languages lived in the Italian peninsula before it was conquered by the Romans. Sabines and Umbrians, for example, lived to the north of Rome, while Apulians and Bruttians were farther south.

Statue of a warrior from an ancient Umbro-Sabellian tomb in central Italy.

the Italian peninsula.
264–146 BC Punic Wars against

Carthaginians of North Africa.
58–51 BC Caesar conquers Gaul.

44 BC Caesar assassinated.
31 BC Octavian defeats

Cleopatra of Egypt and Mark
Antony, ending civil war.

27 BC End of the Roman
Republic.

eventually took control of its empire. The growing gap between the rich patricians (aristocracy) and poor plebeians (ordinary people) led to conflicts among political leaders and to the rise of a great general, Julius Caesar (100–44 BC).

In 58 BC Caesar took command of the armies in Gaul (roughly modern France, the Netherlands, and part of western Germany), and by 51 BC he had conquered the entire region. A general named Pompeii persuaded the Senate to order Caesar to disband his army. Caesar refused, and war broke out. It ended four

years later, when Caesar defeated an army led by Pompeii's sons in Spain. Caesar was now ruler of the Roman world, and he declared himself "dictator for life." On March 15, 44 BC, conspirators who were unhappy at having a single ruler stabbed him to death. Civil war raged until a general named Octavian gained the upper hand and became Rome's first emperor in 27 BC, taking the name Augustus.

1. *Early bronze figure from pre-Roman times.*
2. *Etruscan vessel painted in Greek style.*
3. *Fresco from an Etruscan tomb.*
4. *The* fasces, *the symbol of Republican Rome.*

The Rise of Rome

Roman civilization, which spanned more than 1,000 years, had a humble beginning. The earliest traces of a Roman settlement (c.900 BC) were found on a hill rising above marshy ground near the Tiber River in central Italy. Nearby villages of huts gradually fused with this settlement to become a town. It grew quickly under a series of kings, some of whom were Etruscans. By the 6th century BC Rome was a walled city with fortifications. After a time the citizens decided to take control away from the kings and set up a republic, whose influence spread rapidly around the Mediterranean. But there were conflicts between Rome's rich aristocracy and the poor. The murder in 44 BC of Julius Caesar, the leading citizen, plunged Rome into civil war and led to the first emperor taking power in 27 BC.

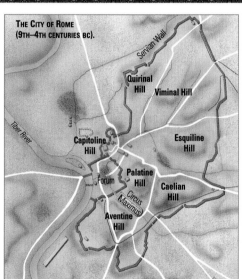

THE CITY OF ROME (9TH–4TH CENTURIES BC).

Servian Wall · Quirinal Hill · Viminal Hill · Capitoline Hill · Esquiline Hill · Palatine Hill · Caelian Hill · Aventine Hill · Forum · Circus Maximus · Tiber River

Romulus and Remus
According to legend, twin babies named Romulus and Remus were washed ashore in a basket on the banks of the Tiber River. They were suckled by a she-wolf, then looked after by a shepherd, and when they grew up they founded a city, in 753 BC. But the brothers argued over who should rule the city, and Romulus killed Remus. This was how Romulus became the first king of Rome.

Above: This Roman stela *or "stone monument" dates from the 5th century BC and shows the earliest recorded use of the Latin language.*

She-wolf suckling Romulus and Remus.

One of the founders of the Roman Republic, Lucius Junius Brutus (below) was one of the first pair of consuls elected after the Etruscan king, Tarquin II, was overthrown in 509 BC.

ROMAN TERRITORY c.120 BC.

SPAIN · ITALY · Rome · GREECE · Carthage · AFRICA · MEDITERRANEAN SEA

The Senate
Under the Roman kings the Senate (below) acted as an advisory council. During the Republic it was made up of 300 men and was headed by two consuls, who were voted in each year. Not everyone could vote, however; women and slaves were excluded. Ordinary working people, called plebeians, were not allowed to become consuls or hold high office in the Republic. These positions were held by patricians, or noblemen, who owned land and traced their origins back to early Rome.

Hannibal and the Carthaginians
By 270 BC the Romans had conquered all the Italian peninsula. They then began a series of wars against the Carthaginians. Hannibal, the Carthaginian commander-in-chief, crossed the Alps with a large army and 37 war elephants to attack Italy. He was finally defeated in 202 BC, and the Romans went on to take Carthage and its territory in North Africa in 146 BC.

An ancient Roman election poster. This piece of wall was used to advertise the name of a politician.

SEE ALSO
p. 28 THE ANCIENT HEBREWS
p. 34 CLASSICAL GREECE
p. 38 THE HELLENISTIC WORLD
p. 44 THE ROMAN EMPIRE
p. 106 THE RENAISSANCE

The Roman Empire

The first emperor, Augustus, ruled as supreme head of the Roman world from 27 BC to AD 14. Subsequent emperors continued to expand the empire until it circled the Mediterranean Sea, stretching from Spain in the west to Asia Minor in the east, and from Britain in the north to Egypt in the south. The new territories, called provinces, were conquered and controlled by the vast Roman army. Imperial society was made up of citizens (patricians and plebeians), freedmen (freed slaves), and slaves. During the 4th century AD Christianity became the official religion of the empire, which later split in two. The Eastern, or Byzantine, Empire was controlled from Constantinople, while Rome continued to rule the Western Empire. Rome itself was soon attacked by invaders, and in AD 476 the last Western emperor was toppled by Germanic armies.

Statue of Augustus, first Roman Emperor.

In 27 BC, 17 years after the death of Julius Caesar, his adopted son and heir, Octavian, became the first Roman emperor and took the name Augustus. The Senate and consuls remained in office, but Augustus ruled over everyone. He made sure that the boundaries of his empire were well defended and that the Roman provinces around Europe were under control. Before he died in AD 14, Augustus groomed his stepson Tiberius (reigned 14–37) to succeed him. This prepared the way for a succession of rulers who would keep the empire strong and secure for almost 500 years.

Emperor worship

From the beginning of the Roman Empire, the people were encouraged to worship their emperor as a god, as they had done Julius Caesar. Having a divine figure for millions of people to focus their loyalty on helped bind the vast empire together. Temples dedicated to the emperor sprang up all over the empire.

At its largest and most powerful, the Roman Empire ruled about 1 million people in the city of Rome, another 5 million in the rest of Italy, and up to 70 million scattered throughout the provinces.

Religion

Roman religion developed from ancient beliefs in spirits who guided people's lives. As time passed, the spirits were worshiped as Roman gods and goddesses. Each one had special powers, such as Mars, the god of war, and Diana, the goddess of hunting and the moon. The Romans also adopted many gods from the Greek pantheon.

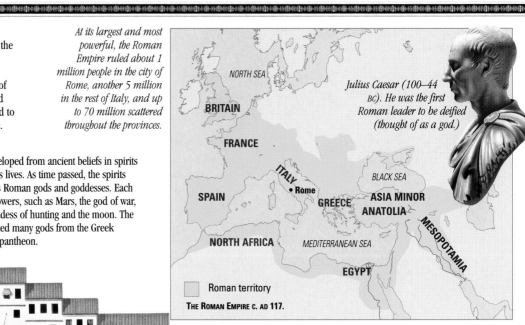

NORTH SEA

BRITAIN

FRANCE

ITALY • Rome

SPAIN GREECE ASIA MINOR ANATOLIA

BLACK SEA

MESOPOTAMIA

NORTH AFRICA MEDITERRANEAN SEA

EGYPT

Roman territory

THE ROMAN EMPIRE C. AD 117.

Julius Caesar (100–44 BC). He was the first Roman leader to be deified (thought of as a god.)

Above: Jupiter was the chief god of the Romans. He was the all-powerful god of the sky, daylight, and weather.

Hairstyles

Women's hairstyles changed with fashion. In the 2nd century AD it was fashionable to tie the hair in a knot (left). Ringlets, curls, and braids were popular, and some women dyed their hair – blonde and red were favorite shades – or wore wigs. Rich women had slaves to help them with their hair, makeup, and jewelry.

Technology

The Romans were master engineers and builders. They built excellent roads throughout the empire, constructed aqueducts, bridges, and innovative public buildings such as baths. Roads and buildings were so well designed and built that many still exist today.

This Roman mill used eight pairs of wooden water wheels to drive grindstones and crush wheat into flour.

Town and country

At the height of the empire, most people lived by farming. They grew wheat, rye, and barley, and tended olive groves and vineyards. Some rich city dwellers grew richer by owning farms, on which they built large country villas. In town they had spacious houses. But most city dwellers lived in an apartment building called an *insula*, or "island," up to five or six stories high (right).

The army

Rome had a huge, well-organized army. It was made up of between 25 and 35 legions, each containing about 5,000 men. A legion was divided into ten groups, called cohorts, which were split into centuries, units of about 100 soldiers. Legionary soldiers were Roman citizens, but other men from the empire could join auxiliary forces and be granted citizenship if they fought well.

The Praetorian Guard was the emperor's personal company of bodyguards. They were the only armed soldiers stationed in Rome.

Christianity the official religion. **330** Constantine moves capital of empire to Constantinople. **395** Empire splits in two: Western, run from Rome, and Eastern from Constantinople. **410** Visigoths sack Rome. **476** Germanic invaders overthrow last Western emperor, Romulus Augustulus.

The third emperor, Caligula (reigned 37–41), was convinced he was a god. He humiliated the Senate by making his horse a consul. In 41 he was assassinated. His uncle, Claudius (reigned 41–54), was a scholarly man who wrote histories of the Etruscans and Carthaginians. His armies invaded Britain in 43, and he added other provinces to the empire. Claudius also improved the Roman civil service, responsible for tax collection and the construction of public buildings. Claudius was poisoned by his third wife so that her son Nero could become emperor. Nero's reign (54–68) descended into

2

tyranny. When a great fire swept through Rome, he blamed the Christians and tortured many to death.

In 69, an army general, Vespasian, became emperor. He was faced with rebellions in Gaul and Judea. He was succeeded by Titus (reigned 79–81) and then Domitian (reigned 81–96), who introduced another reign of terror. Conspirators assassinated Domitian and replaced him with Nerva (reigned 96–98), who ushered in a century of peace and prosperity. The most notable emperor of this period was Trajan (reigned 98–117), who conquered Dacia.

The vast size of the empire made it difficult to run, and from 235 to 284 there was continuous civil war and invasions. The Goths attacked territory in Greece, and the Persians overran Mesopotamia and Syria. In 284 Emperor Diocletian (reigned 284–305) split the empire into eastern and western parts, which were ruled separately. Emperor Constantine (reigned 307–337) reintroduced rule by one emperor and made Christianity the official religion. In 330 he moved his capital to Byzantium, which was renamed Constantinople. In 395 the empire was redivided; the

3

Western Empire was run from Rome, and the Eastern, or Byzantine, Empire was run from Constantinople.

Vandals, Visigoths, and other Germanic peoples invaded the Western Empire. The Visigoths sacked Rome in 410. Then in 476 the Germanic general Odoacer overthrew the last emperor of Rome, Romulus Augustulus, and declared himself king of Italy, bringing the great Roman empire to an end. (The Byzantine Empire survived until 1453.)

1. The eagle was a Roman symbol of power.
2. The arch of Constantine in Rome.
3. Roman model of a vegetable store.

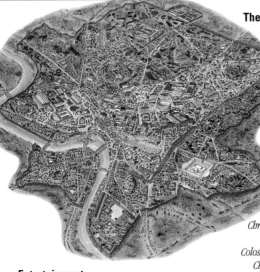

The city of Rome
Ancient Rome was a magnificent city, with forums, amphitheaters, theaters, baths, temples, and aqueducts. All roads led to the Roman Forum in the center of the city; this was the commercial, political, and social center of the entire Roman world. A wall had been built around the city in about 378 BC, but unlike later Roman towns the city was not formally planned.

Free grain
In ancient Rome there was a big gap between rich and poor. Some people found it difficult to feed themselves and lived in appalling conditions. In this mosaic, a Roman official is handing out free grain to some of Rome's poorest citizens. Free grain was distributed to up to 200,000 people, and it ensured that the poor neither starved nor revolted against the state.

Christians were persecuted by the Romans. Some were thrown to the lions in the Colosseum. Peter and Paul (right), who took Christianity to Rome, were both executed. They were later made saints.

Gladiator's helmet.

Entertainment
The Romans loved spectacular, bloodthirsty events. One of the most important buildings in any Roman town was the amphitheater, where specially trained gladiators fought each other to the death. Chariot races were held at the Circus Maximus in Rome. Music and drama also played an important part in Roman life. Romans enjoyed short plays called *mimi*, as well as stories told through music and dancing, called *pantomimi*.

The Colosseum, the largest Roman amphitheater, was built in Rome between AD 69 and 80 on the orders of the Emperor Vespasian. Up to 50,000 spectators thrilled at gladiator contests, animal displays, and even mock sea battles, for which the whole arena was flooded.

SEE ALSO
p. 28 THE ANCIENT HEBREWS
p. 42 THE RISE OF ROME • p. 66 MYTH AND RELIGION • p. 106 THE RENAISSANCE

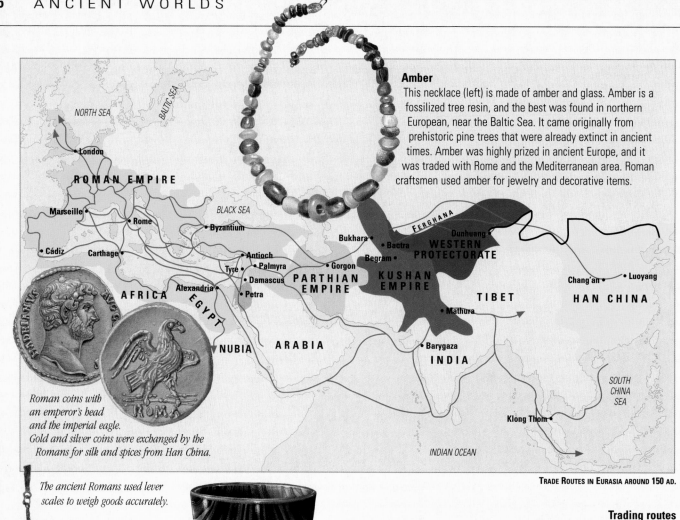

Amber
This necklace (left) is made of amber and glass. Amber is a fossilized tree resin, and the best was found in northern European, near the Baltic Sea. It came originally from prehistoric pine trees that were already extinct in ancient times. Amber was highly prized in ancient Europe, and it was traded with Rome and the Mediterranean area. Roman craftsmen used amber for jewelry and decorative items.

Roman coins with an emperor's head and the imperial eagle. Gold and silver coins were exchanged by the Romans for silk and spices from Han China.

TRADE ROUTES IN EURASIA AROUND 150 AD.

The ancient Romans used lever scales to weigh goods accurately.

The Romans made beautiful bowls, jugs, and other containers from quality glass for export.

Trading routes
Ancient trading routes stretched from the western and northern edges of the Roman Empire to eastern China and the islands of Southeast Asia. The Silk Road was the most important route, covering thousands of miles to connect the ancient Chinese city of Chang'an with Damascus and the Mediterranean. On the way it passed through the Kushan Empire of Afghanistan and northern India, and the Parthian Empire of Persia. Both were happy to control the route in exchange for tolls.

TRADE IN THE ANCIENT WORLD

Trade soon became an important part of life in early civilizations. Individual regions and empires, such as Egypt, Nubia, and Phoenicia, were naturally rich in some resources and poor in others. Rulers and traveling merchants saw opportunities to even up the imbalance. In Eurasia, goods and materials were sent many thousands of miles along the Silk Road and other trade routes, even though Han China at the eastern end and the Roman Empire in the west otherwise had no direct contact with each other. The merchants carried more than the goods on their camels' backs – ideas and skills also traveled along these routes. In this way, for example, Buddhism spread from India to China by the end of the 1st century AD. In the Americas, traders traveled between great cities such as Teotihuacán and Monte Albán, while the Mayan cities traded such materials as jade and obsidian with each other.

Ancient Rome
The Roman Empire was dependent on trade. Helped by their fine network of roads, inland waterways, and harbors, the Romans were able to transport goods throughout the empire. They exported gold and silver – mostly in the form of coins – as well as wine and olive oil. The main Roman imports were silk from China, gemstones, muslin, and spices from India, incense from Arabia, and ivory from Africa.

This Roman sign was used to advertise a bank. Trade throughout the empire was made easy by the use of a common currency, made up of gold, silver, copper, and bronze coins. Beyond the empire, the coins were useful as a source of precious metal.

Han China

During the rule of the Han Dynasty (202 BC–AD 220), ancient China was mainly self-sufficient. Trade was not a fundamental imperial concern, though huge income was gained from the export of silk and lacquerware, such as the tray (below) with mugs and bowls. Certain imports were highly prized, such as spices and mother-of-pearl from Southeast Asia, and horses from central Asia.

Trading cities

The big trading cities such as Chang'an, in China, and Alexandria, in Egypt, had huge populations. At Chang'an trading was carried out in two large markets, where government officials controlled prices and trading standards. Camel caravans followed ancient routes across hills and deserts taking goods to and from the Mediterranean region. On the main route between the Roman and Persian empires, traveling caravans stopped at the oasis city of Palmyra, where citizens grew rich from their services to traders.

MAJOR DATES

c.2700 BC The port of Byblos (in modern Lebanon) is used to ship cedar wood to Egypt.
c.2300 BC The Akkadians make trading contact with "Meluhha," probably the growing cities of the Indus Valley civilization.
c.1500 BC Mycenaean merchants buy amber from northern Europe and ship it around the eastern Mediterranean.
1498–1493 BC During the reign of Queen Hatshepsut the Egyptians sail down the Red Sea to trade with a land called Punt.
814 BC Phoenicians from Tyre found the trading city of Carthage in North Africa.
550 BC Chinese silk reaches Europe.
c.500 BC Darius I (the Great) of Persia improves caravan trails and builds a 1,700-mi. (2,700-km) long Royal Road.
c.280 BC The world's first lighthouse, one of the Seven Wonders of the Ancient World, is built at Alexandria.
135 BC Chinese envoy Zhang Qian visits western Asia and takes back alfalfa, pomegranates, and grapes.
c.110 BC Trade between Han China and western Asia and Europe flourishes along the Silk Road.
c.100 BC Greek navigator Hippalus discovers the monsoon winds of the Indian Ocean.
AD 97 A Chinese ambassador is sent to Antioch (in modern Turkey).

Bronze model of a "heavenly horse" imported to Han China from the Ferghana region of central Asia. The horses were needed by the Chinese cavalry for their struggle with invading nomads from the north.

The Begram treasure

From the 2nd century BC the ancient town of Begram, in present-day Afghanistan, had many public buildings, houses, and shops. It lay across the Hindu Kush mountains from Bactra, a town on the main Silk Road. In 1938 a Belgian expedition discovered two bricked-up storerooms at Begram filled with items that had been stored there since ancient times. There were ivory plaques and statues from India (one of which is shown, above), lacquerwork items from China, and alabaster vessels, bronze statues, and glassware from the Mediterranean region.

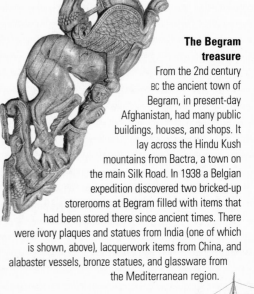

The color purple was rare and expensive in the ancient world. The Phoenicians made purple dye from the murex sea snail (left) which they traded all over the Mediterranean and even farther afield. Our word "Phoenician" comes from a Greek word meaning "people of the purple dye."

Sea routes

About 3000 years ago, the Phoenicians were the greatest sailors of the Mediterranean Sea. Their cedar-wood ships sailed from their ports of Tyre and Sidon, to found trading colonies on the Mediterranean islands, as well as in southern Spain and North Africa. The Romans took up many of these sea routes, and around 100 BC a Greek sailor discovered that the seasonal monsoon winds could be used to sail between Arabia and India. Great ports developed, such as Caesarea (below), which Herod the Great developed from an earlier Phoenician port between 22 and 10 BC.

A Roman merchant ship is loaded with cargo. The largest ships carried huge loads of grain from Egypt and the Black Sea, to feed the Roman people.

A soapstone bust of a bearded man dating from about 2100 BC. It was found in the ruins of the residential area of Mohenjo-Daro. The figure is wearing an emblem on his forehead and an elaborate cloak over one shoulder, and is thought to represent a priest or king.

A terra-cotta model of a two-wheeled ox cart with its driver, from the city of Harappa. Ancient imprints made by wheels have been found in the Indus Valley, and archeologists think the carts used then were similar to some used in the region today.

Trade

Towns may have grown up along the Indus Valley as a result of trade with the kingdom of Akkad in Mesopotamia. According to Mesopotamian records of about 2300 BC, King Sargon of Akkad had contacts with "Meluhha," which experts believe was the Indus Valley. People from the Indus Valley traded metals such as copper. In return, they needed tin, which they mixed with copper to make bronze. They also imported semi-precious stones from present-day Afghanistan. Merchants probably sailed from the port of Lothal, on the coast of modern India, where evidence of a brick-lined harbor has been found.

Indus Valley cities

The Indus Valley cities were made up of two parts: a lower residential town, where most people lived, and a higher fortified citadel, which was built on a raised brick platform and surrounded by a brick wall to protect it from attack. The streets of the residential town were laid out in a neat grid pattern. They had drains running underneath them, which were connected to the washrooms and toilets in people's houses. The citadel probably served as a religious and administrative center. In Mohenjo-Daro there was also a Great Bath that was made watertight by a thick layer of bitumen. It had its own fountain and drainage system.

These pieces of jewelry were found at Mehrgarh, a small settlement of up to a few hundred people that formed one of the earliest farming communities in southern Asia. The items were made of local and imported stones, shells, and bone. The fine craftwork suggests that the Indus Valley people must have used bow-drills.

About 2,500 stone seals have been found in the Indus Valley. They are decorated with pictures of animals, including humped bulls, tigers, elephants, and crocodiles. They also have inscriptions on them, written in the Indus Valley script. Experts have not yet been able to decipher the script. The seals may have been used by merchants to identify goods.

c.4000 BC People settle and farm the Indus floodplain. | Copper in use. **3500 BC** Potter's wheel in use | to make clay vessels. **2600 BC** Cities of Harappa | and Mohenjo-Daro appear; start of Indus Valley civilization.

Ancient India

Almost 5,000 years ago a great civilization developed along the valley of the Indus River in present-day Pakistan and India. It flourished for about 800 years. The centers of authority were the two cities of Mohenjo-Daro and Harappa. Their wealth was derived from trade with people in the north and west of the Indian subcontinent, and also with Mesopotamia. In the Indus Valley farmers grew crops on the river's fertile floodplain. Local rulers lived in citadels overlooking the cities, which were well planned and efficiently run, and had fresh water and good drainage systems. The houses were built from kiln-baked mud bricks. The Indus Valley people had systems of counting, measuring, weighing, and writing, but experts have not yet deciphered their script.

Necklace made in the Indus Valley.

About 6000 BC people started to settle and farm the region of Baluchistan to the northwest of Mohenjo-Daro, an area separated from the Indus Valley by the Kirthar Mountains. About 2,000 years later farmers settled on the Indus floodplain. There is evidence that these settlers were using copper. By 3500 BC craftspeople were using potter's wheels to make clay vessels.

Cities appeared in about 2600 BC, marking the start of what is called the Indus Valley civilization. The two largest cities excavated so far –

The yellow area shows where farming started around 6000 BC. The green arrows show the directions in which it spread.

HIMALAYAS

• Harappa

• Mehrgarh

BALUCHISTAN

Indus River

• Mohenjo-Daro

INDIA

ARABIAN SEA

Lothal •

MAP OF INDUS VALLEY CIVILIZATION

The Indus River rises high in the Himalayas and is joined by several tributaries as it flows 1,800 mi. (2,900 km) through northern India and across Pakistan to the Arabian Sea. It has been suggested that unusually high floods may have been one factor in the civilization's fall. Today the site of Mohenjo-Daro is threatened by a rise in the water table.

AREA OF INDUS VALLEY CIVILIZATION

INDIA

SEE ALSO
p. 22 SUMER AND AKKAD
p. 36 ANCIENT PERSIA
p. 50 FIRST EMPIRES IN INDIA

Left: The decorated terra-cotta lid of an urn found at Harappa. Indus Valley pottery was often red with black geometric designs.

Decorated vases from Baluchistan, the region to the northwest of Mohenjo-Daro. Potters in the Indus Valley first used a wheel to make their pots about 3500 BC.

Houses

At Mohenjo-Daro, the remains of mud-brick houses have been found. This reconstruction (right) shows how one of them may have looked. Houses had a single doorway, and any windows within the house looked onto a central courtyard, which provided privacy and kept the house cool. A washroom (shown to the right of the doorway) contained a well, where fresh water was drawn up; next to it was a bathing platform. Toilets were connected to drains under the street. A wooden balcony on the second floor overlooked the courtyard. In the courtyards of many of the houses, archeologists found brick-lined shafts, which may have been wells or storage places for vases or jars.

a terra-cotta figurine of a mother goddess wearing jewelry and a loincloth. It was found at Mohenjo-Daro and dates from about 2000 BC. Many similar examples have been found. Experts believe that the goddess was probably worshiped in homes or in small, local shrines. No large temples have been found in the Indus Valley cities.

2250–1750 BC Indus Valley cities flourish; civilization grows.

2000 BC Bronze in use.
1800 BC People leave cities;

Indus Valley civilization breaks up into smaller cultures.

c.1500 BC Aryans come to the region from the Iranian plateau

of central Asia and settle. Indus Valley civilization ends.

Harappa and Mohenjo-Daro – have revealed a great deal about this civilization (which is also sometimes called Harappan). The cities flourished between 2600 and 1800 BC, when the Indus Valley civilization covered much of present-day Pakistan and parts of northern India. The heart of the civilization was the vast floodplain of the Indus and Hakra rivers. (The Hakra River flowed parallel to the Indus, but is now dried up.) The main food crops were wheat and barley, which farmers sowed in spring when the floodwaters retreated. Surplus grain was stored in large granaries in the cities. Some farmers also grew rice and cotton,

which was woven at Mohenjo-Daro; this is the earliest evidence of the use of cotton textiles anywhere in the world, outside the Americas. By 2000 BC metalworkers in the Indus Valley were using bronze, probably made from imported tin and local copper.

About 1800 BC the cities began to decline, and 100 years later the Indus civilization broke up into smaller cultures, sometimes

called post-Harappan cultures. This may have been caused by changing river patterns, including the drying up of the Hakra River and changes in the course of the Indus River.

Then, about 1500 BC, a semi-nomadic, Indo-European people came over the passes of the Hindu Kush Mountains from central Asia. These people called themselves Aryans, from a

Sanskrit word meaning "nobles," or "owners of land." Some experts have suggested that the Aryans destroyed the cities and their people, but most believe that they entered a region that was already devastated. Perhaps forests had been destroyed by tree-felling, which would have added to the flood and watercourse problems of the Indus River, on which the people depended. No single civilization took its place until the emergence of the Mauryan Empire in central India in about 320 BC.

1. Indus Valley pendant.

2. Terra-cotta figures on horseback. Dating to before 1500 BC, they are the earliest evidence of the use of the horse in India.

2

c.1500 BC Aryans arrive in northern India. **c.1000 BC** Veda

hymns composed. **c.599–527 BC** Life of Mahavira, founder of

Jainism. **c.563–483 BC** Life of Siddharta Gautama,

founder of Buddhism. **326 BC** Alexander of Macedon

First Empires in India

By the time Aryans migrated to northern India, the earlier ancient Indus Valley civilization had broken up. The Aryans gradually moved down the subcontinent, but they never conquered the southern regions. The mythical story of their migration and wars with the local peoples were recorded in the *Vedic Hymns*, now the most sacred books of the Hindu religion. During the 6th century BC two other religions developed and spread in India – Buddhism and Jainism. The Mauryan Empire came to power in India in 321 BC. It was conquered by the Kushans, a people from central Asia, who were themselves overthrown by native Indian emperors of the Gupta dynasty. Under the Guptas India became a great center of art and learning.

Around 1500 BC migrating bands of Aryans traveled across the Hindu Kush Mountains from central Asia and arrived in northern India. Many of the original Dravidian people living in the region were pushed south by the invaders. The Aryans brought with them a series of Sanskrit hymns, called *Vedas*, which were passed on by word of mouth until they were first written down, in the 6th century BC. Around 1100 BC the Aryans began working iron, and 100 years later

Agni, the god of fire, was one of the most popular Vedic gods.

THE MAURYAN, KUSHAN, AND GUPTA EMPIRES AT THEIR GREATEST EXTENTS.

• Peshwar

• Pataliputra

• Ajanta

→ Aryan invasion

⬦ Mauryan Empire c. 260 BC

Kushan India c. AD 200

Gupta Empire c. AD 400

Bust of the Buddha dating from the period of the Kushan Empire. Before then the Buddha had only been shown in symbolic form, such as a wheel or an empty throne.

Buddhism and Jainism

Two major religions began in India in the 6th century BC. The first was Jainism, which was founded by Mahavira (c.599–527 BC), a member of a Hindu warrior caste. The Jains believe that every living thing has an eternal soul and a temporary physical body. Buddhism was based on the teachings of an Indian prince named Siddharta Gautama (c.563–483 BC), who came to be known as the Buddha or "enlightened one."

The Aryans

The Aryans, who took their name from a Sanskrit word meaning "noble," were originally nomadic herders from the central Asian region. The little we know of ancient Aryan life comes from the Vedas, a series of hymns, spells, and rituals that were composed around 1000 BC and passed down the generations by word of mouth. Though they were only written down much later, the Vedas form the basic Hindu scriptures.

Ashoka put up pillars throughout his empire. They were inscribed with his beliefs and orders. This one was erected at Sarnath, where the Buddha preached his first sermon. Today it is the emblem of the modern state of India.

Ashoka

Ashoka ruled the Mauryan Empire from about 268 to 233 BC. After he conquered the Kalinga region on the east coast of India, Ashoka was unhappy at the bloodshed he had caused. The emperor then converted from Hinduism to Buddhism, rejected war, and asked his people to treat each other with justice and mercy. No living thing was to be harmed unless it was absolutely unavoidable.

The Mauryan Empire

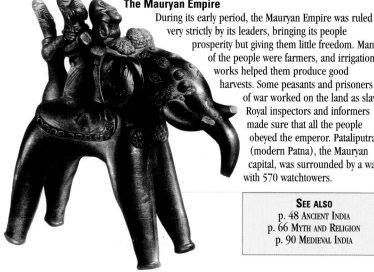

During its early period, the Mauryan Empire was ruled very strictly by its leaders, bringing its people prosperity but giving them little freedom. Many of the people were farmers, and irrigation works helped them produce good harvests. Some peasants and prisoners of war worked on the land as slaves. Royal inspectors and informers made sure that all the people obeyed the emperor. Pataliputra (modern Patna), the Mauryan capital, was surrounded by a wall with 570 watchtowers.

A Kushan gold statue of the Greek goddess Aphrodite made in Bactria.

The Kushans

The Kushans were a group of nomadic tribes who had taken over the ancient Greek kingdom of Bactria in central Asia around 135 BC. Less than 200 years later they crossed the Hindu Kush Mountains and invaded northwest India under their leader Kujala Kadphises. His successors moved further south into the Indus Valley and the Ganges plain. Though most of the early Kushan rulers were Buddhists, they showed respect for a wide range of Greek, Persian, and Roman gods.

> **SEE ALSO**
> p. 48 ANCIENT INDIA
> p. 66 MYTH AND RELIGION
> p. 90 MEDIEVAL INDIA

conquers northwestern India. **321–185 BC** Mauryan Empire. | **c.272–232 BC** Reign of Mauryan ruler Ashoka. **AD 50–320** Kushan | Empire. **c.100–130** Reign of Kushan ruler Kanishka. **320–500** | Gupta Empire. **c.375–415** Reign of Gupta ruler Chandragupta II. | **c.460** White Huns start their invasions of the Gupta Empire.

they settled in villages on the Ganges plain and began farming rice.

By 900 BC small Hindu kingdoms developed across the Ganges plain, and around 500 BC Magadha, ruled by King Bimbisara, emerged as the most powerful kingdom.

In 326 BC Alexander the Great conquered the northwestern region of India, but left again when his troops refused to go on. Five years later a military commander who fought against the new invaders, Chandragupta Maurya

(reigned c.321–293 BC), overthrew the ruling dynasty of Magadha.

The new ruler founded an empire which we call Mauryan, after him. Its most famous emperor was Ashoka (reigned c.268–233 BC). By Ashoka's time the Mauryan Empire extended far into southern India, and Ashoka himself conquered many neighboring peoples. After Ashoka's death the Mauryan Empire broke up into smaller units, and the last Mauryan ruler was overthrown by one of his generals in 185 BC.

In AD 50–75 the Kushans conquered northwest India. Their greatest leader was Kanishka, who ruled from about AD 100. The Kushans ruled over a loosely organized empire until they were overthrown by the Guptas.

Chandragupta I (reigned 320–35) founded the Gupta Dynasty. The Gupta Empire reached its peak during the reign of Chandragupta II (380–414) when it was almost as large as the Mauryan Empire had been. The Gupta ruler Skandagupta (reigned 455–67) fought off an attempted invasion by the White Huns, but then the empire went into decline as smaller tribes reclaimed their independence. Around 500 the

White Huns finally conquered much of northern India.

1. Elephant-headed Ganesha was seen as a god of health, good fortune, and prosperity.
2. Krishna, the eighth incarnation of Vishnu, the Preserver.

Kanishka

Gold coin with the image of King Kanishka.

Kanishka was the greatest ruler of the Kushan Empire, reigning for around 30 years from about AD 100. Kushan culture reached its peak under his leadership. He created a council of Buddhist monks, and at his capital Peshawar (in modern Pakistan) he built a towering monument to house relics of Buddha. Kanishka was a great patron of the arts and encouraged the Gandharan school of sculpture, which produced the first stone images of Buddha.

Above: Hindu monument at Mamallapuram, on the coast of southern India.

The Gupta Dynasty

The Gupta rulers came from a family of rich landowners in the Ganges valley. They favored the Hindu religion, and the Gupta kings revived many of the rituals of the brahmans, or Hindu priests. At the same time they were also tolerant of other faiths, and Buddhist beliefs were widespread. The Gupta kings and other rich people gave large amounts of money to both Hindu temples and Buddhist monasteries.

Gupta arts and sciences

The Gupta rulers were great patrons of the arts and sciences. Chandragupta II encouraged poets and dramatists, including Kalidasa, who wrote in Sanskrit about love, adventure, and the beauty of nature. At the same time many Buddhist monasteries had large libraries. The monastic university at Nalanda attracted visiting scholars from as far away as China. Gupta mathematicians invented the decimal system of counting and the Hindu-Arabic numbers that we still use today.

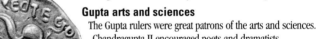

Two gold Gupta coins. Above: a horse is about to be sacrificed in celebration of a victory by Samudragupta, who reigned for about 50 years from 330. Below: Samudragupta plays the vina, an instrument similar to a sitar.

The Ajanta caves

The cave sanctuaries and monasteries of Ajanta are the finest examples of Buddhist rock-cut architecture in India. At Ajanta, to the northeast of modern Bombay, 30 caves were cut into the cliffs of a narrow gorge above a river. Some were first hollowed out around the 2nd century BC, but most were cut and decorated between the 5th and 6th centuries AD. The caves contain wonderfully carved columns and beautiful murals showing the life of Buddha and other scenes.

A mural from Ajanta. The outlines of the murals were first drawn with charcoal, and the background was filled in before the details were finally painted.

Sculpture of the goddess Ganga, personification of the sacred Ganges River.

Imperial decline

The Gupta period was one of peace and prosperity for much of India. At this time the subcontinent became famous for its fine cloth, carved ivory, pearls, and other trading items. The empire was threatened when Huns from central Asia began invading around 460. The Gupta rulers grew weaker, and parts of their empire declared their independence, until finally the Guptas ruled simply as princes in their northeastern Magadha homeland.

c.6500 BC Rice farming begins in the Yangtze Valley. **c.6000 BC** First settlements by the Yellow River in China. **c.4000 BC** Irrigation canals built. **c.1766 BC** Shang Dynasty founded in northern China. **c.1450 BC** Writing developed. **1122 BC** Shang Dynasty conquered by Zhou. **480–221 BC** "Warring

Ancient China and Japan

China is the home of the oldest continuous civilization the world has ever known. It grew from a sprinkling of small farming settlements along the banks of the Yellow and Yangtze rivers. By the Yellow River in the north, the Chinese grew millet. To the south, along the Yangtze River, the main crop was rice. As the population increased, disputes broke out between rival leaders and people moved into walled villages for safety. Some of these villages grew into towns and then into cities, ruled by powerful, often warlike leaders. The ruling families were known as dynasties. Legends tell of ruling dynasties in China from about 2500 BC, but the first dynasty about which anything is known was the Shang Dynasty (founded c.1766 BC). Japan's legendary history began with the first emperor, Jimmu, in 660 BC.

Princess Douwan of the Han Dynasty (202 BC–AD 220) was buried in this funeral suit made from jade plates fastened with gold wire. The tombs of members of the dynasty were richly furnished with bronze, gold, silver, and jade objects.

The Shang Dynasty was founded about 1766 BC and lasted for over 500 years. The Shang built themselves magnificent palaces and public buildings. During their reign, technologies such as bronze-making were discovered, and a form of picture writing was developed. But about 1122 BC a rival dynasty, the Zhou, conquered the Shang and began the longest dynasty in Chinese history, lasting 900 years.

The Zhou divided China into smaller states ruled by lords chosen by the king. The first 400 years were relatively peaceful, with the arts of poetry and song prominent at the Zhou court. But

The birth of agriculture

The choice of crops grown by the early farmers of the Chinese river valleys was dictated by the soil and climate. Beside the Yellow River in northern China the soil is dry and the weather cold. Millet was the chosen crop there. To the south, the Yangtze River flows through wet land where there is heavy rainfall, more suitable for rice farming. Rice was originally cultivated from seeds of wild rice, which grows freely in southern China. An increase in the population and the development of irrigation canals led to rice and millet being grown greater distances from the rivers.

Right: This piece of tortoise shell (a shoulder blade) is inscribed with events from the Shang Dynasty. Picture symbols (below) were also used during the same period.

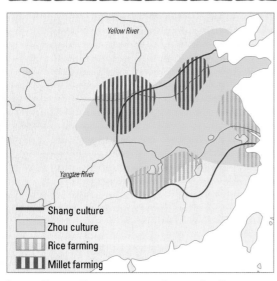

Yellow River

Yangtze River

Shang culture
Zhou culture
Rice farming
Millet farming

ORIGINS OF FARMING IN CHINA AND THE AREAS OF SHANG AND ZHOU DYNASTIES.

Early writing

In the earliest written Chinese, picture symbols were used to represent objects. This kind of writing is called "pictographic." The earliest pictograms date from about 1450 BC, during the Shang Dynasty. It is likely that most writing from this time was done on pieces of wood or fabric, which have not survived. The earliest surviving inscriptions are on pottery, bronzes, and animal bones.

Shang craftspeople made beautiful bronze cups, goblets, and cauldrons. They were probably used in religious ceremonies. This bronze elephant stands over 10 in. (26 cm) high.

The first dynasties

Some Chinese believe that the first dynasty or ruling family was founded about 2200 BC by an emperor named Yu the Great, but there are no historical records of this. The first-known dynasty, the Shang, was founded about 1766 BC by King Tang. The dates of the first two Chinese dynasties, the Shang and the Zhou, are not known exactly.

This bronze figure of a maidservant holding a lamp was found in the tomb of Princess Douwan of the Han Dynasty. It has been dated to before 150 BC.

The chart below shows how China was ruled from about 1766 BC to AD 618. Dynasties were made up of the emperor's extended family and close advisers. During the "Three Kingdoms" period, China was split into Wei, in the north, Wu in the central and lower Yangtze Valley, and Shu round the upper Yangtze.

SEE ALSO
p. 66 MYTH AND RELIGION
p. 86 CHINESE CIVILIZATION
p. 98 JAPAN AND KOREA
p. 124 MING CHINA
p. 194 MANCHU CHINA

Shang c.1766–c.1122 BC | Zhou c.1122–221 BC | Qin 221–202 BC | Han 202 BC–AD 220 | The "Three Kingdoms" 220–581 | Sui 581–618

States" period; China unified.
c.300 BC Rice farms in Japan.

202 BC–AD 220 Period of peace in China under Han Dynasty.

220–589 Warfare between rival states; ends with reunification

under Sui Dynasty.
300–600 Yamato kingdom

dominant in Japan; unification begins, modeled on China.

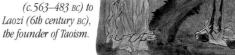

from about 770 BC there were constant wars between the lords. The years from 480 to 221 BC are called the "Warring States" period, because of the constant fighting. In 480 BC there were hundreds of states. By 221 BC the strongest state, Qin, had taken over the rest. The Qin leader, Zheng, set out to make China one nation. Coinage, weights and measures, the writing

system, and even cart sizes were standardized over the whole country, and it was under the Qin that the building of the Great Wall of China began.

In 206 BC the entire royal family was murdered, and soon afterward a new dynasty, the Han, took over. After the downfall of the Han Dynasty in AD 220, China was split into three kingdoms: Wei, Shu, and Wu. Another round of fighting began. At about this time an important influence on Chinese thought began to emerge. This was Buddhism, first introduced to China from central Asia in about AD 100. Along with the Buddhist faith and way of thought came Buddhist art, architecture, and science.

It was not until 589 that the Sui Dynasty came to power and reunified China, paving the way for a long period of prosperity.

Japan's development as a state came much later than China's. As in southern China, the earliest settlements were rice farms. Larger towns and cities only began to develop about 300 BC. By AD 300 the Yamato family had emerged as the leaders, and over the next 300 years they steadily created a unified kingdom of Japan and occupied the southern part of Korea. Chinese influence became strong, and the Yamato encouraged the adoption of Buddhism, a modified Chinese writing system,

Chinese methods of government, and Chinese technology.

1. The wheelbarrow was invented in China in during the Han Dynasty.

2. Ox carts were the most common means of moving goods in ancient China. This ceramic model was excavated from a tomb in the Shanxi province and dates from the mid 6th century.

China is unified

Between 230 and 221 BC, a series of wars enabled the Qin rulers to conquer the whole of China and rule it as one state. King Zheng (reigned 246–210 BC) of the Qin took the name "Shi Huangdi," which means "First Emperor." He was an effective but unpopular ruler with a reputation for cruelty. Millions of Chinese were forced into labor building his palaces, the Great Wall, and other public works. He died in 210 BC.

The First Emperor secretly designed his own tomb, which contained thousands of lifesize clay soldiers that he thought would protect him in his next life. This "terra-cotta army" was equipped with real war chariots and bronze weapons.

This picture is intended to show how the three Chinese religions – Confucianism, Buddhism, and Taoism, – lived in harmony together. Confucius (551–479 BC), on the right, is showing the infant Buddha (c.563–483 BC) to Laozi (6th century BC), the founder of Taoism.

Three religions

The first system of religious belief in China was Confucianism, named after Confucius, who lived from about 551 to 479 BC. He taught kindness toward other people and respect for the family. About 100 AD Buddhism began to spread in China. Buddha, who lived at about the same time as Confucius, taught people to set aside time each day for meditation. A third religion, Taoism, grew rapidly during the Han Dynasty. It was based on the teachings of Laozi, who also lived about 500 BC. Taoists, too, believe in meditation.

The Great Wall

The Great Wall extends for 1,500 mi. (2,400 km) across northern China. It began as a series of earth banks built during the "Warring States" period (480–221 BC) to keep out invaders from the north. Under the rule of Shi Huangdi, the lengths of bank were strengthened and connected into one continuous wall, with garrisons of soldiers stationed along it at intervals. Later dynasties maintained and rebuilt the Great Wall; the structure seen today dates from about the 16th century.

Three ancient Chinese coins. Metal coins date to the 5th century BC. Before then shells were used in some regions. The round coin with a hole in the middle was more convenient as it could be threaded on a string.

Pottery was made in Japan from around 10,500 BC, earlier than anywhere else in the world. This pointed "Jomon" vase stands about 16 in. (42 cm) high and dates from between 10,500 and 7,500 BC.

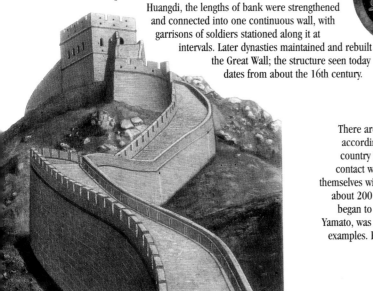

Ancient Japan

There are no historical records of ancient Japan, but according to legend Japan's first ruler, Jimmu, led the country from 660 BC. Until about AD 200 Japan had little contact with the outside world and the Japanese supported themselves with rice growing and coastal fishing. However, from about 200 on, traders started visiting Japan, and Chinese ideas began to influence the Japanese. When the first Japanese state, Yamato, was founded about 300, it was closely modeled on Chinese examples. Buddhism was introduced to Japan by missionaries from Korea in 552, and a great age of temple building began.

ART AND LITERATURE

Museums today are full of splendid examples of art from ancient times. But it is important to remember that the ancients probably did not consider art as we do now; they did not have museums to display it in, and the ancient Greeks did not even have a special word for art. They spoke of *techne*, which is much closer to our word for craft. Objects of beauty were certainly made to be admired, but also, and perhaps most importantly, for more practical reasons, such as to honor a god or goddess who might help win a war or bring a good harvest. The earliest examples of literature date to the times of ancient Mesopotamia and Egypt, but they are probably versions of tales that had been passed down through the centuries orally.

Animals in ancient art

Animals were frequently represented in ancient art. The Egyptians depicted their gods and goddesses as animals, or as humans with animal heads and tails. They also considered some animals, including the cat, as sacred, and made some beautiful statues of them (presumably for worship). The gold statue of a lioness goddess (above) comes from the tomb of the pharaoh Tutankhamun (reigned 1334–1325 BC).

Architecture

Ancient architects used complex technical knowhow to build imposing temples and other buildings. Much of that knowledge was lost during the Middle Ages. For example, European architects were not able to build another dome like the one built by the ancient Romans on the Pantheon in Rome until Renaissance times, over a thousand years later.

This powerful and expressive horse's head comes from the frieze of the Parthenon (Athens). It was sculpted almost 2,500 years ago.

Jewelry

People of the ancient world loved jewelry just as much as we do today. The craftspeople of the times were skilful jewelers and, because metal and stone age well, some stunning pieces of ancient jewelry have been found. Many of the jewels have a religious meaning, while others were worn as charms to ward off evil.

This Egyptian pectoral (breastplate) is made of gold, inset with precious stones. It has a wedjat eye at the top to protect its wearer from harm.

The earliest metal coins were used by Greek traders in the 7th century BC. The idea spread quickly and groups all over the ancient world developed their own distinctive coinage. These examples are 1) Roman, 2) Greek, 3) Celtic.

Left: The Parthenon, in Athens, is probably the most famous building of the ancient world. Built under Pericles in the 5th century BC, It was just one building in an extensive city-panning program Athens undertook after the Persian Wars.

The Parthenon dominates the Acropolis, a walled citadel in the center of Athens.

Literature

Many of the greatest works of literature were written during ancient times. The works of Greek playwrights, such as Aeschylus (see below), Sophocles, and Euripides, are still admired. Many Roman authors too, including Virgil and Ovid, are part of the Western canon of great writers. The Bible, an all-time bestseller, was also written in those times.

Even though few women were taught to read or write, there were still some great women writers. Sappho (610–580 BC) is considered one of the greatest of the Greek poets.

Greek pottery

In Greek pottery the shape of the vase was less important than the way it was decorated. The earliest Greek vases had abstract decorations, but by the 8th century BC they were mainly geometric patterns. This was followed by a period in which black figures were dominant. The more realistic red-figure technique was in vogue in Athens from about 530 BC.

Most vases were jar- or cup-shaped, but some potters gave them more inventive forms, like this painted cup in the form of a donkey's head.

Dance

All of the ancient peoples seem to have enjoyed some form of dance. Some dances, such as the those performed during the Bacchanalia in Roman religion, were frenzied and mystical. Dancing girls also performed to entertain guests at Roman dinner parties and banquets. Egyptian wall paintings also show women dancing and playing musical instruments.

Women in the ancient world often worked as dancers, musicians, and singers.

Scene from a 7th-century BC cup showing Greek soldiers coming out of the wooden horse of Troy.

Music

Music accompanied many activities in the ancient world, not just the obvious ones, such as dancing, but also during athletic competitions, war, and in everyday work situations, such as in a bakery. In ancient Greece boys were taught to play musical instruments and to sing at school. Learning music was thought to have a civilizing effect on the boys' minds. In this image (left) a teacher is instructing two young men how to play the lyre.

Ancient artists also recorded everyday life and historical events. This relief (right) shows the Roman city of Pompeii during the earthquake that destroyed it in AD 62.

MAJOR DATES

3150–2180 BC Early Dynastic and Old Kingdom periods in ancient Egypt. Funerary texts on the walls of private tomb-chapels are written to ensure the survival of the individual beyond death.

1991–1962 BC (12th Dynasty) Earliest manuscripts with literary tales found in Egypt.

2nd millennium BC Five short poems in the Sumerian language recount episodes from the life of Gilgamesh. They probably refer to the King Gilgamesh who ruled at Uruk during the first half of the 3rd millennium BC.

1200–100 BC The Old Testament or Hebrew Bible first written, in Hebrew (with just a few passages in Aramaic).

668–627 BC Reign of Assyrian king Ashurbanipal. The fullest existing text of the Gilgamesh epic was found in his library. It is written in Akkadian on 12 tablets.

c.484–c.420 BC Life of Greek writer Herodotus, author of the first great book of narrative history.

43 BC–AD 17 Life of Latin poet Ovid, author of *Art of Love* and *Metamorphoses*.

AD 143–176 Life of Pausanias.

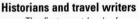

Historians and travel writers

The first great book of history was written by the Greek traveler and author Herodotus. His book recounts the background and events of the Persian Wars. Another Greek – Pausanias – wrote one of the earliest guide books. *His Description of Greece* is an invaluable guide to the ruins of ancient Greece.

Greek theater festivals

The first festival of theater was held in Athens in 534 BC during the great spring festival, the City Dionysia. After that each Dionysia included four consecutive days of theater when spectators sat from dawn until dusk comparing the works of several playwrights. Of the enormous body of work produced over the years, only 35 tragedies and a few comedies have survived.

c.6000 BC Farming settlements along river valleys and coasts.

c.2000 BC Bronze in use in Thailand and northern Vietnam.

c.500 BC Iron being used to make tools in central Thailand.

111 BC Northern Vietnam is made a province of China.

AD 100–550 The kingdom of Funan (southern Vietnam).

Southeast Asia from Neolithic Times

Southeast Asia is made up of two parts: Indochina, which includes Myanmar, Cambodia, Thailand, and Vietnam; and the vast Indonesian archipelago, which consists of the Malay peninsula and over 13,000 islands that make up Indonesia. Early human beings (*Homo erectus*) lived in Indonesia over 500,000 years ago. But the ancestors of most Indonesian peoples moved there from Asia during the 2nd millennium BC. In Thailand, there is evidence that rice was being cultivated from about 6000 BC. By this time settlements had grown up along the rivers and coasts, where fertile soils meant good crops could be grown. In neighboring Myanmar to the west, the first civilizations were the Mon culture in the south, dating from about the 3rd century BC, and founded by the Buddhist Mon people from Thailand and Cambodia; and the Pyu culture, established in the Irrawaddy lowlands of central Myanmar by migrants from Tibet.

By about 1000 BC bronze was in general use throughout Southeast Asia, and within a few hundred years iron was also in common use. These metal-working skills seem to have been developed by the Southeast Asian peoples themselves, rather than being introduced from elsewhere. Pottery was another early development. The independence of the Southeast Asian cultures

This painted pot, found in northeastern Thailand, dates from about 4700 BC.

First civilizations

Early civilizations are defined by their use of stone tools of increasingly efficient design, by the development of metal-working skills, and by the emergence of a structured society. One of the earliest developed civilizations in Southeast Asia was the Dong Son culture of northern Vietnam, dating from the late 1st millennium BC. The Dong Son built well-planned cities and had a wealthy upper class.

Cultivating wild rice

Wild rice is native to Southeast Asia and was the main source of food for the prehistoric population. They learned how to cultivate seeds from the wild plants.

Chinese in Tongking

In 207 BC Tongking (northern Vietnam) was invaded by the Chinese, and in 111 BC it became part of the Chinese Empire. Under Chinese control, northern Vietnam developed in quite a different way to other parts of Southeast Asia.

Left: A bronze lamp-holder from the Dong Son period, northern Vietnam.

MOVEMENTS OF PEOPLES AND THE MAIN CENTERS IN SOUTHEAST ASIA.

In prehistoric times, there were vast movements of peoples across Southeast Asia as populations increased and needed to find fresh sources of food. A long history of invasion and settlement by different peoples created many rich cultures, but also conflict.

Trading routes

Traders sailing through the islands of Southeast Asia brought new ideas and customs as well as cargo. Ships from southern China sailed southward across the South China Sea to reach Vietnam and Indonesia. Indian traders sailed from the Bay of Bengal down the western coast of Myanmar and through the Strait of Malacca.

Traditional Chinese cargo vessels were called junks. They are still used for coastal and river trade today.

This decorated stone from an island off Sumatra, Indonesia, dates from the later megalithic period.

Megalithic structures

Megaliths – huge stone monuments – are widely distributed across Southeast Asia, particularly on the Indonesian islands of Java and Sumatra. They are believed to have been erected during the 1st century BC. Iron Age technology made it possible to carve elaborate decorations onto stone.

First villages in Indonesia

From earliest times, Indonesia, and particularly Java, was the most heavily populated region of Southeast Asia. Equatorial and fertile, from about 5000 BC it attracted migrants who traveled down the Malay peninsula from East Asia. The culture produced by these movements survives in western Sumatra among the Minangkabau people. This Minangkabau barn (left) is used for storing rice. The pointed roof reminds the Minangkabau of their animal hero, the buffalo.

c.200–400 Buddhism from India influences Southeast Asia.

c.500–800 The kingdom of Chenla (Cambodia).

550 Kingdom of Funan is conquered by Chenla.

c.600–900 The kingdom of Champa (southern Vietnam).

800 Borobudur temple on Java, Indonesia – building starts.

faded from the 2nd century BC, when influences from the Chinese civilization to the north and the Indian civilization to the west arrived. The first culture to fall was that of northern Vietnam, which was declared a province of China in 111 BC, after being conquered by a Chinese warlord. It remained a province of China for the next thousand years.

The Indian influence was more peaceful, coming through traders and Hindu and Buddhist missionaries. Ideas from these foreign cultures were added to those of the independent Southeast Asian peoples, and gradually distinctive regional societies evolved. The Pyu culture of Myanmar was one of these. Incomers

from Tibet bringing Buddhist ideas of religion, art, and architecture developed a culture of walled cities, which lasted for 700 years from about AD 100.

In southern Cambodia, the influence was mainly Indian; Hindu temples have been found dating from about 600. Java and southern Sumatra, part of Indonesia, also came under Indian influence, although they had trade links with China too. By 700 there were a number of kingdoms, or states, in Java.

The kingdoms of Funan (c.100–550) and Champa (c.600–900) in southern Vietnam and of Chenla (c.500–800) in Cambodia were also Indian in their style of

government and religion. About 550, Chenla conquered Funan, creating a larger unified state.

In southern Thailand the kingdom of Dvaravati, with strong Buddhist influences, prospered for about 400 years from 600. The relics of all these societies – ruined buildings, statues of Buddha, bowls,

bracelets, and drums – show how the various peoples of Southeast Asia readily accepted foreign ideas but adapted them to fit their own cultures.

1. A ceremonial drum from the Bronze Age. The top is decorated with frogs, perhaps to encourage rain.

2. These cornelian and agate necklaces were found in western Thailand and date from about 390 BC. They are Indian in style and suggest that there was extensive trade with India many centuries earlier than is generally believed.

2

The Ngaju Dayak of Borneo
The Ngaju Dayak, who live deep in the interior of Borneo, are thought to be an indigenous people whose traditions and way of life have survived from the earliest times. They live on the upper reaches of the rivers of southern Borneo, and use dugout canoes carved from a single tree trunk (above).

The kingdom of Funan
The kingdom of Funan in southern Vietnam originated about AD 100 and lasted for about 450 years, until it was conquered by the Khmer rulers of the Chenla kingdom. Accounts by Chinese travelers of the period described Funan as a place of great splendor. The Funanese developed close trading links with India and China, and were highly skilled goldsmiths and jewelry-makers. They extended their farmland by building irrigation channels to take river water to previously dry areas. Probably it was their ingenuity and wealth that made them a target for the Khmers.

Right: A selection of jewelry from the Funanese city of Oc-eo at the southern tip of Vietnam.

Silver coins of the Pyu kingdom, similar to coins minted in India about the same time.

Pyu culture
The Pyu culture began about AD 100, when migrants from Tibet moved south, traveling down the valley of the Irrawaddy River. They brought with them their Buddhist faith, which quickly began to dominate Myanmar life, although the local people blended it with ideas from their older religion of spirit worship. The Pyu built impressive walled cities and brick-built Buddhist monasteries. Their culture lasted until the 9th century.

Hindu and Buddhist influences
From about AD 200 Hindu and Buddhist ideas began to spread through Southeast Asia in the wake of Indian traders. New ideas of religion, art, architecture, and government all took root. The Indian influence is very apparent in these decorations (above) from the mountain temple at Borobudur.

The divinity of kings
Buddhists believed that after death the rulers of Buddhist kingdoms became gods. This tradition dates back to Gautama Buddha, the founder of Buddhism in the 6th century BC. He was a prince who gave up his royal status and became a prophet.

Borobudur
Borobudur in central Java, Indonesia, is one of the most remarkable structures in the world. A large Hindu-Buddhist temple, it has nine terraces – six square and three circular – leading to a central dome, or stupa. The monument represents a Buddhist model of the universe. It was built by the Buddhist Sailendra Dynasty over top of Hindu foundations from about 800.

The kingdoms of Vietnam and Cambodia
Three powerful and well-organized kingdoms developed after AD 500 in Vietnam and Cambodia. The Chenla Kingdom in the Mekong Valley lasted from 500 to 800. It conquered the adjoining kingdom of Funan about 550. The Champa Kingdom on the coast was active in trading with India and China.

This 7th-century scroll painting shows merchants from Champa and Borneo bearing gifts for China's ruler, in return for a blessing on their trading activities.

The Buddhist temple of Shwe Dagon in Rangoon, Myanmar, is 330 ft (100 m) high.

SEE ALSO
p. 18 THE NEOLITHIC REVOLUTION
p. 48 ANCIENT INDIA
p. 52 ANCIENT CHINA AND JAPAN
p. 86 CHINESE CIVILIZATION

c.40,000 BC First people migrate by boat from Southeast Asia to

the Australia-New Guinea-Tasmania landmass.

c.28,000 BC People of northern New Guinea sail east to

Solomon Islands.

c.6000 BC Sea level has risen to

its present level. Aboriginal hunter-gatherer people of

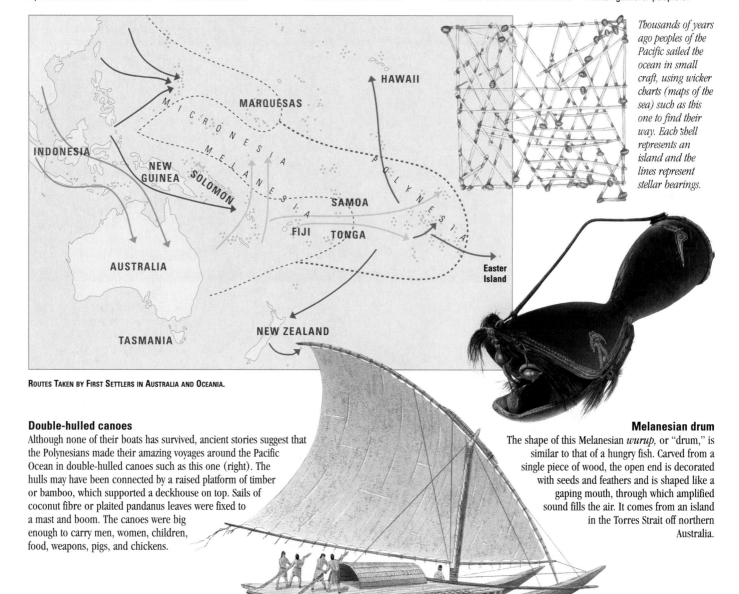

ROUTES TAKEN BY FIRST SETTLERS IN AUSTRALIA AND OCEANIA.

Thousands of years ago peoples of the Pacific sailed the ocean in small craft, using wicker charts (maps of the sea) such as this one to find their way. Each shell represents an island and the lines represent stellar bearings.

Double-hulled canoes

Although none of their boats has survived, ancient stories suggest that the Polynesians made their amazing voyages around the Pacific Ocean in double-hulled canoes such as this one (right). The hulls may have been connected by a raised platform of timber or bamboo, which supported a deckhouse on top. Sails of coconut fibre or plaited pandanus leaves were fixed to a mast and boom. The canoes were big enough to carry men, women, children, food, weapons, pigs, and chickens.

Melanesian drum

The shape of this Melanesian *wurup,* or "drum," is similar to that of a hungry fish. Carved from a single piece of wood, the open end is decorated with seeds and feathers and is shaped like a gaping mouth, through which amplified sound fills the air. It comes from an island in the Torres Strait off northern Australia.

Pacific islands

The first explorers of the Pacific Ocean found thousands of islands of different sizes. Some of the smallest tropical islands are formed from coral and sand. In Polynesia, many of the islands have spectacular scenery: steep cliffs, waterfalls, and forests hidden by cloud. These mountainous islands are the tops of ancient volcanoes that rise from the ocean floor and have their peaks above sea level (below). New Zealand is much larger and has two main islands, with wilderness areas of forest, geysers, hot springs, and several active volcanoes. New Guinea is also mountainous, with tropical forests and lowland swamps.

Skull of an ancestor

In Irian Jaya, the western part of New Guinea, the skulls of ancestors were treated with great respect. A skull was carefully washed, then decorated with feathers and colorful shells.

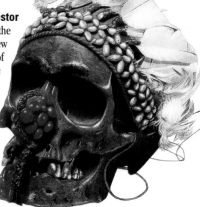

Easter Island statues

The Rapa Nui people from Polynesia arrived on tiny Easter Island – some 2,350 mi. (3,780 km) to the west of South America – about 2,000 years ago. They carved gigantic statues and huge faces known as *Moai* from soft volcanic stone. The largest *Moai* is 65 ft (20 m) tall and weighs 50 ton (50 tonnes.) A completed statue was somehow moved from the quarry where it was carved and lifted onto a stone platform, called an *ahu*, which contained a tomb.

Australia move to interior.
c.2000 BC Lapita-ware people

sail in large canoes from
Moluccas region of Indonesia

to Melanesian Islands.
c.1300–1000 BC First

settlers reach Fiji, Samoa, and
Tonga.

c. AD 800 New Zealand settled
by the Maori from Polynesia.

Ancient Australia and the Pacific

Australia, New Guinea, and the islands of Oceania were probably settled over thousands of years by peoples from Southeast Asia. (The three areas of Oceania are: Micronesia, Melanesia, and Polynesia.) The earliest migrations were made when sea levels were much lower than they are today. Simple rafts or outrigger canoes were probably used. Scientists have proved that the pigs, chickens, and rats that were dispersed over most of the Pacific are of Asian origin. The languages spoken by the peoples of Oceania are similar to one another and to some Southeast Asian languages. New Zealand was settled about AD 800 by the Maori people, who sailed there from Polynesia.

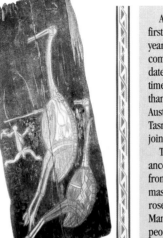

Bark paintings
In Australia, Aborigines made bark paintings (above) to illustrate their stories. First they removed the bark from the stringy bark tree with an ax. Then they painted fine lines using pointed sticks and paints made from black, brown, red, and yellow ochers. Their X-ray style of painting shows the bones and internal body parts of creatures, but no skin or feathers.

Aboriginal hunters
Australia's native people, called Aborigines, hunted with wooden spears. The most deadly spear was armed with twelve sharp, stone barbs. Aborigines ate many kinds of food, including large creatures such as wallabies and wombats, and fish, shellfish, wild honey, and native plants.

New Zealand's flightless Moa
When the Polynesian Maori first arrived on New Zealand about 1,200 years ago, they found the islands supported a number of large, flightless birds. The gigantic Moa stood over 9 ft (3 m) tall on its strong legs. The Maori hunted it for its nourishing meat, made water bottles from its eggs, and necklaces from its bones, and eventually made it extinct about 500 years ago.

Aboriginal dances
This Aranda man from central Australia (left), whose ancestors were threatened by man-eating eagles, is re-enacting an ancient story. The man's body, face, and elaborate headdress are covered in eagles' feathers, and the leaves he holds represent the bird's outstretched wings.

Right: A hei tiki pendant from New Zealand, a symbol of high rank.

Hei tiki
In New Zealand only the highest ranking men and women wore the *hei tiki* as a pendant around the neck. The *hei tiki* was usually made of hard, precious green stone, found only in the remote mountains of the South Island. A craftsperson sometimes took two or three years to carve and polish such an ornament. This humanlike figure is believed to have great Mana, or prestige and power.

Fish trap basket
Fish and shellfish from the seas, rivers, and lakes were important foods to the Maori of New Zealand. Women plaited the tough leaves of the flax plant to make baskets (above), which were used as traps. It was believed that fish were the children of Tangaroa, god of the ocean.

Left: This Karetao puppet, which represents an ancestor, was used by the Maori as they sang songs. The missing arms were manipulated by strings.

Australia was possibly first settled about 40,000 years ago; evidence for this comes from stone axes that date from this period. At that time, sea levels were lower than they are today, and Australia, New Guinea, and Tasmania were one land mass, joined by land bridges.

The first Australians, the ancestors of the Aborigines, sailed from Southeast Asia to this land mass. About 6000 BC the sea level rose, separating the land masses. Many of Australia's Aboriginal people moved into the interior, hunting and gathering a variety of animal and plant foods, and moving with the wet and dry seasons. Others lived along the fertile coast, hunting and fishing. At the heart of the Aboriginal culture are the Dreamtime creation stories, which gave the people a close connection to the natural world and to their spirit ancestors. The Dreamtime was kept alive through songs, dance, and art.

About 30,000 years ago, the Melanesian peoples of northern New Guinea sailed east to the Solomon Islands. Tools dating from this time have been found, with microscopic grains of the taro root vegetable still attached.

About 2000 BC, people who made a finely decorated pottery called Lapita ware sailed with pigs and chickens as far east as Tonga and Samoa. Archeologists are unable to agree whether Lapita ware originated in the islands of Oceania or in Asia. However, it is known that over the next 3,000 years the descendants of the Lapita pottery people – who are today called Polynesians – discovered many islands, including the Marquesas Islands, Easter Island, and Hawaii. Their descendants discovered New Zealand. Historians believe that these voyages were deliberate attempts to colonize new islands as old settlements became overcrowded. The explorers used the stars to navigate across the Pacific Ocean, centuries before European explorers came near.

1. Tangaroa, Polynesian god of the ocean.

2. Bark painting of a pregnant woman in X-ray style.

3. An Aboriginal man using face and body paints made from natural ochers.

SEE ALSO
p. 200 AUSTRALIA AND NEW ZEALAND
p. 234 THE WAR IN ASIA AND THE PACIFIC

c.15,000 BC Probable date of first migrations from Asia.

c.7000 BC Mammoths and mastodons become extinct.

c.2500 BC Migrations of Inuit ancestors from Asia.

c.2000 BC Bows and arrows invented for hunting.

c.1000 BC Maize farming established in southwestern

Ancient North America

The first people to live in North America migrated there from Asia around 17,000 years ago, when large parts of the world's surface were covered in ice. At this time, Asia and America were joined together by a bridge of land and ice that people could walk across. They probably went there following herds of animals in the hope of finding new hunting grounds. The migrations occurred in waves over several thousand years. The early migrants lived as hunter-gatherers. Some roamed the Great Plains hunting the vast herds of buffalo; some pushed their way southward to Central and South America, where they settled; and in time many set up small farming communities. From about 10,000 BC on, the climate warmed up and melted the ice in the south, which caused the sea level to rise and cover the land bridge between the continents. Later migrants from Asia, the ancestors of the Inuit, probably arrived by boat about 2500 to 1800 BC. The first Europeans to reach America were the Vikings, who sailed there from Greenland about 1,000 years ago.

Migrants from the frozen, barren lands of northern Asia found similar conditions in northern North America. Farther south the environment became more varied and generally life was easier. The people who settled the basins of the Mississippi and Ohio rivers developed farming methods and lived in villages. Festivals and ceremonies involving music and dance were an important part of their cultures.

The Pueblo people of the Southwest were also farmers. They built distinctive, terraced villages of multi-story houses made from stone and adobe, and had many ceremonies of their own. They may have had trading links with the Aztecs,

Crossing the land bridge between Asia and Alaska.

North America once supported many large mammals, including mammoths, mastodons, woolly rhinoceroses, buffalo, and camels.

The first people
The Bering Strait is a narrow strip of ocean only 56 mi. (90 km) wide, which separates northeastern Asia and northwestern North America. It was formed when the glaciers melted at the end of the last Ice Age. Before that, the two continents were joined by a "land bridge," across which herds of mammoths and other large animals roamed. About 15,000 BC the first migrants from Asia crossed the bridge into Alaska. They were hunters who followed the herds and depended on them for food. When the ice sheets covering North America melted about 12,000–14,000 years ago, the hunters could spread farther south.

This embossed copper falcon is from a mound site in Ohio.

Mammoths and mastodons
The first Native Americans were nomads, always on the move in search of food. They hunted mammoths and mastodons – huge, elephant-like creatures weighing over a ton. There was enough meat on one animal to feed a whole group for weeks. The hunters caught them in pit-traps. By about 7000 BC mammoths and some other large mammal species had died out from overhunting.

Early settlers captured and trained wild dogs for protection and to carry their possessions.

The mound people
About 100 BC some Native American settlers began to build mounds of earth close to their settlements. There are thousands of such mounds scattered across North America, built sometime between 100 BC and AD 1000. Some are rectangular, some circular, and others are built in the shape of birds or serpents. Some of the sites contain burial grounds, where skillfully crafted copper and stone items have been found.

Fish were an important source of food for Native Americans who lived along the coasts and rivers. The people of the Northwest Coast also caught the salmon that came upriver to spawn each spring.

Hunters
The early migrant hunters learned how to fashion stone into tools and weapons (above). They made stone arrowheads for killing buffalo, which roamed the country in great herds. They also made stone axes, which they used for cutting up the animals they killed, and stone scrapers for cleaning the animal skins. The skins were made into clothing, and were also used to make shelters.

A mask worn by the people of the Northwestern Woodlands during ceremonies to prevent disease.

The beginning of farming
Some of the early Native Americans moved south into Central and South America, where they settled and developed farming methods. Their knowledge of farming slowly spread northward. By 700 BC people in southwestern North America were farming maize. Later they cultivated squashes and beans. The early farmers learned how to improve the land by cutting drainage and irrigation ditches.

The Inuit, who inhabited the far northwest, hunted animals using bows and arrows, which were probably invented about 2000 BC. The arrows had stone arrowheads.

Festivals and ceremonies
Some early North American societies developed beliefs in the supernatural, which they often expressed through dance. At festivals, dancers wearing masks and costumes re-enacted the adventures of various creatures from folklore. Farming communities often held festivals to mark the various stages of the farming season, such as the arrival of the first fruit, the ripening of the corn, or harvest time. Some ceremonies were held to ward off sickness and disease.

North America.
c.100 BC–AD 1000 Mound culture

in Ohio and Mississippi basins.
c.700–1300 Mesa Verde culture

flourishes in Colorado.
c.1000–1250 Small village

farming communities expand in
Eastern Woodlands.

c.1000 Vikings sail to North
America from Greenland.

descendants of a nomadic group of people from northern Mexico who moved south in the 12th century. During the 15th century the warlike Apaches made frequent raids on the Pueblos. One Apache group, the Navajo, settled among them and learned many of their skills.

Many different peoples lived on the Great Plains between the Mississippi River and the Rockies. Some made permanent settlements along the river valleys, where they built walled villages and grew crops. Others were nomads, hunting on foot (horses were only introduced in the 18th century, by Spanish explorers). Groups of up to several thousand lived in tented camps. Their tents, called tipis, were made from buffalo skins stretched across a framework of wooden poles.

Along the Northwest Coast, Native Americans lived mostly by hunting and fishing. Their art forms ranged from weaving and basket-making to wood-carving, including colorful masks. In the Rockies, where the environment was too hostile for farming, people hunted small game.

From the Atlantic to the Mississippi River, an area known as the Eastern Woodlands, farming was important.

There, the Iroquois and Cherokee cleared the land with stone axes and farmed corn, squash, and beans.

In the inhospitable Far North of present-day Canada, nomadic hunters such as the Naskapi followed the herds of caribou. They depended on these animals for food, and used their skins to make winter clothes and shelters. In summer they wore sealskins.

All Native Americans were skilled craftspeople. The arts they practiced depended on the raw materials available. Each group had a distinct character and spoken language of its own. Sometimes local groups joined together into federations, usually for defense. The first Europeans to reach America were the Vikings, who sailed there from Greenland about 1,000 years ago, but did not settle.

1. Ear ornaments worn by a Naskapi woman from the Northern Forests.

2. A club used by the Haida people of the Northwest Coast to hunt halibut.

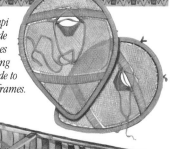

> **SEE ALSO**
> p. 62 PRE-COLUMBIAN CIVILIZATIONS
> p. 114 PORTUGUESE AND SPANISH EXPANSIONISM
> p. 120 COLONIAL AMERICA

Mesa Verde

Mesa Verde, in Colorado, was home to a highly developed hilltop community that lasted from about AD 700 to 1300. Hundreds of people lived in the sandstone houses. As well as farming, they made baskets, pottery, and jewelry, and also wove fabric. Ceremonial meetings were held in underground rooms. The people of Mesa Verde were probably forced to abandon their site because of a series of droughts, which made farming impossible.

The Mississippi basin

On the fertile land of the Mississippi basin, farming communities flourished from about AD 700. The powerful chiefs of the various groups were buried in hilltop burial grounds.

A tomb vessel representing death, from Kentucky.

The Great Plains peoples

On the rolling prairies to the east of the Rockies, the lives of the Great Plains peoples centered on the huge herds of buffalo, several million strong, that grazed there. As well as eating the meat, they used the skins for clothing, the bones for tools, the sinews for thread and bow strings, and the horns for cups. Warrior societies protected the camps from enemy attacks. Each society had its own songs, dances, and costumes.

The Forest Dwellers

In the densely forested country that now forms the border between the United States and Canada, Native Americans lived by hunting, trapping, and fishing. They used canoes made of bark that were light enough to carry overland if the rivers became impassable.

The Northwest Coast

The Native Americans who settled along the rocky, thickly forested Pacific coast from southern Alaska to Oregon lived mainly by fishing for salmon, cod, halibut, and herring. They became expert at carving and painting wood, from houses and "totem poles" to everyday objects such as spoons, tools, and weapons.

The Naskapi made snowshoes by attaching rawhide to wooden frames.

Bark canoes were easy to maneuver in fast-flowing rivers.

The Far North

The Native Americans of the Far North probably arrived some time after the first wave of migrants. They may have come by boat about 2500 BC. With long, bitterly cold winters and few hours of daylight, the search for food was all-important. Hunters and their families were constantly on the move, following the moose and caribou herds on which they depended for survival. They treated nature with great respect; elaborate rituals surrounded the hunting and killing of bears, for example.

1. Inuit hunters and gatherers of the Far North
2. Hunters and gatherers of the Northern Forests
3. Fishers and gatherers of the Northwest Coast
4. Hunters and gatherers of the Great Plains
5. Plains farmers
6. Farmers of the Mississippi
7. Farmers and fishers of Florida
8. Hunters and gatherers of the desert
9. Pueblo farmers

ENVIRONMENTS AND INHABITANTS OF ANCIENT NORTH AMERICA

Wampum belts woven with beads were used by some Native Americans as money.

The Eastern Woodlands

Settled along the Atlantic coast of North America, from the Great Lakes to the Gulf of Mexico, the peoples of the Eastern Woodlands lived mainly by farming.

The peoples of the Eastern Woodlands enjoyed playing sports. They invented lacrosse or stickball (below). In the south a game called chunkey was popular. This involved rolling a smooth stone disk (right) along the ground while players tried to hit it by throwing a wooden pole.

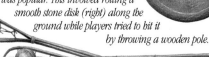

ANCIENT CENTRAL AND SOUTH AMERICA.

GULF OF MEXICO

MEXICO

Teotihuacán
Tenochtitlán
Tikal
Chichen Itza
Monte Albán
Copan
Palenque

CENTRAL AMERICA

- Aztecs
- Olmecs
- Mayas
- Incas

SOUTH AMERICA

Cuzco

Andes Mountains

A temple pyramid at Chichen Itza in Mexico, which was an important Mayan and Toltec center.

The Olmecs

The Olmecs of Mesoamerica were building towns around ceremonial centers soon after 1200 BC. They had a rich artistic culture, which included carving huge stone heads, probably of their rulers. They also invented a hieroglyphic script and a calendar. Their culture was at its peak from 900 to 400 BC. Many later traditions, especially those of the Maya, appear to have developed from the Olmec way of life.

Olmec figurine modeled in white clay.

First peoples

The first people in America were bands of hunter-gatherers who came from Asia about 17,000 years ago. By about 3000 BC their descendants were starting to cultivate plants, and over the next few thousand years farming villages developed in both Mesoamerica and the Andes region. By the same date there were fishing communities on the coast of present-day Peru, and within the next millennium there were permanent settled villages in southern Mexico. The earliest known ceremonial centers were built by the Olmecs about 1200 BC, near the Gulf of Mexico.

A tapestry of a flying figure, possibly a shaman (a priest or witch-doctor). It was woven by the Paracas of coastal Peru, who made intricately patterned woolen cloth to wrap round mummies (preserved bodies) before burial.

The Toltec

The Toltec were a warrior people who dominated central Mexico between AD 900 and 1200. The god Quetzalcoatl ("The snake with feathers of the quetzal bird") was very important to them.

Below: This Moche ceramic spouted jar shows a priest-warrior standing above a prisoner and a guard.

Maize, beans, and squash were the first plants to be cultivated in Mesoamerica. Potatoes were first grown in the Andes region.

A piece of Moche pottery showing women weaving.

Agriculture

The Mesoamerican climate became drier between 7000 and 2000 BC, which probably enabled early farmers to cultivate maize and other plants. In South America the earliest crops were probably potatoes and lima beans. Maize was grown when people started living in settled villages. Early farmers would have grown only enough food for themselves and their families.

Moche civilization

The Moche flourished in river valleys near the coast of Peru from about AD 100 to 600. They used a system of canals to irrigate their land, allowing them to grow food crops. They also raised llamas and guinea pigs to eat, and they fished in the ocean from reed boats. The Moche were master potters and metalworkers; goldsmiths gilded objects so skillfully that they looked like solid gold. They also built pyramids from adobe (a mixture of wet earth and grass dried in the sun), and buried their rulers inside them, together with sacred objects.

---

c.3000 BC Farming begins in Central America.

2500–1500 BC Settled villages in Central America and the Andes.

1200 BC The Olmecs build ceremonial centers.

800–400 BC Chavin culture flourishes in the Andes.

200 BC The Zapotec city of Monte Albán is built.

Pre-Columbian Civilizations

The term "Pre-Columbian civilizations" refers to the Native American cultures that developed in Mexico, Central America, and the Andes region of South America before the arrival in the Americas in AD 1492 of the explorer Christopher Columbus (1451–1506), and Spanish conquerors in the 16th century. The Maya and Aztecs are the best known of the Mesoamerican (Middle, or Central American) peoples, and both built great empires. However, farming communities, ceremonial centers, and great cities such as Teotihuacán existed much earlier. In the Andes region, the Inca replaced earlier cultures, such as the Chavin and Moche, and built a great empire under one ruler, the Inca. The pre-Columbian civilizations were all destroyed by Europeans.

By 3000 BC nomadic hunter-gatherers were cultivating plants in Central America. Over the next few thousand years villages developed there and in the Andes region of South America. Even earlier, around 3500 BC, there were fishing communities on the coast of Peru, and there is evidence of pottery being made in Colombia. The Andean peoples domesticated llamas and alpacas, and started to grow root crops in the highlands. The main crop was potatoes, whereas in Central America maize was the staple crop. By about 2300 BC there were permanent settled villages in southern Mexico. The cultivation of maize spread to South America about 1500 BC. The Olmec people of Mesoamerica probably started farming maize about 1400 BC, and sometime after 1200 BC they were building ceremonial centers. An important feature of Olmec life, and of the Mesoamerican cultures that followed (the Maya and others), was a ceremonial ball game, played on a special court. Two teams of players tried to hit a large, solid rubber ball through a stone ring set high in the wall. This was a

The Aztec Empire

About AD 1200 the nomadic Aztecs from Mexico's northern highlands migrated to the Central Valley, where they built their capital, Tenochtitlán, about 1325. This became a great city of up to 200,000 people, with pyramids, palaces, and temples. As their empire spread throughout Mexico the Aztecs grew rich by collecting payment from conquered peoples. The empire was at its height when Spanish invaders destroyed Tenochtitlán in 1521.

Aztec god Quetzalpapalotl.

Human sacrifice

The Aztecs worshiped hundreds of gods and goddesses. They believed that divine beings needed human blood to remain strong. Sacrifice played an important part in all major ceremonies, and most victims were prisoners of war. Many were killed at the Great Temple of Tenochtitlán. Victims were seized by priests and stretched across a sacrificial stone. A priest slashed open the victim's chest with a knife and tore out his heart, the most precious thing that could be offered to the gods. The heart was placed in a bowl, and the victim's dead body was thrown down the temple steps.

SEE ALSO
p. 60 ANCIENT NORTH AMERICA
p. 112 EUROPEAN VOYAGES OF DISCOVERY
p. 114 PORTUGUESE AND SPANISH EXPANSION

This Aztec double-headed serpent is made of hollow wood and decorated with turquoise mosaic. It may have been worn by a priest.

An Inca silver llama. Llamas were regularly sacrificed to the gods.

The Inca Empire

Inca society developed from about AD 1200. In the 15th century the Incas took over all of Peru and conquered a vast empire that extended from modern Ecuador to central Chile. It had a population of about 12 million people and was ruled from the capital, Cuzco. The people had sophisticated technology and architecture, and were governed by a harsh ruling class.

Machu Picchu was a fortified Inca town high in the Andes. It had a central plaza, a royal palace, and a sun temple. The site was only rediscovered in 1911.

Mayan religion

The Maya were a highly sophisticated people who spread from Guatemala to Mexico about AD 300. They worshiped more than 160 gods and goddesses, many of whom were identified with natural forces such as wind, rain, and lightning. Not only animals such as deer and turkeys were sacrificed to them, but also people. In one ceremony, the Mayan king and queen pierced themselves with a blade, spattering their blood onto bark paper that was burned on a ceremonial fire.

The Chimu people of Peru were skilled at crafts, as this gold and turquoise figure shows.

This mummified man, found in the mountains of Peru, died more than 1,300 years ago. Both the Inca and earlier peoples of the Andes buried their dead in mummy bundles.

Mayan hieroglyphs

The Maya developed a system of writing. It was made up of symbols, called hieroglyphs, which stood for combinations of syllables and sounds. Mayan scribes used quills made from turkey feathers to write on the bark of fig trees. They sometimes wrote on one long strip of bark, which they folded to make pages (left). These Mayan books are called codices. Only four still survive.

AD 250–900 Classic period of the Mayan civilization.

900–1200 Tula is capital of the Toltec Empire.

c.1325 Aztecs' capital built on Lake Texcoco, central Mexico.

1438 Inca ruler Pacachuti embarks on conquest.

1519 Spanish conquistador Hernán Cortés lands in Mexico.

---

sacred ritual to the Mesoamericans; after some games the losing players were sacrificed to the gods.

From about 800 to 400 BC, the influence of Chavin culture spread throughout the Andes region. The Chavin were succeeded by the Nazca and Moche peoples of Peru. The Nazca Lines, huge patterns carved in the desert and identifiable only from the air, remain a mystery.

Between about AD 200 and 600, Teotihuacán (north of modern Mexico City), with its Pyramids of the Sun and the Moon and the Street of the Dead,

became the largest city of the ancient Americas. Its cultural and economic influence spread into Guatemala, and the Teotihuacanos had friendly relations with the Zapotec, whose capital was at Monte Albán in southern Mexico.

At the same time the Maya were starting to build cities such as Tikal, Copan, and Palenque. By the 9th century AD, however, the Mayan Empire was in decline. This may have been caused by overpopulation or by a series of poor harvests. Part of the Mayan Empire may also have been conquered by the Toltecs, whose capital was at Tula. From 1400 on the Aztecs

controlled the Valley of Mexico and the surrounding area.

In South America, the powerful societies of the Huari and the Tiahuanaco controlled much of mountainous Peru and Bolivia from about AD 400 to 900. By about 1200 Inca society had developed. Two hundred years later the Incas embarked on a campaign of conquests. They soon controlled a mighty empire from their capital, Cuzco. Everything changed when the Spaniards arrived. Hernán Cortés (1485–1547) destroyed the Aztec capital of

Tenochtitlán in 1521 (modern Mexico City is built on its ruins). Eleven years later, Francisco Pizarro (c.1475–1541) captured the ruling Inca, Atahualpa. The pre-Columbian civilizations were at an end.

1. Sinu gold figure, from Columbia.

2. Ceramic Moche bowl showing metalworkers at work.

3. Gold pendant, perhaps showing a shaman, from Columbia.

4. Ceramic statue of a Nazca woman chewing on coca leaves.

5. Chavin warrior holding a battleax. The figure is carved into a temple wall in Peru.

c.10,000–9000 BC Warmer climate at end of Ice Age

makes the Sahara habitable.
7000 BC Wavy-line pottery made.

6000 BC Cultivation of millet, sorghum, and rice in the Sahara.

5000 BC Domestic cattle, sheep, and goats reared in the Sahara.

c.2000 BC Bantu-speakers begin to migrate southward.

Ancient Africa

Ancient Egypt became the first great African civilization about 3150 BC, but hunter-gatherers had been roaming the continent for thousands of years before then. South of Egypt, in Nubia, a kingdom called Kush emerged about 1700 BC and lasted until about AD 350. Kush was strongly influenced by Egypt and became a major center of art, learning, and trade. Trade helped spread metalworking, and by about 1500 BC people in the Sahel region were using copper. The Nok culture of present-day central Nigeria used iron from about 500 BC. From about 2000 BC on, the Bantu-speaking peoples of west Africa had started migrating southward. They eventually settled throughout central, eastern, and southern Africa, farming with the use of iron tools.

After the end of the last Ice Age, about 12,000 years ago, nomadic hunter-gatherers roamed most parts of Africa. They first settled about 7000 BC near rivers and lakes, and started making pottery decorated with wavy lines. About 6000 BC farmers in the Sahara region – which was much less dry than it is today – cultivated crops such as millet, sorghum, and rice. Nomads herded cattle, sheep, and goats, driving their animals between seasonal pastures. In the fertile Nile Valley wheat and barley were grown. About 5000 BC farming began in the Ethiopian Highlands; crops included finger millet and a local cereal called *teff*.

From about 3000 BC on, overgrazing in the Sahara region led to soil erosion, and the poor soils turned to desert – a process called desertification. Herders moved south to the Sahel and southeast to the Ethiopian Highlands.

Towns first appeared in Egypt about 3300 BC, and Egypt was united about 150 years later. From about 2000 BC on, Bantu speakers from present-

1

Hunters and gatherers

During the last Ice Age (c.20,000–10,000 BC), the Sahara was even drier than it is today and human survival was impossible. But as the ice sheets to the north melted, wet grassland appeared, and by about 9000 BC hunter-gatherers were living there. They hunted the wildlife, fished in the rivers, and gathered the wild grassland cereals.

Early hunters in the Sahara painted scenes of wild animals, such as giraffes, elephants, rhinoceroses, and hippopotamuses. Later rock art shows them hunting these animals. This rock painting from Jabbaren (left) shows hunters and giraffes.

Herders

By about 5000 BC nomadic herders in the Sahara were tending cattle (above), sheep, and goats. The animals were probably introduced from western Asia through Egypt, although the cattle may have been tamed from local wild stock. As the Sahara became increasingly dry from about 4000 BC on, the herders moved south into the Sahel region.

Left: The earliest pottery in Africa, made from about 7000 BC on, was decorated with wavy-line patterns made by dragging a fish spine over the surface of the wet clay.

Tools included harpoons, fish hooks, and a bone shaft with blades of flint, probably used to cut cereals.

The first farmers

By about 6000 BC the peoples of the Sahara were cultivating sorghum, rice, and millet, which grew wild in the area. Barley and wheat were introduced from western Asia. To the south of the Sahara, tubers and tree crops were domesticated.

Left: Digging sticks were used to uproot tubers such as yams. Reaping knives were used to cut bulrushes and cereals such as finger millet.

Stone bowls used by herders in Kenya about 1500 BC.

Digging sticks and reaping knife.

Cutaway of a 5th-century BC, dome-shaped hut from an excavated village in South Africa. The hut was made from a wood framework covered in grass. It was plastered inside with clay.

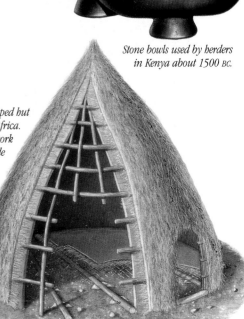

Oil palms were cultivated for the nutritious oil in the palm nuts.

Bulrush Millet.

Finger Millet.

Sorghum.

Yam.

c.1700 BC Kingdom of Kush emerges south of Egypt.

c.1500 BC Copperworking begins in the Sahel region.

c.500 BC Nok culture of west Africa begins ironworking.

AD 1–100 Kingdom of Axum emerges in present-day Ethiopia.

AD 500 Ironworking and cattle rearing reach southern Africa.

day Nigeria and Cameroon started to spread southward and eastward (reaching southern Africa by AD 500). About 1700 BC the kingdom of Kush (in Nubia, south of Egypt) became the first African state outside the Egyptian kingdom. Copper was being worked in the Sahel by about 1500 BC, and bronze was introduced to Morocco from Spain. Ironworking began in the Nok region (present-day central Nigeria) about 500 BC, as well as in Kush, which by then was flourishing; it had rich gold deposits and trade routes to tropical Africa, the source of ebony, ivory, and slaves.

From 770 to 657 BC Egypt was ruled by Kushite kings, until they were expelled by the Assyrians and forced southward. They moved their capital to Meroë in 590 BC. The kingdom of Axum emerged in the 1st century AD; it extended from the Red Sea across northern Ethiopia to the Nile River. The Axumites captured Meroë about AD 350. About this time King Ezana of Axum became the first African ruler to become a Christian. Trade across the Sahara increased after camels were introduced about 100 BC. By AD 500 camel caravan routes linked the Mediterranean with west Africa.

1. These containers are made from dried and hollowed-out gourds, a fleshy fruit. They are used to carry water, milk, grain, or beer.

Ancient Egypt was the greatest of the early civilizations in Africa. This wall painting from about 1450 BC shows some of the African products prized and imported by the Egyptians: leopards, baboons, ebony, ivory (elephant tusks), and ostrich eggs.

Meroë
The kingdom of Kush was ruled from its capital, Meroë (in modern Sudan). The Kushites were strongly influenced by the Egyptians. From 770 to 657 BC Egypt was ruled by Kushite kings.

This wooden sphinx from Kush was carved between the 7th and 4th centuries BC. It originally formed the ornamental leg of a bed or chair.

ANCIENT AFRICAN KINGDOMS AND CULTURES.

Nok culture
The people of the Nok culture lived in mud huts in the lowlands and hills of present-day Nigeria. They flourished for at least 700 years from about 500 BC. The Nok people worshiped their ancestors and had many gods. They made expressive terra-cotta figures of people (left) and animals.

SAHARA

Alexandria •
EGYPT

• Jabbaren

RED SEA

☐ Kingdom of Meroë
☐ Kingdom of Axum
▨ Nok early Iron Age culture
☐ Northwestern Bantu
☐ Eastern Bantu
☐ Western Bantu

NUBIA

Meroë •

Axum •

Nok •

ETHIOPIA

Origin of Bantu-speaking peoples, 2000 BC

Right: This southern African adze – a tool used for shaving wood – has an iron blade. The blade is secured to the wooden handle with a bolt.

Left: A bronze coin from Axum showing a Christian cross.

Below: A Coptic tapestry roundel made from linen and wool.

Iron smelting
People of the Nok culture began to smelt iron about 500 BC. Some furnaces were dome-shaped (left). The iron ore was placed inside and heated with charcoal fuel. High temperatures were needed to turn the ore into metal. These were attained by pumping air into the furnace through clay pipes that went through the holes at the bottom.

The Copts
Christianity was introduced to Egypt by the apostle Mark in AD 70, but few Egyptians converted to Christianity before the 3rd century. Then, Anthony of Thebes introduced a monastic way of life as a Christian ideal, giving rise to the Coptic Church. The Copts added some Egyptian, or demotic, signs to the Greek alphabet, creating a new script called Coptic, used for religious writings. (The word Copt comes from the Greek word for "Egyptian.")

Swahili traders
Swahili traders, who were of mixed Bantu and Arab ancestry, sailed the coast of east Africa in merchant boats called *mtepe* (right). They carried goods between east African markets and Arabia. The name Swahili means "coast people."

The trading kingdom of Axum
Between the 4th and 8th centuries AD the kingdom of Axum in Ethiopia was the largest trading center in northeast Africa. Its merchants traded as far north as Alexandria in Egypt and dominated trade in the Red Sea area. In the 4th century the Axumites invaded the Kushite capital, Meroë, causing its downfall.

SEE ALSO
p. 26 ANCIENT EGYPT
p. 46 TRADE IN ANCIENT WORLDS
p. 96 AFRICAN STATES

MYTH AND RELIGION

Ancient mythology includes all the world's imaginative stories and traditions concerning supernatural forces, gods, and heroes. Many ancient myths tried to explain the origins of the universe, human beings, or a particular culture. In ancient times some of them formed the basis of people's beliefs, or religions, such as Shinto from ancient Japan or Hinduism from India. Other religions, such as Confucianism and Taoism from China, were based more on philosophies of life. The religions of different peoples and places influenced each other, developing, mingling, and spreading throughout the ancient world. As well as helping their followers in their daily lives, they inspired the creation of numerous works of great art, architecture, and literature.

Egypt

The roles of the many Egyptian gods and goddesses developed and changed over the centuries, and very often two or more gods combined. The sun-god Ra was such a powerful influence that most of the important deities were eventually included in the universal sun cult. In this wall painting from about 850 BC (above), the woman is receiving life-giving rays from the falcon-headed sun god, Ra-Horakhty, a combination of Ra and Horus, the god of divine kingship.

Mesopotamia

The praying figure (above) dates from about 2700 BC and comes from the Mesopotamian city of Eshnunna. Temples were an important feature of early Mesopotamian cities, and priests played a major role in organizing the running of the communities. They claimed to be able to persuade the deities to look after their people. Natural processes, such as the flooding of the Tigris and Euphrates rivers, or changes in their courses, were seen as the work of the gods, who governed the world.

Rome

Early beliefs in the divinities of fire, water, and wind were superseded by beliefs in gods with human characteristics. City-dwellers in the Roman Empire built temples to their gods and made offerings to them. As the empire grew, it absorbed many of the religious beliefs of the people it conquered. For example, the Roman deities Jupiter and Diana were associated with the Greek gods, Zeus and Artemis. The Romans also adopted the Egyptian goddess Isis.

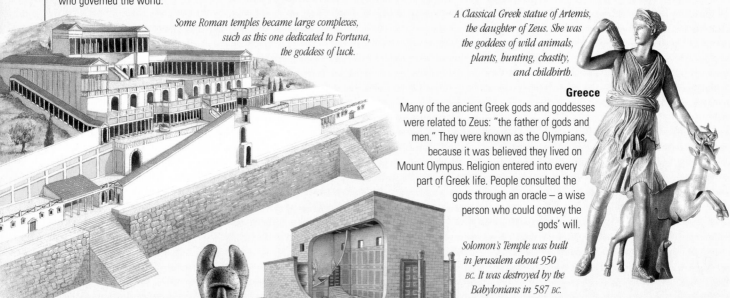

Some Roman temples became large complexes, such as this one dedicated to Fortuna, the goddess of luck.

A Classical Greek statue of Artemis, the daughter of Zeus. She was the goddess of wild animals, plants, hunting, chastity, and childbirth.

Greece

Many of the ancient Greek gods and goddesses were related to Zeus: "the father of gods and men." They were known as the Olympians, because it was believed they lived on Mount Olympus. Religion entered into every part of Greek life. People consulted the gods through an oracle – a wise person who could convey the gods' will.

Solomon's Temple was built in Jerusalem about 950 BC. It was destroyed by the Babylonians in 587 BC.

The Celts

The ancient Celts believed that after death their souls would go to the next world, where they would rest for a time before being reborn on Earth. They believed that an individual's soul was located in his head, and so they kept the skulls of honored ancestors and brave, respected enemies. The Celts often threw prized objects into lakes and streams that were sacred to their gods and goddesses.

Judaism

According to tradition, Judaism – the religion of the Jews – began when Abraham left Mesopotamia and journeyed to Canaan. Most scholars believe that the stories of Abraham and the other patriarchs, or "founding fathers," are set about 2000 to 1750 BC. Judaism's most sacred text is the Torah (Pentateuch), which makes up the first five books of the Hebrew Bible (the Old Testament for Christians).

Celtic statue of a god with horns. Found in Germany, it probably shows Cernunnos who was ruler of the animals and perhaps also of the Otherworld.

The cross and the fish were early symbols of Christianity.

Christianity

According to the Bible, there were only about 120 believers after Christ's death. Seven weeks after Christ's crucifixion they gathered together and their leader, Peter, preached the first Christian sermon. The Bible says that 3,000 new converts were made on that day alone. Christianity then spread quickly, and within 300 years it was known throughout most of the ancient world, and had become the official religion of the Roman Empire.

MAJOR DATES

c.3400 BC Temples dominate the early cities of Mesopotamia.

c.2000 BC Abraham born in Ur; leads his people to Canaan.

c.1500 BC Hinduism founded in India.

1352–1335 BC King Akhenaten of Egypt promotes the worship of a single sun-god, Aten, excluding all others.

660 BC Legendary Jimmu, descendant of the major Shinto goddess Amaterasu, founded the Japanese Empire.

6th century BC Life of Laozi, the founder of Taoism.

c.599–527 BC Life of Mahavira, the founder of Jainism.

c.563–483 BC Life of Siddharta Gautama, the Buddha, founder of Buddhism.

551–479 BC Life of Confucius.

466–456 BC Temple of Zeus built at Olympia in Greece.

c.6 BC–AD 30 Life of Jesus Christ.

AD 118–128 The Pantheon built in Rome as a temple to all the Roman gods.

Confucianism

Confucius (551–479 BC) is a Latin version of the Chinese name Kongfuzi, which means "Great Master Kong." When he was age 22, Confucius became a teacher of history and poetry, and he taught his students to think about the way in which they lived. He believed that every person should be truthful, brave, and courteous to others. If families behaved in this way, governments and rulers would be well ordered, too. He believed society's well-being began in ordinary people's homes. These teachings had great influence in ancient China.

Taoism

Laozi (a name that means "Old Philosopher") lived in China in the 6th century BC, but we know little about him apart from legends. He believed the most important thing was for people to live simple lives in harmony with nature. According to legend, Laozi tried to leave his home state of Honan when he was an old man, but the border guard would not let him pass until he had written down his teachings. Laozi agreed, and wrote 81 short poems, which have been studied ever since.

Laozi traveling on an ox. His Tao, or "Way," reflected the patterns of nature. His followers, called Taoists, tried to live by his teachings.

Hinduism

Hinduism began when Aryans from central Asia invaded India about 1500 BC. The Aryan culture combined with that of the native Dravidians, and Hinduism developed from this blend. The oldest Hindu scriptures are the *Vedas*, which date from about 1000 BC. Hindus worship many gods that represent different sides of Brahman, or pure spirit. Among the most important are Siva, the destroyer; Vishnu, the preserver; and Ganesh, the remover of obstacles.

According to legend, Ganesh has an elephant's head because his father beheaded him and then promised to replace his head with that of the first creature he saw, which was an elephant.

Jainism

Jainism was founded in India in the 6th century BC by Mahavira (c.599–527 BC), who was a princely member of a Hindu warrior caste. After 12 years of self-denial he achieved enlightenment and devoted the rest of his life to teaching his Jainist beliefs. One of his beliefs was that the universe contained six principles: souls, space, time, matter, right, and wrong.

Left: Mahavira gave his first sermon seated on a raised platform in the center of a special circular structure.

Buddhism

The teachings of an Indian prince named Siddharta Gautama (c.563–483 BC), who came to be known as the Buddha, or "enlightened one," formed the basis of Buddhism. At the age of about 29, Siddharta gave up his worldly goods and went in search of enlightenment. According to tradition, he found this six years later while sitting beneath a bo tree (right). Buddhism eventually spread to China, Korea, Japan, parts of central Asia, and to most countries in Southeast Asia.

Shinto

Legends passed down by followers of the ancient Japanese religion of Shinto traced the origins of Japan to divine beings, especially to the sun goddess, Amaterasu (left). She was traditionally seen as an ancestor of the first emperor, Jimmu, who according to legend founded the Japanese Empire in 660 BC. In early Japanese history Shinto was devoted mainly to nature worship.

The Medieval World

From 500 to 1492

In Europe, the first centuries after the fall of the Western Roman Empire were marked by slow economic growth, and frequent invasions and warfare. Feudal kingdoms struggled for control of the largely rural population. To the east, the Byzantine Empire flourished as a center of culture and the arts. In Arabia, Islam appeared and rapidly won a large empire. The Islamic world was a great center of art, science, technology, and learning. Farther east, the Mongol peoples united under Chingis Khan in the 13th century and conquered a huge empire, including the Song Dynasty in China. By the 15th century, the European economy was growing rapidly and invigorating Renaissance ideas were renewing the worlds of art and learning. Although still backward in comparison to China and the Islamic world, Europe was poised to begin a dramatic period of expansion.

Medieval Castles
European kings and lords built themselves fortified strongholds on the territories they controlled. Beginning in the 9th century, the construction of these thickly walled constructions spread throughout Europe. Most castles were circled by one or more moats, with access to the main gates by way of a drawbridge which could be raised in times of danger.

The Mongol Empire
p. 88 *Chingis Khan united the Mongol peoples of Central Asia and set out to conquer the world. His grandson, Kubilai Khan, established the largest empire the world has ever known.*

The Crusades
p. 94 *In 1096 European knights set out on the First Crusade, to win the Holy Land back from the Muslims, and to gain land and riches. After the Eighth Crusade, they admit defeat.*

Japan and Korea
p. 98 *War between feudal states kept Japan disunited through much of the period. Korea was ruled by just two dynasties, the Koryo and the Yi. Both countries gradually threw off Chinese influence.*

Crises in Western Europe
p. 102 *14th-century-Western Europe was hit by famine, the plague, and the Hundred Years' War. Population dropped by one-third, and the feudal system declined in importance.*

The Renaissance
p. 106 *A great flowering of learning and the arts, called the Renaissance, accompanied Western Europe's return to growth and prosperity in the 15th century.*

AD 180 Roman emperor
Marcus Aurelius dies.

284–305 Reign of Diocletian,
who divides empire and

appoints three co-emperors.
330 Constantine moves capital

to Byzantium/Constantinople.
395 Roman Empire is split into

two: Western, run from Rome;
Eastern, from Constantinople.

The Fall of the Western Empire

From about AD 200 on, the mighty Roman Empire became progressively weaker. The Emperor Diocletian (reigned 284–305) divided the empire to make it more manageable, appointing three co-emperors to help him. Less than fifty years later, Emperor Constantine "the Great" moved his capital from Rome to the ancient city of Byzantium, which was rebuilt and renamed Constantinople. Later emperors tried to reorganize the empire, but in 395 it was divided permanently into two parts: the Western Empire and the Eastern, or Byzantine, Empire. Germanic and Slavic peoples from northern and eastern Europe, whom the Romans called "barbarians," continued to threaten the Western Empire, invading in huge numbers during the 5th century. Rome, its capital, was sacked in 410, and in 476 the Western Empire collapsed when the last Roman emperor was overthrown. The invading Germanic and Slavic peoples claimed the empire's territories for themselves.

Emperor Theodosius temporarily reunited the empire in 394.

During the 2nd century AD there was growing disorder in the Roman Empire. Marcus Aurelius (reigned 161–180) had to defend the empire against attacks by Germanic peoples from the north and Parthians from the east. After the death in 192 of his son and successor Commodus, the empire fell into greater confusion. For about a hundred years rival leaders fought to be emperor. Most were army commanders who seized power by force with the backing of their troops.

In 212 all free people within the Roman Empire were granted citizenship,

Diocletian and Maximian

The Roman general Diocletian was proclaimed emperor by his troops in AD 284. He soon realized that one man could no longer successfully govern the empire, so he divided the provinces into smaller units, each of which had its own government and army. In 286 Diocletian appointed a soldier named Maximian to be co-emperor. Maximian ruled the western part of the empire, and Diocletian ruled the eastern part. The co-emperors (left) imposed heavy taxes to pay for the larger government and army.

Dividing the empire

Constantine I (left) was named emperor of Rome's western provinces in 307, but he did not secure his position until he had defeated his rival, Maxentius, in 312. Constantine was said to have had a vision promising him victory if he fought under the sign of the cross. The following year he and his co-emperor, Licinius, who was in charge of the eastern provinces, granted Christians freedom of worship. By 394 Emperor Theodosius had reunited the Roman Empire, but after his death in 395, it was permanently split into two.

Fighting the invaders

Germanic and Slavic peoples entered the Roman Empire in increasing numbers during the 5th century. This Roman (left) is fighting off invaders. Many of the invaders joined the Roman army as paid soldiers or mercenaries.

Right: Ornament from the helmet of the Lombard king, Agilulf (reigned 590–615).

Barbarians

The Romans referred to peoples such as the Goths, Vandals, Franks, Visigoths, and Saxons as "barbarians," because they considered their non-Latin languages uncivilized. This "barbarian" army (above) is armed with swords and spears.

Attila the Hun

The Romans called Attila (c.406–453), joint king of the Huns, the "Scourge of God." He attacked and gained control of lands in the Eastern Empire, and then turned his attention to the Western Empire. In 451 he was defeated in Gaul by a combined army of Romans and Visigoths. This did not prevent him from invading northern Italy in 452, however, and he continued to cause trouble for the Romans until his death.

Britain

From the 5th century on, Angles, Saxons, and Jutes, who came from present-day Germany and Denmark, invaded Britain. The invaders gradually mixed with the local population of Romanized Celts, and their influence spread over much of the islands. The Saxon warrior (left) was depicted on a gravestone.

SEE ALSO
p. 42 THE RISE OF ROME • p. 44 THE ROMAN EMPIRE
p. 72 WARFARE • p. 76 THE BYZANTINE EMPIRE

410 Visigoths sack Rome.
455 Vandals sack Rome.
476 Germanic invaders overthrow last emperor of Rome, Romulus Augustulus.
494 Clovis I, king of the Franks, conquers northern Gaul.
507 Visigoths in Gaul are defeated by the Franks.
568 Lombards invade Italy.

but the empire's vast size made it difficult to control and govern from Rome. In 270 Emperor Aurelian (reigned 270–275) had a new defensive wall built around Rome itself, and he restored some unity by gaining victories over the invading Vandals and other so-called "barbarians."

The Goths invaded Roman territory many times during the 3rd century. In 284 Emperor Diocletian (reigned 284–305), in an effort to restore order, divided the empire into separate parts run by co-emperors. He also banned Christian worship in 303. Just ten years later, however, co-emperors Constantine (reigned 307–337) and Licinius (reigned 308–324) granted Christians freedom of worship. In 324 Constantine defeated Licinius in battle and restored rule by one emperor. In 330 he moved his capital to Constantinople (modern-day Istanbul, Turkey).

After Constantine's death in 337, his sons and nephews fought for control. His nephew, Julian, became emperor in 360. After the death of Theodosius I (reigned 379–395), the empire was divided again, this time into the Western Empire, with its capital still in Rome, and the Eastern, or Byzantine, Empire, governed from Constantinople.

The Western Empire grew weaker as its outer provinces were invaded by Vandals, Visigoths, and other Germanic peoples. In 410 the Visigoths sacked Rome itself, followed in 455 by the Vandals. Then in 476 the Germanic general Odoacer overthrew the last emperor of Rome, Romulus Augustulus (reigned 475–476), and declared himself king of Italy. Odoacer accepted the Eastern emperor as his overlord. In the former province of Gaul, Clovis I (reigned 481–511) founded the kingdom of the Franks. The Franks defeated the Visigoths in 507. By 533 the Vandals had been destroyed by the Byzantines. The Ostrogoth kingdom in Italy collapsed by 562 and the Lombards gained control.

1. Statue of a Celtic warrior god.
2. Pictish stone from Scotland, north of Emperor Hadrian's Wall.
3. Dish with image of Emperor Theodosius I.
4. Mosaic from Aquileia, Italy, sacked by the Huns in 452.
5. Frankish fish, 6th century.

Detail of a mosaic showing the palace of the Ostrogoth king Theodoric the Great (c.454–526), at Ravenna, capital of his kingdom in Italy.

Right: This detail from a miniature shows Queen Radegund of the Franks (518–587) feeding the sick and poor at the abbey she founded at Poitiers, France.

The Visigoths

The Visigoths settled in southern France and northern Spain in the early 5th century. They drove the Vandals from Spain and conquered the entire country, making their capital at Toledo, where this crown (left) was hung above a Christian altar. In 507 the Visigoths lost all their land north of the Pyrenees to the Franks.

Throne of Dagobert I, king of the Franks (reigned 629–639), who made Paris his capital.

The Vandals

The Vandals were a Germanic people who moved southwest from Jutland (present-day Denmark) and across the Rhine in 406, ravaging Gaul for three years before crossing the Pyrenees into Spain. By 442 they had conquered the Roman provinces in North Africa.

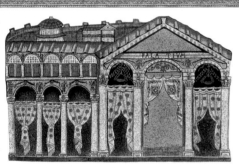
This fragment of a mosaic from Tunisia in North Africa shows a Roman country villa before the Germanic invasions.

SLAVIC AND GERMANIC INVASIONS OF THE ROMAN EMPIRE.

The arrows show the movements of Slavic and Germanic peoples during the 4th to 6th centuries, as they moved into the western part of the Roman Empire.

Huns
Vandals, Sueves
Visigoths
Lombards
Franks
Angles, Saxons, Jutes
Ostrogoths

Londinium (London)
Lutetia (Paris)
Attila's camp
Aquileia
Ravenna
Rome
Neapolis (Naples)
Constantinople (Istanbul)
Toledo
Corinth
Athens
Carthage
Antioch
Alexandria
Jerusalem
Memphis

Western Roman Empire
Eastern Roman Empire

WARFARE IN THE MIDDLE AGES

War was commonplace in medieval times, especially in Europe. The Crusades against the Muslims lasted for almost 200 years, and there was a Hundred Years' War between England and France. There were major invasions for long periods by Vikings, Magyars, and Saracens. Knights were trained to fight on horseback and win battles for the noblemen to whom they had sworn allegiance. Armed knights became the most powerful men in European society, and since warfare was a knight's way of life, he developed his fighting skills to the full. Swords, lances, and longbows were all important weapons. Professional soldiers worked as mercenaries, hiring themselves out to anyone who needed a military force. Since peace was so rare in many parts of the medieval world, fighting men were always highly prized.

Coats of arms, also called shields of arms, date back to the European Middle Ages when they were worn by knights in battle to establish their identity. A heavily armored knight was unrecognizable; the coat of arms served to show enemies and friends who he was. Later they came to show family membership, alliances, ownership of property, and profession.

MAJOR BATTLES
732 Poitiers. Frankish victory over Muslim invaders.
878 Edington. Alfred the Great of Wessex defeats the Danish Vikings.
955 Lechfeld. Magyars defeated by forces of Holy Roman Emperor Otto the Great.
1066 Hastings. Defeat of Harold, king of England, by the Norman army of William the Conqueror.
1071 Manzikert. Byzantine forces beaten by Seljuk Turks.
1096–1272 The Crusades.
1099 Jerusalem. The city is taken by the crusaders.
1187 Hattin. Saladin leads Arab forces to victory over the crusader kingdom of Jerusalem.
1214 Bouvines. Philip II of France defeats the Holy Roman Emperor Otto IV.
1337–1453 The Hundred Years' War between England and France.
1389 Kosovo. Ottoman Turks destroy the Serbian army.
1415 Agincourt. Henry V, king of England, defeats the French.
1429 Orléans. French victory inspired by Joan of Arc.
1453 Constantinople. Turkish Muslims defeat the Byzantines.

Military armor
Medieval knights often wore a full suit of metal armor. Armorers designed the metal plates so that they were jointed, allowing the wearer as much movement as possible. Helmets were of various designs, but most had face guards or hinged visors. Hands were protected by gauntlets, and feet by armored sabotons. A knight's warhorse often wore armor, too. Footsoldiers wore tunics padded with layers of canvas, and finely linked chain mail offered extra protection.

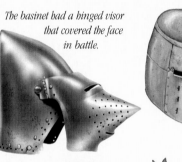

The basinet had a hinged visor that covered the face in battle.

Great helm.

A chain-mail shirt was put on over a quilted tunic to give extra protection.

Chain mail was made up of thousands of small, linked iron rings.

Gauntlet.

Spur with a rotating wheel, called a rowel.

Coat of plates.

Tournaments

Tournaments were competitions between knights that allowed them to practice and show off their fighting skills. The mêlée tournaments of the early Middle Ages were dangerous contests, fought with swords or lances and with few regulations. The general idea was to capture and ransom an opponent rather than kill him, but these mock battles led to many deaths. By the 13th century tournaments had become great attractions, and strict rules were introduced. Knights in armor jousted with lances, trying to knock each other off their horses. Less serious jousts were fought with blunt lances.

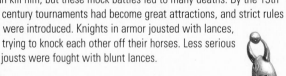

This is the tomb of Edward, the Black Prince (1330–76), eldest son of Edward III of England. He got his name by wearing black armor in the battles he won against France during the Hundred Years' War.

War machines

Various military engines were developed during the Middle Ages. The mangonel hurled rocks up to 650 ft (200 m), using a long arm that was wound up and then released. The 12th-century trebuchet was a much more reliable war machine. It could hurl rocks up to 1,300 ft (400 m), and was used by the crusaders at Acre in 1191.

The trebuchet was a huge wooden catapult used to hurl heavy rocks at enemy walls. It was worked by a counterweight and a sling.

Weapons

The longbow became important during the Hundred Years' War. It was much quicker to load than a crossbow, saving valuable time. Infantrymen carried long spears and two-handed swords. Double-headed axes, balls and chains, and spiked clubs were also used in close combat. The halberd – a combined spear and battleax – was extremely powerful and greatly feared.

Longbowmen fired long wooden arrows with sharp points and feather flights.

Siege warfare

Sieges formed an important part of medieval warfare. An attacking army simply surrounded the enemy town or castle, cut off supplies, and waited for the starving defenders to give in – after days, weeks, or even months. They could also try to force their way in, using battering rams and war machines.

Above: These attackers are using a shelter on wheels to protect themselves from above, allowing them to undermine the castle walls.

England's legendary King Arthur sits with his Knights of the Round Table. Since the table had no head, all the knights were considered to be of equal rank. They were bound by oath to help each other in times of danger.

A new knight

When a young man had been dubbed a knight, he put on his spurs and took up his sword. These actions showed that he was ready to fight on behalf of his lord. The spurs had symbolic significance for a mounted warrior. The investiture ceremony meant a great deal to a young knight. He had already spent seven years in service as a page in a nobleman's household, and another seven years serving another knight as a squire.

A squire was dubbed a knight by his lord, or sometimes even by his king. The investiture ceremony was usually followed by a great feast and celebration.

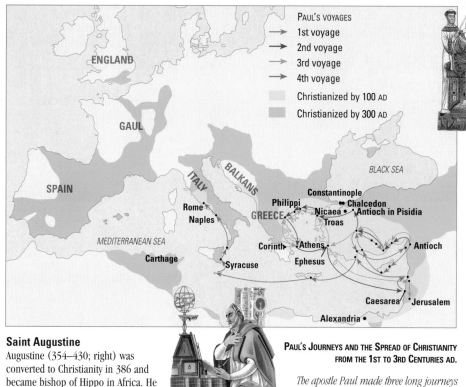

PAUL'S VOYAGES
→ 1st voyage
→ 2nd voyage
→ 3rd voyage
→ 4th voyage
Christianized by 100 AD
Christianized by 300 AD

Constantine the Great

In 313 Emperor Constantine (c.285–337) gave the Lateran Palace in Rome to the bishop of Rome as his official residence (above). He also returned to Christians property that had been seized from them during the persecutions, and allowed them freedom of worship. This resulted in the conversion of thousands of pagans.

Saint Augustine

Augustine (354–430; right) was converted to Christianity in 386 and became bishop of Hippo in Africa. He was one of the greatest thinkers among early Christians and wrote a spiritual autobiography called *Confessions*, which contributed greatly to the development of theology.

PAUL'S JOURNEYS AND THE SPREAD OF CHRISTIANITY FROM THE 1ST TO 3RD CENTURIES AD.

The apostle Paul made three long journeys from Jerusalem and founded Christian colonies all around the eastern Mediterranean. His fourth journey was to Rome, where he was tried by Emperor Nero.

Council of Nicaea

Fearing a split in the Christian Church, Constantine summoned 318 bishops to attend the Council of Nicaea in Asia Minor, in 325. The council condemned the view of a priest named Arius (above) and his followers, the Arians, who argued that Christ was not divine. It also issued the Christian Creed, the official set of beliefs of the Church.

Christian faith

Christians showed their faith in different ways. A Syrian monk named Simeon (c.390–459) became a hermit and sat on top of a 50-ft (15-m) tall pillar for more than 35 years (right). The snake represents the temptations of the world, which Simeon resisted.

Early Christian provinces

During the first centuries AD, the leadership of the Christian Church was given to local pastors, called bishops. The Church organized the Roman Empire into provinces. The main provinces were based on cities with large Christian communities, such as Jerusalem, Rome, Antioch, Alexandria, and Carthage.

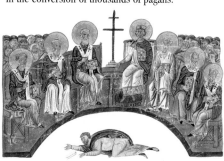

- ▨ Islam
- ▨ Hinduism
- ▨ Buddhism
- → Nestorian Church
- → Coptic Missions
- → Jacobite/Nestorian Missions

THE SPREAD OF CHRISTIANITY OUTSIDE THE ROMAN EMPIRE.

c. AD 50 Paul founds Christian colonies around Mediterranean.

c.70–100 Many of the Bible's New Testament books written.

250 Emperor Decius has thousands of Christians killed.

313 Christians granted freedom of worship in the Roman Empire.

325 Council of Nicaea in Asia Minor – meeting of 318 bishops.

The Spread of Christianity

The earliest Christians – including Jesus's companions Peter and John, and a convert named Paul – traveled widely around the Mediterranean during the 1st century AD, spreading Christianity throughout the Roman Empire. For over 300 years Christians were persecuted by the Romans. In AD 313, however, Emperor Constantine granted them freedom to worship, and bishops were given special privileges. By the late 4th century, Christianity was probably the majority religion in the empire. It continued to spread after the fall of the Western Empire in 476, and by about AD 600 most of the former provinces had been Christianized. Christianity was also well established in the Eastern, or Byzantine, Empire. By 1000 the Slavs of the first Russian state, Kiev, had also been converted.

According to the Bible, there were only about 120 Christian believers when Christ died. After the first sermon preached by Peter, one of Jesus's disciples, 3,000 new converts were made in one day alone. Christianity quickly spread from Jerusalem through the towns of Judea and Samaria, and from there to many of the main cities of the Mediterranean world, including Antioch, Athens, Corinth, Ephesus, and Rome.

The most important of the early converts was Paul (born Saul of Tarsus, c. AD 3–64), who had a vision of Christ while on a journey to Damascus. About AD 50 Paul made several journeys, during which he founded a number of Christian colonies. Paul was executed on the orders of Emperor Nero (reigned 54–68), who chose to blame Christians for a great fire that destroyed much of Rome.

Toward the end of the 1st century many of the books of the Bible's New Testament were written. By the 3rd century the organization of the Christian Church was well established, though Christianity was still a missionary religion. The

Saint Boniface

Boniface (675–754), whose original name was Winfrid, was an English-born Christian missionary who became known as the Apostle of Germany. As archbishop of Mainz, he helped set up an organized church in Germany. He converted many pagans and founded some of Germany's first monasteries. Boniface was killed by pagans during a confirmation service for converts in Friesland (above).

The Celtic Church

In the 6th century, the influence of the Celtic Christians spread from Ireland and Wales to Scotland, where Columba (521–98) founded a monastery on the island of Iona. From there missionaries traveled to northern England.

Large stone Celtic crosses, such as this one (left), were carved with images of saints, as well as animals and swirling designs. The circle around the cross came from a pre-Christian symbol for the Sun.

Russia

Saint Sophia cathedral (below), in Kiev, was named after Hagia Sophia in Constantinople. It was built by Yaroslav the Wise (980–1054) and dedicated by the first metropolitan bishop of Kiev in 1037.

Anthony of Thebes, also known as Saint Anthony of Egypt (left), founded the early Christian monastic movement.

A Nestorian, from a wall painting in China.

The Nestorians

The Nestorians followed the doctrines of the Syrian bishop, Nestorius, who died about 450. In 489 his supporters established themselves in Persia. Nestorianism spread along the Silk Road to China and Mongolia and by sea via the spice trade to India and Indonesia.

Saint George

Saint George (later the patron saint of England) was the subject of many legends in Europe, including the tale of how he saved a king's daughter by slaying a dragon with his lance (left). He may have come from the Middle East or Asia Minor. According to tradition, he became a soldier in the Roman army, but because he was a Christian, he was executed by order of the Roman emperor, Diocletian, during his purge of Christians about AD 303.

The Copts

The Copts of Egypt played an important role in the development of the early Christian Church. The Copts believed in the unity of the human and divine in Christ's nature. In 451 Coptic rulers in Alexandria were condemned for this belief by church leaders from Rome and Constantinople at the Council of Chalcedon, which declared that Christ had two separate natures.

The Franks

Clovis, king of the Franks (c.466–511), was converted by his wife, Clotilda. He also had 3,000 of his warriors baptized. At this time, however, most Franks did not recognize the ultimate authority of the pope.

This 9th-century ivory carving shows Clovis being baptized in 496.

Monastic life

Those who followed the teachings of Saint Benedict joined the order of the Benedictine monks and lived apart from other people. This reconstruction (below) shows the Benedictine abbey of Cluny, in France, founded in 910.

354–430 Life of North African theologian, Saint Augustine.

370 Basil the Great is bishop of Caesarea, in Asia Minor.

480–550 Life of Saint Benedict, a founder of Western monasticism.

800 Charlemagne crowned Emperor of the Romans.

988 Grand Prince Vladimir I of Kiev converts; Slavs follow.

original traveling disciples were gradually replaced by local pastors, called bishops.

In 250 Emperor Decius (reigned 249–251) had thousands of Christians killed for refusing to take part in pagan rituals. In 303, under Emperor Diocletian, the persecutions were even worse. The situation changed under Constantine (reigned 307–337), who extended tolerance to all religions, including Christianity thereby ending persecution. By the time of Theodosius I (reigned 379–395) Christianity was the main religion in the Roman Empire.

In Egypt, a Christian named Anthony of Thebes (c.250–356) formed the early monastic movement that led to the foundation of the Coptic Church. Other monastic communities of the time included those of Saint Basil (c.330–379) in Asia Minor and John Cassian (c.360–435) in France.

By the beginning of the 4th century, Christianity was well established in Britain, and in Ireland Saint Patrick (c.390–460) converted many people.

About this time Church and Christian rulers banished many heretics (people

who did not believe in orthodox doctrine), and this led indirectly to the spread of different forms of Christianity.

By the 5th century missionaries had reached India, and by the 7th century they were in China. In 800, on Christmas Day, Pope Leo III crowned Charlemagne (c.742–814) Emperor of the Romans. His empire was later called the Holy Roman Empire, showing how closely tied it was to the Christian Church.

The Christian religion also flourished in the Byzantine Empire, forming the basis of today's Eastern Orthodox Church. In Russia, in 988, Grand Prince Vladimir I (c.956–1015), ruler of the state of Kiev, became a Christian and most of the Slavs under his rule also converted.

1. A miniature c.800 showing Jesus being arrested.

2. A painting of the Virgin Mary and her son, Jesus Christ.

3. Monks farmed the land, taught people to read and write, and spent much time praying.

4. Saint Bernard of Clairvaux (1090–1153), who helped expand the Cistercian order.

The beautiful church of Hagia Sophia, the Church of Holy Wisdom, was built in Constantinople by Emperor Justinian I. It took 10,000 masons, carpenters, artists, and sculptors over five years to complete. It was dedicated in 537 and remained the center of the Eastern Christian world for more than 900 years.

Roman Empire at Justinian's succession

Area recovered during Justinian's reign

— Byzantine Empire, 1025

— Byzantine Empire, 1204

THE BYZANTINE EMPIRE IN THREE DIFFERENT MOMENTS: 628, 867, AND 1204

Right: The Byzantine Empire was at its height under Emperor Justinian I (482–565). He is most famous for his laws, conquests, and buildings. He is shown here with a Byzantine priest (right) and on a gold coin (far right).

Right: The Sassanids of Persia fought the Byzantines during the 4th century, and they continued to dispute Byzantine territory up to the 6th century. This silver dish shows a Sassanid king hunting lions – a favorite royal pastime.

Below: Byzantine warships, called dromons, were light and fast. They carried a lethal weapon; a chemical mixture that burst into flames when it touched water. The makeup of the mixture was kept a secret, and was known as "Greek fire."

Mosaics

Like the Romans, the Byzantines were expert mosaic makers. The walls, floors, and domes of their churches were decorated with beautiful mosaics made from thousands of small cubes of glass or marble set in plaster (left).

SEE ALSO
p. 70 THE FALL OF THE WESTERN EMPIRE
p. 78 THE RISE OF ISLAM

Icons, or religious images, were important to the Byzantine Church, but the Byzantine Empire banned them from 730 to 843, and many were destroyed. This icon of Christ (left) was disfigured by iconoclasts: people who were against the worship of sacred images.

AD 330 Constantine moves capital of Roman Empire to Byzantium, renamed Constantinople after him. 527–565 Reign of expansionist emperor, Justinian I. 551 Byzantines seize southern Spain from Visigoths. 610–641 Reign of Emperor Heraclius; defeats Persians. 634–642 Muslim Arabs invade.

An ivory panel of Empress Irene (c.752–803).

The Byzantine Empire

The Byzantine Empire, ruled from the city of Constantinople, existed for about 1,000 years until it fell to the Ottoman Turks in 1453. Originally the eastern half of the Roman Empire, its inhabitants continued to think of themselves as Romans and many emperors dreamed of reuniting the old Roman Empire. However, by the 7th century it had developed its own distinctive, Greek-speaking, Christian culture, which modern historians call Byzantine. Throughout its history the empire was continually under attack, first by the Persians, then by the newly-united Muslim Arabs, as well as by Bulgars and Slavic peoples. As the center of Orthodox Christianity, there was ongoing conflict with the Catholic Church in Rome. It was also frequently divided by internal strife, caused by religious and ethnic quarrels. Despite its many problems, Byzantium remained a brilliant center of art, architecture, and literature throughout the Middle Ages.

The city of Byzantium – a port at the entrance to the Black Sea – was founded by the Greeks in the 7th century BC. In AD 330 Emperor Constantine the Great rebuilt the city and made it the capital of the eastern part of the Roman Empire. The city was renamed Constantinople after him. When the western half of the empire collapsed, Constantinople became the capital of the new Eastern, or Byzantine, Empire.

By the 6th century the empire covered Asia Minor, the Balkan Peninsula (the land between the Adriatic, Aegean, and

Left: This miniature of Constantinople shows the strong city walls. At the time of Justinian I the city probably had more than 500,000 inhabitants. In 542, however, an outbreak of plague killed at least half the population. The city was held by the crusaders from 1204 to 1261.

Below: Byzantine administrative officials like this one were called logothetes. *The Byzantine legal and administrative system was originally based on Roman law. In the 6th century Emperor Justinian I appointed a group of lawyers to draw up a set of laws known as the Justinian Code. In 1054 a university was founded in Constantinople to teach law to government officials.*

Right: The Byzantines were expert builders. They built many churches and defensive structures.

Above: A coin with the head of Emperor Heraclius who defeated the Persians at Nineveh in 628.

Trade

Merchants in Byzantine towns imported silks and spices from China, and timber and furs from western and northern Europe. Silkworms were introduced into the empire in the 6th century, when the manufacture of silk textiles became important. These were later exported, along with carved ivory, enamel, and glassware. Trade prospered under powerful emperors such as Basil II (c.958–1025), who was known as Bulgaroctonus, or "slayer of the Bulgars."

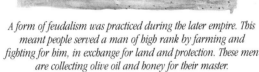

A form of feudalism was practiced during the later empire. This meant people served a man of high rank by farming and fighting for him, in exchange for land and protection. These men are collecting olive oil and honey for their master.

Left and below: Byzantine bread was marked with a special stamp to show that it was pure and of the correct weight.

The fall of Constantinople

On May 29, 1453, the Muslim troops of the Ottoman sultan, Mehmet II (1432–81, right), took Constantinople by storm. They achieved this by carrying 70 ships overland so they could position them behind the Byzantine navy. The last Byzantine emperor, Constantine XI (reigned 1449–53), the eightieth emperor since Constantine the Great, died defending his capital. After his victory, Mehmet went straight to the church of Hagia Sophia and set up a triumphant throne. The great Christian church was turned into a mosque.

730–843 Iconoclast era: icons banned in the empire.

1014 Basil II defeats Bulgars.
1082 Emperor Alexius I

Comnenus gives commercial privileges to Venice.

1204–61 Constantinople is in the hands of the Crusaders.

1453 Constantinople conquered by Turks; Byzantine Empire ends.

Black seas), Egypt, Palestine, and Syria. It reached its greatest extent under Emperor Justinian I (reigned 527–565). He conquered Italy, the southeastern coast of Spain, and much of North Africa. Trade thrived during Justinian's reign, and Byzantine art and architecture flourished.

The empire was always under threat from its warlike neighbors, however, and after Justinian's death it was invaded by Lombards from Germany, who seized parts of Italy, and Slavs and Avars, who invaded the Balkan Peninsula. Persian invaders weakened the empire during the late 6th and early 7th centuries.

Emperor Heraclius (c.575–641) temporarily stopped the collapse by defeating the Persians. But in 634 Muslim Arabs invaded, and by 642 they had conquered Syria, Palestine, and Egypt.

By the 8th century the empire consisted only of Asia Minor, the Balkan coast, Crete and other Greek islands, southern Italy, and Sicily. From 867 to 1025 the empire regained territory in Asia Minor and Bulgaria. In 1054 a dispute over the pope's authority in the empire led to a break between the churches in the West and East. About this time, the Normans seized lands

throughout southern Italy, and in 1071 the Muslim Seljuk Turks defeated a Byzantine army at the Battle of Manzikert, in Asia Minor. Emperor Alexius I Comnenus (reigned 1081–1118) asked Western rulers to help defend the empire against the Turks. They responded by sending Christian "crusaders," whose aim was to repulse the Turks and to liberate Jerusalem from the Muslims.

Later Crusades resulted in increased tension between the Byzantines and the Western Christians, and in 1204 the crusaders sacked Constantinople. With Venetian support, they

established the short-lived Latin Empire. The Byzantines recaptured their capital in 1261, but Ottoman Turks soon invaded Asia Minor, and Serbs advanced in the Balkans. By the late 14th century, Constantinople and part of Greece were all that remained of the Byzantine empire. It finally fell in 1453, when Ottoman Turks captured Constantinople.

1. Emperor Basil I (reigned 876–886) strengthened the empire in Asia Minor and southern Italy.

2. A Bulgar horseman. Bulgars besieged Constantinople in 813 and 913.

3. An icon, or religious image.

c. AD 570 The prophet Muhammad is born in Mecca.

622 Muhammad's flight (called the *Hijira*) to Medina; start of the Islamic era.
632 Death of Muhammad.

632–634 Rule of first caliph, Abu Bakr, known as the "righteous one."

656–661 Rule of 4th caliph, Ali; marries Muhammad's daughter.

The Rise of Islam

The Islamic religion began in the Arabian city of Mecca in about AD 610, when the prophet Muhammad believed he had received revelations from God. The followers of Islam, called Muslims, start their calendar in the year Christians call 622, when Muhammad and his followers moved from Mecca to Medina (both in present-day Saudi Arabia). When Muhammad died in 632, Islam had conquered most of central and southern Arabia. In the hundred years following his death Muslim Arabs conquered and converted the peoples of Mesopotamia, the Levant, North Africa, and parts of southern Spain and France. For almost six centuries Muslim rulers came from just two dynasties: the Umayyads, who made their capital in Damascus, and the Abbasids, who ruled from Baghdad.

Islam was founded by a prophet called Muhammad (c.570–632). Many people in Mecca, in Arabia, where he came from, felt his new religion threatened the old gods, and in 622 he was forced to flee to nearby Medina. There, he was accepted as God's messenger. Muslims count that year as the beginning of the Islamic era. Muhammad returned to Mecca in 630. He died two years later. By then he and his followers had gained control of most of Arabia. After Muhammad's death, various groups revolted. Abu Bakr (c.573–634), the first caliph, or Muslim ruler, overcame them and sent Arab forces into the Byzantine provinces of Syria and Palestine, and the Persian province of Iraq. These so-called "holy wars" continued under the caliphs Omar (ruled 634–644) and Uthman (ruled 644–656). The Muslims occupied the Persian capital of Ctesiphon. The Persians tried to regain their empire during the caliphate of Ali (ruled 656–661), but their attempts failed.

The Umayyad Dynasty of caliphs, who ruled from 661 to

THE EXTENT OF THE ISLAMIC WORLD ABOUT 800.

SPAIN
Cordoba •
Seville •
ITALY
Rome •
BLACK SEA
• Constantinople
Samarkand •
NORTH AFRICA
MEDITERRANEAN SEA
SYRIA
Damascus • • Baghdad
• Jerusalem
PALESTINE
Al-Fusat •
AFGHANISTAN
ARABIA
• Medina
• Mecca
INDIAN OCEAN

☐ Islamic conquests
☐ Byzantine Empire

Above: About 800, the Islamic world covered all of southwestern Asia, the coast of North Africa, the Mediterranean islands, and most of the Iberian peninsula.

This mosaic comes from the court at Damascus, capital of the Umayyad caliphs, who ruled the Arab Muslims. It shows the Garden of Eden as it is described in the Qu'ran.

Muhammad

Muslims believe that the word of God was revealed to Muhammad (whose name means "Praised One") in 610, when he was meditating alone in a cave on Mount Hira, near Mecca. A vision of the angel Gabriel told Muhammad to give God's message to his people in their own language, Arabic. At first Muhammad had doubts about the vision, but his wife Khadijah encouraged him to believe in the revelations. She became his first disciple.

The Qu'ran

This beautifully inscribed page (right) comes from the Qu'ran, or Koran, the sacred book of Islam. About AD 650, Muhammad's followers wrote down the words revealed to him by God, and collected and arranged them into 114 *suras*, or "chapters." The text is written in classical Arabic.

Five pillars of faith

Muslims have five special duties, represented by the fingers of an open hand (right). The duties are: belief in one God, Allah, and in the prophet Muhammad; observance of five daily prayers; fasting during the holy month of Ramadan; giving alms, or donations to charity; and a pilgrimage to Mecca at least once in a lifetime.

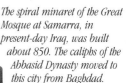

The spiral minaret of the Great Mosque at Samarra, in present-day Iraq, was built about 850. The caliphs of the Abbasid Dynasty moved to this city from Baghdad.

Dating to pre-Islamic times, the Kaaba, in Mecca, is the most sacred Islamic shrine. It contains an ancient black stone, which according to Muslim tradition was given to Abraham by the angel Gabriel. When Muhammad was 35, a flood damaged the Kaaba, and he was chosen to put the stone back in place. Today, Muslims all over the world face the shrine in Mecca when they pray.

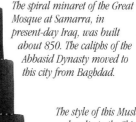

The style of this Muslim's turban shows his loyalty to the Shia branch of Islam. The Shi'ites reject the first three caliphs and regard the fourth caliph, Ali (c.600–661), as Muhammad's only true successor. The leader of Shi'ite Islam must be a descendant of Ali.

661–750 Umayyad Dynasty rules from Damascus. | 711 Muslims invade Spain. | 732 Muslims defeated at Battle | of Poitiers, southern France. | 750 Start of Abbasid Dynasty; | rules from Baghdad. | 756–1031 Umayyad Dynasty | rules Spain from Cordoba. | 1258 Abbasid Dynasty ends.

750, led the Arab Muslims to new victories. The dynasty was founded by Muawiyah (c.602–680), who belonged to the Umayya family, from which the caliphate takes its name. The Umayyads made Damascus their capital. They fought the Turks in Central Asia; sent an expedition into India; and traveled as far as China.

During this period the Muslims also fought the Byzantines in Asia Minor and around the Mediterranean Sea. They captured Cyprus, Rhodes, and Sicily, and completed the conquest of North Africa, where many Berbers were converted to

Islam. The Muslims twice laid siege to Constantinople, but failed to take the city. The Umayyads invaded Spain in 711. From there a Muslim army crossed the Pyrenees and marched through southern France, where they were defeated by Charles Martel's army in 732 at the Battle of Poitiers.

In 750, a family called the Abbasids, descendants of Muhammad's uncle, overthrew the Umayyads and moved the capital to Baghdad, which until then had been a small Christian town. An Umayyad prince

named Abd al-Rahman (731–788) escaped death and traveled to Spain. He pacified rival Arab and Berber factions and established the Umayyad Dynasty of Spain, which lasted from 756 to 1031. Meanwhile, in North Africa and southwestern Asia, the Abbasid Dynasty reached its peak under Haroun al-Rashid (ruled 786–809) and ruled until 1258.

1. *Muhammad, the Muslim prophet.*
2. *Miniature of Charlemagne fighting Muslim invaders in Spain in 778.*
3. *Pottery bowl from Nishapur, Persia.*
4. *A 12th-century candle clock.*

The astrolabe was developed by Muslim astronomers to help traders crossing the desert by camel find their way by studying the stars. It was later used by sailors.

Warfare

Sieges played a major part in Muslim warfare. They were generally more decisive than battles in the field. In this manuscript illustration (left) the forces of Mahmud of Ghazna (ruled 998–1030), the third sultan of the Ghaznavid Dynasty, are attacking a fortress in Afghanistan. Mahmud's soldiers are using a siege engine called a "trebuchet," as well as bows and arrows. Mahmud also led many expeditions to India, supported by 500 war elephants.

The Moors

In the early 8th century the Moors – Arabs, Berbers, and other Muslim peoples from North Africa – invaded and occupied Spain. In 711 the Moors captured the city of Cordoba, and the Umayyads made it their capital in 756. Important scholars were brought to the Muslim court there. In 785 building began on the greatest mosque of the medieval world outside Mecca. The Great Mosque at Cordoba is famous for its beautiful Moorish architecture (right).

Above: Arab Muslim soldiers were extremely effective and their conquests were swift. They believed that they were doing God's will, and this generated a bond of brotherhood among them. The Muslim concept of jihad, *often translated as "holy war," expresses their duty to defend their faith.*

By the 10th century, Muslim scholars had developed astronomy into a science in its own right, despite opposition from theologians. This illustration shows astronomers at work in an early observatory.

Science and learning

The Qu'ran encourages learning, and Muslim scholars were respected wherever they went. They became famous for their discoveries in astronomy, mathematics, engineering (including methods of raising water), medicine, and geography. Muslims built schools, universities, and libraries all over the Islamic world, and schools called *kuttabs* were set up in mosques.

Left: This miniature shows a scene in an Islamic library, where Muslim scholars are reading and discussing ideas.

SEE ALSO
p. 92 THE ISLAMIC WORLD
p. 94 THE CRUSADES

Below: Charles Martel (c.688–741), the grandfather of Charlemagne, ruled northern Gaul. He helped convert Germany to Christianity by supporting the missionary work of Saint Boniface.

Left: This scene shows a medieval kitchen and animal pen typical of Charlemagne's time. The emperor often made surprise visits to his subjects. He was said to have simple tastes, unlike many of his nobles.

Charles the Great

The first emperor of what was later called the Holy Roman Empire was Charles (c.742–814), son of Pepin the Short. In 768 he and his brother inherited the Frankish kingdom, and in 771, when his brother died, Charles took full control and became king of the Franks. He extended his kingdom and forced the Saxons and Avars of central Europe to convert to Christianity. When Charlemagne died in 814 he was succeeded by his son Ludwig, also known as "Louis the Pious," who was a weak leader.

Divided empire

After the death of Louis I, Charlemagne's son, civil war broke out in the empire. This was settled in 843 with the Treaty of Verdun, when the empire was divided between three of Louis' sons. Lothair I received the Middle Realm, which included Italy. Charles the Bald took France, and Louis the German ruled in the east.

Right: A fragment of the Strasbourg Oaths (February 14, 842), an alliance undersigned by Charles the Bald and Louis the German against their brother, Lothair I.

Above: Lothair I (795–855), a nephew of Charlemagne, became king of Italy in 818 and emperor in 840.

Song of Roland

In the summer of 778, Charlemagne's army was returning to France after a failed campaign to reconquer Spain from the Muslims. In the Pyrenees mountains, the Frankish army was attacked by Basques (left). An officer named Count Hruodland was killed. More than 300 years later he became famous as Roland, the hero of the great epic poem, the *Song of Roland*. In the poem, the courageous Roland shows great devotion to Charlemagne, but dies in a battle against the Muslims.

Charlemagne's court became a cultural, educational, and religious center. In 781 the emperor invited the English scholar Alcuin (c.732–804, left) to his court, where science and literature were studied.

Aachen

Between 790 and 805 Charlemagne had a group of buildings erected in his kingdom's capital, Aachen, to serve as his royal court and national church. Among them was the Palatine Chapel (below), which today is the most important example of Carolingian architecture. It was modeled on a church in Ravenna, Italy, and at almost 100 ft (31 m), it was for many centuries the tallest stone building in Germany.

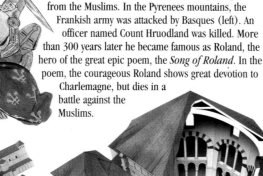

Power of the Church

The pope and the emperor were fierce rivals for political power in Europe. Objects such as this gold-plated reliquary (used to contain a relic of Saint Foy) from the abbey in Conques, France, represented the power of the Church, and made a great impression on ordinary people.

---

800 Charlemagne crowned emperor of Romans by Pope Leo III in St. Peter's, Rome. **843** Treaty of Verdun divides the empire into three kingdoms. **955** Otto I, king of East Francia, defeats Magyars at Battle of Lechfeld, near Augsburg. **962** Otto I crowned emperor. **1024–1125** Salian Dynasty of

The Holy Roman Empire

The official title of Holy Roman Emperor was only used from the 13th century, but the empire had its beginnings in the year 800, when Charlemagne became the emperor. After Charlemagne's death the empire was immediately divided up, but was reunited by Otto I and his successors, who ruled Germany from 919 to 1024. There were constant struggles for power between emperors and popes, and many German princes and Italian factions sided with the pope, which caused a series of civil wars. Frederick I "Barbarossa" of the Hohenstaufen Dynasty restored order to the empire in the 12th century. After a period of further instability, the Hohenstaufens were succeeded by the Habsburgs. Charles V was the last emperor to be crowned by the pope, in 1519. The Holy Roman Empire carried on after the medieval period was over; the last Holy Roman Emperor abdicated in 1806.

A 9th-century bronze statue of Charlemagne.

On Christmas Day in AD 800, Pope Leo III crowned Charlemagne emperor of the Romans. Historians sometimes call his empire – which included most of present-day Germany, France, and Italy – the Western Roman Empire, to show that it was separate from the Byzantine Empire in the East. Later it was referred to as the Holy Roman Empire.

After Charlemagne's death in 814 the empire fell apart, and in 843 was divided into kingdoms ruled by his three grandsons.

THE HOLY ROMAN EMPIRE c.950–1356.

— Boundary of Empire, 1356

Kingdom of Otto I, 936

Kingdom of Burgundy, c.1032

Kingdom of Italy, 12th–13th c.

Territories annexed, 12th–13th c.

Frederick II

Frederick II (1194–1250) was called the "wonder of the world," because he was such a good ruler. He was crowned king of Germany when he was just two years old and became Holy Roman Emperor in 1220. Frederick was a soldier, a scientist, and a patron of poets and artists.

Frederick the II was also an expert huntsman and wrote an illustrated book (right) called On the Art of Hunting with Birds.

Emperor of the world

Otto III (980–1002) became Holy Roman Emperor at age three (his mother and grandmother ruled until he was sixteen). He secured the election of his cousin, Bruno of Carinthia, as Pope Gregory V, the first German pope. Otto lived most of his short life in Rome, where he tried to revive ancient Roman customs. He also took the title "emperor of the world," because he saw himself as the leader of world Christianity.

The Investiture Dispute

Up until 1075 bishops had sometimes been appointed by emperors and kings. Then the pope, Gregory VII, decided that only he should have the authority to appoint them. The Holy Roman Emperor, Henry IV (reigned 1056–1106), disagreed and a feud broke out.

Although centered on investiture, it was really about whether the pope or the emperor should dominate the church.

Right: Henry IV is shown here kneeling, with Matilda of Canossa and the bishop of Cluny in 1077. It is said that Henry had to stand barefoot in the snow for three days while he waited for Pope Gregory VII to pardon him after the Investiture Dispute.

From the beginning of the 11th century, Italian cities such as Florence grew rapidly in size and importance. Popes and emperors fought for authority over these developing city-states until 1250, when Emperor Frederick II died. From then on the city-states ruled themselves, and the pope ruled central Italy.

Emperor Otto II investing a bishop.

Right: Under Pope Innocent III (1160–1216), the power of the papacy was at its strongest.

SEE ALSO
p. 74 THE SPREAD OF CHRISTIANITY
p. 82 9TH- AND 10TH-CENTURY INVADERS

Franconia rules the empire.
1075 Investiture Dispute

between German king, Henry IV, and Pope Gregory VII.

1155–90 Reign of Frederick I "Barbarossa" of the

Hohenstaufen Dynasty.
1273 Rudolf I of the Habsburgs

is elected emperor.
1519–56 Reign of Charles V.

The empire was reunited by Otto I, "the Great" (912–973), who brought the separate German duchies under the control of the monarchy. In 955 he defeated the invading Magyars at the Battle of Lechfeld in southern Germany. Pope John XII asked him for help against his enemies in Italy. Otto was crowned emperor in 962. His son, Otto II (955–83), tried without success to drive the Greeks and Muslim Arabs from southern Italy. Otto III (980–1002) succeeded

him in 996. The next dynasty of German rulers, the Salians of Franconia, were strong emperors from 1024 to 1125. Struggles between emperors and popes led in 1075 to the Investiture Dispute between Henry IV (1050–1106) and Pope Gregory VII (c.1025–85). In 1155 Frederick I (c.1122–90), known as Barbarossa, or "Red Beard," who was a German king of the Hohenstaufen Dynasty, became emperor. Barbarossa forced the Italian city-states to accept governors, but they rebelled and defeated him at the Battle of Legnano in 1176. Barbarossa was

forced to make peace with the pope. Barbarossa's grandson, Frederick II (1194–1250), was a well-educated man who encouraged the arts and sciences. The struggle between emperors and popes allowed German nobles to gain power, and they were very strong from 1250 to 1273, a period called the Interregnum, when a number of dynasties struggled for power. In 1273 Rudolf I (1218–91) was elected emperor, and his dynasty, the Habsburgs, soon gained power over Austria. After Rudolf, the Habsburgs lost power,

however, and the German nobles chose a series of weak rulers for the next 150 years. In 1438 Albert II of the Habsburgs became emperor, and the dynasty ruled again until 1740. Charles V (1500–58), the last emperor to be crowned by the pope, was the most powerful ruler. (The dynasty ruled again from 1745 to 1806, when Napoleon I ordered Francis II to give up the title and the empire ended.)

1. A beautifully embroidered bishop's hat, or miter – a symbol of his office.

2. The gatehouse of the 8th-century monastery of Lorsch, in Germany.

3. The two leaders of the empire, pope and emperor, shown on a joint throne.

800 Frankish king, Charlemagne, is crowned emperor of the

Romans (Holy Roman Emperor).
831 Saracens oust Byzantines

from Palermo, Sicily.
867 Vikings capture Jorvik

(York), in northern England.
886 Danelaw set up in England.

899 Magyars defeat Italian army at Brenta River, Italy.

9th- and 10th-Century Invaders

The Carolingians – Charlemagne and his successors – ruled a large part of Europe throughout the 9th and 10th centuries. Their empire, later known as the Holy Roman Empire, united the continent for the first time since the end of the Roman Empire. This newfound unity and prosperity encouraged invasions from different peoples. From the end of the 8th century on, Europe was invaded from three different directions. From the north came the Vikings, who sailed in their fast longships from Denmark, Norway, and Sweden. They raided coasts and settled in Ireland, England, and Normandy in northern France. At the same time, Arab Saracens attacked from the south and spread their Islamic religion across southern Europe. A third set of invaders, the Magyars, rode in from the east and led successful raids on central Europe. By the 11th century, the Normans were extending their power to Britain and Italy.

Statue of the Viking god Thor with his magic hammer.

From the late 700s on, the Vikings, or Norsemen, made their mark as bold, ruthless raiders. They sailed from their homelands in Scandinavia, probably because their population was growing quickly and there was not enough good farmland at home. Norwegian Vikings began their raids in the 790s, attacking the coasts of England, Ireland, and Scotland. Then in 865 Danish Vikings invaded England. They conquered much of the country, but King Alfred the Great (849–899) only allowed them to settle in the eastern region, which became known as the Danelaw. By that time Norwegians and Danes had also

The Vikings at home

In their Scandinavian homeland, the Vikings lived mainly by farming and fishing. Farmers raised cattle, sheep, pigs, and poultry, and grew wheat, barley, and oats. In Norway the farms were often isolated, but in Denmark they were often grouped in village settlements (below) along the coast, so goods could be transferred to and from ships. The Vikings traded furs, textiles, and iron. Their houses were built of wood and the roofs were covered in thatch or turf. Nearly all everyday items were made by craftworkers; the men worked with wood and metal, and the women spun wool and wove and dyed cloth.

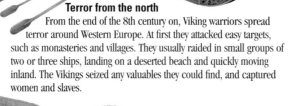

Viking oarsmen rowed their longships near land or when great speed was needed. At sea they used a single square sail.

Terror from the north

From the end of the 8th century on, Viking warriors spread terror around Western Europe. At first they attacked easy targets, such as monasteries and villages. They usually raided in small groups of two or three ships, landing on a deserted beach and quickly moving inland. The Vikings seized any valuables they could find, and captured women and slaves.

Settling Iceland

The Vikings sailed to Iceland in 860 and first settled there 14 years later. They killed or drove out the Irish monks who were already living on the island. The newcomers set up farms near the coast, but they did not make villages of any size. Chieftains met to make laws, and an assembly called an Althing met each midsummer to act as court and parliament.

This scene from the Bayeux Tapestry shows a Norman ship during the conquest of England in 1066.

ICELAND

SCANDINAVIA

ASIA

EUROPE

BLACK SEA

AFRICA   MEDITERRANEAN SEA

Vikings
Saracens
Magyars
Norman kingdoms

ROUTES TAKEN BY THE MAGYARS, SARACENS, AND VIKINGS DURING THE 9TH AND 10TH CENTURIES.

SEE ALSO
p. 72 WARFARE IN THE MIDDLE AGES
p. 76 THE BYZANTINE EMPIRE
p. 78 THE RISE OF ISLAM
p. 80 THE HOLY ROMAN EMPIRE

911 Viking leader Rollo founds the duchy of Normandy.

955 Magyars defeated by Otto I at Battle of Lechfeld.

1000 Stephen crowned first king of Hungary.

1066 Battle of Hastings; Norman conquest of England.

1072 Normans drive Saracens from Sicily.

2 ... looted and burned towns in France, the Low Countries, Italy, and Spain. Norwegian Vikings sailed as far as Iceland and settled there in 874. From Sweden, a group of Vikings known as the Rus traveled east by river and set up trading centers in the Slavic towns of Novgorod and Kiev. Russia takes its name from the Rus.

Meanwhile, in southern Europe, Spain was invaded by Muslims from Arabia, and in 827 Muslim Saracens occupied Sicily – which they ruled for 200 years – ousting the Byzantines from Palermo in 831. The Muslims went on to establish bases on the southern coast of Italy and 3 ...

... to attack Sardinia and Corsica. They raided monasteries and towns in Italy, including Rome itself, before moving on to southern Gaul. European merchants and pilgrims were captured and forced to pay large ransoms for their release.

At the end of the 9th century, the Magyars – nomadic horsemen from Asia – invaded eastern Europe. They made their base in the Hungarian plains, and from there moved swiftly south and west. In 899 they inflicted a heavy defeat on King Berengar of Italy at the Brenta River, and in 907 defeated ...

... the Bavarians at Pressburg (present-day Bratislava, Slovakia). The Magyars continued into northern Germany, and then turned south, reaching Rome in 936. In 955 they besieged Augsburg, but were finally routed at nearby Lechfeld by the army of Emperor Otto I (912–973). The Magyar leaders were killed, and the rest were forced to become Christians. In 1000 Stephen (977–1038), the son of a Magyar prince, was made the first king of Hungary.

During the late 10th century the Normans – descendants of the Vikings who had settled in northern France – invaded neighboring Maine, and in 1066 they conquered England under the ...

4 ... leadership of William I, "the Conqueror" (c.1028–87). In 1072 the Normans drove the Saracens from their Sicilian capital, Palermo, and a Norman named Roger I (1031–1101) was made count of Sicily. The Normans now held power in countries in the south and north of Europe.

1. A 10th-century abbey bell tower in Northern Ireland, used as a lookout post to spot invaders.
2. A Viking longship's bronze weather vane.
3. An 11th-century illustration of Danish Vikings invading England in 866.
4. Sicilian puppet of the Frankish hero, Roland.

Crown of Stephen I of Hungary.

The Norman conquest of England

William, duke of Normandy (c.1028–87), earned the title "the Conqueror" when he defeated England's Anglo-Saxon king, Harold II, at the Battle of Hastings in 1066. William soon captured London and became the first Norman king of England. With the defeat of a northern rebellion in 1069–70 the conquest was complete, and the Normans introduced the feudal system to their new territory. Before the end of the century they had also conquered much of southern Italy and Sicily.

The Magyars: first kings of Hungary

The Magyars were nomadic, horse-riding peoples from Asia. They moved onto the plains of Hungary in the 9th century, and then invaded northern Italy, Germany, and central France, before being defeated by the Holy Roman Emperor, Otto I, in 955. Stephen (left), the son of the Magyar chief, Geza, was brought up as a Christian and defeated a pagan revolt in 998. On Christmas Day, 1000, he was crowned the first king of Hungary, with the approval of Pope Sylvester II.

The Saracens first attacked Sicily in 827, when it was under the rule of the Byzantine Empire. They ruled for about 200 years.

Saracen influence in Europe

The Saracens were Muslim Arabs, originally from the Arabian peninsula, who spread the Islamic religion first to Spain and then, in the 9th century, to Sicily. They went on to make bases in southern Italy, Sardinia, Corsica, and southern Gaul. The Saracens were advanced in learning and technology, and the European regions they conquered were greatly influenced by Islamic art, architecture, literature, and science. The invaders also took their system of irrigation with them and grew fruit and cotton in their new lands.

Above: Tancred was the last Norman king of Sicily.

Lancehead of Otto I.

1066 Battle of Hastings and Norman conquest of England.

1086 The Domesday Book, a survey of the property-holders of England, is produced.

1088 First university founded, in Bologna, Italy.

1094 El Cid defeats the Moors and conquers Valencia, Spain.

1130 First Norman king of Sicily.

European Recovery and the Feudal Kingdoms

After the invasions of the 9th and 10th centuries and the end of Frankish rule, European kings gained in power. They divided their land among the most important noblemen, who in return became their vassals. This system, called feudalism, was particularly strong in France and England during the 12th and 13th centuries. By that time trade and exploration were developing fast, and the first European universities were springing up. A new style of architecture, called Gothic, had developed, and by the end of the 13th century kings were building castles to act as fortified strongholds.

A gargoyle, or water spout, on the Gothic cathedral of Notre Dame, Paris.

EUROPE ABOUT 1180.

The city of Cologne was founded as a Roman settlement. It grew fast after 900, and by the end of the 12th century was the largest German city.

Roman walls
10th century walls
Walls built in 1106
Walls built in 1180
Main churches
River Rhine
Markets
Area occupied c.900

Merchants

By the 12th century, merchants were traveling long distances along the trade routes that linked European cities. Luxury goods began to arrive from Asia and Africa, and cargo ships carried them from the great ports of Venice and Genoa. This illustration (above) shows merchants arriving at a port on the Persian Gulf. They already have an elephant and a camel on board.

Market day

On market day, traders sold all sorts of goods from stalls that they set up in the towns. As trade increased, the markets became more important and medieval towns grew bigger.

Gothic architecture

As building skills advanced, medieval masons were able to build taller, more graceful churches in the Romanesque style. By the 12th century a new style had developed, called Gothic. It lasted until the 16th century. The cathedral at Burgos (left), in Spain, was founded in 1221, but its ornate Gothic towers were added later.

The feudal system

Medieval kings divided their land among their most important noblemen. In return, the nobles acknowledged the king's superiority and became his vassals. They promised to serve the king and fight for him whenever they were needed. For this they, in turn, required the service of knights, who were their vassals. This arrangement is called a feudal system. In this illustration (right) a nobleman kneels before his king to swear an oath of loyalty.

Universities

European universities developed from medieval cathedral and monastery schools. The first university opened in Bologna, Italy. It was founded in 1088 by a group of students, such as these (above), who decided to employ scholars to teach them. In the following century, universities were founded in Paris, France, and at Oxford and Cambridge, in England. The three main subjects taught during the Middle Ages were law, medicine, and theology.

At harvest time, the serfs gathered crops from the master's fields as well as from their own.

1163 Gothic cathedral of Notre Dame, Paris, begun.

c.1200 Commercial and military power develops in Venice, Italy.

1215 King John of England sets his seal to the Magna Carta.

1271 Marco Polo leaves Venice on his journey to China.

1295 King Edward I expands the English parliament.

Robin Hood

According to medieval legend, Robin Hood (left) was an outlaw who lived with a band of loyal followers in Sherwood Forest, in central England. Robin and his "merry men" spent most of their time hunting the king's deer, practicing their archery skills, and robbing the rich to give to the poor. No one knows whether the legendary outlaw really existed, but he was first mentioned in stories in 1377.

SEE ALSO
p. 104 MERCHANTS AND TRADE
p. 108 EUROPE IN THE 15TH CENTURY

Castles

A medieval castle was the fortified stronghold of a king or nobleman. If the castle was attacked, the drawbridge could be raised so that there was no easy way for the enemy to get across the moat. It was almost impossible to capture a castle except by siege. Over the centuries castles got bigger and stronger. King Edward I of England (1239–1307) conquered Wales and had a number of important castles built there. This castle (below), at Beaumaris on the island of Anglesey, northern Wales, was begun in 1295.

In 1297 King Philip IV of France (1268–1314) demanded that Edward I of England do homage to him. Though they had been at war with each other, Edward was Philip's vassal because he was also the duke of Aquitaine. Their long feud was settled when Edward married Philip's sister, Margaret.

Entertainment

Medieval minstrels entertained lords and ladies at banquets and other events. This minstrel (below) is playing a fiddle called a rebec. The diners are sitting at the "high" table, which was raised on a platform to distinguish important guests from those at the ordinary, lower tables. At a banquet, servants would bring several courses of meat dishes, fish, and poultry, followed by sweet puddings.

Parliament

The English parliament developed in the 13th century, when kings consulted nobles and churchmen on important issues. In 1295, King Edward I (reigned 1272–1307) widened the parliament by ordering two knights elected from each county and two people from each town to attend. This assembly was later called the Model Parliament, and was the beginning of the British House of Commons, in which elected members represent their constituents.

When King John of England (1167–1216) put his royal seal to the Magna Carta, or "Great Charter" (left) in 1215, he agreed to respect existing feudal rights and the rights of the church.

El Cid

Rodrigo Diaz de Vivar (c.1043–1099, left) served in the army of the king of Castile, in Spain. In 1081 he was banished by King Alphonso VI after being wrongly accused of disloyalty. Diaz then gathered together his own small army and after successful battles became rich and powerful. He was known as El Cid, from an Arabic word meaning "chief." In 1094, he defeated the Moors and conquered Valencia.

Norman Sicily

The Normans conquered Sicily in the late 11th century, and Roger II (1095–1154, right) became Sicily's first Norman king in 1130. His court was an important center for both Christian and Muslim scholars. By the end of the 12th century Sicily was the richest, most advanced state in Europe.

From about 1000, a system known as feudalism spread throughout much of Western Europe. In a feudal country, lords were granted land by the king in exchange for military service. They, in turn, gave grants of land to sub-vassals or serfs, in return for labor or a large part of their earnings. The serfs were allowed to raise livestock and crops on their small holdings of land. Life for these country peasants was generally hard.

Around the end of the first millennium population began to grow quite rapidly. More food was needed to feed the expanding population and new lands were cleared for farming. Farming methods also improved at this time, and the markets in villages and towns became increasingly important centers of trade.

Townspeople paid taxes to the monarch, and kings became even more powerful. They used their wealth to hire armies and enforce their authority. William the Conqueror (c.1028–87) invaded England from France in 1066. His successors Henry I (1068–1135) and Henry II (1133–89) enforced the king's law and strengthened royal power. In 1215 noblemen forced King John (1167–1216) to sign the Magna Carta and agree to respect existing customs. Edward I (1239–1307), who fought both the French king and the rebellious Scots, created a parliament in order to find ways of raising money.

In France, the Capetian kings (who ruled from 987 to 1328) also struggled with their nobles and defended their country against foreign influences. Just six years after their invasion of England, the Normans also conquered Sicily, and in 1130 Roger II (1095–1154) was made its king.

In Spain, Christians were fully occupied trying to drive out the Muslim Moors. By 1085 they had recaptured Toledo; in 1236 they took the Moorish capital of Cordoba; and in 1248 the Christians marched into Seville.

1. Knights were the most important medieval soldiers. Only wealthy men could afford to become knights because warhorses were very expensive. The lance was the knight's main weapon.

The Silk Route and growing foreign trade

The expansion of the Chinese Empire into Central Asia during the T'ang period strengthened trade routes from China to the West. The most important was known as the Silk Route, a series of tracks across mountains and deserts linking China with western Asia and Europe. Along it traveled countless caravans of camels, taking silk, spices, and other high-value goods westward, in exchange for gold and silver. Walled towns flourished where traders could stop for food and sleep. Traders did not travel the whole route themselves; they exchanged goods with others who had better knowledge of the road ahead.

THE T'ANG EMPIRE WITH OVERLAND TRADE ROUTES

The tracks that made up the Silk Route had been used by for many years. The traders of the T'ang and Song periods increased the number of trade routes and the volume of goods traded.

Highly decorated ceramic models were a feature of the T'ang period and they were often buried with their owners. This 19-in. (49-cm) high camel was modeled on those that traveled the Silk Route.

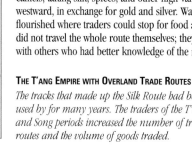

Printed paper money was introduced during the later Song Dynasty. This note is an example. It made buying and selling far easier than handling large numbers of coins, and reflects the growing importance of trade.

Artists and scholars

Art and scholarship flourished during the Song period, when poets, painters, and thinkers had more freedom than before to develop and express their own ideas. This calligrapher (above), a specialist in beautiful handwriting, is wearing a scholar's turban and gown.

Silk

Silk was produced in China as early as 2500 BC. By the time of the Roman Empire it was being imported into Europe. The continuing huge demand from western Asia and Europe for top quality Chinese silk contributed to the trade and prosperity of the T'ang and Song periods. These women (below) are ironing a newly woven length of silk.

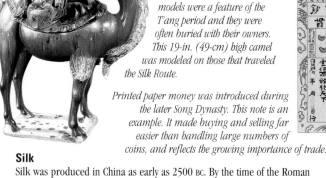

Right: Chinese emperors relied on an army of civil servants to carry out their orders. Officials had to pass a strict examination to join the service. This official is from the T'ang period.

The splendor of China

T'ang and Song emperors spared no expense in building themselves magnificent palaces and surrounding themselves with beautiful buildings and gardens in their capital cities. The Song capital, Hangzhou, was the largest city in the world at that time. It had as many as one million inhabitants. These two ladies of the Song court are out riding (above left).

> **SEE ALSO**
> p. 52 ANCIENT CHINA AND JAPAN
> p. 56 SOUTHEAST ASIA FROM NEOLITHIC TIMES
> p. 88 THE MONGOL EMPIRE
> p. 124 MING CHINA

618 T'ang Dynasty seizes power from the Sui Dynasty.

c. 670 Chinese Empire extends southward from Tibet to Korea.

756 Chinese troops withdraw from Tibet

to fight rebels.

907 Peasant rebellions lead to the fall of the T'ang Dynasty.

Chinese Civilization

The period from the 7th to the 13th centuries was one of great progress in China. Trade was boosted by a network of canals begun under the Sui Dynasty, the increasing use of the Silk Route to western Asia and Europe, and by great fleets of merchant ships. China's military might achieved the conquest of much of mainland Southeast Asia. It was a period when new ways of organizing society were developed, and inventions were made. Paper money was introduced about 1120, for example, making trading easier. During this period the population of China doubled from 50 to 100 million, and at the same time there was a shift of population from the northern plains to the Yangtze Valley. The period ended in disaster, however, with the invasion of the Mongols in 1211.

One of the ambitions that the T'ang Dynasty inherited from the Sui was the wish to expand the Chinese Empire. The Sui had tried unsuccessfully to conquer Korea, but the T'ang had bigger ideas. By about 660 the empire was bigger than it had ever been, extending into Central Asia and southward through Korea. Roads were built to serve this vast empire, and Chinese traders used the Silk Route to reach markets in Europe. Ideas flourished as well as trade, helped by the invention of the printed book in the 9th century.

But this prosperity did not touch most of China's population, who were landless

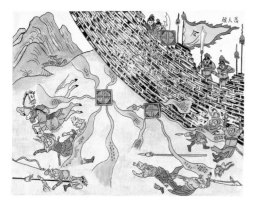

ROUTE OF THE SUI AND T'ANG GRAND CANAL

Part of the Grand Canal was built under the Sui Dynasty (581–618), but the main sections were built in the 7th century during the Song period, and it was completed in the 13th century. It linked the north with the fertile, rice-growing Yangtze Valley in central China.

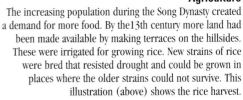

Gunpowder

Gunpowder was first mentioned in an army manual written in 1040. At that time it was used to launch fire-bombs, which were catapulted at the enemy and exploded (above). Later in the Song period, military engineers discovered how to use gunpowder to fire cannons.

The Grand Canal

The Grand Canal provided a trading link and a supply route for the army between the Yangtze Valley and the north. Extensions during the T'ang and Song periods brought its length to 1,550 mi. (2,500 km), linking the present-day cities of Hangzhou and Beijing.

Cargo boats like this one carried Chinese goods along the extensive river and canal system as well as overseas.

Agriculture

The increasing population during the Song Dynasty created a demand for more food. By the 13th century more land had been made available by making terraces on the hillsides. These were irrigated for growing rice. New strains of rice were bred that resisted drought and could be grown in places where the older strains could not survive. This illustration (above) shows the rice harvest.

Printing

The printed book was a Chinese invention. The Chinese first made paper in AD 105. The oldest-known printed book dates from 868 and was made using a single carved wood-block for each page. In 1041, the inventor Bi Sheng began printing books using movable type. Wooden blocks were carved with individual Chinese characters that could be moved and used again and again.

There were three stages to the Chinese printing process. First, ink was brushed onto the type. Then paper was placed over the type and rubbed with a pad. Finally, the printed paper was peeled away.

Science and invention

The T'ang and Song periods saw some great inventions. The clock escapement, or mechanism, was invented during the 8th century and provided the first reliable means of telling the time. The compass, used for navigation, was first mentioned in 1119.

This 30-ft (9-m) high clock tower was built in Kaifeng in 1090. It used an escapement of the type invented three centuries before and still used in all mechanical clocks and watches.

907–960 China splits into 10 states; 5 short dynasties rule.

960–979 Song Dynasty takes over China and reunites empire.

1040 Engineers describe military uses of gunpowder.

1211 Mongols, led by Chingis Khan, invade northern China.

1279 Mongol conquest of China completed by Kubilai Khan.

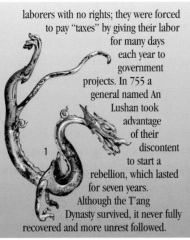

laborers with no rights; they were forced to pay "taxes" by giving their labor for many days each year to government projects. In 755 a general named An Lushan took advantage of their discontent to start a rebellion, which lasted for seven years. Although the T'ang Dynasty survived, it never fully recovered and more unrest followed.

The T'ang Dynasty ended in 907. It was replaced by ten regional kingdoms ruled by local warlords with their own armies. This period of disunity was ended by the first emperor of the Song Dynasty, Taizu, in 960. Unlike the T'ang, the Song Dynasty concentrated on affairs at home and made no attempt to rebuild the greater Chinese Empire. Agriculture and industry prospered as never before. Trade by

sea increased vastly, and the Song built a powerful navy to protect their merchant ships from foreign rivals and pirates.

This prosperity was jolted when, in 1126, rebels from northwestern China overran the north and declared a new dynasty, the Chin. From then on, the Song controlled only central and southern China, and they had to watch the north for fear of further invasions.

In fact, it was the northern kingdom that was invaded when, led by Chingis Khan (c.1167–1227), a huge force of Mongol troops entered northern China in 1211. By 1215 the north had become part of the Mongol Empire. Chingis Khan's grandson, Kubilai Khan (c.1216–94), completed the conquest of China and became emperor in 1279.

1. A T'ang period bronze and iron dragon.

2. An illustration showing the monk Xuanzang on his return from India in 645 with priceless Buddhist icons and manuscripts.

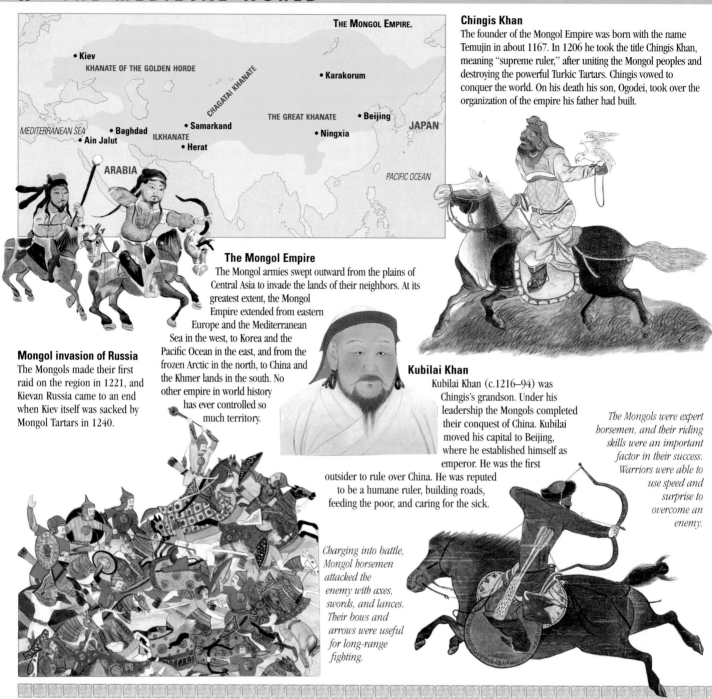

THE MONGOL EMPIRE.

KHANATE OF THE GOLDEN HORDE

• Kiev

• Karakorum

CHAGATAI KHANATE

THE GREAT KHANATE

• Beijing

JAPAN

MEDITERRANEAN SEA

• Baghdad

• Samarkand

• Ningxia

ILKHANATE

• Ain Jalut

• Herat

ARABIA

PACIFIC OCEAN

Chingis Khan
The founder of the Mongol Empire was born with the name Temujin in about 1167. In 1206 he took the title Chingis Khan, meaning "supreme ruler," after uniting the Mongol peoples and destroying the powerful Turkic Tartars. Chingis vowed to conquer the world. On his death his son, Ogodei, took over the organization of the empire his father had built.

The Mongol Empire
The Mongol armies swept outward from the plains of Central Asia to invade the lands of their neighbors. At its greatest extent, the Mongol Empire extended from eastern Europe and the Mediterranean Sea in the west, to Korea and the Pacific Ocean in the east, and from the frozen Arctic in the north, to China and the Khmer lands in the south. No other empire in world history has ever controlled so much territory.

Mongol invasion of Russia
The Mongols made their first raid on the region in 1221, and Kievan Russia came to an end when Kiev itself was sacked by Mongol Tartars in 1240.

Kubilai Khan
Kubilai Khan (c.1216–94) was Chingis's grandson. Under his leadership the Mongols completed their conquest of China. Kubilai moved his capital to Beijing, where he established himself as emperor. He was the first outsider to rule over China. He was reputed to be a humane ruler, building roads, feeding the poor, and caring for the sick.

The Mongols were expert horsemen, and their riding skills were an important factor in their success. Warriors were able to use speed and surprise to overcome an enemy.

Charging into battle, Mongol horsemen attacked the enemy with axes, swords, and lances. Their bows and arrows were useful for long-range fighting.

1206–27 Nomadic Mongol peoples unite under the rule of Chingis Khan. **1218** Chingis Khan defeats Kara-Khitai Empire. **1229–41** Rule of Ogodei Khan. **1238–41** Mongol armies invade Russia, Hungary, and Poland. **1246–48** Rule of Guyuk Khan. **1258** Mongols capture Baghdad.

The Mongol Empire

The Mongols lived in scattered groups across the wide, open grasslands of Central Asia, in the region of present-day Mongolia. They were nomadic peoples who traveled with their herds of sheep and goats in a constant search for new pastures. At the beginning of the 13th century the Mongols were united under a single, powerful leader: Chingis Khan. He set about conquering lands to the east and west, using his fierce army of horsemen to build a vast empire. The empire lasted for 200 years under his successors, but it eventually broke up because the Mongols found such huge territories difficult to control.

In 1206 Temujin (c.1167–1227), the son of a Mongol chieftain, was proclaimed Chingis Khan ("supreme ruler") of all the nomadic groups of the Central Asian steppes. He at once set out on a series of conquests with his fierce army of skilled horsemen. In 1209 he attacked Xixia, on the northwestern border of China, and two years later made the first attacks on the Jin Empire of China. In 1218 Chingis moved west, overcoming the Turkish Kara-Khitai Empire. In the same year, Mongol envoys and merchants were executed on the borders of Khwarizm. The Mongol army took revenge by destroying cities such as Samarkand, Herat, and Merv, and slaughtering entire populations.

With western Asia under their control, the Mongols returned to Xixia in 1226 and destroyed its capital, Ningxia. The following year, as his army pushed into China, Chingis Khan died. He was succeeded by his son, Ogodei, who completed the conquest of Jin China in 1229. Ogodei then declared war on the southern Song Empire and started a new campaign of terror across western Asia. In 1235 he expanded his father's camp at Karakorum into a great walled city that formed the Mongol capital. After defeating Russia in 1238, an army of about 150,000 horsemen swept into

Mongol saddles were highly prized pieces of equipment. They were made of wood and often elaborately decorated.

Born to ride

Mongol nomads grew up with horses, and youngsters learned to ride as soon as they could walk. Scouts at the head of a Mongol army were able to travel up to 100 mi. (160 km) a day, which allowed the army to take unsuspecting neighbors by surprise. The army took with it huge numbers of horses; each warrior had up to five horses, so he could have a fresh mount whenever needed.

Mongol horses were well groomed. In this illustration a warrior braids his mount's tail.

Mongol envoys traveling on official business carried a bronze disk that acted as a passport. Even those who could not read its message knew what it was just by looking at it.

Portable homes

The Mongols lived in portable tents, called yurts (below). A yurt was made by rolling a thick layer of felt made from sheep's wool over a wicker frame. Canvas sheets were then tied over the felt. Each time they moved camp, the Mongols took down their tents and transported them to the next site. The khan's more lavish yurt, however, and those of his wives and generals, were often left fully assembled and hauled on wagons.

In 1269 Kubilai Khan introduced a new script in an attempt to make everyone understand each other throughout the empire. The script was called Phags-pa, after its Tibetan inventor.

Ruling an empire

The Mongols were superb fighters, but they were not experienced administrators. They found it easier to conquer lands than to rule them. In many parts of the empire they relied on others to act as administrators. In China, they brought in foreigners so that they did not have to rely totally on the Chinese. Poor government led to revolts in different parts of the empire. Even when he was at the peak of his power, Kubilai Khan – an enlightened ruler – found it impossible to extend his authority to distant parts of the empire.

In cold weather Mongols lit a brazier in the middle of the yurt, underneath a smokehole. The door faced south, away from the prevailing winds. Some people in Mongolia still live in traditional yurts.

The best-quality Mongol clothes, such as this tunic c.1300, were made of silk, which had been woven in China for centuries.

> **SEE ALSO**
> p. 86 CHINESE CIVILIZATION
> p. 100 RUSSIA AND EASTERN EUROPE

1260–94 Rule of Kubilai Khan, grandson of Chingis.

1275 Venetian merchant Marco Polo arrives in northern China, ruled by Kubilai Khan.

1279–1368 Mongol Yuan Dynasty rules China.

1361–1405 Rule of Timur, or Tamerlane, a descendant of Chingis, from Samarkand.

large parts of Hungary and Poland in 1241. On Ogodei's death the invaders retreated to their homeland.

During five years of rivalry over the Mongol leadership, Ogodei's widow, Toregene, ruled as regent. Her son, Guyuk, was elected great khan in 1246, followed by another grandson of Chingis, Mongke, in 1251. In 1258 Baghdad fell to the Mongols and the last Abbasid caliph was executed. Two years later the Mongols suffered their first major defeat, by the Mamelukes, at Ain Jalut. In 1260 Mongke's brother, Kubilai (c.1216–94), was elected leader.

In 1266 Beijing became the capital of the Great Khanate. Kubilai Khan made unsuccessful attempts to conquer Japan, but in 1279 his forces conquered the Song Empire, and he created the Yuan Dynasty, which ruled China until 1368. When Kubilai died in 1294, the Mongol Empire had already split up into separate khanates. Timur (or Tamerlane, c.1336–1405), another descendant of Chingis, succeeded in uniting some of the empire from his capital, Samarkand. Timur was the last Mongol conqueror.

1. These stirrups were made specially for Chingis Khan.

Games of polo, which involved hitting a moving target while on horseback, often at high speed, provided entertainment and excellent training in horsemanship.

c.500 Invasion of northwest India by White Huns from Central Asia. **606–647** Reign of Harsha in northern India. **711** Muslim invaders conquer kingdom of Sind. **985** Chola Empire expands northward across the Deccan. **1000** Muslim invaders begin conquest of India.

India from 500 to 1526

The decline of the Gupta Dynasty at the end of the 5th century heralded a thousand-year period of India's history that was dominated by wars between rival kingdoms and eventual conquest from outside. The power struggles were generally between the various kingdoms of the north and south. The kingdoms were divided by the Deccan, the plateau of central India, over which they sometimes expanded. But despite the long series of wars, conquests, and reconquests, this was also a period of development for Indian culture, with great achievements in art, crafts, and architecture. Increasing overseas trade brought India into closer contact with other countries. But the greatest outside influence on Indian life came when Turkic and Afghan Muslim invaders arrived in force in the year 1000.

The period of relative peace in northern India under the Gupta Dynasty was shattered about 500 by the invasion of the White Huns from Central Asia. The White Huns, a nomadic people attracted by the great wealth of the northern kingdoms, never gained control, and after about 100 years they had either withdrawn or been absorbed into Indian society. Unity and peace were briefly restored by Emperor Harsha (reigned 606–647) who tried to expand his Kanauj Empire south across the Deccan. His death was followed by another period of internal wars as the small kingdoms fought each other.

Meanwhile, in the south, the dominant power for most of the period was the immensely rich Chola Empire, based in the valley of the Kaveri River near India's southern tip. The Cholas' main rivals were the Chalukyas, who occupied territory to the northwest. The Cholas invaded Ceylon (present-day Sri Lanka) and sent raiding parties by sea to Sumatra in Indonesia, 1,200 mi. (1,900 km) away.

The next milestone in Indian history was the year 1000, when the Muslims attempted to conquer India. Three

INDIA c.750–1081.

KINGDOM OF SIND

GURJARA-PRATIHARAS

PALA KINGDOM

RASHTRAKUTA EMPIRE Deccan plateau

• Kalyani

CHALUKYA EMPIRE

CHOLA EMPIRE

CEYLON

Indus River *Ganges River* *Himalayas*

India: land of rich resources

Throughout its history, India has been the target of invaders attracted by its rich resources. The artifacts that have survived are evidence of great skill and sensitivity over a wide range of arts and technologies. Unlike the nomadic people of Central Asia, Indians chose to settle in cities, towns, and villages, and develop their skills to a high level, from farming to jewelry-making. The Muslim invaders adapted to this way of life.

This 10th-century mosaic from an Indian palace shows the delicacy of Indian art.

Fractured states

With only brief periods of unity and calm, India's history between the decline of the Gupta Dynasty and the arrival of the Mongols was one of small warring regional kingdoms. Rulers exercised enormous power, which they wielded by granting favors in return for homage and tribute, and keeping each layer of society firmly in its place.

Clash of northern empires

After the Kanauji emperor Harsha was murdered in 647 his empire declined and northern India again became a battleground. The three rival powers were the Pala Kingdom along the eastern stretch of the Ganges River; the Pratihara Kingdom of northern India; and the Rashtrakutas to the south. Four centuries of struggles weakened these powers, but no victor emerged. From about 1000, the Muslim invaders took advantage of this.

Struggles in southern India

As in the north, southern India was the scene of fierce struggles between rival powers. Chief of these were the Cholas, established in the south, and the Chalukyas in the west. From 985 the Cholas spread their power into Ceylon (present-day Sri Lanka) and northward across the Deccan plateau. Early in the 11th century they seized the Chalukya capital, Kalyani.

A 13th-century bronze figure of a Chola king. Indian rulers were given a godlike status.

Chess was first played in India sometime before the 7th century. This chesspiece is from the 9th century.

Trade with Arabia and Southeast Asia

Despite internal warfare, the 9th century saw an increase in trading by sea, which exported Indian religions and culture abroad as well as cargoes. The Cholas of southeastern India traded extensively with Arabia to the west, and they also reached Indonesia to the east.

The Cholas used fleets of teak-hulled boats with bamboo sails for trading, which brought them great wealth.

Indian religions

Three religions dominate India's early history. Hinduism mixes Aryan religion with the beliefs of the earlier indigenous population. Buddhism, founded about 527 BC, quickly spread through India. The third religion, Jainism, an offshoot of Hinduism, began in the 6th century BC in the northeast, in protest against some Hindu beliefs.

Shiva, Hindu god of life and "Lord of the Dance."

The beginning of Muslim India

The first Muslim invaders conquered the kingdom of Sind at the mouth of the Indus River in 711. About 1000 there were further Muslim raids, led by the Turkish ruler Mahmud of Ghazna (971–1030), shown here listening to poetry in his court (right). These attacks were aimed at plunder rather than occupation. Then in 1192 Muhammad of Ghur (reigned 1173–1206) and his viceroy, Qutb-ud-din Aibak, conquered northwestern India.

1192 Turk and Afghan Muslims create Sultanate of Delhi.

1321–1412 Tughluq Dynasty rules from Delhi.

1336 Foundation of Vijayanagar Empire in southern India.

1398 Tamerlane raids Delhi.
1526 Moghul invasion of India

led by Babur, a descendant of Tamerlane.

centuries before, Muslims – probably Arabs – had conquered the northwestern kingdom of Sind, but apart from occasional raids on neighboring states for plunder they had not ventured any farther east. The new Muslim invaders were Mongol Turks and Afghans, and they were intent on adding India to their empire. By 1200, Muslim control was established across the Indus and Ganges plains, and the Mongols had created the Sultanate of Delhi to rule over this vast territory. This proved to be difficult because of rivalry among sultans and governors, and from the middle of the 14th century parts of the Sultanate began to break away.

South of the Tungabhadra River in southern India, the powerful new Hindu Vijayanagar Empire was established.

The great Tartar general, Timur, or Tamerlane (c.1336–1405) marched into India in 1398 and reached Delhi, but after a swift and fearsome campaign he returned home. It was not until 1526 that another Muslim general, Babur, began the next invasion. One notable feature of the years following the Muslim invasions is that people of two such different religions, Islam and Hinduism, worked out a reasonable way of living alongside each other. This even extended to the buildings of the time; Hindu temples and Muslim mosques, as well as palaces and

monuments, often combined Muslim and Hindu themes and styles in their ornamentation.

Despite civil wars and invasions, the arts flourished in the period from 500 on. Great works of Sanskrit literature were written, poets were welcomed at the courts of the various kingdoms, and temples and palaces employed thousands of musicians. From about 1000 on, the ideas introduced by the Muslim invaders strengthened Indian culture and led it in many new directions.

1. This sheaf of engraved copper plates holds Chola records and dates to the 11th century.

An 11th-century Hindu temple sculpture celebrating mother love.

Celebrating women
Unlike many other cultures of the period, including Islam, both Hinduism and Buddhism appreciated women's sensuality and displayed it freely in paintings and sculpture. Make-up and hairdressing were highly developed skills among upper-class Indian women.

The Rhajastan leader Prithvaraja Chanana III was defeated by the Muslim army of Muhammad Ghuri at the Battle of Tarain in 1192. This victory opened up Delhi to the Muslims.

Delhi, center of politics
When in 1206 the Muslim general Qutb-ud-din Aibak declared himself "Sultan of Delhi," the city became the center of Indian politics for the next 700 years. He and his successors made it a center of Muslim culture, building richly ornamented mosques and palaces. At its largest, the powerful Sultanate of Delhi extended across northern India from Sind to Bengal. But soon after Aibak's death it began to split up, and in 1290 Delhi faced another army of invaders from the northwest.

The magnificent fort in the city of Jodphur, Rhajastan, founded in 1459 by Maharajah Rao Jodha.

Sultan Qutb-ud-din Aibak (reigned 1206–11) had the Qutb Minar built in Delhi as a symbol of Muslim domination of India.

The accession of the Tughluq
The Tughluq Dynasty ruled the Sultanate of Delhi from 1321 to 1412. The most powerful Tughluq sultan was Muhammad ibn Tughluq (ruled 1324–1351). During his reign the Sultanate expanded to include almost all of India, including the southern kingdoms. It established Muslim settlements in all the territories it controlled. Muhammad's attempt to move the entire population of Delhi to a new capital farther south failed.

Tamerlane in Delhi
In 1398, at the age of 60, the great Central Asian Tartar general, Timur, or Tamerlane, led an attack on India after a lifetime of warfare. He marched on Delhi and won an easy victory over the Tughluq. His army slaughtered the city's population and carried off as much booty as it could take. Soon after this fierce raid, Tamerlane left Delhi and returned home.

An example of art from Vijayanagar in a strongly Hindu style.

Rhajastan
Rhajastan, in northwestern India, was the northern kingdom that held out longest against the Muslims, despite having to give up its claim on Delhi to the Muslims in 1192. It had been controlled by powerful dynasties since the 7th century. Even after the defeat of 1192, Rhajastan continued to resist the invaders. After many years of struggle, some areas of the kingdom were occupied by the Muslims and others reached agreement with them to avoid further bloodshed.

The Vijayanagar Empire
Vijayanagar was a powerful breakaway empire founded in 1336 south of the Tungabhadra River in southern India. Its rulers restored Hindu values and practices, and encouraged Sanskrit literature. The empire became the greatest in southern India and, under three successive dynasties, lasted until about 1616.

Muslims and Hindus
Although Hindus and Muslims fought over territory, their cultures

intermingled and developed a style drawn from the traditions of both religions. The subject of this illustration from a 14th-century manuscript (above) is a traditional Muslim story, but it is illustrated in the style of Hindu art. Later, preachers such as Nanak, the founder of the Sikh religion, declared that Hindu and Muslim ideas of God were similar.

SEE ALSO
p. 48 ANCIENT INDIA
p. 50 FIRST EMPIRES IN INDIA
p. 66 MYTH AND RELIGION
p. 88 THE MONGOL EMPIRE
p. 92 THE ISLAMIC WORLD

INDIA BEFORE BABUR'S INVASION IN 1526.

MULTAN
SULTANATE OF DELHI
Himalayas
Indus River
RAJPUT CONFEDERACY
KINGDOM OF SIND
Ganges River
GUJERAT
MALWA
BENGAL
KHANDESH
GONDWANA
AHMADHAGAR
BERAR
ORISSA
BIDAR
BIJAPUR
GOLCONDA
VIJAYANAGAR
CEYLON

After the death of Muhammad ibn Tughluq in the 14th century, the Sultanate of Delhi shrunk considerably.

750–1258 Abbasid Dynasty rules from Baghdad.

909 Fatimid Dynasty founded in Tunisia, North Africa.

973 Cairo becomes capital of the Fatimid caliphs.

1055 Seljuk Turks from Central Asia capture Baghdad.

1096–99 The First Crusade.
1237 Chingis Khan's Mongol

The Islamic World

The Islamic world – which by 800 extended from Spain in the west across North Africa to Asia Minor in the east – was ruled by the Umayyad and Abbasid dynasties from 661 to 1258. For much of this time, however, rival dynasties fought for power in different areas, and some were more tolerant than others. In the 11th century, Muslim toleration of Jews and Christians ceased. They were persecuted under the Fatimid caliph al-Hakim (ruled 996–1021), and by the Seljuk Turks, who seized Jerusalem in 1071. Christian rulers in Europe responded by sending armies of "crusaders" to the Holy Land to reconquer Jerusalem from the Muslims. In 1250 the Mamelukes came to power in Egypt. A short time later, Osman I founded the small state that eventually developed into the powerful Ottoman Empire. By 1275 most of Spain had been reconquered by Christian armies, and by 1492 Muslim rule there was over.

This vase dates from the last Muslim dynasty in Spain (1238–1492).

The Abbasid Dynasty, which ruled the Islamic world from 750 on, was challenged by a number of rival Muslim dynasties. From 909 on, the Fatimids ruled in North Africa. They were a subsect of the Shi'ite Muslims, who claimed descent from Fatimah, the daughter of Muhammad. The Fatimid Empire was centered on Tunisia, but in 969 the Fatimids conquered Egypt and a few years later made Cairo their capital. They reached their height during the reign of al-Mustansim (1036–94). The Fatimids had a generally peaceful relationship with

Below: This relief of a double-headed eagle comes from the Seljuk capital of Konya, in present-day Turkey.

Greek influence

This Muslim manuscript (left) shows the ancient Greek philosophers Aristotle and Plato. Their works, which had been translated into Arabic by AD 800, greatly influenced Islamic thought. The Muslim philosopher Ibn Rushd (1126–98), who spent most of his life in Cordoba in Spain, wrote books about the Greek philosophers. He believed that religious faith and reason did not conflict with each other, though other Muslims did not agree.

Sunni Seljuks

The Seljuks were the ruling family of the Turkic-speaking Orghuz people, who originated in Turkestan, an area of Central Asia. They were named after their first leader, Seljuk, who converted to Sunni Islam in the late 10th century. Unlike Shi'ites (the other main Muslim sect), the Sunnis accept the first three caliphs as Muhammad's true successors.

Exploration

The Arab geographer al-Idrisi was born in present-day Morocco in North Africa about 1100. He traveled throughout Europe and Asia Minor before taking up a position at the court of King Roger II of Sicily, who asked him to produce a map of the world. Travelers were sent off on journeys of exploration, and al-Idrisi noted down everything they reported having seen. In 1154 he produced this map (above); it shows North Africa, Mediterranean Europe, Arabia, and Central Asia.

Arab ships were called dhows. They had hinged rudders, and sails that ran front to rear rather than side to side. These developments meant the ships could sail fast even in poor winds.

Medicine

Medicine in the Arab world was very advanced. As early as the 11th century, the Persian physician Avicenna (980–1037) wrote a medical encyclopedia. In this miniature (above), a Muslim pharmacist is preparing medicines over a fire. The anatomical plate (left) comes from a Persian medical book.

The dervishes were members of one of the mystical religious orders of Islam in the 12th century. They were later known as the "whirling dervishes," because they danced as part of their worship.

Right: A bazaar is a covered market where all kinds of goods are sold. This early 13th-century illustration shows a jeweler, a pharmacist, a butcher, and a baker.

armies enter Europe.
1250 Mamelukes come to

power in Egypt.
c.1258–1326 Life of Osman, who

founds Osmanli, a small Turkish
state in Asia Minor.

1453 Constantinople conquered
by Seljuk Turks.

1492 End of Muslim rule in
Spain; Christians take Granada.

the Byzantine Empire, ruled from Constantinople, and cooperated with the Turkish rulers of Syria in fighting the crusaders. Saladin (c.1137–93), who led the Muslims against the crusaders in Syria, ended Fatimid rule in 1171.

Another rival to the Abbasids was the Almoravid Dynasty. The Almoravids were Berbers from the western Sahara. In 1056 they conquered North Africa as far as Algiers, founding Marrakesh as their capital about 1070. In 1086 they crossed into Spain, defeating the Christian

army of reconquest. The Almoravids were conquered in turn by the Almohads, another Berber Dynasty, who killed the last Almoravid ruler in 1147.

The Seljuks were a group of nomadic Turkish warriors from Central Asia. They quickly expanded their powerbase, and about 1055 founded their own empire, centered on Baghdad. In 1071 they defeated the Byzantines at the Battle of Manzikert. This victory led to the Seljuk conquest of most of Anatolia, and a weakening of Byzantine power. Seljuk power was at its height during the reigns of Sultans Alp-Arslan (1063–72) and Malik Shah (1072–92). They set up

universities to train bureaucrats and religious officials. A branch of the dynasty established its own state in Anatolia, called the sultanate of Rum. This was conquered by the Mongols in 1243.

Various newly converted Turkish peoples served with the Seljuks. One group, the Ottoman Turks, took their name from their leader, Osman (c.1258–1326). In 1326 his son, Orkhan (c.1274–1362), captured the Byzantine city of Bursa. In 1453 the Ottoman Turks finally put an end

to the Byzantine Empire when they seized Constantinople. In Spain, the Moorish Muslims split into factions as the Christian armies won more victories; Granada finally fell to the Christians in 1492.

1. Arabic was an international language of science, literature, and commerce.

2. A 12th-century candle clock with figures that popped out to mark the hour.

3. This Muslim manuscript from Cordoba shows surgical instruments.

Architecture flowered during this period, and different styles characterize different areas. The mosque of al-Azhar was built in the 10th century in Cairo, Egypt. The dome covers an aisle leading to a prayer niche, which shows the direction of Mecca. From the minarets, or towers, a muezzin calls the faithful to prayer five times a day.

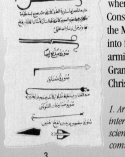

Jerusalem
Jerusalem was always a holy city to Muslims. Early in his mission, Muhammad told his followers to face Jerusalem when they prayed, but after difficulties with the Jews of Medina he changed the direction to Mecca. During the 10th and 11th centuries, several Muslim groups fought for control of Jerusalem. In 1099 it was captured by the Christian crusaders. The Muslims retook the city in 1187. This miniature (above) shows Christian pilgrims paying Muslims for permission to enter a Christian church.

Osman I (c.1258–1326) founded a small Turkish state in Asia Minor called Osmanli. His state expanded at the expense of the Byzantines, and gradually developed into the Ottoman Empire.

Entertainment
Chess (above) was a popular game. It probably originated in India and was taken to Persia. When the Arabs conquered Persia in the 7th century, it quickly spread much more widely. The Moors introduced the game to Europe a century later. The lute (right) was of Moorish origin; "lute" comes from the Arabic *al'ud*. It was also taken to Europe, where it was played by medieval minstrels.

The sacred law of Islam, called sharia, *comes from the Qu'ran. It governs every aspect of a Muslim's life. In the Islamic world it was much more important than the decisions reached by powerful people, such as this governor of a city.*

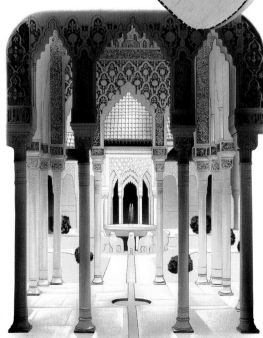

The Alhambra
The Court of the Lions (left) is one of many courtyards and gardens within the citadel of Alhambra, which stands above the city of Granada in Spain. The citadel had the Arabic name Al-Qal'a al-Hambra, meaning "Red Fort," from the color of the sun-dried bricks from which its outer walls were made. Though originally built as a military fortress, the Alhambra became a beautiful Moorish palace.

SEE ALSO
p. 78 THE RISE OF ISLAM

Urban II (c.1042–99) became pope in 1088. His call for a Crusade was made from a desire not only to recover the Holy Land from the Muslims, but also to gain power and prestige for the papacy. He thought that a military expedition would unite Christian knights and nobles, who were constantly fighting each other.

Dates of the Crusades

First Crusade 1096–99
Second Crusade 1147–49
Third Crusade 1189–92
Fourth Crusade 1202–04
Fifth Crusade 1217–21
Sixth Crusade 1228–29
Seventh Crusade 1248–54
Eighth Crusade 1270–72

THE ROUTES OF THE EIGHT CRUSADES.

In 1098, crusaders besieged the Christian principality of Antioch (then in northern Syria; now in Turkey) for seven months before retaking it. It had been occupied by the Turks three years earlier. Many crusaders died, but the survivors were inspired by the discovery of a lance, said to be the one that wounded Jesus on the cross.

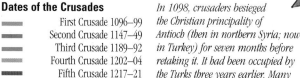

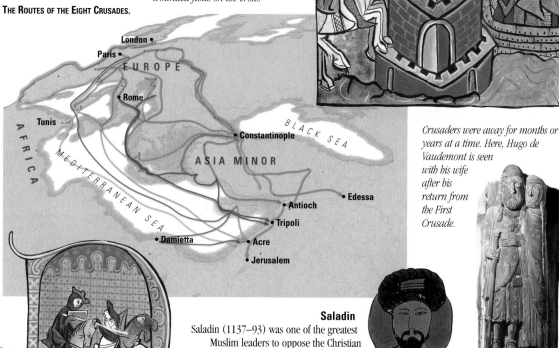

London •
Paris •
EUROPE
• Rome
Tunis
AFRICA
MEDITERRANEAN SEA
• Constantinople
BLACK SEA
ASIA MINOR
• Edessa
• Antioch
• Tripoli
• Damietta
• Acre
• Jerusalem

Crusaders were away for months or years at a time. Here, Hugo de Vaudemont is seen with his wife after his return from the First Crusade.

Jerusalem

Recapturing the holy city of Jerusalem (right) was one of the main aims of the early Crusades. Jerusalem was seen as the center of the Christian world, but it had also been the third holiest city for Muslims – after Mecca and Medina – since the Arabs conquered it in 638. At the end of the 7th century the Muslims built the Dome of the Rock over the place from where they believed Muhammad ascended to heaven. Most Arab rulers allowed Christians to visit their holy shrines in Jerusalem and elsewhere, but in the 11th century the Seljuk Turks changed this policy.

Saladin

Saladin (1137–93) was one of the greatest Muslim leaders to oppose the Christian knights. He was a hero to the Muslims and was respected by the crusaders. Born in Mesopotamia of Kurdish descent, Saladin became sultan of Egypt in 1175. He also ruled Muslim lands in Syria. Most famously, he led the force that recaptured Jerusalem from the crusaders in 1187.

Below: This miniature shows a group of "people's crusaders," led by the French preacher Peter the Hermit (c.1050–1115). With a force of 20,000 peasants, Peter set out for Jerusalem in 1096, but his men were poorly equipped and were massacred by the Turks at Nicaea.

1095 Council of Clermont calls for Crusade to recapture Holy Land.

1096–99 First Crusade led by Godfrey of Bouillon and others.

1147–49 Second Crusade led by Louis VII and Conrad III.

1187 Saladin defeats the Christian army at Battle of Hittin.

The Crusades

Throughout the 12th and 13th centuries the Christian popes, kings, and knights of Europe mounted ferocious military attacks against the Muslim rulers who controlled the holy city of Jerusalem and other important places in the Holy Land. These expeditions were known as the Crusades. There were eight major Crusades, the first five of which were ordered by the pope, who was head of the Christian Church in Rome. The last three Crusades were organized by European kings. Many of the crusaders wished to rid the Holy Land of the Muslims, whom they called "infidels," while others were simply adventurers who wanted to gain riches and land that they could not have at home. The last crusaders were driven out of the Holy Land by the powerful Mameluke rulers in 1291.

During the 11th century, Muslim Seljuk Turks from the Anatolian plateau made it difficult for Christian pilgrims to reach places in the Holy Land. In 1095 the Byzantine emperor, Alexius I Comnenus (1048–1118), asked Pope Urban II for help in fighting the Seljuk Turks. Pope Urban, with the agreement of Church leaders, sent an army of French and Norman crusader knights to his aid, but their main mission was to recover Jerusalem from the "infidel." The Christian armies on this First Crusade (1096–99) defeated the Muslims near

SEE ALSO
p. 74 THE SPREAD OF
CHRISTIANITY
p. 76 THE BYZANTINE EMPIRE
p. 78 THE RISE OF ISLAM

THE CRUSADER STATES

The Crusader states

After the success of the First Crusade and the capture of Jerusalem in 1099, the crusaders gained control of a narrow coastal strip of Palestine. They set up the so-called "crusader states," under the control of European leaders.

Below: In 1142 crusaders captured a Muslim stronghold at Qal'at al-Hosen, in Syria, and began building a large fortress there. It was later called Krak des Chevaliers (French-Arabic for "castle of the knights"). It could hold a garrison of 2,000 soldiers and horses, and enough food for five years.

MEDITERRANEAN SEA

Krak des Chevaliers

☐ Kingdom of Jerusalem
☐ County of Tripoli
☐ Principality of Antioch
☐ County of Edessa
• Jerusalem ☐ Kingdom of Armenia

Below: The crusaders brought back goods from the Holy Land, including sugar and candied fruits, such as apricots and figs.

Byzantine wealth

This 12th-century enameled gold icon of the Archangel Michael (left) was taken to Venice as loot after the Fourth Crusade. The wealth of the Byzantines came as a shock to the Western Christian knights, who captured Constantinople in 1204. The crusaders sacked the city and stole as much of its riches as they could. The episode highlighted the rift between the Western and Eastern Christians.

Warrior monks

The kings of Jerusalem and the rulers of the other crusader states needed a reliable military force for protection. They turned to religious orders of knights, The Hospitalers (above) and the Templars, who had formed communities to protect Christian pilgrims in the Holy Land. The monks took up arms during the 12th century. After the fall of Acre in 1291 the Hospitalers settled first on Rhodes, which they defended from the Turks, then on Cyprus, and finally on Malta.

Crusades against heretics

There were several Crusades against Christian heretic movements. In 1209–29 in southern France, a heretical Christian sect was violently attacked by nobles from the north in the Albigensian Crusade. From 1420–32, a Bohemian "Hussite" leader, Jan Ziska (c.1370–1424, right), and a priest called Procop, were victorious against forces crusading on behalf of Holy Roman Emperor Sigismund (1368–1437).

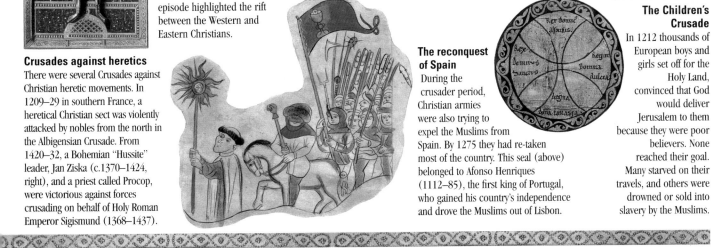

The reconquest of Spain

During the crusader period, Christian armies were also trying to expel the Muslims from Spain. By 1275 they had re-taken most of the country. This seal (above) belonged to Afonso Henriques (1112–85), the first king of Portugal, who gained his country's independence and drove the Muslims out of Lisbon.

The Children's Crusade

In 1212 thousands of European boys and girls set off for the Holy Land, convinced that God would deliver Jerusalem to them because they were poor believers. None reached their goal. Many starved on their travels, and others were drowned or sold into slavery by the Muslims.

1189–92 Third Crusade led by Barbarossa, Richard the | Lionheart, and Philip II. **1202–04** Fourth Crusade | proclaimed by Pope Innocent III. **1217–72** Fifth to Eighth Crusades. | **1229–44** Jerusalem again held by the Christians. | **1291** Muslims finally drive crusaders from the Holy Land.

Nicaea and captured Jerusalem in 1099, after six weeks of fighting.

In 1144, the Turks conquered Edessa, a center of Christianity in southeastern Anatolia. This, and the threat to other Christian kingdoms, brought about the Second Crusade (1147–49). Led by French and German kings, the crusaders reached Asia Minor, but were defeated by Muslim forces before they reached Edessa. In 1187 the great Muslim hero, Saladin, defeated the Christian army and entered Jerusalem, ending an 88-year occupation by the Christians. This led to the Third Crusade (1189–92), led by the

German emperor Frederick I "Barbarossa" (c.1123–90), Richard I "the Lionheart" of England (1157–99), and Philip II Augustus of France (1165–1223). The crusaders failed to capture Jerusalem, but regained control of the coast between Tyre and Jaffa, and Christian pilgrims were allowed to enter Jerusalem.

Pope Innocent III persuaded many French nobles to take part in the Fourth Crusade (1202–04). The plan was to attack Egypt, but,

diverted by the Venetians, the crusaders reached Constantinople in 1204 and sacked the city.

In the Fifth Crusade (1217–21), the Christians briefly captured the town of Damietta in Egypt. Holy Roman Emperor Frederick II (1194–1250) led the Sixth Crusade (1228–29) and negotiated a peace treaty with the Muslim sultan, who gave Jerusalem to the Christians. Jerusalem remained Christian until the Muslims seized it again in 1244, which caused Louis IX of France (1214–70) to lead the Seventh Crusade (1248–54). Louis

attacked cities in Egypt, but the Muslims captured him and his army. He was freed in exchange for a huge ransom. In 1270 Louis led the Eighth Crusade (1270–72), landing at Tunis, where he died. In 1291, the Muslims seized Acre, the last Christian center in Palestine. Further attempts to organize Crusades failed.

1. Crusader crosses on the walls of the Church of the Holy Sepulcher in Jerusalem.

2. Flag of the Almohads, a Muslim dynasty from North Africa.

3. Massacre of the Jews by crusaders.

4. Crusaders learned from the Muslims how to use carrier pigeons as messengers.

Across Africa civilizations developed and thrived through trade. North Africa, once part of the Christian world, was firmly under Muslim power by the 11th century. Traders from the Maghreb (northwest Africa) traveled south and east, where they spread Islam and influenced the development of the local states. West Africa was dominated by three great empires during the Middle Ages. The first, the kingdom of Ghana, flourished from the 8th to the 11th centuries. It was replaced in the mid-13th century by the larger and more powerful Mali Empire. The third empire to control the area, the Songhai, ruled from the 15th century until 1591 when it fell to Moroccan invaders. Other smaller empires also emerged and grew powerful.

In east Africa, the oldest states were the Christian kingdoms of Axum, Alwa, and Makkura in Nubia and Ethiopia. From the 9th to the 14th centuries Swahili-speaking Islamic settlements developed along the coast. Other powerful states arose in the interior, wealthy through cattle and precious metals.

To the south, the Zimbabwe Plateau was rich in grazing areas and gold, iron, copper, and tin. Its capital, Great Zimbabwe, thrived until the 17th century.

The Yoruba in west Africa were among the most skilled craftspeople, and in the 13th and 14th centuries they were famous for their special method of bronze casting. This sculpture is from 12th century Ife.

African States

The first states began to emerge in sub-Saharan Africa during the 7th century. Taking advantage of a vast area rich in natural resources, especially precious metals such as gold, these kingdoms grew wealthy through trade, first with their African neighbors and eventually with merchants from Muslim North Africa, Arabia, and Europe. The kings lived in great splendor and luxury, and gradually developed strong governments and armies. During this time different groups of peoples built cities across Africa, many of which had splendid courts centered around the ruling families. The first states in southern Africa, such as Great Zimbabwe, appeared from the 13th century onward. They were sustained by trade along the east coast. In the northeast, the Christian states of Alwa and Makkura continued until they were overrun by Muslim Arabs.

Ghana sent gold, ivory, and slaves north in exchange for salt (above) – a vital element in tropical societies – and other northern luxuries.

Ghana
Ghana was the first state in west Africa. It was established by the Soninke group of the Mande people north of the Senegal and Niger rivers. Ghana grew rich by trading in gold and, later, by taxing merchants who passed through the kingdom.

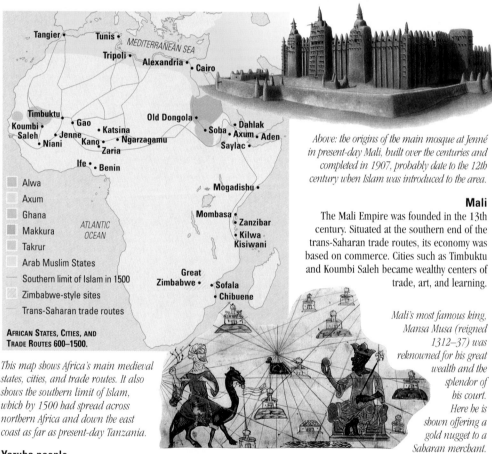

The map

AFRICAN STATES, CITIES, AND TRADE ROUTES 600–1500.

- Alwa
- Axum
- Ghana
- Makkura
- Takrur
- Arab Muslim States
- Southern limit of Islam in 1500
- Zimbabwe-style sites
- Trans-Saharan trade routes

This map shows Africa's main medieval states, cities, and trade routes. It also shows the southern limit of Islam, which by 1500 had spread across northern Africa and down the east coast as far as present-day Tanzania.

Above: the origins of the main mosque at Jenné in present-day Mali, built over the centuries and completed in 1907, probably date to the 12th century when Islam was introduced to the area.

Mali
The Mali Empire was founded in the 13th century. Situated at the southern end of the trans-Saharan trade routes, its economy was based on commerce. Cities such as Timbuktu and Koumbi Saleh became wealthy centers of trade, art, and learning.

Mali's most famous king, Mansa Musa (reigned 1312–37) was reknowned for his great wealth and the splendor of his court. Here he is shown offering a gold nugget to a Saharan merchant.

Yoruba people
The Yoruba people moved to the area west of the lower Niger River sometime before 1000. They formed some of the smaller states in west Africa, such as the Oyo and Ife. Some of these, such as Oyo and Ife-Iodun, still exist. The Yoruba now form one of the largest ethnic groups in Nigeria.

Trans-Saharan trade
Increasingly from about 650, Muslim traders traveled across the Sahara to trade with the peoples to the south. They made the hazardous journey with caravans of camels, and traded salt and luxury goods such as pottery, glass beads, brass, and cloth, for leather products, ivory, slaves, and gold. The export of gold became the mainstay of the major African empires.

11th century gold coins from Pemba, off the coast of Kenya. These coins were traded for goods from the Middle East.

SEE ALSO
p. 64 ANCIENT AFRICA • p. 122 AFRICAN EMPIRES
p. 202 THE SCRAMBLE FOR AFRICA

c. 1076 Ghana invaded by Berber Muslim Almoravids.

c. 1200 Great Enclosure built at Zimbabwe in southern Africa.

c.1250 Mali becomes most powerful state in west Africa.

c.1317 Muslim Arabs destroy Makkura.

c.1464 Songhai Kingdom replaces Mali in west Africa.

Benin

As trade increased, smaller kingdoms began to develop in west Africa. The kingdom of Benin was founded in the 12th century, and at its most powerful probably controlled most of southern Nigeria. The empire was ruled by a series of kings called "obas." During the reign of Ozulua in the 15th century, Benin established a commercial relationship with Portugal, and the empire flourished from European trade from the 15th to 17th centuries.

This brass leopard, a symbol of the king's power served as a royal water vessel. It was filled through an opening in the head and poured out through the nostrils.

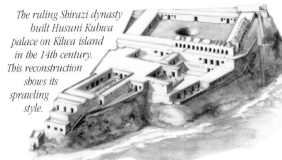

The ruling Shirazi dynasty built Husuni Kubwa palace on Kilwa island in the 14th century. This reconstruction shows its sprawling style.

Below: This gold plated rhinoceros, found at Mapungubwe, South Africa, probably dates from the 12th century. Mapungubwe was the capital of a strong southern African kingdom. It thrived from a trade network along the Limpopo River to the Indian Ocean. This rhinoceros may have been imported from India because unlike African rhinos, which have two horns, it only has one.

Trade on the east African coast

East African peoples began to form trading communities before the arrival of the Muslims from the north and west. By the 8th century Bantu-speaking people began to settle and by the 9th century they became part of the trade network across the Sahara. The Christian Axumite Empire in Ethiopia was destroyed in the 10th century, but Christianity remained strong in the region. Kilwa, which was prominent after 1050, exported gold, ivory, skins, and horns to Arabia and India.

Masks played an important role in many African cultures. Many people believed that masks had their own identities which could be transferred to the wearer. This mask, made of local tin, is from the Ivory Coast and could date from the 12th or 13th century.

African cultures maintained a rich artistic tradition, and the wide availability of precious metals developed the areas of metalwork and sculpture during the Middle Ages. West African sculptures became internationally famous for their technical excellence and naturalistic qualities. In the 20th century archeologists found a treasure trove of bronze artifacts at Igbo Ukwu in eastern Nigeria, dating from the 9th and 10th centuries. This ornate bronze pot, standing 1 ft (33 cm) high, was probably used for sacred water.

Reconstruction of the Great Enclosure at Zimbabwe.

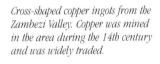

Cross-shaped copper ingots from the Zambezi Valley. Copper was mined in the area during the 14th century and was widely traded.

Great Zimbabwe

More than 100 stone enclosures were built in southern Africa between the 10th and 15th centuries. These formed a trading system linked to the coast. Great Zimbabwe was the largest and most famous of these structures, covering over 60 acres (24 hectares). An oval building in the center, known as the Great Enclosure, is the largest structure of the period found in sub-Saharan Africa. It was protected by an outer wall 820 ft (25 m) long and 30 ft (9 m) high and 15 ft (4.5 m) thick at its base. Archeologists have found many objects such as soapstone carvings and large statues at the site; many of these portrayed the sacred fish eagle, which was revered by the inhabitants. Great Zimbabwe went into decline in the 15th century, but its ruins still stand and are preserved today as a National Heritage Site.

Detail of brickwork from the wall of the Great Enclosure shows the intricate double chevron pattern, a common African motif.

646–710 Nara built, Japan's first capital city. **794** Japanese   capital moves to Heian (Kyoto); imperial style of government   begins. **913** Koryo Dynasty founded in Korea by Wang Kon.   **1185** Start of Shogun period in Japan. **1258** Korea becomes   Mongol vassal state. **1392** Start of Yi Dynasty in Korea. **1467–77**

Medieval Japan and Korea

The early histories of Japan and Korea were greatly influenced by the Chinese. By AD 700 both Japan and Korea had Chinese-style governments and had adopted many of the ideas of Chinese Confucianism and Buddhism. In Japan, these became intermingled with an older religion, called Shinto, which involved ancestor worship. As time went on China's influence was gradually absorbed into the distinctive Japanese and Korean societies. In Japan, many skills and technologies were introduced by volunteer migrants or captured Korean prisoners. For much of their history, until the 19th century, Japan and Korea were isolated from the rest of the world and largely resisted European contact.

The horse was a symbol of military might in Japan. This model, based on a typical Korean design, is from the tomb of a Japanese ruler of the 6th century.

Before 710, when a central capital was established at Nara, there were many unsuccessful attempts to unite Japan which was ruled by rival princes. Although Japan was in theory ruled from Nara, a truly imperial style of government only began after the capital moved to Heian (present-day Kyoto) in 794. Tight controls were introduced on land

The Mongol threat

In 1274 the Mongol emperor Kubilai Khan (c.1216–94), having conquered Korea, sent an invasion force to Japan's southernmost island of Kyushu. The Japanese drove the Mongols away, but in 1281 Kubilai Khan tried again, with a much bigger and better-armed expedition. This time the Mongols sailed into a typhoon and their fleet was destroyed. The threat faded, and by 1392 Korea was once again a self-governing nation.

Chinese influence on Japanese architecture can clearly be seen in the temple of Todaiji at Nara, built at the beginning of the 8th century.

Nara

Before 710, each new emperor of Japan chose a new site for his court, because the place where a previous emperor had died was thought to be unlucky. Nara, built between 646 and 710, was Japan's first permanent capital city. It remained the capital for about 75 years. Nara was a Buddhist city, and its buildings included seven magnificent temples.

Territory gained by Yi Dynasty (after 1392)

CHINA
HOKKAIDO
KOREA
SEA OF JAPAN
• Seoul
JAPAN
HONSHU
Heian • Nara
SHIKOKU
KYUSHU

JAPAN AND KOREA IN 1183.

A ball game popular at court involved keeping a ball in the air for as long as possible. Skilled players could pass it up to 260 times without letting it fall.

Japanese drama

Japan's specialized form of drama, called *No*, dates from the 14th century and is still performed. It combines singing, dancing, and poetry. The actors wear masks and magnificent costumes, and perform on a bare stage without scenery. This *No* mask (right) dates from the 15th century. *No* plays were encouraged and enjoyed by the shogun, who often gave the actors homes in the court.

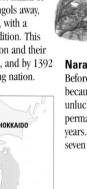

Court life

For the shogun, protected by his military elite, life at the Japanese court was very pleasant. He enjoyed poetry recitals, concerts, dancing, and fine food. Sporting events held outside the precincts of the court included horse racing, archery competitions, and ball games like the one in this illustration (above). Court life was at its most splendid between about 800 and 1000, when Heian was the Japanese capital.

Feudalism in Japan

With the rise of the Kamakura shogunate in 1185, Japan became a feudal society. The shogun, or "great general," was served by a band of military regional governors called *daimyos*, who in turn were served by samurai. During the Ashikaga shogunate (1338–1573) full-scale civil war erupted with the Onin War in 1467–77. The authority of the shoguns declined and the *daimyos* took power. Japan was splintered into hundreds of separate feudal states.

Oda Nobunaga, who unified half of Japan in 1573.

Christianity in Japan

Jesuit missionaries arrived in Japan in 1548. Many Japanese distrusted them because they thought armies of conquest would follow. Resentment grew, and in 1638 some 37,000 Japanese Christians were slaughtered in a furious outbreak of violence (right). After that, Japan began a period of isolation from the rest of the world.

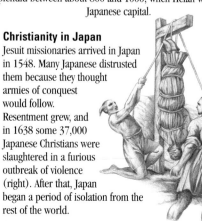

The samurai

Samurai were the "knights" of Japan. They were highly trained warriors who fought with swords. An elite and efficient fighting force on horseback, they were prepared to die for their leaders; if they thought they had failed in their duties, they committed suicide by falling on their swords.

Highly decorated samurai swords were much prized by their owners, who controlled Japan's feudal society.

Onin War in Japan brings civil war. **1548** First Jesuit missionaries arrive in Japan. **1568–90** Oda forces led by Nobunaga, then Hideyoshi, unite central and eastern Japan. **1592–97** Japan attacks Korea. **1639** Japan begins 200-year period of isolation.

ownership, the payment of taxes, and military policing. Despite these measures, the emperor could not prevent wars between regional princes and by the 12th century, power had slipped back into their hands. Civil war splintered Japan into more than 400 feudal states in 1467–77 and the country only regained some unity under the Oda clan in the 1580s. In the mid-16th

century European traders and missionaries arrived in Japan, introducing western muskets, among other things. Before long they became unwelcome, and after 1639 almost all traders were expelled, Christians were persecuted, and Japanese were forbidden to travel abroad. This began over 200 years of isolation.

2

Korea's history was greatly affected by its geographical position between China and Japan. Until 913 it was regarded as a state of the Chinese Empire. That year, however, Wang Kon founded the first ruling dynasty, the Koryo. From 913 until the 20th century, Korea was ruled by just two dynasties: the Koryo (913–1392) and the Yi (1392–1910). In 1258 Korea was attacked by the Mongols and became a vassal state. Mongol

rule was thrown off in 1356 with Chinese help. In the 16th century a large army from Japan invaded, and in the early 17th century China attacked again. These threats made the Koreans seek isolation from the rest of the world. As in Japan, travel abroad was banned and there was very little trade with other countries. Korea's isolation lasted for 300 years.

1. This 17th century painting is a representation of the kamikaze, *or "divine wind," which destroyed the fleet of Mongol ships poised to invade Japan in 1281.*

2. Tax tallies like these were tied to goods in transit during the Nara period in Japan.

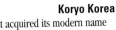

Early Korean and Japanese religion

In 424 Buddhism was introduced to Korea from China. At this time Japan had its own religion, called Shinto, based on a form of ancestor worship. By the 6th century, however, Buddhism reached Japan, too. Relations between Buddhists and the emperor were often uneasy, as the emperor feared that Buddhists had too much power over government.

Southern Korea was a center of metal-working and jewelry-making. This gold crown, recovered from a royal burial chamber, dates from about the 5th century AD.

The Yi Dynasty

Korea's Yi Dynasty came to power in 1392 and controlled the country until 1910. The early rulers adopted the ideas of Confucius, and treated learning and scholarship with great respect. In 1234, the Koreans invented a printing technique that used moveable metal type 200 years before it was re-invented in Europe. This was followed by a boom in publishing, especially in areas of science such as medicine, astronomy, and methods of agriculture. The main center of learning was the royal academy, Chipyonjon, set up in 1420.

Koryo Korea

Korea first acquired its modern name in 913, when a leader named Wang Kon founded the new Koryo Dynasty. Surviving the later Mongol invasions, the dynasty lasted for nearly 500 years. The most well-known artistic achievements of the time were in ceramics, which used new techniques of decoration. This wine ewer (right), from the 12th century, has a gourd-shaped top and is decorated with ducks and a willow tree, inlaid in black and white.

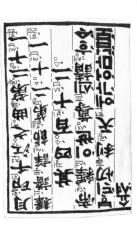

This bronze Buddhist figure is nearly 40 in. (1 m) tall. It was cast in Korea in the 7th century.

> **SEE ALSO**
> p. 52 ANCIENT CHINA AND JAPAN
> p. 204 JAPANESE EXPANSIONISM

This poem was written in the new Korean alphabet in 1497 by the Korean emperor Sejong, as a tribute to his dead wife.

Korea in the 16th century

Toward the end of the 16th century Korea had to fight off two invasions from Japan. The first was in 1592, when the Korean navy, helped by Chinese troops, drove the Japanese back. Five years later the Japanese attacked again. The invasion left much of Korea in ruins and many Korean scholars and craftworkers were taken away to Japan, but Korea remained independent.

The Sejong period in Korea

Sejong, the fourth ruler of the Yi Dynasty, ruled Korea from 1419 to 1450. A strong military leader, he kept both the Chinese and Japanese at bay, allowing Korean culture and learning to flourish. The spread of learning was encouraged by Sejong's support for the invention of a new writing system, called *chongun*. It had fewer characters than the Chinese system previously used, and they were easier to learn. The characters were phonetic, representing the sounds of speech, as in Western alphabets.

Admiral Yi Sun-shin, a national hero in Korea, commanded a fleet that defeated Japanese invaders in 1592. Statues of him stand in public places throughout Korea.

Confucianism and learning

Confucianism developed as a set of beliefs based on the teachings of the great Chinese philosopher, Confucius (551–479 BC). During the Yi Dynasty in Korea it replaced Buddhism as Korea's main religion. It became the basis of Korea's educational and bureaucratic systems. The illustration of a bookshelf screen (above) from later in the Yi period reflects the typical Confucian respect for books and learning.

Russia and Eastern Europe

Bears are the symbol of Russia.

During the 9th century, Swedish Vikings traveled south from the Baltic Sea into present-day Russia. These explorers soon controlled trade routes along rivers and lakes all the way to the Black Sea. They took furs, honey, and other forest products across the Black Sea to Constantinople, where they exchanged them for silks, spices, and gold. The Vikings soon ruled and integrated with the Slavic peoples, who had lived in the region for hundreds of years. Kiev, the capital of modern Ukraine, developed as the most important city, and the region around it had its own prince. During the 13th century, Russia was invaded by Mongols from the east. Moscow emerged as the most powerful city, at the center of the principality of Muscovy. Meanwhile, other states such as Hungary, Poland, and Bohemia had developed in Eastern Europe.

According to a medieval chronicle, groups of Slavs in Novgorod asked Vikings from Sweden to bring order to their settlement. The Swedish Vikings, known as Rus, arrived in 862. They were led by a chieftain named Rurik, who died about 879. The first state, called Kievan Rus, grew up around the town of Kiev in the 9th century, and a Rus named Oleg ruled as its prince. Kiev lay on the main trade route linking the Baltic Sea with the Black Sea. In 988 the grand prince of Kiev and

Trading waterways

Swedish Vikings rowed and sailed down the Dnieper, Volga, and other rivers in the 9th century. The Slavs who lived in the region of present-day European Russia probably welcomed the newcomers as traders. The Dnieper River passes through Kiev, which the Slavs had founded in the 5th century. Across the Black Sea lay Constantinople, which quickly became the main trading partner of the new state of Kiev.

An amber and glass necklace. The best amber came from the Baltic Sea region and was traded throughout early Russia by the Vikings.

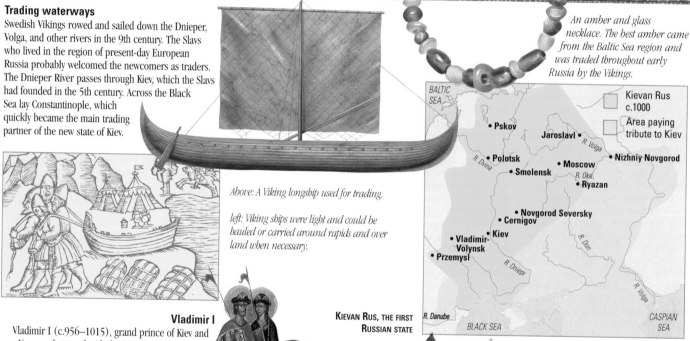

Above: A Viking longship used for trading.

left: Viking ships were light and could be hauled or carried around rapids and over land when necessary.

KIEVAN RUS, THE FIRST RUSSIAN STATE

Left: The first two Russian saints, from an icon painted on wood. Saints Boris and Gleb were sons of Vladimir I. They were killed by their brother, Svyatopolk the Accursed, who then seized power in Kiev.

The conversion of Vladimir I in 988. The Russian Orthodox Church began under his rule.

Vladimir I

Vladimir I (c.956–1015), grand prince of Kiev and Novgorod, agreed with the Byzantine emperor to become a Christian in 988. According to a medieval chronicle, Vladimir had decided that his state needed a major religion. He sent envoys to report on Islam, Judaism, and Roman and Byzantine Christianity, and was won over by news of a magnificent mass held at Hagia Sophia cathedral in Constantinople. This was the start of the Russian Orthodox Church. He also agreed to marry Anna, sister of Byzantine emperor, Basil II.

Right: Alexander Nevsky (c.1220–63), prince of Novgorod and grand prince of Vladimir, acquired his name by defeating the Swedes near the Neva River in 1240. Two years later he defeated the Teutonic Knights at Lake Peipus. He accepted the rule of the invading Mongols, however, and saved the region from being devastated.

The "land of the Rus" was the origin of modern "Russia." In this illustration (left), Slavs are offering a tribute of fur pelts to the Rus. The Vikings took sable, ermine, and other valuable furs from the Arctic north to trade with merchants in Constantinople.

Powerful rulers

The amazing Cap of State (left), a fur hat decorated with precious metals and jewels, was first worn by Vladimir II (1053–1125), grand prince of Kiev, as a symbol of his power. Vladimir II was a strong ruler who fought many successful campaigns against invading princes. Later Russian czars inherited and wore Vladimir's Cap of State.

Kiev and invade Hungary.
1240–42 Alexander Nevsky, prince of Novgorod and grand prince of Vladimir, defeats the Swedes and Teutonic Knights.
1326 Russian Orthodox chief bishop moves to Moscow.
1364 Cracow University founded.
1389 Ottoman Turks defeat the Serbs at the Battle of Kosovo.

Novgorod became a Christian. The rulers of other Kievan Rus principalities gained power and fought many wars.

In 1237, Kievan Rus was invaded by the Mongol Tartars, who swept in from the east. Led by Batu, a grandson of Chingis Khan, their army was made up of over 200,000 men. They destroyed Kiev in 1240 and Russia was absorbed into Mongol Empire where it was known as the khanate of the Golden Horde. Batu forced the surviving Russian princes to pay heavy taxes.

In the early 14th century, Prince Yuri of Moscow married the sister of the Golden Horde's khan, or ruler, and was appointed Russian grand prince. About 1326 Ivan I expanded the Muscovite territory, and then persuaded the chief bishop of the Russian Orthodox Church to move to Moscow. By this move he made Moscow the capital of Russia. In 1380 Grand Prince Dmitri defeated a Mongol force at the Battle of Kulikovo, freeing Moscow from Mongol control.

By this time many other countries had developed in Eastern Europe. By the start of the 11th century, Poland had its first king, Boleslaw the Brave (c.966–1025).

After his death, Poland was invaded by many different peoples.

Stephen I became the first king of Hungary in 1000. Fifty years after his death he was made the country's patron saint. The Mongols invaded Hungary in 1241. Some 150 years later, the Hungarians were fighting the Ottoman Empire.

Bohemia became a kingdom in 1158, when Emperor Frederick I gave the title of king to the duke of Bohemia. The kingdom's golden age was ruled over by Charles IV (1316–78), who was both king of Bohemia and Germany and, subsequently Holy Roman Emperor (reigned 1346–78).

A warrior chief named Stefan Nemanja had formed the first united Serbian state in the late 12th century. Its great emperor, Stefan Dusan (c.1308–55), fought off Byzantine attacks, but in 1389 the Ottoman Turks conquered Serbia and held it until 1879.

1. A 10th-century terra-cotta egg. The egg is an ancient symbol of renewed life, adopted by Christians as a symbol of Easter.

2. The battle belmet of Yaroslav I, grand prince of Kiev (reigned 1019–54).

3. The emblem of the Russian Orthodox Church, found on many Russian buildings.

Poland

The first king of Poland, Boleslaw the Brave (reigned 1024–1025), reorganized the Church in Poland, making it responsible directly to the pope. After Boleslaw's death, Poland went through a period of instability and was invaded by various peoples. It was united again in the early 14th century, especially under the rule of Casimir the Great (reigned 1333–70, left), who extended Polish territory and encouraged learning.

Teutonic Knights

The Order of Teutonic Knights was a German order of crusading monks founded about 1190 in Palestine. In 1211 they traveled to Eastern Europe, where they tried to convert and subdue the people along the Baltic coast. Their influence spread inland, but they lost power during the 14th century and were beaten by the united Poles and Lithuanians at Grunwald in 1410. The order declined rapidly after that.

Building work on the cathedral of the Assumption in Moscow in the 1320s.

SEE ALSO
p. 118 THE RISE OF RUSSIA

The rise of Moscow

Allowed to collect taxes from his Mongol overlords, Ivan I, known as "Moneybags" (c.1300–41), kept some of the taxes and began expanding his principality of Muscovy. Ivan also persuaded the chief bishop of the Russian Orthodox Church to move from Kiev to Moscow in 1326, and so Moscow became the capital.

Hungary

Stephen I (977–1038) was brought up a Christian and became the first king of Hungary in 1000. Stability followed until the Mongol invasions of 1241. About 1396, the Hungarians were fighting another threat: this time the Ottoman Empire. In 1456 the Hungarian military leader Janos Hunyadi fought a successful campaign against the Turks, and his son Matthias Corvinus (c.1443–90, right) became king of Hungary in 1458. Hungary prospered during his powerful reign.

EASTERN EUROPE AT THE END OF THE 14TH CENTURY.

SWEDEN
BALTIC SEA
TEUTONIC ORDER
PRINCIPALITY OF MOSCOW
BRANDENBURG
LUSATIA
POLAND
LITHUANIA
BOHEMIA
Prague •
MORAVIA
• Cracow
• Kiev
AUSTRIA
STYRIA
CARINTHIA
CARNIOLA
• Pest
MOLDAVIA
KHANATE OF THE GOLDEN HORDE
KINGDOM OF HUNGARY
SERBIAN EMPIRE
WALLACHIA
ADRIATIC SEA
KOSOVO
BULGARIA
BLACK SEA
SERBIAN EMPIRE

☐ Bohemian lands
☐ Habsburg lands
■ Venetian territory
— Boundary of Poland-Lithuania after 1386

Serbia

Stefan Nemanja first united Serbia in the late 12th century. Serbia's greatest emperor, Stefan Dusan (c.1308–55), fought successfully against the Byzantine Empire, but Serbia began to break up after his death. In 1389 the Ottoman Turks defeated the Serbs at the Battle of Kosovo (below), though they lost their leader, Sultan Murad I. The Ottoman Empire went on to rule Serbia for nearly 500 years.

Bohemia

The first great ruler of Bohemia, a region in the west of the present-day Czech Republic, was Wenceslas. He became Bohemia's patron saint after his death in 929. In 1158 Holy Roman Emperor Frederick I gave the title of king to the duke of Bohemia. The region's golden age came during the reign of Charles IV (1316–78), who was both king of Bohemia and Holy Roman Emperor. Charles made Prague (left) his capital, and in 1348 he founded the Charles University there.

The Avignon papacy

Pope Clement V (1264–1314, right) was appointed by the influence of King Philip IV of France. In 1309 Clement moved the papal court from Rome to Avignon, in southern France, where it remained until 1377. The following year two rival popes were elected – one in Rome and one in Avignon. This situation divided Europe, making existing political differences even worse.

Joan of Arc (c.1412–31) led the French forces that took Orléans from the English in 1429. This was the turning point in the Hundred Years' War.

Italian city-states

Siena's Town Hall.

Italy's powerful, independent city-states, such as Florence, Milan, and Venice, often argued and fought each other. The leader of the Sienese army, Guidoriccio da Fogliano (below right), was a mercenary, or hired soldier. City-states used hired soldiers to fight their battles. The leaders were ruthless businessmen who made a lot of money out of war. Some of them later conquered territories for themselves.

The Hundred Years' War

This conflict was actually a series of wars fought between England and France from 1337 to 1453. It was triggered by French attempts to regain English lands within France, and fed by the claims of English kings to the French throne. The English won some important battles, including the sea Battle of Sluys in 1340 (above), and the land battles of Crécy (1346) and Poitiers (1356). Henry V (reigned 1413–22) reasserted the claim to the French throne, and won a famous victory at Agincourt in 1415 (below). But by 1453 the French king Charles VII had pushed the English back to Calais.

Left: The legendary hero William Tell came to symbolize the Swiss struggle for independence from the Austrian Habsburgs.

The Swiss Confederation

In 1291 the Swiss cantons of Uri, Schwyz, and Nidwalden formed the Everlasting League to defend their freedom against the rule of the Habsburgs and the Holy Roman Empire. This was the origin of the Swiss Confederation, which later became known as Switzerland (after the canton of Schwyz). Between 1332 and 1353 five more cantons joined the Confederation, and the Swiss twice defeated the Austrians in battle during the 1380s.

Disputed kingship

When Emperor Henry VII of the house of Luxembourg died, the Germans wanted a king from another dynasty. Some supported Ludwig (right), who belonged to the Wittelsbach family, and others wanted Frederick the Fair, a Habsburg. Both were elected king in 1314, and this led to a long war, which Ludwig IV – also called Louis the Bavarian (1282–1347) – finally won in 1322. Pope John XXII wanted to veto Ludwig's election, and when Ludwig denied this right, Pope John excommunicated him in 1324.

1291 Swiss cantons form the Everlasting League, origin of the Swiss Confederation and Switzerland.

1307 Dante begins writing the *Divine Comedy*.

1309–77 The Avignon papacy, beginning with Pope Clement V.

1337–1453 Hundred Years' War.
1347–52 Bubonic plague (Black

Crises in Western Europe

The 14th century was marked by disease and conflict. Climatic change across Europe caused harvest after harvest to fail, and many poor people faced starvation. Weakened by these conditions, a terrible plague called the "Black Death" swept across Europe killing almost one-third of the people. The sharp drop in population caused labor shortages which in turn led to social unrest. The struggle between the popes and state rulers continued, with the papacy losing ground when it fell under the power of the French kings. This led to the Great Schism and between 1378 and 1417 rivals popes sat at Rome and Avignon, in southern France. The Hundred Years' War between England and France cost both sides great losses, while in Italy the city-states and their political factions continued to fight.

As the feudal system began to break down in Europe, many nobles lost power and kings used hired armies to enforce their authority over them. The kings also gained power with the support of townspeople, who were prepared to support them by paying taxes in return for peace and good government.

There were ongoing disputes between Church leaders and state rulers. Some popes surrendered their independence to the kings, and from 1309 to 1377

the papacy was moved from Rome to Avignon, in France. In 1324, the second Avignon pope John XXII excommunicated the Holy Roman Emperor, Ludwig IV (1282–1347), who four years later set up an antipope in Rome. After the papacy returned to Rome in 1377, disputes over papal election divided the Church in the so-called Great Schism. Two churchmen claimed the title of pope. These disputes caused the Church and its teaching to be criticized.

Wars also played a great part in halting European progress. From 1337 to 1453, England and France fought the Hundred Years' War,

The Black Death

The bubonic plague, or Black Death, came to Europe from Central Asia in 1347. It spread rapidly, and after three years had killed millions of people. At least a third of the population of Europe died. The disease was passed to humans by fleas that had bitten the rats that carried the deadly bacteria. People in the Middle Ages had little idea how the plague spread, and it caused great fear and panic. Plague victims suffered a painful, but rapid death.

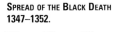

SPREAD OF THE BLACK DEATH 1347–1352.

■ 1347 ■ 1347 ■ 1348
■ 1349 ■ 1350 ■ 1352
☐ area not affected
→ direction of spread

ENGLAND
FRANCE CENTRAL EUROPE
SPAIN ITALY BALKANS
BLACK SEA
MEDITERRANEAN SEA

During the Black Death, groups of Christians roamed Europe beating themselves with whips to atone for their sins in the hope that this would end the plague. In 1349 Pope Clement VI condemned the practice, called flagellation.

Right: Saint Roch, the plague saint, was associated with a supposed miraculous cure for the disease.

Literature

Many major European works of literature were written during the 14th century, including those by Dante Alighieri (1265–1321), Giovanni Boccaccio (1313–75), and Geoffrey Chaucer (c.1342–1400). Dante (below) was born into a noble Guelph family of Florence. He became involved in politics, and was very much opposed to the Church's claims to political power. Such criticism of the Church was only possible in the later Middle Ages. In the *Divine Comedy*, Dante described a journey through Hell and Purgatory to Paradise.

A medieval artist's vision of Hell, from the Baptistry in Florence, Italy.

Right: Peasant rebel-leader Wat Tyler was murdered when a quarrel broke out between Richard II and the rebels.

The Peasants' Revolt

In 1380 King Richard II (1367–1400) made a new law that everyone in England over the age of fifteen had to pay a tax. The peasants rebelled. Led by Wat Tyler and John Ball, they marched to London, where in 1381 Richard granted their demands for an end to serfdom (complete obedience to lords) and better living and working conditions. At a later meeting with the king, however, Tyler was killed by the mayor of London (left). The king later withdrew his concessions.

A merchant's main aim was to make money. Business was conducted from stalls set up in the streets, allowing all the tradesmen of a town to keep an eye on one another. Traders' weights and measures were supervised to prevent cheating.

Scottish independence

Robert the Bruce (1274–1329, left, with his queen) seized the Scottish throne in 1306. Eight years later, at the Battle of Bannockburn, Bruce defeated Edward II of England (reigned 1307–27). This great victory established independence for Scotland and confirmed Robert's claim to the throne. Robert I spent the rest of his life fighting the English in Ireland and along the Scottish borders. In 1328 England formally recognized Scottish independence.

SEE ALSO
p. 108 EUROPE IN THE 15TH CENTURY

Death) sweeps through Europe.
1378–1417 The Great Schism.

1381 Peasants' Revolt in England, led by Wat Tyler.

1386 Chaucer begins writing *The Canterbury Tales*.

1415 King Henry V of England victorious at Battle of Agincourt.

1429 Joan of Arc helps French take Orléans.

---

which began when the English king, Edward III (reigned 1327–77), made a claim for the French throne. There had long been disputes over English territory in France and French support for the Scots, whose independence had been recognized by England in 1328. In 1360 English military successes were recognized in the Treaty of Brétigny, and the Burgundians supported England's King Henry V (reigned 1413–22) after his great victory at the Battle of Agincourt in 1415. His successor, Henry VI (reigned 1422–71), was a weak king, however, and Joan of Arc and others inspired the French so

that by 1453 the English had been driven from all French territory except Calais.

In 1347 the plague known as the "Black Death" swept though Europe and killed about one third of the population. The dramatic drop in population caused prices and rents to fall and wages to rise, weakening the traditional feudal bonds of medieval society. There was increasing social unrest as peasants and workers demanded better conditions and incomes.

In Italy, the powerful city-states continued to fight among themselves. Although weakened by war, the great

cultural blossoming of the Renaissance, began in Italy in the 14th century.

1. A medieval doctor in protective clothing.

2. Medieval depiction of the belief that the sun, moon, and planets moved around the earth.

3. King Edward III's coat of arms combined French fleurs-de-lis with England's lions.

4. A cannon c.1347, used to fire arrows.

5. Murder by Henry II's knights of Thomas Becket, Archbishop of Canterbury from 1162.

c.1000 Population of Europe reaches about 42 million.

c.1100 Guilds of artisans begin to develop in towns.

c.1200 Windmills in common use throughout Europe.

1230 Hamburg and Lübeck found the Hanseatic League.

1250s Florence and Genoa begin to mint gold coins.

Merchants and Trade

The Middle Ages lasted for about 1,000 years from, arguably, 476 to about 1450. In the first centuries of this period, the economy of Europe declined. But from about 1000 on, new farming methods improved yields, the population began to increase, and trade and commerce started to flourish as they had not done since Roman times. Cities and towns grew in number and size, and merchants and traders plied their goods on an ever increasing scale across Europe. International trade routes carried merchandise from as far away as India and China. Bankers, who raised money and financed trade, grew powerful. Many of the largest banking and merchant families, such as the Medici in Florence, Italy, became so powerful that they ruled their cities.

Agricultural improvements in the Middle Ages – such as the widespread use of the three-field system, the introduction of the wheeled plow, and the use of the padded shoulder collar so that horses could be used to plow fields – led to an increase in productivity. The surplus produce was sold at local markets which grew in size and importance. Products such as wool, hides, and dairy produce began to be traded with distant markets.

From the 11th century on, the towns in many parts of Europe grew. Most people in towns were craftworkers, storekeepers, or merchants. As the towns grew in size and importance, the ordinary townspeople began to assert their desire for freedom from rule by royalty and lords. They wanted to supervise their markets themselves and elect their own town government. In some places, most notably in Italy, they were successful. Cities such as Milan, Venice, Genoa, Florence, Pisa, and Siena became self-governing city-states with strong economies based on international trade.

Venice, a city in northwestern Italy, for example, built up a trading empire that extended from China in the Far East to

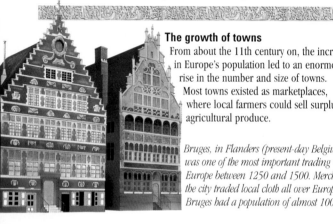

The growth of towns

From about the 11th century on, the increase in Europe's population led to an enormous rise in the number and size of towns. Most towns existed as marketplaces, where local farmers could sell surplus agricultural produce.

Bruges, in Flanders (present-day Belgium), was one of the most important trading cities in Europe between 1250 and 1500. Merchants from the city traded local cloth all over Europe. By 1450 Bruges had a population of almost 100,000 people.

Left: The gold florin was first made in Florence in 1252. It became an important currency for trade in Europe.

Merchants and bankers used small, portable scales to weigh coins, which were mostly made of silver. The weight of the metal was used to determine the coins' value, so it was easy to compare different currencies and difficult for anyone to cheat.

Below: This illustration is based on a beautiful fresco by the Italian artist Ambrogio Lorenzetti. Painted in the 14th century, it shows daily life in the thriving Italian city-state of Siena.

Right: This medieval coin, called a ducat, is from Venice. Venetian merchants traded widely, making Venice a very rich city.

c.1300 New accounting system developed in Italy.

1300 Population of Europe reaches 72 million.

c.1350 Shipping insurance first practiced, in Genoa.

1380 Hans Fugger founds the Fugger bank in Augsburg.

1414 The Medici of Florence become bankers to the pope.

England in the west, amassing great wealth. Venetian traders introduced new technology and products, such as glassware to the West.

Farther south, in Florence, the Medici family controlled one of the largest banking businesses in Europe. The Medici were so powerful that they married into many of the most prestigious royal families of Europe.

Many northern European cities also became important trading centers. Bruges and Ghent in present-day Belgium were the focus of the international cloth trade. During the 13th century in Germany, many trading cities banded together to form a trading group called the Hanseatic League. The European economy declined sharply in 14th century when the plague killed more than a third of the population.

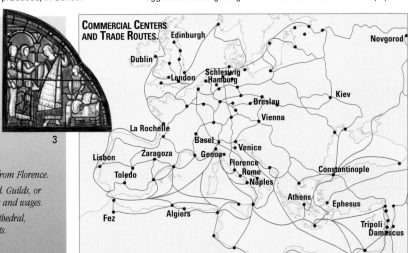

1. A 13th-century nobleman from Florence.

2. The sign of the bakers' guild. Guilds, or trade associations, fixed prices and wages.

3. A window from Chartres cathedral, France, showing fur merchants.

COMMERCIAL CENTERS AND TRADE ROUTES.

Improvements in farming methods

One of the most important improvements in farming took place about 700, when three-field crop rotation was introduced. Each year, peasants planted cereals in one field, vegetables in another, and a third was left uncultivated so that it could regain its fertility. Another major advance was the invention of a plow with wheels. Later on, a harness with a padded shoulder collar was introduced, allowing horses to pull the plow (they were far more efficient than the oxen used previously). These changes boosted agricultural production beyond the levels reached during Roman times.

Trade routes

The map shows the most important towns and trade routes of the Middle Ages. Journeys in medieval Europe took a long time. From Venice, for example, a journey to London normally took 4 weeks; a journey to Lisbon took 7 weeks; and a journey to Damascus took 12 weeks. Luxury goods such as silk, jade, and porcelain came overland all the way from China. Gold from Africa was carried by Islamic merchants across the Sahara Desert. Trading cities grew quickly as regular fairs were held by the merchants.

The growth of commerce

By the 13th century Italian merchants no longer accompanied their goods to markets. They used specialized carriers to transport goods, and agents to oversee their business abroad. The merchants stayed home and developed sophisticated business and financial practices, such as the double-entry accounting system (the basis of modern accounting), credit finance, stocks and shares, and banking.

SEE ALSO
p. 70 THE FALL OF THE WESTERN EMPIRE
p. 84 EUROPEAN RECOVERY AND THE FEUDAL KINGDOMS
p. 102 CRISES IN WESTERN EUROPE
p. 106 THE RENAISSANCE
p. 108 EUROPE IN THE 15TH CENTURY

Leonardo da Vinci's famous sketch of a man was made to show the ideal proportions of the human body.

PEOPLE AND EVENTS

1310–1447 The Visconti family rule the city-state of Milan.

1341 Petrarch is crowned poet laureate in Rome.

1349–53 Giovanni Boccaccio writes the *Decameron*.

1418–36 Filippo Brunelleschi builds the double-shelled dome of Florence cathedral.

1430–35 Donatello produces his bronze statue of *David*, thought to be the first free-standing sculpture since ancient times.

1434–64 Cosimo de' Medici rules Florence and gives large sums of money to Florentine artists.

1450 The Sforza family take control of Milan by force.

1455 Johannes Gutenberg of Mainz prints his *Bible*.

1485–1603 The Tudor Dynasty rules in England.

c.1503 Leonardo da Vinci paints the *Mona Lisa*.

1508–12 Michelangelo paints the ceiling of the *Sistine Chapel* in Rome.

1511 Erasmus attacks church abuses in his *Praise of Folly*.

1515–47 Reign of King Francis I of France, who brings many Italian artists and scholars to his court.

Terra-cotta figure of a boy by Luca della Robbia (1400–82). The idea that childhood was a special stage in a person's lifetime began to be recognized in the Renaissance.

The Renaissance

From the 14th to the 16th centuries, Europe was transformed by a flood of new ideas. The transformation began in Italy, and it included new ways of building, a new style of art, and new ways of living. This period and the changes it brought are now known as the Renaissance, meaning "rebirth." The period saw a great increase in trade and wealth. A new atmosphere of confidence encouraged support of the arts, which began to show the world as it really was rather than in symbolic representations. A revival in classical learning coincided with painting and sculpture showing real people in real places. Artists and writers were seen as important figures in society, and they were supported by noble families who wanted to display their own wealth and importance.

This enameled and gilded goblet was made on the Venetian island of Murano in about 1475. By this time Venetian glassblowers had rediscovered the skills of making fine glass.

Leonardo da Vinci's drawing of an old man dates from about 1514 and is thought to be a self-portrait.

Michelangelo's David, *sculpted from 1501 to 1504.*

Daily life

As more people became wealthy, they had more leisure time to spend as they wished. They were able to take more care with personal hygiene and dress. Privacy and modesty became important in society, and many towns were transformed by major civic projects. By the early 15th century it was becoming normal for families to have their own house or apartment. These were divided up into smaller rooms, so that family members did not have to spend all their time together.

Arts and artists

A great number of masterpieces were produced during the Renaissance in painting, sculpture, and architecture. Some of the great artists of the time were Leonardo da Vinci (1452–1519), Michelangelo (1475–1564), and Raphael (1483–1520) in Italy; Albrecht Dürer (1471–1528) and Hans Holbein the Younger (c.1497–1543) in Germany; and Jan Van Eyck (c.1390–1441) in Flanders. Merchants spent their new wealth on works of art, and artists were encouraged to explore new techniques.

The dome of Florence cathedral was designed and built from 1418 to 1436 by Filippo Brunelleschi (1377–1446), who is often called the founder of Renaissance architecture.

During the Renaissance, music was played for enjoyment rather than only as part of religious services. Instrumental and vocal music both became popular, and were enjoyed in many wealthy homes. In this group of musicians, the man is playing a lute, the woman standing is playing a recorder, and the woman next to her is playing a bass viol. The keyboard instrument is a virginal.

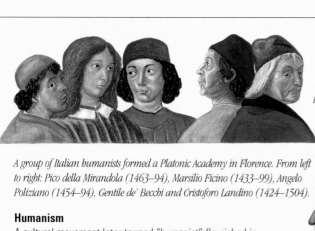

Lorenzo de' Medici, "the Magnificent" (1449–92), was a powerful member of the Medici family, who used their wealth to dominate the government of Florence.

A group of Italian humanists formed a Platonic Academy in Florence. From left to right: Pico della Mirandola (1463–94), Marsilio Ficino (1433–99), Angelo Poliziano (1454–94), Gentile de' Becchi and Cristoforo Landino (1424–1504).

Humanism

A cultural movement later termed "humanist" flourished in Renaissance Europe. Humanist writers and thinkers took a renewed interest in the arts and classical culture of ancient Greece and Rome, bringing classical study into the everyday, non-religious world. Early humanists such as Francesco Petrarch (1304–74) copied the Latin of ancient times, and they especially admired Plato and Cicero. The humanists were concerned with trying to understand human actions and with striving to improve themselves.

Portrait by Piero della Francesca (c.1420–92) of Federico da Montefeltro, the Duke of Urbino.

The increase in trade led to changes in fashion. This 15th-century Italian man is wearing a pleated cape and decorated stockings.

Printing

Printing was a crucial invention of the Renaissance. Johannes Gutenberg (1398–1468) set up the first printing press using movable type in Germany in 1450, and the new methods reached Italy by 1470 and Britain a few years later. Instead of laboriously copying manuscripts by hand one at a time, printers could turn out dozens of copies in a few days.

The printing press of 1450 had a flat base with a frame for holding the metal type. A sheet of paper was pressed against the inked type to make the printed pages.

Princes and patrons

The princes, dukes, and other powerful men who came to dominate the cities in Renaissance times became important patrons of the arts. In Italy, the Medici family of merchants and bankers established a tradition by supporting a brilliant circle of artists and architects such as Michelangelo, Brunelleschi, and Botticelli. The Duke of Urbino (above) was an art patron as well as a great military leader.

Erasmus (c.1466–1536) was a great humanist scholar who was respected by all sides in the religious disputes of the early 16th century. He greatly influenced Sir Thomas More.

Sir Thomas More (1477–1535) was an English lawyer and politician who worked hard to end abuses within the Church of England. King Henry VIII had him executed for treason.

The layout of Palma Nova shows how important up-to-date defense was to Italian cities. The walled city has pointed bastions and is surrounded by a wide moat.

Great cities

The great cultural blossoming of the Renaissance happened first in northern Italy. This may owe something to the great wealth of the city-states, their size, and their great sense of civic pride. The cities of northern Italy were dominated by Roman ruins, which prompted a growing interest in Classical civilization and the desire to bring back to life the values, art, architecture, literature, and language of ancient Rome. Behind their heavily fortified walls, the cities developed prosperous societies and erected magnificent town halls and churches, and they competed with each other to be the most advanced.

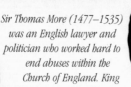

Medicine

By the early 16th century doctors had developed new methods. Ambroise Paré (1510–90), chief surgeon to the French army, discovered the benefits of sewing up wounds rather than cauterizing them with a red-hot iron. In 1543 the Flemish physician Andreas Vesalius (1514–64) published the first accurate descriptions and illustrations of human anatomy.

1442 Alfonso the Magnanimous, king of Aragon and Sicily, seizes the kingdom of Naples. **1453** France and England's Hundred Years' War ends. **1455** Gutenberg Bible printed. **1455–85** Wars of the Roses. **1461** Louis XI king of France. **1465** Charles the Bold rebels against Louis XI.

Europe in the 15th Century

Europe was very unstable in the first half of the 15th century. There was intense rivalry between Castile and Aragon in Spain (and a struggle in both kingdoms between the king and the powerful nobility), and the Hundred Years' War continued on and off between France and England. By the end of the century, however, Spain was united and the French monarchy had started to re-establish its power. Europe's wealth was still concentrated around Italy, where cities such as Naples, Venice, and Milan continued to grow in population and power. In northern Europe the powerful trading association called the Hanseatic League started the century with 160 members, including Lübeck. Families such as the German Fuggers and the Italian Medicis extended their influence over trade and banking.

Burgundy and France

After victory at Orleans at the end of the Hundred Years' War (1337–1453), the French drove out most of the English. Louis XI (1423–83) regained royal power. Charles the Bold (1422–77), duke of Burgundy (right), joined a revolt against the king, conquered Lorraine, and invaded Switzerland. He wanted to create a Burgundian kingdom, but was defeated by Louis and killed during a siege of Nancy.

Practical politics

This period in Europe was marked by the struggle between royal power (mostly on the increase), and the power of the nobility and churchmen (mostly beginning to decline).

Niccolo Machiavelli (1469–1527), a Florentine diplomat, wrote his most famous work, The Prince, *in 1513, and his* Discourses *four years later.*

This illustration shows London being attacked in May 1471 by the Lancastrian forces.

Civil war in England

The Wars of the Roses (1455–85) came about in England when two branches of the royal Plantagenet family claimed the right of descent from Edward III (1312–77) and fought for the throne. The House of Lancaster had a red rose as its emblem. In 1455 Lancastrian Henry VI (1421–71) was king. The House of York, with its white rose, was at first represented by Richard, duke of York. There were many battles and changes of king, until the Lancastrian Henry VII (1456–1509), the first Tudor king, married Elizabeth of York in 1486 and united the two warring Houses.

EUROPE IN THE 15TH CENTURY.

NORWAY · SWEDEN · RUSSIA · SCOTLAND · IRELAND · DENMARK · ENGLAND · LITHUANIA · ATLANTIC OCEAN · HOLY ROMAN EMPIRE · POLAND · KHANATE OF ASTRAKHAN · FRANCE · HUNGARY · MOLDAVIA · KHANATE OF CRIMEA · MILAN · VENICE · WALLACHIA · BLACK SEA · PORTUGAL · NAVARRE · PAPAL STATES · OTTOMAN EMPIRE · SPAIN · ARAGON · CASTILE · CORSICA · GRANADA · SARDINIA · NAPLES · SICILY · MOROCCO · ALGIERS · TUNIS · MEDITERRANEAN SEA · EGYPT

Merchants and bankers

Powerful families controlled trade and finance in different parts of Europe. In Italy, the Medici family, whose power was established by Cosimo de' Medici (1389–1464), dominated the government of Florence from 1434. The Medici were patrons of Renaissance artists such as Botticelli and Michelangelo. The wealth of the German Fugger family (left) was based on weaving. Jakob Fugger (1459–1525) diversified into mining and also handled financial business for the pope.

Naples and Spain

By the mid-15th century, Naples (below) was one of Italy's five most powerful states (together with the papacy, Milan, Venice, and Florence), and one of the largest cities in Europe. During the 1420s, Naples was ruled by Queen Joanna II (1371–1435), supported by King Alfonso the Magnanimous of Aragon (1385–1458). In 1442, however, Alfonso seized the kingdom of Naples himself, and his court became a brilliant cultural center. He established a Spanish connection for the city for the next 300 years.

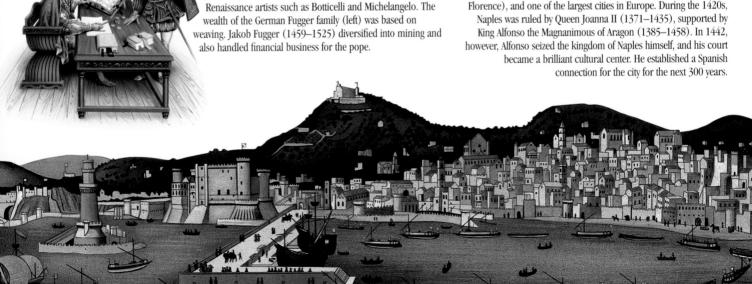

1469 Isabella of Castile marries Ferdinand of Aragon.

1513 Machiavelli writes *The Prince*.

1492 Christopher Columbus makes first voyage to the New World under patronage of Ferdinand and Isabella.

1493 Habsburg Maximilian I becomes Holy Roman Emperor.

Castile and Aragon

The marriage of Ferdinand of Aragon (1452–1516) and Isabella of Castile (1451–1504) united the two largest Spanish kingdoms (right). Isabella gained her nobles' support and Ferdinand was a good military leader. When the two kingdoms joined forces, it marked a turning point in Spain's history. The Muslims who had settled around Granada were driven out. King Ferdinand and Queen Isabella made sure that their children married heirs of other kingdoms, so that Spain gained powerful allies throughout Europe.

Ottoman Turks

Sultan Murad II (1404–51, left) restored unity to the Ottoman Empire after it had been invaded by the Mongol conqueror Timur, or Tamerlane (1336–1405). By 1430 Murad had regained control of Thessaly and Macedonia, occupied Anatolia's Aegean coast, and won Salonika in a war with Venice. In 1444 Murad defeated both a European crusade organized by the pope, and Janos Hunyadi of Hungary at Varna. Four years later he defeated the Hungarians at the second Battle of Kosovo.

Exploring by Caravel

In the late 15th century European shipbuilders changed the design of their hulls to a more streamlined style. The new ships, called caravels (below), were soon sailing for Spain and Portugal on record-breaking voyages of discovery. The caravel *Niña* sailed on three of Christopher Columbus's four voyages to the New World between 1492 and 1504.

Christine de Pisan

The daughter of a court astrologer to Charles V of France, Christine de Pisan (1364–1431), was brought up in Paris. She married and had three children, but when her husband died she was left with no money. In order to support her family she wrote a number of brilliant works, including a biography of Charles V, books of poems, and an educational compendium for women.

Christine de Pisan at work, from a 15th-century illuminated manuscript. Having withdrawn to a nunnery, she wrote about Joan of Arc's successes in 1429.

Stability in China

While there was no dominant state in Europe at the start of the 15th century, the huge Chinese Empire had stable government under the rule of the Ming dynasty. In China paintings and pottery, especially the famous blue and white porcelain (above), were made, and quantities exported to Europe.

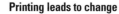

Printing leads to change

Gutenberg's (c.1398–1468) invention of a method of printing using movable metal type greatly speeded up the spread of ideas and gave far more people access to knowledge. When Gutenberg printed copies of the Bible in 1450 he never dreamed that this would eventually lead to the reformation of the Roman Catholic Church.

A late 15th-century statue of Maximilian I. In German folk legend, the Habsburg emperor was known as "the last knight."

Habsburg imperial power

The Habsburg ruler Maximilian I (1459–1519) was Holy Roman Emperor at the end of the 15th century. He tried to increase imperial power and wanted to rule the whole of Western Europe. He married Mary of Burgundy, daughter of Charles the Bold, who was heiress to the Netherlands, but then had to defend his realm against Louis XI of France. The marriage of Maximilian's son Philip to Joanna the Mad of Castile gave his grandson, Charles V, a vast empire.

This farming scene comes from a painting by Brueghel. The development of technology and farming techniques helped agriculture develop during the 15th and 16th centuries.

After the problems and crises of the 14th century in Europe, armies and navies expanded. By the middle of the 15th century, France had the beginnings of a standing army. Louis XI (reigned 1461–1483) was able to fight foreign enemies and his own powerful vassals with the best artillery in Europe. Burgundy was a major power, but the region's desire to become a middle kingdom between France and Germany was ended when it was divided up after the death in battle of Charles the Bold in 1477. Louis XI was succeeded by his son Charles VIII, who ruled until 1498.

In England, during the Wars of the Roses (1455–85) two branches of the Plantagenet family claimed the throne. In 1486 the Lancastrian Henry VII (1456–1509), the first Tudor king, married Elizabeth of York and united the Houses of Lancaster and York.

In Spain, Prince Ferdinand of Aragon married Princess Isabella of Castile in 1469. Isabella became queen of Castile in 1474, Ferdinand became king of Aragon in 1479, and most of Spain was united. Before the end of the century, the last of the Muslims were driven from Granada.

In Eastern Europe, from the middle of the 15th century, the Ottoman Turks and the Muscovites took over large regions from the Black Sea to the Baltic Sea.

In Germany, a series of alliances united the lands owned by the powerful Habsburgs with those of Luxembourg (in 1437) and Burgundy (in 1477). The marriages of Holy Roman Emperor Maximilian I to Mary of Burgundy, and of his son Philip the Handsome to Joanna of Castile, were to make his grandson Charles V (born 1500) the most powerful Christian ruler since Charlemagne.

Many books were beautifully printed to look as much like manuscripts as possible.

SEE ALSO
p. 102 CRISES IN WESTERN EUROPE
p. 104 MERCHANTS AND TRADE

European Expansion
c.1492–c.1800

The 15th to 18th centuries were marked by the expansion of European interests outside Europe. Explorers, especially Portuguese and Spanish, undertook ambitious overseas voyages and established trading and cultural links with civilizations around the world. The arrival of the Europeans was not always beneficial, and millions of people native to the Americas were wiped out by European diseases to which they had no immunity. Land-hungry European settlers also caused grief, as they used any means to expel native owners. But in many other parts of the world the European presence was still limited. In Africa, kingdoms rose and fell, and were only slightly affected by European explorers along the coast.

The Europeans rediscover the Americas
Italian explorer Christopher Columbus believed he could reach China by sailing west across the Atlantic Ocean. Financed by the king and queen of Spain, he set sail in 1492. The tiny fleet sighted land on October 12 and then landed in the Caribbean. Columbus's discovery provoked a spate of journeys and led to the European settlement of North America. However, Columbus was not the first European to set foot in the Americas. This honor goes to the Viking explorers who landed in Newfoundland almost 500 years earlier.

The Mughal Empire

p. 128 *The Muslim leader Babur founded the great Mughal Empire in India in 1526. The empire reached its peak under his grandson Akbar.*

The Ottoman Empire p.130 *The Ottoman Turks were at their zenith in the 16th century.*

The Reformation

p. 136 *Europe was shaken by a great religious revolution after Martin Luther called for the reform of the Roman Catholic Church.*

France

p. 150 *Louis XIV reigned as king of France for 72 years. Known as the "Sun King," the splendors of his court at Versailles dazzled visitors from all over Europe.*

The Scientific Revolution p. 156 *In the 16th and 17th centuries science came to the fore and many important discoveries were made.*

PHILOSOPHIÆ
NATURALIS
PRINCIPIA
MATHEMATICA

1485 The Portuguese reach Angola in East Africa.

1488 Dias rounds the Cape of Good Hope, southern Africa.

1492 Columbus reaches Dominica in the Caribbean.

1497 John Cabot reaches Newfoundland in Canada.

1498 Da Gama crosses the Indian Ocean.

Voyages of Discovery

During the 15th century most Europeans never traveled far from home, and sailors avoided losing sight of land if they could help it. But toward the end of the century a new spirit of adventure started to grow, driven by two main motives: the desire to spread Christianity and to make money from trade. The most valuable trade in Europe was in silk, luxury goods, and spices from the East. In the past, these goods had been carried from the East for thousands of miles along overland routes to Europe, passing hands between merchants many times on the way. They were hugely expensive. But the conquests of the Ottoman Turks, who were also threatening Eastern Europe, had cut off many of the trade routes. Inspired by ancient geography, some people thought that they could renew trade with the East if they could reach it by sea. The advances in all kinds of knowledge, including geography, made during the Renaissance gave the Europeans the technical knowledge for their new undertakings.

During the 15th century most Europeans knew nothing about the other continents. Although the Vikings had landed in North America 500 years before the Italian navigator Christopher Columbus (1451–1506), their voyages had been forgotten, and the accounts brought back by Marco Polo (1254–1324), who went overland to China in the 13th century, seemed so strange that few people believed them. Many of the stories about distant lands were based on legends or superstition. Europeans knew, for

The compass was the most useful instrument that European navigators had. They knew that the magnetized needle always pointed north, but they did not know that magnetic north was different from true north. The apparent misbehavior of their compasses caused explorers such as Christopher Columbus some confusion.

Right: This outline map of the world is believed to have been drawn by Columbus. It shows the world as it was known to Europeans about 1490. Africa, Europe, and Arabia make up the left part of the landmass, and Asia is the right part. The map also shows some islands, real and imaginary, in the Pacific Ocean.

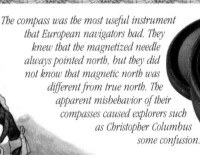

Pepper grew wild on vines in India. It was greatly valued in Europe because it disguised the flavor of old or salted meat and fish.

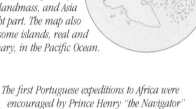

The first Portuguese expeditions to Africa were encouraged by Prince Henry "the Navigator" (1394–1460). He set up a school for navigation and an observatory to train his captains.

Portuguese voyages

Portugal lies at the corner of Europe, with the Atlantic Ocean on its doorstep. The Portuguese had a foothold in North Africa, at Ceuta, where they sought access to the gold that came from beyond the Sahara Desert. Prince Henry "the Navigator" sent the first expedition to explore the African coast in 1418. It went as far as Morocco. More voyages followed, with each captain daring to go a little farther than the one before. They hoped to find a route to the East, but the African coast seemed endless. In 1488, some 70 years after the first expedition, Bartolomeu Dias (c.1450–1500), after sailing south for nearly 5,000 mi. (8,000 km), suddenly found he was sailing eastward. He had passed the southern tip of Africa. Because of stormy weather he called it the Cape of Storms, but the king of Portugal renamed it the Cape of Good Hope.

Christopher Columbus

Christopher Columbus was an Italian captain who believed he could reach Asia by sailing westward. He won support from Spain and, with three small ships, set sail in 1492. After five weeks he arrived at a Caribbean island, believing he was somewhere near Japan. Later, people realized he had discovered a "New World."

To India and beyond

The next Portuguese expedition after that of Bartolomeu Dias in 1488 was led by Vasco da Gama (c.1460–1524, right). His ships, carrying trade goods, rounded the Cape of Good Hope and sailed into the Indian Ocean. On the east coast of Africa they found large Muslim cities that had been thriving on trade with the East for centuries. The ships of Arab and Indian merchants crossed the Indian Ocean daily. Da Gama hired a local captain and arrived at the port of Calicut in India in 1498.

North America

In 1497 John Cabot (an Italian, like Columbus, but working for the English), sailed from Bristol in southwestern England across the North Atlantic to Newfoundland in Canada. Other sailors soon followed: fishermen went there to catch the cod (right) that swarmed off Newfoundland, and explorers went hoping to find a passage to the East, so they could bring back valuable silks and spices for trade.

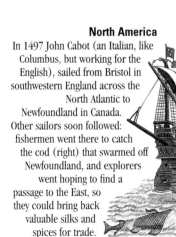

1500 Pedro Cabral claims Brazil for Portugal.

1512 Portuguese reach the Spice Islands (Moluccas).

1519–22 Magellan's westward round-the-world voyage.

1524 Verrazzano explores North American coast.

1535 Cartier sails up the St. Lawrence River, Canada.

example, that a country named India existed in the east, but tales described a fantasy land full of treasure and strange monsters.

For most people the open sea was a frightening prospect; they thought the world was flat, and that ships might sail off the edge and fall into Hell. Others believed that if they sailed too far south the sun would burn them up. Although educated people did not believe these stories, it still took great courage for sailors to venture out into open seas.

What knowledge of the world people had was based on the work of the Greek astronomer and geographer, Ptolemy, who lived in the 2nd century. He wrote a *Geography*, with maps, which became the standard medieval work on the subject. Only three continents were known about: Europe, Asia, and Africa. North and South America and Australasia were not known. It was also thought the world was about one-third smaller than it is.

Sea captains had been using magnetic compasses since the 12th century, so they were able to tell in which direction they were sailing. They could also work

out their position between north and south (latitude), by using a cross-staff to measure the height of a star above the horizon. But they had no way of measuring their position east and west (longitude). For this they depended on "dead reckoning," or guesswork.

Based on this world view, in 1480 Columbus calculated that he could reach Asia by sailing westward across the Atlantic Ocean. He expected to find Japan and China about where he found the Americas. More expeditions to the "New World" followed. In 1508 a Spaniard named Juan Diaz de Solis (c.1470–1516) first visited Central America. On a later trip, in 1516, he sailed up the Uruguay River, but was killed and eaten by Charrua Indians. Subsequent Spanish expeditions in search of gold led to the conquest and destruction of the mighty Aztec Empire in Mexico and the Inca Empire in Peru.

1. A captain uses a crosstaff to measure the height of a star above the horizon.

2. Adzes were used to shape ships' beams.

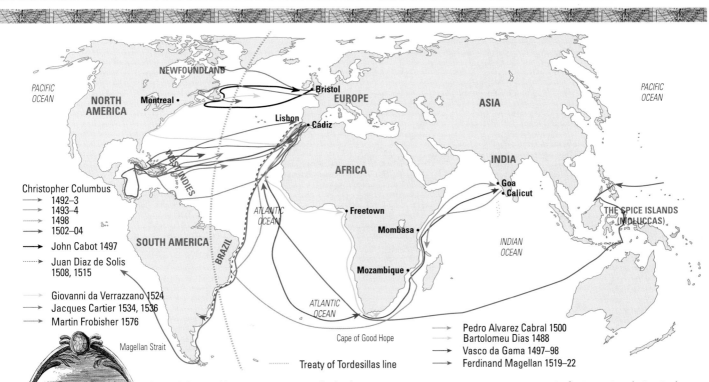

Christopher Columbus
→ 1492–3
→ 1493–4
→ 1498
→ 1502–04
→ John Cabot 1497
······ Juan Diaz de Solis 1508, 1515
→ Giovanni da Verrazzano 1524
→ Jacques Cartier 1534, 1536
→ Martin Frobisher 1576

Magellan Strait

→ Pedro Alvarez Cabral 1500
→ Bartolomeu Dias 1488
→ Vasco da Gama 1497–98
→ Ferdinand Magellan 1519–22

Cape of Good Hope

·········· Treaty of Tordesillas line

NEWFOUNDLAND
PACIFIC OCEAN
NORTH AMERICA
Montreal
Bristol
EUROPE
ASIA
Lisbon
Cádiz
WEST INDIES
AFRICA
INDIA
Goa
Calicut
SOUTH AMERICA
BRAZIL
ATLANTIC OCEAN
Freetown
Mombasa
INDIAN OCEAN
Mozambique
THE SPICE ISLANDS (MOLUCCAS)
PACIFIC OCEAN
ATLANTIC OCEAN

Around the world

Ferdinand Magellan (left) was a Portuguese adventurer. In 1519 the king of Spain commissioned Magellan – who had visited the Spice Islands (the Moluccas) by the Portuguese eastern route around southern Africa – to find a western route, so that Spain, too, could profit from trade with the Spice Islands. Magellan had to sail far to the south of South America before he found a passage, now called the Magellan Strait, near its southern tip. After crossing the Pacific Ocean, he eventually reached the Spice Islands, where he was killed in 1521. Three years after his five ships had left Spain, just one returned, in 1522.

The world divided

To prevent quarrels, in 1494 the pope divided the non-Christian world between Portugal and Spain. He drew a line through the middle of the Atlantic Ocean. Lands to the west of the line (the Americas) were acknowledged as Spanish territory, and lands to the east of it (Africa and Asia) were Portuguese. Later, Brazil, which straddled the line, became Portuguese. Spain and Portugal ratified the pope's decision with the Treaty of Tordesillas in the same year.

A single sea

Between 1492 and 1522, European captains sailed across every major sea and ocean. They made the important discovery that all the seas and oceans are connected. A ship starting from any port in the world can sail to any other port. The Portuguese had succeeded in finding an eastern sea route to India and the Far East, although it was an extremely long voyage. Magellan's westward route was even longer, however, making it impracticable as a regular trade route.

On first impression, the Spaniards thought the Americas were not as rich in goods as Asia. But the New World had many riches of its own: not only silver and gold, but also valuable crops, later grown by European colonists. Among these were tobacco, sugar cane, and pineapples.

Tobacco.

Sugar cane.

Pineapple.

SEE ALSO
p. 106 THE RENAISSANCE
p. 114 PORTUGUESE AND SPANISH EXPANSION
p. 116 DUTCH, ENGLISH, AND FRENCH EXPANSION
p. 132 SOUTHEAST ASIA AND THE SPICE TRADE

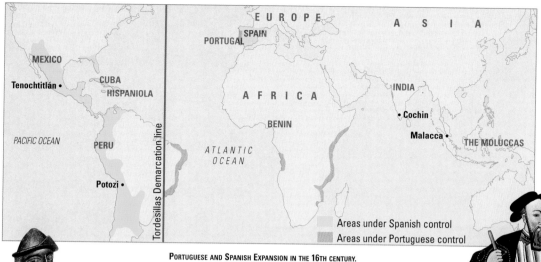

PORTUGUESE AND SPANISH EXPANSION IN THE 16TH CENTURY.

Areas under Spanish control
Areas under Portuguese control

Portuguese and Spanish Empires

As soon as they had discovered a sea route to India, the Portuguese started to build an empire based on sea power. Its purpose was trade. Within 15 years they had control of the Spice Islands (the Moluccas). In the New World of the Americas the Spanish created their own empire. They set up colonies and claimed the right to rule all Central and South America. In Mexico and Peru they settled in large numbers, but in the rest of their empire they had only a few forts and mission stations.

Francisco de Almeida was the first Portuguese viceroy of India (1505–09). He established a base at Cochin in southern India. Almeida killed many Arab rivals for the spice trade at sea before he was killed himself in a fight in South Africa, on his way home.

From the early 15th century on, the Portuguese set up bases in West Africa. This small sculpture of a Portuguese soldier was made in the forest state of Benin to the west of the Niger delta. At first Portugal had good relations with the African states, but these soon deteriorated when the Portuguese started the trade in African slaves.

Cortés

Hernán Cortés (1485–1547) was sent by the governor of Cuba to colonize the Mexican mainland. When he landed, he burned his ships so his men could not desert. As he marched inland, he discovered the towns and cities of the great Aztec civilization. To the Spanish, the Aztecs – who believed it was essential to offer human sacrifices to their powerful gods – seemed a bloodthirsty nation of constantly warring groups. In 1519 Cortés marched on the Aztec capital, Tenochtitlán, where he was received peacefully.

SEE ALSO
p. 112 EUROPEAN VOYAGES OF DISCOVERY
p. 116 DUTCH, ENGLISH, AND FRENCH EXPANSION
p. 132 SOUTHEAST ASIA AND THE SPICE TRADE

This Aztec picture shows the Spanish – on horses, which the Aztecs had never seen before – and their Mexican allies attacking the Aztecs at Cholula. The Aztecs had been ordered by their emperor, Montezuma II, to ambush the Spanish and take prisoners, but they were utterly defeated; 6,000 Aztec soldiers were killed.

1507 Portuguese base at Sofala, Mozambique. | **1510** Albuquerque takes Goa. | Albuquerque. | begins campaign to protect Native
1511 Malacca falls to | **1514** Las Casas |

Portuguese and Spanish Expansion

Between 1500 and 1900 Europeans came to rule half the world, and to control even more. For the first 100 years, Portugal and Spain led the way: Portugal in the east, Spain in the west. Portugal was a small country. It had far too few people ever to conquer or colonize large countries in Africa and Asia. But at sea the Portuguese were supreme. They established trading posts along the coasts, supported from the sea. In the Americas the situation was different. The Native Americans had never seen guns, or horses, or steel. A few determined Spaniards, inspired by religion, patriotism, or greed, destroyed the great Aztec and Inca Empires in Mexico and Peru. After 1600 the Portuguese lost many of their trading bases to the Dutch. The Spanish Empire lasted until the 19th century.

A gold pendant made by the Tairona people of Colombia, who resisted Spanish domination for 75 years.

At the beginning of the 16th century the richest, most advanced countries in the world were in the East: the Ottoman Empire, India, and China. These nations had no desire to investigate the West, whereas Europe was becoming eager to explore the possibilities of trade and conquest in distant lands.

Portugal, one of the smallest and poorest European nations, had already pioneered sea trading routes to West Africa. It quickly followed up the discovery of the eastward sea route to India, and by 1511 had established fortresses and trading posts at Cochin

Right: Francisco Pizarro (1478–1541) was one of hundreds of Spanish adventurers who went to the New World to find a fortune. Hearing of rich lands in the south, Pizarro gathered together 183 men and set off from Central America. Through deceit, he captured the Inca emperor, Atahualpa, demanding as a ransom a roomful of gold. The Incas filled a room with gold and Pizarro took the ransom, but he killed Atahualpa. He and his men then captured the Inca capital, Cuzco, in 1533.

Conquest of Peru

The Inca Empire covered much of South America west of the Andes mountains. Like the Aztecs in Mexico, the Incas were the last of a series of people to form empires with control over a large area. They ruled about 8 million people. Inca walls and buildings were built from huge stone blocks that fitted together perfectly and needed no mortar. Built high in the mountains, their cities were connected by paved roads. Like other Native Americans, they could not survive the guns of the invading Spanish, who were motivated by their desire for gold.

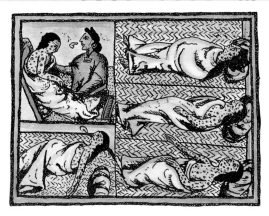

After the Spanish conquest there was a sharp fall in the Native American population. Exposed to European diseases for the first time, the Aztecs and Incas had no inbuilt resistance. Diseases that were mild to Europeans, such as measles (shown above), proved fatal to people who had never known them.

The Spanish forced many Native Americans to work as slaves in gold and silver mines (right). By 1650 the Spanish had shipped 16,000 tons of silver and 180 tons of gold to Europe. This included the ransom of golden artifacts paid – in vain – to save the Inca emperor, Atahualpa, from Francisco Pizarro.

A Dominican missionary

Christian missionaries believed it was their duty to spread Christianity to the Native Americans. One of the first missionaries was Bartolomé de las Casas (1474–1566), a Dominican friar. He wrote a history of Spanish colonization that condemned the practice of slavery in all its forms.

Jesuits

The leading missionaries were members of the Roman Catholic order known as Jesuits (right). Portuguese Jesuits visited the court of the Mughal emperor of India and tried to persuade him to become a Christian. They reached Japan and China soon after the first European sailors had established a sea route there. The Jesuits often wrote detailed reports of the people they lived among. One missionary in India made no converts, but spent ten years making a detailed map of the Ganges River.

Left: A plan showing African slaves packed into a ship for travel across the Atlantic Ocean.

The Slave Trade

The Portuguese first sold captives from West Africa as slaves in Portugal in 1434. Later, the Spanish colonists of the New World bought African slaves from the Portuguese to work in their mines and plantations alongside Native Americans. In spite of some protests, and fierce rebellions by the slaves, the slave trade became big business. By the time it ended in the 19th century, about 20 million Africans had passed through the trade forts of West Africa (right).

Americans from Spanish.
1521 Cortés captures Tenochtitlán, Aztec capital.
1535 Pizarro founds Lima.
1548 Jesuits reach Japan.
1556 Philip II, king of Spain.
1557 Portuguese at Macao.
1571 Spanish found Manila.
1580 Philip II becomes king of Portugal by force.

and Goa on the west coast of India, and Malacca on the Malay peninsula. In 1513 Afonso d'Albuquerque (1453–1515) reached the Moluccas, center of the fabulously valuable spice trade, and Ceylon (present-day Sri Lanka). By 1557 the Portuguese were trading with Japan from bases at Macao in China and Nagasaki in Japan. They never controlled all trade with the East, as they had hoped to do, but no Asian power could challenge them at sea.

The main thrust of the Spanish explorers was to the West. Spain sought not so much to trade as to set up new communities in the New World, first on Hispaniola (present-day Dominican Republic and Haiti) and Cuba in the Caribbean, where they did not thrive, and later in Panama. From there, Hernán Cortés (1485–1547) set out in 1518 to conquer the Aztecs of Mexico. Having forced their king, Montezuma II (1466–1520), to submit to Spain, he tried to

govern fairly; his letters show his fascination with the Aztec culture, whose capital city was larger than any in Europe, but where the wheel was unknown. But Cortés's men were greedy and ill-disciplined; in 1521 the cruelties of his deputy in his absence provoked an Aztec revolt. Montezuma, trying to calm the riot, was killed. Cortés lost many men in evacuating the capital, Tenochtitlán; he regrouped, retook it, and razed it to the ground, building Mexico City in its place.

Thousands of Aztecs later died from smallpox and other European diseases carried by the Spaniards, to which they had no resistance. Francisco Pizarro (1478–1541) was less high-minded than

Cortés in his ruthless conquest of the Inca Empire. Having captured and killed the emperor, Atahualpa, Pizarro looted his empire. He was murdered in Lima, the city he founded, by some of his former followers.

Native Americans died by the thousand in the huge silver mines discovered at Potosí in Bolivia (1545); to obtain more workers, the Spanish turned to Portuguese slave-traders and began to import slaves from West Africa.

1. Afonso d'Albuquerque, who colonized Goa, the Spice Islands, and Ceylon (Sri Lanka).

Discoverers

Although the Portuguese were the first Europeans to sail to India and beyond, and the Spaniards were the first to reach the Americas, explorers commissioned by the English and French – for example, John Cabot (c.1450–99) and Jacques Cartier (1492–1557) – were not far behind. Their interests, however, were in finding a sea route to the Far East, rather than in colonizing North America.

Right: Jacques Cartier reached present-day Montreal, in Canada, in 1535, but French settlement in the region didn't begin until 1608.

Sir Francis Drake (c.1540–96), a criminal to the Spanish, a hero to the English, was the most famous of 16th-century privateers. A fierce Protestant, he hated the Catholic Spanish.

The Northwest Passage

In the 16th and early 17th centuries, many sea captains, mainly English and French, sailed northwestward in the hope of finding a sea route to the Far East. They were disappointed to find North America in the way. Not knowing how wide the landmass was, they looked for a passage through to the Pacific Ocean. Jacques Cartier hoped the St. Lawrence River might take him there, and Henry Hudson (c.1550–1611) tried the Hudson River. They made many discoveries, but they never found a Northwest Passage.

This map of 1576 is the earliest world map printed in England. It shows all the continents except Australasia.

Trading companies

Early trade expeditions were financed by merchants, who pooled their investment in joint-stock companies – the forerunner of today's business corporations. These needed royal approval. A royal charter granted them special rights, such as a monopoly, which made competition in a particular trade illegal. The Dutch East India Company was the most powerful of these companies.

In search of a northeast passage

In 1553 an English ship set out to reach the Far East by sailing round northern Scandinavia and along the Russian coast. After reaching the White Sea, the expedition traveled overland to Moscow, opening the way for trade with Russia. In the 17th century, other merchants continued to the Caspian Sea and Iran. In 1596 a Dutch party led by Willem Barents (c.1550–97) became trapped in the Arctic ice and spent the winter there, escaping the next year in open boats.

A portrait of a Dutch merchant and his family in India in the 17th century. The Dutch liked their own country, and few wanted to settle in colonies abroad.

Traders and raiders

The Dutch, English, and French made profits by supplying Spanish colonies with goods that Spain itself could not provide. In times of war, privateers (licensed pirates) raided Spanish towns and attacked Spanish ships. Trade often continued even in wartime: the Dutch, for example, traded with Spanish colonies while fighting Spanish rule in the Netherlands.

Rise of the Dutch

In 1567 the people of the Netherlands rebelled against their Spanish rulers. The northern (Dutch) provinces gained independence by 1609. Their success filled the Dutch with confidence and energy. A nation of burghers – merchants, bankers, and shipowners – they were less dominated by landowning nobles than other European countries. The Dutch merchants and soldiers set out to build a commercial empire. They soon replaced the Portuguese (ruled by Spain after 1580) as the main European power in the East Indies.

A merchant ship under construction in Amsterdam. The Dutch had more merchant ships than the other seagoing nations put together.

MAJOR TRADE ROUTES AND AREAS AND PLACES CONTROLLED BY EUROPEAN POWERS.

AFRICA — ASIA — CHINA — INDIA — PHILIPPINES — PACIFIC OCEAN — Luanda — Zanzibar — Mozambique — Cape of Good Hope — INDIAN OCEAN — Batavia

Areas and places under control of European powers		Trade routes	
Dutch	Portuguese	Dutch	Portuguese
English	Spanish	English	Spanish
French		French	

1567 Dutch revolt against Spain.
1578 Drake visits California.
1580 Spain takes over Portugal.
1602 Dutch East India Company receives its charter.
1607 English colony established

Dutch, English, and French Expansion

In 1580 Spain was the strongest and by far the richest country in Europe; it had absorbed its only colonial rival, Portugal. Much of Spain's wealth came from the silver mines in its American empire. One hundred years later, however, Spain had become feeble and poor. Part of the trouble lay in the fact that most of its wealth came from its overseas colonies, and this discouraged business enterprise and industrial development. The cost of war also caused Spain's decline. During the 17th century Spain was at war with its chief continental rival, France, and with its Protestant enemies, the English and the Dutch. After a long struggle, in 1610 the Dutch gained independence from Spain. These three countries – France, England, and the Netherlands – challenged Spain's claim to rule the non-Christian world.

Australia and New Zealand

Europeans believed there was a huge southern continent in the Pacific. Dutch ships had touched on eastern Australia, which they thought was part of this continent. In 1642 the Dutch East India Company, looking for new opportunities, sent Abel Tasman (c.1603–1659) on a more southerly route across the Indian Ocean. He discovered Tasmania and New Zealand. In the 18th century, French and English captains discovered more of the Pacific islands.

Abel Tasman and his family. He was the first European to meet the New Zealand Maoris, who quickly drove him away.

Early English colonists in America were in danger of failing until they began to grow local tobacco.

Cloves

Nutmeg

Tobacco

SEE ALSO
p. 132 SOUTHEAST ASIA AND THE SPICE TRADE

Overseas produce

The Americas produced crops previously unknown in Europe, such as tobacco, which became a huge source of profit. The English in India started the profitable trade in tea with China. Like American coffee, tea was new to the Europeans.

West Africa

The Portuguese found some gold in Africa, as well as a coarse form of pepper, and a few luxuries such as ostrich feathers and ivory. But African goods were disappointing compared with those of the East Indies. The European trading stations along the West African coast were built for the slave trade. There were no European colonies in Africa except Cape Town, founded to supply Dutch merchant ships sailing to and from the East Indies.

A European trading for slaves in West Africa (1820). Slaves were supplied to European traders by people from the small coastal states, who seized captives from inland.

North American colonies

The first permanent English colony in North America was founded in Virginia in 1607. It was a commercial venture: the colonists intended to return to England. Farther north, the Puritan colonists in New England were true immigrants, who were determined to create a new society. In Canada, the first French settlers hoped to make enough money in the fur trade to buy property in France. Genuine settlement began about 1608. The Dutch founded a settlement at New Amsterdam (present-day New York City) in 1621, but lost it to the English in 1664.

Virginia Dare was the first English child born in America (1587). Later, the Roanoke colony to which she belonged disappeared.

New France

In 1608 the French settled the St. Lawrence valley in Canada, calling it "New France." Their main centers were Montreal and Quebec. During the 18th century they spread down the Mississippi valley and claimed a large part of the continent, naming their territory "Louisiana." In 1763 the British took over New France, while Louisiana passed to Spain.

Native American totems from the northwest were greatly admired by European explorers.

Colonial contests

By making their base at Batavia, east of Portuguese Malacca, the Dutch gained control of the Spice Islands' trade, and drove out merchants from the English East India Company. They also took Brazil from the Portuguese, but lost it after Portugal regained independence from Spain in 1640. After 1689, with Dutch power fading, the main contest was between France and England.

Dutch and Portuguese fighting in Brazil.

Two discoveries

In 1721 a Dutch captain named Jacob Roggeveen (1659–1729) by chance found tiny Easter Island in the Pacific Ocean. It was so far from land that its inhabitants thought they were the only people on Earth. In 1771, in Canada, an agent of the British fur company on Hudson's Bay reached the Arctic Ocean while trying to find a land route to the Pacific.

Animal and plant life in the New World was strange to Europeans. The anteater was just one of the many new creatures they found.

at Jamestown.
1608 Settlement of Quebec.

1655 English capture Jamaica.
1619 Batavia (Jakarta) founded.

1652 Dutch gain Cape of Good Hope off southern Africa.

1682 Pennsylvania founded.
1718 New Orleans founded.

1775 American colonies rebel against Britain.

Until about 1780 Europeans believed in an economic theory called mercantilism. Mercantilists thought that the world held a certain amount of wealth. The country that gained the greatest share of this wealth would grow rich and powerful. A country that failed would become poor and was likely to be plundered by its more successful rivals. It was widely believed that a country could only increase its wealth from overseas sources. Spain, for example, had amassed great wealth from the silver mines in its South American empire.

With every country trying to gain a larger share of what they believed was a limited amount of wealth, the natural result was fierce competition leading to violence. The Dutch, English, and French, besides their conflicts with Spain, were often at war with each other.

Governments made great efforts to protect their overseas trade from rivals. The Dutch East India Company, for example, was set up in 1602 to protect Dutch merchants in the Indian Ocean. It effectively drove the British and Portuguese out of the East Indies (now mainly Indonesia). The French and English set up similar companies.

Governments also passed laws to protect their own trade from foreign competition. The English Navigation Act (1651) laid down that all English trade should be carried in English ships. It was aimed against the Dutch, who dominated what was called the "carrying trade," supplying transportation for other nations' goods. This resulted in a series of wars between the English and the Dutch (1652–74), which marked the end of Dutch supremacy in overseas trade.

The purpose of colonies was to provide more wealth for the colonizing, or "mother," nation. Colonies also provided valuable products such as tobacco and furs. By 1700 England had large colonies in North America, but its most valuable colony was the tiny sugar-growing island of Barbados. After the decline of the Dutch, England and France were the leading colonial and sea powers. The contest between them lasted for over a century, and ended with the English, or British, dominant. That success was to make Britain the greatest imperial, economic, and political power in the world during the 19th century.

1. A Dutch naturalist's painting of a fig from an expedition to Brazil in the 1630s.

In 1380 Dmitri Donskoi (1350–89), prince of Moscow and grand prince of Vladimir, defeated a Mongol force under Khan Mamai at Kulikovo on the Don River, freeing Moscow for a time from Mongol control.

Ivan the Terrible, the first czar

In 1547 Ivan IV (1530–84), grand prince of Muscovy, was the first ruler to be crowned czar, a Russian title that came originally from the Latin word *caesar*, or "absolute ruler." Ivan earned his reputation as "the Terrible," with a reign of terror that reduced the power of the boyars, the highest aristocracy. Hundreds of aristocrats were murdered and their estates given to landowners serving in the army and the government. They, in return, supplied the army with peasants and horses. Ivan killed church leaders who opposed him, and in a fit of rage he even murdered his oldest son.

A 16th-century portrait of Ivan the Terrible.

Serfdom

Constant warfare reduced Muscovy's peasant population, depriving the army of soldiers and the landowners of people to work the land. During the 16th century the czars passed laws that turned the peasants into serfs, tied to the land. Serfdom became the basis of the Russian economy. This was very different from what was happening in Western Europe, where serfdom was dying out and the growth of trade led to the use of money as royal payment in return for service.

First of the Romanovs

The so-called "Time of Troubles" ended in 1613, when Michael (1596–1645, left), founder of the Romanov Dynasty, was elected czar. Michael was a weak ruler, and serfdom increased during his reign. The Romanov family, however, was powerful, and ruled Russia for the next 300 years.

RUSSIAN EXPANSION FROM 1581 TO 1800.
Most of this enormous area was acquired from native peoples. The illustrations below show some of these people in their traditional costumes.

ARCTIC OCEAN

YAKUTSK

Kamchatka peninsula

RUSSIAN EMPIRE

• St. Petersburg

• Moscow

Ural Mountains

• Surgut

• Tobolsk

Okhotsk •

• Orenburg

• Tomsk

AMUR

CASPIAN SEA

ARAL SEA

• Irkutsk

ACQUISITIONS

| Russian Empire in 1581 | Territory added in 1650s but given up in 1689 to China | 1581–98 | 1618–89 | 1725–62 | Kazakh territory subject to Russia |
| | | 1598–1618 | 1689–1725 | 1762–1800 | |

A Lapp from the Kola peninsula, which Russia acquired in the 15th century. The Lapps are nomadic hunters.

A Mordvinian woman from the Mordovian Republic west of Moscow, which Russia acquired in the 16th century.

A woman from the khanate of Kazan, which Ivan the Terrible captured in 1552.

A Cherkess woman from the Caucasus region.

A woman from Finland, which Russia acquired in 1809.

A merchant from Kaluga, on the Oka River.

1462 Ivan III becomes grand prince of Muscovy.

1480 Ivan III proclaims Muscovy's independence from

Mongol rule.
1547 Ivan IV, the Terrible,

crowned czar of Russia.
1605–13 Time of Troubles.

1613 Michael, first of Romanov Dynasty, becomes czar.

The Rise of Russia

After the state of Muscovy threw off Mongol rule in 1480 and expanded in all directions, its grand prince became known as the czar of Russia. The first czar, Ivan IV, was crowned in 1547, but his brutal regime led to him becoming known as Ivan "the Terrible." He and later czars bound Russia's peasants to the land as serfs, and serfdom became the basis of the Russian economy. Toward the end of the 17th century, Peter the Great adopted Western European ideas and based his new capital, St. Petersburg, on European models. Until this time Sweden had barred Russian expansion to the Baltic Sea, but a series of wars resulted in Swedish lands being ceded to Russia in 1721, making Russia a European power.

During the 15th century Moscow became the most powerful Russian city. Ivan III (1440–1505), the grand prince of Muscovy, known as Ivan "the Great," won control of Moscow's main rival, Novgorod. In 1472 he married the niece of the last Byzantine emperor, and in 1480 threw off Mongol control. Under Ivan's rule, Muscovy expanded eastward into Siberia. This expansion led to Muscovy's grand prince being known as the czar, or emperor, of Russia.

Ivan IV was the first to be crowned czar, in 1547. He became known as Ivan "the Terrible" because of the brutality he showed to his opponents. He fought the Tartars at Astrakhan and

Peter the Great's powerful character matched his stature; he was nearly 2 m (7 ft) tall. This portrait of him was painted in 1698 in England.

Peter the Great

At age 10 Peter I (1672–1725), later called "the Great," was made co-czar with his half-brother under the regency of their older sister, Sophia. In 1689 Peter forced his sister to retire to a convent, and in 1696 his brother died, leaving him sole ruler. The following year Peter set off with a group of envoys on a tour of Europe (1697–98). He visited Austria, Germany, and England, learning about Western technology, which he introduced to Russia. After his return he founded the city of St. Petersburg (1703) on marshy land that had been gained from Sweden. Thousands of serfs died during the city's construction. Peter saw it as his "window on Europe."

While Peter the Great was away in Europe in 1698, a small number of Russia's 20,000 streltsy, or "musketeers," staged a rebellion. On his return, Peter had more than a thousand of the rebels hanged or beheaded in or near Moscow.

Russian envoys

From the 16th century on Russian envoys were received with great interest in Western Europe. The envoys wore fine robes and unusual hats. They rarely carried money, but took with them a wealth of furs. The demand for furs from the West encouraged Russia to expand farther eastward into Siberia. This woodcut from 1576 (left) shows a group of envoys and merchants at the court of Holy Roman Emperor Maximilian II (1564–76).

In this popular woodcut, which circulated widely after Peter the Great's death in 1725, a cat is being dragged to its grave by the mice it tormented. The mice symbolize the many groups of people whom Peter had persecuted.

Charles XII (1682–1718), king of Sweden, died while invading Norway during the Great Northern War.

The Great Northern War

In this series of wars (1700–21), Russia, Denmark, and Poland fought against Sweden for control of the Baltic Sea. Charles XII of Sweden was defeated by the Russians under Peter the Great at Poltava in 1709. He fled to the Turks, who turned against Russia two years later. Finally the Treaty of Nystad in 1721 gave Russia large amounts of land, including access to the Baltic Sea.

As Empress Catherine I, Peter's widow helped the Russian peasants, lowered taxes, and reduced the power of local officials.

A Kyrgyz nomad. Kyrgyzstan became independent again in 1991.

A hunter from the Kuril Islands, off the Kamchatka peninsula. Russia founded a colony there in 1795.

A woman from Estonia, which Russia gained in 1721 after the Great Northern War.

Empress of Russia

Catherine I (1684–1727) was the daughter of Lithuanian peasants. As a young girl she married a Swedish army officer, and in 1702 she was captured during the Great Northern War with Sweden. Three years later she became the mistress of Peter the Great, and in 1712 became his second wife. Peter had her crowned empress a year before he died, but he had not named her as his successor. The guards regiments, with whom she was popular, put her on the throne.

---

took their lands. His forces then crossed the Urals and conquered western Siberia. He was defeated when he tried to win lands neighboring the Baltic Sea.

After Ivan's death Russia suffered weak leadership and in 1605 a former monk pretended to be Ivan's son Dmitri, who had actually died in 1591. This "False Dmitri" invaded Russia with Polish troops in 1604. He was joined by many discontented Russians and became czar in 1605, but he was killed the following year. In 1608 a second False Dmitri turned up, followed by a third in 1611. During this period of political upheaval (1605–13), known as the "Time of Troubles," there were peasant revolts, and landowners and

Cossacks fought each other. Polish invaders were driven out of Moscow in 1612, and the following year Michael Romanov (1596–1645) was elected czar, founding a dynasty that ruled until 1917.

During the 17th century Russia took much of Ukraine and extended its control of Siberia all the way to the Pacific Ocean. Peter I "the Great" (1672–1725) came to full power in 1696. He was influenced by the political and commercial ideas of Western Europe, where he had traveled. During Peter's reign Russia expanded to the Baltic Sea in the Great Northern War with Sweden. In 1703 he founded St. Petersburg and made it his capital in 1712. Peter increased his power over

aristocrats, church officials, and serfs, and turned Russia into a major European force. After his death in 1725 there was a series of struggles for the throne. In 1762 Peter's grandson, Peter III (1728–62), ordered Russia's withdrawal from the Seven Years' War with Prussia, which displeased the army, who deposed and killed him. His wife, Catherine II "the Great" (1729–96), took the throne and ruled until her death in 1796.

> ### SEE ALSO
> p. 82 9TH- AND 10TH-CENTURY INVADERS
> p. 100 RUSSIA AND EASTERN EUROPE
> p. 192 THE RUSSIAN EMPIRE

1. Statue of Peter the Great.

2. Portrait of Catherine II, who continued Russia's expansion.

1584–90 Roanoke, first English colony fails.

1603 First French colonies, in Newfoundland and Nova Scotia.

1607 First permanent English settlement in Virginia.

1608 French found Quebec.
1612 Colonists in Virginia

cultivate tobacco.
1620 Pilgrim Fathers establish

Colonial North America

The continent of North America was a place of dreams for many Europeans in the 1600s. For some it offered the chance to escape religious persecution and to live and worship in peace. For others it was a place where fortunes could be made by trading in goods that were highly prized in Europe: for example, furs, sugar, and tobacco. Above all, European powers saw it as a place where they could lay claim to huge areas of land. Settlers came from England, France, Spain, the Netherlands, Sweden, and Germany. Each group established its own colonies. At first the settlers lived peacefully alongside the Native American peoples of North America and, after suffering great initial hardships, they learned from them how to survive in their new environment. But as the colonies expanded, conflicts broke out.

Pocahontas (c.1595–1617), seen here in European clothes, was a Native American princess.

For some 200 years the history of North America was one of colonization by the powers of Europe at the expense of the native peoples of the continent. An unstoppable tide of people left Europe to begin new lives in a "New World," and traders came in search of goods to buy and sell.

At first the Native Americans and Europeans existed together on friendly terms, and gifts were exchanged between them. Some Native Americans, such as Pocahontas and Tisquantum, were taken by settlers to visit the countries of Europe. The Europeans learned from the local

The first colonies

The earliest colonists in North America were mostly English and French. Between 1607 and the 1730s the first English colonies became established. Known as the Thirteen Colonies, they extended along the east coast from present-day Canada south to the borders of Florida. It was a vast area, some fifteen times larger than that of Britain. The French established their colonies mostly in eastern Canada and in Louisiana, the Spanish in the southwest, and the Germans in the center of the continent. By 1700 there were an estimated one million people of European origin living in North America.

Trade and colonies

The first English colonies in North America were founded in the early 17th century. Many of the colonists were religious refugees anxious to build independent communities, but they were backed by merchants who hoped for profits. For the government, the colonies were useful as producers of raw materials which could not be grown in Britain, and as markets where British goods could be sold. The reason for the empire that Britain had gained by 1763 was, in one word, trade. That included the slave trade, which made many merchants rich at the cost of death and misery to millions of Africans.

The Puritans had turned against the flamboyant European clothes of the early 1600s. Instead, both men and women wore plain styles of clothing. Although escaping from persecution themselves, the Puritans of Massachusetts were not tolerant of others' ways. They laid down rigid rules about dress and conduct in the colony.

The Puritans

The Puritans were originally a group of English Protestants who were dissatisfied with the Church of England. Many emigrated to the American colonies, where they led simple, religious lives. Large-scale settlement began in 1630, when a group of wealthy Puritans founded a colony in Massachusetts Bay.

In the fall of 1621 the English settlers of Plymouth Colony who had survived their first winter harvested their first year's crops. They held a thanksgiving feast and shared food with the Native Americans who had helped them survive.

Plymouth Colony.
1626 Dutch found New

Amsterdam on East Coast.
1642 French found Montreal.

1664 New Amsterdam claimed by England; renamed New York.

1682 France claims all of Mississippi Basin.

1744–48 Britain and France at war in North America.

peoples many things that helped them to survive in their new land. But as the settlers' colonies became established and grew bigger, the Native Americans sensed that their way of life was threatened. Disputes, usually over European land claims, led to frequent and extremely violent wars.

The French, who were primarily traders, did not seize Native American land at the same rate as the English. They formed valuable trading alliances with some groups, such as the Hurons.

In the end, contact with Europeans proved disastrous for the native peoples. Their lands were seized and their traditional ways of life destroyed; some were sold into slavery; and worst of all, European diseases to which they had no immunity, such as smallpox, spread quickly among them. Native settlements and entire nations were wiped out, and colonists moved in to take their land.

From the 1650s onward, North America also became the fighting grounds for conflicts between the European powers – France, Spain, the Netherlands, and England – each of which wanted to control all of North America, not just a part of it. The main rivalry was between France and England and there was ongoing conflict between the two nations.

1. Corn was a new and valuable crop to the European settlers.

2. A Native American bead belt called a wampum. It shows a European and a Native American clasping hands in friendship.

3. Title page from A History of the Indian Wars, published in 1812.

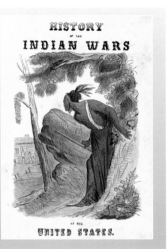

Plymouth Colony

Plymouth Colony in New England was founded in 1620 by a group of about 100 Puritans. They had sailed from Plymouth, England. Many years later this group of settlers became known as the Pilgrim Fathers. The group had originally intended to join an existing colony in Virginia, but were blown off course by a storm and landed on a deserted coast near Cape Cod. In the terrible cold of their first winter, half the settlers died. Had it not been for the help of Native Americans, who taught them about local foods, the colony might have failed. From the Native Americans the settlers learned about new foods such as turkey, squash, and corn.

Above: By 1627 Plymouth Colony had grown into a community of about 200 people. A small fort at the end of the main street guarded the settlement, which was surrounded by a timber palisade, or fence. Within this boundary were the houses and gardens of the settlers.

Several European nations claimed territory in North America, to which they gave names such as New Spain (Mexico), New France (Canada), and New England (the northeastern coastal area).

LAND CLAIMED BY ENGLAND, FRANCE, AND SPAIN IN ABOUT 1750.

□ British
■ French
■ Spanish

Tisquantum, a Patuxet Native American, learned English and acted as an interpreter and guide. He befriended the settlers of Plymouth Colony and taught them how to grow corn, and where to catch fish and eels.

Above: View of the port of Manhattan around 1750. The Dutch New Netherland colony was established in the Hudson River region in 1621. Dutch merchants bought Manhattan Island from Native Americans in 1626. The Dutch colony was overrun by English forces in 1664 and the growing town of New Amsterdam became New York.

Tobacco trade

Some early European colonists hoped to find gold. Instead, settlers were introduced to the tobacco plant, the dried leaves of which were burned and smoked by the Native Americans. The settlers began growing fields of tobacco, exporting the leaves to Europe. For a time, tobacco was more valuable than gold.

The fur trade was a major source of wealth to Europeans. Trappers sold the pelts from beavers, otters, and deer to merchants from Europe. This trapper is wearing snowshoes and smoking tobacco in a small pipe.

SEE ALSO
p. 60 ANCIENT NORTH AMERICA
p. 116 DUTCH, ENGLISH, AND FRENCH EXPANSIONISM
p. 168 THE UNITED STATES OF AMERICA

African Empires

Between 1500 and 1800 several important empires developed in Sub-Saharan Africa. Increasingly people came to live under the rule of a central government, with an economy based on agriculture and trade. Islam, already well established in North Africa, spread farther down the east coast. During this time Europeans began exploring the interior of Africa and expanded trade along the coast. In the early 16th century the Atlantic slave trade was established which would have dramatic consequences for millions of Africans in the centuries to come.

The Songhai Empire

The Songhai Empire was the third great kingdom in west Africa, following the Ghana and Mali empires. It began in the 15th century and survived until 1591 when it fell to Moroccan invaders. Under their leader Sunni Ali, who was known for his bravery and ruthlessness, the Songhai built up their empire, controlling most of the trade across the Sahara and conquering the network of trading cities such as Gao, Jenne, and Timbuktu. These cities also became centers of education and Muslim religion.

The Songhai leader Sunni Ali (died 1492) was known in Arabic as "Sunni Ali Ber" or Ali the Great.

AFRICAN STATES AND TRADE ROUTES 1500–1800.

This map shows many of the kingdoms in Africa during the 15th–18th centuries, as well as the extent of Islamic penetration by 1800.

This 16th century ivory carving from Benin depicts a Portuguese soldier taking slaves for trade. The Portuguese, the first Europeans to visit Africa, arrived in Benin City in 1486.

Portuguese exploration of Africa

The Portuguese first arrived on the west coast of Africa in the mid-15th century. In 1488 explorer Bartolomeu Dias sailed around the southern tip of Africa, and by the mid-16th century Portugal had set up a series of trading posts along Africa's east coast.

Statue of Behanzin, the last king of the Dahomey empire, represented with the head of a bird and body of a shark.

TUNIS
TRIPOLI
CYRENAICA
AIR
KAARTA
KANEM-BORNU
DARFUR
FUNJ
MOSSI STATES
KONG EMPIRE
HAUSA STATES
WADAI
BAGIRMI
AWSA
ASANTE
OLD OYO
BENIN
ETHIOPIA
DAHOMEY
OROMO
KUBA
CONGO
LUBA
LUNDA
LOZI
ROZWI

- ▢ Songhai Empire
- ▢ Kingdom of Adal
- ▢ Kingdom of Mwenemutapa
- ▢ Empire of Kanem-Bornu
- ▢ French territory
- ▢ Dutch territory
- ▢ Ottoman Empire
- ▢ Portuguese territory
- — Southern limit of Islam
- — Trade routes

Southern empires

South of the Congo River in central Africa several Bantu-speaking African states developed, including the Luba and Lunda kingdoms. Southeast of these kingdoms the Mwenemutapa Empire was well known to early European traders.

This statue shows the Luba prince Tshibinda Ilunga. During the 15th century he married a Lunda queen, whose people were so disapproving that they migrated south to present-day Angola, founding new kingdoms.

Small Empires

Small powerful empires also developed along the coast of west Africa. The kingdom of Benin flourished during the 15th–17th centuries and at its height controlled most of modern Nigeria. West of the Niger River was the Yoruba kingdom of Oyo, established in the 17th century. Like Benin it was famous for producing works of bronze and terra-cotta. Further west was the kingdom of Dahomey, which flourished during the 17th–19th centuries. In the early 18th century Dahomey king Agaja became a major supplier of slaves to Europe. He is famous for creating an army of women known as Amazons.

This map was created by Portuguese explorer Diego Homem in 1558. Europeans began arriving in Africa in the mid-15th century, and they soon discovered the continent's wealth of resources. Seeking gold, ivory, wood, and slaves they began to develop and expand trade links to the coasts. Although the Portuguese and Dutch did establish colonies in southern Africa, kingdoms ruled by African leaders continued to develop and expand in most areas.

1592 Britain joins other European nations in the slave trade.

1626 French begin to settle in Senegal and Madagascar.

1652 Cape Town founded by Jan van Riebeck

1701 Rise of the Asante Kingdom under Osei Tutu.

1724 Dahomey is important partner for European slavers.

When Queen Njinga met with the Portuguese they refused to offer her a seat. One of her followers knelt down for her to sit on so that she could meet the Europeans on equal terms.

Islam continues to spread

Between 1500 and 1800 Islam continued to spread. Starting in northwest Africa, it traveled further east and south along the coast of the Horn. Islam permeated all aspects of life, not just politics and religion, bringing new ideas, customs, language, scholarship, art, and architecture.

This beautiful late-17th-century copy of the Qu'ran, the Muslim holy book, combines African and Arabic influences.

Arrival of French and Dutch settlers in Cape Colony

Representatives of the Dutch East India Company established a trade settlement in 1652 at the southern tip of Africa. More Dutch and French settlers soon arrived, and by the 18th century they had taken over almost all of the lands belonging to the native Khoikhoi people. Cape Town became a major port on the way from Europe to the East Indies.

European explorers

Europeans were fascinated by the mysteries of Africa, and during the 19th century exploratory expeditions were sent almost annually. German missionaries Ludwig Krapf and Johannes Rebman, for example, became the first Europeans to see Mt. Kilimanjaro, Africa's highest mountain, in 1848. French explorer Pierre de Brazza founded the country that is now the Congo. English explorers John Speke and Richard Burton discovered the source of the Nile River in 1857.

Opposition to the Portuguese

The Portuguese established a colony in what is now Angola in 1575, and it became a major center for the slave trade with Europe. Queen Njinga, who ruled the kingdom of Ndongo 1624–63, prevented the Portuguese from expanding their empire inland. She took in fugitive slaves from Portuguese Angola, encouraged Africans under Portuguese rule to rebel, and recruited Portuguese-trained Africans into her army. She finally persuaded the Portuguese to sign a treaty enforcing the limits of their power.

The trans-Atlantic slave trade

Portugal began the European slave trade in the early 16th century. It expanded because of the need for agricultural workers in the new colonies in the Americas. The Dutch, French, British, and Danish soon joined the Portuguese, and between 1500 and 1800 around 20 million people were sold as slaves from Africa. Most of the slaves were provided by other Africans, leaders of empires who grew rich from the trade.

Ethiopia

The Christian empire of Ethiopia tried to expand into neighboring Islamic lands in the Horn of Africa, but in 1529, a Muslim religious leader called Ahmad Gran proclaimed a holy war against Ethiopia and won many victories. After this Ethiopia fell victim to southern invaders and went into a period of decline.

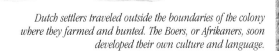

Dutch settlers traveled outside the boundaries of the colony where they farmed and hunted. The Boers, or Afrikaners, soon developed their own culture and language.

Scottish explorer Mungo Park (1771–1806) explored the Niger River.

Kanem-Bornu

The empire of Kanem-Bornu in central Africa lasted for around 1000 years, until the 19th century. Based on trade, the state became Muslim in the 11th century. During the 16th century King Idris Aloma, who got firearms from the Turks in North Africa, greatly expanded the empire.

King Alkemy of Guinea, shown here as a powerful warlord, provided slaves to France.

Empire building in Africa began in the early Middle Ages with the prosperity brought by trade. In west Africa, the great Songhai Empire grew and flourished during the 15th and 16th centuries. Other smaller states, such as the kingdoms of Benin, Oyo, and Dahomey, also expanded their empires during this period. In central Africa, the Kanem-Bornu Empire, established in the 9th century, survived for 1000 years.

Although its lands were greatly reduced, Ethiopia revived during the Gondar period. King Fasiladas built the city of Gondar and this castle, the first fixed royal residence, in 1636.

In southern Africa, several Bantu-speaking states developed, including the Luba Kingdom, which included many tribes. East Africa was almost totally under Islamic control, except for the Christian Empire of Ethiopia, which went into a period of decline but managed to survive.

African leaders continued to build their empires after the arrival of Europeans, who traveled to Africa from the 15th century as explorers, missionaries, and traders. As European countries developed more of a demand for Africa's resources, including slaves, they began to claim more power in the continent. Despite this, during the 18th century the majority of African leaders managed to retain political control of their kingdoms.

Emperor Hongwu

Hongwu, the son of a landless laborer, was born Zhu Yuanzhang. Orphaned at age 16, he went to a Buddhist monastery to learn to read and write. At age 24 he joined a rebel group fighting Mongol rule and soon became one of its leaders. In 1368 he took the name Hongwu ("Vast Military Power") and declared himself emperor. His aim was to drive the hated Mongols from China and repair the damage they had done to the Chinese economy. In this, he was successful.

Hongwu was famously ugly, with a protruding lower jaw, pockmarked skin, and a pig-like face. His enemies made fun of the fact that his family name, Zhu, sounded exactly like the Chinese word for "pig."

Zheng He, the great explorer of the Ming Dynasty, aboard the flagship of his fleet. A Muslim himself, he was able to make friends with the Muslim leaders he met on his travels. His expedition fleets were huge. The first consisted of 63 large ships and 225 small ships carrying 27,000 men.

Admiral Zheng He brought back from his expeditions species of plants and animals unknown to the Chinese. One of these was the giraffe, first seen in China in 1414. In this painting on silk, a foreign visitor is leading a giraffe intended as a present for the emperor.

The Ming capital

The first Ming emperors ruled from Nanjing, but in 1421 Beijing became China's capital city. Beijing was a series of walled enclosures, one inside the other. At the center was the palace, known as the Forbidden City. Movement between the different enclosures was through gates in the walls, which were strictly guarded. During the Ming Dynasty Beijing was greatly expanded by enclosing more areas within defensive walls, and by 1600 it was the largest city in the world. It was home to a vast number of civil and military officials, who supervised the smallest details of the lives of the Chinese people.

The Gate of Supreme Harmony in the Forbidden City, Beijing. In front of it was a large courtyard where the emperor or members of his court would meet visiting Chinese and foreigner.

Exploration and growth

The main purpose of the overseas expeditions of the Ming Dynasty was to set up Chinese colonies. This plan was largely a failure. But the expeditions led to the establishment of trading routes and to trading arrangements with Portugal, then the leading European seafaring nation. The Chinese soon discovered the advantages of overseas trade; they exported Chinese products such as Ming porcelain and silk in exchange for European silver. In 1557 the Portuguese were allowed to set up their own trading post at Macao in southern China. From about 1560, Chinese cargoes were also carried across the Pacific Ocean to Acapulco in Mexico, and from there across the Atlantic Ocean to Europe.

1368 Ming Dynasty founded.
1388 Mongols driven from China.

1405–33 Expeditions to India, Persian Gulf, and East Africa.

1421 Chinese capital moves from Nanjing to Beijing.

1556 Earthquake in Shensi province, northwestern China,

kills more than 800,000 people.
1557 Portugal establishes first

Ming China

The Mongols ruled China for less than 100 years. After their leader Kubilai Khan died in 1294, the Mongol Empire began to fall apart. In 1368 a rebel leader, Hongwu, became emperor of China. His dynasty, the Ming, lasted for just over 300 years. Hongwu's first task was to bring China under his control, and he dealt out fearsome punishments to anyone who opposed him. He died in 1398. From about 1400 onward China saw a period of expansion. Chinese ships undertook a number of great expeditions, and the army invaded Mongolia and Vietnam. These invasions failed, and the Ming Dynasty went on the defensive. The Great Wall was rebuilt, and a fleet was built to defend China's shipping from Japanese pirates. The Ming Dynasty lasted until 1644, when it fell to the Manchus.

A painting on silk of the legendary Chinese warrior Guan Yu. Ming emperors and their families loved to hear and re-tell stories of this hero.

Hongwu (ruled 1368–1398), the first Ming emperor, believed in his own supreme power and in ruthlessly punishing anyone who disagreed with him. He took personal charge and worked hard on the smallest details of government. Hongwu is remembered in Chinese history as a harsh ruler, but one who restored prosperity to a country that had been almost destroyed by the Mongols.

Agriculture was improved by a program of new irrigation works. Huge areas of devastated forest were re-planted. In 1411 the Grand Canal system linking the cities of northern and southern

Chinese traditional medicine

Chinese medicine developed methods of treating illness that were quite different to Western practices. They made great use of medicinal plants such as ephedra, which was boiled to produce a treatment for asthma, hay fever, and coughs. The Chinese understood the circulation of the blood, and the aim of Chinese medicine was to ensure a good flow of *chi*, or "life-force," through the body.

SEE ALSO
p. 86 CHINESE CIVILIZATION
p. 88 THE MONGOL EMPIRE
p. 114 PORTUGUESE AND SPANISH EXPANSION

This illustration from a Chinese medical book shows the twelve pulse positions, which were used to check on a patient's health and flow of chi, *or "life-force."*

A Ming house

A typical Ming house was built of bricks or clay and had a curved, tiled roof. The family living quarters faced south, while the north-facing wall was blank to keep out evil spirits. The inner courtyard was used by the family. Servants and guests shared the outer courtyard and lived in rooms built around its walls.

Ming porcelain

The best-known product of the Ming period was its decorated porcelain, which is still highly prized all over the world. The best was made at Jingdehzen in southwestern China, where the clay was particularly white and smooth. Thousands of craftsmen worked in the potteries there. At first, Ming porcelain was reserved for use by the emperor and his court, but later large quantities were exported to Japan and Southeast Asian countries. By about 1600 Ming porcelain was being collected in the Middle East and Europe.

Ming porcelain was decorated by hand before being glazed. In a set of items, the decoration on each piece had to be exactly alike.

This clay model of the house of a Ming landowner was found in his tomb. The much larger imperial palaces followed a similar pattern.

This ceramic table screen, dating from the first years of the 16th century, carries a verse from the Qu'ran and was probably made for export to a Muslim country.

Trade

In the Ming period, China's main exports were porcelain and silk. Silk was exported both as cloth and as finished articles. Silver from South and Central America was the main import, but Spanish and Portuguese traders also introduced the Chinese to new crops such as sweet potatoes, maize, and peanuts.

The Jesuit missionary Matteo Ricci arrived in China in 1582. He impressed the Chinese by his efforts to learn the language and study classical Chinese literature. They also respected, and benefited from, his knowledge of geography, astronomy, and mathematics.

European trading base in China.
1582 Arrival of first Jesuit

missionary in China.
1627–28 Famine in northern

China leads to rebellion.
1642 Thousands die when rebels

cut banks of Yellow River.
1644 Ming Dynasty replaced by

Manchus, non-Chinese people from north of the Great Wall.

China was perfected. The landless peasants, of whom Hongwu had been one in his youth, were encouraged to own land. The result of this increasing prosperity was that China's population grew from an estimated 60 million in 1393 to 130 million by 1580. Meanwhile, China attempted to

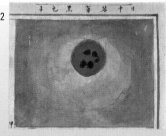

make more contacts with the outside world. Under a brilliant admiral, Zheng He, Chinese ocean-going ships,

or "junks," undertook seven great expeditions between 1404 and 1433, sailing as far west as east Africa.

But when Zheng He died in 1434, China's seafaring ambitions died with him. By 1450, following a number of failed invasions of neighboring states, the Ming Dynasty had become more inward-looking. Mongol armies were still threatening China from the north. To combat this threat the Great Wall was rebuilt and turned into a fortress running across all of northern China. The Ming emperors from the middle of the 16th century proved unable to control

their empire, and a series of floods, famines, and outbreaks of disease led to great discontent, especially in the north. One rebellion followed another, and in 1644 rebels took over the Ming capital, Beijing. The last Ming emperor committed suicide, but before the rebels could set up their own government, invaders from north of the Great Wall, the Manchus, took control. Some of the most important features of the Ming Dynasty were its great flourishing of arts and crafts (notably blue-and-white porcelain); closer contact with the outside world through exploration; the arrival of the first Portuguese traders; and contact with Jesuit missionaries.

1. This ivory figure of a woman from the Ming period was used as a teaching aid for students of medicine. She has very small feet – a Chinese ideal of beauty.

2. The Ming Emperor Zhu Gao-Zhi painted this picture of atmospheric effects round the sun during a period of sunspot activity in 1425.

1500 Safavid Dynasty founded.
1500 Shaybani Khan creates

Uzbek confederation.
1513 Portuguese attack on

Aden repelled. **1516** Ottomans conquer Egypt and Arabia.

1526 Babur defeats Afghans at Panipat.

1571 Ottoman fleet defeated at Lepanto.

Muslim Empires

In the early 16th century four powers were established in the area of Islam comprising west and south Asia. They were the Ottomans in Turkey and the Near East, the Safavids in Iran (Persia), the Mughals in India, and the much smaller federation of the Uzbeks in Turkistan. The first three especially were formidable powers. Their great cities, such as Istanbul, Isfahan, and Agra, proclaimed their wealth and culture. The Ottomans, the strongest military power, penetrated deep into Europe, attacking Vienna, capital of the Holy Roman Empire. Some Europeans felt that their whole continent was in danger of being conquered. But by the 18th century, all these powers had faded. The Ottomans had been driven back to southeast Europe. The Safavids had been overthrown. Mughal rule in India was breaking down, and Uzbekistan had split into separate states, or khanates.

The Muslim empires had many things in common. They were all descended from nomadic Turkic or Mongol tribes. They all belonged to Islam, and educated men all spoke the language of Islam, Arabic. Persian was also spoken – and written by poets – in the Mughal and Ottoman courts, as well as in Iran.

Sharing a religion did not prevent conflict in Islam, especially between the Shi'ite Safavids and the Sunni Ottomans, any more than it prevented conflicts between the nations of Christian Europe. In fact, Muslim conflicts were carried into Europe. The Ottomans allied with France against the Holy Roman Empire. The Safavids allied with Austria against the Ottomans.

But these wars did not prevent co-operation in the region. The rulers of the Muslim empires all supported trade, and the greatest of them devoted their time and wealth not only to war but also to building roads, bridges, and carvanserais (roadside inns), and making the country safe for traveling merchants. To encourage trade, customs duties were low. Something like a limited form of a

The great conquering dynasties were the Ottoman Turks, who expanded into Europe and North Africa, and the Mughals, who conquered India. But by about 1600, both powers had passed their peak.

The Ottomans

The Ottomans reached the height of their success under Suleiman the Magnificent, also known as "the Lawgiver." But Suleiman set up a system of government in which the sultan took little part in everyday affairs. The result, after him, was weak leadership, since even the most gifted sultans knew little of government. The viziers (ministers) of the Kuprili family partly restored Ottoman power in the late 17th century, but the lack of strong, central leadership weakened the empire. Still, though shrinking, it lasted into the 20th century (largely because of the rivalry of its European neighbors.)

A Turkish pistol case. Ottoman power was based on the Janissaries, an elite slave army recruited from Christian children in the Balkans.

The Safavids

The Safavids, Shi'ite rivals to the Ottomans were originally sufis, or holy men. The dynasty was founded in 1501 by Ismail I, the first Safavid shah. He united the Iranian tribes, enforced the Shi'ite faith in his dominions, and defeated the Uzbeks. But he was himself defeated by the Ottoman Turks. Ismail's successors had to struggle not only against the Ottomans but also to keep the loyalty of the tribes. After the revival under Abbas I, "the Great," the Safavids, like the Ottomans, began the custom of isolating the ruler from government. That and the failure to check the ambitions of the *ulama* (the learned elite) led to their downfall.

KHANATE OF KAZAN

MONGOLIA

CRIMEA

Istanbul

Lepanto

Khiva · Khokand

ARMENIA · Bukhara · Samarkand

KHANATE OF CHAGATAY

Baghdad FERGHANA

KHURASAN

· Isfahan

· Delhi
· Agra

Safavid Empire, 1512
Area disputed between Uzbeks and Safavids
Ottoman Empire, 1566
Russia, 1722
Manchus, 1783
Mughal Empire, 1707

THE SAFAVID, OTTOMAN, AND MUGHAL EMPIRES.

Abbas the Great, a ruler of great energy and vision, who built Isfahan, one of the world's most beautiful cities.

The Safavid Empire

The Safavid Dynasty reached its peak under Shah Abbas (reigned 1588–1628). His reorganized army drove out the Uzbeks, regained land lost to the Ottomans, and captured Baghdad. He also encouraged local industry and export trade, run mainly by Armenian merchants who received special protection from the shah. At Isfahan, his capital, he built a fabulous array of mosques, *madrasas* (religious colleges), and palaces.

A ceramic mosaic from Isfahan.

The Uzbeks

The Uzbek khans, like the Mughals, were descended from Chingis Khan and Tamerlane. About 1500 they formed the Uzbek tribes into a confederation. They fought with the Safavids over possession of Khurasan, a rich province, and also clashed with the Mughals. But they never created a centrally governed empire, and in the 17th century, the region split up into separate khanates, chiefly Bukhara, Khiva, and Khokand.

Abdullah Khan II (reigned 1583–98) was the last ruler who tried to convert the Uzbek confederation into an empire like Safavid Iran. Internal divisions among the Uzbeks frustrated his efforts.

SEE ALSO
p. 78 THE RISE OF ISLAM • p. 92 THE ISLAMIC WORLD • p. 128 THE MUGHAL EMPIRE • p. 130 THE OTTOMAN EMPIRE p. 190 DECLINE OF THE OTTOMAN EMPIRE

Samarkand, the city of Tamerlane, was one of many fine religious and cultural centers of central Asia ruled by the Uzbek khans, who were strict Sunnis.

1598 Abbas establishes Iranian capital at Isfahan.

1603 Safavids invade Mesopotamia and take Baghdad.

1722 Safavids defeated by Afghans.

1736 Nadir Shah seizes throne of Iran.

1783 Russians conquer Crimea khanate.

common market existed throughout southwest Asia. Muslim merchants were also the agents who carried Islam into Southeast Asia and China.

The wealthiest of the Muslim powers was Mughal India. Its huge stretches of very fertile land between the Indus and Ganges rivers produced cotton and other export crops, and supported up to 100 million people. The others had fewer resources and smaller populations.

The Safavids relied mainly on the Persian silk industry, and the nomadic Uzbeks on the export of horses. The Ottoman economy was stronger, especially after Egypt was added to the empire, thanks to the prosperous farming lands from Egypt to Iraq, and to lively trade, especially in textiles. By 1540 the Ottomans ruled the largest and most powerful empire in the world, but heavy spending on wars and the construction of cities soon began to weaken the economy.

One feature of the wealth and power of the Muslim empires was the flowering of the arts. Under the great emperors, such as Abbas I in Safavid Iran, Suleiman I in Ottoman Turkey, and Akbar in Mughal India, some of the world's most splendid buildings were built. Their great cities were an expression of the belief that the greatness of a ruling dynasty was reflected in the splendor of its buildings.

1. A 16th-century miniature showing the citadel of the Islamic city of Aleppo in Palestine.
2. Elaborately worked metal helmet made by Safavid craftspeople for Shah Abbas I.

Babur enters Samarkand (1500) during his battles with the Uzbeks. Shaybani Khan Uzbek soon drove him out again.

War

The contest, mainly for land, fought by the Safavids against the Ottomans and Uzbeks was particularly bitter because of religious differences. The conservative Sunnis feared and disliked the Shia Safavids, who encouraged rebellions among Shia tribes under Ottoman rule and whose claim to be the rightful leaders of Islam challenged the supremacy of the the Ottoman sultan. Militarily, the Ottomans were a greater power than Safavid Iran, but they never succeeded in conquering it.

Growing hostility between the Safavids and Ottomans led to all-out war in 1514. At the Battle of Chaldiran, the Ottomans were victorious and seized what is now eastern Turkey.

A Portuguese attack on Muslim merchants off the coast of India. Until 1498, no European ship had entered the Indian Ocean.

Rise of the Mughals

The Mughals had fought a long and unsuccessful war to hold their their land in Ferghana, western Turkistan, against the Uzbeks. Babur, who succeeded his father in 1494, attracted support from a wide range of people, but by 1512, it was clear that he could not regain his power in central Asia. He turned his thoughts to winning new territory in the plains of northern India.

Nadir Shah

A former bandit, Nadir Shah seized the throne of Iran when the last Safavid (a baby) died in 1736. He was a disastrous ruler but a brilliant warrior. He attacked Iran's neighbors and in 1739 seized Delhi, the Mughal capital, slaughtering thousands of people. Campaigns against the Ottomans and the Russians followed, and Iran was almost ruined before Nadir Shah was killed by his own soldiers (1747).

Nadir Shah was the last of the great Asian conquerors in the tradition of Chingis Khan and Tamerlane.

Decline of the Muslim empires

In the 17th century, the power of Islam was in decline. Poor government, costly wars, and inflation undermined the Ottoman Empire which, after over a century of expansion, was forced on to the defensive. After Abbas the Great, the Safavids again began to lose their grip on Iran. All the Muslim empires faced increasing rebellions among their subjects.

One reason for the decline in Muslim government, especially in Iran and Turkey, was "palace politics". The ruler's huge household was too involved with its own affairs instead of the affairs of the nation.

The Manchu

Muslim groups in western China had been founded by merchants and sufis from central Asia. They were generally tolerated by Chinese rulers. When the powerful Manchu gained control of China (1644), they began to expand the empire to include the Muslim khanates farther west, of which the greatest was the Chagatay khanate based in Kashgar. By 1759 this area, much of it desert, was incorporated in the Chinese province of Xinjiang.

Expanding Russia

About 1500 the small Russian state around Moscow began its long expansion. Eventually it would stretch from the Baltic to the Pacific. Early victims were the khanates to the east, which had succeeded the Mongol Empire. When the khanate of Kazan fell in 1552, the Russians gained control of the Volga River, down to the Caspian Sea. That brought them into contact with the Ottomans, Uzbeks, and Iranians. By 1792, the Russians had conquered the Crimea and replaced the Ottoman Turks on the northern Black Sea coast.

An 18th-century Russian arquebus.

Sea power

The Muslim powers could not prevent the Europeans dominating the sea routes and coasts because they did not have powerful navies. The Ottoman Empire was an exception. Under Suleiman, the Ottoman fleet of war galleys ranged through the Mediterranean unchallenged, even using the French port of Marseille as a base. After defeat by a Christian fleet at Lepanto, where they lost nearly 200 ships (the first big victory of the Christians over the Ottomans), they still commanded the eastern Mediterranean.

A member of the imperial guard of the Manchu emperor, Quianlong (reigned 1736–96), in whose reign all of Mongolia was included in the Chinese empire.

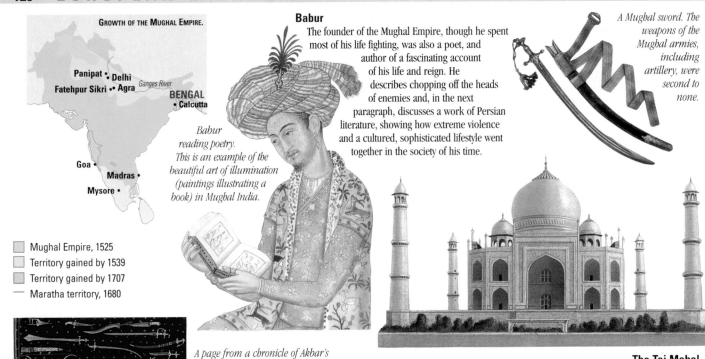

GROWTH OF THE MUGHAL EMPIRE.

Panipat • Delhi
Fatehpur Sikri • • Agra　Ganges River
BENGAL
• Calcutta

Goa •
Madras •
Mysore •

☐ Mughal Empire, 1525
☐ Territory gained by 1539
☐ Territory gained by 1707
— Maratha territory, 1680

Babur reading poetry. This is an example of the beautiful art of illumination (paintings illustrating a book) in Mughal India.

Babur

The founder of the Mughal Empire, though he spent most of his life fighting, was also a poet, and author of a fascinating account of his life and reign. He describes chopping off the heads of enemies and, in the next paragraph, discusses a work of Persian literature, showing how extreme violence and a cultured, sophisticated lifestyle went together in the society of his time.

A Mughal sword. The weapons of the Mughal armies, including artillery, were second to none.

A page from a chronicle of Akbar's reign, showing tools and weapons.

The Taj Mahal

Often called the most beautiful building in the world, the Taj Mahal in Agra was built in glittering white marble by Shah Jahan as a tomb for his wife, Mumtaz Mahal. It is intended to represent the throne of God in paradise. The craftsmen who worked on it came from all over Islam, a sign of the high status of the Mughal emperors.

Left: An illustration showing Akbar meeting with Jesuits to discuss Christianity.

Akbar

The greatest of the Mughals, Akbar was unique in practicing religious toleration – an unthinkable policy anywhere else in Islam or in Christian Europe. Because his childhood was so turbulent (he was only 13 when he succeeded his father), he never had a proper education and could hardly read or write; yet he enjoyed learned debates and respected Sanskrit (Hindu) literature. His reign has always been seen as a golden age in Indian history, and the style and achievements of Mughal civilization have fascinated later generations.

Akbar's court

Akbar built a magnificent, red-sandstone palace complex, which included the Jama Masjid (mosque), at Fatehpur Sikri, near Agra, though he only lived there for a year or two. Like other Muslim rulers, the Mughal emperors had a large household of women, called a harem. But, unlike the Ottomans and the Safavids, the Mughals did not make the mistake of becoming so involved with household affairs, or "palace politics," that they neglected the country they ruled.

Akbar's government

Akbar introduced a system of administration that was perhaps the most advanced in the world at the time. The empire was divided into districts, each governed by a military official, who also held estates in his district. Akbar's administration did not offend the hundreds of local rulers, Muslim and non-Muslim, in India, yet it provided massive revenue for his government. With peace secure, the arts flourished. The Mughal style, a mixture of Persian and Hindu influences, reached its peak in the reign of Akbar's grandson, Shah Jahan (1628–57).

1510 Portuguese found colony at Goa. **1526** Babur victorious at Panipat. **1556** Humayun reclaims Delhi. **1562** Akbar marries a Rajput princess. **1575** Akbar creates a center for all religions at Fatehpur Sikri. **1658** Mughal capital moved from Agra to Delhi. **1674** Sivaji

The Mughal Empire

The Mughal Empire was founded by Babur in 1526, but Mughal control was not firmly established until the reign of his grandson, Akbar. Muslim rule was not new in northern India, but the Mughals came to rule nearly all of the subcontinent of South Asia, and over 80 percent of their subjects were non-Muslims (mainly Hindus). In other ways too, the Mughal Empire was different from the Ottomans or Safavids. It did not depend on the loyalty of particular tribes, and the Mughal emperors saw no need to create a professional slave-army, like the Janissaries, as a safeguard against tribal rivalries. The Mughal emperors were mostly great war leaders, but their success depended on fair, efficient government and economic prosperity, as well as their powerful armies.

1

The heartland of all Indian empires was the fertile "basin" of the Ganges and its tributaries, in north central India. Babur built forts to control this region, but could not create an effective government before his death in 1530. His son Humayun spent much of his reign in exile, but under Akbar (reigned 1556–1605), the struggling Mughal state was transformed into a large and powerful empire. Akbar was not only a successful conqueror, he was a wise ruler. He defeated the Rajputs, his strongest opponents, but then won their support, and turned these proud and independent princes into loyal subjects and the backbone of his army.

Aurangzeb

Quarrels over the succession afflicted all the great Muslim dynasties. Aurangzeb (reigned 1658–1707) imprisoned his father and slaughtered his brothers to secure the throne. Though not a great patron of the arts like his predecessors, he was a tireless warrior, and the Mughal Empire reached its greatest extent in his reign. He moved the capital from Agra to Delhi, but he was seldom there, being almost permanently on campaign in the south.

This superb embroidered hunting jacket belonged to the Mughal emperor Jahangir (reigned 1605–27).

The Mughal collapse

Although there was a Mughal emperor for 150 years after Aurangzeb's death, he had no power beyond the district around Delhi and Agra. The reasons for the collapse lay in Aurangzeb's reign. Above all, his long, unsuccessful wars against the Marathas strained even the Mughal treasury and led to a decline in the standards of government. Aurangzeb alienated some Hindus because he ruled as a strict Sunni, without the tolerance of his great-grandfather, Akbar.

Sivaji, a warrior chief famous for his daring, founded the Maratha Kingdom and established a fair and tolerant government.

The Marathas

The Marathas were a a warlike Hindu people from western India. Their opposition to Muslim rule became a serious threat in the late 17th century, when Sivaji united the various Maratha chiefs into a federation. After the collapse of Mughal power, the Marathas conquered much of north and central India, and seemed the likely successors to the Mughals. But they failed to take Delhi and were defeated by invading Afghans, while the *peshwas* (hereditary ministers) who succeeded Sivaji could not hold the federation together.

The Europeans

The Portuguese established bases at Goa and elsewhere in the early 16th century. In the 17th century they were joined by other Europeans, especially the French and the British. Indian trade brought great profits to the European merchants and also great quantities of silver into India. Before about 1780 Indian industry was just as advanced as Europe's, and in textiles and some other goods (India was the only known source of diamonds until 1725), Europe could not compete with Indian products.

The British and the French

Rivalry between the British and the French trading companies in India broke into open war in the 1740s. The Europeans also became involved in the rivalries among various princes following the collapse of the Mughal government. The Nawab of Bengal, suspicious of British plans, captured Calcutta. It was soon retaken and the Nawab, with his French allies, was defeated by the British general Clive at Plassey. As a result the British gained control of Bengal, one of India's richest regions, and French ambitions in India were ended.

Clive made a pro-British claimant, Mir Jaffa, Nawab of Bengal.

Tipu Sultan

Another expanding Indian state was Mysore, in the south. Its Hindu rajahs were overthrown by Hyder Ali, who quarreled with the British in Madras and fought against them (1781–84). His son Tipu renewed the fight. When Tipu was finally defeated, the British restored the Hindu rajahs but became themselves the effective rulers of Mysore.

The English East India Company retreated to India after its merchants in the Spice Islands were killed by the Dutch. Calcutta (left), was founded in 1690 and eventually replaced Madras as the Company's HQ.

British control

The British were in India to make money, not to rule the Indians. They did not set out to replace the Mughal Empire with a British empire, but that was what eventually happened. With the capture of Bengal, the East India Company became an imperial power. The British had enemies, notably the Marathas, and wars against them led to further conquests.

A mechanical toy of a tiger eating a British East India Company soldier. It belonged to Tipu Sultan, and could make realistic growls and groans.

Warren Hastings, British governor of Bengal (1774–85). Long experience in India made him sympathetic to Indian culture, but he fell foul of his own colleagues and was later charged with misconduct.

SEE ALSO
p. 92 THE ISLAMIC WORLD
p. 126 MUSLIM POWER
p. 130 THE OTTOMAN EMPIRE
p. 190 THE DECLINE OF THE OTTOMAN EMPIRE

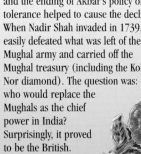

establishes Maratha kingdom. **1690** Calcutta founded by the English. **1739** Nadir Shah sacks Delhi. **1757** British victory at Plassey. **1761** Marathas defeated by Afghans. **1774** Beginning of British-Maratha wars.

He strengthened this alliance by marrying Rajput princesses, but – what made him so different from other Muslim rulers – he did not force them to become Muslims. Akbar knew he could not rule his empire without the support of Hindus. So he practiced religious toleration and restricted the power of the *ulama* (Muslim religious leaders). He was

prepared to listen to people of all religions, including Christian missionaries from Portuguese Goa.

The cash to pay for the army and the many great buildings of the Mughal emperors came mainly from taxes on farming and the export of products such as cotton textiles. Because farming was so prosperous, taxes could be kept quite low.

The wealth and power of the Mughals lasted until the time of Aurangzeb (reigned 1658–1707). Then it quickly collapsed. Like others before it, the Mughal

Empire was stretched too far. Aurangzeb's wars against the Marathas, and the ending of Akbar's policy of tolerance helped to cause the decline. When Nadir Shah invaded in 1739, he easily defeated what was left of the Mughal army and carried off the Mughal treasury (including the Koh-i-Nor diamond). The question was: who would replace the Mughals as the chief power in India? Surprisingly, it proved to be the British.

1. Mughal daggers with ornamental scabbards, handles, and blades.

2. A lady of the harem dressing her hair. In Islam, men could have more than one wife and they sometimes had very large families. Shah Jahan had 15 children with his beloved Mumtaz Mahal.

3. Floral decoration with precious stones inlaid in white marble. From the time of Shah Jahan's reign.

1499 Ottomans at war with Venice and Hungary.

1514 Selim I defeats Safavid Empire at Battle of Chaldiran.

1520–66 Peak of Ottoman power under Suleiman the Magnificent.

1571 Ottomans lose Battle of Lepanto. **1639** Treaty sets

permanent border between Ottoman and Safavid empires.

The Ottoman Empire

The Ottomans and their empire were named after their legendary first leader, Osman. The Ottoman Empire reached the height of its extent and power under the rule of its greatest sultan Suleiman the Magnificent during the first half of the 16th century. Its territories, encompassing much of North Africa, southwest Asia, and the Balkans, were held by a disciplined army. The capital, Istanbul, prospered with merchants coming from all over the world to buy and sell goods there, and the empire was criss-crossed with trade routes. From the 17th century the empire declined, however, as many nations won back their independence. Incompetent sultans and government corruption contributed to the decline, and by the end of the 18th century the empire was severely weakened.

The Ottoman Turks captured Constantinople in 1453 and renamed it Istanbul. Their empire began to grow rapidly after this. Sultan Selim I ("the Grim," reigned 1512–20) conquered Egypt and Syria, gained control of the Arabian Peninsula, and in 1514 beat back the Safavid rulers of Persia at the Battle of Chaldiran. Selim was succeeded by Suleiman I ("the Magnificent," reigned 1520–66), who conquered Mesopotamia and Albania, reduced Hungary to vassal status after his victory at the Battle of Mohacs in 1526, and gained naval supremacy in the Mediterranean. Although his siege of Vienna in 1529 was unsuccessful, Suleiman made the empire one of the great powers of Europe.

Decline set in after his death. The Ottomans experienced their first major defeat by Europeans in the Battle of Lepanto (1571), when its fleet was destroyed by a

THE OTTOMAN EMPIRE.

conquests
- ☐ 1492
- ☐ 1520
- ☐ 1566
- ☐ 1640

Ottoman cavalrymen from the Balkans were known as "Greeks."

The Ottoman army

The strength of the Ottoman army was based on its cavalrymen, who fought in return for income from land that was granted to them. They were always ready to be called into action. By the time of Suleiman the Magnificent in the 16th century, these landed cavalrymen numbered more than 17,000 in Anatolia, and together with their soldiers they made up an army of about 45,000 men. Mercenaries were added to the army when required.

View of Istanbul at the end of the 17th century.

The Ottoman Empire

By the middle of the 16th century the Ottoman Turks had the largest empire in Europe and the Middle East. They were the leaders of the Muslim world and rulers of an empire that stretched from the Atlas Mountains in North Africa to the Caspian Sea and included the Middle East, Anatolia, and the Balkans.

Suleiman the Magnificent

Suleiman I (1494–1566) (right), became known in the Western world as "the Magnificent." But the Ottomans called him "the Lawgiver" because he revised the legal system of their empire, which reached its peak under his rule. He also ensured religious freedom throughout the empire. Not only was Suleiman an able soldier and administrator, but he was also a patron of the arts, all of which flourished during his reign. He was largely responsible for rebuilding Istanbul and other cities such as Mecca and Baghdad.

Suleiman's wife Roxelana (above), was known to the Ottomans as "the smiling one." She had been captured in a raid and sold as a slave in Istanbul before joining Suleiman's harem. She bore him five sons and a daughter, and ensured that she and the harem had a strong influence on the way the empire was run.

Istanbul

When the Ottomans captured Constantinople in 1453 it was almost deserted. Mehemed II moved people into the city from parts of Greece and by 1480 the population had risen to around 70,000. Under the Ottomans the city experienced a long period of peaceful growth. Wealthy Ottomans built fountains, palaces, and mosques and the city was completely transformed.

The Ottoman navy

The Ottomans learned how to build ships and formed a naval fleet which, unlike European navies, was purely military and did not take part in trade. The Ottoman fleet became the largest in the Mediterranean, and was made up of 230 ships at the Battle of Lepanto in 1571. Although they lost 200 ships in that battle, the Ottomans had rebuilt their fleet by the following year.

The Janissaries

The Janissaries (left), whose name meant "new troops," were highly trained professional infantrymen. At first they were made up of carefully selected slaves and prisoners of war, especially from Christian families. They became known for their discipline and their early use of firearms. Janissaries made up the elite troops of the Ottoman army until the 16th century, but then they became a threat to the sultan's authority and were finally outlawed.

Christian Holy League commanded by Don John of Austria. The Ottoman navy soon recovered supremacy of the eastern Mediterranean, but failed to capture Crete from the Venetians in 1645. A Venetian fleet threatened Istanbul in 1648, and Sultan Ibrahim (reigned 1640–48) was deposed by the Janissaries in the crisis that followed.

In 1683 Grand Vizier Kara Mustafa led the empire's last challenge to Christian Europe, which ended with another siege of Vienna. After this failed, the Ottoman army collapsed. Major territories were lost to European powers, and the Treaty of Karlowitz (1699), confirmed lands won by Holy Roman Emperor Leopold I, the Republic of Venice, Poland, and Russia.

In 1711 the Ottomans defeated Peter the Great at Stanilasti, but a few decades later they began to suffer under Russian expansion. From 1768 to 1774 the Ottomans were at war with Catherine the Great, and in 1783 Russia annexed the Crimea. By the end of the 18th century the empire of Suleiman the Magnificent had shrunk considerably and had limited influence outside the Middle East. Sultan Selim III (reigned 1789–1807) tried to reform the Ottoman system by replacing the Janissaries with a new style of army, but they overthrew him and massacred most of the reform leaders.

1. The imperial monogram of Suleiman the Magnificent.

2. The saddle of Kara Mustafa, who was the empire's grand vizier from 1676 to 1683.

3. A man is severely beaten for failing to clean the street in front of his house. Ottoman law and order were strictly enforced.

4. Early 17th-century pendant necklace from Fez, in Morocco, which traded heavily with the western part of the Ottoman Empire. The gold filigree bird is encrusted with pearls, emeralds, and garnets.

Selim II (1521–74) succeeded his father Suleiman I in 1566. Unfortunately he was known for his love of Cypriot wine, of which he drank far too much. During his reign Cyprus was captured, and 30,000 of its inhabitants were massacred.

An 18th-century Jewish woman from Anatolia.

Vienna besieged

In 1529, under Suleiman the Magnificent, the Turks unsuccessfully besieged Vienna, capital of the Habsburg Empire. In 1683 they gathered a huge army for another assault on the city and appeared to be winning until the Austrians were saved by the troops of John III Sobieski, the king of Poland. Forced to retreat, the Ottoman grand vizier, Kara Mustafa, was dismissed from his post and executed.

The Ottoman navy fought the Venetians off Morea (southern Greece) in 1499.

The Jewish community

In the 16th century the Jewish community within the Ottoman Empire became the largest in the world. Istanbul and Salonika each had a community of about 20,000 Jewish people. Many were refugees from Spain and Portugal, and the empire became their haven on condition that they paid a poll tax and acknowledged the superiority of Islam. They were able to trade with Christian Europe and went into trades such as wool-weaving.

Trade

The Ottomans gained great wealth through trade, and the busiest trade routes between North Africa and East Asia ran through their empire – leading all the way from Morocco to China. In addition, European merchant ships unloaded goods at Mediterranean ports such as Tripoli, bound for the Silk Route and the Far East. Caravans brought silk, porcelain, and other Chinese goods the other way.

Sleighs such as this were pulled by horses to carry people and goods across the Asian steppes. The opening-up of Siberia after the 16th century meant that Russian and European traders were able to bypass the Ottoman Empire, which reduced its wealth and influence.

A Greek girl in traditional costume. The Ottomans allowed religious freedom to the Christian Greeks, as they did to other groups. Christians and Jews made up the largest non-Muslim groups, each of which formed a "millet" or nation.

SEE ALSO
p. 92 THE ISLAMIC WORLD
p. 126 MUSLIM POWER
p. 142 CENTRAL AND EASTERN EUROPE
p. 190 THE DECLINE OF THE OTTOMAN EMPIRE

Southeast Asia and the Spice Trade

From 1500 to 1800 mainland Southeast Asia was populated by many different peoples with their own rich cultures, and was ruled by many small kingdoms. Power swung between states ruled by Burmese, Thai, Khmer, Vietnamese, Arakanese, and Laotian peoples. Local rulers had little interest in trading with the Europeans, who had started sending ships across the Indian Ocean in search of precious goods such as spices, which were highly prized in Europe. Attempts by the Europeans to seize power in the late 16th century caused distrust and hatred among the local rulers. The Portuguese led the way, but were soon succeeded by the Dutch as the dominant trading nation in the archipelago.

Myanmar (Burma) lies at the center of mainland Southeast Asia. It has a complex history of kingdoms vying for power with each other and their neighbors. At the beginning of the 16th century Myanmar was made up of four separate kingdoms: Arakan, Ava, Pegu, and Toungoo. In 1539 the Toungoo ruler Tabinshwehti (reigned 1535–50) conquered the Mon and Shan peoples to the north, who had been threatening Burman independence. Then Toungoo invaded the Thai kingdom of Ayutthaya in 1548. Although unsuccessful, this created a tension between Burma and Thailand

The Europeans in Southeast Asia made little impact on the mainland kingdoms, but from 1511 on they greatly affected the islands along the Spice routes.

Vietnam

The state of Dai Viet, or Greater Viet, had a close cultural relationship with China and had to resist many attempts by the Chinese to restore rule. In 1471 the Vietnamese state of Annam conquered the kingdom of Champa to the south and eventually seized the Mekong delta from the declining Khmer Empire. About 1600 Vietnam split into northern Tongking and southern Cochin-China. In 1773 a rebellion started that reunited the kingdom.

Myanmar (formerly Burma)

In the early 1700s the Mon people, who had been conquered by the Toungoo kingdom of Myanmar in 1539, rebelled. They set up a king of their own at Pegu, and in 1752 captured the capital of Ava, another of the Burmese kingdoms. Three years later, however, the Burmese overthrew the Mons and founded a new capital at Rangoon. From 1766 to 1769 the Chinese made four attempts to invade Burma, but these ended in failure.

A finely crafted Burmese puppet of an 18th-century king wearing ceremonial robes.

EUROPEAN TERRITORY AND TRADE ROUTES c.1760.

- ☐ British
- ☐ Dutch
- ☐ Spanish
- ☐ Portuguese

Java

The Hindu Majapahit Empire survived on Java until the early 16th century, but the spread of Islam hastened its decline. In 1596 the first Dutch fleet arrived, landing at Bantam. In 1619 the Dutch East India Company took control of the neighboring state, Batavia, where it based its headquarters.

Above: Traditional Javanese shadow puppet.

Malacca

By 1500 Malacca, on the west coast of the Malay peninsula, was the most important port on the narrow straits that linked the Indian Ocean with the South China Sea. In 1511 the Portuguese, under Afonso d'Albuquerque (1453–1515), captured Malacca and built a fort there (left). This gave them control over the route to the Spice Islands. They held Malacca until 1641, when it was captured by the Dutch.

Angkor Wat is the finest temple of the Khmer city of Angkor.

Cambodia

Angkor was the capital of the Khmer Empire. In 1431 it was captured by the Thais after a long siege. The weakened Khmer court moved south to Phnom Penh. The ruined city of Angkor became overgrown by jungle, and was only rediscovered in 1850. The rest of the Khmer Empire was fought over by the Thais and Cochin-China.

Thailand (formerly Siam)

At the beginning of the 16th century a powerful Thai kingdom controlled much of the east coast of the Malay peninsula from the Thai capital at Ayutthaya. In 1661, the Thai king sought help from France after the Dutch tried to control Thailand's foreign trade.

Ruins of the ancient temples at Ayutthaya, the Thai capital from 1350 to 1767.

1602 Founding of the Dutch East India Company.

1610 Kingdom of Ava conquers kingdom of Toungoo and creates a new Burmese Empire.

1623 English trading base at Amboina, on the Moluccan island of Ceram, is sacked by Dutch.

1641 Dutch take Malacca.

1762–64 British occupy Manila.

that lasted for centuries. In 1610 the Ava Kingdom conquered the Toungoo Kingdom, creating a new Burmese Empire.

On the eastern mainland, the Vietnamese states of Tongking and Annam had expanded southward and captured the Hindu kingdom of Champa in 1471. By 1611 Champa had been absorbed by Cochin-China.

Farther south, on the Malay peninsula, the Portuguese arrived in 1511 and quickly established a base at Malacca, followed by a chain of strategically placed forts and trading bases. They were not interested in controlling the mainland Malay states. Their aim was to dominate the trade in cloves and nutmeg from the Spice Islands (the Moluccas), defending it from Muslim and European rivals. The Portuguese held Malacca until 1641, when it was captured by the Dutch.

In 1521 the Spanish, under Ferdinand Magellan (c.1480–1521), had laid claim to the islands in the east of the South China Sea. The locals were unable to mount any effective resistance. The Spanish later established a permanent settlement on Cebu in 1565, and in 1571 the islands were named the Philippines, in honor of King Philip II of Spain (reigned 1558–98). The economic basis of the Spanish colony was trade in Chinese silk, which they took from China to Manila, and then sold in Mexico in exchange for silver.

In 1619 the Dutch East India Company gained control of the spice trade. They made their headquarters at Batavia, on Java. Sultan Agung of Mataram (reigned 1613–46), who controlled most of the island, twice failed to take Batavia from the Dutch. There was strong competition between the Dutch and the English for the spice trade, but in 1623 the Dutch sacked the English base at Amboina. In 1685 the English set up another base, this time at Benkulen, on Sumatra, for trading pepper. In the 1700s the Dutch introduced coffee cultivation to Java. The colony of Manila prospered until it was occupied by the British (1762–1764).

1. This painted stone sculpture of a spiritual guardian from Annam dates from 1601.

2. Europeans discovered tea in China in the early 17th century. The Dutch and English East India companies spread its cultivation to Java and India. Tea was first sold in England in 1657. By the late 1700s the Duchess of Bedford had introduced to British society the habit of taking tea in the afternoon.

Dutch East India Company

The Dutch East India Company was founded in 1602 to promote and protect Dutch trade in the East Indies, which included the Malay archipelago and present-day Indonesia. Shares to a value of 6.5 million Dutch guilders were issued, and these paid enormous dividends throughout the 17th century. From its headquarters at Batavia (present-day Jakarta) on Java, the company expelled the Portuguese from most of their bases, gaining control of the Spice Islands (the Moluccas). They then fought off English attempts to control the spice trade. The company survived until 1799.

A wooden figure of a Dutch East India Company officer.

> **SEE ALSO**
> p. 114 PORTUGUESE AND SPANISH EXPANSION
> p. 116 DUTCH, ENGLISH, AND FRENCH EXPANSION

Spanish settlement of the Philippines only began in 1571. The settlers built a walled city called Manila, the only significant Spanish harbor in the East. It soon became the center of Roman Catholicism in Southeast Asia. The University of Santo Tomas (above) was founded in 1611.

English East India Company

Eighty London merchants formed the English East India Company in 1599. The following year it was given a charter by Queen Elizabeth I (reigned 1558–1603), empowering it to trade, settle, conquer, and defend overseas territory. A smaller concern than its Dutch counterpart, it was rarely able to resist Dutch naval aggression in the archipelago. Instead it concentrated on trade in cotton and pepper from India, and later tea and porcelain from China. The company survived until 1858.

Symbol of the English East India Company.

This 18th-century Siamese lacquer panel portrays a Dutch merchant as an evil enemy of the Buddha. The Dutch had tried to take over Thailand's foreign trade, and this and the behavior of various adventurers led to a dislike and distrust of Europeans.

Rivalry between the English and Dutch East India Companies was great. This English merchant is being tortured by the Dutch.

Dutch–English tensions

In 1623 the commercial rivalry between the Dutch and English in the East Indies led to one of many outbreaks of violence. The Dutch sacked the English base at Amboina, on the island of Ceram. Ten English merchants were executed. From then on, the English East India Company concentrated its efforts on India and the textile trade.

Rice and coconuts were cultivated on Sumatra just as they are today. European influence had a great effect on the islands of the region, and in most cases local workers were not well rewarded for their labors. During the 18th century the Dutch introduced coffee cultivation to Java, but their trading policies did not help the local population.

1501 Portuguese merchant ships carry spices to Antwerp, in Flanders, from the East Indies. **1557** Partial bankruptcy of Spain hits the financial center of Antwerp. **1581** Revolt of the Netherlands begins. **1609** The Amsterdam Exchange Bank opens. **1618–48** The Thirty Years' War. **1648** Spain

At the end of the 15th century the cities of northern Italy and the Hanseatic League were the most powerful financial forces in Europe. During the 16th century Dutch and English growth put pressure on the Hansa, which declined after 1500. Hanseatic trading privileges ended in England in 1556, and just over a century later the League held its last assembly.

In 1501 Portuguese merchant ships arrived directly at the port of Antwerp, carrying spices from the East Indies and having avoided Italian ports altogether. Antwerp grew rapidly and soon became the main banking and financial city of northern Europe. In 1531 it became the distribution center for Spanish silver from America, but in 1557 the partial bankruptcy of Spain hit Antwerp hard, and Genoa took over the running of Europe's finances. In 1576 Antwerp was severely damaged by mutinous Spanish soldiers, and soon afterwards the independent Netherlands held the Scheldt estuary and did not allow ships to sail up the river to Antwerp. Flemish merchants and bankers moved to Amsterdam.

In 1581, at the start of the so-called Revolt of the Netherlands, the seven northern provinces of the Low Countries

In many parts of Europe farming methods continued as they had done for centuries. This harvest scene by Pieter Brueghel the Elder dates to the 16th century, but could easily have taken place in the Middle Ages.

Crop rotation

Wishing to use their limited land wisely, the Dutch changed the traditional system of leaving land fallow every third year. Instead they rotated their crops so that fields were used differently each year – planted with corn one year, for example, then with root crops such as turnips the next, and perhaps clover in the third year. This system was adopted in 18th-century England, where fields were also enclosed with hedgerows.

The Dutch reclaimed almost 365,000 acres (148,000 hectares) of land from the sea between 1550 and 1715. They built dykes and used windmills to pump water into canals. They used the reclaimed land for growing crops and grazing animals, as shown in this painting of 1590.

The Netherlands and England

By the 1570s Dutch and English merchant ships were breaking the dominance of Italian traders. The two main northern European ports – Amsterdam and London – continued to grow in size and importance. By 1700 the Dutch Republic and England had the largest merchant fleets, the best textile producers, and the most advanced metal manufacturers in Europe. Improved farming methods and the gradual breakdown of the feudal system meant that by the end of the 18th century only about one in three of the population worked on the land.

New machines, such as this drill plow with a seed and manure hopper, helped to make farming more efficient. The seed drill was invented in 1701 by the English agriculturalist Jethro Tull (1674–1741).

Frederick the Great (reigned 1740–86) made Prussia a major European power. Here he is shown encouraging Prussian farmers to grow potatoes.

New crops

In countries other than England and the Netherlands, the greatest farming improvements came from the introduction of new crops, mainly from America. The potato was introduced, starting in Spain and Italy and spreading throughout Europe. American maize was planted in the south, and Russian buckwheat in the north. Asian sugar cane, rice, and citrus fruits were brought to the Mediterranean region.

Model of a Dutch "flyboat." These sturdy merchantmen gave Dutch traders the edge on other European traders.

As new farming systems were introduced and more land was enclosed, many small farmers lost their holdings. Some became farm laborers, and at haymaking time whole families would set out to look for work. They carried their own tools with them (left).

1694 Bank of England is established.

recognizes independent Dutch Republic in Peace of Westphalia.

1701 Jethro Tull invents the seed drill. **1712** Thomas

Newcomen introduces an early steam engine.

1765 James Hargreaves invents the spinning jenny.

(including Holland, Zeeland, and Friesland) proclaimed their independence from Spain as the United Provinces of the Netherlands, under the leadership of William the Silent (1533–84). After the Thirty Years' War (1618–48), Spain recognized the Dutch Republic in the Peace of Westphalia.

English banking developed from the custom of goldsmiths looking after their customers' precious metals. They found that they could safely lend the metals out, giving their customers receipts, which the customers used to pay their own bills. The Bank of England was established privately in 1694 and then chartered by the English government in return for a loan. The bank

was allowed to issue its own notes and it gradually became a form of central bank.

In 18th-century Britain there were further revolutions in industry. The most important mechanical inventions were John Kay's flying shuttle (1733), James Hargreaves's spinning jenny (1765), Richard Arkwright's water frame (1769), Samuel Crompton's spinning mule (1779), and Edmund Cartwright's machine loom (1785). In 1712 the English blacksmith Thomas Newcomen built an early steam engine, which was used for pumping water out of mines.

1. A Dutch windmill used to pump water from land to be reclaimed for farming.

Europe: Agriculture and Trade

The population of Europe more than doubled between 1500 and 1800. Over most of the continent agricultural production kept pace with population growth, increasing gradually mainly due to the new food crops being introduced from the Americas. However, in northwest Europe, especially in the Low Countries and England, an agricultural revolution began in the 16th century which led to the development of an efficient, market-oriented farming system. Improved farming led to greater specialization in food production and increased exports. It also allowed more people to leave the land for jobs in the burgeoning towns, where they were employed in industry. These conditions laid the basis for the industrial revolution shortly to follow.

In 1500 the great trading cities of northern Italy were very powerful. Sienese cloth merchants (shown here) continued to import wool from Spain, but by 1700 they had lost the lead to the textile producers of northern Europe.

As the capitalist financial system grew, there was a growing spirit of free enterprise in towns. Street peddlers offered all sorts of wares, including eyeglasses.

Economic change

In the 17th century the banking system grew in western Europe and broke away from the earlier methods of Italy and the German Hanseatic towns. The Amsterdam Exchange Bank opened in 1609 and became the focus of European trade. The Bank of England was set up in 1694 by a group of London merchants to lend money to William III. Many financial enterprises were unsuccessful, however. The Scottish financier John Law (1671–1729) (below) tried to help the French economy by opening a bank in 1716 to issue paper money. Speculators soon demanded gold for their paper money, however, and the project failed, leaving thousands bankrupt.

Spread of industry

The building of canals allowed coal to be transported in bulk, which transformed industry. Newcomen's mine pump led to the invention of Watt's steam engine, which started to have its effect at the end of the 18th century. The first textile mills appeared in Britain in the 1740s, and great changes were made when Richard Arkwright invented his water-powered spinning frame in 1769. This and other inventions led to the advent of modern factories. By the 1780s there were 120 textile mills in England.

This English lady was painted around 1550. Her French gown with ivory brocade and lynx fur on the sleeves shows a mixture of styles and materials from several different countries.

In France, the silk industry became important during the 16th century. This illustration from 1602 shows women treating cocoons.

MONEY AND TRADE CONSIDER'D; WITH A PROPOSAL For SUPPLYING the NATION with MONEY. By Mr. JOHN LAW, now Director of the Royal Bank at Paris. The SECOND EDITION. LONDON.

John Law's best-known book (left) was published in 1705.

SEE ALSO
p. 108 EUROPE IN THE 15TH CENTURY
p. 162 THE INDUSTRIAL REVOLUTION
BEGINS • p. 172 THE INDUSTRIAL
REVOLUTION IN EUROPE

Martin Luther

In 1517 Martin Luther, a monk who taught at the University of Wittenberg in Germany, published a list of 95 complaints, or "theses," against the Catholic Church. Soon people all over Europe were discussing his ideas. Angered by Luther's attacks on the Church, the Pope made an example of him to others by excommunicating him for heresy. In 1521 Luther was allowed to defend his views at the Diet, or parliament, held at Worms; the session was presided over by the Holy Roman Emperor, Charles V. Luther refused to back down and was declared an outlaw. Later, he attacked the beliefs as well as the government of the Church. All that was vital in religion, he said, was to be found in the Bible; people would not get to Heaven by giving money to the Church and doing good deeds, but only by God's grace and their faith in Jesus. Unable to reach a compromise with the Catholic Church, Luther eventually founded the first Protestant Church.

In Luther's time people used church doors as notice boards. Luther nailed his 95 theses to the church door in Wittenberg.

Luther is shown on the left of this group of reformers. He was often represented at conferences by his humanist friend Philip Melancthon (far right). Some of the reformers, like Erasmus (third from left), wanted reform, but stayed within the Catholic Church.

Printing

The printing press helped the ideas of the reformers to spread quickly. By 1517 there were more than 2,000 printing presses in Europe, each able to print hundreds of copies of a pamphlet in just a few days. The writings of the reformers kept the presses busy. For thirty years Martin Luther alone published a sermon, a pamphlet, or another piece of writing at the rate of one every two weeks.

Luther's Bible

The Bible that the Catholic Church used was written in Latin, a language that only priests and a few educated people could understand. Martin Luther believed that ordinary people should be able to read the Bible, too. While he was in hiding, after the Diet of Worms in 1521, he translated the Bible's New Testament into German (left).

The clergy

By the beginning of the 16th century, clergy made up a large part of the population in Europe. Besides clerks and parish priests, there were monks, who lived in monasteries; nuns, who lived in convents; and friars, who taught and preached as they traveled the land. Many clergy worked as teachers and clerks, and bishops held office as royal ministers or ambassadors. The pope, who ruled the Church from Rome, claimed supremacy over all other rulers: kings, queens, and emperors. By the early 16th century many people had lost confidence in the clergy and were beginning to protest that parish priests were too often ignorant, and bishops more interested in their incomes than their duties.

Not everyone who took holy orders did so for religious motives, and some behaved in an unsuitable way.

Below: A caricature of 1517 showing a friar selling indulgences.

Indulgences

The main reason for Luther's attack on the Church in 1517 was the sale of indulgences. An indulgence was a piece of paper issued by the pope that said that a person would not be punished for their sins. Originally, indulgences were given to people who prayed, fasted, or gave alms; they were not exchanged for money. But by Luther's time, the sale of indulgences was making a great deal of money for the Church. Luther believed it was wrong of the Church to encourage people to think they could buy their way to heaven.

1517 Luther nails his 95 theses to a church door in Wittenberg.

1519 Ulrich Zwingli preaches reform in Zurich, Switzerland;

Charles V becomes Holy Roman Emperor.

1521 Luther excommunicated. He defends his beliefs at the

Diet, or parliament, in Worms. **1524–25** Peasants' War.

The Reformation

For about a thousand years there was only one Christian Church in Western Europe: the Roman Catholic Church. Ruled by the Pope in Rome, it was the most powerful institution in Europe and owned more land than most kings. The local church was the largest building in every town and village. The Church also provided the only schools and ran the only hospitals. People who questioned the teachings and laws of the Church were punished and even tortured. During the 16th century, however, for the first time people with opposing ideas dared to challenge the Church and voiced their objections to what they regarded as abuses of power. The movement for reform began in Germany with Martin Luther, who was the first person to publicly attack the Catholic Church. But other reformers soon followed, founding Churches of their own. The reformers and their supporters were called Protestants. By 1550 many of the countries in northern Europe had national Protestant Churches, while in others there were less official groups of Protestants. Conflict between the Protestants and Catholics plunged Europe into a century of religious wars.

In 1517, when Martin Luther publicly attacked the Catholic practice of selling indulgences, or "pardons," from the pope, he was joining many other thinking people who for years had been criticizing corruption and abuses within the Church. Luther's attack came, however, at a time when there was a general spirit of inquiry and questioning. People were asking how

The Elector of Saxony

John Frederick, grandson of Frederick the Wise, reigned in Saxony from 1532 to 1547.

Martin Luther came from Saxony. After he had been declared a heretic, he would certainly have been killed if he had not been protected by the Elector, or ruler, of Saxony, Frederick the Wise. Frederick admired Luther, but he never became a Lutheran himself. His successors did, however, and they established a Lutheran Church in Saxony. In 1530 the Protestant princes in Germany formed the Schmalkaldic League to defend themselves against the forces of the Catholic Holy Roman Emperor, Charles V.

The Peasants' War

During the early 16th century peasants in Europe, especially in Germany, suffered a succession of poor harvests that pushed prices up. The most grasping landlords were often the monasteries and other Church estates. In 1524 the peasants in Germany rebelled against their greedy landlords in an outbreak known as the Peasants' War (though craftworkers in the towns also took part). The peasants expected support from Luther, who had attacked the abuses of the Church. But Luther wanted only to reform the Church, not to destroy it. He denounced the revolt, which was put down by the German princes with great violence.

John Calvin

The reformer John Calvin was a French lawyer who fled to Switzerland after his preaching got him into trouble in France. He settled in Geneva in 1536. There he put into practice his ideas on Church government and Protestant beliefs. Calvinism was a stricter form of doctrine than Lutheranism. It had a strong influence in the Netherlands, France, and Scotland, where it formed the basis of Presbyterianism. Calvinism also influenced the English Puritans, some of whom later settled in North America.

A French congregation listening to a Calvinist preacher, c.1564.

Pope Leo X

Pope Leo X was a member of the Italian Medici family, who ruled Florence. He was elected pope in 1513. Luther's first attacks on the Church took him by surprise and he tried to persuade Luther to take back his criticisms. By 1519 the standpoint of both men had hardened, however, and in 1520 Pope Leo formally condemned Luther's teaching in a Papal Bull, or declaration. Luther publicly burned it, and in 1521 Pope Leo excommunicated him, making him an outcast from the Church. Pope Leo died later the same year.

Rulers and the Reformation

Some rulers saw a political advantage in the Reformation. By breaking away from Roman Catholicism, they gained independence from the pope's authority in their country. They could also acquire great wealth by confiscating Church property. King Henry VIII of England (1491–1547) was not a Protestant; he had been commended by the pope for a book he wrote attacking Luther. But he wanted to end the authority of the pope in England so that he could obtain a divorce. Henry established a Church of England, independent of the pope, but otherwise essentially still Catholic in doctrine.

The pope refused to grant Henry VIII a divorce from his first wife, Catherine of Aragon, who did not produce a son. Henry made himself head of the Church of England and obtained a divorce from the Archbishop of Canterbury, whom he had appointed.

Destruction of images

Some of the later reformers, such as John Calvin, regarded the works of art that decorated churches as signs of worldly wealth and believed that they distracted people from the worship of God. They thought stained glass and statues of saints had no place in churches. In some Protestant countries, gangs tore paintings from the walls of churches, smashed stained-glass windows, and burned statues and vestments.

> **SEE ALSO**
> p. 138 THE COUNTER-REFORMATION

---

the practice of selling indulgences could be defended. They wanted to know why Church services and the Bible should not be translated from Latin into the languages of ordinary people. They also questioned whether priests were needed to mediate between God and humankind.

After Martin Luther (1483–1546) had made his ideas public, they began to spread rapidly. In Switzerland, the reformer Ulrich Zwingli (1484–1531) introduced Protestantism to Zurich. He did not ally himself with Luther, however, because he did not agree with Luther on some points of doctrine. Luther, in his new Protestant Church, retained the traditional structure of bishops and clergy, and also the form of worship. A Lutheran church building still looked much like a Catholic one.

Some reformers were more radical. John Calvin (1509–64) and his followers in Geneva not only removed all ornaments from their churches; but also they did away with bishops and priests. Calvinist ministers were chosen by the people who attended the church. Elected laymen called elders assisted the minister to instruct the congregation how to live. Calvinists were not allowed to swear, visit taverns, or wear extravagant clothes. Calvin's form of Protestantism spread beyond Switzerland to France, the Netherlands, and particularly Scotland, where it was known as Presbyterianism. There, the founding preacher John Knox (1514–72) helped to establish it as the dominant religion.

In England, William Tyndale (1494–1536) translated the Bible into English from the original Hebrew and Greek manuscripts. To escape Catholic persecution, he fled to the continent to complete his task, but he was arrested near Brussels and in 1536 he was put to death. Some 90 percent of his translation went into the King James Bible (also called the Authorized Version) of 1611.

1. The papal bull, or decree, of Pope Leo X, which excommunicated Luther in 1520.

2. The Church sails into rough seas.

1540 Jesuits founded by Ignatius Loyola.

1545 First Council of Trent held by Pope Paul III.

1555 Peace of Augsburg, which brings peace to Holy Roman Empire, says a ruler's religion should be that of the state.

1562–63 Second and Third Councils of Trent meet under

The Counter-Reformation

Following the period of religious fervor at the beginning of the 16th century that brought about the Protestant Reformation, the Catholic Church made a number of attempts to reform itself – a phase known as the Counter-Reformation. The first meeting of a Great Council of the Church at Trent under Pope Paul III accomplished little, but under Pope Pius IV many far-reaching decisions were taken. At this time both Catholic and Protestant rulers expected to have the last word over their subjects' religious beliefs. Religion and politics were intermingled, and the result was a continual state of conflict in Europe. Sweden became briefly the dominant power, following the victories of its warrior king, Gustavus II Adolphus; Philip II of Spain sent an Armada against his sister-in-law Queen Elizabeth I of England; and Catholic France became allies of the Protestant princes against the Catholic emperor.

Pope Paul III presided over the Great Council at Trent in 1545.

From the beginning of the 16th century pressure on the Roman Catholic Church to reform and improve its practices had mounted from within its ranks, and the rapid rise of Protestantism increased this pressure. When Pope Paul III (ruled 1534–49) was elected in 1534, Emperor Charles V encouraged him to call a Great Council of the Church to bring about reform and make peace with Protestant powers. The pope was reluctant to do this; he did not trust the emperor; he did not want to compromise with heretics; and he was well aware how large a portion of the Church's income came from the sale of indulgences and other abuses.

The Inquisition

The Inquisition was a religious court first created in the 13th century to seek out and punish heretics. In 1542 it was refounded as the Roman Inquisition. Like other courts, it could obtain confessions by torture, but a heretic sentenced to death had to be handed over to the civil authority, as the Church was forbidden to shed blood. The Inquisition was widely used against Protestants in Italy and Spain, especially under Pope Paul IV (ruled 1555–59).

Philip II (reigned 1556–98) succeeded his father, Charles V, as king of Spain, though not as Holy Roman Emperor. He saw himself as the champion of the Roman Catholic Church in Europe.

The Duke of Alba's mass executions of Dutch Protestant rebels only strengthened the determination of the Dutch in their fight against Catholic Spain.

The Jesuits

Ignatius Loyola (1491–1556) was a Spanish soldier who converted to Christianity in 1521. He spent a year as a hermit and studied at four universities before becoming a priest in 1537, 16 years after his conversion. With a group of friends, he went to Pope Paul III with a plan for a new religious order based on total commitment to God. The pope approved, and the Society of Jesus, better known as the Jesuits, was founded in 1540. The Jesuits became well-trained missionaries and teachers. They established hundreds of schools, perhaps the best in Europe, and gained many converts to the Roman Catholic Church. Jesuits traveled as far as America, India, and Japan.

Ignatius Loyola, founder of the Jesuits, died in 1556 and was made a saint in 1622.

The revolt of the Netherlands

As king of Spain, Philip II also ruled the Netherlands. By 1556 the northern provinces of the Netherlands were mostly Protestant, while Spain remained firmly Catholic. Philip was determined to punish these heretics. In 1566 he sent an army commanded by the Duke of Alba to crush the Dutch Protestants. Alba began by executing two popular Dutch noblemen. This provoked a national rebellion, to which Alba reacted extremely harshly. His army destroyed towns and killed their entire populations. After an 18-year struggle, the seven united northern provinces, led by Holland, declared their independence, while the Spanish kept control of the southern Netherlands.

Catholic Spanish and Protestant English ships clash in the English Channel in 1588.

The Armada

In 1588 Philip II of Spain decided to attack the English, who had been helping the Dutch Protestant rebels in the Netherlands. He sent an Armada, a great fleet of 130 ships, to conquer England. The plan was for the ships to sail east along the English Channel to the Netherlands, where they would take on board a Spanish army, which they would land in England. But bad weather and the English navy intervened. Blown by a storm and chased by the English, the Spanish ships fled north round Scotland and returned to Spain. Less than half the ships reached home.

SEE ALSO
p. 114 SPANISH AND PORTUGUESE EXPANSION
p. 136 THE REFORMATION
p. 140 THE MEDITERRANEAN WORLD

Pope Pius IV; further reforms of Catholic Church made.

1562–98 French Catholics fight Protestant Huguenots.

1588 English defeat the Spanish Armada, sent by

Philip II of Spain.
1594–1632 Reign of Gustavus II

Adolphus of Sweden.
1618–48 The Thirty Years' War.

In 1545, however, a Great Council met at Trent (Trento) in northern Italy. On the question of Church teaching, it refused all the changes sought by the Protestant reformers, defining Catholic beliefs more clearly and strongly than ever before. Further meetings of the Council of Trent in 1562 and 1563, however, under the more flexible Pope Pius IV (ruled 1559–65), proved constructive in that he was determined to root out ignorance and corruption. The Council gave him greater powers to hold his bishops accountable and to ensure that the bishops exercised tighter control over the clergy. It also established religious colleges (seminaries) to ensure priests were better educated.

Pope Pius IV also encouraged a number of new religious orders to go out into the world, make converts, and work with the poor. These included the Capuchins, the Ursulines (for women), and above all the Jesuits, who gave absolute loyalty to the pope and worked with Catholic rulers in Germany, Austria, Poland, and France to restore the credibility of the Church.

But reforms within Catholicism did nothing to heal the breach with the Protestants. In England Catholics were executed under Edward VI (reigned 1547–53), and under his successor Mary I (reigned 1553–58) Protestants were killed. Religious differences exacerbated the nobles' quarrels in the French civil wars. In the Holy Roman Empire, where the Reformation had started in 1517, the Peace of Augsburg (1555) laid down that the religion of each ruler should be the religion of that state; Protestant and Catholic alliances were formed, and the disastrous result was the Thirty Years War (1618–48), which left most of Europe devastated and its countries bankrupt.

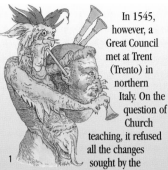

1. Anti-Protestant propaganda: Luther plays the Devil's tune.

2. Detail from a colored woodcut by Lucas Cranach the Elder (1472–1553). Cranach was a friend of Luther and the woodcut sets out to show the corruption of the Roman Catholic clergy (on the right) compared to the purity of the Protestant clergy (left).

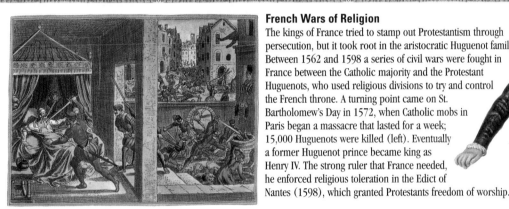

French Wars of Religion

The kings of France tried to stamp out Protestantism through persecution, but it took root in the aristocratic Huguenot family. Between 1562 and 1598 a series of civil wars were fought in France between the Catholic majority and the Protestant Huguenots, who used religious divisions to try and control the French throne. A turning point came on St. Bartholomew's Day in 1572, when Catholic mobs in Paris began a massacre that lasted for a week; 15,000 Huguenots were killed (left). Eventually a former Huguenot prince became king as Henry IV. The strong ruler that France needed, he enforced religious toleration in the Edict of Nantes (1598), which granted Protestants freedom of worship.

Henry IV (1553–1610) succeeded to the French throne in 1589, but had to fight another war and become a Catholic himself before he could be crowned king.

Religion in Europe

Every country in Europe was affected by the Protestant Reformation. Although France remained Catholic, it had many Calvinist Protestants (the Huguenots). There were groups of Protestants of various kinds in Spain, Portugal, and Italy, though fewer than in northern Europe. The Counter-Reformation had some success in preventing Protestantism from spreading farther, and sometimes won back Protestant regions to Catholicism. Poland, for example, had become mainly Protestant, but reverted to Catholicism by 1630.

Rom. Catholic	Anglican
Orthodox	Lutheran/Catholic
Lutheran	Calvinist/Lutheran/Catholic
Calvinist	Muslim/Orthodox

NORWAY
SCOTLAND
SWEDEN
IRELAND
DENMARK
ENGLAND
POLAND
FRANCE
HUNGARY
PORTUGAL
SPAIN
OTTOMAN EMPIRE

RELIGION IN EUROPE IN 1565.

England

England went through many religious changes under King Henry VIII and his three children. Henry established a national church, but kept a Catholic form of worship. Under his son Edward VI (reigned 1547–53) England became Protestant. Mary I (reigned 1553–58) made England Catholic again under the pope.

In 1559 Elizabeth I (reigned 1558–1603, above) chose to make her Church of England a national, Protestant Church, but its form of worship was nearer Catholicism than that of any other Protestant Church of the time.

War in Bohemia

The Peace of Augsburg (1555) brought religious peace to the Holy Roman Empire. For over 50 years there were no religious wars. Then in 1618, in response to the oppression of the Catholic king of Bohemia, who was also the Habsburg emperor, some Bohemian Protestants threw two of his officials out of a window of his castle in Prague. This incident, known as the "defenestration of Prague," (right) contributed to the outbreak of the next major religious war in Europe, the Thirty Years' War.

King Gustavus II Adolphus of Sweden (1594–1632), a Protestant champion in the Thirty Years' War, won many victories over Emperor Ferdinand II. He was killed at the Battle of Lützen.

The Thirty Years' War (1618–48)

In the conflict between the Protestants of Bohemia and its Catholic king, the Holy Roman Emperor, both sides looked for allies. The war soon spread, until every major European country (except England) was involved. The Dutch, for example, helped the Protestants, while the Spanish sided with the emperor. In 1634 France, which had recently been fighting French Protestants, entered the war in alliance with Sweden against the Catholic emperor. When the war finally ended in 1648, France had become the greatest power in a devastated Europe.

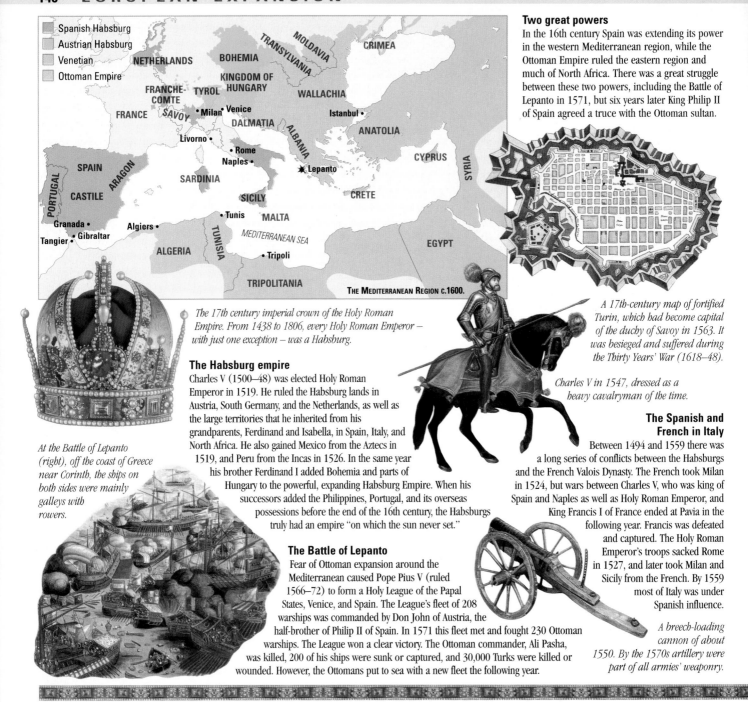

Spanish Habsburg
Austrian Habsburg
Venetian
Ottoman Empire

THE MEDITERRANEAN REGION c.1600.

Two great powers

In the 16th century Spain was extending its power in the western Mediterranean region, while the Ottoman Empire ruled the eastern region and much of North Africa. There was a great struggle between these two powers, including the Battle of Lepanto in 1571, but six years later King Philip II of Spain agreed a truce with the Ottoman sultan.

The 17th century imperial crown of the Holy Roman Empire. From 1438 to 1806, every Holy Roman Emperor – with just one exception – was a Habsburg.

A 17th-century map of fortified Turin, which had become capital of the duchy of Savoy in 1563. It was besieged and suffered during the Thirty Years' War (1618–48).

Charles V in 1547, dressed as a heavy cavalryman of the time.

The Habsburg empire

Charles V (1500–48) was elected Holy Roman Emperor in 1519. He ruled the Habsburg lands in Austria, South Germany, and the Netherlands, as well as the large territories that he inherited from his grandparents, Ferdinand and Isabella, in Spain, Italy, and North Africa. He also gained Mexico from the Aztecs in 1519, and Peru from the Incas in 1526. In the same year his brother Ferdinand I added Bohemia and parts of Hungary to the powerful, expanding Habsburg Empire. When his successors added the Philippines, Portugal, and its overseas possessions before the end of the 16th century, the Habsburgs truly had an empire "on which the sun never set."

At the Battle of Lepanto (right), off the coast of Greece near Corinth, the ships on both sides were mainly galleys with rowers.

The Spanish and French in Italy

Between 1494 and 1559 there was a long series of conflicts between the Habsburgs and the French Valois Dynasty. The French took Milan in 1524, but wars between Charles V, who was king of Spain and Naples as well as Holy Roman Emperor, and King Francis I of France ended at Pavia in the following year. Francis was defeated and captured. The Holy Roman Emperor's troops sacked Rome in 1527, and later took Milan and Sicily from the French. By 1559 most of Italy was under Spanish influence.

A breech-loading cannon of about 1550. By the 1570s artillery were part of all armies' weaponry.

The Battle of Lepanto

Fear of Ottoman expansion around the Mediterranean caused Pope Pius V (ruled 1566–72) to form a Holy League of the Papal States, Venice, and Spain. The League's fleet of 208 warships was commanded by Don John of Austria, the half-brother of Philip II of Spain. In 1571 this fleet met and fought 230 Ottoman warships. The League won a clear victory. The Ottoman commander, Ali Pasha, was killed, 200 of his ships were sunk or captured, and 30,000 Turks were killed or wounded. However, the Ottomans put to sea with a new fleet the following year.

1519 Habsburg Charles V is elected Holy Roman Emperor.

1558 Habsburg Mediterranean possessions pass to Philip II

(1527–98) of Spain.
1571 Battle of Lepanto between

Holy League and Ottoman Turks.
1593 Livorno (Leghorn) is

declared a free port.
1655 The British destroy a

The Mediterranean World

In the 16th century the Italian states lost power as the Mediterranean world saw the rise and expansion of two great empires, which vied for control over the region. The Spanish Habsburgs gained almost total control over southern Europe, from Gibraltar and the Iberian Peninsula to the northern part of the Dalmatian coast on the eastern Adriatic. Apart from Venetian territories in Dalmatia and on islands such as Corfu, Zante, and Crete, the eastern region of the Mediterranean and the north African coast were part of the Ottoman Empire. The two great empires met in conflict and then quickly agreed a truce. In the 17th century European sea power passed to the Atlantic nations, and the Mediterranean became less important in world terms. At the beginning of the 18th century the whole of the western region was affected by the War of the Spanish Succession (1701–14) as Louis XIV tried to increase French power.

Early in the 16th century the Habsburg Empire, under Holy Roman Emperor Charles V (reigned 1519–56), expanded southward to the Mediterranean region. Charles was heir to separate inheritances from his four grandparents, and two of them increased his Mediterranean interests: from Ferdinand of Aragon he gained Aragon, Sardinia, Naples, and Sicily, to which he added Lombardy and Tunis in 1535; from Isabella of Castile he acquired Castile and Granada.

On Charles's death in 1558, his central European territories passed to his brother, Ferdinand I, while his Mediterranean possessions went to his

VENETIA.

Independent Venice

In the 16th century the republic of Venice held large territories in the eastern Mediterranean, including Crete, Cyprus, and the Dalmatian coast (now part of Croatia), as well as the region surrounding the city of Venice itself. The Ottoman Turks were a great threat to the Venetian colonies, however. In 1571 they took Cyprus, and in 1669 they succeeded in gaining Crete after besieging the port of Heraklion for 20 years. Venice itself remained independent until 1797, when Napoleon's forces occupied the city and divided what was left of its empire between France and Austria.

When the French attacked Algiers, Barbary pirates retaliated by making human cannonballs of their captives.

Barbary pirates

Piracy and privateering flourished around the Mediterranean from the early 16th century. Muslim pirates from the Barbary coast of North Africa attacked Spanish, French, and Italian ships from their bases in Algiers, Tunis, and Tripoli. When the Grand Duke of Tuscany declared Livorno a free port in 1593, the pirates also increased their activity.

SEE ALSO
p. 108 EUROPE IN THE 15TH CENTURY
p. 130 THE OTTOMAN EMPIRE
p. 148 GERMANY • p. 150 FRANCE

English naval power

English navy fleets were first sent into the Mediterranean in the 1650s by the Lord Protector, Oliver Cromwell, in pursuit of royalist vessels. Admiral Robert Blake (1599–1657) was one of Cromwell's most successful commanders, and he destroyed Prince Rupert's royalist fleet. In 1655 he destroyed a fleet of Barbary pirates off Tunis. England captured strategic points in the region, which helped keep the balance of power: Tangier in 1662, Gibraltar in 1704 (both securing the entrance to the Mediterranean), and Sardinia and Menorca in 1708.

A detail from a painting by the young Velazquez (1599–1660), who showed everyday Spanish life in a country where poverty struck hard. In the 16th century a series of wars drained the royal treasury and heavy spending ruined the Spanish economy.

A 16th-century Italian scene of a rich man feeding the poor.

Barbary pirate fleet off Tunis. **1669** Ottoman Turks take Crete | from the republic of Venice. **1701–14** War of the Spanish | Succession. **1713** Britain acquires Gibraltar by the Treaty | of Utrecht. **1718** Kingdom of Sardinia founded. | **1797** Napoleon's forces occupy Venice.

son, Philip II, who was King of Spain from 1556 to 1598. Philip, who had married Mary I of England in 1554, also inherited Spanish possessions in America, and in 1580 he annexed Portugal. Spanish Habsburg expansion meant that during the 16th century much of Italy was ruled by Spain, while the many French attempts to gain parts of the Italian peninsula were defeated. Even the independent republic of Genoa was economically dependent on Spain, since most of its trade was with Habsburg territories.

While the Habsburgs were influencing more and more of the European regions of the Mediterranean, the Ottoman Turks were pushing their way farther along the coast of North Africa. The Ottoman Empire included Algiers

(gained in 1529) and Tripoli (1551), and expansion led inevitably to conflict between the two empires. In 1565 the Turks besieged Malta, but the island was relieved. Then in 1571 a combined Holy League force defeated the Ottomans off Lepanto. This did not end the conflict, however, and in 1577 the Spanish king agreed a truce with the Turkish sultan.

During the 17th century Spanish control of Italy was disputed by France, while the Turks generally stayed out of the western Mediterranean. In the east, however, they acquired Crete from Venice in 1669 after a long war. At the same time England was

capturing strategic points in the Mediterranean, including Tangier in 1662, Gibraltar in 1704, and Sardinia and Menorca in 1708. These important bases were soon disputed: Tangier was won by the Sultan of Morocco in 1683; despite Spanish unhappiness, Gibraltar was officially ceded to Britain in 1713 by the Treaty of Utrecht; but the British lost Menorca in 1783. In 1718 the Italian kingdom of Sardinia was created through the duchy of Savoy's acquisition of the island in exchange for Sicily.

1. Sculpture of a winged lion from Venice, Italy. The lion is the symbol of St. Mark, patron saint of Venice.

142   **EUROPEAN EXPANSION**

1526 Ottoman Turks defeat the   at the Battle of Mohacs.   Roman Emperor. **1618–48** The   Peace of Westphalia. **1655**   of Poland's Baltic provinces.
Hungarian and Bohemian army   **1556** Ferdinand I becomes Holy   Thirty Years' War, ends with the   Sweden wins control over most   **1674** John III Sobieski becomes

Central and Eastern Europe: the struggle for power

For a long time after 1500 there was a great struggle in Central and Eastern Europe between the Habsburg Austrians and the Ottoman Turks. The reconquest of Hungary gave the Habsburgs great power, and when the Turks were driven from their siege of Vienna in 1683 with the help of the king of Poland, the Habsburgs were even stronger. When their male line died out in 1740, however, the Habsburgs lost Silesia to the emerging force of Prussia. Just 32 years later, Poland was also divided up among the three powers of Russia, Prussia, and Austria. The map of Central and Eastern Europe had changed dramatically by 1806, when Francis II declared the end of the Holy Roman Empire.

In 1526 Habsburg Charles V's brother Ferdinand I became king of Bohemia and Hungary. He fought against the Ottoman Turks, who had conquered a large part of Hungary at the Battle of Mohacs, and made the region of Transylvania a principality. The Habsburgs took Hungary's western and northern sections. In 1556 Austria and the title of Holy Roman Emperor went to Ferdinand.

In 1618 Bohemian Protestants rebelled against their Roman Catholic Habsburg ruler but were defeated. The revolt triggered the Thirty Years' War, which eventually involved most European nations. The Peace of Westphalia

Habsburg designer

Giuseppe Arcimboldo (1527–93) was born in Milan and moved to Prague in 1562, where he became a designer of court pageants to the Habsburg emperor Rudolf II (reigned 1552–1612).

Arcimboldo was well known for his strange portraits, such as this man made of vegetables entitled "Summer." Rudolf's court was a haven for eccentrics, astrologers, and alchemists.

The Austrian Habsburgs

The Habsburg Dynasty ruled Austria as dukes, archdukes, and emperors continuously from 1282 to 1918. They also ruled Bohemia and Hungary from 1526, though Ferdinand I (brother of Holy Roman Emperor Charles V, who himself became emperor in 1556) had a rival king of Hungary in Janos Zapolya. After 1740 the Austrian dynasty was known as the House of Habsburg-Lorraine.

The Thirty Years' War

The Thirty Years' War (1618–48) developed from bitter rivalries between the Habsburg Empire's rulers and those of other nations, especially France. It was caused by the revolt of Protestants in Bohemia, and though this was put down by imperial forces, the revolt spread to Germany. The war ended with the Peace of Westphalia, which drew up many of the borders of modern Europe.

Holy Roman Emperor Leopold I (1640–1705) loved the theater and opera, and is shown here (left) in costume. Leopold was successful against the Turks, defeating their siege of Vienna in 1683 and freeing most of Hungary from Turkish control by 1699. Under Leopold Vienna became a great center of culture.

CENTRAL AND EASTERN EUROPE IN THE 17TH CENTURY.

POLAND – LITHUANIA

SILESIA

BOHEMIA

BAVARIA   MORAVIA

AUSTRIA   ROYAL HUNGARY   TRANSYLVANIA

HUNGARY

ITALY   CROATIA

OTTOMAN EMPIRE

A Hungarian pandour, one of the notoriously brutal foot soldiers who became part of the Austrian army in the 18th century. The Habsburgs needed a strong army for their countless struggles over territory.

Left: Albrecht von Wallenstein (1583–1634), the Bohemian general who commanded the imperial forces during the Thirty Years' War, was murdered by British officers after rebelling against Emperor Ferdinand I.

SEE ALSO
p. 100 RUSSIA AND EASTERN EUROPE
p. 130 THE OTTOMAN EMPIRE
p. 148 GERMANY

king of Poland. **1683** Turkish siege of Vienna fails. **1740** Frederick the Great becomes king of Prussia. **1740–48** War of the Austrian Succession. **1756–63** Seven Years' War between Austria and Prussia. **1772, 1793, 1795** First, second, and third partitions of Poland by Russia, Prussia, and Austria.

declared that rulers could determine the official religion of their state, and the Habsburgs were able to force Catholicism on the people in their lands. In the late 1600s, Habsburg forces drove the Ottomans out of most of Hungary. Their harsh rule led to an uprising in 1703, which the Habsburgs put down in 1711.

The Polish Empire had reached its height during the 16th century, when it covered a large part of Central and Eastern Europe. Poland and Lithuania were united under a single parliament in 1569. After 1572, Polish kings were elected by the nobles. In 1655, Sweden won control over most of Poland's Baltic provinces.

Charles VI, archduke of Austria, became Holy Roman Emperor in 1711. In 1724 he made a special decree which allowed his eldest daughter, Maria Theresa, to inherit the Habsburg possessions. After Charles VI died in 1740, several states challenged Maria Theresa's right to rule and tried to take her lands in the War of the Austrian Succession (1740–48). The

Austrians lost Silesia to Prussia, but the European powers recognized Maria Theresa as ruler of Austria, Bohemia, and Hungary. In the following Seven Years' War (1756–63), she tried unsuccessfully to regain Silesia.

Frederick the Great had become King of Prussia in 1740, and he made his country a major European power. In 1772 Austria, Prussia, and Russia divided Poland's territory between them. In 1793 and 1795, Prussia and Russia seized additional territory. In 1806 Napoleon forced Francis II to dissolve the Habsburg Empire.

1. Holy Roman Emperor Joseph II (1741–90) encouraged new farming techniques among his people.

Prince Eugene of Savoy (1663–1736) was turned down by the French army because of his small size. He therefore placed himself at the service of Leopold I, and was so successful that he became commander-in-chief of the Habsburg armies. He was wounded 13 times, but became very rich from his exploits.

The War of the Austrian Succession

The War of the Austrian Succession was fought from 1740 to 1748 between the great powers of Austria and Prussia. Britain supported Austria, while France and Spain were on Prussia's side. The war was brought about by the disputed succession of Maria Theresa (1717–80) to the Austrian lands, and started when Frederick the Great (1712–86) of Prussia annexed the Austrian province of Silesia in 1740.

Maria Theresa (right) became Archduchess of Austria in 1740. In 1745 her husband Francis, Grand Duke of Tuscany, became Holy Roman Emperor during the War of Austrian Succession.

Transylvania

In 1619 Bethlen Gabor (1580–1629) (left), the Protestant ruler of Transylvania – which was then a self-governing principality within the Ottoman Empire – invaded Habsburg-controlled Hungary and was elected king. Two years later he gave up the title in exchange for Ferdinand's agreement to allow Hungarian Protestants to worship freely. In 1687 Transylvania (in present-day Romania) came under the rule of Habsburg-controlled Hungary.

Poland

Elected kings followed the death of the last Jagiellon ruler of Poland, in 1572. Nine years later King Stephen Bathory defeated Ivan the Terrible in the Livonian War. In 1772 Poland was divided between Austria, Prussia, and Russia, and in 1793 further areas were seized. Two years later the invaders occupied the rest of the country, and in 1815 the Congress of Vienna rearranged the division, creating the Congress Kingdom of Poland.

A Livonian peasant. Livonia (a region covering most of present-day Latvia and Estonia) was conquered by Ivan the Terrible in the 1560s, and divided between Poland and Sweden in 1583. In 1710 the region was occupied by Russia.

John III Sobieski (1624–96), who became King of Poland in 1674. He was a brilliant military commander who saved Vienna from the Turks.

The bourgeoisie

This class of people referred originally to the merchants who started living in towns at the end of the Middle Ages and who struggled for rights and citizenship against land-owning nobles. The French term "bourgeoisie" meant "people of the bourg, or town." The term "middle class" came into use in the early 19th century, because these merchants, traders, businessmen and townspeople were economically and socially between the lower, working class and the upper, aristocratic class.

A couple from the Dutch bourgeoisie of the 17th century. The Dutch Republic's great trading wealth helped its middle class develop.

London's Royal Exchange burned down in the Great Fire of 1666. It was rebuilt and opened again in 1675. Lloyd's insurance company began in the 1680s in the London coffee house of Edward Lloyd.

The growth of commerce

During the 16th century, the center of European commerce moved away from Italy to the innovative and fast-growing countries of northwest Europe. The Netherlands became a major ship-building region, supplying vessels to the rest of Europe; England controlled important mining and metal-working interests; Sweden exported its rich metal deposits; and France also forged ahead at this time. Easy access to capital and low interest rates encouraged even more growth in these countries.

London financiers plan the Bank of England, which was set up to raise funds from the public and make loans to the British government. The funds were needed by King William III for the costly war with France. Interest payments to investors were secured by taxes on trade and beer.

Joint-stock companies

In the 17th century joint-stock companies were formed in northern Europe, especially by overseas traders who needed to raise money to fund ships and cargo. The funds were obtained by selling shares of stock to individual investors. The English and Dutch East India Companies were famous examples. Many of these companies were very risky, and in 1720 the collapse of the British South Sea Company, which was set up to trade with Spanish America, bankrupted countless small investors.

This satirical illustration shows the fall of investors in the South Sea Company. The company's collapse was known as the "South Sea Bubble." British Treasury minister Sir Robert Walpole's skilful handling of the crisis led to him becoming Britain's first prime minister the following year.

Rise of the Middle Class

The European economy expanded between 1500 and the onset of the Industrial Revolution. As trade increased in northern Europe, so towns grew in both size and number. Townsmen and their families were socially and economically above peasants and laborers, but their position was still beneath that of the landowning nobility. So townspeople, the so-called bourgeoisie, formed the middle class of European society. Most were merchants or craftsmen, and many became involved in financial services. There were also a growing number of lawyers, doctors, apothecaries, and journalists. These professional people increased their political influence during the 18th century. The middle class had its greatest impact on the culture of the Netherlands, Britain, and France.

The expanding economy of Western Europe was based on trade and finance managed by a growing "middle class." At the top of the middle class there was a small group of very wealthy upper middle class bankers and merchants. Kings and other rulers borrowed money from these men: between 1520 and 1560 Holy Roman Emperor Charles V and his son King Philip II of Spain both raised large loans from merchants and bankers in Antwerp by using the security of Spanish American gold and silver. These loans gave the bankers considerable political power. In Britain, for most of the 18th century, the government depended on the financial support of London bankers and merchants, who came to have a decisive influence on government policies. In France, an equally influential group of financiers supported the reign of King Louis XIV. Directly below the upper middle class were an increasing range of occupations (such as storekeepers and artisans), and professions (including doctors, lawyers,

Left: Cutaway design for a wealthy merchant's London town house (1774). Increasing numbers of merchants and professional people adopted the habits of the upper classes in 17th- and 18th-century England, building themselves splendid houses. The landed gentry, many of whom also grew richer because of improved farming methods, began to live half the year in London where they attended an active social round of balls, receptions, and dinner parties, known as the "season."

LONDON.

This panorama shows London in 1588.

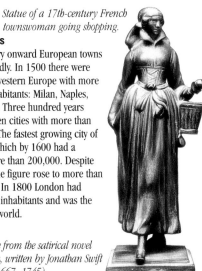

Statue of a 17th-century French townswoman going shopping.

The growth of cities

From the 16th century onward European towns and cities grew rapidly. In 1500 there were just four cities in western Europe with more than 100,000 inhabitants: Milan, Naples, Venice, and Paris. Three hundred years later there were ten cities with more than 200,000 people. The fastest growing city of all was London, which by 1600 had a population of more than 200,000. Despite fire and plague, the figure rose to more than 500,000 by 1700. In 1800 London had about one million inhabitants and was the largest city in the world.

Below: Scene from the satirical novel Gulliver's Travels, *written by Jonathan Swift (1667–1745).*

Genre painting

In the Netherlands of the 17th century the visual arts came to have more meaning and relevance to the middle class. Frans Hals (c.1582–1666) and other Dutch painters invented the group portrait, painting members of guilds and other societies. Hals also painted scenes from everyday life, which are called genre painting. The finest painter of interior scenes was Jan Vermeer (1632–75), who spent his whole life in the Dutch town of Delft but who did not achieve recognition in his own lifetime.

Literature

The new literary form of the novel developed, especially in England, in the early 18th century. It was used to explore social themes, which were of great interest to the middle class. Great English novelists included Daniel Defoe (*Robinson Crusoe*, 1719; *Moll Flanders*, 1722), Samuel Richardson (*Pamela, or Virtue Rewarded*, 1740), and Henry Fielding (*Tom Jones*, 1749).

This Dutch painting shows a poor family receiving a visit from more wealthy citizens. Many peasants who came to the growing towns and cities failed to find work. Life was very different for the comfortable bourgeoisie.

SEE ALSO
p. 134 EUROPEAN AGRICULTURE AND TRADE
p. 146 THE RISE OF THE MODERN STATE

Exchange Bank opens. **1694** The Bank of England is set up in London. **1702** The first daily newspaper, the Daily Courant, appears in England. **1720** The South Sea Bubble (collapse of the British South Sea Company) causes a scandal. **1726** Swift's *Gulliver's Travels* is published.

journalists, and government servants) whose practitioners were rich enough to enjoy leisured lifestyles. These people had a striking influence on the culture of the times. With money and time on their hands they encouraged the growth of new forms of art, such as the novel which developed in Britain and France in the 18th century. Pastimes like the theater and opera became increasingly popular as more people had the money to buy a ticket.

By the end of the 18th century the bourgeoisie made up about 15 percent of the population in England and more than 8 percent in France. Many of the leaders of the French Revolution (1789) came from the bourgeoisie.

Most of these changes took place in the northwestern corner of Europe, especially in Britain, France, and the Netherlands. Elsewhere the economy remained strongly based on agriculture. And even in the northwest where the growth of the middles classes was most obvious, the majority of people were still employed in agriculture and the nobility remained the wealthiest and most powerful group in society.

1. An opera singer in costume. Opera began in 16th century Florence and then spread across Europe. By the mid-18th century it had also become popular in London.

Coffee houses

In the 17th and 18th centuries European coffee houses were centers of cultural and political life, as well as business. This was especially true in London, where middle-class men went several times a day to learn the latest news. In 1730, London had about 500 coffee houses. Newspaper reporters obtained their information there. Many men kept regular hours at their coffee house, so that others knew where to find them.

Catching up on the news in a Viennese coffee house.

In 1603 James VI of Scotland inherited the English throne as James I. The first Stuart king quarreled with parliament because he wanted to rule as an absolute monarch. Under James's son, Charles I, the struggle between king and parliament continued, and Charles did not call a parliamentary session from 1629 to 1640. Civil war broke out in 1642, and Oliver Cromwell emerged as leader. Charles was beheaded in 1649, and England first became a republic, called the Commonwealth, and then a dictatorship, called the Protectorate. In 1660 a new parliament restored the monarchy under Charles II but kept most of the powers it had won. In 1689 William and Mary became joint rulers after accepting the Bill of Rights, which gave the people basic civil rights and made it illegal for the king to keep a standing army, to raise taxes without parliament's approval, or to be a Roman Catholic. In 1707, the Act of Union joined the Kingdom of England and Wales with that of Scotland to form the Kingdom of Great Britain.

In France, the power of the kings and their ministers grew steadily from the 16th century. The actual ruler behind Louis XIII (reigned 1610–43) was prime minister Cardinal Richelieu, who nevertheless increased royal power. Louis XIV was the outstanding example of the absolute French king. After his prime minister died in 1661, Louis declared that he would take the role. But the construction of the Palace of Versailles and a series of major wars drained France's finances. By the 18th century a government bureaucracy had developed to manage a large standing royal army, as well as to collect taxes, while royal courts upheld law and order.

In the Netherlands, the northern provinces had declared their independence from Spain in 1581. The Dutch fought for their freedom until 1648, when Spain finally recognized their independence. The Netherlands fought three naval wars with England between 1652 and 1674. France and England formed a secret alliance in 1670, and attacked the Dutch Republic in 1672. The English suffered major defeats at sea, and made peace with the Dutch in 1674. The French were driven out, and signed a peace treaty in 1678. The Netherlands, England, and other European countries defeated France in two more wars (1689–97 and 1701–14).

1. Soldiers of the English Civil War.

Rise of the Modern State

Uprisings against the state were commonplace throughout the 17th century in both England and France. The English monarch had to contend with the demands of parliament, which did not always coincide with the philosophy of the divine right of kings. In France there were skirmishes between the crown and the aristocracy, as well as with the other two of the three "estates." The upshot was that the French assembly was not convened between 1614 and 1789, and not at all during the long reign of Louis XIV, the epitome of absolute French monarchs. Towards the end of the 17th century, the internal struggles died down in England, France, and the Netherlands, and the three nations started fighting each other.

Dutch Republic 1648
Revolts of the late 16th and early 17th centuries
Town revolts

England, France, and the Netherlands were all plagued by rebellion between 1500 and 1650, as shown on this map.

MAJOR REBELLIONS IN ENGLAND, FRANCE, AND THE NETHERLANDS 1500–1650.

James I (1566–1625) had strong ideas about the role of the kings. In 1598 he wrote a book called The True Law of a Free Monarchy.

The divine right of kings
James VI had been King of the Scots for 36 years before he became James I of England and Ireland in 1603. Now that he ruled over a united Britain, James wished for his subjects "one worship to God, one kingdom entirely governed, one uniformity of laws." But he also believed in the divine right of kings, claiming that monarchs are responsible only to God and that their subjects owe them unquestioning obedience.

The Fronde
The Fronde were a series of uprisings that took place in France between 1648 and 1653. The name was taken from the French word for a sling used in a children's game played in the streets of Paris in defiance of civil authorities. The uprisings, during the regency of Anne of Austria, Louis XIV's mother, were against the monarchy as represented by Cardinal Jules Mazarin (1602–61), who promoted the power of the crown.

Above: The ceremonial costume of the Second Estate – the nobility – of the French assembly, which met regularly between 1347 and 1614, but then not again until 1789. In the intervening period the king ruled as an absolute monarch. The First Estate was the clergy, and the Third Estate the commoners.

Levellers and Diggers
The English Civil War led to several groups campaigning for greater rights for ordinary people. The Levellers, who came mainly from the lower ranks of the army, wanted to abolish the monarchy, have a written constitution, and votes for everyone in an equal society. The Diggers had similar beliefs; they got their name from their attempts to dig up common land and use it as farmland for the poor.

This satire on the Levellers, who saw all occupations as equal, appeared in 1647.

Republic. **1648–53** The Fronde uprisings against the French | monarchy as represented by Cardinal Jules Mazarin. **1653–59** | England is governed by Oliver Cromwell's Protectorate. | **1676** Palace of Versailles begun. **1685** The Edict of Nantes (of 1598) | is revoked by Louis XIV, leading to persecution of the Huguenots.

The Gunpowder Plot

This conspiracy of Catholic gentry, led by Robert Catesby (1573–1605), was intended to blow up the English parliament in 1605. It failed when Guy Fawkes (1570–1606), who placed the explosives in a cellar of the Palace of Westminster, was arrested after another conspirator had warned a relative not to attend parliament that day. Catesby was killed while resisting arrest, and Fawkes was executed.

Men being forcibly recruited to the British army in the 17th century. All the countries of Europe had to work hard to keep up their armies, and they often rounded up petty criminals, drunks, and idlers.

The Gunpowder Plot conspirators. Robert Catesby is second and Guy Fawkes third from the right. In Britain, November 5th is still celebrated with fireworks, and effigies of Fawkes, called "guys," are burned on bonfires.

The Edict of Nantes

This edict of 1598 granting religious liberty to the Huguenots (French Protestants) was revoked by Louis XIV in 1685. This led to persecution of those Huguenots who refused to convert to Catholicism. It also resulted in a weakening of France, however, since many of the country's most productive citizens were driven into exile.

A Protestant "heretic" is forced to sign his conversion in 1686.

The Republic of the United Netherlands

The seven northern Dutch provinces, which were Protestant regions, had rebelled against Catholic Spain for 80 years before the Treaty of Westphalia recognized them as the Republic of the United Netherlands in 1648. The new Dutch Republic, which included the provinces of Zeeland, Holland, and Friesland, was not as large as the southern region of the Spanish Netherlands, however. This region, covering present-day Belgium and including the city of Brussels, did not achieve independence until 1830.

- Holy Roman Empire
- Dutch Republic
- Spanish Netherlands

NORTH SEA — FRIESLAND — HOLLAND — Amsterdam — The Hague — ZEELAND — Bruges — Brussels — Liège — FRANCE

THE NETHERLANDS AND BELGIUM IN 1648.

Prussia

In the late 17th century the Hohenzollern rulers of Prussia succeeded in creating a unified state in north Germany. Prussian serfs were freed in 1719, and the Prussian army was strengthened. Prussian soldiers (shown below in various cavalry uniforms) became famous for their discipline and efficiency. In the 18th century Frederick the Great, who ruled from 1740 to 1786, used his so-called "enlightened despotism" to make Prussia a major European power.

Left: In 1709 a poll tax was introduced in France to pay for the upkeep of the army. Men and women had to pay the tax in person, which meant that tax offices were full of people jostling to pay a tax which they resented.

Louis XIV (right) welcomes the doge of Genoa to the Palace of Versailles, which the Sun King had built as his luxurious residence.

The Sun King

Louis XIV (1638–1715), who was king of France for 72 years, was the greatest European example of an absolute monarch. He believed totally in the divine right of kings, and is supposed to have said, *"L'état c'est moi"* ("I am the state"). Louis chose the sun as his royal emblem and liked to be known as the Sun King, which he felt reflected the splendor of his reign.

Schönbrunn Palace in Vienna was the spectacular summer residence of the Austrian Habsburg emperors. It was meant to rival the French Palace of Versailles.

The Holy Roman Empire

The Holy Roman Empire was more than Germany. In earlier centuries, it had nearly become a single state covering most of central Europe and Italy. The Emperor was also the leading Christian ruler, and after the Reformation he became the defender of the Roman Catholic Church against Protestants.

Above: An eagle with two heads, a symbol of power, became the badge of the Holy Roman Empire in the 15th century and was kept by the Habsburg emperors of Austria until 1918.

Above: A 17th-century musket. Although it took a long time to load and sometimes misfired, it could pierce an enemy's iron breastplate at 300 ft (100 m).

The Peace of Augsburg (1555), established that the religion of any state should be decided by its ruler. This engraving shows the meeting of the German princes at Augsburg.

The Thirty Years' War

Although it began as a religious war, the Thirty Years' War (1618–48) developed into a struggle for power. It was really a series of wars, involving different quarrels. That made it harder to stop. Ambassadors to the peace talks in Westphalia took five years to reach agreement. The chief victims were the people of Germany, although most of them were not directly involved in the war. When it started, the population of Germany was over 20 million. When it ended, the population was only about 12 million. One effect of the war was that the German people began to think of themselves as one people, in spite of their divisions.

Charles V

When he was elected emperor (1519), Charles was already king of Spain. He also ruled the Netherlands, Burgundy, much of Italy, and the Spanish Empire in America. But Charles was not as powerful as he seemed. His different lands were divided. They had different problems, which had to be dealt with separately. There was just too much governing to do, and in 1556 Charles, tired and depressed by his failure to keep Germany Catholic, gave up his crowns and retired to a Spanish monastery. His empire was divided between the Spanish and Austrian Habsburgs.

Charlottenburg castle, Berlin.

Frederick the Great

Frederick the Great (reigned 1740–86) was one of the greatest rulers in European history. He was an "enlightened despot," which means that while he believed that the ruler must do his best for his people, he thought he should also have absolute power. A fair and intelligent ruler, he abolished torture, freed the peasants on his own estates, and gave Catholics and Protestants equal rights. He was the enemy of Austria, stealing Silesia and making war against the Emperor Joseph II (reigned 1765–90), another "enlightened despot," but a less successful one.

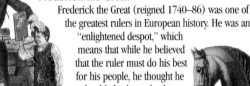

This painting shows Frederick visiting an elementary school. Compulsory education was introduced in Prussia in 1717.

Frederick the Great cared for his army above all. It gave him power to defend and increase his kingdom.

Berlin

Frederick's capital was Berlin, which would later become the capital of the German Empire. It was little more than half the size of Vienna, the Austrian capital, and far smaller than cities like London and Paris. Frederick, a lover of art and architecture, made it a splendid city. Besides his own beautiful palace of Sans Souci, he enlarged Charlottenburg castle (above), built by his grandfather, Frederick I.

1525 The Peasants' Revolt.
1547 Charles V defeats

Protestant princes at Mühlberg.
1555 Peace of Augsburg.

1618–48 Thirty Years War.
1683 The Turks besiege Vienna.

1700–21 Northern War; Sweden loses its German lands.

1701–14 War of the Spanish Succession.

Germany

By about 1500, the kings of England, France, and Spain were building up strong royal governments. Germany also had a king, belonging to the mighty Habsburg family, (he was also Holy Roman Emperor and Europe's senior ruler). But in Germany the opposite happened. Instead of getting stronger, the imperial government grew weaker. Germany remained divided into hundreds of states. Officially, their rulers were subjects of the Habsburg emperor, but in fact they were independent. By far the biggest German state was Austria, which was ruled directly by the Habsburgs. Saxony and Bavaria were also large countries, and in the 18th century they were joined by another, Brandenburg, or Prussia, as it became known in 1701. Under another great dynasty, the Hohenzollerns, Prussia was able to challenge Austria (and even take some of its most valuable territory). As many Germans came to believe, the division of their country slowed down its development. With so many frontiers and customs posts, trade was difficult. Reforms also made slow progress. The German peasants, although they were better off than peasants farther east, were not yet free.

A German soldier of the mid-17th century.

SEE ALSO
p. 136 THE REFORMATION
p. 138 THE COUNTER-REFORMATION
p. 178 UNIFICATION OF ITALY AND GERMANY

Saxony

Augustus the Strong, elector of Saxony (1694–1733) and also king of Poland, hoped to become the greatest monarch in northern Europe. He fought in the long Northern War (1700–21) against Sweden. His statue, known as the Golden Rider (left), stands in Dresden, Saxony's capital and one of the great showplaces of art in 18th-century Germany. Later, Saxony sided with Prussia in the League of Princes (1785), against the Emperor Joseph II, who was trying to expand Habsburg lands by taking over Bavaria.

One industry that was entirely new was the making of porcelain, a secret known only to the Chinese before the Meissen factory opened near Dresden in 1710. This Meissen eagle was made for Augustus the Strong.

Music

Germany produced at least five of the world's greatest composers. Two geniuses, Bach (right) and Handel, were born in Saxony in 1685, though Handel later moved to England. In the next generation, Austria took the lead with Haydn (1732–1809), Mozart (1756–91), who was giving concerts in foreign cities at the age of seven, and finally Beethoven (1770–1827), who was born in the Rhineland but worked in Vienna.

Industry

Modern industry was just beginning in the mid-18th century. In Prussia, Frederick the Great treated industrial development as more important than anything except the army. Berlin became a manufacturing city and industrial zones appeared in other areas as well. Germany had its first steam engine in 1751. New industries, especially in textiles and metals, got underway.

People who were accused of sorcery were sometimes forced to wear iron masks like these.

Witch hunts

The strong religious feelings that brought so much trouble to Germany did not prevent superstition and fear. Fear of witches actually increased after the Reformation. Even Luther once said he was in favor of burning witches. In the late 17th century it was at its worst: hundreds were tortured and killed.

Weimar

One of the princes who favored German unity but opposed Habsburg expansion by joining the League of Princes was the Grand Duke of Saxe-Weimar. Although his state was a small one, Weimar became a kind of capital of German literature and scholarship in the late 18th century. One of his ministers was Goethe (right), who is now regarded as the greatest of all German writers.

Wars

During the 17th and 18th centuries Germany was seldom at peace. One cause of war was the conflict between the Austrian Habsburg emperors and the German princes. Prussia was becoming the leader of resistance to Austria, but alliances often changed, and in 1772 Prussia joined with Austria (and Russia) to divide up Poland. Frederick the Great gained West Prussia which, lying between his divided lands, finally joined them into one.

Farming

the 18th century, most people worked in farming. Enlightened rulers like Frederick the Great tried to improve farming by building roads and bridges, clearing forest, and draining swamps, and encouraging new crops such as turnips and potatoes. Frederick also gave aid to pioneer farmers to start cultivating new land in the eastern provinces.

An iron foundry in Prussia.

A grenadier in Frederick the Great's army. Muskets now had a fitted bayonet, for hand-to-hand fighting. Frederick's army was the best in the world.

1740 Frederick II of Prussia introduces economic and religious reform.
1740–48 War of the Austrian Succession.
1756–63 Seven Years War.
1772 First Partition of Poland.
1785 League of Princes formed.

One of the most important events in German history was Martin Luther's attack on the Church that led to the Reformation. By challenging the rule of the Pope, Luther encouraged the German peasants to rebel (1525) against the landowners. For a short time they controlled half of Germany, but in the end the rebellion was crushed. The Reformation also influenced German rulers. By becoming Protestants, they gained more independence, not only from the Pope but also the Emperor, the guardian of the Catholic Church. Civil war followed, between the Protestant princes and the Emperor. The princes were defeated in battle, but in the Peace of Augsburg (1555) the Emperor agreed that the religion of any

state should be decided by its ruler – a victory for the princes.

Religious wars were still not over. In Bohemia, Czech Protestants disliked the growing power of their Habsburg king (who was soon to be Emperor). In 1618 they threw two of his officials out of a window, and started what became the Thirty Years' War. Most countries in Europe joined in, but nearly all the fighting was in

Germany. After 30 years of war, large stretches of Germany lay in ruins. The German ruler who did best from the war was Frederick William, elector of a smallish state in northern Germany called Brandenburg. Frederick William, called the Great Elector (reigned 1640–1688), strengthened his country, created a permanent army (one of the first in Europe) and greatly increased the power of royal government. He came out of the Thirty Years' War with his lands much enlarged, and later gained control of East Prussia. His successor took the title king of Prussia in 1701.

In 1740 the Habsburg Emperor Charles VI died. He was succeeded by his daughter,

Maria Theresa. There had never been a female emperor, and her position was weak. The Prussian king Frederick II (also called the Great) took his chance to seize the Austrian province of Silesia, and so set off the War of the Austrian Succession (1740–48). Silesia was important because it had large deposits of coal and iron ore.

In the next European war (the Seven Years War, 1756–63), Maria Theresa had the chance of getting Silesia back, because Prussia had no powerful allies on the continent and Austria was fighting alongside France, Russia, Saxony, and Sweden. But Frederick the Great was a brilliant general and Prussia survived – and kept Silesia.

1562 Wars of Religion begin.
1572 St Bartholomew's Day

Massacre.
1598 Edict of Nantes.

1608 French colonists found Québec, New France.

1624 Richelieu becomes chief minister.

1642 Mazarin succeeds Richelieu.

France

In 1500 France seemed to be growing into a strong and united kingdom. But difficulties lay ahead. It was a large country with many different regions, not easy to rule from Paris. France contained many Protestants and for many years civil wars were fought between Catholics and Protestants (the latter were called Huguenots). Strong government returned in the 17th century, and when Louis XIV took over in 1661 he was the most powerful monarch in Europe, and by far the grandest. His large army was almost unbeatable until 1704, and his wars increased the size of France. France was still a great country in the 18th century, the center of European civilization, envied and copied by others. Educated people everywhere spoke French. (King Frederick the Great of Prussia never spoke German at all, except to servants.) But French society was divided. New ideas were stirring, and the royal government was no longer in tune with the times.

Francis I, a true prince of the Renaissance, ruled France from 1515–47. He built beautiful palaces and hired Italian artists like Leonardo da Vinci to work for him.

France in the 16th century had two strong kings, Francis I and his son Henry II. But in 1559 Henry II was accidentally killed in a tournament, leaving the government to his widow, Catherine de Médicis, and their three sons (who all became king in turn). They were unable to prevent a series of nine religious wars between 1562 and 1598. Not until Henry IV, first of a new royal dynasty, the Bourbons, became king was peace restored and freedom of religion granted by Henry's Edict of Nantes. France began to grow rich again.

After Henry IV two clever

Francis I

Francis made an agreement with the pope that gave him control of the French Church and strengthened royal government. He spent much of his reign fighting his great rival, the Habsburg Emperor Charles V, who was also king of Spain. In 1525 he was defeated and captured at the Battle of Pavia. He was released after making promises that he later broke. France was willing to join with Protestants and Muslim Turks to fight the Habsburgs.

Religious Wars

The nine civil wars of the late 16th century were not only about religion. The great noble families, like the House of Guise at the head of the Catholic cause, were struggling to gain control of the royal government, which had become feeble after the death of Francis I's son, Henry II. The man who ended the wars, Henry of Navarre, had been a Huguenot, but became a Catholic in order to gain the crown as Henry IV.

The Massacre of St. Bartholomew (1572) began as a Catholic plot to kill the Huguenot leaders. It got out of control, and ended in the killing of thousands of Huguenots.

Cardinal Mazarin was an Italian, which made him even more unpopular with his opponents in France. He was blamed for the civil wars called the Fronde.

Louis XIV

Louis became king in 1643 when he was five. He took over the government when Cardinal Mazarin died in 1661. Louis believed that he was God's appointed ruler, who answered to God alone. His greatness was the greatness of France because, as he said, the king and the kingdom were the same thing. His reign of 72 years was the longest in European history.

The rule of the Cardinals

The strength of the royal government that Louis XIV enjoyed was mainly the work of Cardinal Richelieu and his chosen successor, Cardinal Mazarin. Richelieu, who was the real ruler of France from 1624 to 1642, also checked the power of the Habsburgs and made France the greatest power in Europe. Mazarin, a brilliant diplomat, put the finishing touches to Richelieu's foreign policy in the peace treaties of Westphalia (1648) and the Pyrenees (1659), bringing peace with Spain.

Versailles

Louis built the palace of Versailles as a home (he had others, including the Louvre in Paris) fit for the world's greatest monarch. It was, and still is, the grandest palace in Europe. Life at Versailles circled around the person of the "Sun King," as Louis was called. When he sat down to dine, hundreds of his subjects queued up to see him, paying a small fee.

Below: A French general's baton from the War of the Spanish Succession (1702–14). The last and greatest of Louis XIV's wars was also the most costly. Although the war was not lost, his armies were now often defeated.

The magnificent gardens of Versailles, planned in the Italian style, had 1,000 fountains. The plan was to change the course of the River Eure to supply them with water.

The wars of Louis XIV

France under Louis XIV took part in many costly wars. Although Louis won more lands for his kingdom in the north and east, he was no great conqueror. His early wars were fought mainly to make France's borders secure. Even his aggressive wars in the Low Countries were caused partly by his fear of Habsburg ambitions. After 1679 he tried to avoid major wars, but other European countries, fearing France's power, were suspicious, and ready to combine against him.

1648–53 The Fronde. **1661** Louis XIV takes over government. | **1685** Louis XIV cancels Edict of Nantes. | **1715** Death of Louis XIV. **1751** First volume of Diderot's | *Encyclopedia.* **1774** Death of Louis XV. | **1789** Outbreak of the French Revolution.

ministers, Richelieu and his successor, Mazarin, greatly strengthened the royal government. Cardinal Richelieu took France into the Thirty Years' War in order to strike a blow against the country's Habsburg rivals, and when Louis XIV began his reign, France had replaced Spain as the strongest and richest country in Europe. But the rule of the cardinals was unpopular. Cardinal Mazarin had to flee the country when revolts, called the Fronde, broke out. By 1652 he was back in control.

This was France's *Grande Siècle* ("great century"). The dazzling splendors of Louis XIV's court astonished foreign visitors. French theater, music, and art enjoyed a

golden age. The successful policies of Louis's minister Jean Baptiste Colbert in trade and industry brought money rolling into the royal treasury. The nobles, who had given French kings so much trouble in the past, were now firmly under royal control. So were the *parlements*.

The provinces were ruled by *intendants*, a new class of officials who depended on the king for their jobs. But later in the reign, after Colbert's death (1683), Louis was less successful. Colbert would have been shocked when Louis cancelled the Edict of Nantes, causing many Huguenots to flee the country. Louis's wars were expensive, and money was running out. In his last and greatest

war, the War of the Spanish Succession, his once-unbeatable armies were thrashed by the English Duke of Marlborough and the Austrian Prince Eugene. Still, he did succeed in making his grandson king of Spain, though he had to agree that Spain and France would never be united. When at last he died, France was still a great country, trade was still growing and, although the poorest peasants lived like animals, many people were rich.

Like Louis XIV, Louis XV tried to be his own chief minister, but he was not a good ruler. Although Louis XIV had warned him not to spend so much money on war, France was again involved in expensive wars that gained nothing. In

the Seven Years War (1756–63), the British took over France's Empire in North America and drove the French out of India. At home, reforms were needed but not made. The laws were complicated, unfair, and out of date. Taxes were so arranged that the rich paid little or nothing and the poor paid a lot. The middle classes, who had grown rich in the days of Colbert, wanted a part in government. The philosophers of the Enlightenment were asking serious questions about the whole nature of royal government. The omens were not good. Said the king's mistress, Mme de Pompadour, *"Après nous, la déluge."*

King Louis XIV with members of the Academy of Sciences, founded in 1666. It was one of the first places where scientists from all over Europe could meet to discuss ideas.

Science and technology

Louis XIV reigned during an exciting time for science, when new ideas were in the air, discoveries were made, and new knowledge put to use in expanding industries. In the next century, one exciting invention was the first successful balloon by the Montgolfier brothers. The first passengers were a sheep and a duck, but in 1783 two men flew over Paris in the Montgolfiers' balloon, the first human beings to fly. At the same time another inventor, Jacques Charles, was experimenting with a hydrogen balloon.

Peasants

Although the largest class of people in France were the peasants, they had few rights and no power. Unlike nobles, they had to pay a tax called the *taille*, as well as other taxes which the nobles managed to avoid. They also had to perform the *corvée*, a kind of tax paid not in money but in labor, usually by repairing the roads. Only the peasants had to do this, although they were the people who needed roads the least.

A high proportion of the many poor farmers had hardly enough land to grow food for their families.

French art and design

Louis XIV's France was a leader of European fashion. The Renaissance style of art and architecture of the 16th century changed to Baroque, an impressive, spectacular style for a spectacular age. In the reign of Louis XV, Baroque gave way to Rococo, especially in the decorative arts and crafts. It was a lighter style with flowing shapes and irregular forms, and it was thoroughly French (as opposed to Baroque which had its origins in Italy).

SEE ALSO
p. 116 DUTCH, ENGLISH, AND FRENCH EXPANSION
• p. 136 THE REFORMATION • p. 138 THE COUNTER-REFORMATION • p. 146 RISE OF THE MODERN STATE

Left: Jean-Baptiste Poquelin (1622–73), better known as Molière, was the greatest French actor and playwright of the times.

The weakness of government

Besides the growing resentment of the Third Estate and the criticisms of the philosophers, the government had serious money problems. In fact it was practically bankrupt. Because of the luxury of the royal court and the laziness of the nobles, the expenses of war could only be paid by borrowing money.

About half the government's income went to pay the interest on its debts. Taxes were not enough, and all efforts to make the nobles pay a fair share failed. Worse, recent wars had been unsuccessful. New France, (Canada) was lost to Britain in 1760. The government had lost not only money, it had lost the confidence and respect of its subjects.

The Three Estates

The people of France could be roughly divided into three classes, or "estates:" the nobility; the clergy; and the rest – the "Third Estate." Government was biased in favor of the nobles and the priests who enjoyed many privileges. The clergy paid no taxes, but levied their own, called tithes, and the nobles too were excused from certain taxes. They were prepared to fight against any government reform that threatened their comfortable situation. The Third Estate was made up of a large middle class of wealthy businessmen, shopkeepers, and the like, who resented the privileges of the higher classes. Because they were not organized, had no spokesmen, and were not represented in government, their complaints could be ignored – for the time being.

This cartoon shows the burdens that were loaded on the backs of the peasants.

The Making of Britain

In 1500 England was a second-rank European kingdom. By 1763 Britain was a leading world power. To achieve this, two things above all were needed: an efficient and stable government, and growing prosperity. By 1500 the English monarchy had finally gained control of the barons and established a strong central government. In the next century, the Stuart monarchy was challenged by parliament and the result was civil war, which led to increased power for the parliament. By the 18th century, now united with Scotland, the country again had a strong and efficient government. It was not seriously threatened by rebellions in support of the exiled Stuarts. Strong government made it possible for the economy to grow. An established British sea-going tradition lay behind the growth of trade and colonies. Rival nations, especially the Dutch and the French, were defeated, and by 1763 Britain was the dominant European power in North America, India, and other centers of trade. The profits of trade in turn provided the money for investment in industry, which made Britain the first truly industrial country.

Henry VIII spent a lot of money building a navy. His flagship, the Henry Grâce à Dieu, *was the largest warship in the world.*

Henry VIII

Henry VIII (reigned 1509–47), famous for his six wives, was an ambitious monarch, who wasted a lot of money on wars with the French and the Scots that gained nothing. The Reformation brought him more money, because Henry confiscated the property of the monasteries, but that too was soon spent. The Reformation was legalized by acts of parliament, which had the effect of making parliament more powerful.

Elizabeth I

People would look back on the reign of Elizabeth (1558–1603) as a golden age. England was growing rich. There was no longer much danger of civil war or rebellion, and gentlemen built fine country houses instead of castles. It was an age of poetry and naval enterprise, when England defied the might of Spain in the Armada of 1588 and Sir Francis Drake sailed around the world. But the Elizabethan government was less successful: it was running short of income, and Elizabeth's ministers failed to make badly needed changes.

Elizabeth, who owned 2,000 dresses, enjoyed being queen, never married, and had no children. She was succeeded by the king of Scots, James VI and I, whose mother had been executed as a traitor in England.

A cameo portrait of Charles I. His execution shocked Europe, and he is still regarded by some people as a martyr.

The Civil War

Relations between king and parliament soon worsened, especially in the reign of Charles I (son of James I). Charles believed that he ruled by the will of God. Parliament believed he was becoming a dictator. When Civil War broke out, the Royalists were at first successful. But Parliament controlled London and the navy, vital advantages, and Charles was defeated. He was later executed (1649) after trying to trick his opponents. England became a republic.

Cromwell

Rule by parliament did not work, and in the end the leading general, Cromwell, was made Lord Protector, in effect king without the title. Although he was a Puritan, always thanking God for his victories, he was more tolerant than most Puritans and a better ruler than most kings. Cromwell was respected by the army, but no one else had his prestige and after his death Charles II, already crowned king by the Scots, returned from exile in 1660.

The Glorious Revolution

Religion played a part in causing the Civil War, because the Puritans disliked the king's Catholic sympathies. The trouble arose again under Charles II, whose heir, his brother (the future James II), actually was a Catholic. When he became king, the tactless James annoyed his Protestant subjects, and on the birth of his son (which meant another Catholic king), they rebelled in the Glorious Revolution (so-called because no one was killed). James was succeeded by his daughter Mary and her husband, William of Orange, both Protestants.

James II is welcomed by the Catholic king of France, Louis XIV, after fleeing England. The existence of James and his descendants in exile gave the French a useful weapon against England.

Parliament

Parliament began as a body that offered advice. Gradually, it gained more power to pass laws and to raise taxes. In 1500, it seldom dared to criticize the royal government. But by 1730 the government was run by the king's ministers (the cabinet) who had to answer to parliament.

Westminster in the 17th century, left to right: Parliament House, Westminster Hall, and Westminster Abbey. Sir Robert Walpole, often called the first prime minister, was in power from 1721 to 1742.

1694 Bank of England founded.
1707 Act of Union between England and Scotland.
1745 Jacobite rebellion.

1765 James Watt invents an efficient steam engine.

1770 Captain Cook lands in Australia.

1776 American Declaration of Independence.

Theater

The first public theaters opened in London in the reign of Elizabeth. Shakespeare, the best among many fine playwrights, was also a professional actor, and owned shares in the Globe Theater, where many of his plays were first performed.

William Shakespeare, the world's most popular playwright, was the son of a tradesman in the provinces.

The Act of Union

In 1707 England and Scotland, who had shared the same monarch for 100 years, joined as one kingdom (above: the act is presented to Queen Anne). The English wanted to prevent Scotland accepting the exiled Stuart monarchy and perhaps aiding France. The Scots wanted to share the growing prosperity of England's trade and empire. Although the Act was very unpopular in Scotland at first, within a few years both English and Scots were firmly united as the nation of Great Britain.

> ### SEE ALSO
> p. 116 DUTCH, ENGLISH, AND FRENCH EXPANSION
> p. 136 THE REFORMATION
> p. 138 THE COUNTER-REFORMATION
> p. 146 THE RISE OF THE MODERN STATE

Left: Although there was no motor traffic, London was as noisy in the 18th century as it is now. This musician finds rehearsal impossible because of the din from the streets.

Most of the old City of London was destroyed by the Great Fire of 1666. It was quickly rebuilt.

Farming

Several things were necessary for industry to develop: new machines, money for investment, and a large workforce. The British population was growing fast in the 18th century, thanks partly to advances in farming, such as rotation of crops, which made it possible to produce more food. In England especially, rich landlords spent much of their time on their country estates. Viscount Townshend, for example, was a government minister, but he was also a progressive farmer, whose nickname was "Turnip" Townshend.

London

London, the capital city, was the biggest city in Europe. It was really two cities: Westminster was the center of government, and the City was the center of trade and business. London was also the chief port, the largest industrial city, and the center of fashion and the arts. It contained large numbers of foreigners and even larger numbers of criminals. Among its inhabitants were some of the poorest people in Europe, and some of the richest. "There is in London," said the writer Samuel Johnson in 1777, "all that life can afford."

Hunting, a popular country sport, allowed landowners, tenants, and tradesmen to meet on equal terms.

The Grand Tour

Among the first tourists were rich people from England who traveled to Italy and other countries from about 1660. Some were young men who went as part of their education as gentlemen, others went to collect works of art to furnish their country houses. They were sometimes gone as long as three years. They were not very popular, because they made no secret of their belief that they were superior to all foreigners.

In this cartoon, an Italian art dealer sells a fake masterpiece to an Englishman on the Grand Tour.

In the Reformation Henry VIII founded the Church of England, making himself the ruler of the church as well as the state. The final settlement of the religious question, under Elizabeth I, created a moderate Protestant Church, but to some Protestants it seemed like Roman Catholicism without the pope. Elizabeth was succeeded by James I, who was already king of Scotland (as James VI). Because Scotland had adopted Presbyterianism, founded on the teaching of John Calvin, these people, called Puritans, hoped he would introduce changes. They were disappointed and religious differences became one of the ingredients of the growing quarrel between king and parliament.

Under James's son, Charles I, the quarrel came to a head. Parliament wanted more say in government, and it could bring pressure on the royal government because it controlled taxes. When Charles's attempt to rule without parliament failed, civil war began. It involved Scotland and Ireland as well as England, and it produced a great leader in Oliver Cromwell. But England's brief experiment with republicanism failed and, after Cromwell's death, the monarchy was restored (1660). Its powers were reduced, especially after the Glorious Revolution (1689), when the English drove out the Catholic James II and put a Dutch prince on the throne as William III.

In spite of all these disturbances at home, England's influence in the world was growing. It produced great writers, like Shakespeare, and great scientists, like Isaac Newton, who finally explained how the universe works. It was a leader in the new developments in farming, which greatly increased food production. Its trade and empire, and the wealth of its merchants, persuaded the Scots to give up their parliament and join with England. Protected by the surrounding sea, Britain was safe from foreign invasion, although the French supported rebellions in favor of the exiled Stuart Dynasty. Even when they took part in European wars, the British did not send large armies to fight in Europe. They concentrated on trade and colonies, where, after they had defeated the Dutch in the late 17th century, France was their chief enemy. In the Seven Years War (1756–63), which was really the first worldwide war, the British drove the French out of North America and India. The French would get their revenge later, when they supported the rebellious American colonists against Britain. But even the loss of its American colonies did not check Britain's growing power and prosperity.

The Struggle for Empire

Between 1500 and 1780, European powers founded bases or settlements across the world. In Asia, where large populations lived in civilizations older than Europe's, they could not create big colonies. In Africa too, they hardly advanced farther than the coast. But the Americas were more thinly populated, and their people could not resist European colonization. In the 17th century, the Spanish and the Portuguese were challenged overseas by northern Europeans. In the East, the Dutch replaced the Portuguese as the leading European power. In the Americas, the huge Spanish Empire was attacked by new rivals, who took over some of the valuable Caribbean islands and established settlements in North America. In the rivalry between the European nations, the winners by 1763 were the British. Spain was a fading power, and the Dutch and Portuguese were too small. France was large and powerful enough, but it was engaged in continental wars; the English were free to concentrate on developing an empire.

Portuguese ships reached Japan in 1543. The Japanese artist has exaggerated features that to him seemed strange – baggy breeches and big noses.

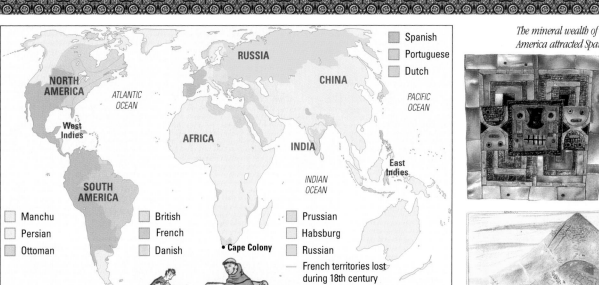

Spanish	
Portuguese	
Dutch	

Manchu	British	Prussian
Persian	French	Habsburg
Ottoman	Danish	Russian

— French territories lost during 18th century

MAJOR WORLD EMPIRES IN 1800.

The European nations that founded bases and colonies around the world were those that bordered the Atlantic. Portugal and Spain, which had led the way, were challenged by England, France, the Netherlands, and the Scandinavian countries. The newly independent Dutch were a great sea power in the 17th century, but Dutch ships had to pass through the English Channel, which England controlled.

The mineral wealth of Central and South America attracted Spanish adventurers. Left: A Huari shell and stone mosaic mirror. Below: At Potosi, in modern Bolivia, the Spanish discovered a mountain of silver. As a result of piracy and smuggling, American silver made up most of Europe's money.

Portugal and Spain in the Americas

In 1783 the Portuguese and Spanish still held their American empires. Although the Dutch seized Brazil from the Portuguese, they were driven out again in 1654. Brazil was valued for sugar-planting, but later provided gold and diamonds. Spain suffered some losses in the Caribbean (the English captured Jamaica in 1655), but remained the leading power. In fact the Spanish Empire revived in the 18th century, through reforms of trade and government. It even expanded, establishing forts as far north as San Francisco.

Above left: A Spanish missionary teaching Christianity to Native Americans in Florida, about 1600.

The Dutch

From its eastern base at Batavia (now Jakarta), the Dutch East India Company controlled the spice trade. It dominated the Portuguese, forced out the English East India Company, and in 1652 established a settlement (right) at the Cape of Good Hope in South Africa, as a halfway house for its merchant fleets. Its smaller companion, the Dutch West India Company was unable to keep Brazil but founded colonies in Guyana and on the island of Curaçao.

West Africa

The Portuguese found some gold in Africa, as well as a coarse form of pepper and a few luxuries, such as ostrich feathers and ivory. But African produce was disappointing compared with the East Indies. The European trading stations scattered along the West African coast were built for the slave trade.

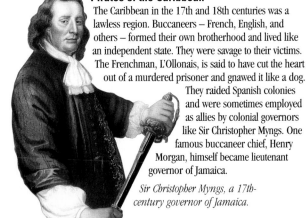

Pirates of the Caribbean

The Caribbean in the 17th and 18th centuries was a lawless region. Buccaneers – French, English, and others – formed their own brotherhood and lived like an independent state. They were savage to their victims. The Frenchman, L'Ollonais, is said to have cut the heart out of a murdered prisoner and gnawed it like a dog. They raided Spanish colonies and were sometimes employed as allies by colonial governors like Sir Christopher Myngs. One famous buccaneer chief, Henry Morgan, himself became lieutenant governor of Jamaica.

Sir Christopher Myngs, a 17th-century governor of Jamaica.

from Ceylon. **1664** The English take New York from the Dutch. **1690** Calcutta founded by the English. **1700–13** War of the Spanish Succession. **1740–48** War of the Austrian Succession. **1754** French and Indian War begins. **1756–63** Seven Years War. **1783** Britain recognizes US independence.

New trade and new settlements were usually paid for and organized by business companies. Governments issued charters to these companies, giving them special privileges. The Dutch East India Company was the most powerful in the 17th century, and controlled all Dutch trade with the East. In the following century, the British East India Company became even larger. The American colonies were also supported by business companies, such as the Virginia Company of London which sponsored the English colony at Jamestown.

By 1700 a string of Dutch, English, and French colonies stretched along the east coast of North America, from the Caribbean to Canada. The new colonial powers sometimes attacked the Spanish colonies on the mainland, but never conquered them, partly because of rivalry among themselves: the Dutch and the English feared France more than Spain. When the last Spanish Habsburg died in 1700, he left his empire to a grandson of the French king Louis XIV; the result was the War of the Spanish Succession, in which the Dutch and British fought to prevent France gaining control of the Spanish Empire. It ended with the Treaty of Utrecht, which gave the British valuable trading rights but left the Spanish Empire alone.

Quarrels between the Europeans over trade and colonies continued. Because the Caribbean was not properly policed, smuggling and piracy flourished, and there was nearly as much fighting in peacetime as in war. An incident in which a Spanish coastguard cut off the ear of a British captain was one of the causes of the war of 1740–48. Trade, legal and illegal, was growing, and so were the colonies. The French in Canada established forts south from the Great Lakes and threatened to cut off the British colonies on the east coast. In the Seven Years War, the contest turned in favor of Britain. The British navy controlled the Atlantic, cutting off France's colonies from reinforcements. The British took over French Canada.

Sea power also played a part in enabling the British East India Company to gain control of Bengal, ending French dreams of an Indian empire. The British Empire was now immense, and difficult to defend. When the American colonists, helped by France, rebelled against Britain, the British were defeated, and the colonies gained their independence as the United States of America.

Thomas Arne composing Rule Britannia, *a patriotic song of 1740 that includes the line "Britannia rule[s] the waves."*

The Treaty of Utrecht
In the War of the Spanish Succession (1700–14) the French armies were defeated in Europe by the Austrian, British, and Dutch alliance. In the treaty ending the war, Britain gained some land in North America from the French, as well as the Mediterranean island of Gibraltar, and the right – greatly valued by British merchants – to sell slaves to the Spanish colonies in America.

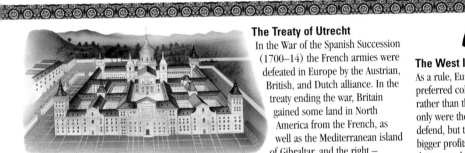

King Philip II's palace-monastery, the Escorial, a monument to Spain's power and glory in the 16th century.

French and English in North America
Trouble with the English began early, and there was serious fighting during the many wars of the 17th and 18th centuries. Native Americans fought on both sides. French settlements in the Ohio-Mississippi valleys threatened New England but, although the French seemed to hold a stronger position, they depended on supplies from France. That proved a decisive weakness when the British blockaded French ports in the Seven Years War.

India
The English East India Company was chartered to compete with the Dutch for East Indies trade. Forced out by the Dutch (1623), it concentrated on India, and later established a highly profitable trade with China. The Dutch had bases in southern India and Ceylon (Sri Lanka), while the Portuguese still had their colony at Goa, but by the 18th century, the main rival to the British was the French East India Company. The divisions of India and the lack of strong government forced the Europeans to become involved in politics to protect their trade.

The British under Wolfe captured Québec (1759) when they surprised the French by climbing steep cliffs from the river at night. Both Wolfe and the French commander, Montcalm (above), were killed.

The Seven Years War
This was truly a world war, fought not only in Europe but in the Americas, West Africa, India, and the Far East. It followed from the War of the Austrian Succession, which had left matters undecided. In America it coincided with what British colonists called the French and Indian War. Overseas, the British were victorious, beating the French in the Caribbean, North America, and India. The defeat of the French fleet at Quiberon Bay off Brittany (1759) ensured British dominance at sea.

The West Indies
As a rule, European governments preferred colonies in the islands, rather than the mainland. Not only were they were easier to defend, but they also turned bigger profits. In the 18th century, the sugar plantations of the West Indies, and the slave trade that supplied them with labor, made many Europeans rich. The plantation owners and the merchants mostly lived in Europe, and their influence was strong enough, especially in England, to affect government policy.

Buccaneers attack a Spanish ship.

Britain and France in India
In 1746 the French captured Madras and began to expand their power in India. But at the Battle of Plassey (1757), the British general Robert Clive defeated the ruler of Bengal and his French allies. Gaining control of Bengal was the beginning of the British Empire in India.

The Treaty of Paris
Although the British gave up some of their conquests, such as Guadeloupe and Martinique, the treaty ending the Seven Years War left them supreme in India and in North America east of the Mississippi. They also gained Senegal in West Africa, and Florida, from Spain. The Spanish regained Cuba and the Philippines, and were also given the French territory of Louisiana (west of the Mississippi).

An officer of the British East India Company, with a young attendant.

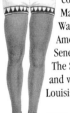

A sword used in the Battle of Plassey.

A cartoon lampooning the negotiators at the Treaty of Paris.

> **SEE ALSO**
> p. 168 THE UNITED STATES OF AMERICA • p. 198 COLONIALISM • p. 202 THE SCRAMBLE FOR AFRICA

1526 Paracelsus lectures at Basel University.

1543 Publication of Copernicus's *On the Revolution of the Heavenly Spheres* and Vesalius's *Structure of the Human Body.*

1628 Harvey publishes treaty on how blood circulates.

1633 Galileo is forced to recant his Copernican views.

The Scientific Revolution

According to Ptolemy's system of astronomy, which was commonly accepted before the 16th century, the sun, moon, planets, and stars moved round the earth, which was at the center of the universe (as shown in this diagram, right).

During the 16th and 17th centuries scholars and scientists increasingly realized the importance of observation and experimentation in science. This realization helped bring about all kinds of advances. Some theologians supported science because they believed that it helped reveal the wonders of God's creation and could be used to improve the quality of life. But many others were unhappy at the development of scientific laws that seemed to govern the physical world without divine assistance. Scientists such as Galileo suffered from the censure of the Inquisition by the Catholic Church. But there was no stopping the scientific revolution, as scientists in various fields continued their successful experiments throughout the 18th century.

Alchemists at work, searching in vain for the philosophers' stone, a substance that they hoped would turn other metals into gold or silver.

Two revolutionary books were published in Europe in 1543: one by Andreas Vesalius (1514–64) showed the anatomy of the human body in accurate detail; and the other, by Nicolaus Copernicus (1473–1543), presented the theory that the earth moved round the sun. Danish astronomer Tycho Brahe (1546–1601) observed the motions of the planets very precisely, and Johannes Kepler (1571–1630) added detail to the Copernican system, establishing astronomy as an exact science.

The great Italian scientist Galileo Galilei (1564–1642) contributed to the improvement of scientific instruments, including the clock and the telescope. In England, Sir Isaac Newton (1642–1727) formulated a law of universal gravitation and laid the foundations for the study of optics. Newton and Gottfried Leibniz (1646–1716) independently developed a new system of mathematics, called calculus.

Modern physiology began with the work of William Harvey (1578–1657), who showed how blood circulates through the human body, and Robert Boyle (1627–91) helped establish experimental methods in chemistry. New ideas about the methods of science arose: René Descartes (1596–1650) proposed that mathematics was the model that all other sciences should follow, while Francis Bacon (1561–1626) viewed experience as the most important source of knowledge. Bacon's ideas inspired the creation of the Royal Society in London in 1660.

One of the major scientific achievements of the 18th century was the creation of modern chemistry. Oxygen was discovered by Carl Scheele (1742–86) and independently by Joseph Priestley (1733–1804) in 1774. Three years later, Antoine Laurent Lavoisier (1743–94) discovered the nature of combustion. In natural history, the Swedish botanist Carolus Linnaeus (1707–78) devised a system for naming and classifying plants and animals.

Paracelsus (1493–1541), whose real name was Theophrastus Bombastus von Hohenheim, disputed that mental illness was caused by demons. He introduced the use of drugs made from minerals, including sulfur, mercury, and antimony.

From alchemy to chemistry

The medieval alchemists had combined ideas of chemistry with magical and mystical views of the universe. From the 16th century on these ideas were combined with more practical chemistry.

The Swiss physician Paracelsus challenged the ancient belief that disease was caused by an imbalance of humors, or bodily fluids. He stressed the importance of chemical compounds in treating disease, and the need for research and observation in medicine.

The Copernican system

The Polish astronomer Nicolaus Copernicus (1473–1543) developed the theory that the Earth is a moving planet. This led him to devise a revolutionary system of the universe – illustrated (right) in his book *On the Revolution of the Heavenly Spheres* (1543) – in which the Earth and planets revolve around the Sun, and the Moon orbits the Earth. Copernicus was not able to prove his theories during his lifetime, but later astronomers – Galileo Galilei and Johannes Kepler – showed him to be correct.

Below: Descartes used a technique of methodical doubt in his Meditations *(1641), arriving finally at his famous statement: "I think, therefore I am."*

The telescope

The Dutch optician Hans Lippershey (c.1570–1619) invented and built the first telescope in 1608. The Dutch government tried to keep the invention a secret, but news of it reached Galileo Galilei (1564–1642) in Italy. Galileo designed his own telescope and used it to study the night sky. He soon made a number of discoveries, including sunspots and the moons of Jupiter, and became entirely convinced of the truth of the Copernican system.

Galileo at work with his telescope. In 1633 he was forced by the Inquisition in Rome to say that his Copernican views were wrong. He was placed under house arrest for the rest of his life.

Scientific method

In the early 17th century many European thinkers and writers contributed to the methods of science. The English lawyer and philosopher Francis Bacon (1561–1626) presented a new classification of the sciences. He argued that knowledge can be gained only from experience. The French mathematician and philosopher René Descartes (1596–1650) claimed that the world was made up of two things: mind and matter. He considered mathematics to be the supreme science. Descartes, the father of modern philosophy, was a sincere and lifelong Roman Catholic.

1641 Descartes' *Meditations.*
1665 Isaac Newton discovers the force of gravity.
1735–53 Linnaeus publishes his systems for naming and classifying animals and plants.
1660 Foundation of the Royal Society in London.
1771–78 Priestley and Scheele independently discover oxygen.

The anatomists

In 1543 the Flemish physician Andreas Vesalius (1514–64) published his *Structure of the Human Body,* which contained the first truly accurate descriptions and illustrations of human anatomy. The illustrations were drawn by skilled artists and reproduced with the latest printing techniques. Almost a century later, in 1628, the English anatomist William Harvey (1578–1657) published his revolutionary discoveries on how blood circulates through the body. He showed that the two halves of the heart are separate, and that blood travels from the left half into the arteries, and returns to the right half through the veins.

The Italian physicist Evangelista Torricelli (1608–47) invented the mercury barometer to measure atmospheric pressure. In his barometer he also created the first human-made vacuum, a space that contains no matter.

This illustration from Harvey's On the Motion of the Heart *(1628) shows the blood flow in the veins of an arm. The valves, which prevent blood in the veins from flowing in any direction other than toward the heart, are shown as raised swellings.*

The microscope

The compound microscope (right), with a system of lenses and an eyepiece, was invented by the Dutch spectacle-maker Zacharias Janssen (1580–1638) in 1609. Later in the century a Dutchman named Antonie van Leeuwenhoek (1632–1723) made his own microscopes and magnified objects up to 300 times with a single lens. He was the first person to study micro-organisms such as bacteria, which he called "animalcules."

Following studies under a microscope, Antonie van Leeuwenhoek sent this detailed drawing of an ichneumon fly to the Royal Society in London.

Newton's Principia *(or Mathematical Principles of Natural Philosophy), containing his theories on the laws of motion and gravity, was published in 1687.*

Sir Isaac Newton

The English physicist, mathematician, and astronomer Isaac Newton (1642–1727) was one of the greatest scientists of all time. Between 1665 and 1667, when Cambridge University, where he studied, was closed by plague, he worked alone at home and made three great discoveries: the law of gravitation, supposedly inspired by watching an apple fall from a tree; the discovery that light is a mixture of different colors; and the invention of a branch of mathematics called calculus (also invented independently by the German mathematician Gottfried Leibniz).

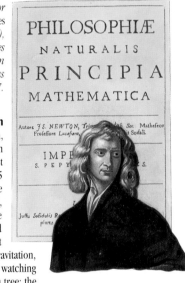

Experiments and matter

The Irish scientist Robert Boyle (1627–91) established experimental methods in chemistry and physics. He disproved the previous theory that air, earth, fire, and water were the basic elements of all matter, arguing that physical properties were due to the motion of atoms, which he called "corpuscles." Boyle is best known for his experiments on gases. In 1660 he was a founding member of the Royal Society in London.

In this experiment, Boyle pumped air out of a jar to create a vacuum. He demonstrated air's importance for life and combustion.

The French chemist Antoine Laurent Lavoisier (1743–94) is regarded as the founder of modern chemistry. He discovered that air is made up of oxygen (which he was first to name) and nitrogen. He was arrested during the French Revolution for his earlier involvement in tax collection and was guillotined.

Joseph-Louis Lagrange (1736–1813) became a professor of mathematics at the royal artillery school in Turin at age 19. He served as a mathematician at the court of Frederick the Great of Prussia, and later taught in Paris. He headed the commission that produced the metric system of units in 1795.

SEE ALSO
p. 164 THE ENLIGHTENMENT
p. 174 THE AGE OF INVENTIONS

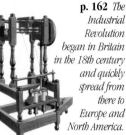
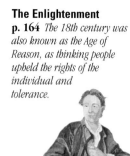

European Dominance
c.1750–1914

Europe was the birthplace of revolution in the 18th and 19th centuries. The intellectual revolution of the Enlightenment was followed by political revolution in France and America, and nationalistic rebellion across Europe. But it was the Industrial Revolution that set European countries on their course to dominate the world. Driven by their search for new sources of raw materials and markets, European companies came to monopolize world trade. When explorers returning from Africa told of its immense untapped wealth, the entire continent was divided up in just a few years. Resistance to colonization, or even to the opening up of local markets, was quickly overcome by European armies whose weaponry was now more advanced than any other in the world.

The Opium Wars
European merchants were prepared to fight for their right to trade. Britian and China clashed twice in the Opium Wars (1839–42; 1856–60) over trading rights in China. At the beginning of the 19th century, Britain began importing opium from India into China. When the Chinese government objected, war broke out. The British won and claimed extended trading rights. These were also granted to other European nations. The Second Opium War was provoked by the British and French and gained them even more rights.

The Birth of the Railroad
p. 172 *The building of railroads across Britain and Europe fueled the Industrial Revolution, leading to even faster economic growth.*

Latin America

p. 180 *The countries of Latin America freed themselves from European rule rapidly, almost all gaining independence between 1818 and 1828.*

The Age of Immigration
p. 210 *In the largest population movement of all time, more than 50 million people left Europe for the New World between 1850 and 1914.*

The Scramble for Africa
p. 202 *During the 19th century the colonial powers of Europe carved up Africa between them.*

Emergence of the USA
p. 206 *In the second half of the 19th century the USA expanded geographically and economically, establishing itself as a world power.*

Plantations

At the end of the 18th century plantations had sprung up along the Atlantic coast of the Americas, all the way from Chesapeake in the north to Brazil in the south, and especially on the Caribbean islands. The plantations produced cacao, cotton, indigo, tobacco, and the most valued produce of all – sugar. Most plantations depended on African slaves for their labor, and increased demand for produce meant a requirement for more slaves.

This late 18th-century Worcester vase shows a fashion for oriental styles.

Local Native American slaves working on a Spanish sugar plantation in the Americas. The workers first ground the cane and then heated the resulting juice in copper cauldrons to purify it.

The fur trade

Native Americans of the frozen north were connected to the Atlantic economy by the fur trade. They traded furs for imported European goods such as firearms and alcohol, both of which changed their way of life fundamentally. By the end of the 18th century the demand for fur had encouraged the Russians to push east right across Siberia, while the French and British went west across present-day Canada.

Seals were a valued but difficult catch for Inuit hunters. Every part of the animal was used, including the skin.

The Atlantic economy

By the end of the 18th century the eastern coastal regions of the Americas had close ties with Western Europe and Africa in both trade and migration. By then the European population of North America was self-sufficient in food but had limited manufacturing. They imported large quantities of manufactured goods from Europe, which had to be paid for by exports. Britain, however, exported three times as much in value to North America than it imported from that region.

At the beginning of the 19th century trade routes all over the world were helping to create the beginnings of a global economy.

→ Main trade in raw materials
→ Main trade in manufactured goods
• Major base and coaling station

Women selling fruit, vegetables, and grains in a market in India, painted around 1850.

Steaming ahead

After 1850, railroads spread rapidly all over the world, helping trade as well as the movement of people. By 1869 there was a transcontinental track across the United States, from New York to San Francisco. In India, the first railroad was constructed from Bombay in 1853. The British governor-general's plan was to develop trade routes connecting the seaports of Bombay, Calcutta, and Madras. This involved tremendous feats of civil engineering, including crossing mountain ranges and the great Ganges and Indus rivers.

Before a bridge was built, this locomotive was ferried across the Indus River.

More than two million slaves were shipped to Central and South America during the last 30 years of the 18th century. This drawing from 1794 shows an iron collar the slaves were forced to wear to prevent them from escaping (it would also have made lying down to rest impossible).

1819 Steamship Savannah crosses Atlantic from New York to Liverpool. **1821** Britain adopts gold as the basis of its currency. **1839–42** First Opium War between Britain and China, results in five ports being opened to British trade. **1846** Slave trade between Brazil and west Africa at its peak. **1848** California gold rush

World Trade

During the 19th century expanding world trade was dominated by the industrialized nations of Europe and increasingly by the United States of America. Plantations along the east coast of North, Central, and South America sent vast quantities of agricultural produce, including cacao, cotton, and sugar, across the Atlantic. Raw materials from the colonies were used by European industrialists to manufacture goods for use at home and abroad. Improving rail and sea transportation helped producers, exporters, and importers. The fastest means of transporting tea and other goods from the Far East remained the clipper ship. By the end of the 19th century the industrialized nations were selling modern technology to traditional societies, including machinery and military equipment, as the age of the motor car was about to dawn.

1. A late 18th-century illustration of the continents of Africa, Europe, and America as three beautiful Graces.

2. Portuguese sanctuary lamp dating from about 1880.

3. Oriental carpets were popular in the west, and many of their patterns were soon copied or adapted by European manufacturers.

By the end of the 18th century many regions that had been colonized by Europeans were closely linked to the economy of Europe. They produced many of the raw materials that industrialized nations such as Britain and France needed for manufacturing.

During the 19th century, world trade continued to be dominated by the industrialized nations of Europe and the United

Bustling ports

The first English colonies in North America were founded in the early 17th century. Many of the colonists were religious refugees, anxious to build their own communities in a New World, but they were backed by merchants, who hoped for profits. For the government, the colonies were useful as producers of raw materials, like tobacco, which could not be grown in Britain, or as markets, where British goods could be sold. The reason for the empire that Britain had gained by 1763 was, in one word, trade. That included the slave trade, which made many merchants rich at the cost of misery to thousands of Africans.

SEE ALSO
p. 194 MANCHU CHINA
p. 196 BRITISH INDIA
p. 198 COLONIALISM
p. 200 AUSTRALIA AND NEW ZEALAND
p. 202 THE SCRAMBLE FOR AFRICA

Asia

At the end of the 18th century the spice and pepper trades had been overtaken by a boom in textiles from India, tea from China, and coffee from Java. Asian imports to Europe were generally paid for with American silver, but there were exceptions. In the Bengal province of India, for example, which the British had captured in the mid-18th century, the locals were taxed by their new rulers.

In 1853 Commodore Matthew Perry steamed into Tokyo Bay in the first steamship the Japanese had ever seen. Many Japanese saw this as a devilish new machine, as shown in the contemporary Japanese illustration.

Many of the staple foods in Europe today, including tomatoes and potatoes, were unknown there before the Europeans reached the Americas. Initially treated with suspicion, their consumption became widespread during the 18th and 19th centuries.

Canton

The southern Chinese port of Canton (or Guangzhou) had traded for many centuries with Hindus and Arabs. From 1759 to 1842 it was the only Chinese port that was open to foreign trade. By the early 19th century British, Dutch, French, and Portuguese merchants controlled most of the trade between Canton and Europe. In 1839–42 the port became the focus of the First Opium War when British opium stores were confiscated there.

This early breech-loading rifle was invented by a British army officer in 1776. Such weapons were used in the American Revolution and were later sold to Native Americans, changing their way of life.

Gold standard

This gold napoleon, worth 20 francs, was issued in France in 1804.

Increasing global trade required an international standard for currencies. Britain adopted the gold standard in 1821, by which different country's currencies were convertible into gold at a fixed rate and international debts were met in gold. If a country had a trade deficit, there would be an outflow of gold, reducing its money supply. This would lead to lower prices, which would encourage exports. Japan joined the gold standard in 1897.

Ships

The introduction of steam made a great impact on trade. The first Mississippi steamboat left New Orleans in 1812, and seven years later the American-built Savannah became the first steamship to cross the Atlantic. By 1835 paddle-steamers were making regular transatlantic crossings. Ports were modernized and enlarged to handle the new, bigger ships and larger cargoes. Clippers were still the fastest ships, however, speeding to Europe with wool from Australia and tea from China.

begins. **1853** US naval expedition opens up Japan to world trade. **1869** First trans-America railroad across USA completed. **1877** Frozen meat shipped from Argentina to Europe for first time. **1895** Malayan rubber plantations start production. **1913** Henry Ford introduces mass production of his Model T. car.

States, which traded manufactured goods and foodstuffs with each other. During the course of the century trade also increased with Latin America, Africa, and Asia, where growing ports had been built for the despatch of raw materials. European farming and marketing methods were introduced in many parts of Africa, India, and Southeast Asia. These often led to exploitation of local traditional societies and the destruction of rural economies.

All over the world railroads were built to speed up the transportation of

goods. Railroads were opened in British Guyana in 1848, Mexico in 1850, India in 1853, Australia in 1854, and South Africa in 1860. By 1850 there were nearly 6,000 mi. (10,000 km) of railroad track in Britain, and by 1869 there was a transcontinental track across North America.

Ship and harbor designs were also radically changed, after the first successful steamship was built in 1807 by the American engineer Robert Fulton. Iron hulls were introduced in 1837 and steel hulls in 1856. Two years later Brunel's Great Eastern was launched: it

was easily the largest ship built up to that time (with propeller, paddle wheels, and sails), and in 1866 was used to lay the first transatlantic telegraph cable. The canals opened at Suez (1869) and Panama (1914) cut voyage times around Africa and South America, and between 1850 and 1914 the world's merchant fleet expanded almost fourfold.

In 1821 gold was adopted as the basis of the British currency, and the gold standard was adopted internationally during the 1870s. Gold rushes in the United States (1849), Australia (1851), New Zealand (1861), South Africa (1886), and Canada (1896) increased

the money supply and encouraged the growth of world trade.

From the 1870s the price of wheat and other staple foodstuffs began to fall, following the development of fertile lands in such countries as Canada, Argentina, Australia, and Russia.

1709 Abraham Darby I smelts iron with coke; the industrial revolution in Britain begins.
1712 Thomas Newcomen (1663–1729) invents a steam-powered pump to drain mines.
1733 John Kay (1704–80) invents the flying shuttle loom, which improves weaving.
1761 First canal built.

The Rocket was the first modern locomotive. Designed by George Stephenson (1781–1848), it won a competition in 1829 at Rainhill, Lancashire, to decide which locomotive should travel on the railway between Liverpool and Manchester. It ran at an average speed of 14 mph (22 km/h).

The industrial revolution marked the start of a new period in world history as countries shifted their economies away from agriculture and toward industry. The term "industrial revolution" was first used by a British historian in 1884. It is a useful way to describe the many changes that took place in industry during the 18th and 19th centuries, although the word revolution is slightly misleading, since revolutions are usually swift and sudden events, whereas the industrial revolution took place over more than a hundred years.

The process began in Britain where the industrial economy was already forging ahead by around 1750. Modernization in Britain can be traced to the agricultural revolution that began in the 16th century and which led to the development of an efficient, market-oriented farming system. This freed more people from agriculture to work in industry.

Other conditions in Britain also favored the development of industry, such as reasonably peaceful social conditions (all the 18th-century wars in which Britain was involved were fought abroad and there were only a couple of Jacobite rebellions to put down at home). Britain was rich in natural

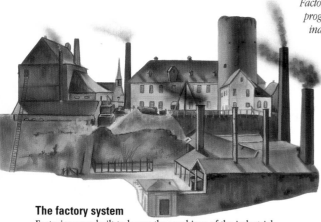

Factories were symbols of progress during the industrial revolution. They made their owners wealthy, provided work for the population, and changed the appearance of towns.

Towns became overcrowded as people moved to them from the countryside. Most working-class people lived in low-quality houses, or "slums."

The factory system
Factories were built to house the machines of the industrial revolution. The textile industry was the first of the large manufacturing industries to build factories, for its spinning and weaving machines. Before factories, workers in the textile industry worked from their homes. But with the arrival of factories full of machines, workers no longer needed to work at home. Instead, workers came together to work in one place – a factory. This method of organizing work is called the factory system. It was pioneered in England in the 1770s by Richard Arkwright.

The rise in population
In the 150 years from 1700 to 1850 the population of Britain trebled, growing from about six million to 18 million. There are many reasons for this. Improved medicine, health care, and diet meant that people lived longer and healthier lives. People had larger families, and more children survived childhood. It was also a time of emigration, when people moved to England from Ireland and Scotland in search of work. Overcrowding was a problem in most towns.

Richard Arkwright (1732–92), inventor of the spinning frame and creator of the factory system. He revolutionized the cotton industry in England.

Arkwright's water frame of 1769 (it got its name because it was powered by a water wheel) was a spinning wheel, twisting fibers into yarn for weaving.

The textile industry
Britain's textile industry was one of the first industries changed by the industrial revolution. Throughout the 1700s inventors found new and better ways to spin fibers and weave cloth. The industry was transformed from a cottage industry, where people worked at their own pace in their own homes, to a factory industry.

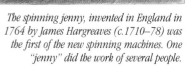

The spinning jenny, invented in England in 1764 by James Hargreaves (c.1710–78) was the first of the new spinning machines. One "jenny" did the work of several people.

resources, including coal and tin, and with its expanding empire had access to other raw materials as well as markets for manufactured goods.

With the introduction of new inventions and working methods, Britain's industries began to change. A gradual process of industrial revolution had begun, and with it came changes in transportation. Roads were improved, canals and rivers provided cheap means of shifting goods, and then railways were built. With these conditions, Britain was set to become the "workshop of the world."

Steam-engines made by Scottish inventor James Watt (1736–1819, left) and his partner Matthew Boulton (1728–1809) were used to pump water out of mines, making it possible for coal to be mined from much deeper locations than before.

The Industrial Revolution Begins

A massive technological change began in Britain during the 18th century. It has become known as the Industrial Revolution, and it marks a long period during which society gradually changed from being based on agriculture to being based on industry. Great Britain was the first country to undergo such a change. From there it spread throughout Europe and Scandinavia, and across to North America. It was a time of invention and discovery. Factories were built in towns, and people moved away from the countryside to work in them. The population of towns grew quickly. New machines, powered by steam, speeded up the manufacturing process, and more goods were made than ever before. New forms of transportation were developed to move the raw materials and finished goods.

The world's first bridge made entirely from iron was completed in 1779. It spanned the River Severn, near Coalbrookdale, in Shropshire, England.

The Wedgwood factory in Staffordshire, England, was a good example of how a factory-owner, in this case Josiah Wedgwood (c.1730–1795) used all the modern methods of science, logical use of labor, and business organization to build the largest pottery factory in the world.

Left: A cutaway illustration of an early steam engine in action.

The iron industry

Iron had many uses, from horseshoes to machine parts. In 1709, the ironmaster Abraham Darby I (1677–1717) became the first person to produce iron using coke (a fuel made from coal) instead of charcoal. He did this at his ironworks at Coalbrookdale. Other "firsts," took place in and around this part of Shropshire in England, and the area has become known as the "birthplace of the industrial revolution."

The harnessing of steam

In 1765 James Watt greatly improved the efficiency of the existing steam engine and by the 1770s it had become the driving power in the factories and mines of industrial Britain. Steam would also revolutionize transportation with steam-powered trains and ships providing much faster and more efficient ways of moving goods.

The coal industry

Coal was the major fuel of the industrial revolution. By 1800 there were about 50,000 coalminers working in the mines of Britain, digging up millions of tons of coal each year. When coal was burned it was used to heat water to make steam to power machines – from pumps to locomotives. People heated their homes with coal fires.

In the early 1800s workers protested when machines took their jobs. In England the Luddites organized attacks on factories at night to destroy machines. One group was shot by an enraged employer. These were only the first struggles between factory owners and workers. Later in the 19th century, workers protested about low pay, long hours, and the atrocious conditions in which many of them were forced to work.

George Stephenson, inventor of the railway locomotive.

Many children, aged four and up, were employed in the coal mines, sometimes working 13-hour shifts in terrible conditions. The youngest worked as "trappers," opening doors to let coal wagons pass through. A law was passed in 1842 which banned children from underground mines.

SEE ALSO
p. 156 THE SCIENTIFIC REVOLUTION
p. 172 THE INDUSTRIAL REVOLUTION IN EUROPE
p. 174 THE AGE OF INVENTIONS
p. 182 NORTH AMERICA INDUSTRIALIZES

John Locke's political ideas were introduced into France by Voltaire. They had even more effect in France than in England, where the king ruled together with Parliament.

John Locke

During the 17th century the English executed one king and drove another into exile. John Locke (1632–1704) argued that they had a right to do so. He declared that governments ruled only with the agreement of the people they governed; that it was the government's business to defend people's rights; and that if a king became a tyrant, he lost the right to govern. Locke also supported religious toleration (with some exceptions) because, he said, what people believe is their own business.

THE ENLIGHTENMENT

The Enlightenment is the term used to describe the ideas of intellectuals, or thinking people, in Europe in the 18th century – a time also known as the Age of Reason. The leading thinkers of the Enlightenment were a group of French philosophers. Their ideas spread widely and affected not only Europe, but also the Americas. The leaders of the Enlightenment believed that the power of reason was capable of solving all life's problems. They argued that a king must take responsibility for his people's welfare, and upheld the rights of the people against tyrannical government and religious intolerance. The ideas of the Enlightenment were among the influences that led to the American and French Revolutions. The Enlightenment marks the beginning of a way of thinking called liberalism.

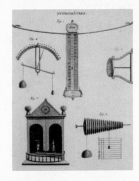

Instruments for measuring humidity invented by H.B. Saussure, a Swiss scientist. He introduced the word "geology" into scientific language.

The Encyclopedists

One of the greatest works of the Enlightenment was the *Encyclopedia* of Denis Diderot and Jean d'Alembert. It was one of the earliest encyclopedias ever written. The writers tried to present in it a summary of all human knowledge. All the leading thinkers of the time, including Voltaire and Rousseau, wrote articles for the *Encyclopedia*, which was published between 1751 and 1755. It eventually grew to 35 volumes.

Denis Diderot (1713–84) translated the works of English philosophers, wrote novels and plays, and struggled for nearly 30 years to produce the great Encyclopedia, *which included magnificent pictures of tools and machines.*

Paris

Paris, capital of France and heart of the Enlightenment, grew rapidly during the 18th century. Many fine new mansions were built, and on the wide avenues cafés and small theaters opened up. This was the great age of the *salon* (right), weekly social gatherings in the houses of aristocrats, where artistic and scientific subjects were discussed. The Encyclopedists often met at these gatherings.

Adam Smith (below) argued against government interference in the economy, and in favor of free trade, private enterprise, and competition. He was a friend of the philosopher David Hume (1711–76) and other leading intellectuals in Edinburgh, Scotland.

Montesquieu

Charles de Montesquieu (1689–1755) was a French nobleman. In his great work *The Spirit of the Laws* (1748), he compared different kinds of government. He admired the system in England where, he explained, each branch of government was kept in check by the other branches. This idea of checks and balances in government later influenced the Constitution of the United States of America.

When Montesquieu was asked to write for Diderot and d'Alembert's Encyclopedia, *he refused to write on politics and instead wrote an article on taste.*

Economics

Many of the Enlightenment thinkers were preoccupied with the subjects of freedom and tolerance. This made them begin to think differently about economics. A group of thinkers in France called the Physiocrats criticized restrictions such as customs barriers, and argued for greater freedom of trade. Their ideas were taken further by the Scottish philosopher Adam Smith (1723–90), in his famous book *The Wealth of Nations* (1776).

SEE ALSO
p. 156 THE SCIENTIFIC REVOLUTION
p. 166 THE FRENCH REVOLUTION
p. 168 THE UNITED STATES OF AMERICA

Voltaire

Courtly and witty, François Arouet de Voltaire (1694–1778) was often in trouble with the Church and the government. He spent a year in prison in the Bastille in Paris, and later moved to Geneva to avoid arrest. Of all the Enlightenment philosophers, he was less certain that progress could be achieved through reason. His novel *Candide* ends with the advice that we should cultivate our garden, rather than try to change the world.

Right: In 1750 Voltaire (seated) became adviser and friend to King Frederick the Great of Prussia. Other European rulers patronized the French philosophers, too. Diderot spent some time in St. Petersburg at the invitation of Catherine II, the Great, of Russia (c.1729–96).

The title page of Rousseau's novel Emile: or, On Education, *published in 1762. This book shocked some religious groups so much that they had it burned. Rousseau was forced to flee to avoid arrest.*

Rousseau often had angry disagreements with the other philosophers. A brilliant and productive thinker, he eventually died insane.

Rousseau

Jean Jacques Rousseau (1712–78) worked with Diderot and, like Voltaire, moved to Switzerland to avoid arrest for attacking religion and the government. His great political work *The Social Contract* (1762) was a strong defense of the freedom of the individual. The state, he argued, represented "the general will of the people, and its purpose is to ensure freedom, equality, and justice." Almost as influential was *Emile*, a book about education in the form of a novel. The French Revolution and the violent years that followed put an end to the era of the Enlightenment. The ideas of the next great movement, Romanticism, were in many ways directly opposed to those of the Enlightenment. Rousseau, who believed in the goodness of people and the importance of nature, belonged to both movements.

Intellectual women

Educated upper-class women played an important part in the Enlightenment. Some, like the Marquise Marie du Deffand (1697–1780, far right) organized *salons*, or "informal meetings" to discuss political ideas. Some were admired writers like Mme. Anne de Staël (1766–1817).

The popular interest in science and scientific instruments in French high society is mocked in this illustration showing a lady looking through a telescope, but through the wrong end, and a gentleman using a magnifying glass to examine a celestial globe.

Science becomes popular

The discoveries of scientists such as Sir Isaac Newton (1642–1727) stimulated a growing interest in science and learning in the 18th century. People began to feel that nature was governed by basic laws, and that it was possible to discover these. It seemed that all problems could be solved by scientific means.

Clocks became fashionable during the Enlightenment period. This finely crafted French longcase clock c.1755 is decorated with gilded bronze.

Scientific journeys

Before the 18th century, the main aim of European explorers had been to find highly prized goods for trade. Gradually, however, exploration was undertaken by people wanting to make scientific discoveries. Charles de la Condamine spent 10 years in South America from 1735 to 1745, and he traveled the length of the Amazon. He was the first trained scientist to lead an exploring expedition.

The wife of a scientific explorer, Isabella Godin set off to join her husband on the Amazon in 1749. All her fellow-Europeans died but, living on roots and helped by the forest people, she survived.

Music

About the middle of the 18th century Western music moved away from the style called "baroque" – controlled, flowing, and often on a religious theme – in which J.S. Bach and G.F. Handel had written. Composers such as Josef Haydn (1732–1809) and Wolfgang Amadeus Mozart (1756–91) wrote in a style that made beautiful, regular patterns, but was also able to express the strongest emotions, especially in Mozart's operas. An important development in musical instruments was the invention of the piano about 1720, though it did not replace the harpsichord until the 19th century.

Wolfgang Amadeus Mozart, at age seven, was already a genius. Audiences listening to this small boy playing with his family could hardly believe their eyes or ears.

1789 Bastille seized; the Revolution begins; Rights of

Man declared; National Assembly formed.

1791 Louis XVI and Marie Antoinette try to leave France,

but are caught.
1792 Louis XVI and Marie

Antoinette imprisoned; monarchy abolished; France

The French Revolution

The social and political upheavals that took place in France between 1789 and 1799 are known as the French Revolution. For more than a thousand years France had been a monarchy, ruled by kings who had absolute power. There was no real parliament and no constitution – the system of laws that guide a country. By the late 18th century the royal family and the nobility enjoyed great luxury, while to a large extent the working people lived in hardship and were made to pay high taxes. In 1789 King Louis XVI faced mounting protests from the people. Harvests had failed and food prices had doubled. Louis tried to control matters by meeting Church leaders, the nobility, and working people, but they could not agree on a course of action and riots broke out. In 1789 the monarchy was overthrown and France became a republic.

Above: Through taxation, the poor paid for the comforts enjoyed by the rich. In this satirical cartoon, a peasant literally supports a bishop and a noble.

Eugène Delacroix's painting of Liberty Leading the People *(1830) shows the Tricolor flag – a symbol of unity in the new republic.*

The king of France

Louis XVI's problems were not all of his own making. The system of privileges for the monarchy and nobility was centuries old. When the mood of the people – many of whom were starving – turned against him, he argued that he was not guilty of any crime, but his life was not spared.

Louis XVI (1754–93) became king in 1774 at a time when France was in debt and taxes were high. The country's troubles were blamed on the royal family, who tried to flee to Austria, but were caught. Louis was guillotined in 1793.

Symbols of the Republic

The French Revolution was a new beginning for France. The idea of a republic – a state without a monarch, where power was in the hands of the people and their elected officials – gripped the nation. They mocked anything connected with the despised monarchy. Words became powerful messengers of the changes that were taking place: the people who fought for the new France believed in liberty, equality, and fraternity. They wore the red and blue of Paris joined with the white of the former flag.

The Bastille – a symbol of monarchy

A highly visible symbol of the monarchy was the Bastille (below), a great medieval fortress in Paris. It became notorious as the place of imprisonment for people who dared to speak out against the state. The Bastille was one of the first casualties of the Revolution. Images of it appeared on everyday objects such as pocket-knives and fans. By carrying these, people showed how much they hated this royal prison. On July 14, 1789, royal troops were seen on the move in Paris. The people, thinking they were about to be attacked, stormed the Bastille, where they hoped to find a store of weapons, but they found none. The Bastille's seven prisoners (none of whom were actually there for crimes against the state) were set free, and the governor and his men were killed.

Left: Revolutionary fighters were called sans-culottes, or "without breeches" by their enemies, because they did not wear the knee-length trousers (breeches) of the nobility. Instead, they wore the ankle-length trousers of working men.

MARCHE DES MARSEILLOIS

Left: Revolutionaries from the town of Marseille sang a song that became known as The Marseillaise. *It became the French national anthem.*

Left: Supporters of the Revolution wore red caps like those worn by freed slaves in ancient Rome. Here a red cap crushes a hated priest.

1789–1799 167

declared a Republic.
1793 Louis XVI and Marie | Antoinette executed;
Robespierre's Reign of Terror | begins; Marat murdered.
1794 Robespierre executed; | Reign of Terror ends.
1796 Bonaparte defeats Austria | in northern Italy.
1799 Bonaparte First Consul.

Left: The decorated title of The Rights of Man, which is still an important political document.

The Rights of Man

In 1789 the French National Assembly issued a statement called the *Declaration of the Rights of Man and the Citizen*. It listed 17 civil rights; for example, there shall be no imprisonment without a fair trial, and people are free to speak openly in public.

Marat, friend of the people

Physician and writer Jean-Paul Marat (1743–93) came to prominence through his news-sheets, which encouraged people to fight authority. Forced into hiding, he took refuge in the Paris sewers, where he caught a skin disease. While easing his pain in a bath he was murdered. His death turned him into a hero of the Revolution.

Jean-Paul Marat published a news-sheet, Ami du Peuple *("Friend of the People"), which demanded changes to the way the country was run.*

Maximilien Robespierre (1758–94) was a politician who supported the Revolution. As his power grew, people feared he was becoming a dictator. He was guillotined in 1794.

Dr. Joseph Guillotin (1738–1814) invented the guillotine, a machine that cut off people's heads quickly and efficiently.

The Reign of Terror

From June 1793 to July 1794 a revolutionary government was set up to rule France, led by a young lawyer, Maximilien Robespierre. Believing the new republic was in danger of falling apart, Robespierre planned to save it by instigating a "Reign of Terror." Any person suspected of treason against the republic was arrested. It became more important than ever to wear the symbols of the revolution, such as the red hat and the tricolor. Thousands were sent to the *guillotine* – 2,639 people were executed in Paris alone. This extreme phase of the Revolution ended when Robespierre was overthrown.

Failed harvests and rising prices had increased people's anger toward the monarchy and nobility, who were never without food. The food shortage continued during the Revolution. People queued to buy bread, which was rationed.

The guillotine was the main instrument of execution during the Revolution. The person to be executed was strapped face down on the wooden bench. When the executioner released a lever, the heavy blade fell, slicing through the person's neck.

The fate of the Revolution

After the king had been killed and Robespierre's Reign of Terror was over, the new French Republic still was not calm. Supporters of the monarchy remained in France, even though thousands had fled abroad. Royalist risings in La Vendée and Lyons had been brutally put down. In 1796 France decided to attack Austria; its victorious young general was Napoleon Bonaparte (1769–1821), and it was he who united France, declaring himself First Consul in 1799. Another new chapter in French history was about to begin.

The late 18th century was a time of change on both sides of the Atlantic Ocean, culminating in the creation of independent nations and new ways of thinking. It was a time of "Enlightenment," when the driving political force of the day was that of revolution. The United States of America was formed in the 1770s as a result of a conflict between Britain and her American colonies. Britain and France were old enemies, so it was no surprise that France supported the new American nation. This support took the form of military aid, with France sending troops to fight alongside the Americans in their struggle for independence from Britain.

The French government found it impossible to pay for an army engaged in a conflict thousands of miles away, and heavily increased taxes. It was a recipe for disaster. In 1788 there were revolts in several French provinces. After the harvest of 1788 failed, starving peasants crowded into Paris. The repeated demands of middle-class intellectuals for reform were taken up with irresistible vigor by the working people.

Expressed in the short term in immense violence, in the long term these demands brought about a much fairer system of government and taxation in France.

1. Marie Antoinette (1755–93), the Austrian-born wife of Louis XVI, made herself extremely unpopular with the people of France.

> **SEE ALSO**
> p. 164 THE ENLIGHTENMENT
> p. 170 NAPOLEONIC EUROPE
> p. 176 NATIONALISM AND LIBERALISM IN EUROPE

1763 French–Indian War ends. **American colonies.** **1774** First Continental Congress **1775** War of the American **leads army. 1776** Declaration of
1767 Import taxes anger the **1773** "Boston Tea Party." seeks recognition of rights. Revolution begins; Washington Independence.

The United States of America

The struggle that resulted in the birth of the United States of America had its origins on both sides of the Atlantic Ocean. While the countries of Europe fought for supremacy on their own continent, a new nation was being forged among the colonies of North America, where Britain was the leading colonial power. No longer content to be ruled from Britain, and unhappy about paying new taxes, the colonies showed signs of increasing unrest. Angry crowds voiced their protests with acts of vandalism and defiance. Alarmed by these events, Britain's army was pressed into action and the War of Independence began. After six years of fighting, Britain renounced its claim to the colonies and the United States of America was born, free to decide its own future.

Sybil Ludington (1761–1839) was a heroine of the Revolution. In 1777 she called on the men of her father's regiment to rally against the British.

The settlers who went from Europe to America in the 18th century did so because they sought a better way of life. By 1775 there were 2.5 million of them, living in thirteen self-governing colonies. Britain interfered with their everyday life very little, except in one vital matter: trade. The British believed colonial trade existed to benefit Britain; goods sent to Europe had to go in British ships and by way of British agents. This was increasingly resented by the outspoken colonists.

After the end of the French and Indian War (Seven Years' War) in 1763, Britain was deep in debt, and one way to raise money was to put a tax (customs duty) on many goods sold to the colonies,

NORTH AMERICA AFTER 1763.

□ British   □ Russian
□ Spanish   — French
□ Unexplored

Left: In 1763 France's North American mainland territory was divided between Britain and Spain.

The French and Indian War

Britain and France fought in North America to decide who should control the continent. In 1763 France was defeated, and by the Treaty of Paris gave up its claim to the North American mainland. France ceded to Britain all its territory east of the Mississippi River, including Canada. Spain ceded Florida to Britain, and received the Louisiana territory and New Orleans from France.

The tough policies of King George III of England (reigned 1760–1820) cost Britain a substantial part of its North American territories.

Rule from Britain

Following the Seven Years' War, Britain's empire in North America expanded beyond the original thirteen colonies to include land as far west as the Mississippi River and north into Canada. The British government tightened control over its American possessions by imposing direct rule from Britain. Maintaining the new empire and keeping an army there was very expensive. To cover the costs, Britain taxed goods that were imported into America. Tea, paper, paint, and glass became expensive. People in Britain also paid higher taxes on goods exported from America, such as sugar.

Below: The first blood of the Revolution was shed on March 5, 1770, when British redcoats killed three men in a riot outside the Boston Customs House.

Right: In 1773 rebels disguised as Native Americans destroyed chests of tea belonging to the British East India Company in an act of defiance that became known as the "Boston Tea Party."

Below: Patrick Henry (1736–99) was an outspoken opponent of British rule. He called for revolution with the words: "I know not what course others may take, but as for me, give me liberty, or give me death!"

Americans prepare for war

After the Boston Tea Party incident, the British tried to restore order. They closed Boston's port and imposed military rule on the colony of Massachusetts. The other colonies rallied in support of Massachusetts, however, and American civilians prepared for war. Known as "Minutemen," they swore to be ready to fight at a minute's notice.

Anti-British feeling grows

Americans became increasingly hostile toward Britain. They objected to the new taxes that were imposed to pay for the army, and resented being ruled by the British government. Street protests showed how much anti-British feeling there was, particularly in the East Coast port of Boston, where trade had suffered. When British troops, provoked by a brawling crowd, opened fire in Boston unrest increased.

Paul Revere (1735–1818), a silversmith, was an American patriot. On the night of April 18, 1775, he rode from Boston to Lexington warning people that British troops were on the move.

SEE ALSO
p. 182 NORTH AMERICA INDUSTRIALIZES
p. 184 THE EXPANSION OF THE USA
p. 186 THE AMERICAN CIVIL WAR

1778 France enters the war.
1779 Spanish and British at war.

1781 British forces surrender at Yorktown, Virginia.

1783 Britain recognizes colonies' independence; colonies

renamed United States.
1789 George Washington

elected first president of USA.
1790 Constitution agreed.

including tea. Most of the tea drunk there was smuggled, so no duty was paid on it. Britain passed a law allowing the British East India Company to take its own tea direct to American ports; the merchants who made money from smuggling denounced the tax on tea as unfair and in Boston £25,000-worth was thrown into the harbor in 1773. The British closed the port and extra troops were sent to Boston.

In April 1775 General Gage sent soldiers on a mission from Boston to Concord, 20 mi. (32 km) away; because of Paul Revere's night ride, they were ambushed and 250 killed or wounded. Britain and its colonies were at war. The British and their Hessian (German) allies faced huge problems with supplies and communications (orders took six weeks to arrive from England). They were used to fighting set battles, not skirmishes with small groups. The colonists had few trained generals and few ships, but they had fine marksmen who were fighting for freedom and their rights, as set out in the Declaration of Independence (1776).

Britain's General Howe was almost defeated at Bunker Hill in 1775, but captured New York in 1776; the American

commander George Washington crossed the Delaware River in a snowstorm to beat the British at Trenton and Princeton. General Howe took Philadelphia, but another part of the British army was badly beaten at Saratoga in 1777 and surrendered. This defeat made the French realize that the colonists might win, so in

1778 France entered the war on their side. It was a turning point. The British campaign in the south ended when the soldiers of General Cornwallis were trapped at Yorktown, Virginia, in 1781. French ships prevented supplies from reaching them and Cornwallis had to surrender. The war was effectively over. In 1783 Britain gave the 13 colonies their freedom. It took six more years for the new states to become the United States, with a written Constitution.

1. The new nation soon had its own currency.
2. An early flag of the USA.

George Washington

Born into a wealthy family in the colony of Virginia, George Washington (1732–99) played a major role in America's struggle for independence. His skill as a military leader brought him to the attention of the British, on whose side he fought in the war with France over control of North America. As anti-British feeling grew, Washington became leader of the American army. In 1775 he embarked on the War of the American Revolution.

British soldiers were known as "redcoats" or "lobsterbacks," because of their scarlet jackets. The main weapon of a redcoat was the musket, which fired a lead ball.

The American Revolution

The clash between British troops and American militia (part-time soldiers) at the townships of Lexington and Concord on April 19, 1775, marked the start of the War of the American Revolution. The British were defeated and withdrew to Boston. They had several successes, but were heavily beaten at Saratoga. After a long campaign in the South, the British army was trapped at Yorktown and on October 17, 1781, it surrendered to General Washington.

In 1776, General George Washington crossed the semi-frozen Delaware River to attack Trenton, New Jersey.

Below: A French nobleman, the Marquis de Lafayette (1757–1834), fought with the Americans against the British.

The Constitution

On September 23, 1783, Britain recognized the United States as an independent country. The thirteen former British colonies became the first States of the new nation. Each one at first governed itself. But this was a weak system; something stronger was needed. In 1790 a set of written rules, called the Constitution, came into force. Beginning with the words "We the People…," it set out how power was to be shared between central government and the States.

France enters the war

The Americans asked for help from France, Britain's enemy. At first France did not want to become involved in a major overseas conflict. But when the Americans beat the British at the Battle of Saratoga (1777), France realized that Britain might be defeated. In 1778 France sent soldiers and ships to fight alongside the Americans. The French blockade of Yorktown was the turning point in the war.

James Madison (1751–1836) earned the title "Father of the Constitution" for his skills in reaching agreements. He was the fourth president of the United States (1809–17).

Thomas Jefferson (1743–1826) and the committee that drew up the Declaration of Independence in 1776 present the finished document to Congress.

CANADA
NEW HAMPSHIRE
VERMONT
NEW YORK
MASSACHUSETTS
RHODE ISLAND
CONNECTICUT
NEW JERSEY
DELAWARE
MARYLAND
NORTH WEST TERRITORY
PENNSYLVANIA
OHIO
VIRGINIA
KENTUCKY
TENNESSEE
NORTH CAROLINA
SOUTH CAROLINA
GEORGIA
MISSISSIPPI TERRITORY
FLORIDA
GULF OF MEXICO
ATLANTIC OCEAN

☐ Original Thirteen Colonies
☐ Territories acquired after 1783
* Massachusetts included Maine until 1820

THE UNITED STATES AFTER 1783 SHOWING THE LAND ACQUIRED TO THE WEST OF THE THIRTEEN STATES.

NAPOLEON'S EMPIRE, 1812.

- French Empire
- States ruled by Napoleon's family
- Other dependent states
- * Battle

Below: Cap worn by a soldier of Napoleon's Grand Army. Men from twenty nations served in the army.

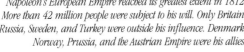

Map labels: NORTH SEA, SWEDEN, BALTIC SEA, Moscow, BRITAIN, PRUSSIA, Friedland, 1807, Borodino, 1812, Eylau, 1807, Beresina, 1812, London, RUSSIAN EMPIRE, Waterloo, 1815, Leipzig, 1813, AUSTRIA, Paris, Jena, 1806, Austerlitz, 1800, ATLANTIC OCEAN, FRANCE, Ulm, 1805, Vienna, Marengo, 1800, BLACK SEA, OTTOMAN EMPIRE, CORSICA, Ajaccio, Rome, SPAIN, ELBA, Trafalgar, 1805, MEDITERRANEAN SEA, ITALY

Napoleon's European Empire reached its greatest extent in 1812. More than 42 million people were subject to his will. Only Britain, Russia, Sweden, and Turkey were outside his influence. Denmark, Norway, Prussia, and the Austrian Empire were his allies.

Napoleon hoped to follow the example of another military leader – Alexander the Great. He planned to build an eastern empire that would include Egypt, India, and other Middle- and Far-East lands. He took Egypt, but unrest at home forced his return to France.

Napoleon I, Emperor of France

In 1795, Napoleon had saved the Revolution when his troops crushed royalists who plotted to restore the French monarchy. From then on, Napoleon's power increased. In November 1799 he overthrew the Directory – an unpopular committee of politicians who governed the country. He moved into the Tuileries Palace, in Paris, the residence of the former kings of France, and assumed power for life as the First Consul of France. He had become a military dictator. In 1804, 3.5 million French people voted in favor of Napoleon becoming their emperor – only 2,580 voted against. He was the people's hero, and in a coronation ceremony in the cathedral of Notre-Dame (right), the dictator crowned himself Napoleon I, Emperor of France. His wife, Josephine, knelt before him and he placed the imperial crown on her head: she became Empress of France.

The French Civil Code (Code Napoléon) listed more than 2,000 principles. It became the basis of a new system of law in France and its territories overseas, such as the State of Louisiana, USA. It became a model for other law reformers.

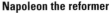

Napoleon the reformer

After years of revolution, the French legal, political, and social systems were in chaos. Through Napoleon's reforms, order was restored to France. He took advice from trusted officials, and his secret police stopped people from speaking against him. He restored friendly relations with the Pope; established the University of France and reformed the educational system; and founded the Bank of France. His greatest improvements were to the law.

1795 Napoleon crushes royalists.
1799 Napoleon becomes dictator.

1798 Napoleon captures Egypt. **1799** Napoleon overthrows Directory;

becomes First Consul of France. **1801** Pope and Napoleon sign Concordat,

re-establishing Catholicism. **1803** Start of the Napoleonic Wars.

1804 Napoleon crowned Emperor; French Civil Code (*Code Napoléon*)

Napoleonic Europe

Napoleon Bonaparte (1769–1821) was one of the greatest military leaders of all time. In the final years of the French Revolution he became dictator of France, and set about gaining an empire for his country. He almost succeeded, and for sixteen years he was master of most of Europe. To his troops he was the "Little Corporal." To the kings whose thrones he overthrew he was "that Corsican ogre." As his power increased, he declared himself Napoleon I, Emperor of France. It was a position he held for eleven years until his ambition to dominate all Europe ended in defeat at the Battle of Waterloo, in 1815. Napoleon's lasting gift to France was the *Code Napoléon* – the first clear statement of French law in modern times.

The future ruler of France and conqueror of much of Europe was born at Ajaccio, a town on the Mediterranean island of Corsica. In 1768, Corsica was given to France by Italy, and when Napoleon was born the following year he automatically became a French citizen. Napoleon grew up hating the French. He disliked the fact that they had gained control of his native land, Corsica. Despite this, he studied at military schools in France and at age sixteen he joined the French army.

Each French regiment had an eagle standard. The eagle was a symbol of honor and strength.

The Napoleonic Wars (1803–15)

Napoleon's attempt to conquer Europe began in 1803, when Britain and France declared war on each other. Russia, Austria, and Sweden fought with Britain, but to no avail. Austria was defeated in 1805, followed by Prussia in 1806. The defeated nations were added to the growing French Empire. Only Britain stood in the way of Napoleon's command of Western Europe. In 1805 he had planned to invade Britain, but the English navy, led by Admiral Horatio Nelson (1758–1805), destroyed the French fleet at Trafalgar. In 1812, Napoleon attempted to conquer Russia, but was driven back by fierce resistance and winter weather. Finally, in 1815 he was defeated at Waterloo, Belgium.

Antiquities were looted by Napoleon's army to glorify Paris. Roman bronze horses came from Venice, Italy, to adorn the top of a triumphal arch (see left). They were later returned. Greek and Roman statues came too, as did treasures from ancient Egypt.

To commemorate his defeat of Austria in 1805, Napoleon ordered a triumphal arch (the Arc de Triomphe du Carrousel*) to be built in Paris. Statues of his soldiers stood on the arch's columns. Copied from an arch built by a Roman emperor, it formed a gateway to Napoleon's palace.*

An emperor in exile

Napoleon surrendered at Waterloo to the British army, led by the Duke of Wellington (1769–1852). In 1815 he was exiled to the island of St Helena in the Atlantic Ocean, 1,200 mi. (1,900 km) off the coast of Africa. Exile was not new to him. In 1814 he had been banished to the Italian island of Elba, from where he had returned to carry on his military campaign. But there was no return from St Helena, and he died there in 1821.

Right: Scene from the Battle of Trafalgar. Napoleon's planned invasion of Britain ended in his defeat at Trafalgar in 1805.

issued. **1805** Napoleon defeats Austria; Napoleon defeated at the Battle of Trafalgar. **1808** Peninsular War in Spain begins. **1812** Napoleon defeated in campaign against Russia. **1814** Napoleon abdicates and is exiled to Elba. **1815** Napoleon returns to Paris, but is defeated at Waterloo. Exiled to St Helena. **1821** Napoleon dies.

In 1792 he was stationed in Paris. It was a crucial time to be in the city: the Revolution was in progress, the monarchy was overthrown, and the French Republic was born. These events gave Napoleon the opportunity to further his career in the army, and by the age of twenty-four he was a general. He was a strong supporter of the Revolution, and when, in 1795, it seemed that royalists were regaining their strength, it was General Napoleon who stamped them out.

As Napoleon's power grew, he gained control of France, setting himself up first as dictator, then as emperor. And with France under his command, he began his attempted conquest of Europe and beyond.

Between 1800 and 1807 his brilliant military campaigns won the Low Countries, northern Italy, and western Germany, and established France as the dominant power in Europe. After 1807 he conquered Spain, southern Italy, northern Germany, and Poland. The tide began to turn against him in 1812 when he failed to conquer Russia.

In 1814 Napoleon abdicated and was exiled to the Mediterranean island of Elba. In an attempt to restore peace and stability after the Napoleonic Wars the major European powers met at the Congress of Vienna in 1914. However,

during the Congress Napoleon escaped from Elba to fight one last campaign. He was finally defeated at Waterloo in Belgium in 1815.

The Congress of Vienna redrew the political map of Europe, restoring many ruling houses (including the Bourbons in France), and recognizing new kingdoms, such as the United Netherlands.

SEE ALSO
p. 166 THE FRENCH REVOLUTION
p. 176 NATIONALISM AND LIBERALISM IN EUROPE

Under Napoleon, the French economy became strong once more. His image appeared on coins, wearing the laurel crown of an emperor.

1825 Trade unions legalized in Britain. **1830–50** Coal industry in Belgium trebles its output. **1830** First railways in France and Germany open. **1838** Steamship service across Atlantic begins. **1839** British engineer James Nasmyth invents steam hammer. **1840** First postage stamps issued, in Britain. **1848** Communist Manifesto

Emigration

In the 1850s, travel by steamship (left) reduced the time it took to sail from Europe to the USA. A new era in fast, reliable and cheap transport had begun. For many Europeans the chance to begin new lives in new countries was a welcome prospect. Millions of people affected by famine (as in Ireland in the 1840s), or who had lost their jobs to machines, emigrated from the ports of Europe. America was the chosen destination for many, and some 13 million people abandoned Europe and sailed to the USA.

Machines forced millions of agricultural laborers from the land. Many found work in factories, but some, like this harvester, became migrant workers moving from farm to farm in search of work.

The Industrial Revolution in Europe

The Industrial Revolution began in Britain in the 18th century. During the 19th century it spread to continental Europe and then to North America. Beginning in Belgium in the 1820s, coal mining and the textile and metal industries took root and quickly expanded and spread. By the 1840s railroad construction across Europe was creating a strong demand for iron and coal. By mid-century, much of northern Europe, especially Belgium, France, Russia, and Germany had well developed factory systems. As in Britain, people left the countryside to find work in the new industrial regions and cities grew rapidly. But far from improving people's lives, industrialization was also the cause of suffering and poverty, and the mid-1800s saw the rise of social movements, especially trade unions, intent on improving the lives of working-class people.

Left: Invented in Britain in 1839, the steam hammer forged, or shaped, iron that was too large to be worked by hand. Their hammers pounded white-hot iron, pressing it into shape.

Below: Rolling mills, such as this one in France, worked day and night. They made long bars of rolled iron and steel, from which finished goods were produced.

Trade unions

As the pace of industrial change quickened across Europe, groups of workers came together to form trade unions. These were associations (unions) of people who worked in the same trade. For example, there were unions for weavers and spinners, nail and chain-makers, miners, and farm laborers. Unions acted on behalf of their members, supporting them in their struggle for better pay and working conditions. Employers were not always happy to have trade union members in their workforce, accusing them of being disruptive people.

The new "iron age"

Iron and steel were the key materials in the rise of Europe's metal-bashing industries. The continent had good supplies of the raw materials needed to make iron (iron-ore, limestone to remove impurities, and coal to power the furnaces). Cast iron (hard and brittle) and wrought iron (soft and malleable) were used to make anything from a nail to the hull of a ship. From the 1850s, steel (an improved type of iron) was widely used by the cutlery and engineering trades.

Trade unions issued membership certificates decorated with images from their industries. This certificate was issued by the Amalgamated Society of Engineers, the first enduring trade union in Britain.

published; Year of Revolutions in Europe. **1850–1870** Coal and steel output trebled in France. **1851** Great Exhibition, London, celebrates Britain's industrial achievements. **1856** British metallurgist Henry Bessemer (1813–1898) discovers how to make large quantities of steel. **1876** Internal-combustion engine invented by Nikolaus Otto.

When gas streetlighting was introduced in Pall Mall in London in 1807 people were both amazed and skeptical. But by 1812 the Gas Light and Coke Company had installed 125 mi. (200 km) of gas pipes in central London.

Left: In the 1860s the International Working Men's Association spread Marx's ideas throughout Europe.

Freidrich Engels (1820–1895) who worked with Karl Marx on the Communist Manifesto.

Rise of the working-class

Workers in 19th century Europe became part of another revolution – and this one had nothing to do with machines. Instead, philosophers, notably the Germans Karl Marx and Freidrich Engels, began a revolution in ideas. They spoke against the system in which a few people (the capitalists) grew wealthy at the expense of the working-class (the proletariat). Marx and Engels proposed a classless society in which the working-classes would be the masters. It would be a society based on the principles of communism.

The rapid expansion of the railroad network, first in Britain and then in Europe, played an important role in the Industrial Revolution. The rapid distribution of goods and materials stimulated economic growth even more. The first passenger trains (below) were not as comfortable as modern trains!

Karl Marx (1818–1883) was a philosopher and economist. He wanted to change the system in which people worked for a low wage, while a few wealthy people owned the factories and the land.

There were few large-scale wars in 19th-century Europe: only civil unrest in several countries in 1848, caused by food shortages, rising prices, and opposition to unpopular leaders, threatened to slow the pace of change. By 1870, Belgium, Germany, France, and Switzerland had joined Britain as industrial powers. The northern region of Italy was in the process of becoming industrialized, Sweden was building up its metal and manufacturing industries, and Norway was developing its textile business. But not every nation could keep up with the changes that swept the continent – the countries of southern Europe, such as Spain, Portugal, and Greece, remained agricultural.

In less than 100 years Europe's leading countries changed their working ways, their means of transportation and communication, and reformed their educational and welfare systems. The workers' revolution, predicted by radical thinkers, would have to wait for the 20th century before it took hold.

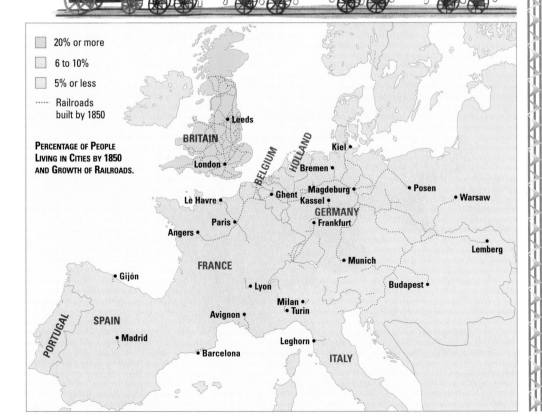

- **20% or more**
- **6 to 10%**
- **5% or less**
- ..... Railroads built by 1850

PERCENTAGE OF PEOPLE LIVING IN CITIES BY 1850 AND GROWTH OF RAILROADS.

Leeds
BRITAIN
London
Kiel
BELGIUM
HOLLAND
Bremen
Le Havre
Ghent
Magdeburg
Kassel
Posen
Warsaw
GERMANY
Paris
Frankfurt
Angers
Lemberg
Munich
FRANCE
Budapest
Lyon
Milan
Turin
Avignon
Gijón
SPAIN
PORTUGAL
Madrid
Leghorn
Barcelona
ITALY

The postage stamp was first used in Britain in 1840. Switzerland introduced stamps in 1843, and other nations followed. Stamps opened a new era in communications.

Alessandro Volta, inventor of the electric battery, and an early electric generator based on the work of Faraday and Ampère: the revolving magnet was cranked by hand.

Electricity

Scientists in the 18th century thought electricity was a fluid. Many people played a part in explaining and capturing this force of nature, beginning with Benjamin Franklin, who realized that electricity causes lightning. About 1800 an Italian, Alessandro Volta, found that a wire connecting two different metals placed in salt water (a voltaic cell) carried an electric current. By connecting many cells together he made a "voltaic pile," the first electric battery. André Ampère gave his name to the unit of measurement of an electric current.

The telegraph

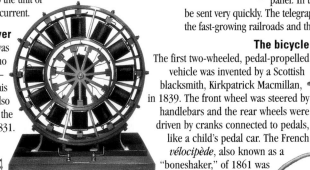

In 1837 two Englishmen, Charles Wheatstone and William Cooke, were granted a patent for an electric telegraph system. Their telegraph (left) had five needles which, powered by electrical impulses transmitted along a cable, could be moved to indicate letters or numbers on an inbuilt panel. In this way messages could be sent very quickly. The telegraph was widely used by the fast-growing railroads and the military.

Electrical power

The decisive step in putting electricity to use was made by Englishman Michael Faraday, who showed that a magnet can produce electricity – the principle of electromagnetic induction. This led to the first electric generator. Faraday also invented the electric motor in 1821, and the dynamo and transformer in 1831.

The bicycle

The first two-wheeled, pedal-propelled vehicle was invented by a Scottish blacksmith, Kirkpatrick Macmillan, in 1839. The front wheel was steered by handlebars and the rear wheels were driven by cranks connected to pedals, like a child's pedal car. The French *vélocipède*, also known as a "boneshaker," of 1861 was an improved design. The first "safety bicycle" (still the basic pattern today) appeared in 1874. The invention of air-filled tires by John Boyd Dunlop in 1888 helped to make cycling a popular pastime.

The "penny-farthing," named after very large and very small British coins, was popular in the 1870s.

Right: The rotary printing press made it possible to print tens of thousands of newspapers in just an hour or two.

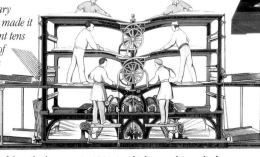

Printing

The invention of the cylinder press in 1811, in which a revolving cylinder was used to press paper against type, was a major advance over the traditional hand press. About 1837 the next step was the web-fed press, which printed onto a continuous role of paper. Finally, the rotary press used two cylinders, the second cylinder carrying the type.

The automobile

A steam-driven truck that moved under its own power was built in 1769. Many other steam-driven vehicles, mostly buses and tractors, were made over the next hundred years. The first automobile – a wooden three-wheeler with a small gas engine and a tiller for steering (right) – was invented by the German engineer Karl Benz in 1885.

Railroads

The first railroads were built in the 16th century; horse-drawn wagons that ran on wooden rails were used to carry rock and coal from mines. Although the steam engine was invented in 1712, it wasn't until 1803 that the first steam locomotive was built, by Richard Trevithick in England. Running on iron rails, the earliest steam locomotives pulled freight trains, but in 1825 the first public railroad, the Stockton and Darlington, opened in England.

Steam locomotives proved popular with passengers. The earliest trains went at nearly 30 mph (almost 50 kph).

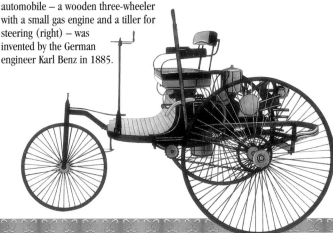

c.1800 Volta invents "voltaic pile," or electric cell battery.

1803 Trevithick invents steam locomotive; runs on metal rails.

1811 Cylinder press advances printing methods.

1821–31 Faraday invents electric motor and transformer.

1837 Wheatstone and Cooke invent electric telegraph.

The Age of Inventions

Since prehistoric times, humans have invented things to make life easier for themselves. Some inventions were the result of a flash of insight, others evolved gradually from the observation of repeated experiments. One of the most significant inventions was the wheel, which was in use over 5,000 years ago. For thousands of years after that life changed very slowly by comparison with recent times. Changes came faster after the Renaissance, when the invention of printing revolutionized all forms of learning, including science. The scientific revolution of the 17th century saw the invention of the telescope, microscope, thermometer, accurate clocks, and other instruments. During the 18th-century Enlightenment, or Age of Reason, thinkers believed that science could explain everything, and the Industrial Revolution encouraged technological advances and new machines.

The Age of Inventions sprang from two connected developments: the rise of modern science and the development of modern technology. Change was rapid. A good example is the history of transportation. Throughout history the fastest way to travel on land was on horseback, but in the hundred years after 1820 came, first railways, then automobiles, and then airplanes.

Scientific discovery and technological invention went hand in hand, but they had different objectives. The job of scientists is to explain the world; the job of inventors is to find ways of improving it. Some scientific discoveries, such as Louis Pasteur's discovery of germs, brought

Electric light

Candles and oil lamps began to be replaced by gas lighting from about 1800 on. Electric arc lamps also appeared then, used mainly in theaters. Electric lighting for houses needed an incandescent bulb (one that produced white heat). One of the earliest successful ones was developed by American inventor Thomas Edison in 1879; it burned for 40 hours continuously.

Among Thomas Edison's many inventions were the electric light bulb and the phonograph, for recording sound.

The telephone

Telecommunications began with the telegraph, which sent messages along a cable carrying an electric current. Samuel Morse's code of dots and dashes was the common method. The telephone, in which actual speech was carried by the cable, was demonstrated in 1876 by Alexander Graham Bell.

On this early telephone the earpiece and mouthpiece are attached by a cable.

The elevator

By about 1850 new building methods and materials made it possible to construct taller buildings. Steam-driven elevators were already in use in industry, but they had no safety device to prevent them falling if they broke down. Elisha Otis invented a safety system and installed the first elevator in a New York store in 1857. Motor-driven elevators were first used in skyscrapers about 1890.

Germs

There were many advances in medicine in the 19th century. One of the most important was the germ theory of Louis Pasteur in the 1860s. He proved that food goes bad because it becomes infected by bacteria, or germs, in the air. This led him to invent the process of pasteurization, which prevents food becoming infected. Influenced by this theory, surgeon Joseph Lister realized that germs caused infections after operations, causing unnecessary deaths. He used a carbolic acid spray (above) on patient's wounds to stop infections.

X-rays were useful in the fight against lung disease.

X-rays

Electromagnetism came to be recognized as a basic force of the universe, present everywhere in the form of waves (including radio waves). One of these waves, X-rays, can pass through some kinds of matter and register on a photographic plate. Wilhelm Roentgen discovered them in 1895 and X-rayed his wife's hand.

Right: The cover of the French magazine Figaro illustré *in 1909 summarized the growth of flying technology.*

Photography and cinema

The principle of making a picture with light was known by Frenchman Joseph Nièpce in 1816, but he was unable to print positive impressions from his negatives. In 1839 several French and British pioneers found ways to make photographs. The process spread rapidly, and improvements came thick and fast. Photographers knew that moving pictures were possible, too. In 1895 the brothers Louis and Auguste Lumière invented their cinematograph. The movies had arrived.

In 1901 the East Kodak Company began selling the "Brownie," the first camera for a mass market.

"Flying machines"

Between the Montgolfier balloon of 1783 and the first aircraft flight by the Wright brothers in 1903, progress was made in airships (right), especially in France. Like balloons, they were basically huge bags filled with a gas lighter than air. Airships, or "dirigibles," could be steered and flown slowly against the wind. Henri Giffard's airship of 1852 was driven by a steam engine.

In 1903 the American brothers Orville and Wilbur Wright made the first controlled flight in a powered aircraft.

1839 Macmillan's pedal bicycle.	**1876** Bell invents telephone.	**1885** Benz builds automobile.	radio transmission.	**1903** Wright brothers make
1860s Pasteur's pasteurization.	**1879** Edison's incandescent bulb.	**1894** Guglielmo Marconi's first	**1896** Roentgen discovers X-rays.	controlled aircraft flight.

---

huge improvements almost immediately. But some, like Isaac Newton's discovery of the law of gravity, had little direct effect on the way people lived.

There were few professional scientists or engineers before the 19th century. Few universities taught science, and there were no research institutes with white-coated scientists working in laboratories. Many of the greatest discoveries were made by amateurs: for example, Joseph Priestley, who discovered oxygen, was a

SEE ALSO
p. 156 THE SCIENTIFIC REVOLUTION
p. 162 THE INDUSTRIAL REVOLUTION BEGINS
p. 172 THE INDUSTRIAL REVOLUTION IN EUROPE

clergyman. Many of the machines in the new factories were invented by ordinary craftworkers looking for a quicker or better way to do a certain job. Machines were invented because they were needed. For instance, in the 17th century coal could only be mined near the surface, because deeper mines became flooded. As consumption of coal increased, the surface seams were worked out. It became necessary to invent a pump to allow miners to work at

deeper levels. This was the origin of the steam engine. The steam engine could have been invented earlier, but there was no urgent need for it.

One invention often led to another. In the textile industry the invention of the flying shuttle made weaving much faster than spinning. This led to technological advances to speed up spinning. Weaving caught up with the steam-driven power loom. In science too, one step led to another. Studies of the fermentation process in making beer led Pasteur to develop his theory of germs.

1. The hot-air balloon invented by the Montgolfier brothers carried two passengers over Paris in 1783 in the first human flight.

2. A poster advertising the Lumière brothers' new invention – the cinema.

Nationalism and Liberalism in Europe

Political events in 19th-century Europe were driven by two powerful forces: nationalism and liberalism. Their origins can be seen in the French Revolution. A "nation" is a group of people who speak the same language and are bound together by a shared history. Liberalism was founded on the ideas of the Enlightenment. It represented the movement toward greater freedom and power for ordinary people in a state ruled by law, whose government is subject to the approval of the people it governs. Eventually, Europe became a continent of democratic nation-states, but early 19th-century liberals were not true democrats because they believed that only men who owned property should be able to vote. Liberalism was strongest among the newly prosperous middle classes.

Right: A cartoon satirizing the diplomatic positions taken by the European leaders at the Congress of Vienna.

As Napoleon marched across Europe from 1804 to 1812, his victorious armies spread the liberal ideas of the French Revolution (1789). Among them was the idea that all people were equal before the law and that they could decide things for themselves, rather than having everything decided for them by an absolute monarch.

After Napoleon's defeat, Europe's rulers tried to reassert their authority. At the Congress of Vienna in 1814 they restored most of the European boundaries that had existed before 1789. They also set up the "Congress System" – regular meetings of the great powers to deal with any future revolutions. But many people wanted to live under a freer system of government; they no longer wanted their countries to be ruled by larger foreign powers such as the Ottoman and Austrian empires.

Between 1820 and 1848 countries throughout Europe became restless for independence. In 1820 uprisings took place in Sicily and Naples against King Ferdinand I (1751–1825), who had introduced measures that restricted personal freedom. Revolts also took place in Spain and Portugal, but these achieved little. In 1830, however, in France, the July Revolution overthrew King Charles X (1757–1836), who had been restored to his throne after Napoleon's defeat. The French example encouraged uprisings in other nations, which were forced to introduce liberal reforms.

During the 1840s harvests failed, unemployment was high, and prices rose. Tensions mounted, and in 1848 revolutions against dictatorial and foreign rule broke out across Europe. Once again France led the way. It expelled King Louis-Philippe (1773–1850), the last of the old Bourbon monarchs, and set up the Second Republic. Prussia was forced to adopt a liberal constitution. Austria had to grant some independence to the Hungarians and Czechs; and republics were declared in Italy. By 1849 the revolts had all been put down, but the governments of Europe had been forced to recognize the importance of nationalist movements.

The Congress of Vienna

The leading figure at the Congress of Vienna in 1814 – the conference following Napoleon's defeat – was the Austrian chancellor, Prince Klemens von Metternich. His aim was to restore the Habsburg Empire to a leading place in Europe and to bring political stability. Austria regained its empire, except for the Austrian Netherlands, and in the Two Sicilies (southern Italy), the Bourbons regained their thrones.

A Polish rebel with his nation's flag. Poland did not gain its freedom until 1918.

Below: The beautiful Mostar Bridge, in present-day Bosnia, built in 1556 by the Turks on the Drina River.

The Balkans

The Balkans (southeastern Europe) had been part of the Ottoman Empire since the 14th century, but the people had kept their own languages, religions, and customs. By 1800 the Ottoman Empire had grown weak, and in 1822 Greece won its independence. Nationalism was also growing among the other Balkan nations. The unwillingness of Europe's major powers to allow Austria and Russia to expand into the Ottoman Empire kept the empire in existence, but by 1900 Romania, Serbia, Bulgaria, and Montenegro had all gained independence.

Eugene Delacroix's Greece Expiring on the Ruins of Missolonghi (after a battle with the Turks) expresses his sympathy toward nationalist feelings.

Greek independence

In 1821 the Greeks rebelled against their rulers, the Ottoman Turks. The European powers were sympathetic and some foreigners, such as the English poet Lord Byron, went to fight for them. Greece declared independence in 1822, but in 1826 was reconquered by Mehemet Ali of Egypt. A combined fleet sent by Britain, France, and Russia destroyed the Egyptian fleet at Navarino in 1827, and Greece regained its independence.

Poland

The kingdom of Poland, revived in 1815, was little different from a Russian province. Polish nationalists rebelled in 1830, but they lacked strong leadership and, unlike the Greeks, had no help from abroad. After nearly a year of fighting they were crushed. They rebelled again in 1846 and in 1863, but Poland did not finally gain its independence as a republic until 1918.

The July Revolution

In July 1830 King Charles X of France (1757–1836) dissolved the national assembly and declared that he would rule alone. Violent riots broke out in Paris and Charles was forced to abdicate. He was replaced by the so-called "citizen-king," Louis-Philippe (1773–1850), who promised constitutional government. But little changed and the poor conditions of the working people worsened. Louis-Philippe lost popular support; as his ideas grew more old fashioned, reformers demanded greater change.

Fighting between citizens and troops at the Porte St. Denis in Paris marked the outbreak of the 1830 July Revolution.

against Russian rule.
1848 Revolutions in France, Austria, Hungary, German and Italian states, Ireland, Switzerland, and Denmark. Communist Manifesto published by Marx and Engels. **1852** French Second Republic overthrown; Second Empire founded by Napoleon III.

Belgium and Switzerland

A nationalist rebellion in the former Austrian Netherlands resulted in the creation of the kingdom of Belgium in 1831. The Belgians chose a German prince for their king, Leopold I (1790–1865). The Swiss had been independent since 1648, living in a confederation of cantons, or states. In 1847 civil war broke out between the Catholic cantons, which wanted to remain independent, and the others, where radicals demanded a government for the whole country. Peace was restored in 1848, when a constitution was agreed for the united cantons.

Above: Brussels became the capital of the newly independent Belgium. The Maison du Roi, or House of the King, in Brussels's main square was restored by Belgium's second king, Leopold II.

1848: Austria

In March 1848, following an uprising in Vienna, the Austrian chancellor Prince Metternich resigned. He abdicated in favor of his nephew, Franz Josef

(1830–1916). The same month the Hungarians rebelled against Austrian rule, claiming independence. A Pan-Slav Congress led by the Czechs demanded self-government for all the Slav peoples – Hungarians, Czechs, Romanians, and Poles – in the Austrian empire. But the Austrian armies gradually defeated the Slavs, who never united because of their nationalism.

In 1849 the Hungarian leader Lajos Kossuth (1802–94) declared Hungary independent and himself president.

Socialism

A new force for change was active in 1848. *The Communist Manifesto* (title page below), by Karl Marx (1818–83) and Friedrich Engels (1820–95), preached revolutionary socialism. It demanded the overthrow of the middle class in a workers' revolution, and the creation of a state where all people were equal and the state owned everything. Other socialists believed this could be achieved through peaceful reform instead of violence.

In this representation of the end of the monarchy in France, Louis-Philippe's throne is burned on a bonfire.

1848: France

In 1848 French democrats and socialists led protests against the government of King Louis-Philippe, which had failed to fulfill expectations. Louis-Philippe abdicated, and the Second Republic was established with Louis Napoleon (later Napoleon III, 1808–73), nephew of Napoleon Bonaparte, as president.

In 1848 revolts against dictatorial rule broke out all over Europe. This time the protesters were working people, not the middle classes, whose aims had largely been met.

Friedrich Wilhelm IV of Prussia (reigned 1840–61), with backing from the army, tries to close the door on liberal reformers.

Louis Napoleon became Emperor Napoleon III in 1852. Although effectively a dictator, he liked to be seen as the "liberal emperor."

Counter-Revolution

The gains of the revolutionary movements of 1848 were quickly lost. In France Louis Napoleon ended the Second Republic and made himself emperor. In Austria the Habsburg government regained control, suppressed the Czechs, and cancelled the new, liberal constitution. The republics in Hungary and northern Italy disappeared. But in future, no government could ever again safely ignore calls for reform.

1848: Germany

In 1815 the 39 German states were formed into a confederation under Austrian leadership. In 1848 popular uprisings took place in most of the states, including the strongest: Prussia. The people's desire for German unification forced Friedrich Wilhelm IV of Prussia to grant a constitution. An elected assembly convened at Frankfurt, and in 1849 offered him the crown of a united Germany. He refused because the offer was made by a popularly elected body. After riots in Berlin, the liberal revolution was crushed by the Prussian army and the assembly was dissolved.

1848: Italy

The three main powers in Italy were Austria in the north, the Papal States in the center, and the Kingdom of the Two Sicilies (Sicily and Naples) in the south. All three regions saw uprisings against the rulers in 1848. Northern Italy and the Papal States gained constitutions as a result. In the Two Sicilies, King Ferdinand II (1810–59) quelled disorder by bombarding his own cities.

Pope Pius IX had to flee Rome when revolution broke out in 1848. He was restored in 1849 by French troops.

Below: The potatoes grown by Irish peasants were almost their only food. Famine resulted from a disease called blight, which rots potatoes.

Ireland

Ireland (then part of Great Britain) had a half-hearted revolt in 1848, but the people were exhausted by the potato famine that had afflicted the Catholic peasants in the south and west since 1845. Starvation, disease, and emigration, mainly to England or North America, reduced Ireland's population by nearly one quarter. A long-term effect of the famine was the growth of Irish nationalism, supported by Irish immigrant communities in North America.

SEE ALSO
p. 170 NAPOLEONIC EUROPE

THE UNIFICATION OF ITALY (1859-70).

SWITZERLAND   AUSTRO-HUNGARIAN EMPIRE
SAVOY
TYROL
PIEDMONT LOMBARDY   VENETIA
KINGDOM
OF SARDINIA   PARMA
NICE LIGURIA   MODENA ROMAGNA
CORSICA   TUSCANY MARCHES   ADRIATIC SEA
UMBRIA PAPAL STATES
Rome
Naples
TYRRHENIAN SEA
SARDINIA   KINGDOM OF THE TWO SICILIES
KINGDOM OF SARDINIA

☐ Kingdom of Sardinia in 1815   ☐ Lost to France, 1860
Territories annexed by:
☐ 1859   ☐ Nov. 1860   ☐ 1866
☐ March 1860   ☐ Nov. 1860   ☐ 1870

Piedmontese soldiers made ready for war with Austria after Cavour's meeting with Napoleon III.

Nationalism in Italy

During the 1820s and 1830s nationalist ideas were spread in Italy by secret societies such as the Carbonari in the south and "Young Italy," led by Giuseppe Mazzini (1805–72), in the north. Mazzini wanted the people of Italy to rise against Austrian rule and create an Italian republic ruled from Rome. He founded a republic in 1848, but it was short-lived.

The republican Mazzini, an Italian hero.

Cavour: Piedmont's expansion

In 1852 Count Camillo di Cavour (1810–61, left) became prime minister of Piedmont. His skilful diplomacy in 1858 secured France as an ally against the Austrians, in a war he was about to provoke in order to try and gain Italian independence. In 1859 Austria demanded that Piedmont stop its military preparations on the frontier of Austrian Lombardy. Cavour refused and war followed. Together the French and Piedmontese troops defeated the Austrians, and Lombardy fell to Piedmont.

The French alliance

Cavour involved Piedmont in the Crimean War in Russia in order to gain influence with Britain and France. The French emperor, Napoleon III (1808–73), met Cavour secretly at Plombières in 1858. He agreed to support Italy in a war against Austria, and that in the event of victory, a northern Italian kingdom should be formed; in return France would gain Nice and Savoy from Italy.

The kingdom of northern Italy

After Piedmont's victories over Austria at the battles of Solferino and Magenta in 1859, nationalism was unstoppable. Rebels offered the throne of Tuscany to Victor Emmanuel II of Sardinia (1820–78), and Modena and Parma followed. A kingdom of northern Italy was declared. But Cavour had no wish to add the undeveloped south to Piedmont's northern Italian kingdom, and opposed the expedition of Garibaldi to Sicily. He feared that Garibaldi might create his own republic or, worse, march on Rome, the pope's city, protected by the French.

Unification

Napoleon III insisted that in all the 13 Italian states, the government must consult the people on the issue of joining Victor Emmanuel's kingdom. The results were huge votes in favor (right), and in less than two years, nearly all Italy, including part of the Papal States, had been brought together under Victor Emmanuel II. Two regions remained outside: Rome, Italy's most important city, but also the pope's, and Venice.

Some of the fiercest fighting in 1848 took place in Milan; Italians drove out the Austrians after a week of street fighting.

The 1848 revolution

In 1848 the people of Milan drove out their Austrian rulers, and Piedmont attempted to expel the Austrians from Italy. But the uprising in Milan was quickly contained by Austrian troops. In Rome, a revolution drove out the pope and a republic was declared. Mazzini was made effective head of government. But the pope appealed to the French for help. French troops soon crushed the republic and the pope was restored in 1849.

Garibaldi

In southern Italy, an ultra-conservative royal government ruled the kingdom of the Two Sicilies (Sicily and Naples). In 1860 Giuseppe Garibaldi (1807–82), an inspiring guerrilla leader, led 1,000 volunteers in an invasion of Sicily. Having taken control, he crossed to the mainland, defeated an Austrian force and, in spite of Cavour's orders to stop, drove the Bourbon king from his capital, Naples. Cavour hastily sent troops south to prevent Garibaldi advancing on Rome.

Garibaldi (on the left) remained a monarchist and freely handed over his conquests to Victor Emmanuel II.

1831 Mazzini's "Young Italy."
1848 Year of Revolutions.

1852 Count Cavour prime minister of Piedmont.

1853–56 Crimean War.
1860 Garibaldi conquers Naples

and southern Italy. **1861** Victor Emmanuel II becomes king of

united Italy. **1862** Bismarck becomes chancellor of Prussia.

Unification of Italy and Germany

National states existed in England, France, Spain, and other countries by 1500. Italy and Germany, however, remained divided into many small states until the late 19th century. In some ways the nationalist movements in the two countries were alike. Although its origins were much older, national unification first became a serious issue in 1848: earlier revolts had generally been in favor of more liberal government. After the 1848 revolutions failed, liberal nationalists changed their ideas and became willing to support strong, expanding powers – Piedmont in Italy and Prussia in Germany – because these powers seemed more likely to be able to unite their countries. In both Italy and Germany, therefore, what came to matter most was the power and influence of a particular state, and the influence of one skilful statesman: Cavour in Piedmont, Bismarck in Prussia. But unification also depended on military force. In Germany that was supplied by the formidable Prussian army. In Italy there was no such force, and success was only possible with the military help of one of the great powers: France.

The composer Giuseppe Verdi (1813–1901), born in Parma, was a strong supporter of Italian independence. He was elected as a member of the first Italian parliament in 1861. Some of his operas, such as Rigoletto, caused trouble with the authorities.

THE GERMAN STATES BEFORE UNIFICATION (1815–71).

Map legend:
- Prussia in 1815
- Acquired by Prussia 1815–66
- Imperial territory of Alsace-Lorraine 1871
- German Empire 1871

The German rivals

After 1815 Germany was still divided into 39 states. Austria was the dominant power, but Prussia was growing stronger. Prussia benefited most from the *Zollverein* (customs union), which most German states (but not Austria) joined by 1834. After the failures of the 1848 revolutions and the collapse of the Frankfurt Parliament, liberal German nationalists became more willing to support Prussian ambitions as a way of gaining German unity.

Bismarck

Otto von Bismarck became Prussian chancellor (prime minister) in 1862. A conservative, and a patriotic Prussian from the old land-owning military class, he became the most powerful figure in Europe for nearly 30 years. Bismarck was not interested in Germany as a nation. His idea of unification was a Prussian Empire. The chief obstacle to Prussian domination of Germany was Austria, but Bismarck was an opportunist, and in 1866 he was able to defeat Austria.

Otto von Bismarck, Germany's "Iron Chancellor" and greatest statesman; he was also noted for his passion for pickled herrings.

The Franco–Prussian War 1870–71

In 1866 Prussia, with Italy's help, defeated Austria in Bohemia. Then in 1868 a Prussian prince claimed the throne of Spain. Napoleon III of France, increasingly alarmed at Prussia's growing power, renewed protests to Germany. Bismarck, the Prussian chancellor, changed a reply (the Ems Telegram) from King Wilhelm to Napoleon, making it more aggressive. France took the bait, declared war on Prussia, and was crushingly defeated at Sedan in 1870.

A German factory forging steel ingots for the manufacture of railroad track.

Right: Statue erected in Berlin after the war of 1870–71. It was meant to symbolize the industrial and military superiority of Prussia.

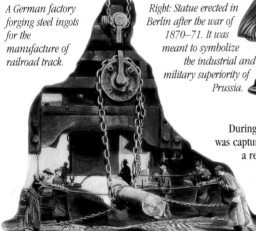

Defeat of Austria

In 1864 Denmark tried to take over the provinces of Schleswig and Holstein, where many Germans lived. Austria and Prussia acted together to prevent this, and the two provinces were placed under joint Austrian and Prussian control. But the governments quarrelled over how they should be governed, and Prussia provoked Austria into declaring war. In just seven weeks, the efficient Prussian army, under Field Marshal von Moltke, won a decisive victory over the Austrians. Prussia was now the dominant power in Germany.

The German Empire

During the Franco–Prussian war Napoleon III was captured at Sedan, and France again became a republic. With the people of Paris under bombardment and almost starving – restaurants served up animals from the zoo – France surrendered. Its northern provinces of Alsace-Lorraine were absorbed by the new German Empire, formed after the Prussian victory in 1871.

Wilhelm I, king of Prussia from 1861; kaiser (emperor) of Germany (1871–88).

The new Europe

From 1871 the newly created German Empire was ruled by its army under the emperor. The united kingdom of Italy, by contrast, was ruled largely by and for businessmen. For Europe, the creation of a powerful Germany promised future problems. Bismarck failed to recognize the bitterness of the French, who never accepted the loss of Alsace-Lorraine; and future rulers of Germany were quicker to use force rather than diplomacy.

FRENCH SATIRICAL MAP OF THE NEW EUROPE.

1866 Austro–Prussian War.
1870 Franco–Prussian War;

Battle of Sedan; Napoleon III taken prisoner; Prussians

besiege Paris; Napoleon III abdicates.

1871 Wilhelm I becomes kaiser (emperor) of Germany;

Rome capital of Italy.

Looking back, it is easy for historians to recognize the series of events that led to the creation of the German Empire and the Kingdom of Italy. But to people at the time, who were unable to foresee the future, events were much less orderly. Neither Camillo Cavour nor Otto von Bismarck set out with a plan to unify Italy or Germany. In fact, neither of them intended this to happen. Their aim was to increase the power and wealth of their own states. Bismarck's motive was to build a greater Prussia, not a new Germany. Cavour

hoped that his king might reign over a larger northern Italian kingdom, but he had no desire to include southern Italy (Naples and Sicily), which was extremely poor and, he thought, likely to cost much more than it was worth.

The two countries achieved unification in different ways. In Germany, all depended on the Prussian army. The result was a German Empire in which the army kept its power, and liberal ideas were discouraged. In Italy, the ordinary people were more closely involved in the struggle. Guerrilla

warfare played an important part, and the south was won not by a professional army but by Garibaldi's 1,000-strong army of red-shirted volunteers. The result was a more liberal state.

German and Italian unification brought dramatic changes to Europe. Until 1870 the main land powers in Europe were Austria and France, with Britain supreme at sea. That balance was destroyed by the creation of a huge new power: the German Empire. Its resources and industry were already challenging Britain's place as top trading nation.

1. An Austrian army helmet, lost at the battle of Sadowa, or Königgrätz.

2. The German composer Richard Wagner (1813–83), whose Ring cycle of operas based on German mythology strengthened German nationalism.

Latin America

The Spanish and Portuguese colonial powers were ousted from Latin America in a remarkably short period of time, from 1818 to 1828, leaving only the strongholds of Cuba and Puerto Rico in the Caribbean. Independence was gained through a combination of local rebellions and events in Europe. Napoleon's invasion of the Iberian Peninsula in 1807 greatly weakened Spain and Portugal. Simón Bolívar and other American liberators quickly took the opportunity to rise against and defeat the Europeans. The liberated Latin Americans did not find it easy to make their new republics work efficiently and peacefully, and ambitious military leaders or wealthy landowners often seized power. Although slaves were freed by the end of the 19th century, independence did not bring much economic benefit to most ordinary people.

In 1807 Napoleon's forces conquered Portugal, and the following year he placed his brother Joseph Bonaparte (1768–1844) on the Spanish throne. Spain's control over its colonies weakened, and many Latin Americans began or intensified their fight for independence. Mexico began its revolt in 1810, called for and led by the Catholic priest Miguel Hidalgo y Costilla. The initial revolt failed, and Mexico did not gain its independence until 1821. Central Americans won freedom in the same year, with Costa Rica, El Salvador, Guatemala, Honduras, and Nicaragua becoming part of Mexico in 1822. The following year they broke away again and formed the

Chileans celebrate independence by raising their new national flag.

Chile

The Chileans began their revolt against Spain in 1810, when a provisional republic was declared. General Bernardo O'Higgins led the fight for independence. In 1814 he joined forces with the army of the Argentinian liberator, José de San Martin. The two men led the "Army of the Andes" from Argentina over the Andes mountains into Chile, and in 1817 defeated the Spanish. Chile gained independence in 1818, and O'Higgins served as "supreme director" until 1823. He made sweeping reforms, but was forced to resign after revolts in the provinces.

Right: Antonio José de Sucre (1795–1830) was born in Venezuela. He was the most able of Simón Bolívar's generals and helped to liberate Ecuador, Peru, and Bolivia. He served as president of Bolivia. The nation's legal capital, Sucre, is named after him.

Bernardo O'Higgins (1778–1842), the main liberator of Chile, was the son of an Irish-born colonial official.

According to legend the Aztecs of Mexico built their capital on an island where they found an eagle perched on a cactus. This became the Mexican national emblem.

Mexico

Mexico's struggle for independence began in 1810 and achieved success 11 years later. The country was still divided, however, between conservatives, who wanted a monarchy, and liberals, who favored a republic. An emperor was appointed in 1822, but he was deposed a year later, and in 1824 a republic was declared. A turbulent period for the new nation ended with the so-called Mexican War (1846–48) with the United States, by which Mexico lost territory to its northern neighbor.

Peru

The treasurehouse of Spain for some three centuries, Peru declared its independence in 1821. The Spanish were defeated by General Sucre's troops three years later. *Caudillos,* or "military leaders," fought for control of the new nation, and stability was only achieved when General Ramón Castilla became president in 1845.

Peruvian patriot José Olaya carried letters between the liberating armies in the mountains and republicans in the Spanish-held capital, Lima. He was killed by the Spaniards in 1823.

Simón Bolívar

Bolívar was South America's greatest general. Known as "the Liberator," he gained independence for Bolivia, Colombia, Ecuador, Peru, and Venezuela. Bolívar became president of Gran Colombia in 1819, and the former Upper Peru took the name Bolivia in his honor. Rather than creating so many independent nations, Bolívar had hoped to form a united Andean republic. But his dream was never realized and he became disillusioned by the political disagreements that put paid to unity.

Simón Bolívar (1783–1830) was the son of a wealthy Venezuelan Creole family. As a young man he traveled in Europe, and it was while in Rome that he vowed to liberate Venezuela.

COUNTRIES OF LATIN AMERICA WITH DATE BY WHICH INDEPENDENCE WAS GAINED.

MEXICO 1821
UNITED STATES
BAHAMAS 1973
CUBA 1902
HAITI 1804
JAMAICA 1862
DOMINICAN REPUBLIC 1844
PANAMA 1903
UNITED PROVINCES OF CENTRAL AMERICA* 1823
GUYANA 1966 (from Britain)
VENEZUELA 1821
SURINAME 1975 (from Holland)
NEW GRANADA 1831
FRENCH GUIANA
GUIANA
ECUADOR 1830
GRAN COLOMBIA 1822
PERU 1824
EMPIRE OF BRAZIL 1822
BOLIVIA 1825
PARAGUAY 1811
CHILE 1818
ARGENTINE CONFEDERATION 1816
URUGUAY 1828
PATAGONIA
FALKLAND

*GUATEMALA 1821–47
BELIZE 1981 (from Britain)
EL SALVADOR 1821 (as part of Mexico); full, 1823
HONDURAS 1821 (as part of Mexico); full, 1838
NICARAGUA 1821 (as part of Mexico); full 1838
COSTA RICA 1821 (as part of Mexico); full 1838

Independent country

COLONIAL POWER:
Britain
Netherlands
Spain
France
Denmark

SEE ALSO
p. 114 PORTUGUESE AND SPANISH EXPANSION
p. 198 COLONIALISM
p. 248 CENTRAL AND SOUTH AMERICA

becomes president of Bolivia.
1830 Death of Simón Bolívar.

1831–89 Pedro II rules as emperor of Brazil.

1846–48 Mexican War against the United States.

1888 Brazil abolishes slavery.
1901 Cuba becomes a republic.

1903 Panama gains independence.

United Provinces of Central America. By 1847 each of the five states was an independent republic. Panama was a Colombian province until 1903, when it rebelled with the help of the United States and became independent. British Honduras (present-day Belize) became a British colony in 1862.

In South America, "the Liberator" Simón Bolívar helped to free New Granada (centered on present-day Colombia) from the Spanish by defeating them at Boyacá in 1819. New Granada was renamed the Republic of Gran Colombia that, after another defeat of the Spanish in 1821, united with Venezuela, Ecuador, and Panama; Bolívar ruled as

1

president. Venezuela left the union in 1829. Peru declared its independence in 1821, and defeated the Spanish in 1824. The following year Upper Peru became a republic, named Bolivia in honor of its liberator.

Another great freedom fighter was the Argentine general José

de San Martin, who liberated Argentina in 1816. Two years later he helped General Bernardo O'Higgins free Chile from Spanish rule.

The largest country in South America, Brazil, won its freedom from Portugal without bloodshed. The Portuguese court had moved to Brazil during the Napoleonic Wars, and in 1815 the colony was made a kingdom. In 1822 independence was declared by Pedro I (1798–1834), who became emperor.

In the West Indies, François Toussaint-L'Ouverture had led African slaves in a revolt against their French rulers in 1791, and in 1804 Haiti had become the first independent nation

in Latin America. Forty years later the other part of Hispaniola island became the Dominican Republic. Cuba gained independence in 1899. The smaller Caribbean islands and Guyana remained under British, Dutch, or French rule.

The population of the new republics was made up of mestizos (of Native American and European descent), Creoles (of African and European descent), mulattos (of African and European descent), Native South Americans, and freed African slaves.

1. Vase showing the three constituents of the Latin American population: Native American, Spanish, and African.

Famous Brazilian sculptor and architect Antonio Francisco Lisboa (c.1730–1814) designed this church in Congonhas.

Pedro I, emperor of Brazil.

Brazil

Brazil declared independence in 1822, and Pedro I (1798–1834), son of John VI of Portugal, became emperor. He was forced to resign in 1831 and left his throne to his five-year-old son, Pedro II (1826–91), who ruled from 1840 for more than 50 years. Despite wars against Argentina and Paraguay, Brazil prospered; agriculture and industry expanded, railroads were built, and between 1870 and 1888 slavery was abolished. Brazil became a republic in 1889.

In Rio de Janeiro, capital of the Portuguese Empire, the European nobility lived in luxury, attended to by Brazilians.

These African slaves are harvesting coffee in Brazil. Between 1800 and 1855 up to two million slaves were taken from Africa to Brazil. Slavery was finally abolished in 1888.

The hacienda

After independence the new Latin American countries were dominated by the huge landed estates called haciendas. These depended on cheap labor, and slavery continued in some regions until the 1840s, and even longer in Brazil. After the eventual abolition of slavery, African blacks still remained very poor, along with mestizos.

Von Humboldt

In 1799 the German scientist Alexander von Humboldt (1769–1859, right) set out for Central and South America. He spent five years studying the geology and biology of Latin America, collecting a vast number of samples. On his return to Europe in 1804 he met Simón Bolívar, and it is said that he told Bolívar that South America was ripe for revolution.

Native South Americans

The newly independent countries had multi-racial populations. Rulers often used force to weld these different peoples into a single nation. Hoping to weaken the loyalty of the Native Americans to their groups, rulers divided their communal lands between individual Native American farmers. As landowners, they had the responsibilities of private citizens.

A Native American leader visiting a local community in Brazil.

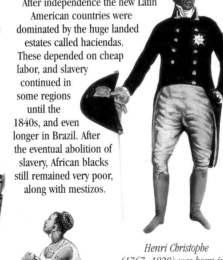

Henri Christophe (1767–1820) was born into slavery on a Caribbean island. He fought in the revolution that led to an independent Haiti in 1804.

Hispaniola and Cuba

The western third of Hispaniola was a French colony: Saint Domingue. It gained independence as Haiti in 1804. The rest of the island, Santo Domingo, gained independence as the Dominican Republic in 1844. Cuba was a Spanish colony divided into large estates worked by African slaves. Slavery was finally abolished in 1886, but independence from Spain was not gained until 1899, following two uprisings. The smaller Caribbean islands remained under European control.

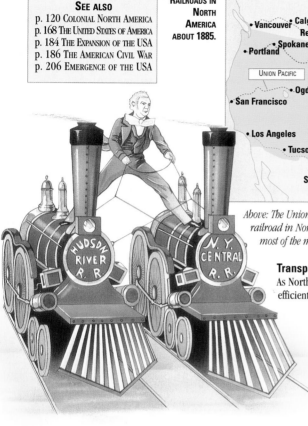

RAILROADS IN NORTH AMERICA ABOUT 1885.

Vancouver • • Calgary
Regina • CANADIAN PACIFIC
• Winnipeg
• Spokane NORTHERN PACIFIC
• Portland Sudbury • Quebec •
• Ottawa
Minneapolis • Boston •
UNION PACIFIC Chicago • New York •
• Ogden Omaha • Washington •
• San Francisco

• Los Angeles
Atlanta •
• Tucson SOUTHERN PACIFIC
• El Paso • Montgomery
New Orleans •
San Antonio •

Above: The Union Pacific was the first coast-to-coast railroad in North America. By 1885 railroads linked most of the major towns of America and Canada.

Transportation unites the continent

As North America began to industrialize, more efficient transportation was needed. Gradually the horse-drawn stagecoaches that carried people and baggage long distances by road were replaced by steam trains. From the 1860s the railroad network spread across the land, eventually uniting the continent from coast to coast.

Farming the prairies

The industrialization of farming in North America had a huge impact on the landscape. The railroad network opened up the prairie lands of the Midwest to farmers, who transformed this region of fertile grassland into the world's largest grain-producing area. Steam engines such as this one (below), which dates from 1869, powered threshers that separated out the grain. So much wheat was produced that the United States became a grain-exporting nation.

Above: Cornelius Vanderbilt (1794–1877) made his fortune in the shipping business and then moved into railroad finance. This cartoon shows him controlling railroads in the northeastern states.

During the 1840s a new horse-drawn reaping machine, invented by Cyrus McCormick (1809–84), revolutionized cereal harvesting. The machines cut wheat five times faster than a person with a scythe. They were widely used on the fertile prairies.

Slavery in the South

Until the mid-1860s the United States was a nation divided by slavery. The Northern states had abolished slavery by 1804, but the Southern states – with an agricultural economy – had come to depend on slave labor. The first slaves had been shipped there from Africa in the 1600s by the British. Slaves worked on the plantations, growing and harvesting crops such as cotton, sugar cane, and tobacco.

Slaves were bought and sold at public auctions. They were even used as "currency" to pay bills and settle debts.

1790s Whitney's cotton gin speeds up production.
1833 National Highway reaches

1830s Settlers move West.

Ohio in the Midwest.
1840s McCormick horse-drawn

reaper comes into general use.
1851 Isaac Singer (1811–75)

patents his sewing machine.
1860s 30,000 mi. (48,000 km) of

North America Industrializes

During the 18th century Britain's North America colonies struggled for independence. During the 19th century the newly independent nation of the United States of America emerged as one of the world's major industrial countries. Rich in natural resources, North America exploited these to the full. Coal, oil, iron ore, cotton, and wheat were vital to the development of the nation's new industries. Skilled industrialists and financiers steered the growing economy, and inventors created machines that could make goods faster and more cheaply than people. For many people it was a time of opportunity and success. But for slaves and the rural poor in the South, for low-paid immigrant workers in the new industries of the North, and for the dispossessed Native Americans there was still great hardship.

Eli Whitney (1765–1825) invented the cotton gin in the 1790s. His "engine" (later called a "gin") separated cotton fibers from the seeds. It revolutionized the textile industry.

If the 1700s saw the birth of the United States of America, then it was the 1800s that witnessed its headlong rush to industrialize. By the end of the 19th century the United States had the fastest economic growth rate in the world. This was combined with a population that doubled in size about every 27 years, the result of a rising birth rate and increased immigration from Europe (some 13 million immigrants arrived during the late 1800s and early 1900s).

Many factors helped the United States to achieve its place as the world's leading industrial power. One of the most important was the availability of land for

John D. Rockefeller (1839–1937) founded the Standard Oil Company in 1870. As his company grew, Rockefeller gained control of 90 percent of the United States' oil trade, making him a multi-millionaire.

The industrial North

Industrial centers developed in the Northern states. Textile mills (left) became a feature of New England, where cotton from the South was turned into cloth for home use and for export. The coal and oil industries were based in Pennsylvania, while Illinois was the center of the iron, steel, and chemical industries.

Millions of immigrants went to North America in search of good jobs and a better standard of living. But for many the reality was a life of hardship, working in poor conditions for little money.

The discovery of oil

Few individuals can claim to have pioneered a major industry, but Edwin Drake (1819–80) is one. When his drilling rig at Titusville, Pennsylvania (above), struck oil at a depth of 69 ft (21 m) in 1859, it set the United States on course to becoming a leading oil producer.

ANDREW CARNEGIE

1. Carnegie Institute, Pittsburg
3. Birthplace of Andrew Carnegie, Dunfermline, Scotland

Carnegie and the steel industry

Born in Scotland, Andrew Carnegie (1835–1919) emigrated to the United States with his family in 1848. He settled in Pittsburgh, Pennsylvania. After several jobs, including one as a railroad clerk, Carnegie formed the Union Mills Company in 1868. Its purpose was to make steel rails for the growing railroad network. He bought coal mines, iron-ore mines, fleets of ships, and rival companies, and turned the United States into the world's leading iron and steel producer.

From the 1820s, travel by steam boat reduced journey times around the Great Lakes, making it possible to ship goods cheaply and quickly to and from the region's industrial centers of Detroit and Chicago.

Designed by German-born American engineer John Roebling (1806–69) and his son Washington (1837–1926), New York's Brooklyn Bridge was the world's first steel suspension bridge. Completed in 1893, it was also the world's longest bridge of its type. Sailors used to heights were employed to rig its cables.

| railroads in eastern US.
1869 First coast-to-coast | railroad (Union Pacific) built.
1877–92 Period of greatest | industrial expansion; factories triple their output. | **1890s** US Railroad network greater than all of Europe's; | USA is world's leading industrial nation. |

---

farming and building new settlements. In Europe the situation was the reverse; most land was already extensively farmed and settled. Many Europeans flocked to the United States during the 19th century in the hope of acquiring land. Between 1840 and 1850 the cotton gin quadrupled cotton production; the use of fertilizers, new strains of cotton, maize, and wheat, and the introduction of farm machinery – from McCormick's reaper in 1831 to rotary plows, steam threshers, and combine harvesters – made the United States the leading agricultural producer in the world.

The main period of railroad-building took place between 1860 and 1900,

and came at the same time as the development of America's industries. The railroads spread across the land at a rapid rate and proved a vital means of transportation and communication. They played an important part in the economic development of the country, transporting raw materials to the factories and finished goods to the markets.

American industry pioneered new manufacturing methods such as mass-production, where identical components are made quickly and cheaply. This labor-saving process began in the armaments industry. From there it spread to other businesses, notably the automobile industry in the

1900s. Methods of mass-production were also used to make ready-to-wear clothes for the first time. Previously clothes had all been individually fitted and sewn by hand. Together, these factors modernized and industrialized the United States.

1. A sewing machine from the 1850s. This new invention made it possible to provide, at prices people could afford, the types of clothes needed for work. The manufacture of ready-to-wear clothing was an industry created by industrialization.

Territorial gains

The map (right) shows how the territory of the United States expanded from coast to coast. Land was acquired by several means: outright purchase, annexation (taking possession), official treaty, claims by settlers, and force. As territory was gained, new states were formed. These eventually became members of the United States of America.

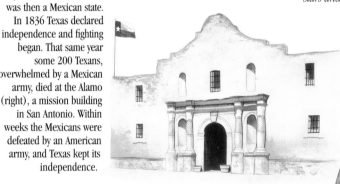

CANADA

Ceded by Great Britain 1818

OREGON
Ceded by Great Britain 1846

LOUISIANA
Purchased from France 1803

CALIFORNIA
Ceded by Mexico 1848

LAND ACQUIRED BY TREATY OF PARIS

13 ORIGINAL UNITED STATES OF AMERICA

TEXAS
Annexed 1845

PACIFIC OCEAN

ATLANTIC OCEAN

Purchased from Mexico 1853

MEXICO

GULF OF MEXICO

LAND ACQUIRED BY THE UNITED STATES AFTER 1783.

Mexico gains independence

In 1821 Agustín de Iturbide (1783–1824), a Mexican soldier and politician (left), broke off relations with Spain, Mexico's colonial power. Mexico became an independent nation supported by the United States.

The Louisiana Purchase

In 1803 the United States purchased from France for $15 million a vast tract of land in the Midwest, extending from the Gulf of Mexico in the south to the Canadian border in the north. This purchase doubled the size of the United States' territory.

The transfer of Louisiana to the United States was marked in New Orleans by the French Tricolor being lowered and the Stars and Stripes hoisted in its place.

The Texas Revolution (1835–36)

By 1830 about 30,000 Americans lived in Texas, which was then a Mexican state. In 1836 Texas declared independence and fighting began. That same year some 200 Texans, overwhelmed by a Mexican army, died at the Alamo (right), a mission building in San Antonio. Within weeks the Mexicans were defeated by an American army, and Texas kept its independence.

The Mexican War (1846–48)

In 1846 war broke out between the United States and Mexico. The United States had annexed Texas, which Mexico claimed as its possession. When Mexico lost the war it gave up its claim to Texas. The United States also gained neighboring territory as a result of the war.

United States' soldiers took Mexico City in 1847, weakening Mexico's claims on Texas, California, and New Mexico.

Right: President James Monroe promoted a "hands off America" policy.

The Monroe Doctrine

A speech given by President James Monroe (1758–1831) is known as the "Monroe Doctrine." He pledged that the United States would not become involved in European wars (unless American interests were at stake); that the United States would not become the target of future European colonization; and that future colonization would be seen as an "unfriendly act."

1803 Louisiana Purchase.
1814 Land granted to soldiers

who fought in the war of 1812.
1816–19 Cotton boom stimulates

settlement of southwest.
1821 Mexican independence.

1823 The Monroe Doctrine.
1830 Indian Removal Act.

1835–38 Cherokees move westward along Trail of Tears.

Expansion of the USA

In 1783 the Treaty of Paris – which marked the end of the American Revolution and the birth of the United States – set the new nation's western limit as the Mississippi River. This boundary remained the same for the next 30 years. West of the Mississippi lay the interior of the continent, stretching westward for thousands of miles to the Pacific Ocean. Spain, France, Britain, and Mexico claimed this land as their territory. During the early 1800s, however, pressure mounted for them to withdraw their claims. The first half of the 19th century was a time of rapid territorial expansion for the United States, and as fast as land was acquired settlers moved in. The frontier was pushed ever westward, but there was a human price to pay. Little regard was given to the Native Americans, who lost both their land and their rights.

Books provided emigrants with information and stories about the almost-unknown West.

A spirit of adventure inspired Americans to venture west of the Mississippi River. Curiosity about their continent led them to explore its unknown interior. Fur trappers ventured far inland, returning to the eastern states with tales of what they had seen. In 1804 the explorers Meriwether Lewis (1774–1809) and William Clark (1770–1838) set out to follow the Missouri River to its source. They crossed the Rocky Mountains and in 1806 reached the Pacific Ocean, an astonishing journey across an unknown continent.

Although still fairly new, the government of the United States began

California Gold Rush

When a carpenter discovered gold in the foothills of California's Sierra Nevada mountains in 1848, "gold fever" gripped the nation. Pamphlets were printed with titles such as *The Emigrant's Guide to the Gold Mines*, and people flocked to the West. Some 100,000 people arrived in 1849, and the town of San Francisco rapidly grew into a city.

Above: Heavier than sand, gold flakes sank to the base of the prospectors' pan.

Settlers move to the West

From the 1840s on, people began to move to the west coast region, west of the Rocky Mountains. Emigrants, who were known as pioneers, followed long-distance trails to Oregon, California, and Santa Fe. To reach their goal they first had to cross the Great Plains, a vast inhospitable area of grassland and few trees. The Great Plains were home to many Native American nations and to vast herds of buffalo.

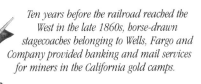

The Oregon Trail

Emigrants who moved west faced a four-month journey across difficult terrain. Arming themselves with guns in case they were attacked by hostile Native Americans, and with guidebooks to show the way, they set out in wagons pulled by oxen. The wagons traveled in long convoys, known as "trains." Between 1840 and 1848 some 11,500 emigrants took the Oregon Trail. Many died from disease and starvation on the way.

Ten years before the railroad reached the West in the late 1860s, horse-drawn stagecoaches belonging to Wells, Fargo and Company provided banking and mail services for miners in the California gold camps.

Right: Between 1835 and 1838, bands of Cherokees were forced to move from lands they held sacred some 800 mi. (1,300 km) westward to Arkansas, along the so-called Trail of Tears (left). Some 3,000 died on the way. They were resettled on land "given" to them by a government treaty and this letter from President Martin Van Buren.

Left: In 1874 gold was found in the Black Hills of Dakota. The United States' government tried to buy the land, but the Sioux rejected the proposal. Little Big Man was the Sioux spokesman.

Native Americans lose land

In the first half of the 19th century the United States' government had an aggressive policy toward the Native American nations. Many were made to sign treaties giving up their rights to the land. In 1830 the Indian Removal Act became law, and the people were forced to move westward. Between 1830 and 1850 about 100,000 Native Americans were moved from their home territories (above). The army was used against any people who resisted.

From 1866 to 1876 General George Armstrong Custer (1839–76) led the 7th Cavalry against the Native Americans. In 1876, in an attempt to force them from their land, Custer fought the Sioux at the Battle of Little Big Horn. Custer and 265 of his troops died.

1836 Texas independent from Mexico; fall of Alamo; Mexico loses Battle of San Jacinto.
1840–60 Pioneers head west.

1846–48 Mexican War.
1848–49 California Gold Rush.

1860–61 Pony Express operates across 2,000 mi. (3,200 km).

1861–65 American Civil War.
1876 Battle of Little Big Horn.

---

planning for westward expansion, and in 1803 the first major step was made with the Louisiana Purchase, which added 827,000 sq. mi. (2,150,000 sq. km) to the nation. In 1812 the United States declared war on Britain in a dispute over trade. Needing to raise an army, the government promised, when the war was over, to give land to men who enlisted. In 1814 peace was made and the government gave 6 million acres (2.4 million hectares) of land to American servicemen who had fought in the war. These men and their families were among the first to head westward to claim their new land. Many traveled along the National Highway, which the

government extended as far as Illinois.

As settlers poured into the West they met with sizeable populations of land-owning Native Americans. Some Native American nations, such as the Cherokees, Creeks, and Choctaws, had a long history of contact with settlers through trade and intermarriage. Some had accepted Christianity and had lived in settled communities for generations. The United States' government regarded them as "civilized," but did not prevent acts of ill-treatment and their wholesale removal from their ancestral homelands. Other Native American nations, such as the Sioux and Cheyenne, had never forged such strong

links with the encroaching settlers, whom they regarded as invaders. In the ensuing conflict, many Native Americans and settlers died. By 1890 the settlers had taken the Native Americans' lands, and the mainland borders of the United States had been set.

1. The Pony Express used riders to carry mail over long distances. Letters from New York took 10 days to reach San Francisco.

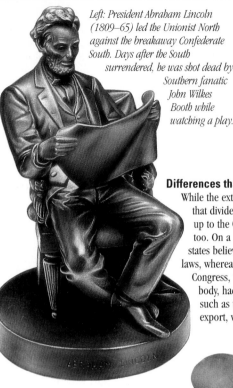

Left: President Abraham Lincoln (1809–65) led the Unionist North against the breakaway Confederate South. Days after the South surrendered, he was shot dead by Southern fanatic John Wilkes Booth while watching a play.

The Civil War 1861–1865.

☐ Union states
☐ Confederate states
☐ Union state with slavery
→ Union campaigns
→ Confederate campaigns
······ Union blockades
• Battle

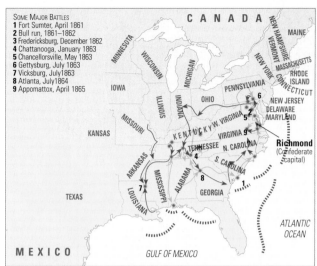

SOME MAJOR BATTLES
1 Fort Sumter, April 1861
2 Bull run, 1861–1862
3 Fredericksburg, December 1862
4 Chattanooga, January 1863
5 Chancellorsville, May 1863
6 Gettysburg, July 1863
7 Vicksburg, July 1863
8 Atlanta, July 1864
9 Appomattox, April 1865

CANADA

MINNESOTA · WISCONSIN · MICHIGAN · IOWA · ILLINOIS · INDIANA · OHIO · MISSOURI · KANSAS · KENTUCKY · W. VIRGINIA · VIRGINIA · TENNESSEE · N. CAROLINA · ARKANSAS · MISSISSIPPI · ALABAMA · S. CAROLINA · GEORGIA · TEXAS · LOUISIANA · MAINE · NEW HAMPSHIRE · VERMONT · NEW YORK · MASSACHUSETTS · RHODE ISLAND · CONNECTICUT · PENNSYLVANIA · NEW JERSEY · DELAWARE · MARYLAND

Richmond (Confederate capital)

MEXICO · GULF OF MEXICO · ATLANTIC OCEAN

Differences that led to war

While the extension of slavery was a key issue that divided North and South during the build up to the Civil War, their were other problems too. On a more general level, the Southern states believed in the right to make their own laws, whereas states in the North said that only Congress, the country's national law-making body, had that right. Economic questions, such as tariffs to be placed on goods for export, were also disputed.

The mess (meal) kit of a Confederate soldier included bags for corn and coffee beans, a water bottle, and tins for cooking. For every hour in battle soldiers spent weeks in camp doing routine work such as mending uniforms, cutting firewood, washing, cleaning weapons, and cooking.

The fall of Fort Sumter

The first shots in the Civil War were fired on April 12, 1861, when the Confederate commander of Charleston, in the breakaway state of South Carolina, opened fire on Fort Sumter. The fort, which lay at the entrance to the town's harbor, was garrisoned by soldiers loyal to the Union. For thirty-four hours the fort was bombarded until its soldiers surrendered. The Confederate flag was raised and the war began. The tattered "Stars and Bars," emblem of Southern independence, continued to fly over Fort Sumter until February 1865.

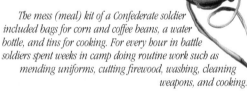

General Robert E. Lee

Commander-in-chief of the Confederate army, Lee (1807–70) was one of the most skilful tacticians of the war. He took the fight into Union territory, threatening to attack the nation's capital city, Washington. Defeat at Gettysburg in 1863 forced him to retreat, and in 1865 he surrendered to the Union commander, Ulysses S. Grant.

During the war both sides issued paper money in place of gold and silver coins. When prices rose, people lost confidence in paper money.

1860 Abraham Lincoln becomes president of the United States.

1861 Southern states set up the Confederate States of America; Confederates attack Federal post of Fort Sumter.

1862 Confederate victories at Richmond and Fredericksburg.

1863 Lincoln's Emancipation Proclamation; Grant takes

The American Civil War

As huge tracts of land were added to the US in the first half of the 19th century, the question arose as to whether slavery should be banned in the new territories. The industrialized states of the North had abolished slavery, but the plantation economy of the South was dependent on its slave workforce. When Abraham Lincoln was elected president in 1860, the Southerners feared that he would not only prohibit slavery in the new territories but also abolish it in the South. The Southern states withdrew from the Union and formed the Confederate States of America with Jefferson Davis as their president. Lincoln refused to accept their withdrawal and provoked them into firing the first shots at Fort Sumter in April 1861. The ensuing war lasted four years and cost hundreds of thousands of lives. When the war ended in 1865, slavery was officially abolished and around 4 million black people gained their freedom.

Soldiers carried leather belts that held sixty rounds of ammunition. They fired rifles and hand guns. The variety of ammunition used by both sides was enormous.

The Civil War was fought mainly in the east and southeast of the United States, between eleven Southern, or Confederate, states and twenty-three Northern, or Union, states. The Confederates, who fired the first shots, began a war which they stood little chance of winning. The South had a population of nine million, one-third of whom were slaves. In comparison, twenty-two million people lived in the North, where there were 3.5 times as many white men of military age as there were in the South. The North had two-thirds of the nation's railroad tracks, and its factories and

Grant pursues Lee

Ulysses S. Grant became commander of the Union forces in 1864. He had a long and distinguished career in the army, and had served in the Mexican War of 1846 to 1848. In a succession of hotly-contested battles at the Wilderness, Spotsylvania, North Anna, and Cold Harbor, he steadily advanced on Richmond, the Confederate capital. The city fell to him on March 26, 1865, and General Lee's army was surrounded. On April 9, 1865, the war ended.

General Ulysses S. Grant (1822–85) was commander-in-chief of the Union army. Later he became President of the United States.

On December 20, 1860 the state of South Carolina voted to leave the United States. In the town of Charleston the local newspaper printed a declaration to this effect on its front page. South Carolina was the first of the southern slave-owning states to separate from the Union. Other states soon followed.

The Confederate army

Soldiers of the Confederacy were called Confederates. The Unionists called them "rebels." At first the Confederate army consisted of volunteers – men who enlisted for one year – but in 1862 conscription was brought in for the first time in American history. All able-bodied white men between the ages of 18 and 35 had to join the army for three years. As the war went against the Confederacy, men between ages 17 and 50 were called up. At its peak the Confederate army numbered 800,000 troops.

Right: The Battle of Gettysburg, July 1–3, 1863, is generally regarded as the turning point of the war. Confederate General Robert E. Lee, at the head of 75,000 troops, tried to invade the North. After three days of fighting, the Confederates were turned back by the Union army, led by General George G. Meade.

The Union army

With an army of 2.1 million soldiers, the Unionists heavily outnumbered the Confederates. Not only was the Union army larger, it was better equipped. The industrial North kept Union troops supplied with weapons, clothes, and food. In contrast, soldiers in the Confederate army were often short of food and badly clothed; they were nicknamed "ragged rebels." As in the South, conscription was the main means of raising troops. All able-bodied white men between ages 20 and 45 could be drafted into the Union army.

Lee surrenders

In the village of Appomattox, General Lee signed the surrender document on April 9, 1865, watched by General Grant. Four days later, soldiers of the defeated Confederate army laid down their weapons. The war was over.

Freedom for slaves

Slavery had been abolished in the North by 1804, but it was retained in the cotton-growing states of the South. President Lincoln's first aim in fighting the Civil War was to save the Union, but he also wanted to end slavery, and in 1863 he issued his Emancipation Proclamation, in which he said that all slavery must end. This pledge changed the course of the war. From then on the Union was fighting a war against slavery. With the defeat of the South in 1865, some 4 million slaves were freed.

Vicksburg; Union victory at Gettysburg; war turns against the South.
1864 Ulysses S. Grant becomes commander of the Union army.
1865 Confederates defeated; General Lee surrenders at Appomattox; slavery abolished; Lincoln assassinated.

heavy industries produced three-quarters of the country's wealth.

But the South also had its strengths. If the Confederacy was to succeed in its struggle for independence, then the Union would have to fight the Confederates on their home ground – and an army that fights on its own territory often has an advantage over an invader. Although the Confederate army met with success in the first two years of the war, the sheer size of the Union army, and its ability to keep itself supplied with food and weapons, proved too much.

The Confederacy was defeated, soldiers from both sides returned home, slavery was abolished, and the United States of America once again became one nation. The four years of war caused more casualties than any other conflict in American history, before or since. The death count stood at 360,000 Union soldiers and 260,000 Confederates.

It was the first war in history in which the railroad played a major role, transporting men, horses, and supplies. New weapons, such as the

repeating rifle, and the Gatling gun (forerunner of the machine gun) were developed, as

were armor-plated ships called "ironclads." It was a war in which women played a key part, too. The new profession of nursing (pioneered by Britain in the 1850s) saw 3,200 nurses at work in the hospitals of both sides. But for every soldier killed in action,

two died of disease.

Despite the bloodshed and damage, the economy was quick to recover after the war, and the paper money that the war had brought about became the nation's national currency.

1. Colt sixshooter (left) and Remington revolver (right). The Union army manufactured large quantities of Remingtons during the Civil War.

SEE ALSO
p. 168 THE UNITED STATES OF AMERICA
p. 182 NORTH AMERICA INDUSTRIALIZES
p. 184 EXPANSION OF THE USA

Novalis (Friedrich von Hardenberg) was a major poet of the early Romantic movement in Germany.

ROMANTICISM

The late 18th century was a time of revolutions – in politics the French Revolution, in economics the Industrial Revolution. There was a third "revolution," a revolution in culture and feeling, which is called the Romantic movement. Like most great cultural movements, it was partly a reaction against the ideas of the preceding age, the Enlightenment. Romantics rebelled against the Enlightenment's belief in reason, logic, and science. Instead, they emphasized the importance of feelings, the human imagination, and the uniqueness of the individual. The *philosophes* of the Enlightenment had concentrated on the human mind. The Romantics complained that they had ignored the human soul. The Romantic movement was complicated and varied. It included people of all beliefs, religious and non-religious, liberals and conservatives, revolutionaries and reactionaries. In fact, it was so various that historians have never found a definition of Romanticism that everyone agrees with.

German Romanticism

Romanticism in Germany began with the *Sturm und Drang* (Storm and Stress) movement of young intellectuals in the 1770s. They included two of Germany's greatest writers, Schiller (1759–1805) and Goethe (1749–1832). Both really belong to the classical tradition, but in their youth they were Romantic rebels against Classicism. The 25-year-old Goethe's novel, *The Sorrows of Young Werther* (left), about a young genius driven to suicide by disappointments, was the first to make a personal effort to express emotion.

Weimar

Weimar became the center of German Romanticism after Goethe moved there in 1775, followed by Schiller, who soon made his reputation as a great playwright. They developed the idea of "culture" as an ideal that society should aspire to. In their writing they tried to find a balance between Classicism and Romanticism, bringing together reason and feeling, science and art.

English Romanticism

The publication of the *Lyrical Ballads* (1798), with poems by Wordsworth (1770–1850) and Coleridge (1796–1849), was a landmark in English Romanticism, an outstanding period for lyrical poetry. Wordsworth lived in the beautiful Lake District, which attracted other Romantics. History and nature inspired many English Romantic writers.

An illustration (above) by William Blake (1757–1827), an extraordinary painter-poet, who was little known in his own time but inspired later artists.

Left: John Keats (1795–1821) wrote some of the most famous poems in English. Like many heroes of Romanticism, he died young.

Later English Romanticism

The second generation of English Romantics were more liberal than their predecessors. Again, the outstanding figures were lyric poets, including Lord Byron (who died on his way to fight for Greek independence), the radical Shelley, and Keats. The outstanding Romantic novelist, besides Jane Austen, was Walter Scott, whose historical novels created a long-lasting image of Scotland as a land of romantic adventure.

Heidelberg, seat of Germany's oldest university, was a center of German Romanticism.

Heidelberg: a center of Romanticism

Many of the second generation of German Romantics gathered in Heidelberg from about 1800–1815. They were less sentimental and more practical, producing poems and songs based on German folklore. Another genius, the poet Heinrich Heine (1797–1856), though he lived later (and not in Heidelberg), was the outstanding figure of the later generation. Like many others, he moved away from Romanticism when he grew older.

Russia

Modern Russian literature was born in the Romantic age. The great figure was the poet Aleksandr Pushkin (1799–1837, right), who opened new horizons for Russian writers by using everyday language and treating history and folklore as subjects of literature. An aristocrat with radical ideas that often got him into trouble with the government, Pushkin was killed in a duel defending his wife's reputation.

Mme de Staël (Anne Louise Necker, 1766–1817), helped develop French Romanticism by her praise of German Romantic writers.

French Romanticism

French Romantic writers like Victor Hugo (*Les Misérables*) and Alexandre Dumas (*The Three Musketeers*) produced vigorous Romantic dramas. Shakespeare, a favorite of all Romantics, was a frequent source. Romantic poetry reached its most extreme form in Baudelaire. Chateaubriand (right), aristocrat, traveler, diplomat, and writer, was, with Mme de Staël, an admirer of Rousseau and a key figure of the early years. His writings show his love of the wild, and a kind of sad, religious longing – both strong features of Romanticism.

France

France was the land of the Enlightenment *philosophes*, and although Rousseau, one of the leading *philosophes*, was a "father" of Romanticism, the movement did not reach a peak in France until the 1830s, when it was already fading in England and Germany. It was bitterly resisted by the classical tradition, and the first night of Victor Hugo's play *Hernani* (1830) ended in a riot between supporters and opponents of Romanticism.

MAJOR DATES

1774 Goethe's *Sorrows of Young Werther.*

1798 Wordsworth's *Lyrical Ballads.*

1798 Napoleon's expedition to Egypt.

1808 Friedrich's painting *The Cross in the Mountains.*

1810 Mme de Staël's *De l'Allemagne* (On Germany).

1813 Jane Austen's *Pride and Prejudice.*

1818 Mary Shelley's *Frankenstein.*

1819 Géricault's *The Raft of Medusa.*

1830 Riot at first night of *Hernani.*

1869–76 Wagner's *Ring of the Nibelungs.*

An illustration from Grimms' Fairy Tales.

Myths and monsters

Romanticism included an interest in the strange and exotic. The brothers Grimm researched German folklore for their famous collection of *Fairy Tales.* (Some of the stories were much too gruesome for children.) Ghosts and the supernatural inspired other writers and artists. Frankenstein (1818), a famous horror story and one of the first works of science fiction, was written by Mary Shelley, the young wife of the English poet. The monster is an example of the popular idea of the Noble Savage – a simple, good creature whose nature is made evil by bad treatment.

Frankenstein's monster, from one of many films of the book.

The Pulse of Enterprise: Friedrich's paintings captured a feeling of vaguely religious, melancholy longing that can never be fulfilled.

Painting: Romantic landscapes

Romantics loved natural scenery, especially rugged mountains, thundering waterfalls, and wild forests. Landscape painting was just becoming, for the first time, an important subject for painters in the 18th century. It was strong in England, especially in the work of Constable (1776–1837), with his wide, blowing skies. Other painters emphasized the personal vision. Among these was the leading German painter, Caspar David Friedrich (1774–1840), whose haunting landscapes are imaginary. The real subject of his painting is personal feeling.

The Swiss/English painter Fuseli painted often shocking subjects from a dream world: this is aptly called The Nightmare.

Ancient Egypt

The Romantic love of the distant past was stimulated by Napoleon's expedition to Egypt, which first made people aware of its ancient civilization. New branches of scholarship, notably archeology, flourished. The young classicist, Jean François Champollion (above), after studying the Rosetta Stone that Napoleon had brought back from Egypt, finally succeeded in translating ancient Egyptian hieroglyphics. He became France's first professor of Egyptology.

Narrative painting

Other painters, notably in France, embraced the Romantic love of great events, sometimes violent ones, from myth or history. Géricault's *The Raft of Medusa,* based on a shipwreck, astonished Europe. He influenced Delacroix, one of the greatest history painters. Delacroix's famous *The Death of Sardanapalus,* inspired by a play by Byron, is a magnificent and luscious painting of a horrible event (a massacre of innocent women).

Opera glasses (binoculars) and fan, essential aids for the fashionable lady opera-goer.

Schubert (left, at the piano), the first great Romantic composer, set poems by Goethe and Heine to music in his emotional Lieder *(Songs).*

Romantic music

In music, the term Romantic covers a longer period, lasting into the 20th century. Romantic music included expressive melody, exciting harmony, and greater freedom in rhythm. Full of feeling, it expressed many Romantic themes – love of youth and nature, individualism, nationalism, and idealism. Romantic composers, like artists, often found their inspiration in Romantic poetry, novels, and plays.

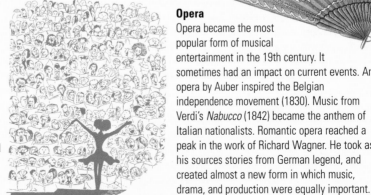

Opera

Opera became the most popular form of musical entertainment in the 19th century. It sometimes had an impact on current events. An opera by Auber inspired the Belgian independence movement (1830). Music from Verdi's *Nabucco* (1842) became the anthem of Italian nationalists. Romantic opera reached a peak in the work of Richard Wagner. He took as his sources stories from German legend, and created almost a new form in which music, drama, and production were equally important.

1798 Napoleon invades Egypt.
1805–48 Mehmet Ali rules

Egypt as viceroy.
1821–32 War of Greek

Independence.
1853–56 The Crimean War.

1869 The Suez Canal opens.
1876–1909 Reign of Sultan

Abdul Hamid II.
1877–78 The Russo-Turkish

Decline of the Ottoman Empire

During the course of the 19th century the Ottoman Empire gradually became smaller and weaker. Several of the Ottoman sultans tried to reform their old-fashioned state, but they faced opposition from within and interference from the powers of Western Europe and Russia. As former Ottoman territories gained independence, political maps in the region were redrawn. These changes also affected the neighboring regions of North Africa and southwest Asia. By 1875 the Ottoman Empire was virtually bankrupt, and internal rebellion forced the opening of an Ottoman parliament two years later. After the First World War, in which the Ottomans sided with Germany, the sultanate was quickly demolished and in 1923 the new republic of Turkey was declared.

After Napoleon's invasion of Egypt in 1798 failed, Mehmet Ali, an Albanian army officer who was part of the force sent by the Ottomans to expel the French, seized power and became viceroy in 1805. At first Mehmet was useful to the Ottomans, helping them in the Greek War of Independence in 1825. Six years later, however, Mehmet and his son Ibrahim Pasha invaded Syria, threatening Ottoman power. European nations, especially the British, stepped in to help the Ottomans, because they feared that problems in the region would threaten their links with India. They also helped the Ottomans against the Russians during the Crimean War (1853–56),

Ottoman reform

During the 19th century Ottoman rulers made attempts at modernization, but these usually meant asking for foreign help and led to European intervention. Sultan Selim III (left) tried to reform the system by replacing the traditional Janissaries with a new-style army, but they overthrew him in 1807 and massacred most of the reform leaders. Other reforms of property, taxation and religious freedom were introduced later, but met with opposition. In 1865 the Society of New Ottomans first called for constitutional government.

DECLINE OF THE OTTOMAN EMPIRE BETWEEN **1800** AND **1914**.

Egypt

Napoleon's expedition to Egypt at the end of the 18th century caused other Europeans to take greater interest in that country. Mehmet Ali (1769–1849; right) was appointed viceroy in 1805 and ruled on behalf of the Ottoman Empire until 1848. After suppressing an Arab revolt, the British occupied Egypt in 1882, turning it into a protectorate. Egypt regained independence in 1922, although it remained under British influence.

The Crimean War

The Crimean War (1853–56) was triggered by the Russians demanding the right to protect the Orthodox subjects of the Ottoman sultans, but was more generally a clash of power for control of the Middle East. The Ottomans declared war and were joined by France and Britain, who were concerned about Russia's expansion. Conditions in the Crimea were appalling and the administration of both armies was very poor. More than a quarter of a million men died on both sides, until Russia accepted peace terms.

British workers built a railroad track at the Crimean port of Balaclava. The railroad was used to move equipment and troops.

Greece

During the War of Greek Independence (1821–32) Britain, France, and Russia became involved against the Ottomans, who were supported by Egypt. Peace negotiations began in London in 1829, and independence was declared three years later. A Greek monarchy was then established. European sympathizers for the Greek cause included the aristocratic English poet, Lord Byron (left).

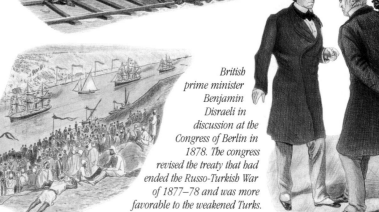

The first ships passed through the Suez Canal in 1869. The canal connected the Mediterranean and Red seas, saving ships thousands of miles on voyages between Europe and Asia. In 1888 the canal became a neutral zone.

British prime minister Benjamin Disraeli in discussion at the Congress of Berlin in 1878. The congress revised the treaty that had ended the Russo-Turkish War of 1877–78 and was more favorable to the weakened Turks.

War, resulting in Congress of Berlin.

1912–13 The Balkan Wars.

1914–18 First World War.
1917 The Balfour Declaration

on the Jewish nation in Palestine.

1923 The independent republic of Turkey is declared.

mainly because they were afraid of Russia's expansionism. The resulting Treaty of Paris (1856) preserved the Ottoman Empire.

French interests in the area grew when it gained the concession to build the Suez Canal in 1854 (it was opened in 1869). Six years later, the Ottoman viceroy in Egypt sold his canal shares to Britain, which eventually occupied Egypt in 1882.

Rebellions in Bosnia-Herzegovina, Serbia, Bulgaria, and Montenegro led to 2

another Russian invasion of the Ottoman Empire in 1877 and resulted in the creation of a pro-Russian "Big Bulgaria." However, the Congress of Berlin in 1878 revised the new frontiers to check Russian expansion, and in 1887 the Bulgarians elected Prince Ferdinand of Saxe-Coburg as their ruler.

In 1909, worried about the empire's decline, rebellious army officers called the "Young Turks" overthrew Sultan Abdul Hamid II and tried to reform the state along

Western lines. But European powers encroached again and in the Balkan Wars of 1912–13, the Balkan League of Bulgaria, Serbia, Greece, and Montenegro defeated the Ottomans, and they lost almost all their European possessions. In 1920 the Treaty of Sèvres stripped the Ottoman Empire of all its non-Turkish regions. The Ottoman sultan was deposed and in 1923 Turkey was declared a republic, with Kemal Atatürk as its first president.

1. Florence Nightingale (1820–1910) led a party of nurses to the Crimean War in 1854. She greatly improved conditions in the British army hospitals. Often on the wards at night, she was known as the "lady with the lamp."

2. Women of Algiers by Eugène Delacroix, painted in 1834. Delacroix visited Morocco and Algiers in the early 1830s and found a rich source of exotic imagery.

3. A woman waves the Zionist flag.

Persia

From 1794 to 1925 Persia was an independent kingdom ruled over by shahs of the Qajar Dynasty. Fath Ali (1797–1834) (left) was the last Persian shah to rule without European interference. During the second half of the 19th century Western influence made itself increasingly felt, especially from Britain and Russia. A reform movement in 1905–06 led to a European-style constitution, and during World War I Persia was used as a battleground by the great powers.

Bulgaria

In the 19th century Bulgaria was the scene of bitter disputes between Russia and the Ottomans. In 1887 the Bulgarians, led by Stefan Stambuloff (1854–95), elected Prince Ferdinand of Saxe-Coburg as ruler. Eight years later Stambuloff was murdered (right), supposedly by Macedonian rebels. In 1908 Ferdinand proclaimed Bulgaria's independence and made himself czar. His army fought the Turks and won in the first phase of the Balkan Wars (1912–13), but he turned against his Serbian and Greek allies, and the second phase ended disastrously for Bulgaria.

Palestine

From the mid-19th century many Jews settled in Palestine. The first Zionist congress was held in Basel in 1897, and by 1914 there were about 90,000 Jews in Palestine. After the First World War, Palestine was captured by the British, and in 1917 they stated in the Balfour Declaration that they supported the establishment of a national Jewish home there.

Left: Zionist leaders – Max Nordau, Theodore Herzl, and Prof. Mandelstamm – are portrayed with their ideals of settling in Palestine.

This French cartoon shows Morocco as a scared rabbit being tugged in all directions by European powers. In 1912 Morocco was split into French and Spanish protectorates.

In 1908 the Young Turks forced the Ottoman sultan to restore parliament, which for them was a symbol of modern political life. A few months later they deposed the sultan.

Below: In this satirical drawing Abdul Hamid (right) fumes helplessly at the loss of Bosnia-Herzegovina to Austria-Hungary and Bulgaria to independence, in 1908.

Father of the Turks

After the First World War the Allies occupied Istanbul and began dismantling the Ottoman state. The Ottoman sultan was deposed in 1922 and Mustafa Kemal (1881–1938; right) created an alternative parliament. In 1923 Turkey was declared a republic, with Kemal as its first president. Eleven years later the president took the name Atatürk, meaning "father of the Turks."

Sultan Abdul Hamid II

Abdul Hamid II was sultan of the Ottoman Empire from 1876 to 1909. After defeat by Russia in 1878 he suspended the constitution and ruled as an autocrat. He opposed Western interference in Ottoman affairs and was notorious for the Armenian massacres of the 1890s. He was finally deposed after an uprising by the revolutionary Committee of Union and Progress, known as the Young Turks.

SEE ALSO
p. 92 THE ISLAMIC WORLD
p. 126 MUSLIM EMPIRES
p. 130 THE OTTOMAN EMPIRE
p. 222 THE PEACE SETTLEMENT

The Russian Empire

Russia has always been a land of contrasts. In 1800, it was backward in every way compared with the countries of Western Europe. Yet it was also a great European power. In the previous century the population had increased nearly four times, largely due to Russian expansion and the acquisition of new territories. Over 95 percent of the people lived in the country, and the majority were serfs. The number of educated people was tiny. Russia continued to expand in the 19th century, especially to the south, where it gained many more non-Russian peoples. Great progress was made in modernizing society: the number of town-dwellers tripled, modern industry was established, and serfdom was abolished. But Russia still lagged behind the West in economic development and in education. Although the arts, especially literature and music, flourished, 75 percent of the people could not read or write in 1900.

Leo Tolstoy, whose immense War and Peace, *is sometimes called the world's greatest novel.*

The greatest problem facing Russia was the need for reform. This was widely recognized, even by the czar. Alexander I (reigned 1801–25) acknowledged it and some progress was made in administration and education under his minister Michael Speransky. Otherwise, little changed. Having a constitution (which gives the people some part in government) was unthinkable in a country ruled by an emperor with unlimited authority and ministers who were his personal servants. Even Alexander II (reigned 1855–81), a genuine

EXPANSION OF THE RUSSIAN EMPIRE, 1802–1914.
The Russian Empire continued to grow in the 19th century. Finland was taken from Sweden in 1809; Bessarabia (northwest of the Black Sea) from the Ottoman Turks in 1812; central Poland was gained in 1815; the Caucasus (Georgia, Armenia, Azerbaidjan) by 1859; the Amur region by 1860; and the Uzbek khanates by 1900.

Map legend:
- ARCTIC OCEAN
- St. Petersburg
- Moscow
- Kotlas
- CRIMEA
- RUSSIAN EMPIRE
- Tashkent
- Kuril Islands
- Vladivostok
- PACIFIC OCEAN
- Russian Empire 1802
- TERRITORIAL GAINS
- 1809–55
- 1855–1914

The Balkans

The aim of Russian policy was to gain access to the Mediterranean via the Black Sea. Russia also saw itself as protector of the mainly Slav and Christian people of the Balkans, under the weakening Ottoman Empire. The other big European powers were determined to prevent Russian expansion at the Ottoman Turks' expense. This conflict produced major crises, one leading to the Crimean War, the other following the Turks' savage suppression of Balkan rebels in the 1870s. Russia invaded (1877) and forced heavy concessions on the Ottoman Turks, but was forced to give up its gains by the international Congress of Berlin.

Defeat of the French

Napoleon invaded Russia in 1812. His Grand Army reached Moscow but was forced to retreat; it was almost destroyed by the freezing Russian winter and fierce resistance by the army and people. Campaigning in Europe brought the Russian soldiers into contact with French liberal ideas. Officers returned home hoping for a constitution, while soldiers, who were mainly serfs, hoped for freedom. Instead, they met fierce repression.

Moscow was burned by its own people when the French army attacked.

A Russian officer's sword.

The Crimean War

In 1853 Russia demanded more rights in the Balkan provinces and, when the Turks refused, occupied them. War broke out, but Nicholas I found no allies in Europe, and British and French forces invaded the (Russian) Crimea. Sevastopol was captured, and the Russians forced to retire from the Balkans and the Black Sea.

The Russian Bear threatens a fearful Ottoman Turkey, with its Balkan chicks.

Rebellions

A large empire, with people of different cultures, was difficult to govern, especially in a time of growing nationalism. Old enemies, such as the Finns and Poles, resented Russian dominance. The small Polish Kingdom established in 1815 was supposed to be self-governing – but its king was the czar! In 1830 the Poles launched a major rebellion, which took a year to crush. Greater repression followed, as the Polish constitution was abolished. After further outbreaks in 1848 and 1863, Poland was reduced to a Russian province.

Jewish survivors of a pogrom, about 1908.

Reform

Alexander II introduced real and far-reaching reforms. He overhauled law and order, banned the worst forms of torture, reduced censorship, and allowed elected assemblies at local level. Above all, he carried out the emancipation of the serfs, a step that earlier rulers had avoided because of the huge practical difficulties. In fact, it did little to improve the condition of the peasants, who were still dominated by landowners, and criticism of the government actually increased.

The Jews

In 1890 the Russian Empire included five million Jews. They lived in restricted areas and ghettoes, and were forbidden to own land. They were treated as "non-Russians" and were persecuted even more than other such groups. Anti-Jewish riots began in the 1880s and, after 1900, developed into murderous pogroms, which the government did nothing to prevent. About one million Jews escaped abroad, mainly to the USA.

1881 Alexander II assassinated.

1881 Pogroms in Russia hit Jewish people especially hard.

1891 Trans-Siberian railroad begun (completed 1916).

1905 Russo-Japanese war.
1905 First Russian Revolution.

1914 Outbreak of First World War.

reformer though not a liberal, would not surrender the czar's autocratic powers.

One result was the growth of revolutionary activity, beginning with army mutinies (brutally punished) and the revolt of the Decembrists (dissatisfied young army officers). They were crushed by the reactionary Nicholas I (reigned 1825–55), who ruled as if he were a general and the people his army. His methods helped to antagonize moderates, creating a dangerous situation in which many people were hostile to the regime on principle. The government became very

unpopular. Most people blamed officials, not the czar, their "father," and some extreme groups, such as the so-called "nihilists," planned revolution. They adopted murder as a political weapon, and Alexander II was one victim.

Other divisions existed within Russian society, especially between Westernizers, who saw Russia as part of Europe, and Slavophiles, who saw Russia as unique by race and religion, different from (and potentially superior to) Europe. Subject peoples often did not like Russian rule, and rebellions occurred in Poland. The later policy of

"Russification" further alienated non-Russian peoples, while it encouraged persecution of the empire's large Jewish minority.

In spite of Russia's huge area, good land was in short supply. But by 1850 Russia had gained the fertile "black earth" region of the southern steppes. As a result, grain became its largest export. Poor communications held back industrial development, but the building of railroads enabled Russia to begin its own industrial revolution about 1880 (a

century after Britain). Iron and coal were the chief resources of the Donets basin, and the newly conquered Caucasus region provided oil.

Banking and business organizations helped to stabilize the Russian currency and attracted foreign investment, especially from France.

1. Silver coin worth 20 copeks from 1861.

2. A five-ruble banknote from 1865; for a long time the Russian peasants refused to accept paper money.

Communications

The difficulty of communications in the Russian Empire held back development. There was not even a proper road between Moscow and St. Petersburg until 1830, and no railroad until 1851. Russian troops took longer to reach the Crimea (in Russian territory) than the French and British. Railroad building speeded up in the late19th century. The Trans-Siberian railroad, begun in 1891, opened up Siberia and was almost complete, across nearly 6,000 mi. (10,000 km) by the outbreak of the Russo-Japanese War.

The Kuril Islands were given to Japan in exchange for the southern half of Sakhalin.

Political prisoners exiled to Siberia at work on the Trans-Siberian railroad.

Expansion in the east

Russian expansion in southeast Europe was checked by the great powers, but control of the Caucasus was established by 1864 and expansion continued in the east. Siberia was opened up, and Vladivostok was founded on the Pacific in 1860. Russian forts were built in Alaska. The Treaty of Beijing (1860) advanced the Russian border with China to the Amur River. China leased land in Manchuria to Russia, including Port Arthur (Lüshun), an ice-free port usable all year round.

Workers in an armaments factory in 1914. Russia was not short of labor, but conscription of men for the army encouraged employment of women.

> ### SEE ALSO
> p. 100 RUSSIA AND EASTERN EUROPE
> p. 118 THE RISE OF RUSSIA
> p. 220 THE RUSSIAN REVOLUTION
> p. 242 SOVIET EXPANSIONISM

Industrial development

Industrial development took off in the 1890s, when production increased at an average rate of eight percent a year. Around 1900 the Caucasus produced more oil than the rest of the world put together. About three million people (only three percent of the population) worked in industry, and towns and factories grew rapidly. These developments did not alter Russia's fundamental social problems, and the industrial working class became a fertile breeding ground for socialist ideas.

Nicholas II

The last Russian emperor, Nicholas II (reigned 1894–1917), was well-meaning but weak and stubborn, a poor leader of 120 million subjects. A conservative, like his father Alexander III (reigned 1881–94), he believed that it was his religious duty to maintain Russian autocracy. Meanwhile, the activities of revolutionaries and government agents (sometimes the same people!) threatened to destroy all government authority. Nicholas's failure to keep Russia out of costly and unsuccessful wars hastened the revolution of 1917.

Writers and artists

Few writers and artists of world class appeared in Russia before the 18th century, but by 1900, Russian literature, of which the poet Pushkin (1799–1837) is called the founder, stood on equal footing with that of France or England. The Russian novel achieved unique status in the works of Dostoyevsky, Tolstoy, and Turgenev; and Russian theater in the works of playwrights Chekhov and Gorky. Russian artists included Kandinsky, founder of abstract painting, and Chagall.

The upper class

In Russia social classes were fixed. The land-owning nobles, although they made up only one percent of the population, were the most influential class. Some were thoroughly "Europeanized," and they included nearly all educated people, apart from some Orthodox clergy and the growing number of government officials. Besides their hereditary estates, they had many privileges – they did not have to pay taxes or serve in the army – because the autocracy depended on their support and co-operation.

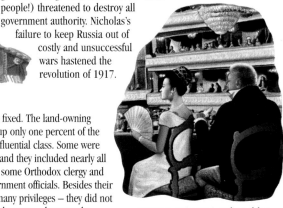

Russian aristocrats at the Bolshoi Theater, Moscow.

Music

Like other arts, music was energized by the interaction of Russian nationalist tradition and European (especially German) influence, represented by composers such as Tchaikovsky, Mussorgsky, Rachmaninoff, and Rimsky-Korsakov. In ballet, Russia astonished the world when the impresario Diaghilev brought the Russian Ballet to Paris in 1908.

Designs for costumes for the ballet Narcissus *by Lev Bakst.*

The Manchus

The Manchu people were descendants of the Jurchens, who occupied northern China in the 12th century. A hunting, fishing, and farming people, during the Ming period several Manchu groups paid tribute to the Chinese Empire. The Manchus were organized by their chieftain Nurhachi (1559–1626), who died in battle while establishing control over Mongol lands to the north of the Great Wall of China. When bandits rebelled against the Ming Dynasty in 1643, a Ming general asked the Manchus to help drive them out.

Mounted bowmen formed the main strike force of the Manchu army, which was organized into units under different colored banners.

The Manchu Empire.

- DZUNGARIA
- Urga
- MANCHURIA
- Kashgar
- MONGOLIA
- XINJIANG
- Mukden
- Beijing
- QINGHAI
- KOREA
- TIBET
- JAPAN
- Lhasa
- Guangzhou
- TAIWAN
- Hong Kong

Manchu expansion
- [ ] By 1644
- [ ] By 1659
- [ ] By 1800

The vast Manchu Empire extended for many thousands of miles from the Manchurian homeland north of Korea, westward beyond Kashgar and south to Hainan Island.

Society and culture

Many leaders of the early Manchu Empire believed that the previous Ming Dynasty had collapsed because it had allowed society to be too open. The Manchu encouraged a more conservative approach, with strict rules and social standards. Women were expected to adopt traditional roles as wives and mothers. Writers and painters, however, were allowed freedom to express themselves without interference.

Right: A 19th-century illustration from the novel Dream of Red Mansions, *written by Cao Xueqin (1715–64) and published in 1791. It is considered a great masterpiece of Chinese literature.*

As a young man Kangxi spent a great deal of time studying. He later commissioned many scholarly works, including histories of the Chinese Empire and dictionaries.

Kangxi and Qianlong

Kangxi (1654–1722) was chosen to succeed as emperor at age eight. This may have been because he had already overcome smallpox and so was likely to survive. He took over sole power of the Manchu Empire in 1669, and ruled for the next 53 years. Kangxi led his army against the Mongols and personally toured his vast empire six times. He also organized engineering works to prevent the Huang He (Yellow River) from flooding. Kangxi's grandson, Emperor Qianlong (reigned 1736–96) also made many tours of his huge empire. An able general, he destroyed Mongol power in Central Asia. Agricultural and industrial developments during his reign made China prosperous.

Jesuit influence

Jesuit missionaries to China presented Christianity in a form that did not conflict with Confucianism, and some influential Chinese were converted. During the 18th century, however, many Jesuits were expelled or imprisoned for undermining traditional Chinese beliefs.

Left: This pocket sundial and compass was made by Adam Schall von Bell (1591–1666), a German Jesuit who became head of the Chinese Imperial Board of Astronomy.

POPULATION GROWTH IN CHINA, c.1368–c.1850.		
		400
		300
		200
		100
MING DYNASTY 1368–1644	MANCHU DYNASTY c.1750	c.1850

Population growth

China's population expanded rapidly during the 18th century, rising from about 150 million in 1700 to twice as many in 1800. By this time the standard of living for most people was beginning to fall as the population outgrew the amount of food being produced. From 1800 on the prestige of the Manchu rulers declined, and the administration became more corrupt and inefficient. Many people were without jobs and everyday life became more competitive. During the 19th century millions of Chinese emigrated, mainly to the countries of Southeast Asia.

The graph shows that by 1850 the Chinese population had reached more than 400 million – about three times as many as at the start of the Manchu Dynasty.

1644 Manchus gain control of Beijing after expelling rebels.

1661–1722 Long reign of Qing Emperor Kangxi.

1689 Treaty of Nerchinsk gives Chinese the Amur region in exchange for Russian trade.
1720 Qing control Tibet.

1736–96 Long reign of Emperor Qianlong; China prospered.

Manchu China

After the Manchus replaced the Ming Dynasty and took power in China in 1644, there was considerable resistance to their new Qing Dynasty and to their ways and customs. Rebellions were ruthlessly put down, however, and the new empire expanded its influence in all directions. Foreign trade was restricted to the port of Guangzhou (Canton), until the Opium Wars forced a series of so-called unequal treaties in favor of Western powers. Foreign influence and internal unrest led to a series of further rebellions in the second half of the 19th century. Though the Manchus attempted reforms, a republican revolution in 1911 led to the establishment of the Republic of China and the end of thousands of years of imperial rule.

In 1644 the Manchus invaded China, gained control of Beijing, and established the Qing (meaning "pure") Dynasty. The first Qing (or Manchu) emperor was named Shunzhi. The Manchus integrated better than the Mongols had done, but there was still some resistance to their rule. In 1674 provincial governors led a revolt that lasted for five years.

The empire continued an aggressive campaign of territorial expansion, and in 1683 the island of Taiwan came under imperial control. Conflicts with the Russian Empire on China's northern borders were settled by the Treaty of Nerchinsk in 1689. In 1720 Tibet came under the

control of the Qing, while to the far west of the empire the Chinese put down a revolt in Dzungaria and conquered the region in 1755.

Three very able and long-lived emperors in the early part of the dynasty – Kangxi, Yongzheng, and Qianlong – who ruled from 1669 to 1799, built up a strong empire.

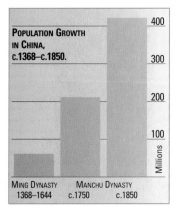

The Opium Wars

To stop the outflow of silver, which the Chinese paid to traders in return for opium smuggled in from India, and to fight the spread of drug addiction, in 1800 the Chinese banned the production and import of opium. In 1813 smoking the drug was made illegal, but smuggled quantities kept increasing. Finally, in 1839 Chinese officials seized 20,000 chests of opium from British merchants in Guangzhou, and the first of two Opium Wars broke out.

The wooden sailing junks of the Chinese forces were no match for the iron steamships of the British in the Opium Wars.

Angered by the large fortunes being made by Western traders, in 1900 Chinese Boxer rebels (whose name derived from their secret society, the "Right and Harmonious Fists,") started attacking Westerners. They wanted to drive out all foreigners. To end the rising, many Boxer rebels were shot.

Trade with Europe

During the 18th century cotton goods became a major Chinese export, along with traditional silk. Europeans were keen to buy Chinese porcelain, furniture, and lacquer ware, and sales of tea to Britain soared. Goods were paid for in silver, but since China bought few goods in return, European merchants increasingly smuggled in opium from India to earn some of the silver back.

Chinese workers packing crates of porcelain bound for Europe.

Hong Kong

At the end of the first Opium War, the Treaty of Nanjing forced the opening of five treaty ports to the British. By the terms of the treaty the island of Hong Kong was also handed over, and the mainland peninsula of Kowloon was added in 1860. In 1898 the New Territories were granted to Britain on a 99-year lease. When the lease ran out, in 1997, the British crown colony was returned and Hong Kong became a special administrative region of China.

The Taiping rebellion

A series of uprisings took place between 1851 and 1864. The Taiping rebellion's leader, Hong Xiuquan, was convinced by a dream that he was Jesus Christ's brother and the savior of China. His preaching gained him many followers, who combined Christian beliefs with communist ideals. They captured Nanking in 1853 and introduced many social policies, such as the abolition of private property. After Hong's death, the Manchus crushed the rebellion, in which 20 to 30 million people had been killed.

SEE ALSO
p. 86 CHINESE CIVILIZATION
p. 124 MING CHINA
p. 234 CHINA TO 1950
p. 256 MODERN CHINA

A painted fan decorated with a scene of Guangzhou, where the flags of different European trading nations are flying.

Hong Xiuquan (1814–64) had failed to get a place in the Chinese civil service before he declared himself "Heavenly King of the Great Peace."

Below: Yuan Shikai (1859–1916), a leading general under the Qing, became president of the Chinese republic in 1912.

End of the empire

At the end of the 19th century the Manchus put through many reforms. They abolished the Confucian civil service examinations and modernized the education system. They also promised to adopt a constitution and gave the provinces more power. But the reforms came too late for many people, who wanted a republic, and in 1912 the last Chinese emperor was replaced by a president.

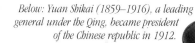

1839–42 First Opium War against Britain.	**1850–64** Taiping rebellion causes millions of deaths.	**1856–60** Second Opium War against Britain and France.	**1862–1908** Regency of the dowager Empress Cixi.	**1911** Chinese revolution. **1912** Republic of China founded.

Kangxi and Qianlong both ruled for at least sixty years. Manchu China reached its peak during this time. Trouble set in during the last years of Qianlong's reign, due to excessive spending and, some suggest, the emperor's encroaching senility. The much less able rulers who followed were unable to resist the double threat posed by internal rebellion and European aggression. Anti-Manchu secret societies, such as the White Lotus and Triad groups, rebelled in several different parts of the country.

The first Opium War (1839–42) with Britain resulted in the Treaty of Nanjing, that gave Hong Kong to the British and opened five treaty ports. The second

Opium War (1856–60) against Britain and France led to further commercial gains for Europe. At the same time the Taiping (or "Heavenly Kingdom") rebellion of 1850–64 brought civil war and millions of deaths.

From 1894 to 1895 China was at war with Japan. It lost control of Taiwan and was forced to recognize Japan's control of Korea. In 1900 the Boxer Rebellion was led by a society called the "Right and Harmonious Fists," who opposed Westerners in China. The rebellion was crushed by an international force. In 1905 several republican organizations formed the revolutionary United League, and in 1911 an army mutiny led to Sun Yat-sen becoming temporary president of a republic, which was formally founded on January 1, 1912. Six weeks later the last Manchu emperor, six-year-old Pu Yi, gave up his throne and Yuan Shikai became president.

1. Carved boxwood figure from Manchu China.

2. Early 18th-century painted enamel teapot.

3. Emperor's court boots.

1784 The India Act says British will not expand further.

1818 Final defeat of Marathas.
1836 Large road-building program

begins.
1849 Punjab annexed.

1853 First railroad in operation.
1856 Oudh annexed.

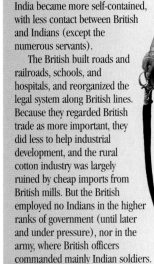

British tiger hunters.

The East India Company was responsible to the British government, which stated, in the India Act of 1784, that territorial expansion was against "the honor and policy of this nation." However, territorial expansion did occur, and by the middle of the 19th century the British effectively ruled India. Early governors believed that British rule would be brief. Then the idea arose that British rule was a great benefit to the Indian people, a "sacred trust." One result was the admission in 1813 of Christian missionaries, whom the Company had kept out until then. By the 1880s the British (or some of them) had become entranced by the sheer magnificence of their Indian empire and were unwilling even to think about giving it up.

At first the British treated Indians as equals and did not interfere with Indian customs. Once the "sacred trust" idea took hold, they began to enforce reforms, many of which were strongly resented by some groups of Indians.

The rebellion of 1857–58 marked a watershed. After that, both the British and the Indians were more suspicious of each other. The Suez Canal (opened 1869) dramatically shortened the voyage to India, and British families joined their men, forming European communities. British society in India became more self-contained, with less contact between British and Indians (except the numerous servants).

The British built roads and railroads, schools, and hospitals, and reorganized the legal system along British lines. Because they regarded British trade as more important, they did less to help industrial development, and the rural cotton industry was largely ruined by cheap imports from British mills. But the British employed no Indians in the higher ranks of government (until later and under pressure), nor in the army, where British officers commanded mainly Indian soldiers. They remained an alien ruling class.

British India

After the British East India Company virtually annexed the state of Bengal in 1765, it began to change from a trading company to a military and political institution. In 1784 the British government had declared that it would not expand further, but by 1805 the East Indian Company was the chief power in the subcontinent. Increasing hostility to British rule led to a widespread rebellion, known as the Indian Mutiny, across north and central India in 1857–8. It took 14 months of bitter fighting to put down. At the end of the rebellion the British government took over from the East India Company, and from that point on India was governed by a tiny minority of British civil servants. The Indians, forbidden to participate in the government of their own country, began to organize themselves to regain their independence.

A detail from a large painting (1830) of a grand procession of the Rajah of Tanjore. The most prominent figure (above) is the British Resident (minister).

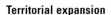

British India, 1914.

AFGHANISTAN
PUNJAB
CHINA
TIBET
Delhi •
NEPAL
OUDH
ASSAM
SIND
MEWAR
BENGAL
• Calcutta
BURMA
ARABIAN SEA
ORISSA
HYDERABAD
BAY OF BENGAL
Goa
MYSORE
MADRAS
Territories
CEYLON
Possessions, 1858
Acquired 1858–1914
Dependent Indian states

Territorial expansion

Partly through their own provocation, the British in 1780 were confronted with three enemies: the Marathas, the Nizam of Hyderabad, and Tipu Sultan of Mysore. It took three wars to defeat the Marathas and establish British supremacy, while other campaigns resulted in British authority stretching, in the east, from Bengal to Ceylon (Sri Lanka). Other states were taken over when the ruler died without – according to the British, but not Hindu, interpretation – leaving a direct heir.

The British

In the early days, many of those employed by the East India Company retired to England with huge fortunes. This profiteering was later stopped, but life in India, though it had drawbacks, was very comfortable for the ruling British. A young nobody in London, sent out as a clerk for the Company, found himself with a large house and 20 servants. Some Britons came to love and understand Indian ways and chose to stay on after retirement, but others were bored, superior, and increasingly racist.

The princely states

One third of British India was made up of nominally independent states. The British recognized the value of maintaining the Indian princedoms, and until 1858 many areas experienced little contact with Europeans. But British reluctance to interfere was combined with reforming zeal. (The custom of killing baby girls, for example, was unacceptable, so the British made it a capital crime, yet failed to end it entirely.) After 1858, under the rule of the Crown, the princes felt more secure. They generally remained firm allies of Britain.

A "memsahib" (meaning "the lady of a sahib," a man of high status) with her servants.

Trade and industry

The British saw India as a market for its booming industry and did not invest in Indian industry, which might compete. The industrial revolution was a disaster for India's cotton workers (as it was, earlier, for Britain's hand-weavers). Hindu ritual and the caste system also hindered technological progress. However, India was brought into the world capitalist system, with great benefits for the merchants and bankers of the growing middle classes, who became closely identified with British rule.

Making block-printed cotton cloth. The collapse of India's cotton trade brought severe hardship.

After the death of Ranjit Singh (1839), the Punjab fell into disorder. Invasion of British territory resulted in war and annexation under Ranjit's successor, Duleep Singh (left).

Communications

Industrial development, like trade, depended on communications. No roads existed before 1830. The famous Grand Trunk Road between Calcutta and Delhi was begun in 1839. Railroads were built from the 1850s, partly through private investment. Nearly 40,000 mi. (70,000 km) of track were working by 1914. They provided the means for development, encouraging trade and new industries (such as coal-mining) and stimulating modernization of others – for instance textiles. By 1914 India was again a major cotton exporter.

Hindu reformers

The British could not have ruled India without the co-operation, active or passive, of most Indians. While Muslims in general kept themselves apart from Western influences, a growing number of Hindus identified with them. They spoke English (the official language) and studied European history and literature. Many government reforms were brought about by pressure from Hindus.

Ram Mohun Roy (1772–1833) was a Hindu liberal reformer who opposed the caste system and adopted aspects of Christianity. He founded the Brahmo Samaj (Society of God, 1828) and the Hindu College in Calcutta (1817), and had great influence on the British as well as Hindus.

The end of East India Company rule

The rebellion ended the rule of the East India Company. After 1858 India was placed directly under the British government, with a viceroy and a council, responsible to the London government. Indian involvement in government was increased by later acts, but the concessions were minor (though resented by many British).

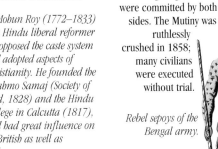

In 1876 Queen Victoria was made "Empress of India," partly because she wanted a title like the German and Russian emperors.

Burma and Tibet

British annexations did not cease entirely after 1858. Following clashes with the Burmese Empire (1824–26, 1852, 1885), Upper Burma was annexed. The motive was the desire to balance French expansion in Indochina. Fear that the Russians were gaining influence in Tibet prompted an unjustifiable military expedition to Lhasa (Tibet) in 1903, which led to effective British control.

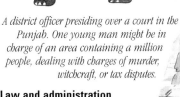

The royal elephant, carrying the king of Burma.

A district officer presiding over a court in the Punjab. One young man might be in charge of an area containing a million people, dealing with charges of murder, witchcraft, or tax disputes.

Law and administration

In 1852 the Company had just 2,000 officials in India. They understood little of Indian customs and less of Indian languages, but had to work out compromises between Indian and Western custom. By 1900 the British had established an administration which, though often rough and ready in practice, was relatively fair and administered evenly throughout India. The trouble was that the administrators and judges were almost entirely British.

The Mutiny

New practices introduced in the army offended Indian soldiers (called "sepoys"), both Hindu and Muslim. In 1857 several regiments mutinied against their British officers. Rebellion, including many civilians, spread across much of northern India, fuelled by hostility to European influences. Delhi was captured and fighting was fierce (right). Horrible atrocities were committed by both sides. The Mutiny was ruthlessly crushed in 1858; many civilians were executed without trial.

Rebel sepoys of the Bengal army.

The meaning of the Mutiny

The rebellion was more than a mutiny, but it was not a nationalist rising. Few Indians yet thought of an all-Indian "nation," and no great leader emerged to unite resistance to the British. The motives of the rebels were conservative. They feared that modernization was destroying ancient culture. The British also stood for a system (imperialism) which, though it lasted another 90 years, was doomed to destruction.

Famine

Local famine was a continual curse in India. It could wipe out half the people in a town or region. Relief usually arrived too late. The 1866 famine in Bengal, with over a million dead, was made worse by monsoon rain preventing transportation and merchants hoarding grain. In 1883 the government set up an elaborate plan, the Famine Code, to deal with the problem. It was an unusually large social-welfare program for the time, and brought improvement, but did not stop famines.

In later times, opponents of the British blamed them for outbreaks of famine.

B. G. Tilak (1856–1920) led the extreme wing of Congress. He first had the idea of opposing the British by massive civil disobedience, or non-cooperation, the policy later adopted by Gandhi.

Congress

The Indian National Congress was founded by educated Hindus and Muslims in 1885, with British support. Its original object was to press the government for a greater share of power for Indians, but national independence was not part of the agenda. A more extreme wing soon emerged and gained control of the party. It advocated self-government for India as a dominion of the British Empire, like Canada or Australia.

The Muslim League

Muslims in the Congress feared that, in a more democratic India, they would be swamped by the Hindu majority. They founded the separate Muslim League (1906), which reached an agreement with Congress (the Lucknow Pact) for certain seats to be reserved for Muslims in future elections. Members of the League took part in the non-cooperation movement and some Muslims remained members of Congress.

SEE ALSO
p. 128 THE MUGHAL EMPIRE
p. 154 THE STRUGGLE FOR EMPIRE
p. 198 COLONIALISM
p. 236 ASIA TO THE 1960S

COLONIALISM

European powers greatly expanded their empires during the 19th century, when a large part of the world fell under their control. Britain, for example, gained power over a fifth of the world's surface, and added 88 million subjects to its empire. France, Germany, Italy, Belgium, Portugal, as well as the United States and Japan claimed vast areas across the world. Although the imperial powers developed many of their colonies, bringing international trade and infrastructure (railroads, for example), the colonists often treated the local peoples badly, seizing their land and depriving them of some of their most basic human rights.

How colonialism was achieved

The imperial powers usually had well organized armies and modern technology to take their colonies by force. With their modern weapons, European armies were able defeat armies that far outnumbered them. The invention of the machine gun in 1884, for example, enabled 320 French troops to overpower 12,000 African soldiers in Chad during a battle in 1899.

A poster advertising cocoa, one of the goods in demand from the colonies

This picture shows convicts in Tasmania who were forced to walk great distances carrying heavy loads.

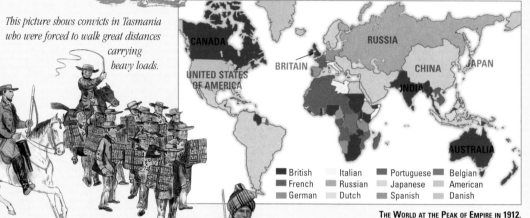

THE WORLD AT THE PEAK OF EMPIRE IN 1912.

British	Italian	Portuguese	Belgian
French	Russian	Japanese	American
German	Dutch	Spanish	Danish

Commerce and power

There were many reasons why the imperial powers were interested in expanding their empires. One was strategic: to keep their rivals from becoming too powerful. Another was to increase trade. As Western powers industrialized, they needed to look further afield for raw materials and markets. Many of the colonies had excellent climates for growing products such as sugar, tea, coffee, fruit, and cocoa, and were rich in natural resources.

Early colonies: Australia

For many years rough seas prevented explorers from visiting Australia, but in 1770 British Captain James Cook landed there and claimed the east coast for Britain. The British did not look for trade opportunities in Australia, but they found another reason to colonize it: to establish a place far away from Britain to send their criminals.

Afridis tribesmen from Afghanistan, who showed fierce resistance to the British.

The Indian Mutiny

By the early 19th century, the British East India Company had become the most powerful force in India, complete with its own army. In 1857, however, many of the company's Indian soldiers rebelled against their British officers, and soon the mutiny turned into a general rebellion against the British. After the Indian Mutiny, the British brutally punished the rebels and decided to make India a British colony.

An English army commander in India.

Colonialism becomes a European obsession

From 1870 European powers rushed to expand their empires. During this time two major continents, Africa and Asia, were almost completely carved up. Missionaries, traders, and military officers all saw enormous potential in these areas and pressed their countries for imperial advances. Britain and France, as well as emerging powers such as Germany and Italy, concerned about the strategic advances of their rivals, scrambled to seize new territories. They also raced to claim areas rich in natural resources for the new wave of industrialization. Britain made the greatest gains to its empire during this time, seizing lands all over Africa as well as strategic points in the Pacific.

Afghans resist Britain

During the late 19th century, both Britain and Russia wanted to control Afghanistan. The competition between the two imperial powers was called the Great Game and resulted in two wars: the First Anglo-Afghan War of 1839–42 and the Second Anglo-Afghan War of 1878–80. The Afghan tribesmen, who were fiercely independent, managed to resist the British, and the British finally signed a border agreement and an agreement to recognize Afghanistan's independence. Afghanistan became a buffer between the British and Russian empires.

In this cartoon an evil serpent, symbolizing imperialist Britain, squeezes the globe, squashing traditional cultures.

Algerian patriot Abd al-Qadir surrendering to the French governor general. It took the French until 1847 to capture and exile him.

Asia gets carved up: Burma
To protect their interests in India and to gain a strategic advantage over their French rivals, the British colonized Burma during the mid-19th century. After a series of three wars, in 1824–26, 1852–53, and 1885–86, the British secured all of Burma and governed it as part of India.

Right: In Indochina a group called the Black Flags, led by De Tham (top right), resisted French domination.

The French in Algeria
The French army captured the port of Algiers in 1830 and then began to colonize the rest of Algeria. They met fierce resistance, however, from the Muslim hill tribes led by Abd al-Qadir, a holy man claiming to be a descendent of Muhammad. Algeria officially became a part of France in 1871.

China resists European colonization
After partitioning the whole continent of Africa, the European powers, as well as Russia, turned their interests to China, which seemed likely to suffer the same fate. Indeed Germany, France, Great Britain, Russia, and Japan were able to gain economic control of China, where they built railroads and controlled natural resources. The Chinese government, however, was more centralized than the separate African states, and were able to resist major colonization.

Chinese government officials in the late 19th century.

European explorers
European explorers traveled extensively in Africa before it was colonized. On returning to Europe, many encouraged their governments to begin colonization. In the words of British-American explorer Henry Morton Stanley, it was their duty "to put the civilization of Europe into the barbarism of Africa."

Left: French explorer Count Pierre Savorgnan de Brazza sold photographs of himself to help finance expeditions north of the Congo River in the 1880s.

The Pacific is colonized
The Pacific Islands were colonized during the 19th century by the Dutch, French, British, and Germans. The British gained strategic areas such as Singapore, Malaya, and Fiji. Although some Europeans, such as French painter Paul Gauguin, romanticized the traditional culture and people of the islands, colonists imposed Western religion and customs, and spread Western diseases such as syphilis.

Gauguin was inspired by his beautiful tropical surroundings to develop a new style of painting.

Japanese Colonialism
By adopting Western-style government, military, and technology, Japan was able to avoid colonization and become a major colonial power itself. Successful wars against China 1894–95 and Russia 1904–05 resulted in Japan gaining control of Korea, Taiwan, southern Manchuria, and half of Sakhalin.

Colonialism feeds into nationalism
The imperialist fervor that marked the late 19th and early 20th centuries affected all levels of society. Popular culture instilled a nationalist sentiment in many Europeans, who viewed the scramble for empire as a contest to increase economic and strategic power, outdo their rivals, and dominate "inferior" peoples and cultures. Only in the 20th century did increasing numbers of Europeans question the morality of colonialism.

Africa is carved up
After British explorers traveled inland in Africa, claiming new areas for the queen, Britain began to colonize vast areas of the continent. Between 1880 and 1914 the British gained Egypt, the Sudan, Uganda, Kenya, Nigeria, and Northern and Southern Rhodesia. They also consolidated their rule of South Africa with their victory in the Second Boer War of 1899–1902.

Emperor Meiji, who took the throne in 1868, modernized Japan and began its transformation into a world power.

This board game glorifies an expedition of adventurer Henry Morton Stanley to rescue Sudan's governor from Muslim rebels.

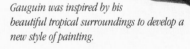

Right: Burke and Wills crossed the continent of Australia in 1860-61, but starved to death on their way back.

Captain James Cook

In 1768 Cook was given command of HMS Endeavour, and ordered first to sail to Tahiti in the Pacific Ocean to observe the transit of Venus and then to go on as far as 40 degrees south to search for the Great South Land. In October 1769 the ship's boy sighted land. Cook explored and charted New Zealand's coastline, and used his Tahitian interpreter to speak with the Maori people. After sailing west, the southeast coast of Australia was sighted in April 1770. Cook landed at Botany Bay and named the land New South Wales.

Exploration

By 1804, Matthew Flinders in his sloop "Investigator" had circumnavigated Australia and proved it was an island continent. In 1813, explorers crossed the Blue Mountains west of Sydney and found land suitable for crops and cattle. Between 1820 and 1850, inland explorers discovered more pastoral land in eastern Australia as well as large rivers such as the Murray and the Darling. Others discovered hot, arid regions, unsuitable for farming. Burke and Wills, with their camels and horses, first crossed the continent in 1860–61.

Aborigines

The Australian colony's first Governor, Arthur Phillip, treated the Aborigines with respect, but most of his successors did not. There was much violent conflict. In their search for farming country, the Europeans invaded Aboriginal food-gathering and hunting territories, and forcibly occupied their lands. The Aborigines had no choice but to give up their traditional way of life. Infectious European diseases such as influenza and measles, as well as extreme poverty, caused the deaths of many Aborigines.

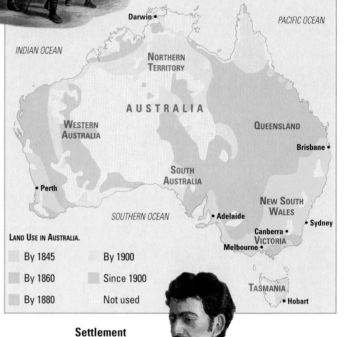

LAND USE IN AUSTRALIA.

By 1845	By 1900
By 1860	Since 1900
By 1880	Not used

Goldrush

The discovery of gold in New South Wales and Victoria in 1851 attracted prospectors from Europe, North America, and southern China. Even most of Victoria's police force resigned to join the rush. In the 1850s, over 600,000 immigrants arrived in Australia and by 1860 Australia's population was over one million.

Settlement

The first British immigrants arrived in New South Wales in 1788 and settled at Sydney Cove. They were people convicted of a variety of crimes and were transported in the rat-infested ships of the First Fleet. Other early convict settlements were on Norfolk Island, and in Van Dieman's Land (modern Tasmania).

White Australia

One of the first laws passed by the new Federal Government forbid non-European people, such as Asians, from settling permanently in Australia. In 1974 the Labor Government, under Prime Minister Whitlam, changed many laws, and people of any race were allowed to immigrate to Australia.

1770 James Cook lands at Botany Bay. 1778 First British convicts arrive on the First Fleet. 1801-1803 Flinders circumnavigates Australia. 1829–36 Free colonies established in Australia. 1851 Goldrush in New South Wales and Victoria. 1901 British colonial rule of Australia ends.

Australia and New Zealand

In his first voyage of discovery of the Pacific, the English explorer James Cook claimed New Zealand and New South Wales (in Australia) for Britain. The arrival of the British in Sydney Cove resulted in catastrophic changes for the ancient Aboriginal culture. The British claimed New South Wales was unoccupied, largely based on Cook's incorrect reports that the Aboriginals were not settled there. Britain, at least officially, recognized Maori ownership of the land in New Zealand, although many wars were fought over it. In the 1850s, as the number of settlers and their demand for land increased, race relations in New Zealand deteriorated.

After the loss of the American colonies, New South Wales was established by the British as a penal settlement. Van Diemen's Land, founded in 1825, was infamous for its brutal prison at Port Arthur. Western Australia and Queensland were also founded as penal colonies, but free settlers colonized South Australia and Victoria. Convicts built roads, churches, and government buildings until as late as 1868, even as growing numbers of immigrants arrived from 1830 onward. They were attracted by the opening up of grazing land for merino sheep and beef cattle, and later by the gold rush.

When Charles Darwin visited New South Wales in 1836, he observed that the settlers were obsessed with money and sheep. Darwin also noted the continual push for "fresh pastures." Successive colonial governors failed to control the grab for land. However, by 1850 these so-called "squatters" had seized millions of acres (hectares) of land, were growing politically influential, and were responsible for killing many Aboriginals.

For most of the 19th century, the Australian colonies existed separately. Gradually, however, the colonials came to see themselves as Australians rather than as Victorians or Queenslanders. Australians worried about the French troops in the New Hebrides, and German

European discovery of New Zealand

In 1642, Dutch explorer Abel Tasman reached New Zealand's South Island. While anchored offshore, Tasman was greeted by tattooed Maori men in double canoes. At first the Maori seemed friendly, but when Dutch sailors approached in a row boat, the Maori attacked and killed four of Tasman's men. The place was named Murderer's Bay and Tasman sailed quickly away without ever landing. At this time it was thought that the west coast of New Zealand might be the edge of a great southern continent.

Territory purchased from Ngai Tahu 1844–64
Center of Maori King Movement 1858
Maori land confiscated by Government 1864–67

European Settlement

From 1790, sealers and whalers from North America, Australia, Britain, and France set up temporary camps around New Zealand. Early settlements were established in the Bay of Islands and Hokianga Harbor in the North Island. Hokianga was close to the great kauri forests that provided timber for British shipbuilding.

> **SEE ALSO**
> p. 58 ANCIENT AUSTRALIA
> AND THE PACIFIC
> p. 112 EUROPEAN
> VOYAGES OF DISCOVERY

Settlers and the Maori

At first, most Maori welcomed the new arrivals, trading their decorative wooden carvings, food, flax mats, and shrunken human heads for metal products such as nails, axes, and guns, as well as rum. In the 1820s some Maori chiefs, including Hongi Hika, traded goods for muskets, with which they attacked and killed their tribal enemies. Musket use spread south, in a series of tribal wars that disrupted the traditional Maori way of life. Christian ideas were introduced by the Reverend Samuel Marsden.

Treaty Of Waitangi

In 1840, the Treaty of Waitangi appointed Queen Victoria as the supreme ruler, or sovereign, of New Zealand. In return, Maori chiefs were promised protection and possession of their property and fishing grounds if they agreed to sell land only to the Crown. However, such transactions created problems, as Maori land was held communally rather than individually owned, and some chiefs refused to sign the Treaty. Under the Treaty, the Maori people became British subjects.

Relationship with Britain

Most permanent settlers in New Zealand were British immigrants, and New Zealand society, like that of Australia, was based on British law and customs. This continued into the 20th century, and during both World Wars Australian and New Zealand troops fought and died in support of Britain. For many years, New Zealand was very dependent on Britain as an export market.

Transportation and Technology

Until 1870 people traveled by coastal ship, on horseback, or on foot. After that time, the government spent large sums of money building new roads and bridges and the new capital city Wellington in the North Island was linked to many other towns. Railroads, the telegraph, and postal services also began to lessen the isolation of many settlements.

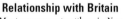

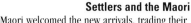

1642 Abel Tasman reaches New Zealand. **1769-70** James | Cook circumnavigates New Zealand. **1800** First European | settlement. **1840** Treaty of Waitangi. **1860s** Land Wars. | **1865** Wellington becomes the capital. **1907** New Zealand | becomes a Dominion of the British Empire.

---

interest in New Guinea. As no single colony could produce a defence force, protecting the coastline required a national strategy. In 1898 a new constitution was agreed, with the British monarch retained as head of state. British colonial rule ended in 1901 when Edmund Barton became prime minister of the Commonwealth of Australia with its new capital in Canberra.

During early contact with Europeans, most Maori warriors in New Zealand scoffed at the trading of muskets, preferring traditional hand to hand combat. However, in the 1820s, the Ngapuhi tribe waged war on many

longstanding enemies, armed with muskets, and other tribes thought they too must own guns.

In the 1830s, Englishman Edmund Wakefield formed the New Zealand Company, which bought Maori land cheaply to sell to wealthy settlers. When the British Government heard of this, the Treaty of Waitangi was hastily drawn up and Captain William Hobson appointed Lieutenant Governor. (At that time, New Zealand was administered from New South Wales.) Increasing numbers of British settlers (later called Pakeha), caused the Maori to fear for their land.

In 1856, New Zealand became a self-

governing colony with an elected parliament. Wellington became the capital in 1865. Most Maori, however, were barred from voting and unable to voice their grievances over land disputes. The Land Wars of the 1860s, fought in Waikato and Taranaki, led the British to confiscate large tracts of the best Maori land. In the South Island, sheep and dairy farms owned by Pakeha grew steadily. The discovery of gold in Otago in 1861 created a short-lived boom, and the European population rose again. The government borrowed huge sums of money to build roads and railroads, and assisted over 100,000 immigrants. The economy expanded, and refrigerated

ships opened the British market to New Zealand butter, meat, and cheese.

The rebuilding of Maori society, led by Princess Te Puea Herangi and others, encouraged cooperation, education, and traditional arts. Most native-born Pakeha opposed joining the Australian Federation and in 1907 New Zealand became a Dominion within the British Empire.

1. Until the invention of the chronometer (ship's clock), it was difficult to record the location of newly discovered lands. A chronometer accurately times the distance sailed each day and calculates longitude or east-west distance from Greenwich, England. Cook used a chronometer on his Antarctic voyage.

2. Maori carving.

1830 French invade Algeria.
1853–56 David Livingstone
follows Zambezi River to
Victoria Falls.
1867 Diamonds discovered at
Kimberley in South Africa.
1881 Transvaal defeats British
in First Boer War.
1884–85 Conference of Berlin
on European claims in Africa.

The Scramble for Africa

During the early 19th century most of Africa, then known to Europeans as the "Dark Continent," was free from outside imperialist powers. During the course of the century explorers, adventurers, and Christian missionaries journeyed widely through the continent, including the northern deserts and central rainforests. The Europeans became aware that there were vast, untapped resources in Africa, including diamonds and gold. During the last quarter of the century they sent armed expeditions to claim exclusive rights over vast territories. Several African peoples resisted, but the Europeans used their advantage of superior weapons to dominate and divide up the continent. By the end of the century most of Africa was under European control.

The Scottish explorer and missionary David Livingstone (1813–73) rides an ox on his travels across Africa. Livingstone made several difficult journeys into the interior of the continent and spread the idea that Africans needed Christianity and commerce in order to become "civilized."

By the end of the Napoleonic Wars in 1815, the British had taken over Cape Province from the Dutch Boers, beginning a long period of opposition and disagreement between the two colonial powers in southern Africa. In the north of the continent, the French invaded and occupied Algeria in 1830.

European explorers gradually made their way through the rest of the continent. From 1853 to 1856 David Livingstone followed the Zambezi River to the Indian Ocean, and from 1858 to 1864 he went inland again, exploring Lake Nyasa. In 1835–36 the Boers left the Cape and set out on their Great Trek northward, making new settlements in

This political map of Africa in 1913 shows how the continent had been divided up among seven foreign powers over a very short period of time.

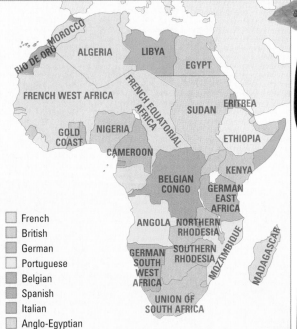

AFRICA IN 1913.

French
British
German
Portuguese
Belgian
Spanish
Italian
Anglo-Egyptian

A Zulu shield and spears.

Exploration
The best-known African explorers were David Livingstone (left) and Henry Morton Stanley (1841–1904), a British–American journalist. Livingstone first crossed the continent in the 1850s. In 1871 an American newspaper hired Stanley to look for Livingstone, of whom nothing had been heard for some time. When he met Livingstone on the shores of Lake Tanganyika, Stanley greeted him with the famous words: "Dr Livingstone, I presume?"

Mining
The discovery of Africa's mineral wealth attracted all the imperialist powers. The diamond fields of South Africa were discovered in 1867, when a farmer's son found a "pretty pebble" on the bank of the Orange River. More finds were soon reported and before long land rights were being disputed by native Africans, Boer settlers, and British and other fortune hunters.

A map showing holdings at Kimberley in South Africa, in 1883. The town of Kimberley was founded in 1871 following the discovery of diamonds (left). Gradually, independent miners sold out to small mining companies, which then merged to become huge organizations.

Early colonization
Before 1880 only two African regions were colonized by Europeans on a large scale. Northern Algeria was invaded by the French in 1830, and in southern Africa the original Dutch Cape Colony had been seized by the British. Then came the formation of the Afrikaner states of Transvaal and Orange Free State. Apart from this, there were Portuguese territories in Angola and on the east coast, as well as Spanish, British, and French trading stations and those slaving ports that still existed.

This wooden model of Queen Victoria was made by a Yoruba craftworker in the late 19th century.

This cartoon of Cecil Rhodes (1853–1902), the British statesman and businessman, shows his desire to see Britain bestriding Africa. Rhodes made a fortune in the diamond industry. Rhodesia (now Zambia and Zimbabwe) was named after him.

The Zulu War
The kingdom of the Zulus, a Bantu people, was formed in the early 19th century. The Zulus clashed with the Boers in 1838, and with the British in 1879, by whom they were finally defeated at Ulundi. The Zulu king was exiled and former Zululand was divided into 13 chieftaincies. The end of the Zulu military threat encouraged the Boers to shake off British power in Transvaal and led to the first Boer War (1881).

1885 King Leopold II of Belgium establishes Congo Free State
1886 Gold found in Transvaal.

1899–1902 Second Boer War ends; British defeat Afrikaners.

1900 British finally overcome Asante of West Africa.

1913 Native Lands Act; whites take 87 percent of South Africa.

Transvaal and Orange Free State.

Two discoveries changed the European attitude to southern Africa: in 1867 diamonds were discovered on the banks of the Orange River, and in 1886 prospectors struck gold near Pretoria. Fortune hunters descended on the region, including Englishman Cecil Rhodes, who gained control of the diamond mines and became prime minister of Cape Colony. The English defeated the local Zulus in 1879, but in the first Boer War the Boers rebelled and regained Transvaal. In the second Boer War, the British defeated the Boers and the two Afrikaner states became British colonies.

In the rest of the continent, by 1880 there was great rivalry between European powers as they made claims to profitable regions. In 1881 Tunis accepted a French protectorate, and by this time the French were also moving inland from Senegal. They began a conquest of Madagascar in 1883, and the island became a French protectorate two years later. French Equatorial Africa was added to French West Africa (bordering Algeria) in 1910, to form a vast territory. In 1885 the Congo region became the personal colony of

Leopold II of Belgium (1835–1909). Germany's two largest gains were German Southwest Africa in 1884 and German East Africa in 1885. The Italians gained Eritrea and part of Somaliland in 1889, but Emperor Menelik II of Ethiopia (1844–1913) fought off an Italian invasion in 1896.

In 1884–85 the European nations met in Berlin to settle rival claims, but the conference only

established the broad principles of the "scramble for Africa." By 1913 the European colonial powers of Belgium, Britain, France, Germany, Italy, Portugal, and Spain had divided almost all of Africa between them.

1. An early machine gun, such as those used by 320 French troops to defeat a Chad army of 12,000 in 1899.

SEE ALSO
p. 122 AFRICAN EMPIRES
p. 240 DECOLONIZATION OF AFRICA
p. 268 AFRICA TO THE PRESENT

The Boer Wars

Beginning in 1880, the British and the Boers (from the Dutch for "farmers") fought a series of wars for control of southern Africa. In the first Boer War (1881) the Boers rebelled against British rule and regained the Afrikaner state of Transvaal. In the second Boer War (1899–1902), the Boers were successful at first, besieging Ladysmith, Mafeking, and Kimberley. The British, under Lord Kitchener and Lord Roberts, brought in many more troops and finally defeated the Boers. The two Afrikaner states became British colonies.

The Boers had no uniforms and little training, but used guerrilla tactics to hold off the British.

French gains

The French marched inland from Senegal in the late 1870s, and by 1895 had colonized the large region that they named French West Africa. They added French Equatorial Africa in 1910. Together with Algeria, this gave France a large proportion of northwestern Africa. In addition, they took control of the island of Madagascar after many battles against the local Merina people.

Below: Behanzin, the king of Dahomey (present-day Benin). The French had a trade agreement with Dahomey, but war broke out in 1892 and the kingdom became part of French West Africa.

A French soldier plants his flag on the Madagascan capital of Tananarive. Madagascar became a French colony in 1896.

These carved figures show a Yoruba artist's representation of a Catholic missionary arriving in West Africa. The traditional Yoruba religion included worship of sky gods and ancestral spirits. Many converted to Christianity or Islam.

Belgian Congo

In 1879–84 King Leopold II of Belgium hired Henry Morton Stanley, who had extensively explored the Congo River region, to set up Belgian outposts along the river. In 1885 the region became Leopold's personal colony, named Congo Free State. The king's harsh rule brought protests, however, and the Belgian government took over control in 1908, renaming the colony the Belgian Congo.

Right: Leopold II (1835–1909), whose chief interest was the expansion of Belgium in Africa. He made a fortune from rubber and ivory.

Emperor Menelik II (1844–1913) united and expanded Ethiopia and fought off an Italian invasion in 1896. The Italians had already gained Eritrea and part of Somaliland.

German protectorates

Germany's two largest gains were German Southwest Africa (1884, covering present-day Namibia) and German East Africa (1885, covering present-day Tanzania). In 1884 the Germans also took Kamerun (present-day Cameroon) and Togoland (Togo). In East Africa the Germans made many Africans work on plantations, and they recruited Swahili soldiers to fight against other local Africans (right).

Despite the official ban on foreigners in force until 1854, European traders visited Japan during the early 19th century. The USA was particularly keen to establish trade links with Japan, and in 1853 the US government sent a formal mission, headed by Commodore Matthew Perry, to negotiate with the Japanese

government. Perry was able to force Japan to open two of its ports to US trade. Trade agreements with European countries such a Britain and France soon followed. As more foreign ships arrived in Japanese ports, major clans began to resent the foreign presence, and some of them rebelled against the Tokugawa *shogun*, weakening his rule.

In 1867 Prince Mutsuhito came to power when the last *shogun*, Tokugawa Yoshinobu, resigned. Prince Mutsuhito chose the name Meiji, meaning "enlightened government," and this became his title as well as the name for the government during his rule. The royal capital was moved from Kyoto to

Edo, which was renamed Tokyo, meaning "eastern capital."

Emperor Meiji thoroughly modernized Japan and began its transformation into a world power. By reversing the long-standing policy of isolationism, the Japanese government was able to compete with Western powers and avoid colonization. The Japanese adopted Western-style political, financial, social, and military systems and embraced modern technology.

By growing economically and militarily, Japan was able to begin its period of expansion. In 1879 it took over the neighboring Ryukyu

Islands. In 1894–95 it fought its first modern war, against the Chinese, whom it defeated to gain control of Taiwan and the Pescadores. Ten years later Japan became the first Asian country to defeat a European power when it swiftly crushed Russian forces in Manchuria. From this Japan was awarded the Liaodong Peninsula and the southern

Right: In traditional Japanese society women called geishas were employed to attend parties and entertain men with singing, dancing, poetry, and conversation.

Commander Perry arrives in Japan

In 1853 Commodore Perry arrived in Tokyo Bay and presented a treaty of friendship and commerce to the emperor's representatives, implying that he would use power if the Japanese did not comply. He returned in 1854 with an even more powerful fleet of ships and the government signed the Treaty of Kanagawa, which opened up two ports to US trade.

The Meiji restoration

Prince Mutsuhito's accession to the throne marked the beginning of what is called the Meiji restoration. Influential Japanese and Westerners helped to strengthen the government and unify the country. Meiji abolished the feudal system of *shoguns*, *daimyos*, and *samurais*. During this time new political, economic, and social systems were established and Western-style systems of law, administration, and taxation were introduced.

The end of the Tokugawa Dynasty

Even before Commodore Perry's arrival in 1853, many of the great clans of Japan resented the Tokugawa government and supported the emperor in Kyoto. After Japanese ports were opened up to trade, the presence of foreign ships enraged these clans even further. Young *samurai* attacked the ships, but their attacks were quelled by a multinational force in 1863–64. Civil war followed in 1867–68, further weakening the shogunate. Tokugawa Yoshinobu, the last *shogun*, resigned in 1868, and Emperor Mutsuhito began the Meiji government.

Japanese pistol used during the civil war of 1867–68.

Left: Commodore Perry meets a representative of the emperor.

Right: A samurai warrior's suit of armor, from the 1870s. It was during this time that the Japanese government officially abolished the samurai *class of professional warriors.*

Industrialization

Japan was one of the few Asian countries not colonized by the West. This was mainly due to industrialization, which began in 1873 when the Meiji government formally abolished the old feudal system. The Japanese government invited Western industrialists and engineers to advise Japan on how to modernize. Japanese businessmen set up coal mines, steel mills, shipyards, and factories.

New factories with modern machines replaced home spinning wheels for silk production. By the end of the 19th century, Japan was producing a large proportion of the world's silk.

A Japanese army helmet from the late 19th century. The Japanese army quickly adopted Western styles of administration and technology.

Army reforms

Japan reorganized, strengthened, and modernized its military in order to compete with Western powers. In 1872 the emperor decreed a universal military service, and four years later the *samurai* class of warriors was abolished. The Japanese government brought in French officers to remodel the army and British seamen to help create a new navy equipped with modern ships. With its stronger military, Japan was able to look for new territories to colonize.

Increase in trade

The Japanese realized that they must increase trade in order to avoid European domination. A new central bank financed the building of railroads, factories, and telegraph lines. Businessmen opened mines and factories to produce silk, textiles, metals, wood, and ships, all using modern Western technologies. In just over 30 years Japan became a strong economic power. During the Meiji restoration Japanese foreign trade increased dramatically. By 1917 exports far outweighed imports.

1889 Western-style constitution and parliament   are introduced.

1894–95 Japan defeats China in the Sino-Japanese War

1904–05 Japan defeats Russia in the Russo-Japanese War

1910 Japan annexes Korea

Japanese Expansionism

The military government established by Tokugawa Ieyasu at the beginning of the 17th century remained in force until the mid-19th century. Under this system, political power lay with the *shogun* at Edo, who controlled the *daimyo,* or local barons. All contact with foreigners was shunned, and despite repeated attempts by Russian and American ships to trade with Japan, the country maintained its isolationist position. During the 1850s American ships tried to force trading contacts, which led to conflict. Anti-foreign feelings eventually caused a civil war in Japan (1867–68) and the overthrow of the *shogun*. He was replaced by the emperor. Under the emperor, Japan decided to compete with the West and began a rapid program of industrialization. It also built a powerful army and navy and set out to dominate East Asia. In wars against China and Russia, it gained more territories, including Taiwan (1895) and Korea (1910). By 1914 Japan was a major power in the region.

half of Sakhalin. Russia was also forced to recognize the predominant interests of Japan in Korea, which was formally annexed to Japan in 1910.

Japan continued to develop its sphere of influence through World War I, and today remains one of the world's strongest economic powers.

1. This cartoon shows the Japanese emperor baiting a bear (symbol of Russia).

2. Container made of lacquered wood and coral   **2**

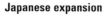

Japanese expansion

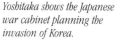

With a strong military force in place, in the late 19th century Japan began a period of expansion. Beginning with the neighboring islands of Ryukyu, Kuril, and Bonin, it embarked on a more aggressive foreign policy. Successful wars against China in 1894–95 and Russia in 1904–05 resulted in Japan gaining control of Korea, Taiwan, southern Manchuria, and half of Sakhalin. By 1914 Japan was a major colonial power in East Asia.

Well-equipped and organized Japanese troops fend off the Chinese during the Sino-Japanese War of 1894–95.

The Sino-Japanese war

In 1894 a growing economic crisis in Korea prompted the Tonghak revolt. China and Japan intervened, but then began a struggle themselves for domination of the area. The Japanese navy crushed the Chinese at the Battle of the Yellow Sea, while the army defeated the Chinese in Manchuria. Under the Treaty of Shimonoseki, Japan gained Taiwan and the Pescadores, while Korea became briefly independent. Japan was also awarded the Liaodong Peninsula in southern Manchuria, but Russia, France, and Germany forced Japan to accept a payment instead.

This painting by the artist Yoshitaka shows the Japanese war cabinet planning the invasion of Korea.

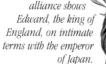

Right: This satirical French cartoon symbolizing the Anglo-Japanese alliance shows Edward, the king of England, on intimate terms with the emperor of Japan.

The Anglo-Japanese alliance

On January 30, 1902 Britain and Japan signed an agreement to help safeguard Britain's interests in China and Japan's interests in Korea. The two countries formed the alliance specifically to stop Russia from gaining power in East Asia. The alliance helped Japan in the Russo-Japanese War of 1904–05 by discouraging France, an ally of Russia, from entering the war against Japan. Based on this alliance, Japan entered World War I on the side of the Allies. The alliance ended in 1923.

Japan defeats Russia

In 1898 Japan and Russia signed a treaty pledging Korean independence. In 1900, however, Russian armies began to enter northern Korea. Japanese forces attacked the Russian controlled Port Arthur in southern Manchuria, starting the Russo-Japanese War. The Japanese defeated the Russians in less than 18 months. In the treaty of 1905, Japan was awarded the Liaodong Peninsula and the southern half of Sakhalin. Russia was also forced to recognize the predominant interests of Japan in Korea.

Left: When Japan defeated Russia in 1905, it became the first Asian country to defeat a European power. Great celebrations took place all over Japan, like the one shown here.

Japan dominates East Asia

Japan transformed itself from an isolated, conservative country to a great economic and military nation in just over 30 years. From acquiring its surrounding islands, it went on to fight modern wars to gain a mainland empire. In 1910 Japan extended its empire by formally annexing Korea, which it renamed Chosen. Japan continued to expand its realm and by the end of World War I gained commercial rights in Mongolia and Manchuria.

Japan embarked on an aggressive foreign policy after 1868. After acquiring its neighboring islands it fought to expand its realm to the mainland.

JAPANESE TERRITORIAL EXPANSION 1895–1914.

- ☐ Japan
- ☐ Territory acquired by 1910

SAKHALIN
KURIL IS.
JAPAN
Port Arthur
KOREA   Edo
Kyoto
RYUKYU IS.
PACIFIC OCEAN
TAIWAN

1862 Homestead Act: farmers move to settle Great Plains.

1867 USA buys Alaska from Russia.

1869 Union Pacific railroad links East and West coasts.

1891 Basketball is invented.
1898 USA gains territories

after defeating Spain.
1900–14 More than 13 million

US economic power

By the end of the 19th century the United States was a major industrial power. It had vast natural resources, including coal, oil, iron ore, and timber, and was self-sufficient in food. Its farmers also grew cotton and tobacco for export, as well as for the rapidly growing home market. The populations of cities such as New York expanded quickly. To save space on the ground, tall skyscrapers – incorporating newly invented elevators – were built as homes and offices. The steel used in their construction was in plentiful supply.

The 20-story Flatiron Building in New York City was completed in 1902 at the junction of Broadway and Fifth Avenue. Built from a steel frame and limestone blocks, its triangular shape made it a symbol of modern architecture.

In the 50 years from 1867 to 1917 the United States turned itself into a major world power. Although the Civil War had severely disrupted trade and industry, the country's vast natural resources – including the coal and iron ore needed for iron and steel production – enabled the economy of the North to recover quickly as peace returned.

Meanwhile the Homestead Act of 1862 encouraged settlers to start farming land west of the Mississippi River by offering them 160 acres (65 hectares) of land for a small fee, in exchange for a promise that they would live on the land for at least five years.

Large areas of land were also given to the railroad companies to enable them to link the East and West coasts. The railroads carried passengers and took manufactured goods to the settlers; they also took cattle and foodstuffs from the rural towns to the cities.

In 1867 the United States expanded the territory under its control by buying Alaska from Russia, and in 1898 gained Cuba, Puerto Rico, Guam, and the Philippines after defeating Spain. Between 1898 and 1916 it also gained control of the Hawaiian Islands, the Panama Canal Zone, and the Danish West Indies.

The population of the United States

Concentration of wealth

By 1914 the concentration of wealth in just a few large businesses began to alarm many Americans. They felt it was unfair that any one company, such as Standard Oil (left, shown here as an octopus wrapping itself around the US government) should have a monopoly on trade. In 1914 the Clayton Antitrust Act prevented businesses from growing too big.

Catalog sales

The Montgomery Ward Company, based in Chicago, produced the world's first mail-order catalog. It included furniture, clothes, tools, and toys. All items were sold with a money-back guarantee. People in small rural communities could now shop almost as easily as people in the cities. A few years later Sears, Roebuck and Co., also of Chicago, brought out their mail-order catalog (left), which was even more successful.

Henry Ford and the automobile

Henry Ford founded the Ford Motor Company in 1903. His most famous automobile was the Model T. Fifteen million were produced between 1908 and 1927. Assembly line production meant that skilled workers were no longer needed, and it became easier for employers to hire and fire.

The assembly line

The assembly line was introduced to the Ford factory in Detroit in 1913 to produce the Model T. Each person on the line had just one specific job to do. This speeded up production and, as more automobiles were produced, prices fell sharply.

The Model T. Ford was the first automobile to be mass-produced.

The Spanish–American War (1898)

War broke out between the United States and Spain in 1898 after the USS Maine (above) was sunk in Havana harbor in Cuba during the Cuban struggle for independence from Spain. The United States navy easily defeated the Spanish. In the peace agreement that followed, Cuba gained its independence and the United States took control of Spain's former territories.

After the California Gold Rush of 1848, people wanted a faster route from the East Coast to the West. The Panama Canal project was started by a French engineer in 1879, but was stopped in 1889. The United States took it up in 1903 during the presidency of Theodore Roosevelt, shown here symbolically digging.

The Panama Canal

In 1903 the United States helped Panama secure independence from Colombia in return for long term control of the Panama Canal Zone. Construction began in 1904 and the canal opened to traffic in 1914, making a journey from East to West faster and easier. About 50 mi. (82 km) long, the Canal links the Caribbean Sea and the Pacific Ocean. Locks lift or lower ships from one level to the next.

immigrants arrive in USA.
1906 T. Roosevelt wins Nobel | Peace Prize for making peace between Russia and Japan. | **1913** Henry Ford sets up first assembly line in Detroit. | **1914** Panama Canal opens.
1917 USA enters World War I. | **1920** USA is world's leading industrial nation.

continued to increase as more and more immigrants arrived from Europe and other parts of the world. The cities in the northeast expanded as trade, industry, and commerce increased.

By 1900 the United States was the richest country in the world, producing more food than it needed and exporting goods to all parts of the globe. Not everyone shared in this wealth, however. Most workers in the booming cities were no better off than their counterparts in Europe, while African Americans had little chance of improving their lives. Worst off were the Native Americans, who had been driven from their own territories and forced by the government to live on reservations, while their land was sold to settlers.

1. The Teddy Bear was named after President Theodore "Teddy" Roosevelt.

SEE ALSO
p. 168 THE UNITED STATES OF AMERICA
p. 182 NORTH AMERICA INDUSTRIALIZES
p. 184 EXPANSION OF THE USA
p. 186 THE AMERICAN CIVIL WAR

Emergence of the USA

As peace returned after the Civil War (1861–65), industry and the economy of the United States began to grow again. The country also expanded geographically, buying Alaska from the Russians in 1867, and gaining overseas territories after defeating Spain in the Spanish–American War of 1898. At the same time, large numbers of immigrants arrived from all over the world. Some came to work in the factories of the northeast; others joined the steady stream of pioneers crossing the Great Plains to settle in the West. In 1917, after years of isolationism, the United States was drawn into World War I. When peace was declared in 1918, the United States had established itself as a major world power.

USA TERRITORIAL GAINS BETWEEN 1867–1916.

ALASKA
UNITED STATES
HAWAIIAN ISLANDS
GUAM
PHILIPPINES
CUBA
PANAMA CANAL ZONE
PUERTO RICO

Territorial acquisitions

During the 19th century the United States developed its western frontier. It bought Alaska from Russia in 1867 for $7.2 million and took control of Cuba, Puerto Rico, Guam, and the Philippines, after defeating Spain in 1898. In the same year it acquired the Hawaiian Islands and in 1903 it gained the Panama Canal Zone. In 1917 it purchased the Danish West Indies.

Alaska

The first Europeans to settle in Alaska were Russian fur traders in 1784. From 1799 to 1867 the Russian-American Company controlled trade. The cartoon (left) shows the US secretary of the interior negotiating with the Russians for the purchase of Alaska.

Advertising

The advertising industry grew quickly during the early 20th century. Advertisements appeared not only in newspapers and magazines, but also on colorful billboards and posters (left). Uncle Sam (above) became a popular symbol for American goods.

Land of opportunity

The United States attracted immigrants from all over the world, especially Europe. They saw it as a land of opportunity; its symbol was the huge Statue of Liberty holding a torch of freedom (left), erected in New York harbor in 1886.

Baseball

Baseball first became popular among soldiers in the American Civil War. Professional players started to appear after the war ended. By 1876 baseball was a national sport with teams organized into leagues and star players treated like heroes.

Teddy Roosevelt

Theodore Roosevelt was president of the United States from 1901 to 1909. Taking a moral approach to politics, his Square Deal program helped ordinary people by improving labor conditions and food quality. He was also keen to conserve the nation's natural resources.

The Industrial Workers of the World (founded 1905) became a revolutionary organization in 1908. It had most support in the mining and timber industries.

Unions and Socialism

The American Socialist Party showed its contempt for the capitalist system in this cartoon showing the workers supporting everyone else. Only a small proportion of the workforce ever joined trade unions, however.

New France

The St Lawrence River, the gateway to Canada, was explored by Jacques Cartier, who sailed as far as modern Montreal in 1535. Fishermen and fur traders followed him, but permanent French settlement did not begin until Champlain arrived in "New France" in 1603. He spent his first years in Canada exploring its rivers and lakes searching for the best sites for colonies. In 1613, the king of France, Louis XIII, appointed him commandant of New France.

Samuel de Champlain (1567–1635) was the "father" of New France. He founded Quebec (1608), laid the basis of the fur-trading system, and encouraged permanent settlement.

Anglo-French rivalry

The Hudson's Bay Company in 1670 was formed when two French traders, fed up with the high French taxes on fur, fled to New England. From there they went to London where they persuaded English merchants to set up the Company in an attempt to gain control of the Canadian fur trade. The ensuing rivalry between England and New France continued for over a century.

French Franciscan friar, Father Hennepin, raises his arms to bless the Niagara Falls. Hennepin was probably the first white person to see the falls.

1763 – France cedes all of Canada to Britain

In the Anglo-French war (1754–63) the British supported the colonies against France. (This war was known in North America as the French and Indian War and in Europe as the Seven Years' War.) British military successes began in 1785 when they captured and razed Louisbourg. With the surrender of Montreal to General Amherst in 1760, the conquest of Canada by Britain was completed. On February 10, 1763, the Treaty of Paris was signed which removed all French claims to land in North America. Britain was then left with a large and rather reluctant group of French-Canadian settlers.

The war of 1812

The United States and the British North American colonies in Canada went to war in 1812 because of rivalry over the fur trade and the advancing US frontier. However, the main reason they fought was for the control of Canada. The war ended with no clear victor, although it did confirm the boundary between Canada and the US.

US-British rivalry continued after the war of 1812. Right: Fatally wounded, James Lawrence, the captain of the American frigate Chesapeake, is carried below decks by his crew to die (1813).

The British finally seized the city of Quebec (left) after the famous Battle of the Plains of Abraham in 1759.

1500 onward European cod-fishing fleets visit Newfoundland. **1534** France claims Canada. **1608** Quebec founded. **1650** Company of New France formed. **1670** Hudson's Bay Company formed. **1713** Queen Anne's War, first French losses. **1763** Treaty of Paris, French expelled from North

Canada

Canada was inhabited by Native American and Inuit peoples before the arrival of Europeans. After Cabot's landing in 1497, European fishing fleets came to catch the cod off the coast and explorers traveled inland on the rivers and bays. Although the French laid claim to Canada in 1534, serious settlement did not begin until the mid-16th century. By the end of the century the French and the British were fighting for control of Canada. The rivalry continued for over a century, until the French were expelled from North America in 1763 after the French and Indian War (Seven Years' War). The colonies of British Canada continued to flourish until they were united in 1867. After confederation, Canada embarked on a westward expansion and internal development not unlike that of the United States.

1

The original inhabitants of the territories we now call Canada were the Inuits and the Native Americans. The latter were divided into quite distinct cultural groups, such as the settled Northwest Coast people or the migratory tribes of the Eastern Woodlands. The Inuits were far fewer in number and they shared a common culture based on hunting.

The first Europeans to discover the northern sea route to North America were the Norsemen in about 1000 AD. Their journeys are recorded in the Icelandic sagas and recent archeological evidence discovered in Newfoundland has

confirmed that they lived there, at least for a time.

Almost 500 years later, in 1497, an Italian explorer, known in English as John Cabot, landed in Newfoundland. Cabot followed a very direct route to North America and some people have suggested that he had local knowledge from fishermen on the east coast of England who had probably been fishing off the coast of Canada for centuries.

In 1534 the Frenchman Jacques Cartier explored the St. Lawrence River. He told the king of France to set up colonies there. But, even though the French were anxious to gain territories in the New World, their first attempts at founding

SEE ALSO
p. 60 ANCIENT NORTH AMERICA
p. 120 COLONIAL NORTH AMERICA
p. 168 THE UNITED STATES OF AMERICA
p. 198 COLONIALISM

Map legend:
- Canada, 1867
- Territory added 1870
- Province added by 1873
- Territory added 1880
- British crown colony
- Canadian territorial claim surrendered to USA

Russian and Canadian traditions mingle on the islands between North America and Asia. This Orthodox priest (above) is blessing a local fishing fleet.

The Dominion of Canada

The expansion of the United States to the south caused the Canadians to press for coast-to-coast union to ensure national security. In 1867 the British North America Act united Nova Scotia, New Brunswick, Quebec, and Ontario in the self-governing dominion of Canada. Manitoba joined in 1870, British Columbia in 1871, and Prince Edward Island in 1873. Ottawa was chosen as the capital of the new dominion and Sir John A. MacDonald was appointed its first prime minister.

The Land rush

Immigrants rushed to settle the prairies in western Canada. As their numbers grew, the territories were extended both to the west and the north. Two new provinces – Alberta and Saskatchewan – were created in 1905. Both provinces extended northward to the 60th parallel.

Quebec became the capital city of Lower Canada (later Quebec province) in 1791. The Château Frontenac (right) is named after Louis de Baude Frontenac (1622–98), governor of New France.

Quebec

By the terms of the Treaty of Paris in 1763, all land east of the Mississippi passed to the British. Although the province of Quebec fell into this area, a special Quebec Act in 1774 allowed this region to keep French as a native language (along with English). It also recognized the Roman Catholic Church. The modern province of Quebec maintains these traditions today.

Gold fever and mineral wealth

In 1896 gold nuggets were found near a tributary of the Yukon River, called the Klondike Creek. A great gold rush began the following year, with miners streaming north from the US. But Canada was also rich in other minerals, including copper, lead, zinc, nickel, silver and coal. in the end these were far more important for the Canadian economy than the gold rush.

Klondike was the last of the great gold rushes. Stories of the difficult climb over the Chilkoot Pass and of the red-coated Mounties keeping law and order became legends.

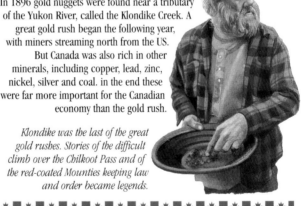

America. **1812** Anglo-American war between US and British North America. **1818** 49th parallel agreement creates undefended US-Canadian border to Rockies. **1867** Dominion of Canada formed. **1885** Canadian Pacific Railroad links east and west Canada. **1896** Klondike gold rush.

---

colonies in Canada did not succeed. It was not until the early 1600s that permanent settlements were established. In 1608 Samuel de Champlain founded Quebec as a market town for the lucrative fur trade. The Company of New France was formed in about 1650 to manage the fur trade.

The English formed the Hudson's Bay Company in 1670 in response to French activity. They wanted to control the fur trade in the Hudson Bay. The resulting rivalry for control of Canada lasted until 1763 when the French were finally ousted.

In 1791 Britain divided the colony into Upper and Lower Canada and extended British institutions and rights to both. The French population of Lower Canada rebelled in 1837. The two provinces were united in 1841 and had gained self-government by 1848. Like their neighbors to the south, the Canadians expanded westward. By the mid-1800s Britain was tired of defending them and in 1867 the dominion of Canada came into being.

Canada continued to grow and was a thriving and prosperous nation as it entered the 20th century. However, conflict between the British and French inhabitants continued. Louis Riel led several rebellions against the British in western Canada which, although unsuccessful, gave the French a hero and a martyr.

1. Bronze pin of Viking origin, found in Newfoundland. Vikings settled briefly at L'Anse-aux-Meadows in about AD 1000.

2. The Royal Canadian Mounted Police, known as Mounties, were founded in 1783 to protect Native Americans in Alberta against unruly US traders.

3. The Inuit people survived to the present, although very few live in traditional ways.

1840–50 First wave of mass
European emigration to the USA.

1845–48 Potato famine in Ireland
creates more than one million

emigrants. **1867** Transportation
of convicts to penal settlements

in Australia ends. **1881–82**
Persecution leads to mass

emigration of Jews from Russia.
1882 US immigration forbids

Out of Europe

During the 19th century the overall population of Europe more than doubled to about 420 million, and in many parts of the continent the increase was much higher. During the course of the century many people began to feel that they could make a better life for themselves on another continent and decided to emigrate. Some did so because they were persecuted as a result of their religious or political beliefs, while others simply felt that life was so difficult that they and their families had nothing to lose by leaving. In the first half of the century most European emigrants came from Britain and Germany; later they were joined by others from Italy, Scandinavia, and the Balkans. In the USA the flood of immigrants rose so sharply that the authorities felt they had to try and stem it.

In this 1880s cartoon by Joseph Keppler, the United States is shown as a safe, generous haven for all those who wish to enter. Cartoons such as this appeared in print to remind people of how it used to be before restrictive laws against immigration were brought in. The welcoming sign beside the door reads: "Free education, free land, free speech, free ballot, free lunch."

Percentages of people leaving the countries of Europe between the years 1846 and 1915.

1846–50	
1851–55	
1856–60	
1861–65	
1866–70	
1871–75	
1876–80	
1881–85	
1886–90	
1891–95	
1896–1900	
1901–05	
1906–10	
1911–15	

Many emigrant families were forced to sell most of their possessions to raise the money for their fare.

Dringende Warnung an auswandernde Mädchen!

Nimm keine Stellung im Auslande an, ohne sichere Erkundigung! Wende Dich in Not und Gefahr an den Kapitän dieses Schiffes!

EMIGRATION 1846–1915.

- Great Britain
- Germany
- France
- Portugal
- Italy
- Sweden
- Norway
- Spain
- Austria-Hungary
- Russia
- Other countries

Brazil and Argentina

Portuguese colonists had been settling in Brazil since the 16th century. From the mid-19th century the mix of Native American, Portuguese, and African peoples was added to by many thousands of immigrants from Germany, Italy, and other European countries. The European influx continued as 3.6 million European migrants entered Brazil between 1880 and 1915. Huge numbers of immigrants also entered the former Spanish colony of Argentina, as well as other smaller South American countries.

This German poster warns girls emigrating not to accept any position without first making detailed inquiries. "If in need or danger," it reads, "apply to the captain of this ship." The poster was issued at the beginning of the 20th century by the German branch of the International Campaign against the White Slave Trade.

During the early years of the 20th century, US immigrants increasingly came from the troubled regions of southern and eastern Europe. These five portraits show just how wide the mix was.

Jewish Man from Armenia, where people suffered terribly from war and persecution.

Youth from Finland, which was under the rule of Russia.

Woman from Syria, which was trying to free itself from the weakened Ottoman Empire.

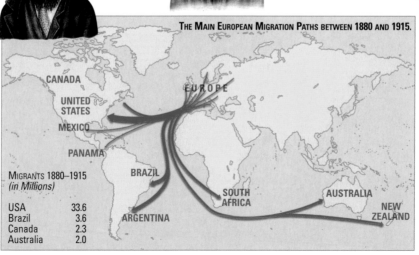

THE MAIN EUROPEAN MIGRATION PATHS BETWEEN 1880 AND 1915.

CANADA
UNITED STATES
MEXICO
PANAMA
BRAZIL
SOUTH AFRICA
ARGENTINA
EUROPE
AUSTRALIA
NEW ZEALAND

MIGRANTS 1880–1915 (in Millions)

USA	33.6
Brazil	3.6
Canada	2.3
Australia	2.0

Woman from Albania, which was under Ottoman rule until 1912, before gaining independence during the First Balkan War.

Elderly woman from the Czech region of Austria-Hungary. Czechoslovakia came into existence immediately after the First World War.

SEE ALSO
p. 172 THE INDUSTRIAL REVOLUTION IN EUROPE
p. 200 AUSTRALIA AND NEW ZEALAND
p. 208 CANADA

entry to "any convict, lunatic, or idiot." **1890** Irish population of New York is double that of Dublin. **1892** Ellis Island immigration center opens in New York. **1901** Australia becomes a Commonwealth. **1910** Angel Island immigration center opens in San Francisco. **1924** US Immigration Act.

Ellis Island

The US government began using Ellis Island in New York Harbor as a reception center for immigrants in 1892. All newcomers were questioned in the main building on the island and examined by doctors. Altogether more than 12 million people first entered the United States via Ellis Island, which was conveniently close to the Statue of Liberty – first unveiled in 1886. The island's busiest years were between 1918 and 1924, but the immigration station did not close completely until 1954. Today the island is a museum.

There were health checks on immigrants to the USA. Only healthy people were allowed to stay, and those who were suffering from any serious or infectious diseases were sent back.

The charts show the percentage of immigrants arriving in different parts of the Americas over three periods between 1901 and 1915.

1901–05   1906–10   1911–15

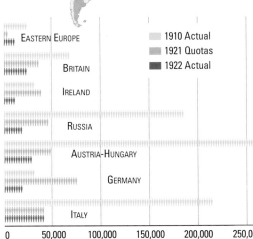

	1910 Actual
	1921 Quotas
	1922 Actual

EASTERN EUROPE

BRITAIN

IRELAND

RUSSIA

AUSTRIA-HUNGARY

GERMANY

ITALY

0   50,000   100,000   150,000   200,000   250,000

IMMIGRATION TO THE US, BEFORE AND AFTER LEGISLATION.

These New York strikers' placards are written in a number of different languages. Many immigrants had little or no knowledge of English. Those who made no attempt to learn alienated others who had been in the country longer.

Not all emigrants traveled in cramped conditions. Wealthier people crossed the world's oceans on luxurious liners, eating fine food on the best china, and sleeping in spacious private cabins. The new ocean liners of the early 20th century were like vast floating hotels, with ballrooms, swimming pools, and sports courts.

US limits

In the last 20 years of the 19th century, more than 9 million people entered the United States. The sheer numbers of the new arrivals began to worry some and in 1921 Congress set limits on how many people could enter the country. The limits were in the form of a quota: the number of aliens who could emigrate to the US each year was limited to three percent of the number of that nationality already in the US in 1910. At the time almost three-quarters of foreign-born US citizens came from Britain, Ireland, and Germany, so the quotas were particularly aimed at those from southern and eastern Europe, the so-called "new" immigrants. The quota law of 1921 had an immediate effect. It was followed up by the Immigration Act of 1924, which limited the number of immigrants from outside the western hemisphere to about 150,000 a year.

The Titanic

In 1912 the Titanic was the world's largest, fastest, and most luxurious ship, and it was thought to be unsinkable. However, the famous ocean liner struck an iceberg off the North American coast in the early hours of April 15. At first the crew thought that the damage was slight, but about two hours later the ship plunged to the bottom of the Atlantic and 1,500 people drowned. There had not been enough room for everyone in the lifeboats, and many of those who drowned were emigrants who had been planning to start a new life in the USA.

This US inspection card was issued to a passenger from Liverpool in 1913.

About one person in ten left Europe between 1850 and 1914. It was the largest population movement of all time, involving more than 50 million people. A few emigrants went to Australia and New Zealand, but the vast majority ended up in the Americas.

The first wave of mass European emigration – mainly of Germans and Irish – to the USA occurred between 1840 and 1850. It was caused by economic hardship, and in the case of Ireland, by the potato famine. Due to a blight, the Irish potato crop failed between 1845 and 1848. About one million people died of hunger and another million emigrated.

Many impoverished Europeans were attracted to the New World by the discovery of gold. The California gold rush of 1848 made headlines around the world, and the discovery of gold in New South Wales, Australia, in 1851, and in Otago, New Zealand, in 1861, stimulated interest in migrating there too.

The main incentives for Europeans, especially Britons, to emigrate to Australia and New Zealand were the cheap fares offered by shipping lines and the expected high standard of living when they arrived. When refrigerated holds were introduced to steamships in 1882, it meant that meat and dairy produce could be shipped in bulk back to Europe, which enriched the economies of the Antipodes and South America.

In Victorian Britain, some wealthy liberals and charities helped poor people move to British colonies; this was not pure altruism – it was cheaper than paying for the poor to be kept in workhouses. Australia also offered free transport to families with useful skills.

In the 1880s economic problems in newly united Italy led many southern Italians to emigrate to North and South America. Canada received its fare share of migrants. The Canadian Pacific Railway was completed in 1885, and the new transcontinental railroad led to a rush to settle Canada's western prairies.

1899 Freud's *Interpretation of Dreams* published.
1901 First vacuum cleaner.
1901 First Nobel Prizes

awarded in Oslo, Norway.
1904 Revived *Entente Cordiale*

between Britain and France.
1906 Morocco crisis ends in

compromise. **1906** A British government publication states

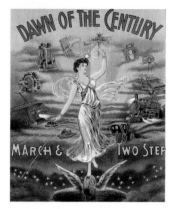

A record cover from 1900 shows technology at the time; railroads were the main form of transportation and cars were in their infancy.

Dawn of the 20th Century

In the early 20th century Europe, especially Western Europe, seemed unusually peaceful and prosperous. Except among the tangled nationalities of Eastern Europe, the continent had settled into a system of nation states, some of them (like France and Britain) long-established, others (such as Italy and Germany) recent. Although the past century had not been free of wars, no general European war had been fought since the defeat of Napoleon in 1815. In North America the United States had recovered from the Civil War and was growing with astonishing rapidity. Immigrants from Europe flocked to the region and the economy was vibrant. In Asia, Japan was expanding rapidly too, while China was in the grips of becoming a republic.

Europe was at the height of its power and influence at the beginning of the 20th century. It was the economic, intellectual, and artistic center of the world, and when people spoke of "the civilized world" they meant Europe and countries of European origin (notably the USA). The rest of the world was either dominated by Europeans, as in most of Africa and Asia, or guided by European ideas and values.

People generally believed in the march of progress, and expected a continual rise in their standard of

This French poster titled "Revenge" records the bitter memory of the loss of Alsace-Lorraine to the Germans in 1871. French hostility to Germany was an unchanging ingredient in international relations from 1871 to 1914.

France
Along with others, France was prospering. The Third Republic was firmly established, though the economy was growing at a relatively slower rate than France's neighbors. No longer Europe's leading power, France was divided by the Dreyfus Affair and a series of political scandals. She compensated for her reduced status in Europe by a burst of empire-building in Africa (in competition with Britain) and Southeast Asia.

Germany
After 1890, Germany seemed intent on exercising its new muscle by dominating Europe and challenging the imperial powers, chiefly Britain and France. By 1910 its steel production was double Britain's; by 1914 its army was the largest and best-trained in Europe. At home the emperor blocked all progress towards democracy – the Reichstag (parliament) had little real power – and opposition was growing.

The German emperor, Wilhelm II (reigned 1888–1918), was determined to lead the government himself. Keen intelligence and strong character were required, but Wilhelm had neither.

Britain
British foreign policy was guided chiefly by imperial concerns, especially the need to maintain safe communications with India. Germany's challenge to British naval and imperial supremacy encouraged the *Entente Cordiale*, an alliance with the old enemy, France, the only other genuine democracy among the great powers. It was followed by the Triple Entente that included another old opponent, Russia.

The veteran Habsburg emperor, Franz Josef (reigned 1848–1916), discusses Balkan policy with his ministers.

Russia
Russia experienced rapid industrialization and scientific progress in the late 19th century, and it had large reserves of manpower. But it was still backward compared with Western Europe, and it was badly shaken by defeat by Japan and the Revolution of 1905. The czarist regime seemed increasingly unstable. When Russian relations with Germany soured after 1887, Russia was naturally drawn towards a defensive alliance with France.

Laying an oil pipeline in Iran: preserving the interests of the Anglo-Persian Oil Company (founded 1909), was another imperative in British foreign policy.

Serbs in traditional dress. The Serbs, who had been under foreign rule for most of their history, were fired by nationalism and dreams of a Greater Serbia.

Russia (in the person of Nicholas II) pays court to France: a satirical cartoon.

Austria-Hungary
The Austrian Empire had shrunk since the days of the Holy Roman Empire, but it still commanded large resources (and it was still ruled by a Habsburg emperor). As a conservative power, it was wary of republican France, and it feared Russia's efforts to increase its influence in the Balkans. With Great Britain also linked to France and Russia, Austria's natural ally was Germany, with which German Austrians shared a common culture.

The Balkan Wars
In 1912 the Balkan League (Greece, Serbia, Montenegro, and Bulgaria), encouraged by Russia, captured the remaining Turkish territory in southeast Europe (except Istanbul). At the Treaty of London the European powers mediated a settlement favoring Bulgaria. Serbia and Greece formed a dissatisfied alliance. Bulgaria struck first but was defeated in the second Balkan War. The larger Serbia that resulted was seen as a threat to Austria, which had already annexed Bosnia-Herzegovina (1908) to prevent a Serbian takeover there.

that the British Empire has over 400 million people.

living. Science and technology had made astonishing advances that seemed likely to continue. Between 1900 and 1914 electricity, telephones, and motor cars became common. Most people – even, at last, the working class – were better off than ever before. People were living longer, and population was rising (mainly because fewer babies were dying). Literature and the arts were especially lively, although many features of the "Modern movement" were unpopular.

Despite problems and anxieties, there was good reason for confidence. Most people foresaw a golden age, and

2

although a few feared that European civilization was heading for trouble, they did not realize that it was heading for self-destruction.

The creation of the German Empire destroyed the balance of power in Europe. Germany, which had overtaken Britain as the leading industrial power by 1900, was the largest and most powerful country in Europe. After the fall of Bismarck (1890), Germany fell into less responsible hands, and adopted a more aggressive policy. A crisis developed over Morocco (1905–06) when Germany decided to challenge the imperial powers. By 1908,

concern over national security had resulted in the chief powers forming two, potentially hostile, blocs: the *Triple Entente* (France, Great Britain, and Russia) and the Triple Alliance (Germany, Austria-Hungry, and Italy). These two power blocs were more or less evenly balanced and, despite internal conflicts and the fear of revolution, stable. The danger area was the Balkans, the small countries of southeast Europe which were in the process of finally breaking free from centuries of Turkish rule.

1. King Camp Gillette invented the first disposable razor blade in 1901 .

3

2. The fight against crime took a step forward in 1901 when the first fingerprints were taken to identify criminals in London.

3. The pizza crossed the Atlantic in 1905 when the first pizzeria was opened in New York.

Urbanization

Towns were growing, but at different rates in different countries. The drift to the towns was fastest in Germany and Britain, slower in France. The main reason was employment in the growing industries, though towns had other attractions, such as better transportation and facilities. By 1900 improvements in transport, such as underground railroads, encouraged the growth of large suburbs.

Electricity in the home was still rare in 1900. This advertisement shows a woman using an early electric cooker.

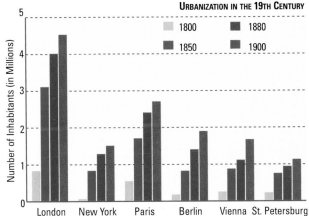

URBANIZATION IN THE 19TH CENTURY

- 1800
- 1850
- 1880
- 1900

Number of Inhabitants (in Millions) — London, New York, Paris, Berlin, Vienna, St. Petersburg

Large cities appeared in comparatively few countries. Of 23 cities in Europe with over 500,000 people in 1910, 6 were British, 3 German, and 3 French.

Freiheit-Recht-Friede!

Reformers and revolutionaries

By 1914 Europe seemed to be progressing towards liberal democracy. All governments agreed that in some way they had a responsibility towards their people. All states had some sort of national assembly or parliament, but its actual power varied: neither Russia nor Germany were genuine constitutional states. Political discontent existed everywhere. Socialism and anarchism competed for the loyalties of the working class; strikes and riots were common.

Crossword puzzles

On December 21, 1913, the readers of a New York newspaper were surprised to find a new word game in the Sunday supplement – it was the first crossword puzzle. Crosswords caught on quickly and soon became a favorite pastime with both young and old.

SEE ALSO
p. 184 EXPANSION OF THE USA
p. 216 THE SHADOW OF WAR
p. 218 THE FIRST WORLD WAR

The Modern Movement

Revolutionary changes were talking place in the arts and literature. The term "modern movement" included many other "-isms," such as expressionism or cubism, which generally rejected old values that went back to the Renaissance. They were influenced by new ideas about human nature among anthropologists, such as Sir James Fraser (in *The Golden Bough*, 1890) and psychologists such as Sigmund Freud (left), whose *The Interpretation of Dreams* (1899) marked the beginning of psychoanalysis.

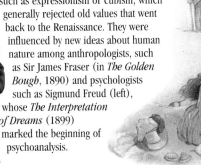

The Belle Epoque

For the well-off, this was a time of great hotels and casinos, ocean liners (including the disastrous Titanic), and regular vacations in fast-growing resorts such as the Mediterranean Riviera. Ordinary middle-class people could afford parties and dances (the Cake Walk was one dancing craze), and a trip abroad with Cook's Tours. Working-class families could be seen at the seaside, if it were not too far away, and the first movies provided a new form of entertainment that most people could afford.

The Modern World
1914 Onward

Two global wars in the first half of the 20th century (World War I in 1914–17 and World War II in 1939–45) killed millions and caused mass destruction, especially in Europe. This was followed by a period known as the "Cold War," when the world was divided between two superpowers – the Soviet Union and the United States of America – and their respective communist and capitalist spheres of influence. The final decades of the 20th century were marked by vigorous economic growth in North America and Western Europe, as well as in many countries of East Asia. Strongly linked to this was the revolution in communication systems (internet, mobile phone, laptop computers, etc.) that occurred in the 1990s. The beginning of the 21st century was marked by economic downturn and a dreadful wave of international terrorism.

Destruction of the Berlin Wall
For much of the second half of the 20th Century, Berlin, Germany, and Europe itself, were divided into Communist and Western blocs. The collapse of communism in Europe at the end of the 1980s brought renewed unity to a city, a country, a continent, and even to the whole world, as the Cold War finally drew to a close. On November 9, 1989, people came from all over Europe to help dismantle the Berlin Wall, a physical symbol of the hated division.

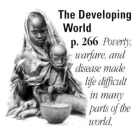

The Developing World
p. 266 *Poverty, warfare, and disease made life difficult in many parts of the world, although by the end of the 20th century substantial progress had been made in Asia and Latin America.*

Science and Technology
p. 272 *The 20th century was marked by dramatic progress in science and in technology. The benefits were especially apparent in the developed world.*

Africa
p. 268 *South Africa threw off apartheid in 1991. The rest of sub-Saharan Africa struggled with poverty, disease, and war.*

North America and Western Europe
pp. 258, 264 *The economy of the USA boomed into the 21st century, while Western Europe grappled with the problems of unifying trade and currencies.*

The Global World
p. 274 *The world seemed to shrink as frequent travel and improved communications increasingly linked people across the globe.*

Assassination in Sarajevo

In June 1914, Archduke Franz Ferdinand of Austria and his wife paid an official visit to Sarajevo in Bosnia. He was the heir to the Austro-Hungarian Empire, of which Bosnia was then a part. However, many people there wanted their country to be independent, like its neighbor Serbia, and during the visit a protester threw a bomb at Franz Ferdinand's car. It bounced off and exploded under the next car in the procession, injuring its occupants. Later in the day, Gavrilo Princip, a 19-year-old Serbian who wanted Bosnia to be united with Serbia, darted from the crowd and shot the archduke and his wife. A month later Austria declared war on Serbia. Soon much of Europe was involved.

Archduke Franz-Ferdinand and his wife were shot and killed in their car on a visit to Sarajevo on June 28, 1914.

Not everyone agreed with the war. Many women, including these delegates from the USA, joined the International Women's League of Peace and Freedom, which was founded in The Hague in the Netherlands in 1915.

Recruiting posters, such as these (below) from Australia and Germany, helped persuade young men to volunteer to become soldiers.

A new recruit being given his equipment at a recruiting office for the US army. The USA entered the war on April 6, 1917 and many men volunteered to go and fight before conscription was introduced in May 1917. Volunteers and conscripts alike joined the army for the duration of the war.

Volunteering to fight

When war broke out, it was soon obvious that both sides would need many more soldiers than they already had, so volunteers were called for. Britain in particular had only a small army, as its strength was in its navy. It had a vast empire, however, and soon men were coming to fight from as far away as Australia, New Zealand, Canada, and India.

Conscription

Before the outbreak of the First World War, most European countries had a system of compulsory military service for their young men and so had large numbers of trained men, in addition to their regular armies. Britain and its empire and the USA had no such system, however, and relied on comparatively small professional armies. When war broke out, thousands of men volunteered to fight, but the fighting was on such a large scale that conscription had to be introduced in Britain in May 1916 to keep the numbers up. From that date on, all men between the ages of 18 and 41 could be called up to serve in the army.

1882 Austria-Hungary, Germany, and Italy form the Triple Alliance. **1894** France and Russia agree to defend each other. **1904** Britain and France sign *Entente Cordiale*. **1907** Russia forms Triple Entente with Britain and France. **1908** Austria-Hungary occupies Bosnia-Herzegovina. **1913** Serbia gains more territory after Balkan Wars.

Archduke Franz Ferdinand was the nephew of the Austro-Hungarian emperor, Franz Joseph.

The Shadow of War

Throughout the late 19th and early 20th centuries, there was increasing rivalry among the industrial nations of Europe. Britain and France felt threatened by the growing power of Germany, while the Austro-Hungarian empire felt threatened by the newly-independent Serbia. Both Britain and Germany added bigger and better battleships to their navies and most nations began to increase the size of their armies in case there was a war. By 1914 the situation was very tense and the assassination of the heir to the Austro-Hungarian throne by a Serbian student was all that was needed to trigger a war which eventually involved most of the nations in Europe and many more from beyond its shores.

1

At the outbreak of the First World War, motorized vehicles such as this ambulance were still rare. Railroads were used to take men and equipment over long distances, while mules and horses were used to haul heavy guns or carry provisions and other items around the battlefields.

As German submarines made it more difficult for food supplies from abroad to reach Britain, rationing was introduced. People were issued ration cards, like the one below.

SEE ALSO
P. 212 DAWN OF THE 20TH CENTURY
P. 218 THE FIRST WORLD WAR
P. 222 THE PEACE SETTLEMENT

DON'T WASTE BREAD !

SAVE TWO THICK SLICES EVERY DAY, and **Defeat the 'U' Boat**

Nursing the wounded

Around 20 million soldiers were wounded in the First World War. Those with slight injuries could be treated in the trenches and return to the fighting, but the more seriously wounded needed the care of doctors and nurses. They were taken from the battlefield to nearby casualty clearing stations, which were usually set up in large tents. Here their wounds were assessed and they were given emergency treatment before being sent on to hospitals. In spite of this care, many died from their wounds, while others became physically disabled or mentally scarred by their experiences.

Edith Cavell, an English nurse working in Belgium, treated wounded soldiers from both sides, until she was executed by the Germans on a spying charge in 1915.

By 1917 there were shortages of basic foods in Britain. Posters like this told people not to waste food and also reminded them of the dangers that sailors were facing at sea.

Women at work

As more and more men left civilian life to join the armed forces, many women took over their jobs in shops, offices, and factories to keep the economy running. Other women were employed in the rapidly expanding munitions factories, making shells and bullets to be sent to the battlefields. For many of them, it was the first time they had gone out to work and earned money of their own.

The First World War affected the lives of large numbers of civilians, especially in France and Belgium. Many fled from their homes at the start of the war, taking as many of their possessions as they could carry. Others had to leave later when their towns, farms, and villages were destroyed in the fighting.

Ferdinand of Austria. **July 28, 1914** Austria-Hungary declares war on

Serbia. **Aug. 1, 1914** Germany declares war on Russia. **Aug. 3,**

1914 Germany declares war on France. **Aug. 4, 1914** Germany

invades Belgium to attack France. Britain declares war on Germany.

In the last quarter of the 19th century new powers began to emerge in Europe. The newly unified Germany soon became a major industrial and military power to rival Britain and France, while in the east the Ottoman Empire, ruled from Turkey, began to break up. After 1878, when it became independent from the Ottomans, Serbia also became more powerful and gained more land. The Austro-Hungarian Empire saw this as a threat and, in 1882, joined with Germany and Italy to form the Triple Alliance to defend each other in the event of a war. France and Russia made a similar alliance in 1891, while in 1904 France

and Britain formed the *Entente Cordiale* for the same reason. Three years later this became the *Triple Entente* when Russia allied itself with France and Britain.

Meanwhile Germany and Serbia were growing in strength and both countries were hungry for more land. To try and prevent Serbia from taking further control of the Balkan lands, Austria-Hungary occupied Bosnia-Herzegovina in 1908, but five years later Serbia gained more territory to the south following its victory in the Balkan Wars.

When the Serbian Gavrilo Princip assassinated Archduke Franz

Ferdinand on June 28, 1914, in protest against Austro-Hungarian rule in Bosnia, the Austro-Hungarians had an

BRITAIN·NEEDS

YOU·AT·ONCE

2

excuse to declare war on Serbia, which they did on July 28. The Russians then mobilized their armies to defend Serbia. Germany saw this as a threat to Austria-Hungary and declared war on Russia on August 1. Two days later, Germany declared war on Russia's ally, France, and on August 4 German armies marched through Belgium to attack France. This brought Britain into the war, not only as an ally of France but also because it had made an agreement in 1830 to defend Belgium if it was ever attacked.

1. Recruiting poster for the US army.
2. Recruiting poster for British forces.

Sept. 1914 Allies halt German advance at Battle of Marne.

1915 British and German navies begin submarine blockades.

April 1915 Germans use poison gas for first time; **May 1915** First Allied

landings in Gallipoli. **May 1915** Italy joins Allies. **1916** Massive losses of

Allied troops at Verdun and Somme. **April 1917** USA enters war.

The German pilot Baron von Richthofen shot down 80 Allied aircraft in less than two years before being shot down and killed himself in April 1918. He was nicknamed the Red Baron after the color of his Fokker Dr-1, shown here.

The First World War

The First World War was fought between the Allied forces, made up of Britain, France, and Russia, and the Central Powers, made up of Germany, Austro-Hungary, and Turkey. When war started in the summer of 1914, many people thought it would be over by Christmas that year. Instead it went on until November 11, 1918, drawing in other countries and costing the lives of millions of men on both sides. Apart from an Allied attack on Gallipoli in Turkey in 1915, most of the fighting took place in two main areas. These were the Western Front, which ran through Belgium and France, and the Eastern Front, which ran along the Russian border. Weapons that were more powerful and accurate than any known before brought a new kind of warfare in which both sides dug long lines of trenches parallel to each other and attacked from there, rather than fighting battles in the open. Despite the use of new weapons such as poison gas, airplanes, and tanks, the situation remained a stalemate until fall 1918, when the Allies began to be victorious.

Trench warfare

By fall 1914 the British, Belgian, and French armies had stopped the German advance through Belgium and northern France. Neither side had a clear victory, however, so a stalemate developed. Both sides began to dig lines of trenches along the edge of their territory. Running parallel with each other, they were separated by an area of ground known as "No Man's Land" which was only 45 ft. (15 m) wide in places. Extending 500 miles (800 km) from Ostend in Belgium to the Swiss border, this was known as the Western Front. Each side kept launching attacks on the other in the hope of breaking through, but little was achieved until August 1918.

Each side's trenches were made up of two parallel trenches, with communicating trenches in between. Nearest the enemy was the frontline trench, from which all attacks were launched. Behind it was the support trench, where men could sleep and eat when they were not on duty.

Both sides used increasingly large guns throughout the war. One of the largest, known as Big Bertha, was used by the Germans to shell Paris from a distance of 75 miles (120 km).

Portable field telephones were the only way that isolated detachments of soldiers could keep in touch with their commanders. If the telephone failed, then the fastest runner would have to risk his life to carry a message.

Both sides fired large shells into each other's trenches and used snipers like these to shoot at anyone who appeared over the top of the enemy's trench. The parapet of the trench protected the sniper's body, but he was always in danger of being shot in the head by a sniper from the other side.

Many soldiers spent their spare time writing letters and postcards to their loved ones at home. In order not to upset their families and to avoid army censorship, they sent cheerful messages and did not mention the terrible conditions they had to endure. Friends and relatives at home replied with postcards and letters to the front in an attempt to keep up the soldiers' morale.

Submarines

Unable to defeat the Allies on the Western Front, Germany planned to force Britain to surrender by using submarines to attack merchant ships bringing food and other much needed supplies across the Atlantic to Britain. At first they only attacked British ships, but in February 1917 they decided to attack all ships heading for Britain. In April that year they sank a total of 430 Allied and neutral ships, including many from the USA. However, this action led to the USA entering the war on the side of the Allies and, as merchant ships began traveling in convoys escorted by destroyers, the submarines became less successful and the plan eventually failed.

German submarines, known as U-boats, could sink to a depth of about 325 feet (100 m). At first this made them undetectable. When Allied ships began to travel in convoys, however, their escorting destroyers had hydrophones which could hear a U-boat's engines running underwater. This made it possible to locate the U-boat and attack it with depth charges.

March–July 1917 Last German offensives on Western Front defeated. **July–Nov. 1917** Battle of Passchendaele. **March 1918** Fighting stops on Eastern Front: Russia and Germany sign Treaty of Brest-Litovsk. **Aug. 1918** Allied forces breakthrough, German army begins to retreat. **Nov. 11, 1918** Germany signs armistice; war ends.

Zeppelins were around 540 ft. (165 m) long and filled with hydrogen gas. The crew of about 20 men, including the steersman, were carried in a gondola underneath the airship.

L 32

War in the air

At first both sides used airplanes to spy on each other and gather information on what was happening behind the front lines. Airplanes were also used to drop grenades and small bombs into the trenches. Once guns were fitted, they could also be used in battles in the air. The Germans also used Zeppelins to drop larger bombs on London and eastern England.

More than 10 million soldiers were killed in the First World War.

Britain declared war on Germany on August 4, 1914, and sent an army of over 80,000 men to join forces with the French to try to stop the German advance through Belgium and France. Although they succeeded at this, they could not force the German armies back, and both sides began to dig trenches from which to defend their positions. Meanwhile, in the east, the Germans were having more success against the Russians, defeating them in battle and forcing them back toward their own border, where a second line of trenches was soon set up. Battles then took the form of attacks launched from the trenches in an attempt to overrun the enemy and gain ground, but nearly every attack failed and hundreds of thousands of lives were lost in exchange for a few miles of ground. The Allied generals thought that they eventually would win because Germany would run out of men with having to fight on two fronts.

The invention of the gas mask helped save many lives on the Western Front. However, they were hot and uncomfortable to wear, and soldiers were sometimes tempted to take them off before the gas had cleared.

At first the Allied troops had nothing to protect them from gas attacks. Many died from lung damage. Others were blinded or had breathing problems for the rest of their lives.

New weapons on land

The First World War saw new weapons on land, as well as in the air and at sea. From early 1915 both sides used poison gas attacks to kill or disable their enemies, by damaging their lungs, their eyes, and their skin, In September of the following year, the British introduced the first tanks at the Somme. Although not very successful there, they were used to great effect at Cambrai in November 1917, when 474 British tanks broke through the German lines.

In March 1918, however, Germany and Russia signed a peace agreement, and Germany was able to bring many more troops to the Western Front. But new German offenses were defeated with heavy losses. By August the Allies, now supported by increasing numbers of US troops, began to drive the Germans back. By the end of October Italy had defeated Austria, and the British had defeated the Turks. The German people were running out of food and fuel, and their navy mutinied. On November 9, amid widespread unrest, the German ruler Kaiser Wilhelm II, abdicated. The war ended two days later.

1. The first tanks were used by the British at the Battle of Somme in September 1916.

To the surprise and disapproval of their officers, some German and British troops called a brief cease fire on Christmas Day 1914. They got out of their trenches and went to meet each other in No Man's Land, where they talked and shared cigarettes.

As the flags and uniforms in this picture show, the Central Powers were made up of a coalition that included Turkey and Bulgaria, as well as Germany, and Austria-Hungary.

Europe at war

The map (left) shows the European countries involved in the First World War and the two main battlefronts. The Germans and the Allied forces stood facing each other along the Western Front, while on the Eastern Front the Germans were facing the Russians. Heavy fighting also took place on the Gallipoli Peninsula in Turkey from April 1915, when Allied forces tried to knock the Ottoman Empire out of the war. The Allies were badly defeated, however, losing over 250,000 men, mainly from Australia and New Zealand, before they withdrew in January 1916.

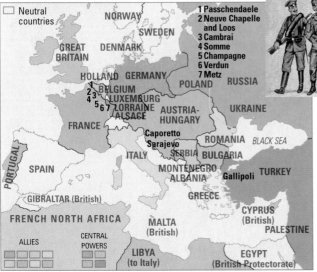

THE WAR IN EUROPE.

Neutral countries

1 Passchendaele
2 Neuve Chapelle and Loos
3 Cambrai
4 Somme
5 Champagne
6 Verdun
7 Metz

NORWAY
SWEDEN
GREAT BRITAIN
DENMARK
HOLLAND
GERMANY
BELGIUM
LUXEMBURG
POLAND
RUSSIA
LORRAINE
ALSACE
AUSTRIA-HUNGARY
UKRAINE
FRANCE
Caporetto
Sarajevo
ROMANIA
BLACK SEA
ITALY
SERBIA
BULGARIA
MONTENEGRO
ALBANIA
Gallipoli
TURKEY
PORTUGAL
SPAIN
GREECE
GIBRALTAR (British)
CYPRUS (British)
FRENCH NORTH AFRICA
MALTA (British)
PALESTINE
ALLIES
CENTRAL POWERS
LIBYA (to Italy)
EGYPT (British Protectorate)

The Russian Revolution

At the beginning of the 20th century, most people in Russia were poor and had no civil rights. They were ruled by a harsh government, led by the czar and wealthy aristocrats. The majority still lived in the country, but rapid industrialization had brought many to live and work in towns and cities. Riots and strikes kept breaking out, and in 1905 the czar promised some reforms. But he did not keep his promise and, when the First World War began, conditions worsened for the Russian people. The railroads were used to take men and supplies to the front, so food and fuel could not get to the cities. People began to starve, and there was serious rebellion in March 1917. The czar abdicated and a temporary government was set up, but this was overthrown in November by the Bolsheviks, who were led by Lenin.

1

In the second half of the 19th century, Czar Alexander II realized that Russia was lagging behind the rest of Europe, so he started a program of reform and modernization. He freed the serfs, improved education, and encouraged industrial development. Some felt that his reforms were not enough, and there were many riots and strikes during his reign. After he was assassinated in 1881, his son, Alexander III, reversed all the reforms, increased police power, and censored books and newspapers.

In 1894 Alexander was succeeded by Nicholas II, but the situation did not improve. The government remained

The 1905 Revolution

In 1898 the Russian Social Democratic Workers' Party was formed to try to improve life for the majority of Russian people. Vladimir Ilyich Ulyanov – later known as Lenin – became leader of the party's militant wing, called the Bolsheviks. Among other things, he wanted the land to belong to the people, and the banks and factories to be owned by the Russian state. He began to organize action against the government, and on January 22, 1905, 200,000 people marched to the Winter Palace in St. Petersburg, to ask the czar to listen to their complaints. Instead, they were attacked by the czar's soldiers and many were killed. Lenin had to flee and spent the next 12 years in exile.

The poor people of Russia came out onto the streets to support the Revolution. Like the Bolsheviks, they wanted an end to the poverty and injustice they had suffered under the czars.

Serfs and peasants

Serfs were at the bottom of Russian society and were treated almost like slaves. Above them came the peasants, but, although they farmed the land, they did not own it. Both groups were nearly always in debt because any money they had went to pay their taxes and their rents.

The children of serfs and peasants were nearly always cold, dirty, hungry, and short of clothes. The conditions they lived in caused many of them to die from simple childhood illnesses. Some even starved to death.

The November Revolution

After the March Revolution, most Russian people still did not have enough food or fuel. The First World War was going badly for them, and many soldiers mutinied. Support for the Bolsheviks grew and on November 7 (October 25 in the Russian calendar) groups of soldiers and armed revolutionaries marched on the Winter Palace and overthrew the government.

Detail from a Soviet painting, showing a Red Guard in the Throne Room at the Winter Palace after the November Revolution.

After the March Revolution, the new government put soldiers on the streets of Petrograd – as St. Petersburg had been renamed in 1914 – to try and prevent any further trouble from rioters or from supporters of the czar.

SEE ALSO
p. 192 THE RUSSIAN EMPIRE
p. 242 SOVIET EXPANSIONISM
p. 262 THE DECLINE OF COMMUNISM

abdicates after March (February, Russian calendar) Revolution. **1917** Bolsheviks seize power in November (October, Russian calendar) Revolution. **1918** Russia withdraws from First World War in March. **1921** Red Army wins civil war. Millions face starvation. **1924** Lenin dies and a struggle for leadership begins.

harsh, and Japan's defeat of Russia in the Russo-Japanese war (1904–05) proved it was also inefficient. When riots broke out in the streets of St. Petersburg in 1905, Nicholas II promised more civil rights for his people and a new national parliament called the Duma. However, since Nicholas, influenced by his wife and a priest called Rasputin, kept getting in the way of the reforms to protect his own rights, he never kept any of the promises he made to the people.

The unrest continued and support for political groups, like the Russian Social Democratic Workers' Party grew. When Russia entered the First World War on the side of the Allies, the czar believed that this would help to calm the unrest in Russia, but instead it became worse. The Russian soldiers were badly prepared for war and suffered huge casualties, while the enormous cost of fighting the war caused even greater hardship for the civilian population. The czar and his government became even less popular, and in March, 1917 rioting broke out and Nicholas II was forced to abdicate.

A new government was set up, but it was overthrown in July and a lawyer named Alexander Kerensky became prime minister. His government was also unpopular, and in November 1917 it was overthrown by the Bolsheviks, led by Lenin. Renaming themselves Communists, they set up a new government in Moscow and made peace with Germany. They gave the land to the peasants to work on, while the workers took control of the factories, and the state took over the banks. Civil war broke out in 1918 and lasted until 1921. By this time the Communists were firmly established and in 1922 Russia became the Union of Soviet Socialist Republics (USSR).

1. Poster of the 1917 March Revolution.

2. Bolshevik propaganda poster shows White Russians being defeated by the Revolutionaries.

3. The new Soviet Union adopted the hammer, representing industry, and the sickle, representing agriculture, as its symbol, as shown on this plate.

Grigor Rasputin (1871–1916) was a priest, but he was also greedy and scheming and told the czar's wife Alexandra, that he could cure her son of a deadly disease. This gave him great influence at court, especially when Nicholas II went to the front with his army in the First World War. Rasputin was hated by the Russian people and he was murdered in 1916.

Czar Nicholas II, his wife, and their five children were executed by the Bolsheviks at Ekaterinburg in July 1918 to stop the White Russians, who opposed the Revolution, from rescuing them.

Lenin was born in 1870 in Simbirsk on the Volga River. His family lived in comfort, but Lenin was aware of the problems in Russia. His strong personality and powerful speeches helped to persuade many ordinary people that they could improve their position by revolution. Many statues of Lenin were erected after the Revolution. In this one he is shown making one of his rallying speeches.

Lenin and Karl Marx

Karl Marx (1818–83) was a German philosopher who set out his political and economic theories in various books, including *Das Kapital*, published in 1867. This book – an analysis of the economics of capitalism – was his most important theoretical work. Marx's writings made a great impression on Lenin when he read them in the late 1880s after he had been expelled from Kazan University for taking part in a student protest there. He later based his ideas for Russia's government on Marx's teachings and hoped they would spread to the rest of the world.

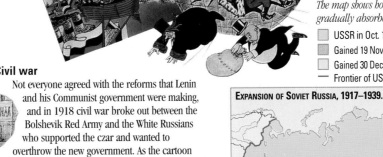

Posters were a good way of spreading propaganda. From left to right these show the Bolsheviks refusing to surrender, Lenin sweeping the world clean of capitalists, and the first anniversary of the Revolution.

The map shows how the Soviet Union (USSR) gradually absorbed many of its neighbors.

- ▨ USSR in Oct. 1922
- ▨ Gained 19 Nov. 1922
- ▨ Gained 30 Dec. 1922
- — Frontier of USSR in 1923
- ▨ Gained by 1925
- ▨ Japanese until 1925
- ▨ Other Communist states

Civil war

Not everyone agreed with the reforms that Lenin and his Communist government were making, and in 1918 civil war broke out between the Bolshevik Red Army and the White Russians who supported the czar and wanted to overthrow the new government. As the cartoon (left) shows, they believed that Lenin and his revolutionaries were destroying the spirit of what they called Mother Russia. Britain, France, the USA, Germany, and Japan supported the White Russians, but the Bolsheviks had the bigger army and finally defeated the White Russians in 1921. Over 100,000 people were killed, and around two million more emigrated during the conflict.

Expansion of Soviet Russia, 1917–1939.

SOVIET UNION

MONGOLIA

CHINA

The end of the war, as announced by the Evening Standard in London on November 11, 1918.

The Paris peace conference

In addition to the peace settlement with Germany, delegates at the Paris peace conference drew up peace settlements with Austria and Bulgaria in 1919. They also produced a covenant in February 1919 to help set up an international body that would work for world peace in the future. This was the League of Nations, which came into being on January 16, 1920, and had its headquarters in Geneva, Switzerland. The forming of the League of Nations brought the Paris peace conference to an end, but later that year peace settlements were signed between the Allies and Turkey and between the Allies and Hungary.

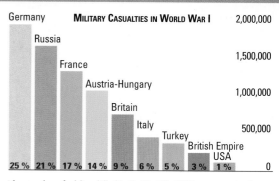

	MILITARY CASUALTIES IN WORLD WAR I	
Germany		2,000,000
Russia		
France		1,500,000
Austria-Hungary		
Britain		1,000,000
Italy		
Turkey		500,000
British Empire		
USA		
25% 21% 17% 14% 9% 6% 5% 3% 1%		0

The number of soldiers killed in the First World War was greater than in any war before or since. As this graph shows, Germany lost the most, followed by Russia, and then France. Many more were left disabled or suffered mentally from the horrors they had seen.

American and British signatures on the Treaty of Versailles, which was signed by most of the world's leaders on June 28, 1919. The master copy was kept in the French archives and was publicly destroyed by the Germans when they occupied Paris during the Second World War.

Under the terms of the treaty, the German army had to be reduced to 100,000 men and most of their equipment, such as this tank, had to be destroyed, to make it difficult for them to go to war again quickly.

Reparation and humiliation

The Treaty of Versailles blamed Germany for starting the First World War, and its terms were intended as a harsh punishment for this. As a result, Germany lost its overseas colonies, as well as losing territory in Europe to France, Belgium, Denmark, and Poland. It also had to demilitarize the entire area west of the Rhine and for 30 mi. (50 km) to the east of it. Worse still from the Germany point of view were the clauses requiring Germany to make huge payments, known as reparations, to the Allies to compensate for starting the war.

From left to right, this picture shows the American President, Woodrow Wilson, the French Premier, Georges Clemenceau, and the British Prime Minister, David Lloyd George. They had the most influence on the terms of the treaty.

Jan. 1918 US President Wilson draws up his 14-point plan for peace. **Oct. 1918** German negotiations for peace start.

Nov. 1918 Signing of the armistice ends the fighting.

Jan. 1919 The Paris peace conference starts.

June 1919 Treaty of Versailles is signed.

The Peace Settlement

When Germany and the Allies signed the armistice on November 11, 1918, the First World War came to an end but there were still many problems to be solved. For this reason, the Paris peace conference was convened in January 1919. It continued until the following January and was attended by the heads of government of Britain, France, the USA, and Italy, plus representatives from other countries who had supported the Allies. Delegates from the defeated nations also attended, but were not allowed to contribute. Its main purposes were to persuade Germany to sign a peace settlement, known as the Treaty of Versailles, and to make it difficult for anyone to start another war on such a scale in the future. Instead, it created a great deal of bitterness in Germany and paved the way for the rise of fascism there in the 1930s.

After four years of stalemate on the Western Front, the end of the First World War came quite suddenly. The German economy began to collapse from the strains of war. Defeat on the battlefield and food shortages led to rising discontent at home. By early October, the German imperial chancellor realized that his country could not win and contacted the US president, Woodrow Wilson, asking for an immediate armistice and the opening of peace negotiations. He wanted these to be based on the 14-point plan for a peace settlement that Wilson had outlined in January 1918.

Among other things, this plan proposed independence for the nations which were part of the Austro-Hungarian and Ottoman empires, the setting up of an independent Polish state, and the return to France of the French territory that Germany had occupied since 1871. It also proposed the reduction of arms by all nations and the setting up of an association of nations to try to prevent future wars.

Fighting continued for another month, however, before the armistice was signed on November 11. Although that stopped the fighting, the war was not legally over until a peace settlement had been drawn up and signed. Discussions for this started in the

This French poster is called "The Emperor Wilhelm II Is Vanquished." Wilhelm was cousin of George V of Britain and had been emperor of Germany since 1888. When Germany realized it was defeated in November 1918, he was forced to abdicate and spent the rest of his life in exile in Doorn in the Netherlands. The French were particularly pleased about this because Germany had defeated them in the Franco-Prussian War in 1871.

SEE ALSO
p. 218 THE FIRST WORLD WAR
p. 226 THE GROWTH OF FASCISM
p. 246 UN AND AID ORGANIZATIONS

Many men who had been permanently disabled by their war injuries were unable to find jobs in civilian life and were forced to beg for a living.

The cost of the war

Besides the cost in human lives, the First World War cost vast amounts of money. Governments on both sides had to pay for the large numbers of guns, ships, and aircraft that were made, and also had to pay their fighting forces, equip them with uniforms, and provide them with food and transport. France and Belgium had the additional problems of rebuilding towns and villages that had been destroyed in the fighting and reclaiming farmland that had been used as battlegrounds. Reparation payments from Germany were meant to compensate the Allies for this.

After the war, Germany was hit by extreme inflation. By November 1923 the German mark was worth so little in relation to other currencies that it cost five million marks to mail a letter, and children, like the ones shown here, used bundles of marks as playthings.

After the war, nearly every town and village built a memorial to those who had died.

Redrawing the map

After the defeat of the Central Powers, the German, Austro-Hungarian, and Ottoman empires broke up and many countries that had been ruled by them became independent states. Germany also had to give back the French territory it had conquered in 1871, and it lost the Sudetenland to Czechoslovakia. The former Russian Empire also underwent changes, with Finland regaining independence in 1917, followed by Estonia, Latvia, Lithuania, and Poland in 1918. Many of the new boundaries were disputed, however, which would cause problems later in the century.

THE POSTWAR SETTLEMENTS.

- New states
- Disputed areas
- Temporarily independent
- Turkey

FINLAND independent 1917
NORWAY
SWEDEN
NORTH SEA
ESTONIA
DENMARK
LATVIA
LITHUANIA
U.S.S.R.
IRISH FREE STATE
HOLLAND
BRITAIN
LUXEMBURG
BELGIUM
GERMANY
POLAND
UKRAINE independent 1917–20
BASQUE REPUBLIC autonomous 1936–37
FRANCE
CZECHOSLOVAKIA
AUSTRIA HUNGARY
SWITZERLAND
Kingdom of Serbs, Croats, and Slovenes
ROMANIA
GEORGIA (1918–21)
AZERBAIJAN (1918–20)
BLACK SEA
ARMENIA (1918–21)
PORTUGAL
ITALY
BULGARIA
SPAIN
CATALONIA autonomous 1932–38
GREECE
TURKEY
ALBANIA
MEDITERRANEAN SEA

Sept. 1919 Allies sign a peace treaty with Austria.

Nov. 1919 Allies sign a peace treaty with Bulgaria.

Jan. 1920 League of Nations is inaugurated.

1920 Allies sign peace treaties with Turkey and Hungary.

1923 Germany is hit by massive inflation.

Palace of Versailles near Paris in January 1919 and were attended by representatives of the Allies and of the Central Powers. The latter were only allowed to listen and, although all the Allies were represented, Woodrow Wilson of the USA, Georges Clemenceau of France, and David Lloyd George of Britain were the only ones with any real influence.

Both Clemenceau and Lloyd George wanted Germany to be so firmly punished that it could never start another war and so, when the draft of the treaty was drawn up in the spring of 1919, it was far more severe than the Germans had expected. At first they refused to sign, saying that it would not only wreck their economy but also humiliate them. In response, the Allies continued to blockade German ports, as they had during the war, bringing millions of Germans to the point of starvation.

Recognizing defeat, Germany signed the treaty in June 1919. Known as the Treaty of Versailles, the peace settlement between the Allies and Germany took effect on January 10, 1920. The harshness of its terms caused great resentment in Germany, however, and this eventually led to another world war.

1. Jubilant Londoners celebrate the end of the War from the top of a bus.

2. Copy of the Treaty of Peace signed at Versailles.

1925–1929 US stock prices more than double.

Oct. 1929 New York Stock Exchange crashes, triggering Depression.

1930 Recession starts to spread beyond the USA.

1932 Over 12 million people are unemployed in the USA.

1932 Franklin D. Roosevelt is elected as US President.

The long-term unemployed received food from soup kitchens set up around the USA.

Many European countries faced economic chaos after the First World War. Germany struggled to pay reparations to Britain and France, while countries that had fought on the Allied side had to try to repay the money they had borrowed to pay for their war effort, leaving little over to invest in industry or new technology.

Much of this money had come from the USA, where, in the early 1920s, the economy was doing well enough for share prices to start rising steadily by 1926. This encouraged people with money to spare to start investing on the stock market in the hope of

making a big profit, and this in turn pushed share prices even higher. They reached a peak in August 1929 and then started to drop.

One reason was that prices were artificially high and did not represent the true value of the companies. Another reason was that people were investing so much in stocks that they had no money left to buy the goods that were being produced, and so businesses made lower profits. When stock

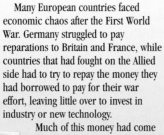

prices were still falling in October, investors began to panic and sell their shares, and on October 24, 1929 (which became known as "Black Thursday") the New York Stock Exchange crashed. The international loan system collapsed, and a severe economic crisis began. Many banks and businesses closed, and millions lost their jobs.

At first North America and Europe were the worst affected, but soon recession spread to other countries. Those

The Roaring Twenties

The 1920s are often known as the Roaring Twenties because people threw themselves into having a good time after the horrors and hardships of the First World War. Dance halls, nightclubs, movie houses, and theaters were all popular, as were eating out and traveling for those who could afford to. Improved public transportation meant that most people could afford an occasional day trip to the beach or country, while others walked or cycled for pleasure.

The Charleston was the most popular of the dance crazes that came to Europe from the USA in the 1920s. It could be danced with a partner or by oneself.

The graph (right) shows how prices fluctuated on the New York Stock Exchange in Wall Street between 1926 and 1936. After the big crash of October 1929, prices continued to drop, hitting their lowest point in 1932.

The development of commercial airlines made traveling quicker and easier in the 1920s, though sailing on a luxury liner was still the favorite method of crossing the Atlantic.

The Chrysler Building in New York is a fine example of the 1920s' Art-Deco style. Started in 1926, it was completed in 1930 at which time it was the world's tallest building.

Travel comfortably
IMPERIAL AIRWAYS
Europe — Africa — India — China — Australia

During the Depression people would do almost anything to try to make some money. This cartoon shows a formerly rich man trying to sell apples alongside a poor man and a poor woman.

Women's fashions in the 1920s were smooth and sophisticated. Dresses were straight with short skirts and looked best on a boyish figure. Hair was worn cut fashionably short in bobs or shingles and makeup became popular.

SEE ALSO
p. 222 THE PEACE SETTLEMENT
p. 226 THE GROWTH OF FASCISM
p. 228 THE BUILD UP TO WAR

that produced food and raw materials for Europe and America were very badly affected, because they lost their markets.

Unemployment reached its peak in 1932, when there were 12 million unemployed in the USA alone. When Roosevelt became president in 1933, however, he introduced a "New Deal" to create jobs and improve the economy. This helped many people, but unemployment remained a major world problem throughout the 1930s.

1. This cartoon shows the economic crisis as an evil octopus spreading its tentacles across the globe.

Franklin D. Roosevelt, US president, 1933–1945.

The Great Depression

The Great Depression started in October 1929, when the price of shares on the New York Stock Exchange in Wall Street fell rapidly. Investors began to panic and sold their shares as fast as they could. This made prices drop even further, however, and on October 24 around 13 million shares were sold for next to nothing. Many investors lost all their money in what became known as the "Wall Street Crash." A huge recession followed and soon spread around the world, reaching its worst point in 1932. Every kind of business was affected and millions of people lost their jobs.

Unemployment

The graph (left) shows the massive increase in unemployment in just five countries between 1929 and 1932. The rest of the world was similarly affected, and many people who lost their jobs in the early 1930s did not find permanent, full-time employment again until the start of the Second World War.

UNEMPLOYMENT (AS PERCENTAGE OF POPULATION).

Britain, Sweden, Belgium, Germany, USA

30%, 20%, 10%, 0%

□ 1929   ■ 1932

The problem of unemployment in the 1930s affected everyone from unskilled laborers to the highly qualified, such as this man using a sandwich board to advertise his need for a job.

Some of the people who had lost all their money in the Wall Street crash could not cope with the situation and committed suicide.

Coping with poverty

During the Depression there was little government help for the unemployed, and many had to beg to survive. Lucky ones found occasional casual jobs, such as clearing snow in winter. In towns and cities soup kitchens provided free food, while hostels provided basic accommodation for some of those who had lost their homes. Others, especially in the USA, moved to shantytowns on the edges of cities.

I KNOW 3 TRADES
I SPEAK 3 LANGUAGES
FOUGHT FOR 3 YEARS
HAVE 3 CHILDREN
AND NO WORK FOR
3 MONTHS
BUT I ONLY WANT
ONE JOB

$100 WILL BUY THIS CAR MUST HAVE CASH LOST ALL ON THE STOCK MARKET

Above: Many wealthy people invested heavily in the stock market when prices were going up, hoping to make a good profit. When the prices crashed, those who had not sold in time lost everything.

The Democrats won the 1932 presidential election by promising to kick out depression, as shown on this campaign badge.

The New Deal

President Roosevelt's New Deal was a system of social and economic reforms that helped get millions of Americans back to work. One of the most successful projects was the creation of the Tennessee Valley Authority, which helped develop farming and industry in a backward area. The New Deal also brought in new regulations for banks and credit suppliers, and gave financial help to farmers, while new welfare and labor laws improved working conditions.

Kick out DEPRESSION WITH A DEMOCRATIC VOTE

The Dust Bowl

The economic situation in the USA was made even worse in the 1930s by droughts that turned the agricultural states of the Midwest into a Dust Bowl. Years of overfarming had ruined the once-rich topsoil, and when the rains failed, it turned to dust and blew away in the wind. Unable to grow any more crops there, many farmers abandoned their homes and their land. With their families, they took what they could carry and moved to California. The story was chronicled in a famous novel called *The Grapes of Wrath* by American author John Steinbeck.

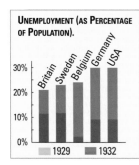

The logo of the Tennessee Valley Authority reads "electricity for all." It became a strong symbol against the Depression.

TVA
ELECTRICITY FOR ALL

The building of dams along the Tennessee Valley created many new jobs. It also helped to control floods, generate electricity, and provide irrigation.

In the political and economic turmoil that followed the First World War in Europe, many people who owned land, property, or businesses worried that the communist revolution, which had swept through Russia in 1917, might spread to other countries. Fascism appealed to them because it stood firmly against communism. Fascism also appealed to many of those who were out of work, because it promised full employment through rearmament and public works. Above all, however, it appealed to national pride, especially in those countries that had come out of the First World War feeling weakened and impoverished.

Italy fell into this group, even though it had fought on the side of the Allies, and it was the first to have a fascist government when Benito Mussolini marched his followers into Rome in October 1922 and threatened to overthrow the government by force if he was not made prime minister. The king of Italy agreed to this demand and Mussolini and his followers then terrorized or killed members of opposing political groups to make the Fascist party the only political party in the country by 1925.

Meanwhile, Adolf Hitler was starting his rise to power as leader of the Nazi party in Germany. By 1934 he had become *fuehrer* and set out to avenge what he saw as Germany's humiliation by the Treaty of Versailles. To do this, he planned to make Germany a great empire, called the Third Reich, which would eventually dominate Europe.

The Growth of Fascism

Fascism was a political movement that started in the years immediately after the First World War. It took its name from the *fasces*, the bundles of rods bound around an ax that were a symbol of authority in ancient Rome. Its leaders promised strong government and a return of national pride in countries that were suffering from the after effects of the war and from increasing unemployment. In the 1920s and 1930s, fascism had supporters in most European countries, but in both Italy and Germany fascist governments took control. Both had powerful leaders (Benito Mussolini in Italy and Adolf Hitler in Germany) who ruled as dictators and used a mixture of terrorism and propaganda to get rid of any opposition. Many of those who disagreed with fascism escaped to other countries, but many more were imprisoned or killed.

The Fascist Benito Mussolini (on the left) became "Il Duce" (undisputed leader) of Italy in 1925, while in 1934 the Nazi Adolf Hitler (on the right) became fuehrer (undisputed leader) of Germany.

A tripartite alliance

By the mid-1930s, Germany, Italy, and Japan all had repressive, right-wing governments. All three countries also wanted to control more territory and defeat communism. It therefore made sense for them to promise to support each other if war broke out. This Italian poster shows the flags of the three countries in the shape of a V for the victory they thought they might achieve by fighting alongside each other if necessary.

In Germany the National Socialist (or Nazi) party promised its members work, freedom, and bread in a time of poverty and unemployment.

As this map shows, by 1938 large areas of Europe were controlled by either extreme right- or left-wing governments. Only those colored green were true democracies.

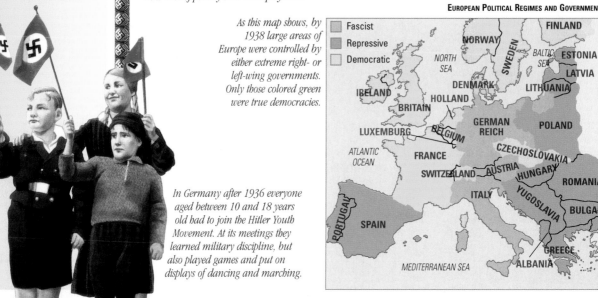

In Germany after 1936 everyone aged between 10 and 18 years old had to join the Hitler Youth Movement. At its meetings they learned military discipline, but also played games and put on displays of dancing and marching.

EUROPEAN POLITICAL REGIMES AND GOVERNMENTS IN 1938.

Fascist
Repressive
Democratic

of Germany. **1933** Spanish Fascist party, called

Falangists, is formed.
1934 Germany becomes a one-

party state under Hitler.
1935 Italy invades Abyssinia

1935 German Jews are stripped of all their civil rights.

1936 German rearmament begins.

SEE ALSO
p. 222 THE PEACE SETTLEMENT
p. 224 THE GREAT DEPRESSION
p. 228 THE BUILD UP TO WAR
p. 230 THE WAR IN EUROPE
p. 232 WAR IN THE PACIFIC

Fascism took its name from fasces, an ancient Roman symbol of authority made up of a bundle of rods and an ax, shown here supporting the Italian flag from fascist times.

Using the slogan "The Spirit of Italy," fascism appealed to people who wanted their country to be rich and strong and have an empire.

Fascism in Italy

Italy was the first country in the world to have a fascist government when Benito Mussolini became its prime minister in 1922. Three years later, he was ruling as a dictator, and all opposition had been wiped out. In addition to revitalizing Italy, he planned to rebuild the ancient Roman Empire, by force if necessary. Over the next decade he became increasingly aggressive, and in 1935 his troops invaded Abyssinia (Ethiopia) and made it part of Italian East Africa.

The swastika on this Nazi party membership badge later became the national emblem of the Third Reich. Its German name was Hakenkreuz *which means "crooked cross."*

While in prison for trying to overthrow the Bavarian government, Adolf Hitler – shown here trying to win support in a tavern – set out his political ideas in a book called Mein Kampf ("My Struggle"). It encouraged people to join the Nazi party, and became a bestseller.

China and Japan at war

In the years following the First World War, Japan changed from being a backward feudal nation into an industrialized power with a rapidly increasing population. Wanting to bring more territory under their control, the Japanese invaded Manchuria in China in 1931. Five years later, the emperor of Japan allowed his army to take control of the Japanese government. They started a campaign of massive rearmament, and in 1937 they took advantage of the civil war in China to attack Chinese cities and gain control of more Chinese territory. They treated the defeated Chinese brutally, killing 250,000 civilians in Nanjing alone.

Japanese territory 1914
Expansion to 1933

JAPANESE EXPANSION TO 1933.

Left: This cartoon represents the struggle between Japan (shown as the warrior) and the Soviet Union (shown as the bear) for control of China. Although the Japanese managed to occupy much of eastern China by 1938, the Soviet army stopped their westward expansion in 1939.

An American cartoon showing Japan breaking all the treaties it had signed. Japan left the League of Nations in 1933 after the League recommended Japanese withdrawal from Manchuria.

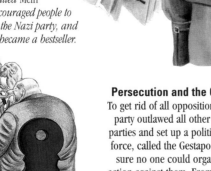

Persecution and the Gestapo

To get rid of all opposition, the Nazi party outlawed all other political parties and set up a political police force, called the Gestapo, to make sure no one could organize any action against them. From 1933 on, people were encouraged to boycott Jewish stores and businesses. Trade unionists, gypsies, and the disabled were also persecuted.

One of the most famous people to leave Germany in the 1930s was the actress Marlene Dietrich who went to Hollywood. From 1943 to 1946 she entertained Allied troops.

1936 Spanish Civil War between Nationalists and Republicans.

1936 Rome-Berlin Axis set up.
March 1938 Germany invades and

annexes Austria. **Sept. 1938** Italy, Germany, France, and Britain sign

Munich Pact and give Sudetenland to Germany.

Nov.1938 Kristallnacht: Nazi thugs attack over 7000 Jewish businesses

The Build up to War

After 1936 the likelihood of another large-scale war in Europe increased. Both Germany and Italy were determined to expand the territory under their control, and the League of Nations did little to stop them. France and Britain tried to appease Hitler by allowing him to take control of the Sudetenland, but could do nothing when he went on to annex Czechoslovakia in March 1939. At the end of that month, however, France and Britain promised Poland, Greece, and Romania that they would fight for them if either Hitler or Mussolini invaded their countries. When Hitler invaded Poland on September 1, 1939, Britain and France had no choice but to declare war on Germany.

By the mid-1930s political tension was building up in many parts of the world. In China the Communists and Nationalists called off their civil war in 1937 to fight together against the invading Japanese. In Europe the democratic countries kept a wary eye on the growing right-wing dictatorships.

Civil war broke out in Spain in 1936 between the right-wing Nationalists and the left-wing Republicans. To show their power, Italy and Germany supported the Nationalist cause, while the Republicans were supported by the

The Spanish Civil War

In 1936 Spanish army generals in Morocco, led by Franco and calling themselves Falangists or Nationalists, revolted against the newly elected Republican government in Spain. The revolt spread to the mainland and led to a bitter civil war that lasted until 1939. Men and women took up arms, and there were many civilian casualties.

During the Spanish Civil War, the Nationalists were supported by the right-wing governments of Italy and Germany, while the Republicans were supported by the Soviet Union and left-wing volunteers from many different countries.

Los Nacionales

THE SPANISH CIVIL WAR, 1936.

La Coruña • • Oviedo • • Guernica
BASQUE TERRITORIES
FRANCE
• Valladolid
Barcelona •
PORTUGAL
• Guadalajara
• Gandesa
Brunete • • Madrid
• Teruel
Valencia •
• Mérida
• Seville
• Granada
• Ceuta
SPANISH-MOROCCO

Nationalist territorial gains by:
- July 21, 1936
- Dec 31, 1937
- February 1939
- Republican March 1939
- Important battles

When the civil war broke out, the Nationalists controlled southern and western Spain, while the Republicans controlled the north and east.

General Franco saw himself as a crusader, saving Spain from communism. After defeating the Republicans, he ruled as dictator until 1975.

ES LEBE DIE AXE ROM - BERLIN

In the mid-1930s alliances of left-wing groups in France set up popular fronts to combat fascism.

VOTEZ FRANÇAIS

Anti-Semitism in Germany

Large-scale persecution of Jews in Germany started in 1935. Those who could afford to leave emigrated to other parts of Europe, the USA, or Palestine. Those who stayed had to have their passports stamped with a large J, and wear a yellow star on their clothes. They lost most of their civil rights and many were forced to live in ghettos, making persecution easier.

The Rome-Berlin Axis, an alliance between Italy and Germany, was set up in 1936.

A Popular Front narrowly won the French general election of 1936 and Leon Blum (above, left) became prime minister with a coalition government. He was firmly against fascism and was imprisoned in 1940 when France fell to the Germans.

Soviet Union, and by left-wing idealists from all over the world.

At the same time, both Italy and Germany, who in 1936 had signed an agreement to support each other in case of war, continued their programs of rearmament and planned to expand the territory they controlled. Having conquered Abyssinia in 1936, Mussolini planned an Italian Empire in Africa, while Hitler planned his Third Reich.

France and Britain became increasingly alarmed over these aggressive policies, but did little to stop them. Even the League of Nations was powerless.

In March 1938 Hitler threatened to annex Austria by force, even though the Treaty of Versailles forbade any union between the two countries. The Austrian chancellor resigned and was replaced by the leader of the Austrian Nazi party. He invited the German army to invade Austria, and so German expansion began.

Realizing there was no way they could defeat Germany if war broke out at that time, the British and the French met with Hitler and Mussolini in Munich in September 1938, and tried to appease Hitler by allowing him to annex the Sudetenland in Czechoslovakia. Not satisfied with this, however, Hitler then annexed all of Czechoslovakia, and invaded Lithuania in March 1939. Italy invaded Albania the following month.

At the same time, Hitler threatened to invade Poland at the end of the summer, even though France and Britain had said they would declare war on Germany if he did so. Hitler carried out his threat on September 1 and two days later Britain and France declared war on Germany.

1. Ordinary men and women took up arms to fight in the bloody civil war that tore Spain apart in 1936.

2. Hitler addressing a rally in Vienna in 1938, following his successful annexation of Austria.

The Nazis used the 1936 Olympics in Berlin to show off their strength and power. When the American athlete Jesse Owens won four gold medals there, Hitler refused to congratulate him because he was black.

BERLIN 1936
1-16 AUG
OL...SCHE SPIELE

SEE ALSO
p. 222 THE PEACE SETTLEMENT
p. 226 THE GROWTH OF FASCISM
p. 230 THE WAR IN EUROPE
p. 232 WAR IN THE PACIFIC

Uniting Germany and Austria

One of Hitler's early ambitions was to unite Germany and Austria, something forbidden by the Treaty of Versailles, because the other countries thought it would make Germany too powerful. But by the 1930s, many people in both Austria and Germany were in favor of a union (called *Anschluss* in German) between the two countries. In 1938 Hitler put pressure on the Austrian chancellor, Kurt von Schuschnigg. He resigned in favor of Arthur Seyss-Inquart, leader of the Austrian Nazi party, who then invited German troops to occupy Austria.

After meeting Hitler and Mussolini in Munich in 1938, British prime minister Neville Chamberlain said that the agreement they had reached would mean "peace in our time."

At 9 a.m. on September 3, 1939, Britain sent an ultimatum, telling Germany to stop its attack on Poland. When no reply was received by 11 a.m., Britain declared war.

As war came closer, many British children were evacuated from the cities to the country for safety. They each had a few belongings, their gas masks, and a label with their name on.

EXPRESS
SPECIAL LATE NEWS
BRITAIN DECLARES WAR

The beginning of the Second World War

As Hitler rose to power in Germany, both Britain and France tried to avoid going to war against him. Following a strategy known as appeasement, they signed the Munich Agreement in 1938, allowing Germany to take control of the Sudetenland, a German-speaking part of Czechoslovakia. In March 1939 German troops annexed the rest of Czechoslovakia, and on April 6 of that year Hitler announced that he would invade Poland at the end of the summer. France and Britain warned him that if he went ahead with this plan they would declare war on Germany. But Hitler ignored the threat and invaded Poland on September 1, 1939.

The War in Europe

The Second World War began in Europe on September 3, 1939, when Britain and France declared war on Nazi Germany. It lasted almost six years and eventually involved almost every country in the world. Over 50 million people died. Many members of the armed forces who died were killed in battles on land, at sea, or in the air, but others died of diseases or ill-treatment in prisoner-of-war camps. Many civilians were killed in huge bombing raids on towns and cities, while in the USSR many died of starvation when their cities were besieged by Nazi forces. But the largest number of civilian deaths occurred in the Nazi concentration camps where an estimated six million Jews and about the same number of other "non-Germans" were killed because the Nazis believed they were inferior.

Britain and France declared war on Nazi Germany over its invasion of Poland in September 1939, but they could do nothing to help the Poles at that time. Instead, a large contingent of the British army went to France expecting the Germans to invade from the east.

Little happened until April 1940, when the Nazis invaded Norway and Denmark. In May they swept through the Netherlands and Belgium and into France. The French army was overwhelmed, and the British army of 350,000 men had to be evacuated back to Britain from Dunkirk on the Channel coast. The French then had to

sign a cease-fire, which divided their country in two. At the same time, Italy declared war on the Allies, which included the British Empire, and Hitler planned to invade Britain with Operation Sea Lion. To do this, he first had to defeat Britain's Royal Air Force (RAF). Since his Luftwaffe (air force) had twice as many planes, he thought this would be easy, but in the Battle of Britain fought from July to October 1940, the Luftwaffe was defeated.

During that winter British cities were heavily bombed in what became known as the Blitz, but in 1941 Hitler turned his attention

1

Flying bombs and rockets

By 1944 German rocket scientists had developed the V-1, or Flying Bomb, and the V-2, which had a rocket engine. Both carried around 2,000 lbs (900 kg) of high explosives and were used against the Allies, in Britain, Belgium, and the Netherlands. Many V-1s were shot down, but the V-2s were more successful. When the war ended, both the USA and the Soviet Union offered jobs to the scientists who had worked on the V-2, which was the basis for the development of space rockets and nuclear missiles.

Warhead
Liquid oxygen tank
Control department
Fuel pump
Alcohol tank
Rocket motor

The V-2 rocket was fueled by a mixture of liquid oxygen and alcohol. This burned for 70 seconds, sending the rocket and its warhead into the atmosphere at a speed of over 1,000 mi. (1,600 km) per hour.

Tank battles were a major feature of the Second World War. The largest was at Kursk in the Soviet Union in 1943 and involved around 6,000 tanks.

The home front

Life was difficult for civilians in the Second World War. In Britain food, clothing, furniture, and fuel were all rationed to try to make sure everyone got their fair share. No lights were allowed outside during the hours of darkness, and there was a constant risk of air raids, especially in cities and industrial areas.

People handed in their spare pans, containers, buckets, and even iron railings in the drive to collect more scrap metal to make weapons, tanks, planes, and ships.

Many people built air-raid shelters in their yards from sheets of corrugated iron, arched over and covered with soil. They put in as many home comforts as possible, often including beds, chairs, and a portable stove.

Resistance groups were also active in Germany. This poster shows the White Rose group, based at Munich University.

Soldiers carried some emergency supplies with them, including dehydrated food, chewing gum, cigarettes and matches, and a mess kit and a cup, all of which fitted into a small pouch.

Right: People who had enough money could buy extra food and other items on the illegal black market for very high prices.

The Resistance

Anti-Nazi groups sprang up in the countries occupied by the Nazis. Known as the Resistance, or partisans, they worked in secret to sabotage the German war effort by wrecking equipment, disrupting troop movements, and even launching guerrilla-style attacks. They also gathered information for the Allies and helped people who were in danger to escape.

MARCHÉ NOIR
CRIME CONTRE LA COMMUNAUTÉ

WIR MAHNEN ZUM FRIEDEN
GEDENKTAG FÜR DIE OPFER DES FASCHISMUS
11·SEPT·1949

declare war on USA. **1942** Axis forces defeated at El Alamein in Egypt. **Sept. 8, 1943** Italy surrenders. **June 6, 1944** D-Day. Allies land in France. **April 30, 1945** Hitler kills himself. **May 7, 1945** Germany surrenders. **May 8, 1945** Peace declared in Europe.

In July 1943 the Allies landed in Sicily and began their long, slow campaign to drive the Germans out of the Italian peninsula. The following June Allied troops landed on the coast of France, and began to push the Germans back toward Germany. At the same time, Soviet troops were heading toward Germany from the east and German cities were being heavily bombed by the Allies. On April 30, 1945, Hitler committed suicide and Germany surrendered on May 7.

eastward. In April his troops invaded Greece and Yugoslavia to support Mussolini, and in June they invaded the USSR. It seemed that the Nazis would take control of all of Europe, but in December 1941 the USA entered the war on the Allies' side and over the next year the situation began to change. The Allies gained their first major victory against the Axis forces at El Alamein in Egypt in November 1942.

1. Container for gas used by the Nazis in the Death Camps.

2. Cup and container from an Allied soldier's mess kit.

The B-17 was equipped with 13 heavy machine guns and could carry 6,000 lbs (2,750 kg) of bombs.

There was bitter fighting in the Soviet Union after Germany invaded in June 1941. Hundreds of thousands died before the Germans were finally defeated there in 1943.

ВОЙНЫ КРАСНОЙ АРМИИ! КРЕПЧЕ УДАРЫ ПО ВРАГУ! ИЗГОНИМ НЕМЕЦКИ ФАШИСТСКИХ МЕРЗАВЦЕВ С НАШЕЙ РОДНОЙ ЗЕМЛ

This American playing card shows what happened to Hitler when he came up against the might of the Soviet Union.

SEE ALSO
p. 226 THE GROWTH OF FASCISM
p. 228 THE BUILD UP TO WAR
p. 232 WAR IN THE PACIFIC

The Flying Fortress

The British made bombing raids over Germany by night, but the Americans preferred daylight attacks. Their bombers included the B-17 Flying Fortress (above). It had 13 machine guns on board to defend itself, but was slower than the German fighter planes sent to intercept it, and so flew with an escort of fighter planes.

Shown right at the 1945 Yalta Conference are (from left to right) Winston Churchill, Franklin D. Roosevelt, and Joseph Stalin.

The Yalta Conference

Between 1943 and 1945 the Allied leaders – Churchill, Roosevelt, and Stalin – met several times to decide what would happen in Europe when the war was over. By the Yalta Conference in 1945 most of Eastern Europe was occupied by Soviet troops. Stalin promised that there would be free elections two years after the war ended, but he later changed his mind and introduced Soviet-controlled communist governments throughout Eastern Europe.

Allied troops began landing on the coast of Normandy, France, on June 6, 1944. Despite fierce opposition from the Germans, the Allies reached the German border by September.

One victim of the concentration camps was Anne Frank, a 15-year-old German Jewish girl. She and her family had hidden in Holland for two years before the Nazis found them. During this time she kept a diary which was later published.

ARBEIT MACHT FREI

Allied victory in Europe

The war started to go in the Allies' favor after they defeated the Axis troops at El Alamein in November 1942. Italy surrendered to the Allies in September 1943, and in June 1944 Allied troops, including Americans, landed in France from Britain in an operation known as D-Day.

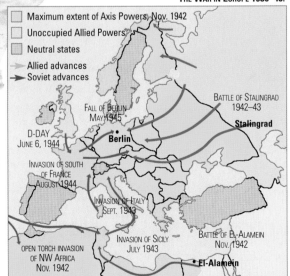

THE WAR IN EUROPE 1939–45.

Maximum extent of Axis Powers, Nov. 1942
Unoccupied Allied Powers
Neutral states
→ Allied advances
→ Soviet advances

FALL OF BERLIN
MAY 1945
D-DAY
JUNE 6, 1944
Berlin
INVASION OF SOUTH OF FRANCE
AUGUST 1944
INVASION OF ITALY
SEPT. 1943
INVASION OF SICILY
JULY 1943
OPEN TORCH INVASION OF NW AFRICA
NOV. 1942
BATTLE OF STALINGRAD
1942–43
Stalingrad
BATTLE OF EL-ALAMEIN
NOV. 1942
• El-Alamein

Dec. 7, 1941 Japanese attack Pearl Harbor. USA declares war on Japan. **Dec. 11, 1941** Germany declares war on USA. **1942** Japanese expansion begins in Southeast Asia and the Pacific. **1942** US navy defeats Japanese navy at battles of the Coral Sea, Midway Island, and Guadalcanal. **1944** US has recaptured Gilbert,

風 ● 神

Kamikaze pilots wore headbands based on those worn by Samurai warriors to symbolize their courage. The writing on this one says "Divine Wind," the English translation of kamikaze.

War in the Pacific

The Japanese attack on Pearl Harbor in Hawaii on December 7, 1941 turned the conflict between the Allies and the Axis Powers into a real global war; Japan had allied itself with Germany and Italy, and they both declared war on the USA on December 11, 1941. It also signaled the beginning of the defeat of the Axis Powers, since the USA had the wealth and power that the Allies lacked. Although Japan continued its conquests of Southeast Asia and the islands of the South Pacific for the next six months, by May 1942 the US navy was able to prevent any further expansion and by June 1945 all the occupied territories had been recaptured. Believing surrender to be shameful, however, the Japanese refused to admit defeat until August 15, 1945 after two atomic bombs had been dropped on their country.

The attack on Pearl Harbor
On December 7, 1941, around 360 Japanese bombers made an unexpected attack on the US Pacific Fleet which was at anchor in Pearl Harbor, Hawaii. They completely destroyed two battleships, sank another three, damaged many more ships, and killed about 2,500 people. At the same time, they attacked US bases in the Philippines and on Guam and Wake Islands. Fortunately the Pacific Fleet's aircraft carriers were at sea on exercises and so were unharmed.

The December 7 edition of the Los Angeles Times announcing the Japanese attack on Pearl Harbor.

Images like this one, of an American sailor killed with a Japanese sword, were published to convince the American people that they should go to war.

On July 26, 1945, the Allies warned the Japanese that they would face "prompt and utter destruction" unless they stopped their aggression and surrendered.

War in the jungle
Fighting against the Japanese on the Pacific islands and in Southeast Asia was very difficult. The climate was hot and humid, sapping the energy of those who were not used to it. Stinging insects carried deadly diseases, and poisonous snakes could kill with a bite. Thick vegetation provided good cover, especially for the occupying Japanese forces, who knew the area better than their enemies did.

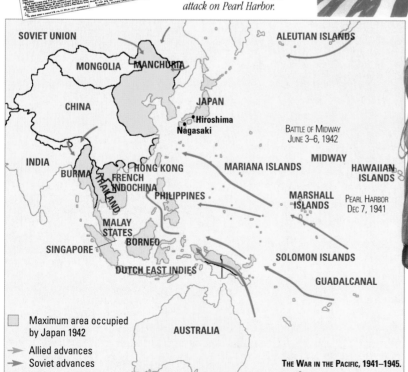

Two American soldiers showing a flag they have captured from fleeing Japanese soldiers, many of whom preferred to die rather than be taken prisoner.

Maximum area occupied by Japan 1942

➔ Allied advances
➔ Soviet advances

THE WAR IN THE PACIFIC, 1941–1945.

Japanese troops overran most of Southeast Asia and many islands in the Pacific before the US navy stopped their progress at the Battle of Midway in June 1942.

SEE ALSO
p. 226 THE GROWTH OF FASCISM
p. 228 THE BUILD UP TO WAR
p. 230 THE WAR IN EUROPE
p. 236 ASIA TO THE 1960S

Marshall, Caroline, and Mariana Islands. **Oct. 1944** Allies

recapture Philippines. **March 1945** US captures Iwo Jima.

June 1945 US captures Okinawa. **Aug. 6, 1945** USA drops atomic

bomb on Hiroshima. **Aug. 9, 1945** USA drops atomic

bomb on Nagasaki. **Aug. 15, 1945** Japan surrenders.

After the USA declared war on Japan, over 100,000 Japanese-American men, women, and children in the USA were moved into makeshift resettlement camps, even though most were US citizens and many were from families who had been in the USA for generations.

Left: Kamikaze pilots died by deliberately crashing their planes onto enemy warships to try to destroy them. They had a few successes, but most ships were able to get back to port for repairs.

Japanese expansion

Between December 1941 and May 1942, Japanese forces overran Thailand, Burma, Hong Kong, Singapore, Malaya, the Dutch East Indies, and the Philippines. They also invaded New Guinea, from where they threatened the northern coast of Australia, and many of the islands in the South Pacific.

The defeat of Japan

Japanese expansion had been stopped by the summer of 1942, but they still had to be driven out of the territories they had occupied. Bitter fighting followed, but by September 1944 the smaller islands in the Pacific had been liberated, and US forces had started to recapture the Philippines. The British then attacked through Burma, and the Soviet Union attacked through China, but Japan refused to admit defeat until mid-August 1945.

Japan must have seemed very much like an octopus pulling everything into its grasp to the people of Southeast Asia and the Pacific islands in early 1942.

The first atomic bomb was known as Little Boy. It was just over 10 ft (3 m) long, but caused an explosion equal to about 22,000 tons (21,000 tonnes) of high explosives.

The atomic bombs that were dropped on Hiroshima and Nagasaki sent huge, mushroom-shaped clouds towering 5 mi. (8 km) into the sky.

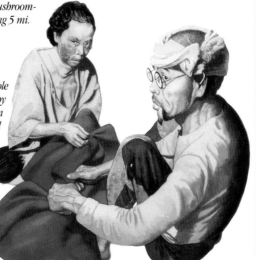

Thousands of people were killed outright by the bombs in Hiroshima and Nagasaki. Many thousands more suffered from burns and radiation sickness.

During the 1930s relations between the USA and Japan worsened. At the same time Japan became more militaristic, and in 1940 it allied itself with the Axis Powers in Europe. Its invasion of Manchuria in 1937, followed by its occupation of French Indochina in July 1941, led to the USA imposing trade sanctions. These included stopping oil supplies to Japan, which had no oil of its own.

In late November 1941 the Japanese government decided to go to war against the USA, and on December 7 the Japanese airforce made an unexpected attack on the US Pacific Fleet anchored at Pearl Harbor in Hawaii. The USA then declared war on Japan, an action that also brought the USA into the war in Europe.

Over the next six months, the Japanese seemed unstoppable, as their forces quickly overran Thailand, Burma, Hong Kong, Singapore, Malaya, the Dutch East Indies, the Philippines, and New Guinea, as well as many smaller island groups in the South Pacific. But by the summer of 1942 the US navy had recovered from the attack on Pearl Harbor and was able to defeat the Japanese navy at the battles of the Coral Sea, Midway Island, and Guadalcanal. This prevented any further Japanese expansion, and the task of recapturing the occupied territories began. By June 1945 this had been completed, but Japan would not surrender.

Then on August 6 the USA dropped an atomic bomb on the city of Hiroshima, followed by another on Nagasaki on August 9. Threatened by more of the same, Japan finally surrendered on August 15, 1945.

1

1. The atomic bomb was developed at Los Alamos in the 1940s. To set up a chain reaction of colliding and splitting atoms, an explosive charge inside the bomb fired a small piece of uranium into a larger piece at a speed of around 2,800 ft (850 m) per second.

1911 Manchu Dynasty is
overthrown. **1921** Chinese

Communist Party founded.
1925 Jiang Jiesh becomes

leader of China. **1926** Defeat of
the northern warlords.

1927 Start of civil war between
Guomindang and Communists.

1931 Communists set up a rival
government in the south.

China to 1950

After years of turmoil, the weakened Manchu Dynasty was finally overthrown in 1911. In 1912 Pu Yi, the last emperor, abdicated and China became a republic, led by Sun Yixian and the Nationalists. But continual fighting among warlords and other groups soon tore the republic apart. In 1927 civil war broke out between the Nationalists, who mainly represented the educated and middle class Chinese, and the Communists, whose party, founded in 1921, had gradually won the support of the peasants, most of whom lived in great poverty. Between 1937 and 1945 the Communists and Nationalists joined forces to fight against the Japanese. Then civil war broke out again, ending with a victory for the Communists in 1949. Their leader, Mao Zedong, became chairman of the new People's Republic of China.

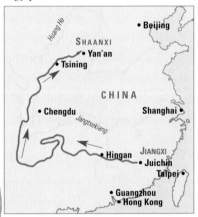

Those who wanted to modernize China by copying Western ways thought the Manchu government was weak and backward. One symbol of this backwardness was the wearing of ponytails by court officials, such as Yuan Shikai who is shown here having his cut off in 1912.

Poverty

Many Chinese people suffered from great poverty at this time. Peasant farmers often struggled to grow enough crops to feed themselves, but they also needed to grow extra to sell in the market to earn money to pay their rent, and buy clothes, simple farming tools, and other basic necessities.

Left: This poster, printed by the Red Army during the Long March, was meant to encourage peasant farmers to give food, lodging, and assistance to the people on the March as they passed through their territory.

Below: Many peasants were so poor that they could not afford to keep draught animals and so had to pull their plows themselves.

Civil war

In 1927 war broke out between the Guomindang, led by Jiang Jiesh and with their capital at Nanjing, and the Communists, who were based in Shanghai. Jiang Jiesh had hundreds of Communists executed and drove the rest out into the province of Jiangxi, where they set up a rival government. Jiang Jiesh's army began to attack them in 1933. After resisting for a year, around 100,000 Communists set out on what became known as the Long March. Fighting continued until 1937, when the two sides united to fight the invading Japanese.

Of the 100,000 men and 35 women who set out on the Long March on October 15, 1934, only around 20,000 reached Shaanxi.

The map (above) shows the route of the Long March from Jiangxi in the south to Shaanxi in the north, a distance of about 6,000 mi. (9,700 km). It took 568 days and claimed many lives.

Mao Zedong led the Long March at a rate of 40 to 60 mi. (60–100 km) a day. Many died from cold, hunger, or attacks by the Guomindang during the March.

Mao Zedong talking with a peasant in 1939. Born into a peasant family himself, he encouraged strong links between the peasants and the Communist Party.

War with Japan

Taking advantage of the civil war in China, the Japanese invaded the Chinese province of Manchuria in 1932. They were much better equipped than the Chinese and, by 1938, they had taken control of much of eastern China, including Shanghai, Nanjing, Wuhan, and Guangzhou. They remained there until 1945 when Japan was defeated in the Second World War.

1933 Jiang Jiesh attacks Communists in Jiangxi.

1934–35 The Long March. Mao Zedong becomes leader of Communist party.
1937 Japan invades China.

1945 Japan surrenders. Civil war breaks out in China.

1949 Civil war ends in victory for Communists.

By the beginning of the 20th century, China had become a poor and backward country. Its economy was based on agriculture, but most of its peasant farmers struggled to grow enough food to feed themselves. The government of the Manchu emperors was weak and much of the country was dominated by foreign powers, such as Russia, France, and Britain. Many educated Chinese people wanted reforms which would modernize their country along European lines and began to plot ways of bringing this about.

Various groups were formed, the most important of which was founded by Sun Yixian in 1905 and eventually became the Chinese Nationalist Party, or Guomindang. The Manchu government gradually lost even more control and in 1911 the Nationalists rebelled against it. They had the support of Yuan Shikai, a powerful general in the army, and the Manchu government collapsed. China then became a republic, with Sun Yixian as its provisional president. He resigned in 1912 and Yuan Shikai took his place.

Sun Yixian returned in 1916 and ruled until 1925, when he was succeeded by Jiang Jiesh. With the help of members of the Chinese Communist Party, Jiang Jiesh put down a rebellion of the northern warlords in his first year in office. In 1927, however, relations between the Communists and the Guomindang broke down and a struggle for power began. Guomindang troops attacked the Communists, who were based in Shanghai, forcing them to retreat south to Jiangxi province, where, in 1931, they set up a rival government.

Two years later, the Guomindang attacked them again. The Communists resisted for a year, but in 1934 were forced to set out on the Long March in order to escape.

The civil war continued until 1937, when the two sides united to fight against the Japanese who had invaded China. This war lasted until 1945, then the civil war started again. By this time the Communists, led by Mao Zedong, had gained the support of many of the peasants and were in a much stronger position than the Guomindang. After fighting a guerrilla war, they took control of mainland China in 1949. The Nationalists fled to Taiwan where they set up a rival government.

The United Fronts

Despite their rivalry, the Guomindang and the Communists twice formed United Fronts to fight against a common enemy. The first time was in 1926 when the warlords of northern China tried to overthrow the new government. The second time was in 1937 when a full-scale war broke out against the invading Japanese. On each occasion the United Front was successful, but the civil war started again as soon as the other enemy had been defeated.

Conditions for soldiers conscripted into the Nationalist army were very bad. Their diet was so poor that many suffered from anemia and eye diseases.

The map shows how the Communist Party gradually took control of China, from their lowest point in 1934 to their victory in 1949.

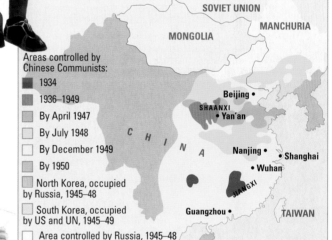

Areas controlled by Chinese Communists:
- 1934
- 1936–1949
- By April 1947
- By July 1948
- By December 1949
- By 1950
- North Korea, occupied by Russia, 1945–48
- South Korea, occupied by US and UN, 1945–49
- Area controlled by Russia, 1945–48

SOVIET UNION
MONGOLIA
MANCHURIA
Beijing •
SHAANXI
• Yan'an
C H I N A
Nanjing • • Shanghai
• Wuhan
JIANGXI
Guangzhou •
TAIWAN

Poster showing Sun Yixian, who founded the Chinese Nationalist Party, or Guomindang, and some of his army.

After invading Manchuria, the Japanese set up Pu Yi (left), the last emperor of China who had abdicated in 1912, as a puppet ruler in the province.

Victory for the Communists

After the Japanese were defeated in 1945, civil war broke out again in China between the Nationalists and the Communists. By this time, the Nationalist government was weak and divided, while the Communists, led by Mao Zedong, had gained the support of vast numbers of peasants. Moving from their stronghold in the northwest, the Communists gradually pushed the Nationalists further and further south. Finally, by October 1949, the Communists had taken control of the whole of the Chinese mainland and the Nationalists had fled to Taiwan.

Left: Chairman Mao Zedong announcing the birth of the People's Republic of China in Tiananmen Square, Beijing, on October 1, 1949.

Left: This postage stamp shows Jiang Jiesh, head of the Nationalist Party from 1926 to 1949, then head of the Nationalist government in Taiwan.

Right: This poster shows Chinese people parading in Beijing with flags and banners showing Mao Zedong's picture as they celebrate People's Republic Day.

1947 Jinnah becomes first governor general of Pakistan.

1947 Burma (now Myanmar) becomes independent from Britain and leaves

Commonwealth. **1948** Mahatma Gandhi is assassinated by Hindu

extremist at peace rally in Delhi. **1948** Ceylon (now Sri Lanka)

becomes independent from Britain. **1954** Vietnamese

Mohandas Gandhi (below) was the leader of the Indian nationalist movement from 1920. His policy of a non-violent struggle against British rule earned him the name Mahatma which means "Great Soul."

The first prime minister of India was Jawaharwal Nehru. He had been one of the leaders in the struggle for independence from Britain and made many social reforms.

Most of Asia, except China, Japan, and Thailand, was colonized by Western powers during the 19th and early 20th centuries. Apart from India, these same countries were invaded and occupied by Japanese troops during World War II.

When the war ended, the colonial powers expected to take control again, but the colonies had decided they wanted their independence back. The Philippines achieved freedom peacefully in 1946, but other countries had to wait longer or even take up arms before they could control their own affairs once more.

On regaining their independence, some countries were then divided along religious or political lines. For example, the Indian subcontinent was divided into India, mainly a Hindu country, and East and West Pakistan (modern Bangladesh), which were predominantly Muslim countries. Korea and Vietnam were both divided into a communist north and a

Indian independence

The campaign to free India from British rule expanded greatly during the pre-war period. During the war, the Indian Congress was appalled at becoming involved in a European war without even being consulted about taking part. In 1945 the British economy was exhausted by the war effort and it was unable to enforce its rule in India by force. Independence was achieved in 1947, although the country was immediately torn apart by the bloodshed of partition.

The partition of India

Religion was one of the biggest problems to Indian independence because, although the majority of people in India were Hindus, there were two large areas to the northeast and northwest where people were mostly Muslims. The British government agreed to divide India, making the two Muslim areas into one independent country known as Pakistan. This led to a bitter religious war and mass migrations as over 15 million people moved between the new states.

Right: This women is working on an assembly line in a Japanese factory in the early 1960s, making high-tech items for export.

ASIAN INDEPENDENCE 1946–75.

PEOPLE'S REPUBLIC OF CHINA

• Islamabad

(WEST) PAKISTAN 1947

• New Delhi

BHUTAN

Dhaka •

INDIA 1947

BANGLADESH (EAST PAKISTAN) 1947

MYANMAR (BURMA) 1948

• Rangoon

THAILAND

Bangkok •

NORTH VIETNAM 1954
• Hanoi

LAOS 1954

CAMBODIA 1954

SOUTH VIETNAM 1954

PHILIPPINES 1946

• Manila

Japanese recovery

The Japanese economy was devastated by World War II and, after its defeat, the country was occupied by US forces until 1951. During this time a new constitution was set up and the emperor no longer claimed to be a god. New technology was then introduced to all major industries and the economy quickly recovered.

Burma

Burma (now Myanmar) regained its independence from Britain in 1948. Its democratic government was overthrown by a military coup in 1962 and, despite many upheavals, democracy has not yet been restored. Pagan (right) was once its capital.

SRI LANKA (CEYLON) 1947

MALAYA 1957

• Kuala Lumpur

SINGAPORE 1965

INDONESIA 1949

• Jakarta

PAPUA NEW GUINEA 1975

In 1963 the Malaysian Federation was made up of Malaya, Sarawak, Singapore, and Borneo. This bird was its national emblem.

The Malay Federation

The Malayan struggle for independence from Britain started after World War II, but was not achieved easily. The Federation of Malaya was created in 1948, but it remained a British colony until independence was granted in August 1957.

communists defeat French at Dien Bien Phu. **1960s** Japan starts selling cars on world market. **1961** South Vietnamese ask the USA for military advice to combat the Viet Cong guerrillas. **1962** War between India and China. **1965** War between India and Pakistan. **1966** Indira Gandhi becomes first woman prime minister of India. **1969** Death of Ho Chi Minh.

capitalist south and both countries went through periods of bitter warfare as the two sides fought for control.

The fear of communism spreading across the whole of Asia made the USA see Japan as a possible useful ally. The Americans spent a lot of money to help rebuild Japan's economy after World War II. Japan responded well, and grew by making military equipment for the Korean War. It then went on to making consumer goods, such as cameras and watches, using all the latest technology. A period of massive economic growth followed that gradually spread from Japan to Taiwan, Hong Kong, Singapore, and South Korea. Heavier industries,

such as steel production, ship-building, and car making, followed, again using modern equipment and cheap labor with which the old industrial nations of the West could not compete. But although these countries were doing well by the 1960s, other parts of Asia were still struggling with poverty, political unrest, and civil war.

1. When the first elections were held in India in 1952, many people could not read or write and so the ballot papers used symbols to represent the different parties.

Asia to the 1960s

Between 1945 and 1960 many of the Asian countries that had been colonized by Western powers regained their independence. In the same period, the Communists took control of mainland China, Korea was freed from Japanese control, and Japan itself was occupied by troops from the USA until 1951. Some countries, such as the Philippines, achieved independence peacefully, but others, such as Vietnam, had to take up arms and fight for their freedom. In an effort to stop the spread of communism, the USA helped to restart the Japanese economy after World War II. This was achieved during the 1950s and started an economic boom which soon spread across much of Southeast Asia.

Singapore
One of the world's busiest ports, Singapore was also a major commercial and trading center. Built on an island, it was a British colony from 1824, but was occupied by the Japanese from 1942 to 1945. It gained its independence from Britain in 1959 and joined the Federation of Malaysia in 1963. Two years later, however, it left the Federation and became an independent republic.

The Philippines
The Philippines are made up of over 7000 islands, around 880 of which are inhabited. They were controlled by the USA from 1898 and occupied by the Japanese in World War II. They gained independence in 1946.

The Philippines, first colonized by Spain in the 16th century, were passed to the US after the Spanish-American War of 1898. European influence remained strong, and many people were Roman Catholics.

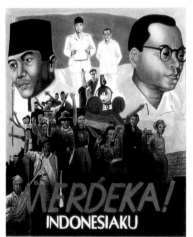

Indonesian independence
The Republic of Indonesia was a colony of the Netherlands from 1798 to 1945, when it was known as the Dutch East Indies. Following the defeat of the occupying Japanese forces in 1945, it declared itself a republic, led by Dr Sukarno, although it did not achieve formal independence until 1949. Dr Sukarno's government was overthrown in 1965 by General Suharto who set up a military dictatorship.

Indochina achieves independence
The French colony of Indochina was made up of Cambodia, Laos, and Vietnam. From 1946 to 1954 they fought the First Indochina War against the French to regain their independence. Vietnam was then divided into communist North Vietnam, led by Ho Chi Minh, and non-communist South Vietnam. The Second Indochina War, or Vietnam War, broke out between the two in 1955. The USA sent forces to help South Vietnam in 1965. Following widespread pressure at home, the US withdrew its forces in 1973. Vietnam was reunited under communist rule in 1975.

Monument to the Vietnamese independence leader and statesman Ho Chi Minh (1890–1965).

A Buddhist monk receives a gift.

Thailand
In 1939, Siam changed its name to Thailand, meaning "Land of the Free." Thailand was never a colony, although it was occupied by the Japanese in World War II. During the Cold War, the USA poured financial and military aid into Thailand. This helped to modernize the country, but traditions and the Buddhist religion remained strong.

The Korean War (1950–53)
In 1945, the Korean peninsula was taken from the Japanese, who had controlled it since 1910. The northern half was then controlled by the USSR and the southern half by the USA. This was meant to be a temporary arrangement, but in 1950 Communist forces from North Korea invaded South Korea, starting a bitter war that lasted for three years and killed four million people. The UN backed the USA in the South, while China helped the North Koreans.

SEE ALSO
p. 196 BRITISH INDIA
p. 198 COLONIALISM
p. 232 WAR IN THE PACIFIC
p. 234 CHINA TO 1950
p. 254 ASIA TO THE PRESENT

1946 Television production and broadcasting starts again.

1947 The Marshall Plan is launched to aid European recovery.

1947 First microwave oven goes on sale.

1949 Formation of NATO. **1953** Coronation of Queen Elizabeth II.

1953 Mount Everest is climbed for the first time.

After the War in Europe and the USA

As most of the world settled down to a time of peace again after the Second World War, many countries experienced an economic boom. Full employment returned, with plenty of jobs available in manufacturing, building, and service industries. Factories began to manufacture consumer goods, including large numbers of cars and televisions, using techniques of mass production which brought prices down. This meant that most families could now afford items such as washing-machines, electric irons, and refrigerators, all of which had previously been luxuries. The idea of supermarkets spread from the USA to Europe at this time, while improvements in transportation and large-scale refrigeration meant that food could be carried over longer distances, making a greater variety available all year round. There was also an improvement in living conditions for many as new houses were built to replace pre-war slums and those which had been damaged or destroyed in the war.

PROSPERITY

In the early 1950s, countries in Western Europe realized they had to co-operate if they were to prosper. This led to the founding of the European Economic Community (now the EC) in 1957.

THE FRUIT OF CO-OPERATION

People on the move

The late 1940s and 1950s saw many people on the move, especially in Europe. Some were refugees who had lost their homes, and often their families, during the war. Others were moving to escape communist rule in their homelands. People from the poorer countries of southern Europe and from former colonies in Asia, Africa, Central America, and the Caribbean moved to northern Europe or the USA in search of work, while many Britons emigrated to Canada, Australia, and New Zealand, as well as the USA.

The Nuremberg Trials

In August 1945 representatives from Britain, the USA, France, and the USSR signed an agreement to set up an international military court in Nuremberg, Germany, to try Nazi individuals and groups for war crimes. The trials started on October 18, 1945 and ended on October 1, 1946. Twenty-one of the twenty-four former Nazi leaders who were charged with war crimes were found guilty. Of these, twelve were sentenced to death by hanging, three were jailed for life, and four were imprisoned for between 10 and 20 years.

Caricature of Nazi war criminals on trial in Nuremberg. The tribunal held that war crimes were the responsibility of the individual and not just of the state.

SEE ALSO
p. 230 THE WAR IN EUROPE
p. 244 THE COLD WAR
p. 258 USA TO THE PRESENT

THE DIVISION OF GERMANY AFTER THE WAR.

- British zone
- American zone
- Soviet zone
- French zone
- Polish admin.
- Soviet admin.

This map shows how Germany was divided into four separate zones immediately after the war. Berlin was also divided into four, although it was in the Russian controlled part of Germany.

The Marshall Plan

The Americans helped rebuild Europe after the war with economic aid in what became known as the Marshall Plan. It was devised by George C. Marshall, US Secretary of State from 1947 to 1949, and won him the Nobel Peace Prize in 1953.

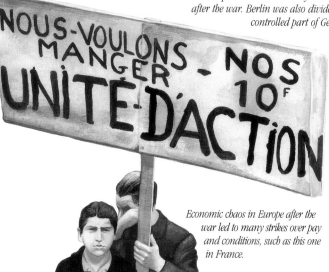

Economic chaos in Europe after the war led to many strikes over pay and conditions, such as this one in France.

After the Second World War, the USA offered aid to its Allies and former enemies alike. But first of all the countries that would benefit from it had to submit a joint plan to make sure they would all co-operate with each other. This pie-chart shows how the aid was then divided up.

AMERICAN AID TO EUROPE.

1 United Kingdom	$3,176m	7 Austria	$677m	13 Yugoslavia	$109m
2 France	$2,706m	8 Belgium/Luxembourg	$556m	14 Sweden	$107m
3 Italy	$1,474m	9 Denmark	$271m	15 Portugal	$50m
4 West Germany	$1,389m	10 Norway	$254m	16 Trieste	$32m
5 Netherlands	$1,079m	11 Turkey	$221m	17 Iceland	$29m
6 Greece	$694m	12 Ireland	$146m	**Total**	$12,970m

1956 *Heartbreak Hotel* is Elvis Presley's first hit record.

1957 The European Economic Community is set up.

1959 There are now over 50 million TV sets in USA alone.

1959 General de Gaulle becomes President of France.

1961 Marilyn Monroe makes her last film.

During the war, General Charles de Gaulle was leader of the Free French in London and a symbol of French patriotism. When France was liberated from the Nazis, he became head of a temporary government, but resigned in 1946. He was then President of France from 1959 to 1969.

This map shows the 12 original members of NATO. They were joined by Greece and Turkey in 1952, West Germany in 1955, Spain in 1982, and the newly reunited Germany in 1990.

NATO adhering countries by
- 1949
- 1952
- 1955
- 1982

President Truman of the USA signed the document that formally ratified the North Atlantic Treaty Organization (NATO) in March 1949.

The foundation of NATO

By 1945 the USSR dominated Eastern Europe and by 1948 all the countries there had communist governments. The communist parties also grew stronger in France and Italy, leading to a fear that communism might also take over Western Europe while its countries were still weakened by the aftermath of war. In March 1948 these countries agreed to co-operate to fight the USSR if necessary. But they were not strong enough to do this on their own and so, in 1949, the USA and Canada agreed to join them to form NATO.

As World War II came to an end, much of Europe lay in ruins. Millions of houses, shops, factories, and offices had been destroyed or badly damaged. So too had hospitals, schools, roads, railroads, and bridges, making it difficult for normal life to start again. To make it worse, countries such as Britain and Germany had put so much money into the war effort that there was nothing left over to pay for all the necessary repairs and rebuilding. The USA was still wealthy, however, and in 1947 the US Secretary of State, George C. Marshall, proposed the European Recovery Plan (also known as Marshall Aid) to help rebuild Europe. As a result, full employment soon returned, especially in building and manufacturing, and both Western Europe and the USA experienced an economic boom over the next decade.

There was also a "baby boom" as soldiers returned home to their wives and an above average number of babies was born between 1946 and 1948. Full employment gave people money to spare for day-trips and holidays and, as cars became cheaper, many families bought their own.

The development and spread of television began to change people's lives, while teenagers began to develop a culture of their own as the music known as rock and roll came out of the USA and spread out across the world.

It was also a time of new scientific discoveries and expeditions, including the discovery of DNA, the development of rocket power, the first climbing of Mount Everest, and the establishment of scientific stations in Antarctica.

Consumer goods

The post-war years saw a great increase in the production of consumer goods, such as refrigerators, washing-machines, and televisions, especially in the USA. Although the first television sets took up a lot of space, they had tiny screens and only showed programs in black and white. However, they soon became popular and there were one million in use in the USA by 1949. By 1953 the first program guides were published.

The scooter became a popular form of transportation after the war, especially in Italy where this Vespa model was first made in 1946.

In the boom years of the 1950s and 1960s, many Americans moved from their city apartments and went to live in new suburban homes, where they had their own backyard, space for the family car and, if they could afford it, a swimming pool. This way of life was reflected in television shows and movies all around the world.

The American film star Marilyn Monroe was the great sex symbol of the 1950s. Born in 1926, she died of a drug overdose in 1962.

The start of youth culture

The 1950s saw the birth of rock and roll. A mixture of rhythm and blues and country music, it started in the USA and soon spread to Europe. Young people especially loved it and it led to a whole new culture aimed almost exclusively at teenagers. Films such as *Jailhouse Rock* and *Rock Around The Clock* drew in huge audiences, while records by performers such as Elvis Presley, Jerry Lee Lewis, Little Richard, Chuck Berry, and Buddy Holly sold millions of copies.

In 1953 Francis Crick and James Watson discovered the structure of the molecule deoxyribonucleic acid (known as DNA). DNA, which contains the hereditary information that is passed down the generations, is present in the cells of all living things.

As this cartoon shows, many Africans believed that capitalism was tearing their continent apart and so many of the new governments tended to be left-wing.

The African countries' campaign for independence started at a time when European powers were finding it increasingly difficult to maintain their overseas colonies. Two world wars in 30 years, with the Great Depression in between, had left Europe economically and militarily weakened. At the same time, political ideas were changing and people who had fought against the Nazi domination of European countries began to realize that countries outside of Europe were also entitled to freedom and self government.

The process of decolonization began, and by the mid-1960s most African countries had regained their political independence. But European powers still had influence over the economies of many of their former colonies, providing markets for cash crops, such as tea, coffee, cocoa, peanuts, and cotton, and for minerals, such as gold, diamonds, and oil. They also influenced the setting up of governments in countries where decolonization went smoothly.

In many countries in Sub-Saharan Africa, however, democratic governments were overthrown and military rulers or dictators took control. Many stayed in power by having their opponents imprisoned or murdered. Others used bribery and corruption, which enabled them to amass great personal wealth while their countries and their people became more and more impoverished. This helped to cause problems which were still unsolved at the beginning of the 21st century.

Decolonization of Africa

From around 1950, the countries of Africa began to campaign for independence from the colonial powers that had controlled them for over half a century. Many achieved independence peacefully by the mid-1960s, but others had to fight long and hard for their freedom. Some of the bitterest struggles were in the French colony of Algeria and the Portuguese colony of Angola, where many were killed before independence was achieved. Once the former colonial powers left, however, the governments of the newly independent countries had to face up to fresh problems. As well as deciding how to run their countries and their economies, they had to raise and collect taxes to pay for things like education, health care, and the armed forces. Many also had to cope with civil wars and ethnic conflicts as the national boundaries set out by the European colonists were disputed. As a result, there was a great deal of political instability in many countries, with many coups and assassinations as military rulers and dictators struggled for control.

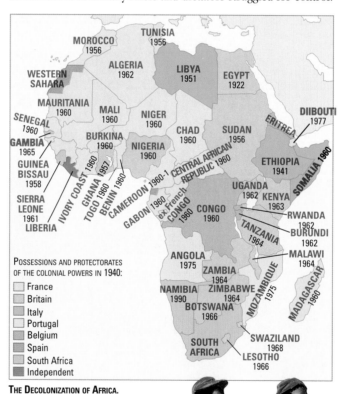

THE DECOLONIZATION OF AFRICA.

This map shows all the countries of Africa, the colonial powers that formerly controlled them, and the dates on which they achieved their independence. Egypt became fully independent in 1922, while Ethiopia regained its independence from Italy during World War II, after only six years as a colony. The Portuguese colonies of Angola, Mozambique, and Guinea-Bissau had to wait until 1975 for their freedom. Most of the other colonies achieved independence between 1956 and 1964, with 1960 being sometimes known as the "African Year" because 17 countries regained their independence then.

Above: French journal from 1911: the colonial powers believed they were bringing the blessings of civilization, wealth, and peace to Africa.

Colonial power's attitudes

Most European colonists saw Africa as a land full of riches waiting to be exploited. They also saw themselves and their way of life as superior and believed they were bringing "civilization" to the continent. Because of this, they had no qualms about taking over the land and using it to grow cash crops, such as tea and coffee, with the help of a poorly-paid African workforce.

Corrupt leaders

Some of the new leaders were as bad, or even worse, than the former colonial powers had been and used their positions for personal gain, rather than for the good of their people. Others acted as dictators, often imprisoning or killing anyone who opposed them. As a result, assassinations and coups, often by the army, were frequent, especially in the early days of decolonization. Some countries still lack stable leadership many years after independence.

Women as well as men were recruited into the Algerian National Liberation Front to fight for their country's independence from France between 1954 and 1962. Independence was finally won in 1962, following referenda in both France and Algeria.

finances building of Aswan Dam in Egypt. **1961** South Africa leaves British Commonwealth. **1965** President Ben Bella of Algeria is overthrown. **1966** In Ghana, President Nkrumah is overthrown in a military coup. **1974** Emperor Haile Selassie of Ethiopia is assassinated. **1975** Tanganyika and Zanzibar unite to form Tanzania.

Joseph Kasavubu and Patrice Lumumba (left) led the Congo to independence from Belgium in 1960. Kasavubu then became president. Lumumba became prime minister, but he was deposed and murdered in 1961.

Below: Following a coup in 1965, Mobuto Sese Seko became president of the Congo (renamed Zaire in 1971). He is said to have amassed a personal fortune, before he was also ousted in 1997.

Many African countries celebrated their independence by issuing special stamps, such as these from Ghana, Gambia, Nigeria, and Congo.

Egypt became a British protectorate in 1914, but gained independence under King Fu'ad I in 1922. Britain continued to have great influence in the country until 1952 when a military coup overthrew the monarchy and brought Gamal Abdel Nasser (left) to power. His nationalization of the Suez Canal in 1956 established him as a leader of the Arab world.

The Bandung conference

(Left) In 1955 representatives from 29 African and Asian countries held a conference at Bandung in Indonesia to voice their opposition to colonialism. Representing half the population of the world, they believed countries from the two continents could work together to achieve their independence from colonial powers. Other conferences were planned, but none took place as friction developed among the members.

Freedom movements

Freedom movements were organized in many countries during the struggle for independence. They were often formed in secret and used non-co-operation with the colonial power as a means of protest. Those who used violence were seen as terrorists by the colonial powers, however, and many were imprisoned or even executed.

Kwame Nkrumah, whose picture is shown here on a woman's dress at a political rally, used a policy of non-co-operation to gain his country's independence from Britain in 1957. Formerly known as the Gold Coast, it was then renamed Ghana.

Civil wars

When the Europeans colonized Africa, they made their own boundaries, instead of acknowledging natural or traditional boundaries between different areas or groups of people. At decolonization, this led to civil wars in some areas because people wanted to reunite their former territories which had been divided by the Europeans.

Jomo Kenyatta (right) campaigned tirelessly for Kenya's independence from Britain. Born into the Kikuyu tribe in 1894, he studied anthropology in London. On independence in 1963, he became Kenya's first prime minister, then its president from 1964 until his death in 1978.

The new governments' problems

The new governments faced many problems as they tried to change the former colonies into independent states. Most members of the new governments had no previous experience of government. They had to learn to work together to set up a new infrastructure for their country. This included organization of the armed forces, a new civil service, a system of taxation, plus health care, transportation, and education, all of which had previously been managed by the colonial powers.

Most African countries achieved their independence by peaceful means, but others had to fight for their freedom. One of these was Angola which was a Portuguese colony until 1975.

SEE ALSO
p. 198 COLONIALISM
p. 202 THE SCRAMBLE FOR AFRICA
p. 266 THE DEVELOPING WORLD
p. 268 AFRICA TO THE PRESENT

Women

As the Soviet Union tried to turn itself into a major industrial nation, both single and married women were encouraged to go out to work in factories, often doing what had previously been thought of as "men's work." As this poster shows, children were looked after in state-run crèches and nurseries while their mothers were at work and the factory canteen provided hot meals for the workers.

Women worked on the collective farms, as well as in industry. But in the early 1930s famine struck again and millions died of hunger.

Andrei Vyshinsky was a professor of law and chief prosecutor in Stalin's Purge trials (1934–1938). He was nicknamed Stalin's Hangman.

The Great Purge

In the mid-1930s Stalin decided to rid the Soviet Union of anyone that he thought was opposed to him, his ideas, or his regime. This included all his political opponents, around 30,000 officers from the Red Army, and the many peasants who had refused to hand over their land to the state to be worked collectively. Millions were sent to *gulags* (labor camps) where conditions were atrocious and many died from overwork, beatings, accidents, malnutrition, and disease.

Joseph Stalin (1879–1953) was born in Georgia and trained to be a priest before joining the Bolsheviks in 1903. He became secretary- general of the Communist Party of the USSR in 1922. By 1929 he was the absolute leader of the Soviet Union.

Monumental Moscow State University (left) was built by Stalin after World War II to honor the Soviet ideal.

Below: The caption on the placard in this French cartoon reads "We are very happy." People had to pretend they were happy with their terrible conditions if they wanted to keep out of the labor camps.

NOUS SOMMES BIEN HEUREUX

Agricultural reform

In 1929 Stalin ordered the collectivization of agriculture. Peasants were forced to give up their land and work on collective farms. Many peasants preferred to slaughter their livestock and grow only enough food for themselves. When this food was requisitioned, millions died of hunger.

1922 Stalin secretary-general of the Communist Party of the USSR. **1924** Death of Lenin. Power struggle between Stalin and Trotsky begins. **1929** First Five-Year Plan for industrial growth. **1932** Two years of famine in which millions die. **1933** Start of the Great Purge of all Stalin's opponents. **1939** Stalin signs non-

Soviet Expansionism

After Lenin died in 1924, there was a struggle for power between Joseph Stalin and Leon Trotsky, who had led the Red Army to victory in the civil war. By 1929 Stalin had won and Trotsky went into exile. Ruling like a dictator, Stalin set out to modernize industry and agriculture in the USSR with a series of Five Year Plans. The plans for industry were largely successful and industrial production was vastly increased, but the plans for agriculture were a disaster and millions died in the famines of 1932–33. Millions more were killed or sent to labor camps in the 1930s because they were opposed to Stalin and his ideas, but by the time of his death in 1953 he had turned the USSR into a modern industrial nation and made it one of the world's two superpowers.

While Lenin was alive, Leon Trotsky was the second most important man in the USSR. He had played an important role in the Russian Revolution and in the civil war that followed and was expected to become leader of the USSR when Lenin died in 1924. However, Joseph Stalin, who had been appointed secretary-general of the communist party in 1922, was determined to overthrow Trotsky and become leader of the USSR himself. A

1935 Soviet statue representing industry and agriculture.

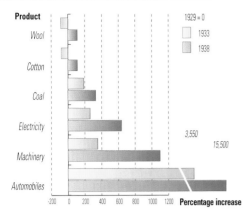

Product   1929 = 0
Wool   1933
Cotton   1938
Coal
Electricity
Machinery   3,550   15,500
Automobiles
-200 0 200 400 600 800 1000 1200 **Percentage increase**

Industrial production rose swiftly in the Soviet Union between 1929 and 1938. As this graph shows, the production of coal, electricity, machinery, and automobiles all increased massively in this period.

After 1945, Stalin was seen as a threat to Western Europe. Here he is dancing towards France to music played by leading French communists.

SEE ALSO
p. 220 THE RUSSIAN REVOLUTION
p. 244 THE COLD WAR
p. 262 THE DECLINE OF COMMUNISM

A model worker called Alexei Stakhanov was invented to encourage people to work harder and produce more. He was said to be a coal miner who had cut fifteen times more coal than normal in a six-hour shift.

AREAS UNDER SOVIET INFLUENCE DURING STALIN'S TIME.

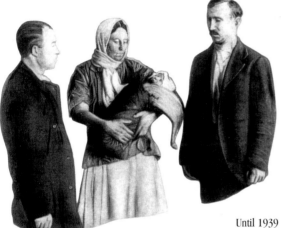

A year after he took control of the USSR, Stalin began a program of massive rearmament and a rapid expansion of the Red Army. Ten years later it was the largest army in the world. The many Tupolev aircrafts, like the one shown here, were the pride and joy of the Russian airforce.

Soviet sphere of influence

Until 1939 Soviet influence was limited to the lands which had made up the former Russian Empire. Then the Soviet Union annexed the eastern half of Poland, followed by Lithuania, Estonia, and Latvia in 1940. They all fell to the Nazis in 1941, but by 1945 they were back in Soviet hands. By 1948, communist governments controlled from Moscow had been set up in all the countries of Eastern and Central Europe, which became known collectively as the Eastern or Communist Bloc.

Soviet rites in place of religion

The Bolsheviks under Lenin aimed to rid the Soviet Union of religion as they saw it as part of the old regime. Stalin shared this belief, even though he had originally trained to be a priest. Thousands of churches and monasteries were closed and religious ceremonies, such as weddings, funerals and baptisms, were replaced by secular rituals. The ceremony at this Soviet baptism included a pledge of loyalty to Stalin's regime.

Annexed by Russia 1940–45
Communist states from 1945–48
Yugoslavia gains from Italy 1945
— Border of Germany in 1937
Cities divided into four occupation zones
Br. = British Fr. = French
Ru. = USSR

---

aggression pact with Hitler. **1940** Death of Trotsky in exile in Mexico.   **1941** German forces invade the USSR, which then enters World   War II on the side of the Allies. **1945-8** Communist governments,   dominated by the USSR, are set up in the countries of Eastern Europe.   **1953** Stalin dies and Nikita Kruschev comes to power.

---

five year struggle for power followed until, in 1929, Stalin emerged as victor and Trotsky was sent into exile.

Originally called Joseph Dzhugashvili, Stalin's adopted surname meant "man of steel," and he ruled his people harshly. He was not interested in the original communist ideas of justice, equality, and fairness and would not tolerate any opposition to his views. He was determined to turn the USSR from a backward, peasant society into a modern industrial nation. To do this, he implemented a series of Five Year Plans in which new steelworks, power plants, coal mines, engineering works, and other factories were quickly built.

Industrial output increased massively and the cities expanded as more and more people moved from the countryside to take up new jobs. However, working and living conditions were often grim and food and fuel for heating homes was frequently in short supply.

In contrast to his industrial plans, Stalin's Five Year Plans for agriculture were a disaster because many peasants refused to hand over their land to the state and then work on it collectively. When they were forced to do so, they were resentful. They also lacked the necessary machinery to farm on a large-scale and, as a result, there were

serious famines in 1932 and 1933 during which millions of people died.

This period also saw the start of the Great Purge in which Stalin rid the USSR of all his opponents by having them killed, exiled, or sent to labor camps. Millions died, including peasants and soldiers, as well as political opponents. Although Stalin succeeded in turning the USSR into a superpower, the cost in human suffering was great and, after his death in 1953, his rule was officially criticized as too repressive by the new Soviet leaders.

Leon Trotsky (1879–1940) was assassinated in Mexico in 1940, presumably by Soviet agents.

1947–48 Eastern European states become communist and pro-Soviet. **1948–49** Berlin airlift stops USSR taking over Berlin. **1949** USA, Canada, and Western European states form NATO. **1950** Start of McCarthy era in USA. **1950–53** Korean War. **1953** Death of Stalin. **1955** USSR and Eastern European countries form

The Cold War

The USA and the USSR emerged from World War II as the world's two superpowers. They had fought as allies during the war, but the rapid expansion of communism in Eastern Europe after 1945 turned them into enemies in what became known as the Cold War. The situation worsened after 1949 when the USSR exploded its first atomic bomb and an arms race started between the two countries as each tried to have bigger and more deadly weapons than the other. Although it was called the Cold War, there was never any actual fighting. Instead, both sides used propaganda and political and economic means to try and gain superiority. At its worst in the early 1950s, the Cold War only really ended in the late 1980s when communism collapsed in Eastern Europe.

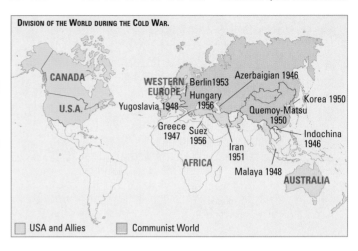

DIVISION OF THE WORLD DURING THE COLD WAR.

CANADA · U.S.A. · WESTERN EUROPE · Berlin 1953 · Azerbaigian 1946 · Hungary 1956 · Korea 1950 · Yugoslavia 1948 · Quemoy-Matsu 1950 · Greece 1947 · Suez 1956 · Iran 1951 · Indochina 1946 · AFRICA · Malaya 1948 · AUSTRALIA

☐ USA and Allies   ☐ Communist World

The arms race

After the USSR exploded its first atomic bomb in 1949, an arms race began between the two superpowers, as each tried to keep or gain the lead in military power. In 1950 the USA had 350 warheads, while the USSR had five. These numbers rapidly increased, however, as did the numbers of traditional weapons, such as guns, tanks, and fighter aircraft.

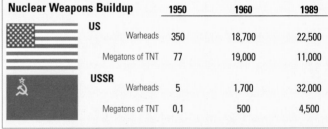

Nuclear Weapons Buildup		1950	1960	1989
US				
	Warheads	350	18,700	22,500
	Megatons of TNT	77	19,000	11,000
USSR				
	Warheads	5	1,700	32,000
	Megatons of TNT	0,1	500	4,500

This American cartoon shows Stalin peeping through the keyhole of an American research center to learn how to make an atomic bomb.

The McCarthy era

In 1950 Joseph McCarthy, a Republican senator, claimed to have a list of communist spies and agents who were working in the USA. In the following four years, many innocent people were ruthlessly persecuted. They included artists and intellectuals, as well as government officials, but McCarthy's claims could not be proved.

During the Cold War both sides were obsessed with international spies and secret agents, both real and imaginary, and many books and films were produced with a background of espionage. Among the most successful were Ian Fleming's novels about James Bond, the British superspy who was also known as Secret Agent 007.

RED ALERT

How well do you know thy neighbour?

A TPU PICTURE

The fear of communism, especially in the USA, grew stronger after 1945. Posters, and even films, such as Red Alert, warned people to be on their guard against the Soviet Union (known as "the Reds") and China (known as "the Yellow Peril").

Both East and West continued experimenting with nuclear weapons during the Cold War. At first scientists (like these two at Bikini Atoll in 1962) watched from what was thought to be a safe distance with only sunglasses for protection.

By the 1950s, fear of the nuclear bomb reached such a level that people invested in fallout shelters and even protective suits, with respirators and filters.

Mutually Assured Destruction

Throughout the 1950s, nuclear weapons grew ever bigger and more deadly as the arms race accelerated. People began to realize that, if a war broke out between the two superpowers, each side had enough power to destroy the world many times over. But John Foster Dulles, US Secretary of State, explained that this "mutually assured destruction" (MAD) was the reason why the arms race really deterred the outbreak of another world war.

SEE ALSO
p. 230 THE WAR IN EUROPE
p. 242 SOVIET EXPANSIONISM
p. 248 CENTRAL AND SOUTH AMERICA
p. 262 THE DECLINE OF COMMUNISM

Warsaw Pact. **1956** Suez Crisis in Egypt. **1956** Revolt against Soviet power in Hungary ruthlessly crushed. **1957** USSR launches first satellite. **1958** USA launches first satellite. **1961** USSR sends first man into space. **1961** Berlin Wall is built. **1962** Cuban missile crisis threatens world peace. **1962** First James Bond film shown.

During World War II, the USA and Britain had made an uneasy alliance with the Soviet Union to defeat Germany. When the war ended, however, the situation changed. In order to defeat Germany, the Soviet Union had liberated the countries of Eastern Europe from Nazi control and put in its place communist governments controlled from Moscow. At the same time, some communists were winning places in democratically elected governments in countries such as France and Italy, and the communists were also poised to take control of China. This rapid spread of communism especially alarmed the USA.

The alarm deepened in June 1948 when the Soviet Union decided to isolate Berlin – which was entirely within Soviet-controlled East Germany – from the West, in an attempt to take complete control of the city. To prevent this happening, an airlift was organized to take vital supplies into West Berlin. It continued until May 1949 when the Soviet Union lifted its blockade. By that time Europe was firmly divided, with the western half allied with the USA and the eastern half allied with the Soviet Union.

Both sides distrusted each other and, since the USSR now also had atomic weapons, both expected to be attacked at any time. There were spies and counter-spies on each side as they tried to find out what the other was planning. In the USA there was a communist witch hunt, led by a senator called Joseph McCarthy who was convinced there were communists in all areas of public life.

The situation eased slightly after the death of the Soviet leader Joseph Stalin in 1953, but both sides continued to stockpile vast quantities of weapons until there were enough to destroy the whole world many times over. The US kept their weapons aimed directly at the Soviet Union while the Russians pointed theirs at the USA.

The situation deteriorated again in 1962, when the Soviet Union decided to install nuclear missiles in Cuba, (which had become communist in 1959) just off the coast of Florida. The USA reacted by putting a naval blockade around the island on October 22 and for the next few days the world hovered on the brink of nuclear war. Finally, on October 28, the USSR agreed to remove the missiles and war was averted.

In 1963 the USA, Britain, and the USSR signed the first Nuclear Test-Ban Treaty, but vast numbers of nuclear and conventional weapons were still produced and, although the two sides never again came so close to war, they both became involved in armed conflicts in many parts of the world for the next quarter of a century.

Left: Looking over the wall: In 1961 the East Germans built a wall along the boundary between East and West Berlin to stop people escaping from the East to the West. Anyone seen trying to cross over the wall was shot.

The rockets used for early space travel were based on those used for launching nuclear warheads.

The Space race

To prove their technological and military superiority, both superpowers raced to conquer space. The USSR took the lead when it launched Sputnik I, the first satellite to orbit the earth in October 1957. Then, in 1961, the USSR sent the first man into space. This made the USA determined to put a man on the moon before the end of the decade.

The first animal to go into space was a dog called Laika who orbited the earth for eight days in November 1957 in the Soviet satellite, Sputnik II.

Europe divided

After its surrender in May 1945, Germany was occupied by the Allied Powers, with Britain, France, and the USA in the west and the USSR in the east. By 1948 the USSR had imposed Soviet-style governments on Poland, Romania, Czechoslovakia, Albania, Bulgaria, and Hungary. As relations between East and West cooled, the USSR built up a military barrier to separate Eastern Europe from the West. This barrier was referred to as the Iron Curtain.

In 1948 the USSR blockaded Berlin, cutting it off from the West. An airlift of 275,000 flights was then used carry supplies to the Western zones of the city and prevent it falling into Soviet hands.

The Suez Crisis

The Suez Canal was built by the French and opened in 1869. In 1888 it became a neutral zone, with Britain guaranteeing to keep it so. In 1956, however, President Nasser of Egypt nationalized the canal. A combined force of British, French, and Israeli troops then invaded Egypt, demanding the canal's return. This led to an international outcry, with both the USA and the USSR putting pressure on the invaders to withdraw. Once they had done so, a UN peacekeeping force was sent to the area to try and prevent war breaking out in the Sinai between Egypt and Israel.

This Soviet poster about the Suez Crisis shows France (the rooster) and Britain (the lion), fleeing before an Egyptian sphinx.

The end of Stalinism

The Cold War eased a little in 1953 when the Soviet leader, Joseph Stalin, died. He had shown increasing hostility to the noncommunist world in the years after World War II, but after his death many of his policies were denounced by the new Soviet leader, Nikita Khruschev. A slightly more liberal time followed in the USSR, but the Cuban missile crisis of 1962 brought a sharp return to Cold War conditions.

A protestor smashing a gigantic head of Stalin during the 1956 revolt in Hungary. Hungarian leader Imre Nagy had promised multi-party elections and withdrew from the Soviet military alliance. The revolt was crushed by 250,000 Soviet troops with 5,000 tanks and Soviet power was reimposed.

Nikita Khrushchev, leader of the Communist Party after Stalin's death in 1953. At the Party's 20th Congress in 1956 he denounced Stalin for his "intolerance, brutality, and abuse of power."

UN AND AID ORGANIZATIONS

Two world wars in the 20th century led to the founding of two international organizations dedicated to maintaining world peace. The first, called the League of Nations, was formed in the aftermath of World War I. It had only limited success in the 1920s and 1930s. It was replaced in 1945 by the United Nations Organization, or UN; by the dawn of the 21st century nearly every country in the world had become a member. As well as trying to maintain world peace, both these organizations did humanitarian work, often aimed at refugees and children. They were joined in this work by many other aid organizations of varying sizes and from many different countries, all of whom were dedicated to helping the victims of war, famine, poverty, and natural disasters.

On this poster, the UN is shown as a tree with its leaves made up of the flags of member nations.

The United Nations

The UN was founded on October 24, 1945 as the successor to the League of Nations. There were 50 founder members, including the USA. They have now been joined by almost every country in the world. The headquarters are in New York and each member nation has one vote in the General Assembly which meets there for three months each year.

This postage stamp commemorates the UN in four different languages.

The League of Nations

The League of Nations was an international organization founded in 1920 with the aim of maintaining world peace. Its covenant was incorporated into the peace treaties negotiated at Versailles after World War I. The USA did not ratify these, however, and so it was excluded from the League. The League did much good work in the 1920s, but it was not strong enough to deal with the growing aggression of Japan, Italy, and Germany during the 1930s.

The League of Nations is shown here as a scared rabbit confronted by international strife in the form of a snake.

THE LEAGUE OF NATIONS 1920–39.

CANADA, ICELAND, SOVIET UNION, U.S.A., ATLANTIC OCEAN, CHINA, JAPAN 1920-33, INDIA, SIAM, INDIAN OCEAN, NEW GUINEA, AUSTRALIA, NEW ZEALAND, SOUTH AFRICA, URUGUAY, ARGENTINIA

1 Albania
2 Austria
3 Bulgaria
4 Estonia
5 Latvia
6 Lithuania
7 Hungary
8 Germany
9 Belgium

☐ Founder member
☐ Subsequent members (with dates of membership)
☐ Colonies of member states
☐ Possessions of member states
☐ Never members

THE 50 FOUNDER NATIONS OF THE UN.

AMERICAS: 21
Argentina, Bolivia, Brazil, Chile, Colombia, Costa Rica, Cuba, Dominican Republic, Ecuador, El Salvador, Guatemala, Haiti, Honduras, Mexico, Nicaragua, Panama, Paraguay, Peru, United States of America, Uruguay, Venezuela

CONTINENTAL EUROPE: 9
Belgium, Denmark, France, Greece, Luxembourg, Netherlands, Norway, Poland, Yugoslavia

MIDDLE EAST: 7
Egypt, Iran, Iraq, Lebanon, Saudi Arabia, Syrian Arab Republic, Turkey

COMMONWEALTH: 5
Australia, Canada, India, New Zealand, United Kingdom of Great Britain and Northern Ireland

SOVIET REPUBLICS: 3
Belarus, USSR, Ukraine

AFRICA: 3
Ethiopia, Liberia, South Africa

EAST ASIA: 2
China, Philippines

MAJOR DATES

1864 The Red Cross is set up to care for people wounded during war, regardless of which side they are on.

1920 The League of Nations is founded to try and maintain world peace.

1945 The United Nations Organization replaces the League of Nations.

1950 The UN faces its first major challenge when war breaks out in Korea. Troops from 16 member nations are sent to support South Korea.

1961 Amnesty International is founded in London to defend freedom of speech and religion throughout the world. It also campaigns for the release of prisoners of conscience, and against torture. By 2000 it has over one million members in 150 countries.

1971 *Médecins sans Frontières* is founded by a group of French doctors.

Peacekeeping forces

Within the UN, the Security Council has the responsibility for trying to maintain peace in the world. It has five permanent members, plus ten more who are elected to serve for two-year terms. If international peace is breached somewhere, the Security Council may send military forces, made up of soldiers from different countries, to try and re-establish peace there.

This UN soldier from India wears a blue turban instead of a blue beret because he is a Sikh.

The aims of the UN

The UN was founded with the aim of maintaining world peace after the Second World War by encouraging international co-operation to resolve social, cultural, economic, and humanitarian problems which might otherwise lead to the outbreak of war. Through its various agencies, it also encourages the worldwide development of education, protects refugees, encourages international trade and economic growth in developing countries, protects the environment, provides aid in emergencies, and promotes better health through the WHO.

The UN International Children's Emergency Fund.

Médecins Sans Frontières.

The Red Crescent and the Red Cross.

Amnesty International.

Médicins du Monde.

The Unesco.

Aid Organizations
There are many different aid organizations operating in the world. UNICEF and UNESCO, both run by the UN, are among the largest organizations. They are both actively involved in promoting health and education in developing countries (among other things). British-based OXFAM is one of many that provides food and clothing in emergencies. It also runs long-term projects to help people become self-sufficient. Amnesty International helps political prisoners throughout the world, while the International Red Cross (Red Crescent in Muslim lands) provides doctors and health care.

UNITED NATIONS
WORLD HEALTH ORGANIZATION

Based in Geneva, Switzerland, the WHO (World Health Organization) was established in 1948 to help all people attain better health.

PEOPLE AND PLACES
Swedish-born **Dag Hammarskjold** (1905–1961), Secretary General of the UN from 1953 until his death in a plane crash in 1961, is awarded the Nobel Peace Prize for the way he deals with the Suez Crisis (1956) and the civil war in the Congo (1960).

J.E. Salk (1914–1995), a virologist from the USA, develops the first successful anti-polio vaccine in 1954.

Albert Sabin (1906–1993) develops an oral vaccine against polio in 1956.

Mother Teresa, an Albanian-born nun, is awarded the Nobel Peace Prize in 1979 for her work among the poor of India.

The Hague in the Netherlands is the seat of the **International Court of Justice**, set up by the UN to pass judgment on disputes between member states.

Health organizations
Some aid organizations were formed to provide health care and advice, both in times of emergencies and natural disasters, and on a longer term basis in countries which are too poor to organize large scale health care for themselves. One of the best known is the French charity *Médecins sans Frontières*. Other charities are set up to help people with one specific disease. For example, Lepra was set up to help people with leprosy.

Providing food and other aid
Most charities provide aid at two levels. The first is emergency aid, supplying food, clothing, medicines, and temporary shelter for people suffering from the effects of famine, war, or natural disasters, such as earthquakes or floods. This is followed by long term aid to help people to be self sufficient once more. Many charities provide seeds, plants, animals, and tools, so that people can start farming again. They also dig wells which will provide water even in times of drought.

Aid parcels mean the difference between life and death for many people.

Missionaries
Both Protestant and Catholic missionaries still go to parts of the developing world, but in smaller numbers than they did in the past. Although they do some preaching, they are more valued for teaching literary, practical, and medical skills.

At the start of the 20th century, missionaries such as Charles de Foucauld (above) set out to convert the Africans to Christianity.

The struggle to beat diseases went on in both rich and poor countries. In 1953 the March of Dimes encouraged Americans to donate to the fight against polio. The first successful vaccine was introduced a year later.

Irish rock star Bob Geldof sang with the Boomtown Rats before becoming involved with raising money for famine victims in Ethiopia.

Live aid concerts
In 1984 Ethiopia was struck by famine as the crops failed and civil war made it difficult for other supplies to get through. Many people were moved to help, but rock star Bob Geldof reacted by organizing two massive concerts – one in Britain and one in the USA – in the summer of 1985. Known as Live Aid, the charity he set up raised over £50,000,000 in Britain alone.

You can help, **too!**

JOIN THE MARCH OF DIMES
THE NATIONAL FOUNDATION FOR INFANTILE PARALYSIS · FRANKLIN D. ROOSEVELT, FOUNDER

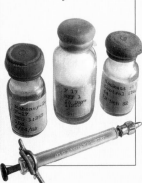

Panama regained control of the Canal Zone from the USA in 1979. Money received from ships using the Panama Canal makes up a large part of the country's economy, together with tourism and agriculture.

Caribbean Sea
• Colon

PANAMA
• Panama
Gulf of Panama

Emiliano Zapata (below) was the leader of the peasant uprising during the Mexican Revolution. He was often helped by the bandit, Pancho Villa (poster, below right).

Right: When the new government in Cuba took control of the banks it issued new bank notes with portraits of the men who had brought about the revolution.

Cuba

Cuba became a socialist republic in 1959 when Fidel Castro came to power after his second attempt at overthrowing the island's government. Relations between Cuba and the USA were strained and the situation worsened after the US supported Cuban exiles who unsuccessfully tried to invade Cuba in 1961. The Soviet Union was a close ally and supporter, but Cuba lost much of its export market when the Soviet Union collapsed.

A Cuban exile in the USA watches news of the 1962 Cuban missile crisis on television.

Fidel Castro (below) was the leader of the revolution in Cuba which overthrew the dictator, Fulgencio Batista, and set up a socialist government.

Right: The revolutionary, Che Guevara, became an icon for left-wing youth around the world in the 1960s.

Bolivia

In 1952 an alliance of mine workers and peasants overthrew the military government of Bolivia and started the Bolivian National Revolution. It nationalized the tin-mining industry, gave all adults the right to vote, and gave land back to many of Bolivia's native inhabitants. However, the economy collapsed in the late 1950s and the resulting period of unrest and instability lasted until the 1980s.

BOLIVIA
No será otra
CUBA

Cuban Missile Crisis

In the autumn of 1962, the Soviet Union began installing launch pads for nuclear weapons in Cuba. To prevent this from happening, the US Navy blockaded the island. For several days in October, the world stood at the brink of nuclear war, but finally the Soviet Union backed down.

PROCLAMATION
$5,000.00 REWARD

FRANCISCO (PANCHO) VILLA

Mexican Revolution (1910–1920)

From 1876 to 1910 Mexico was ruled by a dictator, Porfirio Diaz. He was overthrown and Francisco Madera was elected president. He was a wealthy landowner, but promised reforms to give land back to the peasants. When he went back on his word, the peasants rebelled and the revolution started.

Nicaragua

From 1933 to 1979 the government of Nicaragua was dominated by the Somoza family. Opposition to them led to a civil war which was won by the Sandinistas, led by Daniel Ortega. His left-wing politics brought him into conflict with the USA who backed an army of Somoza supporters, known as Contras. Continuing conflict in the country led to Ortega's downfall in free elections in 1990. Peace returned to the country in 1993.

1952 Evita Peron dies, aged 34. **1966** Guyana gains its independence from Britain. **1967** Che Guevara is killed while trying to start a revolt in Bolivia. **1975** Suriname gains its independence from Netherlands. **1976** Venezuela nationalizes its oil industry. **1980** The Shining Path, a Marxist guerrilla movement, is founded in

Central and South America

Most of the countries of Central and South America regained their independence from their European colonizers in the 19th century. They did not sever their connections with them, however, but kept strong economic and social ties with Europe throughout the 20th century. They also developed stronger links with the USA during this period. But, although the region was largely free from direct European rule, its countries were still controlled by powerful land-owning families who often rigged elections to stay in power. This situation lasted until the 1920s when a series of military coups brought army-backed dictators into power in many countries. Some of these were overthrown in the 1960s and 1970s following Fidel Castro's successful revolution in Cuba. A period of political instability followed, but by the early 1990s most countries had democratic governments. However, rapid population growth and the huge numbers of people moving to the cities kept a large proportion of the population in poverty and dismal living conditions.

GUYANA SURINAME
🛡 Military regime
VENEZUELA
✳ Military coup
COLUMBIA
FRENCH GUIANA
❋ Revolution
ECUADOR

PERU

BRAZIL

BOLIVIA

PARAGUAY

ARGENTINA
PERU URUGUAY

MILITARY REGIMES, MILITARY COUPS, AND REVOLUTIONS IN SOUTH AMERICA FROM 1930.

Juan Peron's first wife, Evita, was responsible for many reforms, including votes for women, during his first presidency.

Argentina

For most of the 20th century, Argentina was ruled by a series of military dictators. One of the best known was Juan Peron who was elected president in 1946. He was overthrown in 1955, but returned to power in 1973, dying a year later. His second wife, Isabel, succeeded him until 1976 when a three-man junta came to power. This was overthrown in 1981 by General Galtieri. Military dictatorship ended in 1983.

Chile

When Salvador Allende was elected president of Chile in 1970, he introduced land reforms and nationalized the mining industry, most of which had been owned by US companies. After his overthrow in 1973, Chile was ruled by a military junta, led by General Pinochet. All political opposition was banned and many human rights were violated. Democracy returned in 1988 when Pinochet was voted out in a referendum.

General Pinochet (right) led the military coup in which the socialist president Salvador Allende (above) was overthrown and killed.

Getulio Vargas of Brazil

Getulio Vargas (1883–1954) was a lawyer who started his political career in 1906. Elected president of Brazil in 1930, he brought in many economic and social reforms before he was overthrown in 1945. He was then elected president again from 1951 to 1954.

The Disappeared

In Argentina, between 1976 and 1983 over 30,000 political opponents of the military dictatorship were killed. They became known as the "disappeared." When democracy returned to Argentina, their mothers (above) campaigned for those responsible to be punished.

Colombia

Colombia is an agricultural country, but it is also rich in minerals, including gold, silver, copper, lead, and emeralds. Its chief export is coffee, but there is also widespread trafficking in cocaine which is made from the leaves of the coca plant (left) which grows wild in Colombia. From 1948 to 1962 its people were involved in a civil war between the liberals and the conservatives. A period of dictatorship followed. Since 1975 there has been much unrest, with strikes, riots, kidnappings, and assassinations.

Brazil

Brazil is South America's largest country and its most densely populated with most people living in large cities on the coast. As these became more and more overcrowded, the government attempted to open up the interior of the country by building a new capital city, Brasilia, and making new roads to develop areas covered by rain forest. However, there has been an international outcry against the ecological damage this is causing.

In 1960 the Brazilian capital moved to a new city called Brasilia. Many buildings, including the cathedral (above), were designed by the Brazilian architect, Oscar Niemeyer.

Rigoberta Menchú

Between 1944 and 1954 there were huge social reforms in Guatemala to improve conditions for the native Amerindian population. When these were reversed, many of their supporters were tortured and killed, including the family of Rigoberta Menchú (right). She became an active campaigner for Amerindian rights in her country and in 1992 was awarded the Nobel Peace Prize.

Peru. **1982** War between Argentina and Britain over

Falkland Islands. **1992** Rigoberta Menchú is awarded Nobel Peace

Prize. **1998** General Pinochet is arrested in Britain and charged

with crimes against humanity. **2001** Argentina defaults on

international debt repayments and plunges into dire economic crises.

Under the leadership of Simón Bolívar, much of South America freed itself from Spanish control in the early 19th century, while Brazil became independent from Portugal a few years later. But in both cases European influence remained strong and Spanish and Portuguese (in Brazil) were kept as official languages. Most of the big landowners were of European descent and they formed the governments of the newly-independent countries, while the majority of the native Amerindian population lived in great poverty, with very few rights or possessions. The landowning families kept control until the 1920s; they were often corrupt and rigged elections to keep their positions. By the mid-1930s, however, most of these landowning families had been overthrown and replaced by dictators who were backed by the army. For the next twenty years, most of these dictators followed right-wing policies and also did nothing to help the increasing numbers of poor people in their countries. The exception was Eva Peron, wife of the Argentinian dictator, Juan Peron, who, having been poor herself, persuaded her husband to help the poor in his country by building orphanages, schools, and hospitals.

More political instability followed in the 1960s as left-wing groups – inspired by the revolution in Cuba – tried to take control. In some countries, such as Chile and Guatemala, they succeeded briefly, bringing about land reforms to help the poor and nationalizing major industries to bring more wealth into their countries. But most of them were also overthrown, often with the help of the USA which was afraid of communism. As the 20th century ended, a degree of democracy had finally been established in many parts of South America, but as in other developing countries many problems still remained, including poverty, disease, and poor economic growth.

1. Brazil was the world's largest coffee producer until overproduction forced a cut back.

SEE ALSO
p. 58 ANCIENT NORTH AMERICA
p. 112 EUROPEAN VOYAGES OF DISCOVERY
p. 114 SPANISH
AND PORTUGUESE EXPANSION

The Middle East

At the dawn of the 20th century, most of the Middle East was part of the Ottoman Empire, ruled from Turkey. When this empire collapsed after World War I, Britain and France took control. By the mid-1940s, all the Arab nations had regained their independence and formed the modern states of the Middle East. The Arab states were united in their opposition to the Jewish state of Israel, which was founded in 1948 in what was formerly Palestine. At the same time, they were often at war with each other for religious, political, or economic reasons, and frequent civil wars, coups, and revolutions made the area unstable. The peace process in Israel was halted abruptly in 2000 by episodes of extreme violence amounting to civil war. In 2003, the Third Gulf War was fought when the USA, acting largely against international opinion, invaded Iraq.

In 1993 President Clinton of the USA (center) brought together the Israeli prime minister, Yitzhak Rabin, and Palestinian Liberation Organization leader, Yasser Arafat, to discuss self-rule for the Palestinians in Gaza and Jericho.

THE MIDDLE EAST IN 1973
(The yellow-shaded areas are members of OPEC).

Caspian Sea · USSR · TURKEY · SYRIA · Mediterranean Sea · LEBANON · IRAQ · ISRAEL · JORDAN · IRAN · AFGHANISTAN · PAKISTAN · KUWAIT · LYBIA · EGYPT · SAUDI ARABIA · BAHRAIN · The Gulf · Red Sea · QATAR · Gulf of Oman · UNITED ARAB EMIRATES · OMAN · SUDAN · YEMEN ARAB REPUBLIC · PEOPLE'S DEMOCRATIC REPUBLIC OF YEMEN · ETHIOPIA

Iran

After years of increasing opposition to his rule, the Shah of Iran was overthrown in 1979 by Ayatollah Khomeini. He ruled the country according to strict Islamic laws and tried to stamp out all Western influence. When he died in 1989, however, a more moderate government came to power and by the late 1990s Iran's international relations had improved.

After the Islamic Revolution in 1979, Ayatollah Khomeini (right) became Iran's religious and political leader until 1989.

Jordan

Transjordan (later known as Jordan) became an independent kingdom in 1946. In 1949 it took control of the West Bank of the Jordan River, but lost the land to Israel in 1967. Jordan then relinquished claims to it in 1988 when the PLO declared it a Palestinian state.

Anwar Sadat (left) was president of Egypt from 1970 to 1981. He negotiated a peace agreement with Israel in 1979, but was assassinated by Islamic extremists in 1981.

King Hussein of Jordan (reigned 1952–1999) played an important role in negotiations between the West and Iraq following the invasion of Kuwait in 1990.

Lebanon

Lebanon became completely independent from France in 1945. Power in the new state was then divided between Muslim and Christian groups. Civil war broke out between them in 1975, lasting for 19 months. Unrest continued and in 1982 the Israelis invaded Lebanon, staying until 1985. UN troops then tried to bring peace among rival militia groups, but this was not achieved until 1991, by which time Lebanon's former prosperity had been destroyed.

Egypt

Egypt became a British protectorate in 1914 and an independent kingdom in 1922. After the king was overthrown in 1952, Gamal Abdel Nasser took control. He waged two unsuccessful wars with Israel (1956 and 1967). His successor Anwar Sadat also went to war against Israel in 1973, but later negotiated a peace treaty with help from the USA. Its terms were followed by his successor, Hosni Mubarak, who regained control over the Sinai peninsula which Israel had taken in 1967.

Syria

Syria gained its independence from France in 1946. It then underwent a period of economic growth and political instability. With Egypt it formed the United Arab Republic (1958–61). Hafiz al-Assad (left) ruled from 1971 until his death in June, 2000. His regime was repressive, with opponents being arrested, tortured, or executed. He was succeeded by his son, Bashar.

SEE ALSO
p. 190 THE DECLINE OF THE OTTOMAN EMPIRE • p. 222 THE PEACE SETTLEMENT • p. 246 UN AND AID ORGANIZATIONS

As life returned to normal in Lebanon after 1991, children played among the abandoned guns and tanks in the streets.

Lebanon to expel PLO. **1988** PLO declares new Palestinian state. **1990–91** Second Gulf War. **1993** Israel and PLO sign Oslo Accords. **1994–99** Limited Palestinian self-rule in Gaza and West Bank. **2000 onward** Civil war in Israel. **2003** USA invades Iraq and overthrows Saddam Hussein.

After Turkey's defeat in the First World War, the Ottoman Empire was broken up and the League of Nations set up a series of mandates (agreements by which one country becomes the trustee of another) giving Britain and France control of the former Turkish possessions. Britain became responsible for Iraq (1920–1932), Transjordan (1920–1946), and Palestine (1922–1948), while France became responsible for Syria (1920–1946). This included Lebanon until 1926 when it became independent from Syria. By 1946 all the countries except Palestine had regained their independence.

In Palestine, however, there was conflict between the Arabs who had lived there for centuries and the Jews who had been settling there since the end of the 19th century. During the First World War Britain had promised to help to establish a Jewish homeland in Palestine, but this led to conflict with the Arabs as the number of Jewish immigrants increased. To try and keep the peace, Britain restricted the number of settlers allowed in after World War II, but Jewish terrorists then attacked both the Arabs and the British.

In 1947 the UN voted to divide Palestine into an Arab state and a Jewish state, but, although the Jews agreed, the Arabs did not. When Britain gave up its mandate on May 14, 1948, the Jews proclaimed the state of Israel. The Arab states promptly declared war, but were defeated. A ceasefire was negotiated in 1949, but further wars broke out in 1967 and 1973. From 1964 there was also conflict between Israel and the Palestine Liberation Organization (PLO), founded to oppose Israel and to secure a homeland for the Palestinians who had left Israel in 1948 and become refugees.

There were also wars among the Arab states, including one between Iraq and Iran. Known as the First Gulf War, it began as a dispute over border territory in 1980. It escalated into a full-scale war and there were huge casualties on both sides before peace was achieved with the help of the UN in 1988. In 1990 Iraqi troops invaded Kuwait, igniting the Second Gulf War in which Iraq was defeated by a multinational force, led by the USA. In 2003, US and UK troops invaded Iraq and overthrew Saddam Hussein's government in the Third Gulf War.

1. Golda Meir was prime minister of Israel from 1969 to 1974.

The foundation of Israel

Jerusalem was the spiritual home of the Jewish people, but in the early 20th century most of them lived elsewhere and Jerusalem itself was in Palestine. Britain promised its support for a Jewish homeland within Palestine, but this led to conflict as increasing numbers of Jewish families moved there. The UN decided to divide Palestine into two states, one Jewish and one Arab. The Jews accepted this, but the Palestinians did not. Then on May 14, 1948 Israel declared itself an independent state. The surrounding Arab states immediately declared war, but Israel was victorious and increased its territory by a quarter as a result.

State of Israel as proclaimed 1948

Subsequent acquisitions

South-Central Lebanon 1982 only

South Lebanon, occupied 1982

Kuneitra Strip 1967, returned to Syria 1974

Gaza Strip, occ. 1967

Jerusalem

Golan Heights, occupied 1967

West Bank, occupied 1967

Sinai 1967, returned to Egypt 1982

East Jerusalem, annexed 1967

Suez Perimeter 1973 only

EGYPT

Occupied territories

Temporary acquisitions

ISRAEL FROM 1948.

Red Sea

Jerusalem

The city of Jerusalem is a holy center for three of the world's major religions – Judaism, Christianity, and Islam. In 1948 it was divided between Jordan and the new state of Israel, and became capital of the latter in 1950. Seventeen years later Israel took control of the whole city, leading to periods of ethnic unrest.

The Arabian peninsula

The Arabian Peninsula is divided into seven countries, of which Saudi Arabia is by far the largest. The land is largely desert, but has vast reserves of oil. In 1973 Saudi Arabia was one of the Middle East countries to raise oil prices sharply, causing an economic downturn in many industrial countries as fuel bills increased rapidly.

Saddam Hussein became president of Iraq in 1979. His repressive regime ended in 2003, leaving Iraq in a volatile and uncertain situation.

In times of crisis in their country, some Israeli citizens carry sophisticated weapons as they go about their daily business.

Tension in the Gulf

The Gulf War started in 1990 when Iraqi troops invaded oil-rich Kuwait. They were defeated by a multinational force in 1991. In 1998 Iraq was bombed again by a combined US and British force because the Iraqi government would not allow UN inspectors to check that disarmament was being maintained. Unresolved tension between Iraq and the West seemed likely to continue into the 21st century.

Iraq

After becoming a kingdom in 1921, Iraq suffered from years of political instability, ethnic and religious unrest, and frequent coups. Saddam Hussein's policies after the Second Gulf War caused the UN to impose harsh economic sanctions. His refusal to demonstrate disarmament to the satisfaction of the USA, along with other political and economic factors, led to his overthrow in 2003.

As defeated Iraqi troops withdrew from Kuwait in February 1991, they set fire to hundreds of oil wells, devastating the country and causing large-scale pollution.

MAJOR ART MOVEMENTS

1905–30 Expressionism. A movement, especially in German art, that rebelled against naturalism and expressed the force of human emotion.

1907–20 Cubism. A movement in painting, and to a lesser extent sculpture, which showed subjects from many different angles.

1

1909–14 Futurism. An Italian art movement which aimed to break with the past and celebrate modern technology, dynamism, and power.

2
1916–25 Dada. Named after the French for "hobby horse," this movement emphasized the illogical and absurd in order to overcome complacency.

1915–37 Suprematism. A Russian movement in abstract art, which limited itself to basic geometric shapes and a narrow range of colors.

1917–44 Neo-Plasticism. A term coined by Dutch painter Piet Mondrian for his style of abstract art, using straight lines, right angles, and primary colors.

1924–69 Surrealism. Influenced by Dada, the Surrealists, tried to free the creative powers of the unconscious mind and overcome reason.

1946–60 Abstract Expressionism. A movement that developed in New York and mainly used the techniques of action painting.

1950- Minimal Art. An impersonal style of painting and sculpture in which only the most basic geometric forms are used.

1957–70 Op Art. A form of abstract art that used optical techniques of patterns and colors to give an impression of movement.

1957–70 Pop Art. A movement based on popular culture, using images from comics, packaging, advertisements, and television.

1960 Conceptual Art. A form of art (often using photographs or video) in which the concept, or idea, is thought to be the most important part.

1. Picasso's Les Demoiselles d'Avignon *(1907) was an early Cubist work.*
2. Fountain by Marcel Duchamp (1887–1968) is an example of his so-called "ready-mades" – mass-produced articles displayed as works of art.

A NEW ART

In the early years of the 20th century, innovative painters and other artists began questioning traditional artistic views. Influenced by developments in photography, more and more artists turned away from producing realistic pictures and looked for new ways of expressing themselves. The movement called Expressionism reflected this change, as expressionists tried to reproduce their emotional experiences to create an effect on the viewer. This was followed by an upsurge in abstract art, including geometric shapes and action painting, and new styles also developed in architecture and commercial design. At the same time pioneers in literature, music, and other artistic fields experimented with new styles, many of which influenced and inspired each other.

Bronze figure entitled Unique Form of Continuity *by Umberto Boccioni (1882–1916), who published a manifesto of Futurist sculpture in 1912.*

Pablo Picasso (1881–1973) was one of the most inventive and influential artists of the 20th century.

Virginia Woolf (1882–1941) was a central figure in the literary and artistic circle known as the Bloomsbury group. Her best-known novels are Mrs Dalloway *(1925) and* To the Lighthouse *(1927).*

Stream of consciousness

In the early 20th century novelists such as James Joyce (1882–1941) and Virginia Woolf began writing in an experimental style known as "stream of consciousness." This involved recording characters' thoughts, feelings, and reactions exactly as they occurred in their minds, without comment or explanation. Joyce used the technique in his masterpiece *Ulysses* (1922).

Cubism

In this style and movement in modern art objects were represented by an assembly of two-dimensional geometrical shapes. The Spanish painter Picasso and Frenchman Georges Braque (1882–1963) developed this great turning point in art, having been influenced by African sculpture and the later paintings of Paul Cézanne. The idea was to show many different aspects of the same object in one work of art.

Classical music

The Russian composer Igor Stravinsky (right, 1882–1971) had a revolutionary effect on classical music at the beginning of the 20th century. His music influenced many others, including the Austrian-born Arnold Schoenberg (1874–1951) who introduced atonality into his works.

Surrealism

This movement showed a whole new way of thinking and acting; it was a way of life rather than just a style. Artists such as René Magritte (1898–1967) and Salvador Dali (1904–89) (*Persistence of Memory,* below) were strongly influenced by Freudian psychology. They tried to express the subconscious mind. The eccentric Dali had a great talent for self-publicity.

Below: The Schröder House in Utrecht was designed by Dutch architect Gerrit Rietveld (1888–1964), who belonged to an artistic group called De Stijl. Mondrian was also a member of the group.

Dutch painter Piet Mondrian (1872–1944) was one of the most important figures in the development of abstract art (above), with his straight lines and use of primary colors. His work had a great influence on decorative and commercial artists.

Le Corbusier

Swiss-born Le Corbusier (1887–1965) was one of the most inventive architects of the 20th century. One of his best known works is the pilgrim church of Notre-Dame-du-Haut in Ronchamp, France (above), built in the 1950s. Like Rietveld, Le Corbusier was a supporter of functionalism, but he moved away from a geometrical style of architecture.

Minimal art

This abstract style of painting and sculpture uses simple, geometric shapes and basic colors. Minimalist artists try to keep self-expression to a minimum, so that their works are impersonal. One of the most famous minimalist artists is Carl André (1935-), whose work *Equivalent VIII* (below) is made up of 120 bricks. There was a public outcry when the work was exhibited at the Tate Gallery, London, with many visitors saying that this could not be called art.

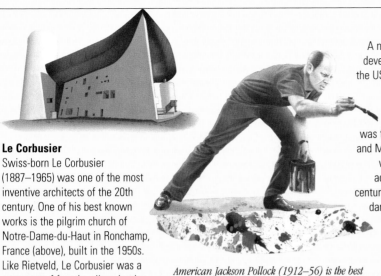

American Jackson Pollock (1912–56) is the best known representative of the style called action painting, in which paint is splashed, sprayed, or dripped onto a large canvas.

Singer and songwriter John Lennon (1940–80) and conceptual artist Yoko Ono (1931–) performing a happening in 1969. Happenings are a form of spontaneous artistic entertainment.

Danish architect Jørn Utzon (1918–) won an international competition to design the Sydney Opera House, which was completed in 1973.

Modern dance

A new form of theatrical dance developed in central Europe and the USA in the early 20th century. It was pioneered by the American dancers Isadora Duncan (1878–1927), who was famous for her "free dance", and Martha Graham (1893–1991), who founded her own dance academy in 1927. Later in the century, many choreographers and dancers were happy to work in both modern dance and classical ballet.

The Russian Ballets Russes company pioneered modern dance at the beginning of the 20th Century.

Pop art

This movement was based on the imagery of popular culture and consumerism. It rejected any distinction between good and bad taste, and took much of its inspiration from television and mass advertising. This meant that pop art was a critical comment on traditional art values. The movement's most famous exponent was the artist and film-maker Andy Warhol (left, 1928–87).

International style

After the First World War a rebellion against tradition led to the development of a new style of architecture. It used simple, geometric lines and new materials such as concrete, steel, and glass. The style's leaders were Walter Gropius (1883–1969), who founded a school of art called the Bauhaus, Le Corbusier, and Ludwig Mies van der Rohe (1886–1969), who also ran the Bauhaus and went on to design the Seagram building in New York. In the 1930s this new movement was called the "international style."

In 1989 this glass pyramid was added to the Louvre national museum in Paris, which was originally opened in 1793.

The Petronas Towers, two 88-story office blocks in Kuala Lumpur, Malaysia, are joined together by a high walkway. At 1,483 ft. (451.9 m), they are the tallest buildings in the world.

Millions of children from all over Asia have first-hand experience of war. Young people in some countries, such as Cambodia, have known little else but war.

Since the mid-1960s many of the countries in East Asia were transformed by economic growth. From being exporters mainly of agricultural products and minerals, they developed a strong industrial base, exporting finished manufactured goods, including electronic and electrical goods, footwear, and clothing to markets across the world. The growth was sponsored by investment from Japanese, European, and American multinational companies which took advantage of a large workforce and lower wage costs. The spurt of economic growth was accompanied by rapid urbanization. Cities grew very quickly, and because many were unable to provide housing and infrastructure for the new arrivals, many ended up living in slums on the outskirts of the cities. At the same time, a growing urban middle class appeared with money to spend. This stimulated the economy even more.

The long economic boom came to an abrupt halt in 1997. Beginning with the Thai baht, many of the region's currencies collapsed. Stockmarkets crashed and many companies and banks were forced into bankruptcy. The crisis caused huge unemployment and

Vietnam

From the mid-1980s, the Vietnamese government enacted a series of economic reforms, including more liberal policies toward private enterprise. Following the dissolution of the Soviet Union in 1991, Vietnam improved relations with a number of Asian and Western nations. In 1995 relations with the US were normalized and the Vietnamese economy began a period of expansion.

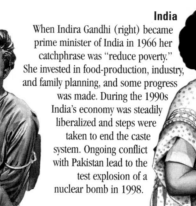

Left: The illustration shows Vietcong soldiers who were captured on the Mekong River in 1967.

Below: Soviet poster in support of North Vietnam during the war.

India

When Indira Gandhi (right) became prime minister of India in 1966 her catchphrase was "reduce poverty." She invested in food-production, industry, and family planning, and some progress was made. During the 1990s India's economy was steadily liberalized and steps were taken to end the caste system. Ongoing conflict with Pakistan lead to the test explosion of a nuclear bomb in 1998.

Right: Benazir Bhutto, elected prime minister of Pakistan in 1988, became the first female leader of a Muslim country.

Pakistan

Pakistan was formed in 1947 as a separate state for the Muslim inhabitants of India. Its powerful military forces gained full nuclear capacity in the 1990s. Throughout the 1980s and 1990s Pakistan was plagued by corruption and the growth of fundamental Islamic law. The strength of the military came to the fore when there was a military coup in late-1999 led by General Pervez Musharraf. In May 2000, Pervez vowed to restore democracy to Pakistan with free elections within three years.

Bangladesh

Formerly East Pakistan, Bangladesh became an independent country in December 1971 after prolonged conflict with West Pakistan. Ten million refugees flooded into India, putting great strain on the Indian region of West Bengal. At the beginning of the 21st century Bangladesh remained one of the poorest countries in the world. Its low-lying river plains were prone to flooding causing the deaths of millions of people.

Philippines

The mixed Indo-Malay, Chinese, and Spanish people of the Philippines elected Ferdinand Marcos president in 1969. Democracy ended in 1972 when he declared martial law. Marcos won elections held in 1986, although he was driven from power when the elections were declared fraudulent. Corazon Aquino took over as president. She was followed by Fidel Ramos, who ruled until 1998. Ramos was regarded as one of the best presidents in the nation's history. He purged the police force of corrupt members, encouraged family planning, and liberalized the economy. His administration reached peace agreements with two long-active guerrilla groups, the communist New People's Army and the Muslim separatists of the Moro National Liberation Front (above).

Cambodia

Political power fell to the communist Khmer Rouge led by Pol Pot in 1975. Inspired by Mao Zedong in China, Pol Pot tried to eliminate all opposition to his regime, and about 20 percent of the population (around 2 million people) were exterminated. The Khmer Rouge was overthrown by the Vietnamese who invaded Cambodia in 1978.

Right: Ruthless Cambodian dictator Pol Pot died in 1998.

The end of the Vietnam War

US troops were withdrawn from Vietnam following a ceasefire agreement signed in 1973. However, the civil war soon resumed and in 1975 North Vietnam launched a full-scale invasion that resulted in the collapse of the South Vietnamese government. On July 2, the two Vietnams were united as the Socialist Republic of Vietnam.

SEE ALSO
p. 196 BRITISH INDIA
p. 198 COLONIALISM
p. 232 THE WAR IN ASIA AND THE PACIFIC
p. 234 CHINA TO 1950
p. 236 ASIA TO THE 1960S

Philippines. **1987** Democratic elections held in South Korea.

1988 Military government comes to power in Myanmar.

1991 Prodemocracy leader Suu Kyi imprisoned in Myanmar.

1997 East Asian economic crisis.
2002 Terrorist bombing of

nightclub in Bali kills 187.
2003 Outbreak of SARS.

economic hardship for many. In some countries, especially in Indonesia, this led to social unrest and political changes. The economic meltdown had a variety of causes, including widespread corruption and over-ambitious spending plans. By 2000, many countries were well on the road to recovery.

A few countries, notably Myanmar, Laos, and Cambodia, did not take part in the economic "miracle." They were held back by repressive governments and lack of basic infrastructure.

Following the terrorist attacks in 2001, US forces invaded Afghanistan, removing the Islamic Taliban government which US President Bush accused of harboring Osama Bin Laden and his Al Queda terrorist group held responsible for the attacks on the US.

1. The Sikh flag. The Sikhs are one of many groups in India seeking independence.

2. An American soldier and a Vietnamese boy drink a coke together in the final days of the Vietnam War.

Asia to the Present

The history of Asia, especially East Asia, in the final decades of the 20th century was marked by unparalled economic growth. Beginning in Japan in the 1950s, economic expansion spread to Taiwan, Hong Kong, Singapore, and South Korea, and from there to Thailand, Indonesia, the Philippines, and Malaysia. Asian lifestyles reflected the increasing economic well-being, and the area, initially an exporter, became an important market for its own and imported goods. A severe economic crisis slowed growth markedly in 1997–99, but the resilient economies of the region bounced back much more quickly than expected. Economic growth in South Asia (the Indian subcontinent) was more contained, but the terrible poverty of at least some of its people was relieved.

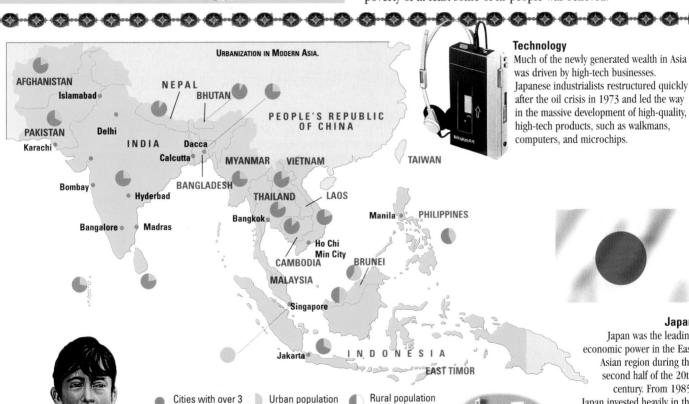

URBANIZATION IN MODERN ASIA.

AFGHANISTAN
Islamabad
NEPAL
BHUTAN
PAKISTAN
Delhi
PEOPLE'S REPUBLIC OF CHINA
Karachi
INDIA
Dacca
Calcutta
MYANMAR
VIETNAM
TAIWAN
Bombay
BANGLADESH
Hyderbad
THAILAND
LAOS
Bangalore
Madras
Bangkok
Manila
PHILIPPINES
Ho Chi Min City
CAMBODIA
BRUNEI
MALAYSIA
Singapore
Jakarta
INDONESIA
EAST TIMOR

● Cities with over 3 million inhabitants
◗ Urban population
◖ Rural population

Technology
Much of the newly generated wealth in Asia was driven by high-tech businesses. Japanese industrialists restructured quickly after the oil crisis in 1973 and led the way in the massive development of high-quality, high-tech products, such as walkmans, computers, and microchips.

Japan
Japan was the leading economic power in the East Asian region during the second half of the 20th century. From 1985, Japan invested heavily in the economies of the countries of Southeast and East Asia, stimulating their growth. The Japanese economy slowed a little toward the end of the 20th century.

The 1997 crash
The racing economies of the East Asian region faced a severe crisis beginning in July 1997. Thailand was the first country to suffer; from there the crises spread throughout the region. However, against all expectations, the worst was over by 2000.

Aung San Suu Kyi, leader of the opposition to the brutal military government of Myanmar.

Right: Singapore, one the of original "Tigers."

Below: the movie industry in India turned out more movies per year than Hollywood.

Myanmar (previously Burma)
Myanmar's nondemocratic military government was voted out of power in 1990 in favor of the National League of Democracy, led by Aung San Suu Kyi. However, the army-led government refused to go, and Suu Kyi, winner of the Nobel Peace Prize in 1991, continued (unsuccessfully) to fight for democracy into the 21st century.

Indonesia
The world's fifth most populous nation, Indonesia is an archipelago of more than 13,000 islands. With 360 tribal and ethnic groups and more than 250 different languages and dialects, the country's unity has often been threatened. Indonesia was badly hit by the Asian crisis and this led to an increase in civil unrest. East Timor became independent in 2002, while other territories, such as Aceh in Sumatra, continue to seek independence.

Modern China

When the Communists came to power in 1949 they reunited China under a powerful central government. Led by Mao Zedong, they wanted to establish a new society that would give more power to peasants and workers and limit that of landowners, intellectuals, and foreigners. Massive projects for modernization were begun; some were successful and many new factories, hospitals, schools, and railroads were built. Others proved disastrous. Increasingly, the government controlled every aspect of peoples' lives; land was collectivized and people were denied basic rights, such as where they could live or what they could read. Economic conditions improved in the final decades of the 20th century, and people were allowed more freedom. But political freedom was still vigorously denied.

中国
东方红

The Communist government simplified Chinese writing to make it easier for people to learn to read and write. These symbols say "China – the East is Red."

In 1949 the Chinese Communist Party (CCP) established a "democratic dictatorship" led by Mao. The economy was in bad shape after 12 years of war and civil war and their first priority was to increase agricultural production. In September 1950 the Agrarian Reform Law took land from the rich landowners and gave it to 300 million peasants. This was followed in 1953 by a series of Five-Year Plans that set production targets for farming and industry. The first of these, from 1953 to 1958, was fairly successful, but the second was a disaster. Known as the Great Leap Forward, it saw the production of steel as the key to

Food shortages had always been a problem in China. A typical greeting in China even today (equivalent of the English "How are you?") is "Have you eaten yet?" However, the famine that followed the Great Leap Forward was terrible even in Chinese terms – somewhere between 20 to 30 million people died of hunger.

The Great Leap Forward

In February 1958 Mao announced the Great Leap Forward, a plan to steeply increase industrial and agricultural output. By November the countryside was organized into 26,000 communes, each of which was expected to deliver enormous increases in production. Steel, for example, was to be produced using small furnaces in backyards in villages (above) where scrap metal could be melted down. But this steel was of such poor quality that it was useless. With so many people occupied in industry and building projects, agricultural production dropped sharply and a great famine followed.

Mao's Five-Year Plans were an attempt to modernize China, increasing industrial and agricultural output. Many factories were built (above), while farms were collectivized and run as communes (below).

Left: The Little Red Book contained quotations from Chairman Mao and was published to gain support for the Cultural Revolution.

During the Cultural Revolution, schools closed and armed students were recruited into the Red Guards.

Left: This cartoon from 1976 shows the Gang of Four being roasted over a fire after they failed to seize power in 1976.

The Cultural Revolution

By 1966 Mao felt that China had lost its revolutionary zeal, so he began the Cultural Revolution. In the anarchy and chaos that followed Mao got rid of all his opponents. Young people were encouraged to criticize their elders and thousands were murdered. The Cultural Revolutionary Committee was led by Chiang Ch'ing, Mao's wife. By 1968 the violence threatened the collapse of Chinese life and some order was restored. Chiang Ch'ing remained powerful, and when Mao died in 1976 she and her "Gang of Four" tried to seize power.

success. Millions of peasants were instructed to make steel in small backyard furnaces. Agriculture suffered as a result and a series of floods and droughts wiped out what few crops had been planted. Famine followed and millions died. The Great Leap Forward was abandoned in 1961.

The Great Leap Forward was followed in 1966 by the Cultural Revolution which proved to be an even greater disaster. China did not recover until after Mao Zedong's death in 1976. There was a brief struggle for power after Mao's death between his wife Chiang Ch'ing and her "Gang of Four." They were defeated and Mao was succeeded first by the more

moderate Hua Guofeng.

From about 1978 power passed to Deng Xiaoping, who had been with Mao Zedong on the Long March in 1934. Deng was a pragmatic leader who moved toward more liberal economic policies, including the creation of special economic zones along the coast of China. He also reformed the peasant communes in 1979, introducing the Responsibility System which gave farmers individual plots of land on 15-year leases and allowed them to keep or sell any surplus produce. Ten years later the communes had almost all disappeared. Agricultural production doubled and China became a net exporter of food.

Liberalization of the economy led to calls for more political freedom. These were firmly crushed in 1989, however, when a peaceful, pro-democracy demonstration in Tiananmen Square was crushed by the army and many demonstrators were killed or imprisoned. Another peaceful protest movement called Falun Gong, based on the practice of breathing and meditation, emerged as a challenge to political oppression in 1999. It also met with strong opposition.

The 2003 outbreak of SARS (Severe Acute Respiratory Syndrome) beginning in mainland China threatened to slow China's economic growth.

Hong Kong was returned to China in 1997, after almost 100 years as a British colony. It remains a center of world trade.

Special economic zones

Beginning in 1978 under Deng Xiaoping, attempts were made to rebuild the Chinese economy. Special Economic Zones were set up along the southern coast of China to encourage financial investment and technology transfer from the West. Deng also encouraged foreign trade, allowed private businesses to be set up, and leased individual plots of land to farmers.

By the 1960s, the Chinese and the Soviet governments had drifted apart. The Chinese saw their version of communism as superior and supported revolutions by oppressed people all over the world. The poster (above) dates from this time.

After Mao Zedong met Henry Kissinger, American Secretary of State, in 1970, China was more open to the West.

Population control

China already had a large population in 1949, but improvements to health care and sanitation after that date helped more people live longer and the population kept increasing. Despite government attempts at encouraging birth control in the 1950s and 1960s, the population had reached 1 billion by the early 1980s. After 1970, however, people were encouraged to marry late and have fewer children. Beginning in 1979 a policy of just one child per family was introduced.

Although in exile, Tibet's leader, the Dalai Lama, continued to fight Chinese domination of Tibet.

Ongoing repression

Despite the many economic reforms in China in the final decades of the 20th century, all attempts at political reform to establish a more democratic government were severely crushed. The biggest was in 1989 when thousands of students and dissidents occupied Tiananmen Square in Beijing for six weeks. Many were killed when the army was sent in to remove them (left).

THE ECONOMY OF CHINA, 1979–92.

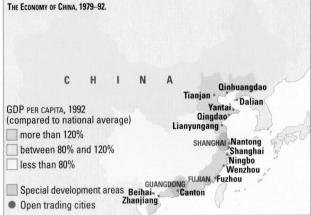

C H I N A

GDP PER CAPITA, 1992
(compared to national average)

☐ more than 120%
☐ between 80% and 120%
☐ less than 80%

☐ Special development areas
● Open trading cities

Qinhuangdao
Tianjan
Yantai · Dalian
Qingdao
Lianyungang

SHANGHAI · Nantong
Shanghai
Ningbo
Wenzhou
GUANGDONG · FUJIAN · Fuzhou
Beihai · Canton
Zhanjiang

This poster shows a duck enjoying some of the benefits of capitalism after economic reforms at the end of the century.

Tibet

Before the Chinese took control in 1950, Tibet was isolated from the rest of the world and kept its traditional economy and society. The Chinese wanted to change this. They built roads, schools, and hospitals, but they also outlawed Buddhism, the Tibetan religion, leading to an unsuccessful revolt in 1959. Tibet's leader, the Dalai Lama, and thousands of refugees fled. More recently, some religious and economic freedom has been restored.

SEE ALSO
p. 86 CHINESE CIVILIZATION p. 124 MING CHINA p. 194 MANCHU CHINA p. 234 CHINA TO THE 1950s

1963 Kennedy assassinated.
1964 Civil Rights Act passed.
1965 Voting Rights Act passed.
1968 Martin Luther King
assassinated.
1973 Fuel crisis as oil prices
rise rapidly. End of US
involvement in Vietnam war.
1975 The USA and the USSR
co-operate for the first time on

John Kennedy (right) was elected president in November 1960. Aged 43, he had a young wife and family and was very popular. He was good on television and planned major social and economic reforms, including new civil rights laws, but was assassinated in 1963.

USA to the Present

The 1960s and 1970s were strongly marked by the protest movement against the Vietnam War, the women's movement, and the search for alternative ways of living. The Civil Rights Act of 1964 did much to improve conditions for African-Americans who had suffered from segregation and discrimination, especially in the southern states. The 1980s saw the beginnings of the electronic revolution that would explode in the new economy boomtime of the late 1990s. But conditions sombered early in the new century as the economy slipped into recession and the terrorist attacks on New York and Washington on September 11, 2001, killed almost 3,000 people.

The United States, Canada, and Mexico

During the 20th century the US increasingly dominated both its neighbors – Canada to the north and Mexico to the south – economically and, to a lesser extent, socially. In 1988 Canada and the US signed the North American Free Trade Agreement (NAFTA). The agreement, which eliminated tariffs and other barriers to trade over several years, was extended to include Mexico in 1992.

Richard Nixon became President in 1969. He ended the war in Vietnam and improved relations with China, but resigned in 1974 over the Watergate scandal.

Above: Former movie star Ronald Reagan was elected president 1980. Strongly patriotic, he promised to revive the national spirit. He cut taxes and increased defense spending, but later held successful arms control talks with the USSR.

The oil crises

Between October 1973 and January 1974 OPEC raised the price of oil from $1.50 a barrel to $11.56. People and governments panicked. Speed limits were lowered and people were urged to save electricity which was generated by oil. The crisis ended in March 1974, but its effects were long lasting as the industrialized world realized it could no longer rely on cheap energy supplies.

Right: In 1992 Bill Clinton was elected president. A former lawyer and state governor of Arkansas, he was involved in peace deals between Israel and the PLO and in Northern Ireland. His presidency ended in November 2000.

Hippies

The hippie movement started among young people in the Haight-Ashbury district of San Francisco in the 1960s. Its ideals of freedom, peace, and love spread across the USA and to many other parts of the world. In the USA the hippies were among the main protesters against the war in Vietnam. Many thousands of them also went to the famous free rock festival at Woodstock in 1969.

The New York Times
MEN WALK ON MOON
ASTRONAUTS LAND ON PLAIN;
COLLECT ROCKS, PLANT FLAG

Walking on the moon

When the Soviet Union took the lead in the space race in 1961 by sending the first man into space, President Kennedy promised that the USA would land a man on the moon by the end of the decade. This was achieved in July 1969 when Neil Armstrong, commander of Apollo 11, became the first man to walk on the moon. Another five moon landings followed.

Hippies wore brightly-colored clothes and long hair. They used drugs, especially LSD and marijuana. A favorite hippie saying – Tune in, turn on and drop out – encouraged many to live in rural communes where they shared their possessions.

SEE ALSO
p. 238 AFTER THE WAR IN NORTH
AMERICA AND EUROPE
p. 244 THE COLD WAR
p. 274 THE GLOBAL WORLD

Right: These Soviet stamps commemorate the first meeting in space between American and Soviet astronauts on July 17, 1975 when a module, designed by NASA, allowed each nation's craft to dock for a meeting that lasted for two days.

a space project. **1991** End of Cold War. **1995** Terrorist bomb in Oklahoma City shocks the US. **1999** US-led NATO forces bomb Kosovo, in former Yugoslavia. **2001** Terrorist attacks in September lead to war with Afghanistan. **2003** US invades Iraq, overthrowing dictator Saddam Hussein.

Martin Luther King won the Nobel Peace Prize in 1964 for his non-violent campaign for civil rights.

Right: The words of Martin Luther King's most famous speech lived on long after his assassination in Memphis, Tennessee, in April 1968.

Social problems

One of the biggest problems facing the USA at the start of the 1960s was racial inequality, especially in relation to the African-American population of the southern states, where many suffered from poverty, unemployment, and poor living conditions, as well as segregation. Protests, which had begun in the 1950s, culminated in the March on Washington in 1963, led by Martin Luther King. After the passing of the Civil Rights Act in 1964 the situation slowly improved.

Left: Despite the great wealth in the USA, homelessness was still a problem for the poorest members of society, especially in the cities.

Right: In 1971 the USA hit a financial crisis. The gold reserves were shrinking and inflation and unemployment were rising. To solve it, the dollar was devalued. Driven by a booming economy, during the first months of the 21st century the US dollar rose against every other currency in the world, only to decline again in 2003.

Bill Gates (left) became one of the richest men in the world through sales of his computer software, known as Microsoft, which is used by millions of computers across the world.

Below: Steven Spielberg made some of the best known movies of the 20th century. They included E.T. in 1982 and Jurassic Park and Schindler's List in 1993.

The US economy

In the late1990s the US economy was growing at the rate of 4 percent a year. This brought about a great upsurge in the number of jobs available and unemployment fell to less than 5 percent. The stock markets boomed, driven particularly by high tech and new media companies. But by the turn of the century the so-called "new economy" had faltered, stock market values had dropped markedly, unemployment had risen, and by 2003, even the strong dollar had weakened considerably.

September 11

On the morning of September 11, 2001, four airplanes were hijacked by terrorists shortly after take off from US airports. Two were crashed into the Twin Towers of the World Trade Center in downtown Manhattan, causing the towers to collapse. The third airplane hit the Pentagon building in Washington D.C., while the fourth crashed in a field in Pennsylvania. Almost 3,000 people lost their lives in the attacks.

Sport and leisure

Most Americans love sports, either as participants or as spectators. Among the most popular individual sports are jogging, athletics, skiing, tennis, hunting, and fishing, while the most popular team sports are baseball, basketball, and football. Apart from watching the game, spectators are usually entertained by cheerleaders and marching bands. The most important matches are shown on television and attract millions of viewers.

The World Trade Center area in New York (right) was the site of the greatest number of casualties. It came to be known as "Ground Zero." In the days following the attacks, rescue workers and firemen worked round the clock searching for survivors.

With the collapse of the Soviet Union in 1991, the USA emerged as the single most powerful nation on earth. The children born in the boom years following the Second World War (appropriately called the "baby-boomers") grew up in a period of sustained economic growth and prosperity. By 1960 almost 40 percent of American families fell into the professional or skilled workers categories. Many of the baby boomers, raised in middle-class homes in the suburbs of the so-called "American Dream," joined the student, women's, or hippie movements in the 1970s. They were of fundamental importance in ending US participation in the Vietnam War and also in changing the social mores of the 20th century.

However, although the economy continued to grow steadily, not everyone had equal access to the wealth it produced.

Even in the boomtime conditions of the early 21st century, around 20 percent of the US population was living below the poverty line. African-Americans, whose lives were improved by the passing of the Civil Rights Act in 1964, followed by the Voting Rights Act in 1965, still experienced discrimination. Immigrants continued to arrive from all over the world (a quota system allowed entrance to around 500,000 legal immigrants each year; a further 500,000 were believed to arrive illegally). Illegal immigrants had a much tougher time than the legal ones, and in some states they were denied access to education and health care.

The US dominated the other countries in North and South America both politically and economically. Its role in world affairs was crucial; and its high profile attitude was often deeply resented by many countries.

The USA fought an ongoing war against illegal drugs and the crimes associated with them. By the late 1980s the biggest problem was crack, a relatively inexpensive but very addictive form of cocaine. In the inner cities, street gangs use violence, and often murder, to keep control of their drug-dealing areas.

By the 1950s, many women were becoming discontented with their traditional roles.

SOCIAL CHANGE

The 20th century was a time of great social change in many parts of the world as people campaigned for more civil rights. In the industrialized countries, women first demanded the right to vote in national elections, then, from the 1950s, greater equality with men. This became easier to achieve after the 1960s when the introduction of the contraceptive pill gave women the choice of whether to have children or not. Black and gay people also campaigned for their civil rights, as did women in the poorer countries of the world. By the end of the century, much had been achieved, but there were still parts of the world where women and members of minority groups were discriminated against.

Birth control

The first family planning clinics opened in Britain and the USA in the 1920s, but women were not able to take full responsibility for preventing unwanted pregnancies until the contraceptive pill was introduced in the 1960s. Some religious leaders still try to ban its use.

Marie Stopes (left) opened the first birth control clinic in Britain in 1921.

MAJOR DATES

1920 French law bans sale of contraceptives.

1933 Treaty on equal rights for women is signed by 11 nations.

1961 Contraceptive pill gives women control over when to have children.

1970s Many countries in Western Europe legalize abortion. Abortion becomes legal in the USA in 1973.

1974 US passport office allows married women to use their maiden names.

1976 UN proclaims International Women's Year.

1988 Swedish government adopts five-year plan to attain equality for women.

1996- In Afghanistan the ruling fundamentalist Islamic Mujahidin abolish almost all basic rights for women.

1893 New Zealand
1901 Australia
1906 Finland
1913 Norway
1915 Denmark, Iceland
1917 Russia
1918 Britain, Austria, Canada, Ireland
1919 Germany, Netherlands, Luxembourg
1920 United States

Women and the vote

In 1893 New Zealand became the first country to allow women to vote in general elections. This encouraged women in other countries to campaign for the same right. Many campaigned peacefully, but others – such as Emmeline Pankhurst (right) – used more violent methods and were often arrested and imprisoned in the years leading up to World War I.

Women in many Islamic countries wear veils when they go out in public. Although some Islamic women defend the custom, most do not have the right to choose.

Sexual harassment

In the USA the offense of sexual harassment in the workplace was taken seriously after 1991 when Anita Hill (below), a law professor at the University of Oklahoma, accused Clarence Thomas, a Supreme Court nominee, of harassing her ten years earlier.

Feminism

In the 1960s a new women's movement started in the USA and soon spread across the world. It became known as feminism, and its followers demanded the same opportunities as were given to men.

Feminists took their protests onto the streets in the late 1960s.

EQUAL PAY FOR EQUAL JOBS

Women's rights today

In many parts of the world women are still treated as second-class citizens. They have fewer rights and opportunities than men. As children, fewer girls are enrolled in schools and women's illiteracy rate is still higher than men's. In some societies wives can be beaten or even killed for disobeying their husbands. They can also be divorced if they fail to produce male heirs.

REPEAL ABORTION LAWS N.O.W.

This poster for International Women's Day (March 8) is from India where women have campaigned for more rights since the 1940s.

Some Islamic women receive good educations, but they are a minority.

Divorces per 100 Married Couples.

	1920	1990	
	0,6	34	Austria
	0	7	Italy
	9,8	22	Japan
	2,1	43	UK
	13,6	48	US

Divorces were rare at the start of the 20th century, but by its end as many as 50 percent of marriages ended in divorce in some countries.

Caring fathers

In the late 20th century, child care was no longer seen as the sole responsibility of the mother in many parts of the developed world. In Sweden, fathers are given paid "paternity leave" of up to 12 months from work to look after young children. After divorces, some fathers now share custody of their children, rather than them being given automatically to the mother.

Gay rights

At the start of the 20th century gay people were discriminated against in most parts of the world and many were jailed for their homosexual activities. By the 1960s, however, they began to campaign for more rights, especially in Europe and the USA. Britain decriminalized homosexuality between consenting adults in 1967 and by the year 2000 gay couples were allowed to marry in some countries.

Map showing Laws on Homosexuality around 1995.

- Countries with laws protecting gay people from discrimination.
- Male and female homosexuality illegal.
- Male homosexuality illegal; female homosexuality ignored by laws.
- No data or unclear.

Sects and creeds

At the end of the 20th century in the Western world there was a sharp drop the number of people going to traditional churches. At the same time, many new sects sprang up, often attracting young people. One of the best known is the Unification Church, founded in Korea by Sun Myung Moon and introduced to the USA, Britain, and other countries in the 1960s. Known as "Moonies," Moon's followers see him as the head of a family of perfect children and obey him absolutely.

The beliefs of many religious sects seem strange and even threatening to outsiders.

The white supremacist Ku Klux Klan was a secret society which had over 4 million members in the USA in the 1920s. Membership has declined since then, but new white supremacist groups have appeared.

Sun Myung Moon and his wife.

MAJOR DATES

1951 First major anti-apartheid demonstration in Johannesburg, South Africa. 18 people killed.

1954 Moonie Church founded.

1958 Campaign for Nuclear Disarmament founded in Britain.

1961 World Wildlife Fund founded.

1963 BBC ban on mentioning sex, religion, politics, or the royal family withdrawn.

1964 Sidney Poitier first black actor to win an Oscar.

1969 The Stonewall rebellion in New York marks beginning of gay rights movement.

1974 Referendum in Italy makes divorce legal.

1991 Italian football star Maradona banned for cocaine use.

1996 Same-sex marriage banned in USA.

As internet use soars many people wonder what the social consequences will be. Side effects could include feelings of isolation, and inability to communicate except through a protective "screen."

Face painting, tattooing, and body piercing became popular with both sexes in many parts of the Western world at the end of the 20th century.

Drug use and abuse

The last half of the 20th century saw a great increase in the use of illegal drugs, especially by young people at nightclubs and rave parties where ecstasy and other new drugs were popular even though they were known to have caused several deaths. There was also a vast international trade involved in the production and smuggling of heroin and cocaine worth billions of dollars.

THE RUSSIAN FEDERATION AND THE NEWLY-INDEPENDENT STATES OF THE BALTIC AND CENTRAL ASIA.

LITHUANIA LATVIA ESTONIA
BELARUS
UKRAINE
MOLDOVA
GEORGIA
ARMENIA
AZERBAIJAN
TURKMENISTAN UZBEKISTAN
KAZAKHSTAN
KYRGYZSTAN
TAJIKISTAN
RUSSIAN FEDERATION

EAST GERMANY · POLAND
CZECHOSLOVAKIA
SLOVENIA · HUNGARY
CROATIA · ROMANIA
YUGOSLAVIA
BULGARIA
ALBANIA

☐ Independent 1989
☐ New state 1992
☐ New state 1992
☐ United with West Germany 1990

The countries of Eastern Europe started to break free of the USSR in 1989, and Germany was reunited in 1990. By 1991 the republics which had formed the USSR were also independent of Moscow, but worked together as the Commonwealth of Independent States (CIS).

Even after Joseph Stalin's death, Soviet leaders kept strict controls over all aspects of people's lives. They stuck firmly to the communist ideals of collective farms and state-owned factories and businesses, and spent vast amounts of money on weapons to hold their own in the arms race with the USA. In the 1980s, this led to unrest in the USSR and also in the communist-controlled countries of Eastern Europe. Earlier revolts against the system, in Hungary in 1956 and in Czechoslovakia in 1968, had been savagely crushed by the USSR, but now Soviet leaders realized that changes would have to be made if the problems were to be solved.

Yuri Andropov began in 1983 by trying to improve transportation and basic living conditions, but he did nothing to reform the economy or political system, and the situation steadily worsened. When Mikhail Gorbachev came to power in 1985, he made much more sweeping reforms and by 1988 the USSR was a limited democracy. This gave the countries of Eastern Europe the encouragement they needed to break free from Soviet control in 1989 and overthrow their communist governments.

In Hungary and Czechoslovakia, this happened with little protest and no bloodshed, but in other countries the struggle for democracy was harder. In

Under the old regime, the Soviet Union showed its military strength every May Day by holding a great parade of rockets, missiles, tanks, and soldiers in Red Square, Moscow.

1945 1968

The people of Czechoslovakia welcomed the Soviet army in 1945 as it gave them the hope of freedom. But when democratic reforms were introduced in 1968, the Soviet army was used to crush them.

Where are all the weapons?
In 1991 the USSR and the USA agreed to sign a treaty (to be known as START II) by which the number of nuclear weapons in the two countries would be cut by two-thirds by 2003. But when the treaty was signed in 1992, the USSR had broken up and many of its weapons were in the independent republics. They agreed either to destroy them or hand them over to Russia, but it is thought that many are still in existence.

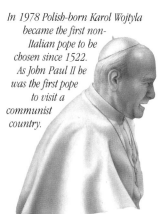

In 1978 Polish-born Karol Wojtyla became the first non-Italian pope to be chosen since 1522. As John Paul II he was the first pope to visit a communist country.

Poland
Poland's bid for independence started in 1980 in the Lenin shipyards of Gdansk where Lech Walesa, an electrician, was one of the founders of a trade union known as *Solidarnosc* (Solidarity). In 1981 the union was accused of trying to overthrow the government, but, although it was then banned, its members continued to campaign for reform. In June 1989, free elections were held for the first time in 40 years. *Solidarnosc* won a huge victory and Lech Walesa was elected president in 1990.

After 1991, many ethnic groups within the former USSR sought independence. Among them were the Chechens (below). Russian troops attacked their homeland Chechnya and brutally crushed their revolt.

Soviet troops occupied Afghanistan in 1979 to support the Marxist government there. Mujaheddin rebels fighting a guerrilla war forced them out in 1989.

Germany reunites
Although the relationship between East and West Germany improved in the 1970s and 1980s, living conditions in the East lagged far behind the West. As the East German leader, Eric Honecker, resisted improvements, he was faced with mass demonstrations and, when Hungary opened its borders with Austria in May 1989, many East Germans used that route to flee to the West. Honecker was forced to resign and in November 1989 the East German government opened its borders with West Germany. Both sides then wanted Germany to be reunited and this took place formally on October 3, 1990.

When East Germany opened its borders in November 1989, people came from all over the country to pull down the Berlin Wall. It was a time of great joy and hope for the future.

Germany are reunited. **1991** Republics of USSR become independent. USSR ceases to exist. **1992** Civil war in Bosnia-Herzegovina, part of former Yugoslavia. **1994** Russian troops sent to Chechnya to suppress rebellion. **2000** Berlin capital of Germany again. Putin elected president of Russian Federation.

Poland the trade union known as *Solidarnosc* had fought against the government since 1980 and many of its members were imprisoned before free elections were allowed in June 1989. In Romania several thousand people were killed before the repressive communist regime of Nicolae Ceaucescu was toppled and Ceaucescu himself was executed by an army firing squad on Christmas Day 1989. And, while the two parts of Germany were reunited after the end of communism in East Germany, the collapse of communism in Yugoslavia led to the break up of that country, followed by bitter civil war. By 1991 the Soviet Union itself had broken up

into its individual republics, but its problems were far from over as attempts to reform the economy along Western lines led to increased hardship and even food shortages for many ordinary people by the end of the century.

1. A matrjoska doll showing a common feeling about Russian politics among Russians: (from left to right) Eltsin contains Gorbatchev, who contains Breznev, who contains Stalin, who contains Lenin.

The Decline of Communism

By the 1970s it was clear that the USSR had serious problems. Lack of political freedom and poor economic growth had led to stagnant living conditions, popular unrest, and a bleak outlook for the future. When Mikhail Gorbachev came to power in 1985 he began a series of far-reaching economic and political reforms that led to the end of communism throughout Eastern Europe and, eventually, to the collapse of the USSR. By 1988 political reforms in the Soviet Union had made it a limited democracy. The following year, within just a few months of each other, all the countries of the Eastern bloc overthrew their communist governments. By 1991 the republics of the USSR had become independent and the USSR itself had been replaced by a loosely-based Commonwealth of Independent States (CIS).

Mikhail Gorbachev (left) was the leader of the Soviet Union from March 1985. On August 22, 1991 he faced a bitter confrontation with his former ally Boris Yeltsin (right) and was forced to read out a statement calling for the end of communist rule.

The new Russia

The collapse of the Soviet Union led to the formation of the Commonwealth of Independent States (also known as the Russian Federation), which cooperated on military and economic issues but were no longer directly controlled from Moscow. Boris Yeltsin, elected president in 1990, introduced Western-style economic reforms which led to real hardship for many Russians. He was replaced by Putin in 2000.

Right: As communism collapsed throughout Eastern Europe, many of its old symbols, such as statues of Lenin, Marx, and Stalin, were torn down and smashed.

The people of the Baltic states of Lithuania, Latvia, and Estonia gained independence from Russia in March 1991. This man's banner (below) compares the Russian takeover of Lithuania in 1940 with the Iraqi invasion of Kuwait in 1990.

These two young Romanians have cut the communist symbol out of their flag to celebrate the overthrow of communism in a bloody revolution which claimed several thousand lives.

The Balkans

The many different ethnic groups in Yugoslavia were held together by a strong leader, Tito, until his death in 1980. Serbia and Croatia declared themselves independent in 1990, and Bosnia and Hercegovina in 1992. This led to a series of brutal civil wars in which many people were killed or forced to flee their homes. Tensions ran high in 1998 when Serbia invaded Kosovo committing atrocities against the local population. In 1999 NATO forces decided to intervene and began bombing raids on Kosovo.

As Yugoslavia split apart into its various ethnic groups, many people had nowhere to go apart from makeshift refugee camps.

The ancient bridge at Mostar became a symbol of the fighting between Muslims and Croats which lasted from 1992 to 1994.

Eastern Europe re-emerges

By 1990 multi-party elections had brought coalition governments to power in the former communist states of Eastern Europe. They were committed to democratic reforms and economic liberalization. Exposure to a capitalist market-based system led to rapid economic decline with high unemployment and economic hardship for many people. However, by the year 2000 most countries had learned to cope and their economies were growing at steady rates.

SEE ALSO
p. 220 THE RUSSIAN REVOLUTION
p. 230 THE WAR IN EUROPE
p. 242 SOVIET EXPANSIONISM
p. 244 THE COLD WAR

European car industry

The European car industry lost sales to imports from Japan and other Asian countries during the 1970s and 1980s. It recovered in the late 1990s, however, and is now especially good at making luxury models and small cars which do not need much petrol.

The Swinging 60s

Having followed American youth culture for years, Britain developed its own style after The Beatles' first record was released in 1962. It marked the start of a period that became known as the Swinging Sixties. As British pop music and British fashion, by designers such as Mary Quant, dominated the world, the boutiques in the King's Road, Chelsea, and Carnaby Street in central London were the places where anyone who was fashion-conscious went shopping.

In 1962 a new group, The Beatles, shot to fame in the UK with their first record, Love Me Do. They went on to achieve worldwide popularity.

Mary Quant's creation of the mini-skirt in the 1960s made London a leading fashion center.

The widespread use of credit cards has made traveling and shopping easier across Europe as they can be used for any currency.

FIAT 500
la nuova

The protest movement

In 1968 there was a wave of anti-government protests by students in Europe, with the most serious taking place in France and Germany. Posters (like the French one here) encouraged students and workers to occupy factories and universities, as well as taking to the streets. In France General de Gaulle's position as President was so weakened that he resigned in 1969.

MAI 68
DÉBUT D'UNE **LUTTE, PROLONGÉE**

Immigration

Borders within the European Union are now more open and it is relatively easy for inhabitants of the member states to live and work in each other's countries. It is more difficult for people from outside the EU, especially those from Eastern Europe, Asia, and Africa, to enter legally. However, as European economies picked up again at the beginning of the 21st century, some countries looked to the developing world to find workers and opened quota systems.

Western Europe is growing

Before communism collapsed in 1989, Western and Eastern Europe were divided by the Iron Curtain. Once this went, however, many Eastern European countries wanted to join the EU. The first to be accepted was the former East Germany, which became part of the EU when Germany was reunited in 1990. Another 12, including Poland and Hungary, have applied for membership.

THE GROWTH OF THE EUROPEAN COMMUNITY, 1957–2000.

EEC founding members, 1957
Subsequent adhesions: 1973 1981 1986 1990 1995
Countries seeking EU membership.

1963 France vetoes Britain's entry into the Common Market.

1968 Student and worker demonstrations in Europe.

1969 British government sends troops to Northern Ireland.

1973 UK, Denmark, and Ireland join EC. **1981** Greece joins EC.

1986 Spain and Portugal join EC. **1990** Germany reunited. **1992**

Western Europe to the Present

By 1960 most of Western Europe had recovered from the devastation caused by the Second World War. New houses, shops, and factories had been built to replace those destroyed in bombing raids and there was plenty of work for everyone. In a decade that became known as the Swinging Sixties, youth culture centered on British pop music and fashion, rather than following the USA as it had done in earlier decades. Meanwhile, some countries in Western Europe began to realize that they would be more successful if they worked together in areas such as trade and agriculture. This led to the setting up of what became known in 1993 as the European Union (EU). In 2003 the 15 member states voted to admit 10 new members, beginning in May 2004. Most of the new members were previously satellite states within the Union of Soviet Socialist Republics (USSR).

The history of Western Europe in the second half of the 20th century was one of steady economic growth following the chaos and destruction of World War II. Aid from the USA from 1948 to 1951 helped to restart industries which had been disrupted by the war, while many towns and cities took the opportunity to build new homes to replace old and inadequate ones, as well as those which had been destroyed by bombing.

Then in 1952, France, West Germany, Italy, Belgium, Luxembourg, and the Netherlands set up the European

From 1968 to 1992 West Germany was terrorized by an anarchist group called the Red Army Faction. Also called the Baader-Meinhof Gang, its aim was the violent overthrow of capitalist society.

Independence movements

Since 1950, several parts of Europe have tried to become independent nations with their own parliaments. Greenland achieved it peacefully in 1979, while Scotland and Wales gained their own assemblies within the UK in 1998. The Basque (or Euskaldunak) people of Spain and France are still campaigning for their independence, however, and since 1968 two nationalist groups, ETA (left) and Enbata, have used guerrilla tactics to try and achieve this.

Terrorism

Acts of terrorism were quite common in parts of Western Europe from the 1960s onward. Planes were hijacked and in Germany and Italy groups of anarchists used bombs and guns to try and destabilize their governments. In Northern Ireland, Republicans and Loyalists carried out atrocities and also operated in mainland Britain.

Some members of the EU were opposed to monetary union. Posters like this (below) tried to persuade people that it would be simpler to have just one currency.

On January 1, 1999 the new European currency, known as the Euro, was introduced for trading among the eleven EU members who had agreed to monetary union.

·Burned out buses and cars were a frequent sight on the streets of Northern Ireland as the Irish Republican Army (IRA) fought a guerrilla war against the Loyalists on behalf of the Roman Catholics there.

Economic growth

Although there were occasional downturns, most of Western Europe enjoyed steady economic growth in the second half of the 20th century. This fuelled a growth in service and leisure industries as Europeans became wealthy consumers as well as producers.

A united future

The Maastricht Treaty, named after the town in the Netherlands where it was signed in 1992, changed the name of the European Community (often also known as the Common Market) to the European Union. In 2003 the European parliament voted overwhelmingly in favor of admitting 10 new countries — Poland, Lithuania, Estonia, Latvia, Hungary, the Czech Republic, Slovenia, Slovakia, Malta, and Cyprus.

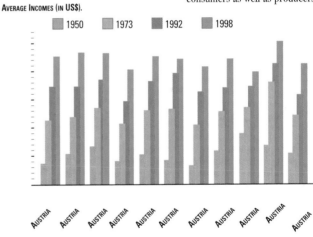

AVERAGE INCOMES (IN US$).

| 1950 | 1973 | 1992 | 1998 |

AUSTRIA AUSTRIA AUSTRIA AUSTRIA AUSTRIA AUSTRIA AUSTRIA AUSTRIA AUSTRIA AUSTRIA AUSTRIA

SEE ALSO
p. 238 AFTER THE WAR IN EUROPE AND NORTH AMERICA
p. 270 POPULATION AND THE ENVIRONMENT
p. 275 THE GLOBAL WORLD

Signing of Maastricht Treaty brings Europe nearer to economic unity. **1993** European Community renamed European Union (EU). **1994** Austria, Finland, and Sweden join EU. **1999** Euro launched as new EU currency. **2003** Relations between America and Germany and France damaged over US and UK invasion of Iraq.

Coal and Steel Community to co-ordinate the production of coal and steel. Five years later, these same countries signed the Treaty of Rome to create the European Economic Community, which established a common market among its members. In 1967 this became known as the European Community, and in 1973 the original six members were joined by Denmark, Ireland, and the United Kingdom. Greece joined in 1981, followed by Spain and Portugal in 1986. In 1993 the name was changed again, this time to the European Union, as the signing of the Maastricht Treaty in 1992 had paved the way for all the members'

eventually form a single, frontierless market, with a common currency (the Euro) and a shared central bank.

The EU gained three more members in 1994 when Austria, Finland, and Sweden joined. They were also members of the European Free Trade Association (EFTA) which set up an agreement with the EU in 1994 to create the European Economic Area,

which is the richest open market in the world. But, although the EU has dealt successfully with manufacturing industries, many farmers and fishermen have had problems coming to terms with its policies on agriculture and fishing.

1. Model wearing Italian designer clothes in the 1990s. As more people became wealthy enough to buy designer clothes, the fashion houses increased their ready-to-wear lines, making high fashion even more accessible.

2. Euro coins will replace current European coins from January 2002.

3. The idea of a tunnel beneath the English Channel to link Britain and France was first suggested by Napoleon in 1802 and work was twice started and then abandoned. The link was finally made as a railroad tunnel in 1994 at a cost of £10 billion.

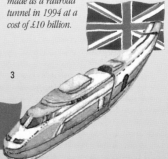

THE DEVELOPING WORLD

As former European colonies in Africa and Asia regained their independence during the 20th century, they looked forward to a better standard of living as well as political freedom. This was not always achieved, however, as their new governments often had to deal with corruption and civil wars, as well as poverty, overpopulation, and large-scale illiteracy in countries where the underdeveloped economy often still depended on the former colonial powers. There was little money for building infrastructure, such as hospitals, roads, and schools, and so the new governments borrowed heavily from countries in the developed world. Paying these loans back added to their problems toward the end of the century. Despite this, many countries, especially in Asia, made substantial progress.

GDP PER CAPITA, 1992.
- Over $15,000
- $5,000–15,000
- $2,000–4,999
- $500–1,999
- $0–499

Above: As the map shows, most of the world's poor people live in Africa and southern Asia. The wealthiest people live in North America, Europe, and Australia.

Left: Using posters like this one, the Indian government promoted sterilization and contraception to try and control population growth.

MAJOR DATES

1980 The World Health Organization (WHO) announces the eradication of the killer disease smallpox after a program of mass vaccination.

1993 The WHO declares global tuberculosis emergency. Strains of the disease have developed that are resistant to antibiotics.

1997 UNICEF reaches agreements to end child labor in the clothing industry in Bangladesh and in the soccer ball industry in Pakistan.

1999 It is estimated that it would cost $7 billion per year to give an education to all children. This is less than is spent annually on cosmetics in the USA.

2000 The world finally awakes to the magnitude of the AIDS crisis in Africa. Of the estimated 45 million people infected worldwide, the vast majority live in Africa.

International aid

International aid organizations help people in the developing world in various ways. Apart from emergency supplies of food and clothing, they provide health care and education. They also provide plants, animals, and farming tools to solve problems of famine in the longer term, and technical advisers and financial aid for large projects, such as sinking wells and building dams.

The water problem

Access to safe drinking water is a major problem in the developing world. In many places there are no adequate drains and drinking water is often polluted with raw sewage. Diseases spread rapidly this way, causing the deaths of more than 25,000 people every day. In other places, the water supply dries up in times of drought and people and their animals have to walk long distances to an alternative supply. Aid organizations in many countries are working with local people to dig deeper wells which will not dry up or become polluted.

Poverty and hunger

Poverty is the major cause of hunger, disease, and a host of other ills. Poor people live in inadequate houses and don't get enough nourishing food. This makes them more vulnerable to disease and less able to cope with natural or man-made disasters. Usually, it is the children who suffer most.

Right: This image shows the top half of a rich Western banker standing on the impoverished legs of a person in the developing world.

Debt and the developing world

In the 1970s and 1980s international banks encouraged countries in the developing world to take out massive loans to finance infrastructure and growth. Many countries were unable to repay the loans, and some even found the interest payments crippling. In 2000 the Group of Seven countries (leaders of the developed world), agreed to write off some of the outstanding debts.

Villagers in India queue up at the settlement's only well. Lugging the heavy containers back to the house is typically a woman's job.

Diseases cured

Aid programs and medical progress led to improvements in health in the developing world. Some diseases, including smallpox, were wiped out, and large-scale vaccination programs brought diseases such as polio under control. However, many people still died from leprosy, malaria, and sleeping sickness, while AIDS, the plague of the 21st century, was pandemic in Africa.

The graph shows a comparison of illiteracy levels in 1980 and 1995 in the developing world and in industrialized nations.

This Ethiopian government worker is helping a Maji mother to weigh her baby to make sure it is thriving.

Health

Staying healthy was a major problem in countries where people lacked the most basic facilities, such as clean water, adequate shelter, and sufficient food. Many governments could not afford health care programs or medicines. This meant that curable illnesses, such as the dehydration caused by diarrhea, killed millions of children each year when just one inexpensive injection would have saved their lives.

Graph:

1980 / 1995

Industrialized nations | Developing world

10% 0 10% 20% 30% 40% 50% 60%

Women
Men

Some schools in the developing world lacked even the most basic facilities. These little Indian girls learned to read while sitting on the floor.

Education and literacy

Great progress in education was made in the final decades of the 20th century in the developing world. Many more children were enrolled in elementary school and literacy was on the increase worldwide. However, there was still discrimination against girls, with fewer girls than boys being enrolled. Class size, teacher training, and adequate learning facilities (including books, classrooms, desks, and chairs) remained problems in poor nations.

Rich world and fair trade

For centuries the developed countries of the world exploited the people of their overseas colonies, forcing them to grow food for export at very low prices. Even when the colonies became independent countries again, most of the growers were no better off than they had been before, as they did not get a fair price for their crops. In the late 20th century, however, a system of fair trade was set up to try and improve the situation.

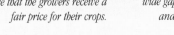

Fair trade products ensure that the growers receive a fair price for their crops.

In the developing world there is a wide gap between the lives of the rich and the poor.

Environmental problems

In some parts of the world the deserts grew by several miles each year. This was caused partly by the changing climate, but also by people overusing the land on the edge of the desert by cutting down trees for firewood and overgrazing their cattle. Many local inhabitants then had to move to more fertile land or face a life of extreme poverty.

People who help

Charity workers from richer parts of the world tried to solve the problems of the developing countries. One of the best known was Mother Teresa (1910–1997) who founded a charity dedicated to helping the poor on the streets of India.

Child labor

Throughout the developing world, many children from poor families worked instead of going to school. They were employed in mines and factories, on farms and construction sites, and as servants in private homes. They worked long hours for poor pay and sometimes for no pay at all. Working conditions were often hazardous, and included using dangerous machinery and even handling corrosive substances without protective clothing. Because they did not go to school, the children usually remained illiterate and were trapped in poverty for the rest of their lives.

Africa to the Present

By 1980 all the African countries except Namibia had regained their independence from European colonial powers. Many of the new governments, freely elected at the time of independence, then fell victim to military rule or dictatorship as rival groups struggled for power. This political instability, together with overpopulation, long periods of drought, and the gradual spread of desert conditions, led to many problems, especially in the countries of sub-Saharan Africa. The South African government's policy of apartheid that separated people according to their skin color, denying most human rights to the non-white majority, finally ended in 1991. Some progress had been made by the end of the century, particularly in North Africa, but war, hunger, disease, and poverty still affected many people across a wide area.

Not all African countries regained their independence in the first wave of liberation that took place in the late 1950s and the early 1960s. The Portuguese colonies of Mozambique and Angola had to wait until 1974. The white minority government in the British colony of Rhodesia (now Zimbabwe) proclaimed its independence from Britain in 1965, but did not achieve black African rule until 1980. Namibia only won its independence in 1990, while in South Africa black citizens had to wait until 1994, when the apartheid

Apartheid

In 1948 the South African National Party introduced a policy of separate development for the white and the non-white populations of the country. It established separate residential and business areas for four groups: whites, blacks, Asians, and coloreds. To enforce the system, non-whites were required to carry a "pass" when out of their areas. The vast majority of South Africans were non-whites; and this system was a blatant violation of their human rights.

In the British colony of Rhodesia, the white minority wanted independence, but they also wanted to keep control of the country. They declared themselves independent in 1965, but legal independence was only achieved in 1980. The country's name was then changed to Zimbabwe.

Below: Idi Amin, a commander in the Ugandan army, overthrew the country's president, Milton Obote, in 1971. Idi Amin then became president, ruling the country directly. In an attempt to keep his country just for Ugandans, he expelled all Asians in 1972. He was also alleged to have had up to 300,000 Ugandans murdered before he was overthrown in 1979.

The African National Congress started the campaign against apartheid in 1948, but international protests only began after Nelson Mandela was imprisoned. Among other things, all-white South African sports teams were banned from international events, while overseas entertainers refused to go to South Africa to perform to white-only audiences.

South Africa after Apartheid

Following international sanctions and unrest in South Africa in the 1980s, a new president, F.W. de Klerk, was elected in 1990 and he began to dismantle the apartheid system. He freed Nelson Mandela and in 1991 the apartheid laws were repealed. In 1992 a majority of whites voted to continue the reforms and in 1993 all South African adults were given the right to vote. A black majority government, led by Nelson Mandela, was elected in 1994, but although the apartheid laws had gone, there were still many social and economic problems to be solved.

Economic development

Africa suffered a major crisis in the 1970s due to the massive increase of oil prices. Many countries took out huge foreign loans which, by the mid-1980s, some were unable to pay off or even meet the interest payments due. Many countries were forced to accept programs decided by the International Monetary Fund (IMF) that remodeled their economies on Western, capitalist principles. By the 1990s income levels in some countries were rising.

UN peacekeeping forces have been called into Africa many times to try and prevent local conflicts escalating into full-scale wars.

Democracy in Africa

After independence, many African states became politically unstable and often fell victim to the rule of a dictator. Some, such as Idi Amin of Uganda and Laurent Kabila of Congo, came to power by force, but others, such as Robert Mugabe of Zimbabwe, were freely elected and gradually turned into dictators. But by the end of the 20th century many countries had democratically elected governments.

Nationalist and socialist leader Agostinho Neto, was one of the founder of the MPLA, popular Movement for the Liberation of Angola. Angola obtained independence from Portugal in 1975 and Neto was its first president (1975–1979).

1990 Namibia is the last African country to regain independence.

1994 Over 500,000 die as ethnic conflict erupts in Rwanda and Burundi.

1997 Zaire is renamed Democratic Republic of Congo.

1999 Thabo Mbeki takes over from Mandela as president of South Africa.

2002 16 killed in terror attack on Israeli-owned hotel in Kenya.

system was finally dismantled, to vote in free elections.

Apartheid, which comes from an Afrikaner word meaning "separate development," was introduced in South Africa in 1948 and reached its climax in the 1970s and 1980s. From that time onward there was increasing protest within the townships, as well as from abroad. In 1986 both the European Community and the USA imposed economic sanctions. This damaged the economy at a time when the internal protest movement, backed by the ANC and the Pan-African Congress, was rising and the white minority government was forced to

introduce reforms. In 1990 banned opposition parties were legalized and Nelson Mandela was released from prison. A new constitution was drafted and in April 1994 all adult South Africans voted in free elections for the first time. The new government was led by Nelson Mandela until Thabo Mbeki took over in June 1999.

In other parts of Africa civil wars were frequent and devastating. In Sudan, the war between the Islamic north and the Christian south has gone on since independence. In Angola, various factions have also been at war since the country achieved independence. In the Horn of Africa,

Eritrea, Ethiopia, and Somalia have also experienced ongoing war.

But at the beginning of the 21st century the most disturbing problem facing Africa remained the AIDS crisis.

1. A Poster in Arab and English calling for independence of Africa from colonial powers.

SEE ALSO
p. 122 AFRICAN EMPIRES
p. 202 THE SCRAMBLE FOR AFRICA
p. 240 DECOLONIZATION OF AFRICA
p. 266 THE DEVELOPING WORLD

Nelson Mandela (below) became the first black president of South Africa in 1994. He had campaigned long and hard against apartheid and was sentenced to life in prison in 1964 on a charge of treason. Local protest and international pressure forced the government to release him in 1990.

CIVIL WAR AND FAMINE IN AFRICA SINCE 1960.

☇ Civil war

☠ Famine

Economic growth
Economic growth in many parts of Africa was severely restricted by drought, flood, and warfare that disrupted food production and made many countries dependent on overseas aid. Exports included gold, diamonds, and petroleum. Cash crops such as tomatoes, bananas, and coffee were also grown for export, while tourism was important in some areas. Despite some growth, the economic prospects of many African countries were bleak at the turn of the 21st century.

The map shows some of the most devastating civil wars and famines that have struck in Africa in the last 40 years.

Famine, poverty, and lack of clean water are just three of the problems that much of Africa has to face in the 21st century. Where the land has been overworked, the soil has lost its fertility and, when the rains fail, the crops cannot grow. Civil wars and overpopulation add to the problem.

The scourge of AIDS
AIDS has hit the African continent much harder than other parts of the world. More than 12 million African children have already lost one or both parents to the disease. In 16 countries, all of them in sub-Saharan Africa, more than one adult in ten is infected with the HIV virus. Botswana is the worst affected, with almost 36 percent of the adult population testing positive. Although there is no cure for AIDS, treatment has been available in the West since the early 1990s. However, poverty in Africa and indifference in the West have meant that most African sufferers do not receive any treatment at all.

In many parts of Africa women traditionally play strong roles in the local economy. They run the farms and in many countries control the local markets. Because of this, international aid and development agencies have begun to make loans to women rather than men.

Nomadic peoples
Some people in Africa still lead nomadic lives. The best known are the Tuaregs, a Berber people who traditionally herded their sheep, goats, and camels across much of eastern North Africa. Wearing blue turbans and veils to protect their skin from the sun, they are often known as Blue Men because the dye often stains their faces. In recent decades, governments have tried to restrict their movements and force them to settle down, so that fewer and fewer of them are able to follow their traditional lifestyles.

Literacy and education
Education is compulsory in many African countries, but not in all of them. Even so, most governments realize that children need at least to be able to read and write and understand mathematics if they are going to have any chance of escaping from poverty in the future. Limited economic resources hindered some countries and children were forced to study without the aid of books or, in some cases, even classrooms.

POPULATION AND ENVIRONMENT

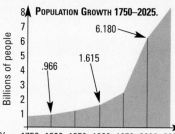

Population growth 1750–2025.

.966 1.615 6.180

Population growth
The world's population did not reach one billion until the early years of the 19th century. It took almost another 150 years for it to reach two billion, but by the end of the 20th century it had passed six billion and was still rising at the rate of one billion every ten years.

The world's population increased rapidly in the second half of the 20th century. In developed countries more people lived longer, while in the developing world many more babies survived beyond childhood. This increase put pressure on the environment in many different ways, as more space was needed for housing, farmland for growing food, and factories to produce the goods the soaring population needed. Pollution increased and many species of animals became endangered as their natural habitats were cleared for farmland. Some scientists began to recognize the problems in the 1960s, but they were not taken seriously until the 1970s when environmental pressure groups and "green" political parties were formed.

Family planning in China
In China, the government tried to limit population growth from the 1950s. After 1979 each family was only allowed to have one child. This gave China a low population growth rate.

MAJOR DATES

1971 Foundation of Greenpeace, an international organization concerned with environmental issues.

1986 Radioactive material from an explosion at Chernobyl nuclear power station in the Ukraine spreads as far as Italy, Scandinavia and the UK.

1987 Scientists discover the hole in the ozone layer above the North and South Poles.

1991 The world's population is estimated to be 5.3 billion and still increasing.

1992 The UN organizes the Earth Summit in Brazil to discuss the future of the planet.

As the chart shows, nearly two-thirds of the world's people live in Asia. As well as being the biggest continent, Asia also has some of the world's most densely populated countries.

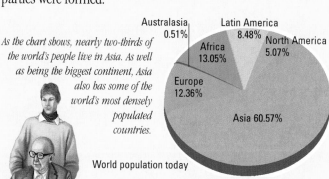

Australasia 0.51% · Latin America 8.48% · Africa 13.05% · North America 5.07% · Europe 12.36% · Asia 60.57%

World population today

By the year 2000 many European countries had zero or negative population growth (where the numbers of births and deaths are equal, or there are more deaths than births).

The graying of the Western world
Falling birth rates in the developed world meant that by the end of the 20th century there was an increasing proportion of old people in the population of many countries. This may well lead to financial problems in the 21st century as, in general, older people need more care, but there will be fewer people of working age to contribute to the health care and pension funds needed to look after them.

The graph (left) compares age profiles of Malaysia, a typical country in the developing world, and Japan, a typical country in the developed world. Malaysia has a high proportion of young people, while Japan has a much smaller number of young people and many more elderly.

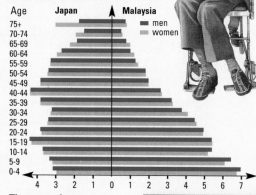

Age — Japan — Malaysia — men/women — % of population

Endangered species
Many animal species face extinction because of overhunting and the destruction of their natural environments. Attempts to save some species, such as the tiger, have been successful and numbers were on the rise again by 2000.

The ozone layer
The ozone layer is between about 12 mi. (20 km) above the earth's surface and protects the earth from excessive ultraviolet radiation from the sun. In the late 1980s scientists discovered there were holes in it above both poles, caused by pollution from fluorocarbons.

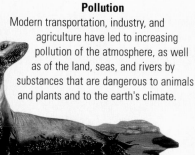

Huge oil spills caused by leaking oil tankers kill thousands of animals.

Pollution
Modern transportation, industry, and agriculture have led to increasing pollution of the atmosphere, as well as of the land, seas, and rivers by substances that are dangerous to animals and plants and to the earth's climate.

1950
1975
2000

- Conifer and deciduous forests
- Rain forests
- Rest of earth's surface

As these graphs show, the area of the world covered by forests shrank rapidly between 1950 and 2000. The rain forests were the worst affected.

Towards the end of the 20th century millions of trees in Europe were killed by acid rain caused by pollutants in the air from vehicles and industry.

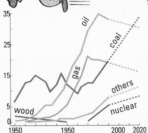

The shrinking rain forests

Most tropical rain forests are found in the developing world. They developed over thousands of years and are home to an enormous variety of plants and animals. In the last fifty years, however, vast areas have been cleared for farmland and timber, and for roads to give better access to forestry and mining operations. Scientists fear that the loss of forests will adversely affect world climate.

This graph shows the change in fuels used in the USA in the 20th century. It also predicts that the use of oil and gas will continue to decline.

This model of the overburdened earth appeared at the Earth Summit, organized by the UN, in Brazil in 1992.

PEOPLE AND PLACES

Rachel Carson, an American scientist, draws attention to the problems of pollution in 1962 with her book *The Silent Spring*.

Bhopal, India over 2000 people die in 1984 following the escape of poisonous gas from an American-owned factory.

Fernando Pereira, a photographer, is killed when the Greenpeace flagship, Rainbow Warrior, is blown up in New Zealand in 1985 during a protest against French nuclear bomb tests.

To try and protect the **African elephant** from extinction, many countries agree to a ban on ivory trading in 1989.

Alternative fuel

When scientists realized that the carbon dioxide given off by fossil fuels might alter the climate, they began to look for alternative ways of generating power for homes, transportation, and industry. The most successful is hydro-electricity, using waterpower to generate electricity. The sun, the wind, and the tides have also been used, but only on a small scale.

Solar power and wind power can both be used to generate electricity with very little pollution.

Nuclear power

In the 1950s and 1960s it was thought that using nuclear energy would be a clean and efficient way of generating electricity. However, after an explosion and fire at the nuclear plant at Chernobyl in the Ukraine released about 8 tons (tonnes) of radioactive material into the atmosphere in 1986, many people decided that the risks far outweighed the advantages.

Ecological products

To cut down on pollution and preserve natural resources, many environmentally-friendly household products have become available. They include bio-degradable washing-powders and liquids, paper products made from recycled paper, and packaging made from recycled plastic.

Electric vehicles are ideal for use in cities as they cause no pollution. By the end of the 20th century, many cities in Europe had introduced electric buses to lower levels of noise pollution and smog.

Organic products

In the 1970s, it was realized that pesticides used in farming were entering the food chain, while fertilizers were draining or blowing off the field and entering water supplies. This led to a small-scale, but increasing, return to organic farming in which crops and vegetables were grown using only natural products, such as farmyard manure, to enrich the soil.

Recycling

Recycling is one way of solving the problem of excess waste and also helps to preserve some of the world's limited resources. Newspapers, aluminum cans, plastic bottles, and glass containers are just some of the items that are collected and recycled again and again, rather than being burned in massive incinerators or buried in landfill sites where they take years to rot away.

SCIENCE AND TECHNOLOGY

The 20th century was marked by rapid progress in almost all areas of life. Great discoveries were made and pioneering work was done in the sciences, laying the foundations for entirely new branches of knowledge. Spectacular achievements, from the Wright brothers' first successful powered flight in 1903, to the first human walking on the moon in 1967, to the communications explosion in the 1990s, made some people wonder whether we were not moving ahead too quickly. Modernization and progress in industry, technology, communications, and living conditions brought increasing prosperity and made everyday life more comfortable. They also increased the wealth gap between the developed and the developing worlds.

The theory of relativity

In 1905 the young German scientist Albert Einstein (1879–1955; above) revolutionized ideas about time and space with his theory of relativity. The theory was verified in 1919 and two years later Einstein was awarded the Nobel Prize for Physics. As a German Jew who escaped from Nazi Germany, he worked hard to help other people escape from the Nazi regime.

Above: The discovery of penicillin by Alexander Fleming (1881–1955) in 1928 was a major breakthrough in the war against infectious diseases.

Left: Dolly, the first animal to be successfully cloned (1997). The possibilities (and the dangers) offered by genetic engineering were much discussed as the world entered the 21st century.

Below: Continental drift.

Radio

On December 12, 1901, Italian engineer Guglielmo Marconi (above) transmitted the first wireless radio signal across the Atlantic. Radio waves were already known, but it was thought that because the electromagnetic waves ran in a straight line they could not follow the curvature of the earth over a great distance. Several more years passed before the first radio programs were broadcast.

A French woman, Marie Curie, was one of the most outstanding scientists of the 20th century. She was twice awarded the Nobel Prize. In 1903 she won the Physics prize jointly with her husband, Pierre Curie, and Henri Becquerel, for the discovery of radioactivity. In 1911 she was the sole winner of the Nobel Prize for Chemistry for the isolation of pure radium.

The theory of continental drift

In 1912 Alfred Wegener, a German physicist and geologist, developed a theory to explain why, if the continents were pushed toward each other on a map of the world, their outlines would fit almost exactly. He started by assuming that millions of years ago a single land mass had formed. This ancient continent, which he called Pangaea (from the Greek: "all earth"), gradually broke up and the different parts of the earth's crust then slowly drifted away from each other. Wegener's theory was thought absurd at first, but fossils of similar species found in different parts of the world have since confirmed it.

Scientific discoveries were important for their own sakes. But the knowledge they generated filtered down to everyday life. Domestic appliances, such as the radio, the refrigerator, and the TV could not have existed without them.

MAJOR DATES

1957 The Medical Research Council in Britain establishes a direct link between cigarette smoking and lung cancer.

1962 Researchers in the Philippines crossbreed two strains of rice to produce a new one, called IR-8, which doubles the yield of most other Asian rices.

1970 The microprocessor silicon chip is invented. Computers are reduced in size leading, in 1976, to the first PC (personal computer).

1987 First criminal conviction made based on genetic evidence.

1990 Game Boy, first hand-held computer console launched by Japanese company Nintendo.

1992 Astronomers discover remains of the Big Bang from which the Universe was born 20 billion years ago.

1997 US space probe *Pathfinder* lands on Mars and beams back pictures of the Martian landscape. The robot *Sojourner* collects rock samples to bring back to earth.

2000 The supersonic Concorde is grounded following a terrible accident.

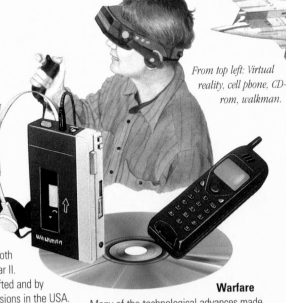

From top left: Virtual reality, cell phone, CD-rom, walkman.

Entertainment

The British Broadcasting Corporation (BBC) started transmitting radio programs in 1922, giving people a new form of entertainment in their homes. Television broadcasting began in 1936 in the UK and in 1939 in the USA. Both were shut down during World War II. After the war restrictions were lifted and by 1951 there were 10 million televisions in the USA. Home entertainment systems were big business worldwide by the end of the 20th century.

Aviation

The search to make journeys faster led in 1969 to the supersonic Concorde, a joint British-French project, which could make the transatlantic journey from London or Paris to New York in just 3 hours 20 minutes. A terrible accident in 2000 led to major restructuring of the Concorde service.

Right: Watch from Hiroshima, frozen at the moment the bomb struck.

Warfare

Many of the technological advances made during the 20th century were a direct result of research done by the military to improve their weaponry and communications systems. Some of the most sinister discoveries included the splitting of the atom, to create the atom bomb, and research in the field of chemical warfare.

The pioneers of flight

American aviator Charles Lindbergh (right) became an international hero on May 21, 1927, when he became the first person to make a solo nonstop flight across the Atlantic from New York to Paris in his plane Spirit of St. Louis. The 3,600-mi. (5,750-km) flight took 33 hours and 39 minutes, giving an average speed of 106 mph (170 kph), and earned him a prize of $25,000.

Above: Tanks were first used during World War I.

Genetic science

After scientists had discovered DNA they began to "map" genes (units of DNA carrying hereditary traits) and to modify information on them. This was a breakthrough for medical science, since it meant that hereditary diseases could be cured or prevented.

Technology and agriculture

Agricultural output was greatly increased during the 20th century by the use of modern farm machinery and technology. In the developed world, tractors and other mechanized farm implements replaced the horse and ox-powered machinery prevalent at the beginning of the century. Agricultural science also made real progress in many other fields, such as crop storage, irrigation, flood control, and drainage. By the end of the century computers and other high-tech products were also being used by modern farmers to increase yields.

The use of chemicals in agriculture to control pests and weeds was introduced in the 20th century. (In the developing world damage by pests can cause crop losses of up to 75 percent.) This helped to increase yields, although it sometimes created environmental problems if the chemicals used were toxic.

Communications

By the beginning of the 21st century people around the world were connected by the internet, cell phones, and e-mail. Millions of people signed up for these new services each year creating a communications boom hitherto unknown.

THE GLOBAL WORLD

In the second half of the 20th century, travel became easier and faster, making the world seem smaller as more and more people traveled by air. International trade flourished, conducted first by telex and fax, then increasingly by mobile phone, e-mail, and the Internet. More people from all over the world also came into contact through increasing tourism and international sports events, as well as through business and trade. Some companies built factories in the developing world where labor costs were lower. Most of the wealth remained in the developed world, however, leading to protests in the late 1990s. Crime, corruption, and terrorism also became globalized and in the mid-1990s the international trade in illegal drugs was worth an estimated US $500 billion.

Communications
During the last decade of the 20th century, technological advances in the electronics industry made worldwide communications easier and cheaper. The development of computers which were small enough to be held in the hand, together with mobile phones, allowed people to keep in touch while they were on the move.

Desk top publishing, using computers and laser printers to produce reports and magazines in the office or at home, was part of the computer revolution.

Satellites orbiting the earth have many different uses. Some are for telecommunications and broadcasting. Others monitor the planet and send the information back to earth.

Against globalization
Protests against globalization increased, with some meetings slipping into street violence (Seattle,1999; Genoa, 2001). The large numbers of protesters included animal and human rights activists, protesters about sweatshop labor, and workers who felt their jobs were threatened.

Left: This cartoon shows the problem of protesting against globalization; the protestor does not realize that he is dressed in clothing made in many different countries. For example, his watch was made in Japan, his shoes in China, his T-shirt in the Philippines, his jeans in Indonesia, his hat in Bangladesh, and his sweater in Malaysia.

Factories in the developing world
By the end of the 20th century many large businesses from the developed world had moved at least some of their manufacturing plants to the developing world where the cost of land and labor were much lower. At first many people had to work in sweatshop conditions, but with international regulation the situation was slowly improving.

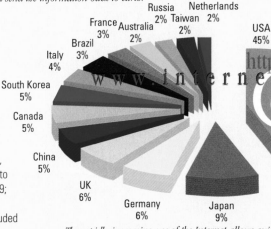

Russia 2% Taiwan 2% Netherlands 2%
France 3% Australia 2%
Brazil 3% USA 45%
Italy 4%
South Korea 5%
Canada 5%
China 5%
UK 6%
Germany 6% Japan 9%

The rapidly increasing use of the Internet allows quick and easy access to information all around the world. The graph (above) shows the number of households with internet links in 1999.

Below: Unemployment in the West was still a problem, mainly for workers without qualitifications to work with new technology.

Above and right: Terrorism is a relatively new problem. In 1993 a terrorist bomb exploded in the car park under the World Trade Center in New York, killing six people and injuring over 1,000 others. High security at airports seeks to stop hijackers boarding airplanes.

MAJOR DATES
1957 The first year in which more people cross the Atlantic by air than by sea.

1969 The supersonic Concorde and the Jumbo Jet both fly for the first time, making way for a revolution in air travel.

1972 Israel withdraws from the Olympic Games in Munich after Palestinian terrorists kill two Israeli athletes there.

1981–2 First PCs launched; leads to evolution and wider use of internet, mainly by academics and researchers.

1992 World Wide Web released. Number of internet hosts passes 1 million.

1993 The USA is shocked when a terrorist bomb explodes in the World Trade Center in New York as it is the first time they have been attacked in their own country.

1999 Protesters take to the streets of Seattle when the World Trade Organization meets there. They include environmentalists worried about the damage being done to the earth, and people from the developed world who are frightened of losing their jobs to people in the developing world.

Global culture

Until the early 1970s most movies shown in cinemas around the world were made in the USA. But, as television became more widespread in the industrialized world, fewer films were made in the USA and by the 1990s India, where far fewer people have televisions, led the world in the number of films produced for the cinema each year.

Immigration

In the first half of the 20th century most migration was from Europe to the New World. By the end of the century, the main migrations were from the developing world to the industrialized countries of North America and Europe. Most migrants sought a better life for themselves and their children, others were refugees.

The cultures of Europe were enriched by the arrival of people from the Middle East, Asia, and Africa. They brought their own foods and customs with them.

Endangered peoples

During the 20th century, many ethnic groups faced extinction, because their traditional way of life was threatened or destroyed by changes in agriculture or industry, or by war or border disputes. In the last decades of the century, however, many of them, including the Ainu people in Japan (above), began to fight back to preserve their languages, religions, and cultures.

Jeans were first produced by Levi Strauss in San Francisco after 1850. They spread all over the world.

Popular culture is global

Movies, television, books, magazines, increasing travel, and the use of the internet have all helped to spread popular culture around the world, especially among young people. Most of it is American-based and nearly all major cities across the world now have at least one burger bar and several shops selling jeans, trainers, and sweatshirts.

World sporting events

World sporting events attract competitors and spectators from all around the world, as well as massive television audiences. One of the most important is the Olympic Games, whose symbol of five rings (right) represents the five major continents. They are held every four years and have both summer and winter competitions.

Fast food became popular in the USA in the first decades of the 20th century. By the 1970s fast-food chains selling hamburgers and pizza were to be found throughout the developed world.

Tourists in the Old World flocked to art galleries, museums, and historic places, as well as enjoying the sunshine, scenery, and food.

Tourism

Tourism and leisure were both rapidly-growing industries at the end of the 20th century as many people in the industrialized world had more free time and more money to spend. Tourism became an important source of income for many countries and they developed special facilities for visitors. There was a slight downturn in tourism after the dramatic terror attacks in the first few years of the new century.

As the two graphs show, many more people speak Chinese than English, but English is used more for official purposes.

MOTHER TONGUES (millions of speakers)

Chinese, English, Hindi, Spanish, Russian, Arabic, Bengali, Portuguese, Malay-Indon., Japanese, French

OFFICIAL LANGUAGES (millions of speakers)

English, Chinese, Hindi, Spanish, Russian, French, Arabic, Portuguese, Malay, Bengali, Japanese

English as a world language

The English language was originally spoken in Britain and emigrants from there took it to the USA, Canada, Australia, and New Zealand. In the 19th century it also spread across the vast British Empire and as Britain, and later the USA, traded with almost every country in the world, making it the most widely used language for trade and other official purposes.

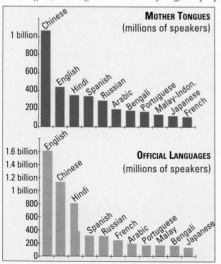

Tourists in the New World enjoyed visiting huge theme parks, such as Disney World in Florida, as well as soaking up the sun.

INDEX